ION

GLOBAL EDITION

Language Development

An Introduction

Robert E. Owens, Jr.

College of Saint Rose

PEARSON

Boston Columbus Indianapolis New York San Francisco Upper Saddle River
Amsterdam Cape Town Dubai London Madrid Milan Munich Paris Montreal Toronto
Delhi Mexico City São Paulo Sydney Hong Kong Seoul Singapore Taipei Tokyo

Vice President and Editorial Director: *Jeffery W. Johnston*
Executive Editor: *Ann Castel Davis*
Editorial Assistant: *Janelle Criner*
Executive Field Marketing Manager: *Krista Clark*
Senior Product Marketing Manager: *Christopher Barry*
Senior Acquisitions Editor, Global Edition: *Sandhya Ghoshal*
Senior Project Editor, Global Edition: *Daniel Luiz*
Manager, Media Production, Global Edition: *M. Vikram Kumar*
Senior Manufacturing Controller, Production, Global Edition: *Trudy Kimber*
Project Manager: *Kerry Rubadue*
Program Manager: *Joe Sweeney*
Operations Specialist: *Deidra Skahill*
Text Designer: *Jouve*
Design Director: *Diane Ernsberger*
Cover Art: © *knysh ksenya / Shutterstock*
Media Producer: *Autumn Benson*
Media Project Manager: *Tammy Walters*
Full-Service Project Management: *Jouve*
Composition: *Jouve*

Pearson Education Limited
Edinburgh Gate
Harlow
Essex CM20 2JE
England

and Associated Companies throughout the world

Visit us on the World Wide Web at:
www.pearsonglobaleditions.com

Authorized adaptation from the United States edition, entitled Language Development: An Introduction, 9th edition, ISBN 978-0-13-381036-3, by Robert E. Owens, Jr., published by Pearson Education © 2016.

ISBN 10:1292104422
ISBN 13:9781292104423

British Library Cataloguing-in-Publication Data
A catalogue record for this book is available from the British Library.

10 9 8 7 6 5 4 3 2 1
14 13 12 11 10

Typeset in Stone Serif Std by Jouve.

Printed and bound by Vivar, Malaysia.

"Say that again. I didn't hear you. I was listening to my toast."

Jessica Owens, age 4

To my gran'kids, Cassidy, Dakota, and Zavier.

Preface

There is no single way in which children learn to communicate. Each child follows an individual developmental pattern just as you did. Still, it is possible to describe a pattern of general communication development and of English specifically. This text attempts such descriptions and generalizations but emphasizes individual patterns, too.

New to This Edition

For those readers familiar with older editions, you'll find much has changed and, hopefully, much that you'll like. The changes in the ninth edition of *Language Development: An Introduction* are as follows:

- Continued distribution of bilingual and dialectal development throughout the text rather than in a separate stand-alone chapter. It seemed time to bring these speakers in out of the cold and put them where they belong in recognition of their importance and also the increase in bilingualism in the United States.
- Expanded discussion of children from lower-SES families, including those living in homeless shelters.
- Chapter 4, which carries the burden of explaining cognition and its relationship to speech and language, has been substantially reorganized to aid learning.
- Consolidated information on Theory of Mind in one chapter, as some professors recommended, so the discussion is more coherent.
- Improved readability throughout with more thorough explanations and clarification/simplification of terms, and increased use of headings and bulleted points.
- Weeded out redundancies and asides to make the text less dense.
- Provided more child language examples throughout to better illustrate language structures.
- And, of course, updated research. I spent over eight months just reading before I ever began to edit. For those compulsive types who count number of bibliographic entries, you'll find several hundred new references along with several retirements.

Phew! That list even makes me tired. My hope is that you'll also find the new edition very useful.

Those of you who will one day become parents should appreciate the value of this text as a guideline to development. If you plan to work with children with disabilities and without, you'll find that typical development can provide a model for evaluation and intervention. The developmental rationale can be used to decide on targets for training and to determine the overall remediation approach.

In recognition of the importance of the developmental rationale as a tool and of the changing perspectives in child language development, the ninth edition offers expanded coverage of preschool and school-age language development. Pragmatics receives increased attention, as does the conversational context within which most language development occurs. If you're a prospective speech-language pathologist, you will find these developmental progressions valuable when making decisions concerning materials to use with children who have speech and language impairments. As consumers of educational and therapeutic products, you must be especially sensitive to the philosophy that governs the organization of such materials. Many materials claim to be developmental in design but are not. I recall opening one such book to find *please* and *thank you* as the first two utterances to be taught to a child with deafness. These words violate many of the characteristics of first words.

Experienced teachers, psychologists, or speech-language pathologists need not rely on such prepackaged materials if they have a good base in communication development. An understanding of the developmental process and the use of a problem-solving approach can be a powerful combination in the hands of creative clinicians.

Acknowledgments

A volume of this scope must be the combined effort of many people fulfilling many roles, and this one is no exception.

My first thanks go to all those professionals and students, too numerous to mention, who have corresponded or conversed with me and offered criticism or suggestions for this edition. The overall organization of this text reflects the general organization of my own communication development course and that of professionals with whom I have been in contact.

The professional assistance of several people has been a godsend. The College of Saint Rose is an environment that encourages collaboration and individual professional growth, and it's a wonderful place to work. This attitude is reflected in the policies and practices of Dean of Education Margaret McLane and my department chair, James Feeney. Other great faculty members include, in alphabetical order, Dave DeBonis, Colleen Karow, Jessica Kisenwether, Megan Overby (now at DeQuesne University), Jack Pickering, Anne Rowley, and Julia Unger, and fellow clinical faculty members Director of Clinical Education Jackie Klein, Marisa Bryant, Sarah Coons, Colleen Fluman, Elaine Galbraith, Julie Hart, Barbara Hoffman, Kate Lansing, Jessica Laurenzo, Melissa Spring, and Lynn Stephens. You have all made me feel welcome and valued.

Others included in my list are

- Dr. Addie Haas, retired professor in the Communication Disorders Department at State University of New York at New Paltz, is a dear friend; a trusted confident; a good buddy; a fellow hiker; a skilled clinician; a source of information, ideas, and inspiration; my go-to person to bounce ideas around; and a helluva lot of fun. I will never forget our adventures "Down under."
- My former department chair, Dr. Linda House, created an environment at SUNY Geneseo in which I enjoyed working and growing.
- Irene Belyakov's suggestions; ideas; and, more important, her loving understanding have been a welcome source of encouragement.
- My dear friend Omid Mohamadi has kept me alert to new possibilities and given me a fresh perspective on the field of speech-language pathology. I look forward to more collaborations.

Additionally, I would like to thank the reviewers of this ninth edition: Brenda L. Beverly, University of South Alabama; Sloane Burgess, Kent State University; Elizabeth

Hunter, Regent University; Tobias A. Kroll, Texas Tech University, Health Sciences Center; and Steven Long, Marquette University.

I would also like to express my love and appreciation to my children, Jason, Todd, and Jessica, who are as beautiful as adults as they were as youngsters; to my gran'kids, Cassidy, Dakota, and Zavier, whose language is sprinkled throughout this book; and to my colleague at O and M Education, Moon Byungchoon.

I'm also indebted to the student researchers who helped me analyze over 175 language samples from which much research continues to flow. The now-SLPs and audiologists are Katherine Allen, Lynda Feenaughty, Annie Feldman, Erin Filippini, Marc Johnson, Andrew Kanuck, Jessica Kroecker, Zhaleh Lavasani-Leliberté, Stephanie Loccisano, Katherine Lyle, Jordan Nieto, Catherine Sligar, Kathryn Wind, and Sara Young.

Robert E. Owens, Jr.

Pearson would like to thank the following people for their work on the Global Edition:

Contributor:
Medha Bhattacharyya, Bengal Institute of Technology, Kolkata

Reviewers:
Annesha Dutta, Institute of Engineering and Management, Kolkata
Aditi Ghosh, Calcutta University
Sonia Sahoo, Jadavpur University

Contents

8 *Preschool Pragmatic and Semantic Development* 222

9 *Preschool Development of Language Form* 263

10 *Early School-Age Language Development* *309*

11 *School-Age Literacy Development* *349*

12 *Adolescent and Adult Language* *371*

Monkey Business Images/Shutterstock

1 The Territory

OBJECTIVES

Before we can discuss language development, we need to agree on what language is and what it is not. Don't worry; as a user of language, you already know a great deal about it. This chapter will organize your knowledge and provide some labels for the many aspects of language you know. Don't panic—introductory chapters usually contain a lot of terminology so that we can all "speak the same language" throughout the text. When you have completed this chapter, you should understand the following:

- Differences among speech, language, and communication
- Differences among nonlinguistic, paralinguistic, and metalinguistic aspects of communication
- Main properties of language
- Five components of language and their descriptions
- What a dialect is and its relation to its parent language
- Major factors that cause dialects to develop
- Important terms:

antonym
bilingual
bound morpheme
code switch
communication
communicative competence
deficit approach
dialects
discourse
free morpheme
language
linguistic competence
linguistic performance
morpheme
morphology
nonlinguistic cues
paralinguistic codes
phoneme
phonology
pragmatics
register
selection restrictions
semantic features
semantics
sociolinguistic approach
speech
suprasegmental devices
style shifting
synonym
syntax
vernacular
word knowledge
world knowledge

Language and its processing in your brain are so complex that specialists devote their lives to investigating them. These specialists, called *linguists*, try to determine the ways in which we use language to communicate. The linguist deduces rules and patterns demonstrated when we, as users of a language, communicate with one another. In a sense, each child is a linguist who must deduce the rules of his or her native language.

You're already a mature language user but let's imagine that you encounter human language for the first time. Even if you had the most sophisticated computer-based code-breaking software, it would be impossible to figure out the many ways in which humans use language. For that task, you would need to decipher each of the 6,000 human languages and gain extensive knowledge of human interactions, emotions, and cultures. In other words, language is more than the sum of these parts. To understand language, we must consider it in the natural contexts in which it occurs.

Language is the premier achievement of humans, and using it is something that all of us can do. For example, the average adult English speaker produces about 150 words per minute, selecting each from between 30,000 and 60,000 alternatives stored in the user's brain, choosing from a myriad of English language grammatical structures, and making less than 0.1% errors! That's impressive!

This becomes all the more amazing when you realize that the typical 4-year-old child has deciphered much of American English and already has well-developed speech, language, and communication skills. Truly remarkable given the complexity of the task!

You probably don't recall much about your own language acquisition. One statement is probably true: Unless you experienced difficulty, there was no formal instruction. Congratulations, you did most of it on your own. Now, we're going to attempt something almost as momentous . . . trying to explain it all!

It's important to understand the significance of language for humans. Watch the first 2:08 minutes of this video for an interesting introduction. http://www.youtube.com/watch?v=PZatrvNDOiE

To appreciate the task involved in language learning, you need to be familiar with some of the terminology that is commonly used in the field. All the terms introduced in this chapter and throughout the text are summarized for you in the Glossary. The remainder of this chapter is devoted to an explanation of these terms. First, we discuss this text in general. Then we distinguish three often confused terms—*speech*, *language*, and *communication*—and look at some special qualities of language itself. Finally, we'll examine dialects.

This Text and You

Although the full title of this text is *Language Development: An Introduction*, it is not a watered-down or cursory treatment of the topic. I have attempted to cover every timely, relevant, and important aspect of language development that might be of interest to the future speech-language pathologist, educator, psychologist, child development specialist, or parent. Of necessity, the material is complex and specific.

No doubt you've at least thumbed through this book. It may look overwhelming. It's not. I tell my own students that things are never as bleak as they seem at the beginning of the semester. Within the last 36 years, I have taken more than 5,000 of my own students through this same material with a nearly 100% success rate. Let me try to help you find this material as rewarding to learn as it is to teach.

First, the text is organized into two sections. The first few chapters provide a background that includes terms, theories, and information on the brain and language. I know it's difficult to have to read this material when you really want to get to the development part, but believe me, all this background is necessary. The main topics of development are contained in the remaining chapters, which are organized sequentially from newborns through adults. Yes, adults are still learning language and adapting to changes.

As with any text, there are a few simple rules that can make the learning experience more fruitful.

- Note the chapter objectives prior to reading the chapter and be alert for this information as you read. That's the key information.
- Read each chapter in small doses then let it sink in for a while. The worst thing to do is put it off until the night before the test.
- Find the chapter organization described at the end of each chapter's introduction. This will help you know where we're going and follow me through the material.
- Take brief notes as you read. Don't try to write everything down. Stop at natural divisions in the content and ask yourself what was most important. Periodic summarizing is a great learning strategy.
- Review your notes when you stop reading and before you begin again the next time. This process will provide a review and some continuity.
- Try to read a little every day or every other day. That's a good long-term learning strategy. I say long-term because if you are a speech-language pathology student, you'll be seeing a lot more about language in your studies.
- Note the key terms in the chapter objectives and try to define them as you read. Each one is printed in boldface in the body of the chapter. Please don't just thumb through or turn to the Glossary for a dictionary definition. The terms are relatively meaningless out of context. They need the structure of the other information. Context is very important.
- Try to answer the questions throughout each chapter. They'll help you think more deeply about the material.
- I have tried to de-emphasize linguists, authors, and researchers by placing all citations in parentheses. Unless your professor calls your attention to a specific person, she or he may not wish to emphasize these individuals either. It may be a waste of time to try to remember who said what about language development. "He said–she said" memorization can be very tedious. The exceptions, of course, are individuals mentioned specifically by name in lecture and in the text.
- Make ample use of the weblinks and videos to enhance your reading. Additional information is always good.

I hope that these suggestions will help, although none is a guarantee.

Roll up your sleeves, set aside adequate time, and be prepared to be challenged. Actually, your task is relatively simple when compared to the toddler faced with deciphering the language she or he hears.

Speech, Language, and Communication

Child development professionals study the changes that occur in *speech, language,* and *communication* as children grow and develop. You might interpret these terms as having similar meanings or as being identical. Actually, they're very different and denote different aspects of development and use.

SPEECH

Speech is a verbal means of communicating. Other ways of communicating include but are not limited to writing, drawing, and manual signing. The result of planning and executing specific motor sequences, speech is a process that requires very precise neuromuscular coordination. Each spoken language has specific sounds or **phonemes**, plus sound combinations that are characteristic of that language. In addition, speech involves other components, such as voice quality, intonation, and rate. These components enhance the meaning of the message. For example, we talk faster when excited.

A highly complicated acoustic or sound event, speech is unlike any other environmental noise. Not even music achieves the level of complexity found in speech. Take a simple word such as *toe* and say it very, very slowly. The initial sound is an almost inhuman "tsch." This is followed by "o . . . w" in which your rounded mouth gradually tightens. Now say *toe* at normal speed and note how effortlessly this is done. Say it again and note how your brain integrates the signal as it comes in, creating the unified *toe*. You are a truly amazing being!

Speech is not the only means of face-to-face human communication. We also use gestures, facial expressions, and body posture to send messages. In face-to-face conversation, nonspeech means may carry up to 60% of the information exchanged.

Although humans are not the only animals that make sounds, to my knowledge, no other species can match the variety and complexity of human speech sounds. These qualities are the result of the unique structures of the human vocal tract, a mechanism that is functional months before the first words are spoken. Infants spend much of their first year experimenting with their vocal mechanisms and producing a variety of sounds. Gradually, these sounds come to reflect the language of the child's environment.

LANGUAGE

Individual speech sounds are meaningless noises until some regularity is added. The relationship between individual sounds, meaningful sound units, and the combination of these units is specified by the rules of a language. **Language** can be defined as a socially shared code or conventional system for representing concepts through the use of arbitrary symbols and rule-governed combinations of those symbols. In other words, the symbols or words are arbitrary but speakers know the meanings of these symbols, which are, in turn, organized in certain ways to convey ideas.

English is a language, as is Spanish or Navajo. Each has its own unique symbols and rules for symbol combinations. Languages are not monolithic. They contain **dialects**, subcategories of the parent language that use similar but not identical rules. All users of a language follow certain dialectal rules that differ from an idealized standard. For example, I sometimes find myself reverting to former dialectal usage in saying "*acros**t*** the street" and "open your ***um**brella*."

Languages change and evolve. Interactions between languages naturally occur in **bilingual** communities. Under certain circumstances, language mixing may result in a new form of both languages being used in that community (Backus, 1999). When I was a child, we said "tidal wave"; now we say "tsunami."

Languages that don't evolve, grow, and change become obsolete. Sometimes, for reasons other than linguistic ones, languages either flourish or wither. At present, for example, fewer than 80 individuals fluently speak Seneca, a western New York Native American language. The death of languages is not a rare event in the modern world. Languages face extinction as surely as plants and animals. When Kuzakura, an aged woman, died in western Brazil in 1988, the Umutina language died with her. It is estimated that as many as half the world's 6,000 languages are no longer learned by children. These languages will die. Many others are endangered. Most of these have less than a few thousand users. Only strong cultural and religious ties keep languages such as Yiddish and Pennsylvania Dutch viable. How long they will be secure is anyone's guess.

This century may see the eradication of most remaining languages. Sadly, it is doubtful that many of the 270 aboriginal languages of Australia—possibly some of the earth's oldest languages—will survive. The one that gave us the name for the cuddly-looking koala is already gone. Of the 154 Native American languages now in use, nearly 120 are each spoken by less than a thousand individuals. Other endangered languages include OroWin, an Amazonian language with only three surviving speakers; Gullah, spoken by the descendents of African slaves on islands off the coast of South Carolina and Georgia; and Nushu, a southern Chinese language spoken only by women. The worldwide loss of languages is the result of government policy, dwindling indigenous populations, the movements of populations to cities, mass media, and lack of education of the young. The Internet is also a culprit in the demise of some languages. The need to converse in one language is fostering increasing use of English.

Each language is a unique vehicle for thought. For example, in many Native American languages, the Great Spirit is not a noun as in European languages but a *verb*. This concept of a supreme being is totally different from that of Europeans. As a speaker of English, can you even imagine *god* as a verb? It changes the whole concept of a supreme being.

In the rain forest of northwestern Brazil, a language called Pirahã is so unique that it almost defies accepted notions of language. Spoken by approximately 350 people and reflecting their culture, Pirahã consists of only eight consonants and three vowels. Yet it has such a complex array of tones, stresses, and syllable lengths that speakers dispense with their sounds altogether and hum, sing, or whistle using relatively simple grammar by linguistic standards. Instead, meaning of words and phrases depends on changes in pitch and tone.

When we lose a language, we lose an essential part of the human fabric with its own unique perspective. A culture and possibly thousands of years of communication die with that language, the study of which might have unlocked secrets about universal language features, the origins of language, or the nature of thought. Within oral-only languages, the very nature of language itself is different. Words that have been passed on for generations acquire a sacredness, and speech is somehow connected to the Divine.

The death of a language is more than an intellectual or academic curiosity. After a week's immersion in Seneca, Mohawk, Onondaga, and other Iroquois languages, one man concluded:

> These languages are the music that breathes life into our dances, the overflowing vessels that hold our culture and traditions. And most important, these languages are the conduits that carry our prayers to the Creator. . . . Our languages are central to who we are as a native people.

"Come visit sometime," he offers. "I will bid you 'oolihelisdi' " (Coulson, 1999, p. 8A).

English is a Germanic variation of a much larger family of Indo-European languages as varied as Italian, Greek, Russian, Hindi, Urdu, Persian, and ancient Sanskrit. Although the Indo-European family is the largest family, as many as 30 others may exist, many much smaller.

Languages can grow as their respective cultures change. English has proven particularly adaptive, changing slowly through the addition of new words. According to the *Oxford English Dictionary*, approximately 8,000 English words predate the 12th century, including *laugh* and *friend*.

What is language and what is not? Watch minutes 4:05–11:50 in this video as Dr. Steven Pinker of Harvard University answers this question. http://www.youtube.com/watch?v=Q-B_ONJIEcE

Already the language with the largest number of words—approximately 700,000—English adds an estimated half dozen words per day. While many of these are scientific terms, they also include words popular on college campuses, such as *selfie* (smartphone self-photo), *cholo* (macho), and *dis* (scorn). English dictionaries have just recently added *24/7, bubba, blog, headbanger, gaydar, pumped (up), megaplex, racial profiling, slamming, brownfield, piercing, homeschool, netiquette,* and *sexting*. Some words have new meaning. For example, previously only Moses had *tablets*, now everybody does. These words tell us much about our modern world.

Although most languages can be transmitted by speech, speech is not an essential feature of language. To some extent, the means of transmission influences processing and learning, although the underlying concepts of signing are similar to spoken languages (Emmorey, 1993; Lillo-Martin, 1991).

American Sign Language is not a mirror of American English but is a separate language with its own rules for symbol combinations. As in spoken languages, individually signed units are combined following linguistic rules. Approximately 50 sign languages are used worldwide, including one of the world's newest languages, Nicaraguan Sign Language, invented by children with deafness to fill a void in their education. On the other side of the earth in Al-sayyid, a Bedouin village in the Negev desert of Israel, another sign language has arisen without the influence of any other spoken or signed languages. Within this village approximately 150 individuals are deaf and use their language to communicate with each other and with hearing members of the community (Boswell, 2006).

Following is the American Speech-Language-Hearing Association definition of *language* (Committee on Language, 1983). The result of a committee decision, this definition has a little of everything, but it also is very thorough.

- Language is a complex and dynamic system of conventional symbols that is used in various modes for thought and communication.
- Language evolves within specific historical, social, and cultural contexts.
- Language, as rule-governed behavior, is described by at least five parameters—phonologic, morphologic, syntactic, semantic, and pragmatic.
- Language learning and use are determined by the intervention of biological, cognitive, psychosocial, and environmental factors.
- Effective use of language for communication requires a broad understanding of human interaction including such associated factors as nonverbal cues, motivation, and sociocultural roles.

Languages exist because users have agreed on the symbols to be used and the rules to be followed. This agreement is demonstrated through language usage. Thus, languages exist by virtue of social convention or use. Just as users agree to follow the rules of a language

Monkey Business Images/Shutterstock

Humans use language to communicate through a number of means, such as reading, writing, speaking, and listening.

system, they can agree to change the rules. For example, the *eth* found as an ending on English verbs (ask*eth*) in the King James Version of the Bible has disappeared from use. New words can be added to a language; others fall into disuse. Words such as *DVD* and *blog* were uncommon just a few years ago. Users of one language can borrow words from another. For instance, despite the best efforts of the French government, its citizens seem to prefer the English word *jet* to the more difficult, though lyrical, *avion de reaction*.

English also has borrowed heavily from other languages, while they have felt free to borrow in return. Here are a few English words taken from other languages:

- *Raccoon* (Powhatan, a Native American language)
- *Jaguar* (Tupi-Guarani languages of the Amazon)
- *Immediate* (French)
- *Democracy* (Greek)
- *Tycoon* (Japanese)
- *Sofa* (Arabic)
- *Piano* (Italian)

In the process, meanings and words are changed slightly to conform to linguistic and cultural differences. More recently, English has incorporated words such as *tsunami* (Japanese), *barrio* (Spanish), *jihad* (Arabic), *sushi* (Japanese), and *schlep* (Yiddish).

Even strong, vibrant, firmly entrenched languages struggle against the embrace of the Internet and its accompanying English. Formal Spanish has given way to Cyber-Spanish with words such as *escapar* (escape) instead of *salir* and *un emilio* or *imail* (an e-mail) instead of *un correo electronico*.

English has become the language of worldwide commerce and the Internet. Possibly a billion people speak English as a second language, most in Asia. As they learn English, these speakers are making it their own, modifying it slightly with the addition of words from their languages and incorporating their own intonational and structural patterns. In the near future, it may be more appropriate to think of English as a family of similar languages.

Braj Kachru, a professor in India, questions the very idea that English is inevitably linked to Western culture. He hypothesizes that English can be as adaptable to local culture as a musical instrument is to music. More succinctly put, English no longer belongs to the English. According to Professor Kachru (2005), the over 500 million Asian speakers of English should direct the language's course because the number of speakers in traditionally English-speaking countries is declining. The "Englishes" of the future may be hybrids or even new languages that may not be mutually understood by users from different cultures.

The socially shared code of English or any language allows the listener and speaker or writer and reader of the same language to exchange information. Internally, each uses the same code. The shared code is a device that enables each to represent an object, event, or relationship. Let's see how this is done.

Close your eyes for a few seconds and concentrate on the word *ocean*. While your eyes were closed, you may have had a visual image of surf and sand. The concept was transmitted to you and decoded automatically. In a conversation, listener and speaker switch from encoding to decoding and back again without difficulty. Words, such as *ocean*, represent concepts stored in our brains.

Each user encodes and decodes according to his or her shared concept of a given object, event, or relationship; the actual object, event, or relationship does not need to be present. Let's assume that you encounter a priest. From past experience, you recognize his social role. Common elements of these experiences are *Catholic, male,* and *clergy*. As you pass, you draw on the appropriate symbol and encode, "Morning, Father." This representational process is presented in Figure 1.1. The word may also suggest a very different meaning, depending on the experiences of each party. Let's assume for a moment

FIGURE 1.1 **Symbol–Referent Relationship**

The concept is formed from the common elements of past experiences. The common elements of these experiences form the core of the concept. When a referent is experienced, it is interpreted in terms of the concept and the appropriate symbol applied.

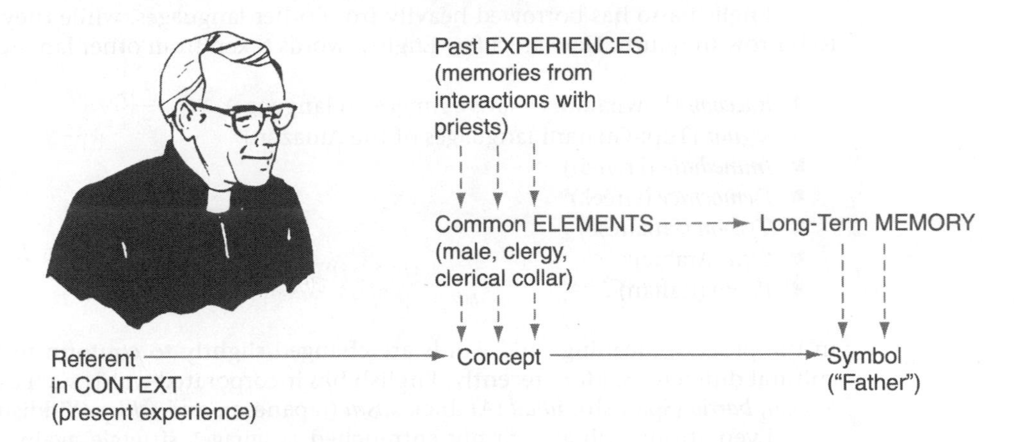

that your biological father is an Episcopal minister. You see him on the street in clerical garb and say, "Good morning, Father." A passerby, unaware of your relationship, will assume something very different from the meaning that you and your father share. Coding is a factor of the speaker's and listener's shared meanings, the linguistic skills of each, and the context in which the exchange takes place.

Individual linguistic units communicate little in isolation. Most of the meaning or information is contained in the way symbols are combined. For example, "Teacher Jim a is" seems a meaningless jumble of words. By shifting a few words, however, we can create "Jim is a teacher." Another modification could produce "Is Jim a teacher?"—a very different sentence. Language rules specify a system of relationships among the parts. The rules for these relationships give language order and allow users to predict which units or symbols will be used. In addition, the rules permit language to be used creatively. Symbols and rules governing their use help us to create utterances.

Language should not be seen merely as a set of static rules. It is a process of use and modification within the context of communication. Language is a tool for social use.

COMMUNICATION

Both speech and language are parts of a larger process called communication. **Communication** is the exchange of information and ideas, needs and desires, between two or more individuals. The process is an active one that involves encoding, transmitting, and decoding the intended message. Figure 1.2 illustrates this process. It requires a sender and a receiver, and each must be alert to the informational needs of the other to ensure that messages are conveyed effectively and that intended meanings are preserved. For example, a speaker must identify a specific female, such as "Have you seen Catalina?" prior to using the pronoun *she*, as in "She was supposed to meet me." The probability of message distortion is very high, given the number of ways a message can be formed and the past experiences and perceptions of each participant. The degree to which a speaker is successful in communicating, measured by the appropriateness and effectiveness of the message, is called **communicative competence**. The competent communicator is

FIGURE 1.2 **Process of Communication**

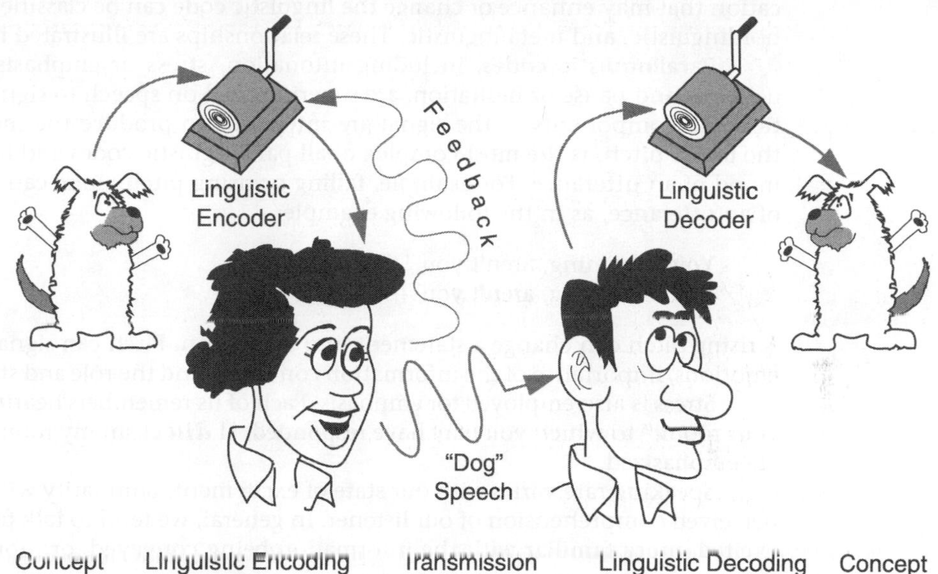

able to conceive, formulate, modulate, and issue messages and to perceive the degree to which intended meanings are successfully conveyed.

Human communication is a complex, systematic, collaborative, context-bound tool for social action. Complexity can be demonstrated by the multifaceted and multifunctional aspects of the process. These include all aspects of communication and language plus additional mental processes, such as memory and planning, exercised within the cultural beliefs, situational variables, and social conventions of the individual participants. Although complex, communication is a systematic pattern of behavior.

Conversations don't consist of disconnected, independent utterances. Instead, communication is collaborative. Partners actively coordinate construction of a joint dialogue as they negotiate to understand each other's meanings.

This process occurs within a specific cultural context that influences interpretation of linguistic units and speaker behaviors. The context is variable, changing minute by minute as the physical setting, partners, and topics change. I once introduced myself to a young Korean boy as *Bob*, unaware that *bob* means *rice* in Korean and that being someone's rice is an idiom for being his servant. Imagine how thrilled — and misinformed — he was when I, his supposed servant, subsequently hoisted him upon my shoulders as his mother and I headed down the street.

Finally, communication is a tool for social action. We accomplish things as we communicate. Let's eavesdrop on a conversation:

SPEAKER 1: Are you busy?
SPEAKER 2: No, not really.
SPEAKER 1: Well, if you could, please take a look at my lesson plan.
SPEAKER 2: Okay.

Speaker 1 used politeness to accomplish his goals. By prefacing his request with a question, he invited speaker 2 to respond in a positive way. That's why gran'ma told you that you could catch more flies with honey than with vinegar.

Paralinguistic Cues

Speech and language are only a portion of communication. Other aspects of communication that may enhance or change the linguistic code can be classified as paralinguistic, nonlinguistic, and metalinguistic. These relationships are illustrated in Figure 1.3.

Paralinguistic codes, including intonation, stress or emphasis, speed or rate of delivery, and pause or hesitation, are superimposed on speech to signal attitude or emotion. All components of the signal are integrated to produce the meaning. *Intonation*, the use of pitch, is the most complex of all paralinguistic codes and is used to signal the mood of an utterance. For example, falling or rising pitch alone can signal the purpose of an utterance, as in the following example:

You're coming, aren't you.↓(Telling)
You're coming, aren't you↑(Asking)

A rising pitch can change a statement into a question. Pitch can signal emphasis, asides, emotions, importance of the information conveyed, and the role and status of the speaker.

Stress is also employed for emphasis. Each of us remembers hearing, "You ***will*** clean your room!" to which you may have responded, "I ***did*** clean my room!" The *will* and *did* are emphasized.

Speaking rate varies with our state of excitement, familiarity with the content, and perceived comprehension of our listener. In general, we tend to talk faster if we are more excited, more familiar with the information being conveyed, or more assured that our listener understands our message.

Pauses may be used to emphasize a portion of the message or to replace the message. Even young children recognize that a short maternal pause after a child's request usually signals a negative reply. Remember asking, "Can Chris sleep over tonight?" A long silence meant that your plans were doomed.

Pitch, rhythm, and pauses may be used to mark divisions between phrases and clauses. Combined with loudness and duration, pitch is used to give prominence to certain syllables and to new information.

FIGURE 1.3 Relationships of Speech, Language, and Communication

Communication is accomplished through linguistic and paralinguistic codes and many means of transmission, such as speech, intonation, gestures, and body language

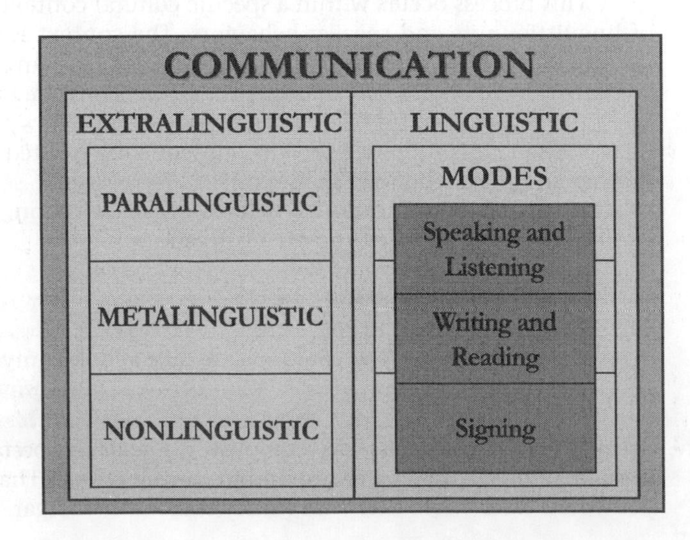

Paralinguistic mechanisms are called **suprasegmental devices** because they can change the form and meaning of a sentence by acting across elements, or segments, of a sentence. As mentioned, a rising pitch can change a statement into a question without altering the arrangement of words. Similarly, "I did my homework" and "I *did* my homework" convey different emotions.

Nonlinguistic Cues

Gestures, body posture, facial expression, eye contact, head and body movement, and physical distance or proxemics convey information without the use of language and are called **nonlinguistic cues**. The effectiveness of these devices varies with users and between users. We all know someone who seems to gesture too much or to stand too close while communicating. Some nonlinguistic messages, such as a wink, a grimace, a pout, or folded arms, can convey the entire message.

As with language, nonlinguistic cues vary with the culture. Perfectly acceptable gestures in one culture may be considered offensive in another. Table 1.1 presents a list

TABLE 1.1 Nonlinguistic Cues

Gesture	Other Interpretations	Countries in Which Unacceptable
Thumbs-up		Australia, Nigeria, Islamic countries, such as Bangladesh
A-OK	Japan: *money* France: *zero, worthless*	Latin American countries
Victory or peace sign		England (if palm toward body)
Hailing a waiter (one finger raised)	Germany: *two*	Japan
Beckoning curled finger		Yugoslavia, Malaysia, Indonesia, Australia
Tapping forehead to signify "smart"	Netherlands: *crazy*	
Stop		Greece, West Africa
Hands in the pockets		Belgium, Indonesia, France, Finland, Japan, Sweden
Strong handshake	Middle East: *aggression*	
Good-bye	Europe and Latin America: *no*	
Crossing legs and exposing sole of the foot		Southeast Asia
Nodding head for agreement	Greece, Yugoslavia, Turkey, Iran, Bengal: *No*	

Source: Information from Axtell (1991).

of common American gestures considered rude, offensive, or insulting in other cultures. Luckily, the smile is a universal signal for friendliness.

Metalinguistic Skills

The ability to talk about language, analyze it, think about it, judge it, and see it as an entity separate from its content or out of context is termed **metalinguistics**. For example, learning to read and write depends on metalinguistic awareness of the component units of language—sounds, words, phrases, and sentences. Metalinguistic skills also are used to judge the correctness or appropriateness of the language we produce and receive, thus signaling the status of the transmission or the success of communication.

The Beginnings of Human Communication

As you can see, like language, communication is quite complex, yet it is almost impossible not to communicate. Even if you tried not to communicate, your behavior would communicate that you do not want to communicate.

When and how did human communication diverge from other primate communication? Unfortunately, speech doesn't leave any tangible evidence. Our best guess is that spoken language appeared around 50,000–100,000 years ago. The first "words" may have been imitations of animal sounds or may have accompanied emotion, such as crying, and actions, such as a grunt when attempting to move something heavy.

Although we can't answer the question more precisely, language itself may offer a place to begin an explanation. If we look back at the characteristics of language, the first was that language is a social tool. If we take this further, we can conclude that language is a social means for achieving social ends based on shared understanding and purpose (Tomasello, 2008). Thus, human communication is fundamentally cooperative. Herein may be our answer.

The cooperative nature of human communication and the cooperative structure of human social interaction and culture are closely related. Early forms of communication were most likely gestural in nature, including pointing and pantomiming (Tomasello, 2008). The cooperative nature of these gesture differs qualitatively from other primate communication, which is primarily requesting to fill immediate needs. In contrast, cooperative communication requires socio-cognitive skills of shared intentionality. While chimpanzees, with whom we share a common ancestor, do have and understand individual intentionality, most do not have the skills of shared intentionality, such as joint goals and joint attention that are necessary for cooperative communication.

Early humans were probably driven to cooperate because of fear of hunger or the high risk of being eaten by predators (Bickerton, 2003). Thus, human cooperative communication resulted from a biological adaptation for collaborative activities; reciprocating could help ensure your survival.

Vocal communication probably emerged after conventionalized gestures. Most likely the earliest vocal accompaniments to gestures were emotional or added sound effects to some already meaningful action-based gestures or other actions. Some vocalizations may have accompanied specific acts such as mourning or imitated animal sounds. At some point, the vocalizations took on meaning of their own. Unlike ape communication, human vocalization is not context-bound or involuntary and this characteristic may be related to the need for vocal communication. While pointing works in context, we must rely on some other signal to communicate about something that is not present. In addition, vocal communication freed the hands for other purposes (Goldin-Meadow, 2005).

When we compare a gorilla skull to a Neanderthal skull from approximately 60,000 years ago, one striking difference can be noted in the vocal tract of the early human. The reconfigured vocal tract suggests that some consonant-like sounds were possible. More modern vocal tracts appear about 35,000 years ago. When compared to other primates, humans have more vertical teeth, more intricately muscled lips, a relatively smaller mouth, a greater closure of the oral cavity from the nasal, and a lower larynx or "voice box." All of these adaptations make speech as we know it possible. Most importantly, humans possess a large and highly specialized brain compared to their overall size.

It is the rules that enable humans to communicate. Sounds can be combined, recombined, broken down, and combined another way to convey different meanings. A dog's bark cannot be manipulated in this way and is a relatively fixed form.

Grammar arose to express more complex relationships. This is especially important as communication moves from requesting to informing and information sharing (Tomasello, 2008).

Properties of Language

Linguists attempt to describe the properties or characteristics of language. In general, language is a social interactive tool that is both rule governed and generative, or creative.

LANGUAGE IS A SOCIAL TOOL

It does little good to discuss language outside the framework provided by communication. While language is not essential for communication, communication is certainly an essential and defining element of language. Without communication, language has no purpose.

As a shared code, language enables users to transmit ideas and desires to one another. In fact, language has but one purpose: to serve as the code for transmissions between people.

Overall, language reflects the collective thinking of its culture and, in turn, influences that thinking. In the United States, for example, certain words, such as *democracy*, reflect cultural meanings and emotions and, in turn, influence our concepts of other forms of government. The ancient Greek notion of democracy was somewhat different and similarly influenced the Greeks' thinking.

Likewise, at any given moment, language in use is influenced by what precedes it and influences what follows. The utterance "And how's my little girl feeling this morning?" only fits certain situations that define the appropriate language use. It would not be wise to use this utterance when meeting the Queen of England for the first time. In turn, the sick child to whom this is addressed has only limited options that she can use to respond. Responses such as, "Go directly to jail; do not pass Go" and "Mister Speaker, I yield the floor to the distinguished senator from West Virginia," while perfectly correct sentences, just don't fit the situation. The reason is that they do not continue the communication but rather cause it to break down.

To consider language without communication is to assume that language occurs in a vacuum. It is to remove the very raison d'être for language in the first place.

LANGUAGE IS A RULE-GOVERNED SYSTEM

The relationship between meaning and the symbols employed is an arbitrary one, but the arrangement of the symbols in relation to one another is nonarbitrary. This nonarbitrary organizational feature of language demonstrates the presence of underlying rules or patterns that occur repeatedly. These shared rule systems allow users of a language to create and comprehend messages.

Language includes not only the rules but also the process of rule usage and the resulting product. For example, a sentence is made up of a noun plus a verb, but that rule tells us nothing about the process by which you select the noun and verb or the seemingly infinite number of possible combinations using these two categories.

A language user's underlying knowledge about the system of rules is called his or her **linguistic competence**. Even though the user can't state many of the rules, performance demonstrates adherence to them. The linguist observes human behavior in an attempt to determine these rules or operating principles.

If you have ever listened to an excited speaker or a heated argument, you know that speakers do not always observe the linguistic rules. In fact, much of what we, as mature speakers, say is ungrammatical. Imagine that you have just returned from the New Year's celebration at Times Square. You might say the following:

> Oh, wow, you should have . . . you wouldn't be-believe all the . . . never seen so many people. We were almost . . . ah, trampled. And when the ball came down . . . fell, all the . . . Talk about yelling . . . so much noise. We made a, the mistake of . . . can you imagine anything as dumb as . . . well, it was crazy to drive.

It's ungrammatical but still understandable. So is much of what we say.

Linguistic knowledge in actual usage is called **linguistic performance**. A user's linguistic competence must be deduced from his or her linguistic performance, such as that of our New Year's reveler. You cannot measure linguistic competence directly.

There are many reasons for the discrepancy between competence and performance in normal language users. Some constraints are long-term, such as ethnic background, socioeconomic status, and region of the country. These account for dialects and regionalisms. We are all speakers of some dialectal variation, but most of us are still competent in the standard or ideal dialect. Dialectal speakers do not have a language disorder, just a different way of saying things.

Even though much that is said is ungrammatical, native speakers have relatively little difficulty decoding messages. If a native speaker knows the words being used, he or she can apply the rules in order to understand almost any sentence encountered. In actual communication, comprehension is influenced by the intent of the speaker, the context, the available shared meanings, and the linguistic complexity of the utterance.

A sentence such as "Chairs sourly young up swam" is ungrammatical. It violates the rules for word order. Native speakers notice that the words do not fall into predictable patterns. When rearranged, the sentence reads "Young chairs swam sourly up." This is now grammatical in terms of word order but meaningless; it doesn't make sense. Other rules allow language users to separate sense from nonsense and to determine the underlying meaning. Although "Dog bites man" and "Man bites dog" are very similar in that each uses the same words, the meanings of the two sentences are very different. Only one will make a newspaper headline. Likewise, a single sentence may have two meanings. For example, the sentence "The shooting of the hunters was terrible" can be taken two ways: either they shot poorly or someone shot them. Language users must know several sets of rules to make sense of what they hear or read.

Learning the Rules

Children learn language rules by actually using them to encode and decode. The rules learned in school are the "finishing touches." For example, a preschool child demonstrates by using words that he or she knows what a noun is long before he or she can define the term or even name it.

On one family trip, we passed the time with a word game. My 5-year-old daughter was asked to provide a noun. Immediately, she inquired, "What's that?" In my best teacher persona, I patiently explained that a noun was a person, place, or thing. She replied, "Oh." After some prodding, she stated, "Then my word is 'thing.'" Despite her inadequate understanding of the formal definition of a noun, my daughter had demonstrated for years in her everyday use that she knew how to use nouns.

LANGUAGE IS GENERATIVE

Language is a generative system. The word *generative* has the same root as *generate*, which means to produce, create (as in the word *Genesis*), or bring into existence. Thus, language is a productive or creative tool. A knowledge of the rules permits speakers to generate meaningful utterances. From a finite number of words and word categories, such as nouns, and a finite set of rules, speakers can create an almost infinite number of sentences. This creativity occurs for several reasons:

- Words can refer to more than one entity.
- Entities can be called more than one name.
- Words can be combined in a variety of ways.

Think of all the possible sentences you could create by combining just the nouns and verbs you know. When this task is completed, you could modify each sentence by adding adverbs and adjectives, articles and prepositions, and by combining sentences or rearranging words to create other variations.

The possibilities for creating new sentences are virtually endless. Consider the following novel sentence:

Large elephants danced gracefully beneath the street lights.

Even though you have probably never seen this utterance before, you understand its meaning because you know the linguistic rules. Try to create your own novel utterance. The process will seem difficult, and yet you form novel utterances every day and are not consciously aware of using any effort. In fact, much of what you said today was novel or new.

I don't mean to imply that sentences are never repeated. Polite social or ritualistic communication is often repetitious. How frequently have you said the following sentences?

How are you?
Thank you very much.
Can I, Mom, please?
See you soon.

These utterances aside, you create whatever sentences you desire whenever you want.

Children do not learn all possible word combinations. Instead, they learn rules that govern these combinations. As a young child, you deduced the rules by hearing others and trying out different types of sentences yourself. Knowing the linguistic rules enables you to understand and to create or *generate* an infinite variety of sentences.

OTHER PROPERTIES

Human language is also *reflexive*, meaning we can use language to reflect on language, its correctness and effectiveness, and its qualities. We referred to this aspect of language previously as *metalinguistics*. Other animals cannot reflect on their own communication. Without this ability, this book would be impossible to produce.

What are the distinctions among speech, language, and communication? And what are form content and use? In this video, Dr. Lydia Soifer answers these questions in the segments 4:51–11:06 and 14:01–23:27. http://www.youtube.com/watch?v=TzpkRZvdOCw

An additional property of language is *displacement* or the ability to communicate beyond the immediate context. As far as we know, your dog's bark is not about something that he remembers of interest from last week. You, on the other hand, can discuss tomorrow, last week, or last year, or events in the dim past of history in which you were not a participant.

Although not always obvious from inside a language, the symbols used in a language are *arbitrary*, another property of language. There is, for example, nothing in the word *cat* that would suggest the animal to which it applies. Except for some words, such as *squash* and *cuckoo* that suggest a relationship between the sound and the action or thing to which a word refers, there is no naturally obvious relationship. The relationship is arbitrary.

Components of Language

An exceedingly complex system, language can best be explained by breaking it down into its functional components (Figure 1.4). We typically divide language into three major, although not necessarily equal, components: form, content, and use. Form includes syntax, morphology, and phonology, the components that connect sounds and symbols in order. Content encompasses meaning or semantics, and use is termed pragmatics. These five components—syntax, morphology, phonology, semantics, and pragmatics—are the basic rule systems found in language.

As each of us uses language, we code ideas (*semantics*); that is, we use a symbol—a sound, a word, and so forth—to stand for an event, object, or relationship. To communicate these ideas to others, we use certain forms, which include the appropriate

- sound units and sequences (*phonology*),
- word order and relationships (*syntax*), and
- words and word beginnings (*un-*, *non-*) and endings (*-s*, *-ed*) (*morphology*).

FIGURE 1.4 Components of Language

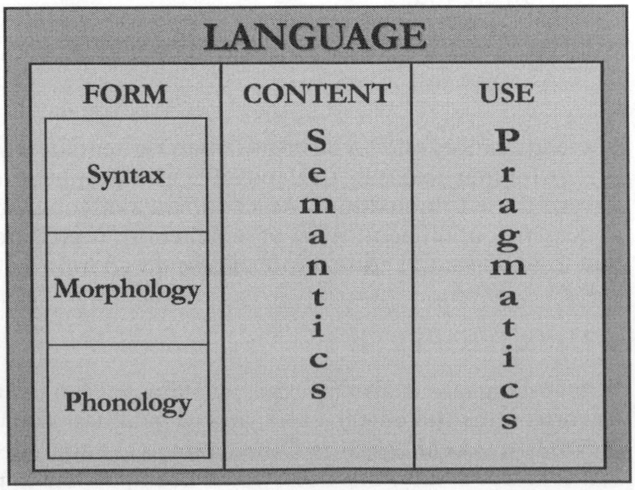

Speakers use these components to achieve certain communication ends, such as gaining information, greeting, or responding (*pragmatics*). Let's examine the five components of language in more detail.

SYNTAX

The form or structure of a sentence is governed by the rules of **syntax**. These rules specify word, phrase, and clause order; sentence organization; and the relationships among words, word classes, and other sentence elements. Syntax specifies which word combinations are acceptable, or grammatical, and which are not. For example, the syntax of English explains why "Maddi has thrown the ball" is a possible sentence, while "Maddi the ball has thrown" sounds awkward.

Sentences are organized according to their overall function; declaratives, for example, make statements, and interrogatives form questions. The main elements of a sentence are noun and verb phrases, each composed of various word classes (such as nouns, verbs, adjectives, and the like).

Each sentence must contain a *noun phrase* and a *verb phrase*. The mandatory features of noun and verb phrases are a noun and a verb, respectively. The short biblical verse "Jesus wept" is a perfectly acceptable English sentence: It contains both a noun phrase and a verb phrase. The following, however, is not a complete sentence, even though it is much longer:

> The grandiose plan for the community's economic revival based on political cooperation of the inner city and the more affluent suburban areas

This example contains no verb and thus no verb phrase; therefore, it does not qualify as a sentence.

Within noun and verb phrases, certain word classes combine in predictable patterns. For example, articles such as *a*, *an*, and *the* appear before nouns, and adverbs such as *slowly* modify verbs. Some words may function in more than one word class. For example, the word *dance* may be a noun or a verb. Yet there is no confusion between the following sentences:

> The *dance* was attended by nearly all the students.
> The children will *dance* to earn money for charity.

The linguistic context of each sentence clarifies any confusion.

Syntax can be conceptualized as a tree diagram (Figure 1.5). Each noun phrase or verb phrase included in a sentence contains various word classes. In a given phrase, word classes may be deleted or added. As long as the noun and verb remain, a sentence is possible. This hierarchical structure permits boundless elaboration within the confines of the syntactic rules. Obviously, the tree diagram in Figure 1.5 has only limited use. Flexible use of language would require hundreds, if not thousands, of other possible diagrams. Children don't memorize diagrams; rather they learn rules for ways of constructing them.

As language users, we sometimes get into difficulty when we must follow prescribed language rules. This usually occurs in writing. Spoken language is much more informal than written language and less constrained. In the 19th century, formal grammar guides were written, often prescribing rules used by the upper class. As a result, today we are saddled with the distinction in formal writing between *who* and *whom*, the incorrectness of using *since* to mean *because*, the inadmissibility of the split infinitive (*to finish quickly* is fine, but not *to quickly finish*), and the don't-end-a-sentence-with-a-preposition rule.

FIGURE 1.5 Hierarchical Sentence Structure

Within the noun and verb phrases, a number of different word classes can be arranged to form a variety of sentences. Many words could be used within each word class to form sentences such as "The young man ate his hamburger quickly" or "The mad racer drove his car recklessly."

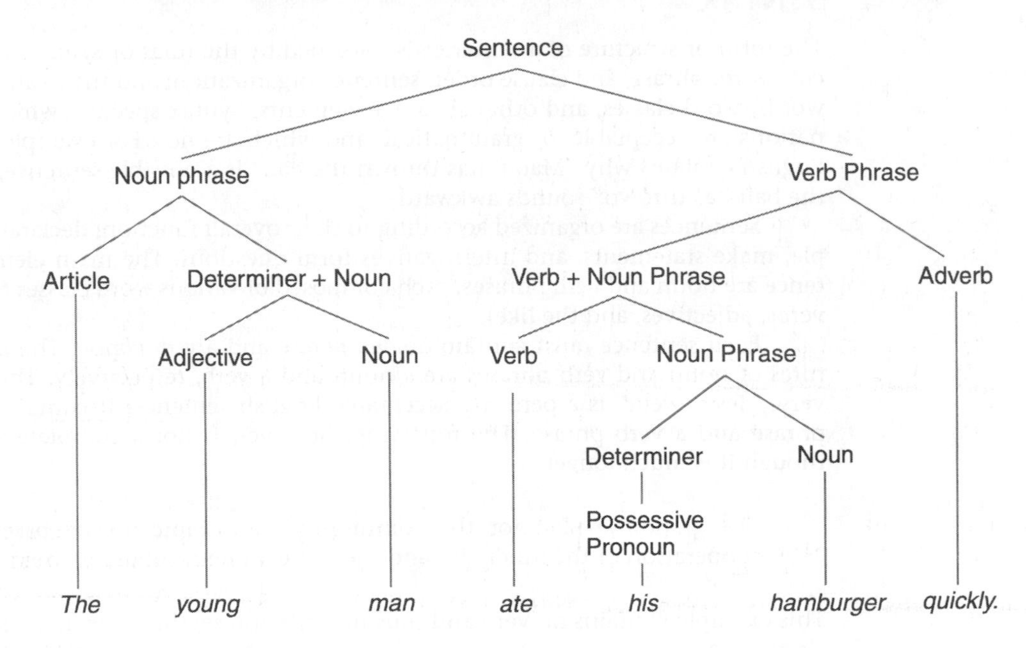

Regarding the latter, Winston Churchill quipped, "That is the type of arrant pedantry up with which I shall not put." Grammatically, he's correct, but boy, is it awkward.

Languages can be divided roughly into those with so-called free word order and those with word-order rules. The Australian aboriginal language, Warlpiri, is relatively free. The same sentence may be expressed with several different word orders. Among word-order languages, rules fall into three classes based on the order of the subject, the verb, and the object. English is an example of the basic subject-verb-object (SVO) word order (*She eats cookies*). In contrast, Dutch, Korean, and Japanese have a basic verb-final form (SOV). The third type, represented by Irish, is verb-subject-object (VSO).

MORPHOLOGY

Morphology is concerned with the internal organization of words. Words consist of one or more smaller units called *morphemes*. A **morpheme** is the smallest grammatical unit and is indivisible without violating the meaning or producing meaningless units. Therefore, *dog* is a single morpheme because *d* and *og* are meaningless alone. If we split the word into *do* and *g*, we have a similar situation because there is nothing in *dog* that includes the meaning of *do*, and *g* is meaningless alone. Most words in English consist of one or two morphemes. In contrast, Mohawk, found in northern New York and southern Quebec, constructs words of several morphemes strung together.

Morphemes are of two varieties, free and bound (Figure 1.6). **Free morphemes** are independent and can stand alone. They form words or parts of words. Examples of free morphemes are *dog*, *big*, and *happy*. **Bound morphemes** are grammatical markers that cannot function independently. They must be attached to free morphemes or to other

FIGURE 1.6 Morpheme Classes and Examples

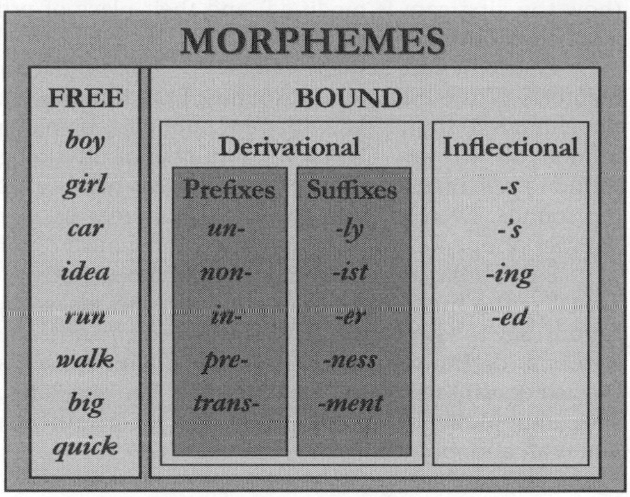

MORPHEMES

FREE: *boy*, *girl*, *car*, *idea*, *run*, *walk*, *big*, *quick*

BOUND

Derivational
- Prefixes: *un-*, *non-*, *in-*, *pre-*, *trans-*
- Suffixes: *-ly*, *-ist*, *-er*, *-ness*, *-ment*

Inflectional: *-s*, *-'s*, *-ing*, *-ed*

bound morphemes. Examples include *-s*, *-est*, *un-*, and *-ly*, meaning plural, most, negative, and manner, respectively. By combining these free and bound morphemes, we can create *dogs*, *biggest*, and *unhappily*. Bound morphemes are attached to nouns, verbs, and adjectives. Furthermore, bound morphemes can be either *derivational or inflectional* in nature.

English derivational morphemes include both prefixes and suffixes. Prefixes precede the free morpheme and suffixes follow. Derivational morphemes change whole classes of words. For example, the suffix *-ly* may be added to an adjective to create an adverb, and *-ness* may be added to an adjective to create a noun: *mad, madly, madness*.

Inflectional morphemes are suffixes only. They change the state or increase the precision of the free morpheme. In English, inflectional morphemes include tense markers (such as *-ed*); plural markers; possessive markers (*-'s* , *-s'*); and the third person, singular present-tense verb ending *-s* as in "she walks."

Languages differ in their relative dependence on syntax and morphology. In English, word order is used more than morphological additions to convey much of the meaning of a sentence. Hungarian, in contrast, has an extensive morphological system and considerable word-order variability. Sentences can be expressed in almost every possible order. Chinese has no inflectional markings of any kind and still permits considerable word order variation. Listeners must rely on probability, context, intonation, and common sense.

PHONOLOGY

Phonology is the aspect of language concerned with the rules governing the structure, distribution, and sequencing of speech sounds and the shape of syllables. Each language employs a variety of speech sounds or phonemes.

A phoneme is the smallest linguistic unit of sound that can signal a difference in meaning. There is an obvious difference in the initial sounds in *pea* and *see* because each begins with a different phoneme. When transcribing phonemes we place them within slashes, such as /p/. This practice follows the International Phonetic Alphabet. The /d/ and /l/ phonemes are different enough to be considered as distinct phonemes. Each can signal a different meaning if applied to other sounds. For example, the meanings of *dog* and *log* are quite different, as are those of *dock* and *lock* and *pad* and *pal*. Phonemes are classified by their acoustic or sound properties, as well as by the way they are produced (how the airstream is modified) and their place of production (where along the vocal tract the modification occurs).

Phonemes are actually families of very similar sounds. Allophones are individual members of these families of sounds. Each allophone differs slightly from another but not enough to sound like a different phoneme. If you repeat the /p/ sound 10 times, each production will vary slightly for a number of physiological reasons. In addition, the /p/ sound in *pea* differs from that in *poor* or *soup* because each is influenced by the surrounding sounds. Even so, each /p/ sound is similar enough so as not to be confused with another phoneme. Thus, as mentioned previously, /p/ is a distinct English phoneme.

English has approximately 43 phonemes, give or take a few for dialectal variations. Actually, the human speech mechanism can make approximately 600 possible speech sounds. Say the word *butter* at normal speed and note the middle "tt" sound. It's not really a /t/ or a /d/, but somewhere in between, with elements of both. Except in rapid speech, English doesn't recognize this difference. The Thai language does and treats this sound as a separate phoneme. In English, it's just a convenient way to pronounce words quickly and is an allophone of /t/.

Phonological Rules

Phonological rules govern the distribution and sequencing of phonemes within a language. Without the phonological rules, the distribution and sequencing of phonemes would be random and most likely meaningless. The organization of phonemes is not the same as speech, which is the actual mechanical act of producing the sounds.

Distributional rules describe which phonemes can be employed in various positions in words. For example, in English the *ng* sound, which is found in *ring* and considered to be a single phoneme(/ŋ/), never appears at the beginning of an English word. In contrast, sequencing rules determine which sounds may appear in combination. The sequence /dn/, for example, may not appear back to back in the same syllable in English.

Sequencing rules also address the sound modifications made when two phonemes appear next to each other. For example, the *-ed* in *jogged*, pronounced as /d/, is different from the *-ed* in *walked*, which is pronounced as /t/. On other occasions, the distributional and sequencing rules both apply. The combination /nd/, for example, may not begin a word but may appear elsewhere, as in *hand*. The word *stew* is perfectly acceptable in English. *Snew* is not an English word but would be acceptable; *sdew*, however, could never be acceptable because in English words cannot begin with *sd*.

SEMANTICS

Semantics is a system of rules governing the meaning or content of words and word combinations. Some units are mutually exclusive, such as *man* and *woman*; a human being is not usually classified as both. Other units overlap somewhat, such as *female*, *woman*, and *gal*. Not all females are women; some are girls. Many women would find it offensive to be called "gal."

It is useful at this point to make a distinction between *world knowledge* and *word knowledge*. **World knowledge** refers to an individual's autobiographical and experiential understanding and memory of particular events. In contrast, **word knowledge** contains word and symbol definitions and is primarily verbal. Word knowledge forms each person's mental dictionary or thesaurus called a *lexicon*.

The two types of knowledge are related. Word knowledge is usually based, in part, on world knowledge. World knowledge is a generalized concept formed from several particular events. In part, your concept of *dog* has been formed from several encounters with different types of dogs.

With more life experience, our knowledge becomes less dependent on particular events. The resultant generalized concepts form the base for semantic or word knowledge. Events become somewhat generalized, or separated from the original context. Thus, the general word *dog* does not refer to any particular type.

As we mature further, concepts in world knowledge may be formed without firsthand experience. For example, very few of us have experienced a tornado firsthand but we know what the word means. Mature language meanings reflect individual knowledge and the cultural interpretation placed on this knowledge.

As we converse with other users of the same language, we sharpen our concepts and shape them to resemble more closely similar concepts in others. In this way, we come to share definitions with others, thus making clear, concise, comprehensible communication possible.

Concept development results in increased validity, status, and accessibility. *Validity* is the amount of agreement between a language user's concept and the shared concept of the language community. *Status* refers to alternative referents: For example, *canine* can be substituted easily for the concept *dog*, and *dog* can be used to refer to the dry, hot, dog days of summer; to a dog-eared book; or to being dog-tired. *Accessibility* relates to the ease of retrieval from memory and use of the concept. In general, the more you know about a word and the more you use it, the easier it is to access.

Each word meaning contains two elements—semantic features and selection restrictions—drawn from the core concept. **Semantic features** are aspects of the meaning that characterize the word. For example, the semantic features of *mother* include parent and female. One of these features is shared with *father*, the other with *woman*, but neither word contains both features. **Selection restrictions** are based on these specific features and prohibit certain word combinations because they are meaningless or redundant. For example, *male mother* is meaningless because one word has the feature male and the other the feature female; *female mother* is redundant because biological mothers are female, at least for the foreseeable future.

In addition to an objective denotative meaning, there is a connotative meaning containing subjective features or feelings. Thus, whereas the semantic knowledge of the features of *dog* may be similar, I may have encountered several large, vicious examples that you have not and may therefore be more fearful of dogs than you. In this way, our meanings differ slightly. Throughout life, language users acquire new features, delete old features, and reorganize the remainder to sharpen word meanings.

Word Relationships

Word meanings are only a portion of semantics and are not as important as the relationships between symbols. One important relationship is that of common or shared features. The more features two words share, the more alike they are. Words with almost identical features are called **synonyms**. Some examples are *abuse* and *misuse*, *dark* and *dim*, *heat* and *warmth*, and *talk* and *speak*.

Antonyms are words that differ only in the opposite value of a single important feature. Examples include *up* and *down*, *big* and *little*, and *black* and *white*. *Big* and *little* both describe size but are opposite extremes.

Knowledge of semantic features provides a language user with a rich vocabulary of alternative words and meanings. To some extent, this knowledge is more important than the overall number of words in a language user's vocabulary. Because words may have alternative meanings, users must rely on additional cues for interpretation of messages.

Sentence meanings are more important than individual word meanings because sentences represent a meaning greater than the sum of the individual words. A sentence represents not only the words that form that sentence but also the relationships among those words. Mature language users generally recall the overall sentence meaning better than the sentence's specific form.

PRAGMATICS

When we use language to affect others or to relay information, we make use of pragmatics. **Pragmatics** concentrates on language as a communication tool that is used to achieve social ends. In other words, pragmatics is concerned with the way language is used to communicate rather than with the way language is structured.

When we go beyond individual isolated sentences to look at how a set of utterances is used to convey a message, we are in the realm of something called **discourse** (Ska, Duong, & Joanette, 2004; Ulatowska & Olness, 2004). Think of discourse as a language activity, such as having a conversation or telling a narrative. That's pragmatics too.

Pragmatics consists of the following:

- Communication intentions and recognized ways of carrying them out
- Conversational principles or rules
- Types of discourse, such as narratives and jokes, and their construction

More than in the other components of language, successful pragmatics requires understanding of the culture and of individuals.

In order to be valid, speech must do three things:

1. Involve the appropriate persons and circumstances.
2. Be complete and correctly executed by all participants.
3. Contain the appropriate intentions of all participants.

"May I have a donut, please" is valid only when speaking to a person who can actually get you one and in a place where donuts are found.

Sometimes the very act of saying something makes it so:

I *apologize* for my behavior.
I *christen* this ship the U.S.S. *Schneider*.
I now *pronounce* you husband and wife.

Again, certain conditions must be met before each is valid. When someone apologizes but is overjoyed by another's discomfort or when a child or nondesignated adult pronounces a couple husband and wife, the act is invalidated.

Not all speech performs an act. For example, saying "John should apologize for his behavior" doesn't make the apology. In this case, it is an expression of opinion.

Pragmatic Rules

Pragmatic rules govern a number of conversational interactions: sequential organization and coherence of conversations, repair of errors, role, and intentions. Organization and coherence of conversations include taking turns; opening, maintaining, and closing a conversation; establishing and maintaining a topic; and making relevant contributions to the conversation.

Repair includes giving and receiving feedback and correcting conversational errors. The listener attempts to keep the speaker informed of the status of the communication. If the listener doesn't understand or is confused, he or she might assume a quizzical expression or say, "Huh?"

Role skills include establishing and maintaining a role and switching linguistic codes for each role. In some conversations you are dominant, as with a small child, and in others you are not, as with your parents, and you adjust your language accordingly.

Roles in a conversation influence the choice of vocabulary and language form. For example, you might be very formal in your role as student presenter at a professional conference but very informal in the role of copresenter with the other students when you celebrate your success later. In another example, your role as grandchild requires different language features than your role as a young parent, lover, or roommate.

Intentions are what a speaker hopes to accomplish by speaking. When I say, "How do you spell 'conqueror'?" my goal is to acquire information. When you respond, "Look it up online," your intention is to deflect having to answer because you don't know either. Speakers have a wide variety of intentions or ways to use their language.

Conversation is governed by the "cooperation principle" (Grice, 1975): Conversational participants cooperate with each other. The four maxims of the cooperation principle relate to quantity, quality, relation, and manner. Quantity is the informativeness of each participant's contribution: No participant should provide too little or too much information. In addition, the quality of each contribution should be governed by truthfulness and based on sufficient evidence. The maxim of relation states that a contribution should be relevant to the topic of conversation. Finally, each participant should be reasonably direct in manner and avoid vagueness, ambiguity, and wordiness.

Three general categories of pragmatic rules concern

1. Selection of the appropriate linguistic form
2. Use of language forms consistent with assumed rules
3. Use of ritualized forms

Selection of form between "Gimme a cookie" and "May I have one, please" is influenced by contextual variables and the speaker's intention. One choice may work with a school friend, whereas the other works best with the teacher. Listener characteristics that influence speaker behaviors are gender, age, race, style, dialect, social status, and role.

Speech may be *direct* or *indirect* as reflected in the syntactic form. "Answer the phone" is a direct order or request to perform that act. In contrast, an indirect syntactic form such as "Could you answer the phone?" is a more polite way of requesting. As a mature language user, you know that the expected outcome is for you to answer the phone, not to answer the question with a "yes."

Speech may also be *literal, nonliteral*, or both. In literal speech, the speaker means what she or he says. After a 10-mile hike, you might exclaim, "My feet really hurt," and no doubt they do. In contrast, nonliteral speech does not mean what the speaker has said. Upon discovering that transportation home has not arrived, the same tired hiker might state sarcastically, "Just what I need, more walking." Both literal and nonliteral meanings might be heard in the comment of a mother as she enters her child's messy room: "Mommy really likes it when kids pick up their room." She does like it, but she's also being sarcastic.

The wheels of social interaction are greased by ritualized sequences, such as "Hi, how are you?" and "Wha's up?" These predictable forms ease social interactions and individual participation. We can all recall an occasion when we felt close to death and yet responded, "I'm fine! How are you?"—a response that has become ritualized in casual greetings.

RELATIONSHIP OF LANGUAGE COMPONENTS

The language components we just discussed may be artificial, merely an analytical device for linguists to use in discussing language. For example, some linguists emphasize the intimate relationship between semantics and syntax rather than the structural

FIGURE 1.7 **Model of Language**

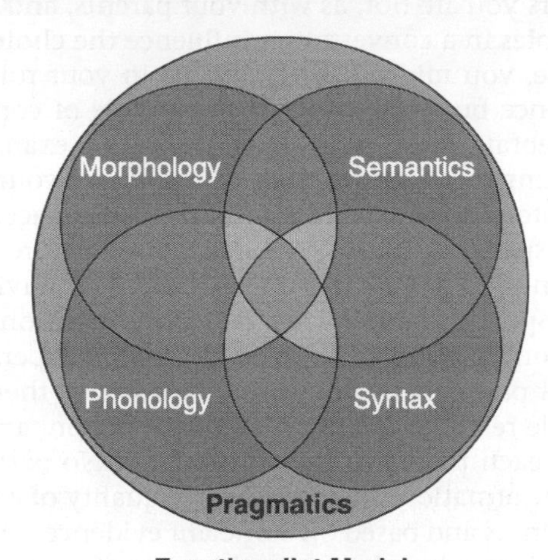

Functionalist Model

Pragmatics is the overall organizing aspect of language.

independence of each. These linguists, called *emergentists*, stress the similarity and causal relationship between meanings and syntax, suggesting that grammar grows out of semantics.

That said, the components of language do provide a convenient framework for us to discuss language development. It may be helpful to think of the relationship between language components as presented in Figure 1.7, in which pragmatics is the organizing principle of language. In other words, language is heavily influenced by context. Context, both situational and linguistic, determines the language user's communication options.

BananaStock/Thinkstock/Getty Images

Bilingual children who learn both home languages simultaneously are able to become proficient in both languages by preschool age but then may shift dominance, sometimes losing the ability to be bilingual by the teen or adult years.

Languages are not monolithic and static. They change and grow and consist of dialects. In this video, explore the relationship between languages and dialects. http://www.youtube.com/watch?v=J0phq7litTc

We might also add that a need to communicate exists prior to the selection of content and form. It is only when the child desires a cookie and is in an appropriate context to receive one that he or she employs the rules of syntax, morphology, phonology, and semantics in order to form the request "Can I have a cookie, please?"

Obviously, all the components of language are linked in some way. For example, the syntactic structure ("Yesterday I . . .") may require the morphological marker for past tense (*-ed*), which, in turn, changes phonetically (/t/) to accommodate the affected word (*walk*). In development, components may also influence one another in that changes in one may modify development in another.

Dialects

The United States is becoming an increasingly pluralistic society in which cultural and ethno-racial groups contribute to the whole but retain their essential character. One characteristic of these groups may be linguistic and/or dialectal. Most groups continue to embrace their culture and, when non-English, their language.

A CHANGING DEMOGRAPHIC

It is conservatively projected that the population of people of color will increase in the United States to 63 million by 2030. At the same time, the white, non-Latino population will increase at a slower rate and will thus become a smaller segment of the entire U.S. population. If current trends continue, white non-Latinos will be the largest *minority* by the year 2050.

At present, in the United States approximately one in four Americans identifies as other than white non-Hispanic. In the states of California, New Mexico, Hawaii, and Texas and in a score of cities and several counties, people of color represent more than 50% of the population. This situation reflects traditional demographics and a population shift that is the result of recent immigration, internal migration, and natural increase.

Within the last twenty years, 80% of the legal immigrants to the United States have come from Asia and Latin America. Approximately 40% of all recent legal immigrants are Asian. As a result, there are over 12.5 million Asians and Asian Americans residing in the United States. Although this number represents only about 4% of the total U.S. population, it does not indicate the impact of Asians and Asian Americans on the country. Asians and Asian Americans tend to settle in coastal states, especially in the West, where they form large segments of the population. In addition, Asians and Asian Americans represent the fastest-growing segment of the U.S. population. Approximately three fourths of the legal Asian immigrants come from the five countries of Vietnam, the Philippines, Korea, China, and India. These individuals speak several languages and dialects of those languages.

There are approximately 52 million Latinos in the United States. These include recent immigrants as well as U.S. citizens with Spanish surnames who identify with Latino culture to a lesser degree. Approximately 40% of all recent legal immigrants are Latino. These immigrants come primarily from Mexico and Central America, Cuba, and South America and speak various dialects of Spanish. Many U.S. citizens from Puerto Rico also move to the United States. Most of the recent increase in the numbers of Latinos is due to increased births not immigration.

In addition, there are approximately 80,000 legal black immigrants per year from the Caribbean, South and Central America, and Africa. This group represents slightly less than 1% of the U.S. population. This minority represents a number of languages, as is evident from the many geographic areas of origin.

The exact number of illegal immigrants is unknown. Estimates range from 5 to 15 million.

The largest internal migration is and has been that of African Americans who number 35 million, or 12% of the U.S. population. Reversing the trend of the early to mid-twentieth century, African Americans began returning to the South in the early 1970s. Many of these individuals speak regional and/or ethno-racial dialects, such as African American English.

To a smaller extent, Native Americans, totaling 2 million or 0.7% of the U.S. population, have also experienced internal migration. At present, just over 20% of Native Americans live in reservations and Off-Reservation Trust Lands, compared to 90% in 1940. Their speech may reflect their native language or the specific dialect of American English they learned.

Currently, the 1.2 million Native Americans who are affiliated with some native community are divided among approximately 450 nations varying in size from the Cherokee Nation of over 300,000 to groups of just a few individuals. In addition to representing a variety of cultures, Native Americans speak over 200 different languages. Some 78% of Native Americans live in urban areas, leading those in the majority culture to perceive them as of little consequence.

Birthrates differ across groups and also contribute to the changing demographics of the U.S. population. The majority white birthrate is 1.4, inadequate to maintain the relative proportion of whites in the United States. Birthrates for other populations are higher, for example, 1.7 for African Americans, 2.4 for Hispanic Americans, and 1.7 for Asian Americans (National Center for Health Statistics, 2004).

A language is especially changeable "around the edges," where its speakers interact with speakers of other languages. For example, in many bilingual communities, speakers develop new varieties of communication incorporating both languages, and these varieties function as the basic vernacular, or everyday speech, of the community.

DIALECTAL DIFFERENCES

A child born and raised in Boston will not sound like a child from Charleston, South Carolina. In turn, a poor child and a wealthy preparatory school child from Charleston will not speak in the same way. These differences are called *dialectal differences*. In general, the language of these children and their families reflects the environmental influences of the language spoken around them. No child learns dialect-free English.

We cannot adequately discuss American English without considering dialectal variations, such as African American English and what we shall call Latino English and Asian English, and their effect on the learning of American English and on the learner. To some extent languages are theoretical entities. The view of a monolithic, unchanging, immutable language does not fit reality. As mentioned, languages are fluid and changing.

Not all speakers of a language use the same language rules. Variations that characterize the language of a particular group are collectively called a dialect. Each of us is a dialectal speaker. A dialect is a language-rule system used by an identifiable group of people that varies in some way from an ideal language standard. Dialects usually differ in the frequency of use of certain structures rather than in the presence or absence of these structures. The ideal standard is rarely used except in formal writing, and the concept of a standard spoken language is practically a myth. Because each dialect shares a common set of grammatical rules with the standard language, dialects of a language are theoretically mutually intelligible to all speakers of that language.

No dialect is better than any other, nor should a dialect be considered a deviant or inferior form of a language. To devalue a dialect or to presume that one dialect is better ultimately devalues individuals and cultures. Each dialect is a system of rules that should be viewed within its social context. A dialect is adequate to meet the demands of the speech community in which it is found. Thus, it's appropriate for its users. Like languages, dialects evolve over time to meet the needs of the communities in which they are used.

Despite the validity of all dialects, society places relative values on each one. The standard, mainstream, or a majority dialect becomes the "official" criterion. Mainstream speakers of the language determine what is acceptable, often assuming that their own dialect is the most appropriate. In a stratified society, such as that of the United States, some dialects are accorded higher status than others. But, in fact, the relative value of a dialect is not intrinsic; it represents only the listener's bias. Dialects are merely differences within a language.

The two ways of classifying dialects—the **deficit approach** and the **sociolinguistic approach**—are illustrated in Figure 1.8. In the diagram, dialects that are closer to the standard in the frequency of rule use are separated by less distance. Under the deficit approach, each dialect has a different relative status. Those closer to the idealized standard are considered to be better. Status is determined relative to the standard. The sociolinguistic approach views each dialect as an equally valid rule system. Each dialect is related to the others and to the ideal standard. No value is placed on a dialect. Dialectal variations that might be considered to represent Nonmainstream American English (NMAE) include Southern American English, Creole English, Latino English, and African American English. Designation as NMAE represents degree of difference, not qualitative judgments of better or worse.

RELATED FACTORS

Several factors are related to dialectal differences. These include geography, socioeconomic status, race and ethnicity, situation or context, peer-group influences, and first- or second-language learning. The United States was established by settlers who spoke many different languages and several dialects of British English. Members of various ethnic groups chose to settle in specific geographic areas. Other individuals remained isolated by choice, by force, or by natural boundaries. In an age of less mobility, before there were national media, American English was free to evolve in several separate ways.

A New York City dialect is very different from an Ozark dialect, yet both are close enough to Standard American English (SAE) to be identified as variants of SAE. As children mature, they learn the dialect of their home region. Each region has words and grammatical structures that differ slightly. What are *sack* and *pop* to the Midwestern American are *bag* and *soda* to the Middle Atlantic speaker. The Italian sandwich changes to *submarine, torpedo, hero, wedge, hoagie,* and *po'boy* as it moves about the United States. Within each region there is no confusion. Order a *milkshake* in Massachusetts and that's

FIGURE 1.8 **The Relationship of the Idealized Standard Language and Its Dialects**

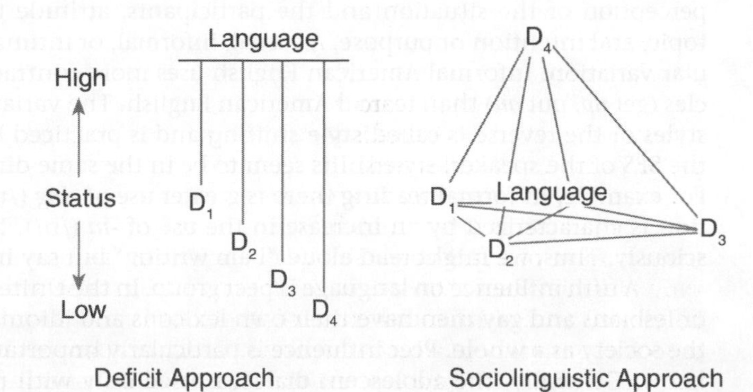

what you get—flavored milk that's been shaken. If you want ice cream in it, you need to ask for a *frappe*.

Some regions of the United States seem to be more prone to word invention or to novel use than others. In the southern Appalachian region, for example, you might encounter the following:

> A man might raise enough corn to *bread* his family over the winter.
> To do something without considering the consequences is to do it *unthoughtedly*.
> Something totally destroyed would be torn to *flinderation*.
> Long-lasting things are *lasty*.

Note that the form of each word follows generally accepted morphological marking rules, such as the *-ly* in *unthoughtedly*.

As a child, my daughter was given a vivid example of regional dialectal differences while conversing with a child from the southern United States. Although she was white, the child's older half brother was the product of a racially mixed marriage. Trying to figure out this situation, my daughter ventured the opinion, "Your brother is really *tan*." She was corrected quickly with, "No he ain't; he's *eleven*."

A second factor in dialectal differences is socioeconomic status (SES). This factor relates to social class, educational and occupational level, home environment, and family interactional styles, including maternal teaching and child-rearing patterns. In general, people from lower-SES groups use more restricted linguistic systems. Their word definitions often relate to one particular aspect of the underlying concept. Those with higher SES generally have more education and are more mobile, which generally contribute to the use of a dialect closer to the mainstream. For example, among African American children, boys from lower-income homes are more likely than middle-class African American boys or girls to use features of a dialect called African American English (AAE; Washington & Craig, 1998). Many lower-SES English speakers change the final "ing" /ŋ/ to /n/, producing *workin'* for *working*.

Racial and ethnic differences are a third factor that contributes to dialect development. By choice or as a result of de facto segregation, racial and ethnic minorities can become isolated, and a particular dialectal variation may evolve. It has been argued that the distinctive Brooklyn dialect reflects the strong influence of Irish on American English. Yiddish influences have also affected the New York City dialect. The largest racial group in the United States with a characteristic dialect is African American. African American English is spoken by lower-SES African Americans, primarily in large industrial areas and in the rural South. Not all African Americans speak African American English.

Fourth, dialect is influenced by situational and contextual factors. All speakers alter their language in response to situational variables. These situationally influenced language variations are called **registers**. The selection of a register depends on the speaker's perception of the situation and the participants, attitude toward or knowledge of the topic, and intention or purpose. A casual, informal, or intimate register is called a **vernacular** variation. Informal American English uses more contractions (*isn't, can't*) and particles (get *up*, put *on*) than formal American English. The variation from formal to informal styles or the reverse is called **style shifting** and is practiced by all speakers. Regardless of the SES of the speaker, style shifts seem to be in the same direction for similar situations. For example, in formal reading there is greater use of *-ing* (/ŋ/), while informal conversation is characterized by an increase in the use of *-in* (/n/). Most shifts are made unconsciously. Thus, we might read aloud "I am writing" but say in conversation "I'm writin'."

A fifth influence on language is peer group. In the United States, groups such as teens or lesbians and gay men have their own lexicons and idioms that are not understood by the society as a whole. Peer influence is particularly important during adolescence as you know. Generally, the adolescent dialect is used only with peers. Linguists have labeled two strains of the current teen dialect as "mallspeak" and "texting." Minimalist and repetitive, the rather imprecise mallspeak is a spoken dialect that overuses words such as *like*, *y'know*, and *whatever*. In contrast, text messaging is minimalist "code" that you use on your smartphone. On chat lines and when instant messaging, communicators use a shorthand including letters for words, such as "u" for *you* and "r" for *are*; numbers for words, such as "4" for *for*; phonetic spelling, such as "sum" for *some*; and combinations, such as "sum1" for *someone* or "b4" for *before*. Whole phrases such as *by the way* may be reduced to "BTW."

Finally, a dialect may reflect the primacy of another language. Speakers with a different native language often retain vestiges of that language. They typically **code switch** from one language to the other. The speaker's age and education and the social situation influence the efficacy of code switching.

AMERICAN ENGLISH DIALECTS

Standard American English (SAE) is an idealized version of American English that occurs rarely in conversation. It is the form of American English that is used in textbooks and on network newscasts. All of us speak a dialect of English or another language. When making comparisons, it may be more appropriate to speak of Mainstream American English (MAE).

There are at least 10 regional dialects in the United States (presented in Figure 1.9): Eastern New England, New York City, Western Pennsylvania, Middle Atlantic, Appalachian, Southern, Central Midland, North Central, Southwest, and Northwest. In general, the variations are greatest on the East Coast and decrease to the West. Each geographic region has a dialect marked by distinct sound patterns, words and idioms, and syntactic and prosodic systems. Regional dialects are not monolithic. For example, within Southern American English, racial differences exist. This is further complicated by the use of Cajun/Creole American English in Louisiana (Oetting & Wimberly Garrity, 2006).

The major racial and ethnic dialects in the United States are African American English, Spanish-influenced or Latino English, and Asian English. In part, these dialects are influenced by geographic region and by socioeconomic factors. Spanish influences also differ depending on the country or area of origin. Colombian Spanish is very different from Puerto Rican Spanish. Asian English differs with the country of origin and the native language.

FIGURE 1.9 Major American Geographic Dialects

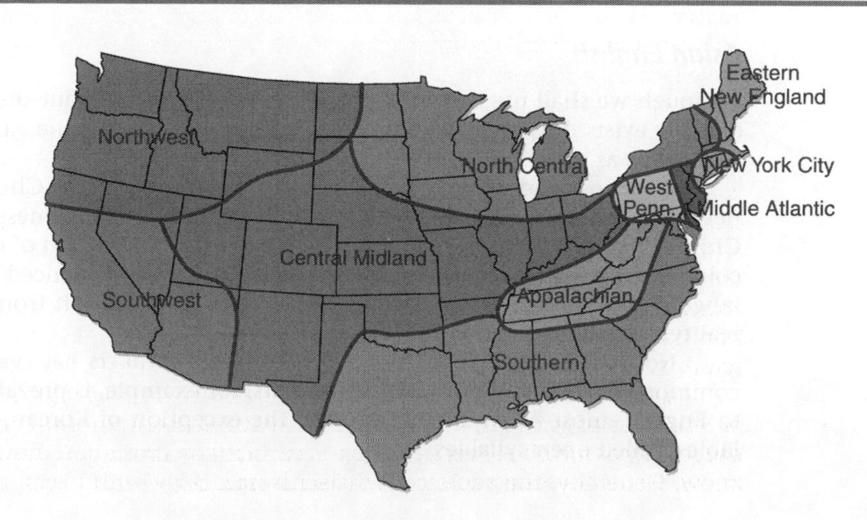

African American English

For the purposes of description, we shall consider African American English (AAE) to be the relatively uniform dialect used by African Americans in the inner cities of most large urban areas and in the rural South, when speaking casually. In short, it is the linguistic system used by lower-SES African American people within their speech community. As such, AAE shares many of the characteristics of Southern and other lower-SES dialects. Obviously, not all African Americans speak the dialect. Even among speakers of AAE, a difference exists in the amount of dialectal features used by different individuals. Conversely, white speakers who live or work with speakers of AAE may use some of its features. It is also important to remember that there are variations of AAE that its speakers use for certain situations. As with other dialects, there is a formal–informal continuum. Individual differences may be related to age, geographic location, income, occupation, and education.

AAE is a systematic language-rule system, not a deviant or improper form of English. Its linguistic variations from Mainstream American English (MAE) are not errors. The linguistic differences between AAE and MAE are minimal. Most of the grammatical rules and underlying concepts are similar. Variations are the result of AAE's different and equally complex rule system. Although it shares features with other dialects, AAE has some features—such as the use of *be* in the habitual sense, as in "She *be* working there since 1985," and the triple negative, as in "Nobody don't got none"—that are primarily characteristic of AAE. Much of the sense of this dialect can also be found in its intonational patterns, speaking rate, and distinctive lexicon.

Latino English

Within the United States, the largest ethnic population is Hispanic. Not all people with Spanish surnames speak Spanish; some do exclusively; and still others are bilingual, speaking both Spanish and English. The form of English spoken depends on the amount and type of Spanish spoken and the location within the United States. The two largest Hispanic groups in the United States are of Puerto Rican–Caribbean and Mexican–Central American origin. Although both groups speak Spanish, their Spanish dialectal differences influence their comprehension and production of American English. The dialect of American English spoken in the surrounding community also has an effect. For ease of discussion, we will refer to these dialects collectively as *Latino English* (LE).

Asian English

Although we shall use the term *Asian English* (AE) throughout this text, no such entity actually exists. It is merely a term that enables us to discuss the various dialects of Asian Americans as a group.

The most widely used languages in Asia are Mandarin Chinese, Cantonese Chinese, Filipino, Japanese, Khmer, Korean, Laotian, and Vietnamese. Of these, Mandarin Chinese has had the most pervasive influence on the evolution of the others. Indian and colonial European cultures, as well as others, have also influenced these languages. Each language has various dialects and features that distinguish it from the others. Thus, in reality there is no Asian English as a cohesive unit.

Nonetheless, the English of Asian language speakers has certain characteristics in common. The omission of final consonants, for example, is prevalent in AE. In contrast to English, most Asian languages, with the exception of Korean, have vowel-final syllables, called open syllables.

Conclusion

LANGUAGE IS A SOCIAL TOOL consisting of a very complex system of symbols and rules for using those symbols. Native speakers of a language must be knowledgeable about the symbols employed and the acceptable usage rules, including concept, word, morpheme, and phoneme combinations.

Humans may be the only animals with a productive communication system that gives them the ability to represent reality symbolically without dependence on immediate contextual support. Although animals clearly communicate at some level, this communication is limited in topic and scope and usually is dependent on the context. For example, bees have an elaborate system of movements for conveying information, but it is extremely iconic (it looks like what it conveys) and unitopical (the topic is always where to find nectar).Whether higher mammals, such as chimpanzees and other primates, are capable of complex symbolic communication will be discussed in the next chapter. In any case, it is only after intensive, long-term training that these animals learn what the human infant acquires in a few short months with little or no training.

Dialectal differences can pose special problems for a language-learning child, especially when the child enters school. Yet children who speak with significantly different dialects of American English seem to understand MAE. These young children, if motivated, follow a developmental sequence and learn a second language or dialect relatively easily. They already have a language-rule system that enables them to understand other dialects and learn other languages. Although different from MAE, other dialectal systems are not deviant. The U.S. district court for eastern Michigan, in a ruling known as the *Ann Arbor decision* (Joiner, 1979), determined that AAE is a rule-governed linguistic system. Furthermore, educators must develop sensitive methods for teaching MAE to dialectal speakers so they have the same educational and employment opportunities.

Hopefully, this introductory chapter has given you an appreciation for the complexity of the topic we'll be discussing. Imagine the enormous task you faced as a newborn with the entirety of language acquisition before you. In the following chapters, I'll try to explain as clearly as I can how you did it. Along the way, you'll gain the knowledge to become an observant parent, guiding teacher, or competent speech-language pathologist.

Discussion

WELL, I DID WARN YOU! Yes, you're right; this is complicated and it can be confusing. It's good to reflect on what we've read at the end of each chapter and to ask ourselves, "So what?"

The highlights in the chapter are the distinctions among speech, language, and communication. Too many speech-language pathologists (SLPs) are still referred to as the "speech teacher" despite the fact that in school caseloads, the largest percentage of cases are now language impairments. If you told someone that you worked with language impairments, not speech, and he or she replied, "Aren't they the same thing?" how would you respond? Think about it. You have the ammunition from this chapter.

Other important aspects of this chapter include the characteristics of language. It's a social tool that's rule based, and those rules enable it to be used in a generative fashion. Language can also be characterized by its five areas: syntax, morphology, phonology, semantics, and pragmatics. Of these, pragmatics seems to be the organizing area because context determines the other four. All areas are interdependent, and changes in one area, either because of development or the dynamics of language use, will result in changes in the others.

This last item—the interdependence of the five areas of language—has important implications for development and also for intervention. When an SLP intervenes with a child or an adult with a language impairment, there may be unforeseen consequences. For example, working on writing with an adult with aphasia or language loss, often due to stroke, may have a beneficial and unintended effect on spoken language. Likewise, adding too many new words to a child's language lesson may increase phonological precision but slow the child's delivery and decrease sentence length. The effect will vary with

Hopefully, this chapter has impressed you with the importance of language and the challenge that language learning presents for children. In this video, Dr. Barbara Lust of Cornell University further explores these topics. http://www.youtube.com/watch?v=z9gATksP8xc

the amount of change, the individual child, and the type and severity of the impairment.

As we travel through this text, note the changes that occur and the overall effect on communication. Where appropriate I will characterize change based on the five areas of language.

I know, I know . . . you sound fine, but everyone else has an accent or a dialect! Not so fast. If nothing else, please take from this chapter that a standard American English really doesn't exist in your daily use of language. You speak a dialect . . . only I use the standard.

I'm having fun with you.

We all speak a dialect, especially me. The important thing to recognize is that no one dialect is better than any other. They are all rule-based variations. And they're all valid.

In the real world, however, some dialects are rewarded, while others are punished by the culture as a whole. Still, within a given community, a dialect that is punished by the larger society may be rewarded and may give status to its user. It is very difficult to separate a dialect or a language, for that matter, from its culture.

Main Points

- Speech is a motor act and a mode of communication, but not the only one.
- Language is the code used in communication. More specifically, it is a set of symbols and the rules for using them.
- Communication is the act of transferring information between two or more people. Speech and language are two of the tools used to communicate.
- Characteristics of language. Language is
  - A social tool
  - Rule governed
  - Generative
- Language has five parameters: syntax, morphology, phonology, semantics, and pragmatics.
- Pragmatics is considered by some sociolinguists to be the organizing principle of language that determines the other four aspects when communicating.
- We all speak a dialect of the language ideal.
  - A dialect is a language-rule system spoken by an identifiable group of people that varies from the ideal language standard.
  - The deficit approach to dialects assigns status based on the amount of variation from the standard. In contrast, the sociolinguistic approach recognizes all dialects as valid and related forms of a language with no relative status assigned.
  - Factors related to dialectal differences are geography, socioeconomic level, race and ethnicity, situation or context, peer-group influences, and first- or second-language learning. Examples include African American English, Latino English, and "Asian English."
  - Dialectal considerations affect education, employment, and perceived status.

Reflections

1. Differentiate between the terms speech, language, and communication.
2. Define paralinguistic, nonlinguistic, and metalinguistic aspects of communication and explain their functions.
3. What is the relation between linguistic competence and linguistic performance?
4. Language is reflexive, arbitrary, and causes displacement. Explain these three properties of language with examples.
5. Briefly describe how dialects are a component of language.
6. What factors contribute to the development of dialects? Relate these to the dialects found in the United States.

Bill Aron/PhotoEdit, Inc.

2 Describing Language

OBJECTIVES

Models of language development help us understand the developmental process by bringing order to our descriptions of this process and providing answers to the questions *how* and *why*. Of the many linguistic theories proposed, we will examine the two main theoretical positions. Each contains a core of relevant information and reflects divergent views of language and child development.

Our knowledge of child language development is only as good as the research data that we possess. In turn, these data reflect the questions that researchers ask and the studies they design to answer these questions. When you have completed this chapter, you should understand the following:

- Relationship of Generative or Nativist theories and Constructionist theories
- Effect of the method of data collection on the resultant data
- Effects of sample size and variability on the resultant data
- Issues of naturalness and representativeness
- Collection and analysis procedures
- Value of cross-language studies
- Important terms:

child-directed speech (CDS)
Constructionist approach
Emergentism
Generative approach
Nativist approach

If you're like me, philosophical theories and arguments often result in a headache. I know it isn't very academic of me, but my mind naturally wants to describe rather than theorize. Because I look for ways to unite rather than divide, trying to defend a notion that two theories are diametrically opposed has been always difficult. And here we are in the present chapter, trying to explain the development and use of language from a theoretical point of view.

Admittedly, linguistic theories have a place. They help explain the overall processes we'll describe in this text. For researchers, theories provide an explanation and also a framework for investigating language development and use. It is through these investigations that we collect the linguistic data from which this text is created. In this chapter, I will try to explain the primary theoretical approaches to the study of language. We will then explore how language data are gathered and explored. I'll try to do all this without inducing a headache on your part or mine.

Linguistic Theory

The study of language and language development has interested inquiring persons for thousands of years. Psammetichus I, an Egyptian pharaoh of the seventh century BCE who had a difficult-to-pronounce name, supposedly conducted a child language study to determine the "natural" language of humans. Two children were raised with sheep and heard no human speech. Needless to say, they did not begin to speak Egyptian or anything else that approximated human language. Throughout history, individuals as different as Saint Augustine and Charles Darwin published narratives on language development. Several modern researchers have devoted their professional careers to the study of language development and use.

People study language development for a variety of reasons. First, interest in language development represents part of a larger concern for human development. Scholars attempt to understand how development occurs. People who specialize in early childhood education are eager to learn about this developmental process in order to facilitate child behavior change. Special educators and speech-language pathologists study child language to increase their insight into normal and other-than-normal processes.

A second reason for studying language development is that it is interesting and can help us understand our own behavior. There is a slightly mystical quality to language. As mature language users, we cannot state all the rules we use; yet, as children, we deciphered and learned these rules within a few years. Few of us can fully explain our own language development; it just seemed to happen.

Finally, language-development studies can probe the relationship between language and thought. Language development parallels cognitive development. Hopefully, the study of language development may enable language users to understand the underlying mental processes to some degree.

Because language and language development are so complex, professionals are often at odds as to which approach provides the best description.

- The linguist is primarily concerned with describing language symbols and stating the rules these symbols follow to form language structures.
- The psycholinguist is interested in the psychological processes and constructs underlying language. The psychological mechanisms that let language users produce and comprehend language are of particular concern.
- The sociolinguist studies language rules and use as a function of role, socioeconomic level, and linguistic or cultural context. Dialectal differences and social-communicative interaction are important.

As with any field of inquiry, there are major theoretical differences. In this video, Dr. Barbara Lust of Cornell University outlines the major theoretical approaches in minutes 6:35–8:52. http://www.youtube.com/watch?v=z9gATksP8xc

- The behavioral psychologist minimizes language form and emphasizes the behavioral context of language, such as how certain responses are elicited and how the number of these responses is increased or decreased.
- The speech-language pathologist concentrates on disordered communication including the causes of disorder, the evaluation of the extent of the disorder, and the remediation process.

The study of how children learn language is like many other academic pursuits in that different theories which attempt to explain the phenomenon compete for acceptance. Occasionally one theory predominates, but generally portions of each are used to explain different aspects. Part of the problem in designing an overall theory is the complexity of both language and communication behavior.

NATURE VERSUS NURTURE

If you've had an introductory course in psychology or development, you have no doubt been introduced to the nature versus nurture debate. In its simplest terms, the discussion centers on whether some aspect of development occurs because

- it is a natural and inherent part of being human, *or*
- it occurs because of nurturance and learning from the environment.

In other words, is our destiny in our genes, in some aspect of being human, or do environment and learning mediate our biological inheritance?

This debate is alive and well in linguistics (Galasso, 2003). The way in which children acquire linguistic knowledge has been the focus of intense interest and debate in cognitive science for well over half a century. There are two primary approaches, representing nature and nurture, respectively:

1. Generative, or Nativist
2. Interactionist, which is characterized chiefly by Constructionism and Emergentism

Within this chapter we'll explore these approaches, examining their overall theories, limitations, and contributions. I've tried to give you the main points of each theory and to highlight the grains of truth in each. Look for similarities and contrasts. You might find it helpful to read each theory separately and allow time for processing before going on to the next.

GENERATIVE APPROACH

In this video, Dr. Steven Pinker of Harvard University discusses the contributions of linguist Noam Chomsky at minutes 15:25–18:35. http://www.youtube.com/watch?v=Q-B_ONJIEcE

The **Generative approach**, or **Nativist approach**, assumes that children are able to acquire language because they are born with innate rules or principles related to the structures of human languages (Chomsky, 1965a, 1965b; de Villiers, 2001; Lenneberg, 1967; Wexler, 1998, 2003; Yang, 2002). Generativists assume that it is impossible for children to learn linguistic knowledge from the environment given that the input children hear is limited and full of errors and incomplete information (Chomsky, 1965a, 1965b). Even with these limitations, children are still able to acquire linguistic knowledge quickly because of the guidance of innate linguistic hypotheses. Something innate or inborn guides a child's learning. According to Chomsky, "To come to know a human language would be an extraordinary intellectual achievement for a creature not specifically designed to accomplish this task" (1975, p. 4).

Basic Theory

Beginning in the late 1950s, Noam Chomsky and others, working from the assumption that language is a universal human trait, tried to identify syntactic rules that applied to all human languages. These rules were assumed to be present in each human at birth in a location of the brain theoretically called the language acquisition device, or LAD. Nativists then attempted to describe the syntactic rules that enabled adult language users to generate a seemingly endless number of sentences in their specific language.

It seemed only natural to apply the new adult linguistic models to child language acquisition. Known by various names, the resulting models basically assumed that children used the universal language rules found in their LADs to figure out the rules of the language to which they were exposed. In 1973, Roger Brown—we'll meet him later—reviewed and evaluated these models, concluding that none of them was totally satisfactory in explaining children's development of language. The basic problem was that the early Generativist theories were adult-based and there was no evidence that children used, or even needed, the adultlike linguistic categories and rules to acquire language. Many linguists concluded after looking at languages across different cultures that no single formal grammar was adequate to account for the acquisition process in all of the world's many languages (Slobin, 1973).

Several theorists suggested that, instead of syntax, a semantic-cognitive basis existed for children's early language (Bloom, 1973; Brown, 1973; Schlesinger, 1971; Slobin, 1970). Called the Semantic Revolution, the position held that the semantic-syntactic relations apparent in children's early language correspond rather closely to some of the categories of infant and toddler sensorimotor cognition. Instead of the subjects and verbs used by adults to produce sentences, children used meaning units, such as *agents*, which caused action (*mommy, daddy*); *actions* (*eat, throw*); and *objects*, which received it (*cookie, ball*). These linguistic units that children know nonlinguistically might form the basis for a linguistic unit such as *agent-action-object* (*Mommy eat cookie; Daddy throw ball*). Other combinations included *possessor-possessed* (*Mommy sock*) and *object-location* (*Key table*). Although these rules explained some child utterances, they failed to explain others. In addition, it was difficult to explain how children moved from these semantic-based rules to the more abstract syntactic rules of adults.

As a consequence, a group of theorists began to advocate a return to adult syntactic models (Baker & McCarthy, 1981; Hornstein & Lightfoot, 1981; Pinker, 1984). These linguists argued that the discontinuity of semantic and syntactic models of language learning posed genuine problems of explanation. They argued instead for a continuity assumption in which children operated with the same basic linguistic categories and rules as adults (Pinker, 1984). At this point, these theorists had returned to a linguistic nativism, which assumed that throughout our lives, all human beings possess the same basic linguistic competence, in the form of universal grammar (Chomsky, 1980).

Language Learning

Generative grammar assumes that natural languages are like formal languages, such as mathematics. As such, natural languages are characterized by two things:

1. A unified set of abstract algebraic rules that are meaningless themselves and insensitive to the meanings of the elements (words) they combine
2. A set of meaningful linguistic elements (words) that serve as variables in the rules (Tomasello, 2006)

To learn a language, each child begins with his or her innate universal grammar to abstract the structure of that language. Think of the universal grammar as a set of mental modules largely dedicated to language.

Acquisition has two components:

1. Acquiring all the words, idioms, and constructions of that language
2. Linking the core structures of the particular language being learned to the universal grammar

In this short video, Dr. Steven Pinker of Harvard University discusses how children learn language according to the Generative, or Nativist, approach. http://www.youtube.com/watch?v=ir7arlLiqxg

Although the language a child hears contains errors, the child acquires the rules because he or she has a genetically determined capacity for acquiring language. The universal grammar contains a limited set of possibilities for how language fits together. These narrow possibilities help the child interpret the language input correctly and will later provide the model for the child's own language output (Pinker & Ullman, 2002).

Being innate, universal grammar does not develop but is the same throughout a person's life span. In other words, there is a continuity in language acquisition and use. The assumption, therefore, is that when a child says, "I'm eating a cookie," she has an adultlike understanding of the present progressive (*be + verbing*) form and can *generate* similar forms. Knowing the rules enables the child to generate novel sentences.

Theoretical Weakness

One problem for generative grammar involves fixed and semi-fixed structures that are not based on abstract grammatical categories but on particular words or fixed expressions, such as *How's it going?* A large portion of human linguistic competence involves the mastery of these routine expressions, plus idioms. Those learning English as a second language will experience difficulty with expressions in which the meanings are nonliteral, such as *He's starting to get to me* and *Hang in there*. These expressions are not part of a core grammar that can generate grammatical rules. Instead, they seem to be memorized like words.

Constructionists would see these language structures as examples that structure emerges from use. Subsequently, a language community may conventionalize or adopt these linguistic structures from their language use.

INTERACTIONALIST APPROACH

In contrast to the Generative approach is the Interactionalist approach that emphasizes the combination of biological and environmental influences. Children learn linguistic knowledge from the environmental input to which they are exposed (Christiansen & Charter, 1999; Goldberg, 2006; MacWhinney, 2004; Reali & Christiansen, 2005; Tomasello, 2005). According to this theoretical approach, children figure out the linguistic structures of the input language based on sufficient information from that language (Tomasello, 2000, 2003). Although there are variants, the two main Interactionalist approaches are Constructivism and Emergentism.

As with Nativists, Constructionists are interested in language structure, but there is less theoretical commitment to language form and to ages of acquisition. To learn language, children rely on the general cognitive mechanisms they possess (Abbot-Smith & Tomasello, 2006; Elman et al., 1996; Gomez, 2002; Tomasello, 2003). Note that this process is not accomplished by a specific language mechanism or LAD but by general brain processes. Although a child may not be born with a bias for grammatical patterns as in a universal grammar, the brain is organized and functions in a way that results in an ability to learn language associations. We are always in danger of overstatement when we simplify, but we could say that Nativists assume we have a brain designed for learning and processing language, while Interactionalists assume we can learn and use language because we have a large, complicated brain.

In this BBC video in *Language Acquisition,* we discuss the rationale for studying language acquisition. Specifically, minutes 2:17–7:03 look at the work of cognitive scientist Deb Roy of the Massachusetts Institute of Technology. http://www.youtube.com/watch?v=PZatrvNDOiE

questions asked, the specific language features studied, and the overall design of a study. Because it is difficult for any of us to explain our own learning process, researchers form hypotheses about language learning and test these hypotheses against actual child language data. There is always the possibility that research may be based on a theoretical approach that does not reflect the actual language hypotheses children employ when attempting to learn and use language. Thus, the research runs the risk of not describing a child's actual operating principles, hypotheses, or linguistic performance. For this and other reasons, child language research must be carefully designed and carried out.

There are many considerations that influence the data gathered through research. Let's briefly explore issues related to child language study, such as the method of study, the population and language sample size and variability, the naturalness and representativeness of the language sample, data collection, and data analysis. Crosslinguistic studies and data will also be discussed.

Issues in the Study of Child Language

While the notion of collecting and analyzing child language data may seem simple, in fact it is quite complex. Several decisions must be made prior to data collection. The methods and procedures used can influence the resultant data and may unintentionally color the conclusions drawn from these data.

METHOD OF DATA COLLECTION

To a great extent the method of collection is driven by the aspect of language being studied. Let's explore this briefly. Three general areas of interest might include speech perception, language comprehension, and language production.

In general, speech perception studies are interested in the speech discrimination of children, especially infants, and the ways in which these abilities may aid language learning. Recent advances in technology, especially digital recording and computers, have assisted researchers in isolating, reproducing, and combining sounds for research (Gerken & Asline, 2005; Karmiloff & Karmiloff-Smith, 2001). Infants can even be tested while still in the womb for their responses to speech sounds in isolation and in connected speech. Infant responses may consist of changing state, moving, or kicking. With older children and adults, speech perception is often assessed with more specific responses, such as pointing. One new approach is called online or real-time research in which responses are paired with brain-imaging techniques, such as magnetic resonance imaging (MRI), to identify areas of the brain where perception occurs. These techniques are also used in language comprehension and expression research.

Language comprehension studies are interested in our understanding of language. Subjects usually respond to structured procedures by looking, pointing, acting out, or following directions in response to a spoken or written stimulus. Of necessity, this type of research requires a standardized, structured experimental design to ensure that all subjects have the same input. As mentioned, these studies may also include neural imaging. For example, a researcher conducting a study of comprehension of sentences might be interested in the contributions of different types of memory that are stored in different areas of the brain.

Expressive language studies can take a number of forms. The primary difference is the degree of control the experimenter has over the context. We'll be primarily discussing expressive language studies in the following sections.

Expressive language-development data are usually collected in two ways:

1. Spontaneous conversational sampling or natural observation
2. Structured testing or experimental manipulation

Each method raises issues of appropriateness for the language feature being studied. Either one alone may be insufficient to describe a child's linguistic competence, that is, what he or she knows about language. Data yielded in one context may not appear in another. For example, in a study of pronouns in which I participated, children produced a wider variety in conversation and produced more advanced forms in more formal testing. Other researchers have also found that formal elicitation tasks, such as testing procedures, produce more advanced child language than conversational sampling. Ideally, the linguist would employ both informal and formal or structured approaches, using the structured procedures to obtain more in-depth information on the data collected by the more broad-based naturalistic or informal procedures.

Structured Collection Methods

Some researchers prefer testing or experimental manipulation in order to control for some of the variables inherent in more naturalistic collection. Within a test or experimental procedure, various linguistic elements may be elicited using verbal and nonverbal stimuli in a structured presentation. Such control of the context, however, may result in rather narrow sampling.

Formal procedures enable researchers to gather data that may not be readily available using conversational or observational techniques. For example, it is difficult to assess either children's comprehension or their metalinguistic skills without direct testing. Some hypotheses cannot be tested directly, however, so researchers must test indirectly or observe some features of language development.

Language and experimental factors must be manipulated with caution. One aspect of language can affect others, even though the researcher does not intend for this to happen. For example, among both children and adults, new information is introduced into a conversation in a consistently more phonologically accurate manner than older, shared information. Thus, pragmatics influences phonology.

Likewise, experimental factors can have unintended consequences. For example, a researcher may highlight an item in a picture in an attempt to ensure a child's accurate comment. Unfortunately, although the accuracy of the message does not seem to increase when one item is marked, the amount of redundancy or inclusion of irrelevant information does increase (Lloyd & Banham, 1997).

In addition, testing and experimental tasks do not necessarily reflect a child's performance in everyday use. For example, in an experimental task, a child may rely on different problem-solving techniques than in everyday tasks.

Results can be misread. For example, noncompliance with testing or experimental procedures doesn't necessarily mean noncomprehension or lack of knowledge. Especially with preschoolers, incorrect responding may indicate a lack of attention or interest.

The results of testing can be especially suspect unless they are analyzed thoroughly. Test scores alone tell researchers nothing about performance on individual items. Two children may have the same score and very different responses. Scoring of individual items may be limited to a wrong-or-right dichotomy, with little analysis of the types of incorrect responses and the underlying processes that these answers may reflect. Testing contexts may provide more or fewer stimuli than are found in the real world, thus modifying the difficulty of the task for the child.

Language processing is not a single unitary operation, as is often assumed in test construction, but consists of component operations, such as lexical or vocabulary access, syntactic decoding, and discourse processing, that are engaged at different times and with varying degrees depending on the linguistic task. So-called *offline test tasks*, such as fill-ins or providing a missing word, measure only the end points of several linguistic processes.

During offline testing, components of the overall process may be overlooked. For example, the process of guessing a missing word may be the reverse of what happens in conversation. Conscious guessing is too slow in conversation. Rather than context aiding in predicting the next word or phrase of the speaker, contextual information seems to provide a check that correct items have been uttered. Although such offline language collection techniques may tell us what children know, they may also tell us little about how children process or access language.

In contrast, *online tasks* attempt to measure operations at various points during processing and describe individual and integrative components (Shapiro, Swinney, & Borsky, 1998). For example, at what point in the cue "Mary has a blue dress and a red dress; she has two ———" does the child access the word *dresses*? We might be able to determine this information by the online technique of asking a child to paraphrase or answer yes/no questions after only limited information is presented. For example, if we say, "Mary has a blue dress and a red dress," a child may access *dresses* based on *and* or *red* or *dress*. Online techniques reflect an interest in discovering at which point this occurred. Techniques can be much more elaborate than this simple example suggests. Although still in their infancy, online techniques are beginning to provide valuable linguistic-processing data (Maas & Nailend, 2012).

In short, testing and experimental data may be very accurate but very limited. The results must be examined within the context of the specific tasks designed to elicit certain behaviors. A better measure is the consistency of use of a language feature across various tasks.

Sampling and Observation

Jerome Bruner, renowned child development specialist, began his career studying language in controlled situations, analyzing discrete bits of language. The model was confining, and the language data felt artificial to him. He then began studying children at home, videotaping open-ended interactions with their families. As a result, his later data had a more authentic quality to it. Naturalistic studies, such as language samples, may yield very different data than experimental manipulations (Abu-Akel, Bailey, & Thum, 2004; Wilson, 2003).

Sampling spontaneous conversation is more naturalistic and, ideally, ensures analysis of real-life behaviors. Such collection is not without its problems. For example, the data collected may be affected by several variables, such as the amount of language, the intelligibility of a child, and the effect of the context. To date, linguists have not identified all the possible variables that can affect performance or the extent of their influence. As a result, certain linguistic elements may not be exhibited even when they are present in a child's repertoire. Some linguistic elements occur infrequently, such as passive-voice sentences, and others are optional, such as the use of pronouns. Usually, a single conversational sample is inadequate to demonstrate the full range of a child's communication abilities. It is difficult to estimate a child's competence or ability based on informal behavior. In addition, information on the child's production provides only a general estimate of comprehension.

Sampling techniques exist along a continuum from unstructured, open-ended situations to more structured, restrictive ones in which the researcher attempts to control or manipulate one or more variables. For example, the researcher interested in narratives may want to elicit a particular variety, such as recounts, and directs a child to provide a story about something that happened to him or her. Pictures also might be used to elicit narratives. All such manipulations affect a child's language. For example, pretend play involving routine events facilitates communication with more topic maintenance and less miscommunication among children than in less familiar interactive situations (Short-Meyerson & Abbeduto, 1997).

Child language data may also be obtained from the CHILDES system of database transcripts. The system includes programs for computer analysis, methods of linguistic coding, and systems for linking these transcripts to digitized audio and video. A corpus of language samples is available along with studies from English and other languages. The Internet address for CHILDES is given at the end of the chapter.

Any given naturalistic situation may be insufficient for eliciting a child's systematic knowledge of language. Nor is there certainty that a given test situation will represent a child's naturally occurring communication. Thus, it is best to have data from a combination of collection procedures. In either case, the linguist is sampling the child's performance. The child's linguistic competence—what he or she knows about language—must be inferred from this performance.

SAMPLE SIZE AND VARIABILITY

The researcher must be concerned about two samples: the sample or group of children from whom data are collected and the sample of language data from each child. In both samples, the researcher must be concerned with size and variability. Too small a sample will restrict the conclusions that can be drawn about all children, and too large a sample may be unwieldy. The two samples, subjects and language, also interact, one influencing the other.

Size

The number of children or subjects should be large enough to allow for individual differences and to enable group conclusions to be drawn. The overall design of the study will influence the number of subjects considered adequate. For example, it may be appropriate to follow a few children for a period of time, called a *longitudinal study*, but inappropriate to administer a one-time-only test to the same limited number of children (McGowan, McGowan, Denny, & Nittrouer, 2013). Other considerations will also influence the number of children studied. In a longitudinal study, for example, as many as 30% of the children may be lost because of family mobility, illness, or unwillingness to continue over the length of the study, which may last several years. It might be better, in this case, to adopt an overlapping longitudinal design with two different age samples, each being observed for half the length of time that would have been needed in a longitudinal study. Unfortunately such studies have their own issues.

Wells (1985), for example, sampled 128 children for two years each, using such an overlapping longitudinal model. In contrast, Roger Brown (1973) studied three children intensively for 10 to 16 months. Wells recorded each child for analysis for 27 minutes at three-month intervals throughout the study, collecting an average of 120 utterances on each occasion. In contrast, Brown averaged two hours of sampling each month. More recently, Hart and Risley (1995) collected monthly audio samples of parents and children in their homes for two years.

Variability

The sample of children should accurately reflect the diversity of the larger population from which they were drawn. In other words, the children sampled should represent all socioeconomic, racial and ethnic, and dialectal variations found in the total population, and in the same proportions found there. Other variables that may be important include size of family, gender, birth order, presence of one or both parents in the home, presence of natural parents in the home, and amount of schooling. Some variables, such as socioeconomic status, may be difficult to determine, although parental education and employment seem to be important contributing factors. Mixed-race children may force the researcher to make decisions about racial self-identity that are not appropriate.

Research on the development of spoken language has focused largely on middle-class preschool children. In contrast, lower-class children whose mothers have less education tend to be slower and less accurate than children of comparable age and vocabulary size whose mothers have more schooling. In general, these slower rates of language learning reflect children's disadvantaged backgrounds. This trend is true for Latino preschool children learning Spanish as well as preschoolers in the United States learning English as their first language (Hurtado, Marchman, & Fernald, 2007).

Characteristics of the tester, experimenter, or conversational partner are also important. In general, preschool children will perform better with a familiar adult. There is also some indication that children of color may perform better with adults with the same identity.

Some children found in the general population may be excluded when the study attempts to determine typical development. These may include children with known handicaps; bilingual children; twins, triplets, and other multiple births; and children in institutional care or full-time nursery school. Children may also be excluded who are likely to move during the course of the study, such as children of migrant workers or military service members, or whose parents were deemed uncooperative or unreliable (Wells, 1985). With each exclusion, the "normal" group becomes more restricted and, thus, less representative.

In order to draw group conclusions, subjects must be matched in some way. Although the most common way to group children is by age, such matching of subjects in language-development studies may be inappropriate because many language differences reflect developmental changes in other areas. Therefore, reliable age-independent measures of development, such as level of cognitive development, may be a better gauge of real developmental differences and may allow more appropriate comparisons of children's language development.

Amount of Language Collected

The problem of the appropriate amount of a child's language to sample becomes especially critical with low-incidence language features, such as passive sentences. Usually at least 100 utterances are needed in order to have an adequate sample, although the sample size depends on the purpose for which it is collected. High reliability on measures such as number of different words and mean utterance and sentence length in morphemes may require at least 175 complete and intelligible utterances. Elements that occur less than once in 100 utterances may not occur within the typical sample of that length. In addition, a single occurrence is very weak evidence on which to base an assumption that a child has acquired a linguistic feature. This assumption is strengthened, however, if a large proportion of the individuals being studied exhibit this linguistic element.

As mentioned, the amount of language collected will vary with the language feature being studied. Pragmatic aspects of language, which vary with the context, may require the inclusion of several contexts to provide an adequately varied sample. Such language uses as conversational openings, which occur only once in each conversation, would require varied contexts in order to enable a researcher to reach even tentative conclusions.

Resources such as personnel, time, and money are always limited. A researcher must decide on an appropriate sample size and an adequate level of analysis. In general, the larger the sample of children and/or speech, the fewer data it is possible to analyze. Conversely, the more detailed the analysis, the fewer children or the smaller the amount of speech it is possible to sample.

NATURALNESS AND REPRESENTATIVENESS OF THE DATA

Any sample should fulfill the twin requirements of naturalness and representativeness. Even testing should attempt to use familiar situations with a child in an attempt to meet these two requirements. A conversational sample will be more natural if the participants are free to move about and are uninhibited by the process of sample collection. A representative sample should include as many of the child's everyday experiences as possible. Unfortunately, little is known about the range and frequency of children's activities. To address this issue, Wells (1985) sampled randomly throughout the day for short periods.

Each day of collection, Wells collected 24 randomly scheduled samples of 90 seconds' duration each. Samples were scheduled so that four occurred within each of six equal time periods throughout the day. Eighteen of the 24 samples, totaling 27 minutes of recording, were needed for analysis. This allowed a possible 25% of the samples to be blank as a result of having been recorded while the child was beyond the range of the microphone. Two samples from each of the six time blocks were randomly chosen for transcription. After these had been transcribed, the process continued randomly with the remaining six samples until 120 intelligible utterances had been amassed. The remaining utterances were not transcribed for analysis. This procedure was followed once every three months for two years for each child.

As you can see, it is not always easy to obtain natural and representative language data. At least three potential factors may be problems. One problem is the *observer paradox*. Stated briefly, the absence of an observer may result in uninterpretable data, but the presence of an observer may influence the language obtained, so that it lacks spontaneity and naturalness.

The presence of an observer can also affect the type of sample collected. The behavior of the child and the conversational partner may be influenced by the presence of another person. For this reason, Wells (1985) collected samples on a tape recorder, with no observer present. The recorder was programmed to begin taping at randomly assigned times throughout the day. In contrast, Brown (1973) included two observers: one to keep a written transcript of the linguistic and nonlinguistic behaviors of the parent and child and the other to tend the tape recorder and to be a playmate for the child.

The absence of an observer may also complicate the process of determining the exact context of the language sample. At the end of each recording day, parents might be asked to identify contexts by the activity and participants present, although the reliability of such recalled information is doubtful (Wells, 1985). In addition, the immediate nonlinguistic context of each utterance cannot be reconstructed from audiotape alone. Digital audio and video recording may address this concern.

A second problem is a child's physical and emotional state at the time the information is collected. Usually, a child's caregiver is asked to comment on the typicalness of the child's performance.

A third problem relates to the context in which the sample is collected. Quantitative values—such as mean or average length of utterances (MLU) or the number of utterances within a given time, or the number of root words—vary widely across different communication situations and partners (Bornstein, Painter, & Park, 2002). For example, a play situation between a mother and child elicits more language than one in which a child plays alone. Productivity, or the amount of language, may be even more affected by a child's conversational partners than by different situations (Bornstein, Haynes, Painter, & Genevro, 2000).

Occasionally, information is collected in experimental or test-type situations. The rationale for collecting this type of data is that, through manipulation of the context, a linguist can obtain language features from a child that may not be elicited in conversation. Unfortunately, the language obtained is likely to be divorced from meaningful contexts in the child's experience and thus does not represent the child's use of language to communicate with familiar conversational partners in everyday contexts. Theoretically, the most representative sample should be elicited in the home for preschoolers and in the home or classroom for older children, with a parent, sibling, or teacher as the conversational partner.

Language samples should be representative in the two ways discussed previously. First, the population sample from which the language is collected should be representative of all aspects of the total population. Second, each child's language sample should be representative of his or her typical language performance. This is best ensured if the sample is collected in a variety of typical settings in which a child is engaged in everyday activities with his or her usual conversational partners.

COLLECTION PROCEDURES

Questions relative to collection of the language sample must of necessity concern the presence or absence of a researcher and the actual recording method. Wells (1985) attempted to minimize observer influences by having the child wear a microphone that transmitted to a tape recorder preprogrammed to record at frequent but irregular intervals throughout the day. Of course, there are problems with this process, such as the compactness and sensitivity of the microphone transmitter. In contrast, Brown (1973) used two researchers in the setting, while data were recorded on a tape recorder. This concern is somewhat addressed by the compactness of modern digital recording devices.

Several collection techniques exist, such as diary accounts, checklists, and parental reports, as well as direct and digitally recorded observation. The first three are alternatives to researcher observation and have been used effectively in the study of early semantic and morphologic growth. Such methods enable researchers to collect from more children because they are less time-consuming and have been pronounced reliable and valid while remaining highly representative.

Electronic means of collection seem essential for microanalysis. Videotaping, while more intrusive, is better than recording audio alone because it enables the researcher to observe the nonlinguistic elements of the situation in addition to the linguistic elements. Although useful, collecting written transcription within the collection setting is the least desirable method for microanalysis. First, it is easy to miss short utterances. Second, it is nearly impossible to transcribe the language of both the child and the conversational partner because of the large number of utterances within a short period of time. Third, transcription within the conversational setting does not enable the researcher to return to a child's speech for missed or misinterpreted utterances.

The language sample should be transcribed from the recording as soon after it is collected as possible. Caregivers familiar with a child's language should be consulted to determine if the sample is typical of the child's performance.

Because transcription offers many opportunities for error, studies should ensure intra- and inter-transcriber reliability. This is not always easy to accomplish. Several factors contribute to transcription errors, including the type of speech sampled, the intelligibility of the child, the number of transcribers, the level of transcription comparison, and the experience of the transcriber(s). In general, factors such as (1) the more defined the speech sampled, the better the intelligibility; (2) the greater the number of transcribers, the larger the unit of comparison; and (3) the more experienced the transcriber result in a better the chance of having an accurate transcript. The type of speech sample may range from individual words to whole conversations. Larger units are more difficult to transcribe accurately. The use of more than one transcriber reduces the possibility of errors if the transcribers compare their transcriptions and resolve their differences in a consistent manner. Finally, lower levels of comparison, such as phonemes, increase the likelihood of error because of the precise nature of such units.

ANALYSIS PROCEDURES

Actual analysis may be ticklish, especially when trying to determine the bases for that analysis. For example, MLU is still the most common quantitative measure of language growth, although its value is questionable. In general, quantitative measures, such as numerical scores and MLU, are inadequate for describing language development in detail. Other quantitative values might include total number of words, number of words per clause, or clauses per sentence. Such values collapse data to a single figure. Breadth of behavior might be obtained by the number of different forms used by a child, such as number of different words and number of unique syntactic types (Hadley, 1999).

In contrast, qualitative research uses a variety of methods within natural situations or contexts to describe and interpret human communication. Given the interwoven character of communication and social interaction, it seems logical to study the two together. As a result, language is studied as a social tool used within the complex relationship of context and communication. Thus, qualitative research is holistic and emphasizes communication's synergistic nature.

By their nature, qualitative research methods change the units being studied. A single word or utterance cannot be analyzed as a separate entity but must be examined in the context of surrounding utterances, topics, or conversation or between partners.

Determining Age of Mastery

It is also difficult to determine when a child or group of children actually knows or has mastered a language feature. Criteria for establishing that a child knows a word or a feature have not been established. For example, with word knowledge, the researcher must have clear evidence that a child comprehends the word. In contrast, production criteria would probably be based on spontaneous use and consistent semantic intent. With young children, a researcher would also note consistent phonetic form and semantic intent, with decisions of knowledge not necessarily based on whether the form and meaning are related to an adult word.

Usually, mastery is based on children using a feature in 90% of the obligatory locations or based on 90% of the children using the feature consistently, but these percentages vary among individual researchers. Some researchers consider the average age for acquisition to be that point at which 50% of children use a language feature consistently. Of course, such measures are complicated by the complex nature of most language features and the extended period of time often needed for mastery. For example, forms such as correct use of *be* may take several years from first appearance to full, mature use.

An example of one real-life analysis difficulty may be illustrative. In a study of preschool pronoun development (Haas & Owens, 1985), a colleague and I were very surprised to find no errors in pronoun use in conversations among children even as young as 2. The children had adopted the rule *when in doubt, use a noun*. Thus, analysis that focused on pronouns only yielded no errors. When analysis expanded beyond pronouns, however, we found overuse of nouns.

Cross-Language Studies

Cross-language studies are usually undertaken in order to investigate universality, linguistic specificity, relative difficulty, or acquisitional principles. Studies of universality attempt to determine which aspects of language, such as nouns and verbs, appear in all languages.

Researchers also look for developmental similarities across different languages. For example, although children in countries with lower standards of living tend to have smaller comprehension or production vocabularies, there are similarities in vocabulary growth. Across children ages 2 to 9 years, comprehension slightly exceeds production and both increase with age (Bornstein & Hendricks, 2012).

Studies of linguistic specificity attempt to determine whether development is the result of universal cognitive development or unique linguistic knowledge. The development of spatial (location) and temporal (time) terms, for example, seems to be based on cognitive knowledge as well as on specific linguistic forms used to mark that knowledge. English uses *in* for containment and *on* for support. In contrast, Spanish

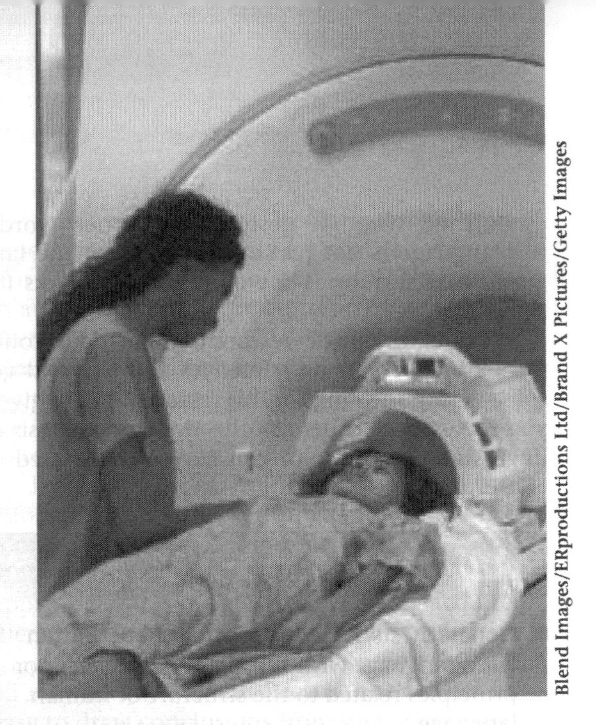

Blend Images/ERproductions Ltd/Brand X Pictures/Getty Images

3 Neurological Bases of Speech and Language

OBJECTIVES

The brain is the only primary organ in the body concerned with processing linguistic information. The study of the manner and location of this processing is called neurolinguistics. In this chapter, you will learn about the structures and functions of the brain relative to language. When you have completed this chapter, you should understand the following:

- Three basic brain functions
- Major brain areas responsible for linguistic processing
- Major theories of brain lateralization
- Processes of language comprehension and production
- Models that help explain linguistic processing
- Information processing
- Important terms:

angular gyrus	motor cortex
arcuate fasciculus	neurolinguistics
Broca's area	neuron
central nervous system (CNS)	neuroscience
cerebellum	peripheral nervous system (PNS)
cerebrum	prefrontal cortex
corpus callosum	reticular formation
cortex	supramarginal gyrus
executive function	synapse
Heschl's area	thalamus
information processing	Wernicke's area
	working memory

After exchanging greetings with a preschool child with whom I had been acquainted previously, he eyed me suspiciously for several seconds. When I inquired if anything was wrong, he asked, "Do I remember you?" In our study of language, we might ask our brains similar questions regarding incoming and outgoing linguistic messages and the ways in which this information is processed. And that's exactly what we're going to do in this chapter. We're going to try to describe how our brains process language.

The study of **neuroscience** focuses on two aspects of the nervous system:

1. Neuroanatomy, or where structures are located
2. Neurophysiology, or how the brain functions

As sciences go, neuroscience is relatively new and relies extensively on the recent advances in neural or brain imaging.

Neurolinguistics, as the name implies, is concerned with neurology and linguistics. More specifically, **neurolinguistics** is the study of the neuroanatomy, physiology, and biochemistry of language. Neurolinguists try to identify the structures in the nervous system involved in language processing and to explain the process.

In this chapter, we will examine the main structures of the central nervous system, specifically those involved in processing language. We will also discuss the functioning of these structures and construct a model for language processing. Finally, we'll discuss the related topic of information processing as a way to explore the how of processing.

Central Nervous System

Your nervous system is complicated. Our discussion must necessarily include both human anatomy and physiology as well as the processes at work. Let's begin with the basic unit, the neuron, and work our way up.

NEURONS

The **neuron**, or nerve cell, is the basic unit of your nervous system. A nerve is a collection of neurons. There are approximately 100 billion neurons in your nervous system. Each neuron consists of three parts: a cell body, a single long *axon* that transmits impulses away from the cell body, and several branchy *dendrites* that receive impulses from other cells and transmit them to the cell body (see Figure 3.1). Axons vary greatly in length from 1 millimeter to 1 meter. Neurons do not actually touch each other but are close enough to enable chemical-electrical impulses to "jump" the minuscule space, or **synapse**, between the axon of one neuron and the dendrites of the next. In short, the electrical charge of one neuron is changed by the release of neurotransmitters at its axon, which in turn affects the release of other neurotransmitters at the dendrite end of the second neuron. And it all happens instantaneously.

COMPONENTS

Your nervous system consists of your brain, spinal cord, and all associated nerves and sense organs. Your brain and spinal cord make up your **central nervous system (CNS)**. Any neural tissue that exists outside your CNS is part of your **peripheral nervous system (PNS)**, which conducts impulses either toward or away from your CNS. Your nervous system is responsible for monitoring your body's state by conducting messages from the senses and organs and responding to this information by conducting messages to the organs and muscles. These messages are transmitted through nerves.

FIGURE 3.1 A Basic Neuron

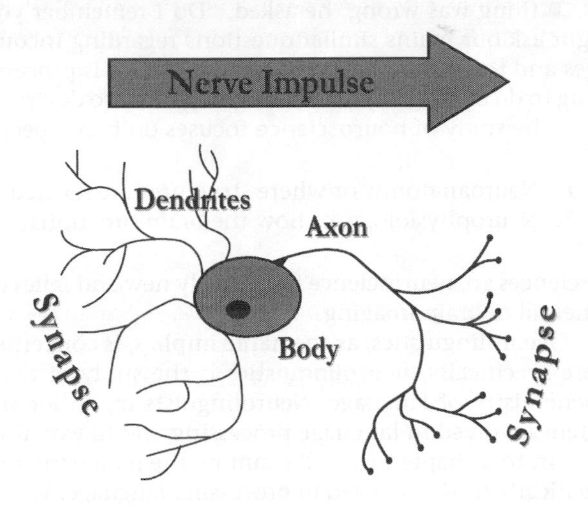

Although we will concentrate on the CNS in this chapter, we should comment on the PNS before we move on. The PNS consists of 12 cranial and 31 spinal nerves that interact with the CNS. The cranial nerves are especially important for speech, language, and hearing and course between your brainstem and your face and neck.

Most of your nervous system's neurons (approximately 85%) are concentrated in the CNS. At its lower end, your CNS contains the spinal cord, which transmits impulses between your brain and the peripheral nervous system. So important is the CNS to functioning that it is encased in bone and three membranous layers called the *meninges*. At the top of the spinal cord is your brainstem, consisting of the medulla oblongata, the pons, the thalamus, and the midbrain. These structures regulate involuntary functions, such as breathing and heart rate. Within the brainstem is a compact unit of neurons called the **reticular formation**. This body acts as an integrator of incoming auditory, visual, tactile, and other sensory inputs and as a filter to inhibit or facilitate sensory transmission. The **thalamus**, also in your brainstem, relays incoming sensory information (with the exception of smell) to the appropriate portion of your brain for analysis and prepares your brain to receive input.

The **cerebellum**, or "little brain," located at the posterior base of your brain, consists of right and left hemispheres and a central region called the *vermis*. Although the cerebellum coordinates the control of fine, complex motor activities, maintains muscle tone, and participates in motor learning, neuroimaging indicates that the cerebellum also has considerable influence on language processing and on higher-level cognitive and emotional functions (Highnam & Bleile, 2011). The cerebellum's posterior lobe modulates this nonmotor processing, which may include the following:

- Executive functioning or the ability to manage several cognitive tasks to reach a particular objective
- Working memory, critical for storage and manipulation of information during processing
- Divided attention or attention to more than one stimulus or to a stimulus presented in more than one modality, such as visual and auditory
- Modulation of affect or emotion

Information flows from the upper portions of the brain to the cerebellum and back again in the form of feedback on the progress of the communication. In this way, the cerebellum acts as a check on communication success. Although the role of the cerebellum in the processing of language is apparent, the exact nature of this role is unknown.

Cerebrum

Atop the brainstem and the cerebellum is your **cerebrum**, which is also divided into left and right hemispheres. The cerebrum is the largest portion of your brain, accounting for 40% of your brain's total weight.

Most sensory and motor functions in the cerebrum are *contralateral*, which means that each hemisphere is concerned with the opposite side of the body. With a few exceptions, the nerves from each side of the body cross to the opposite hemisphere somewhere along their course. Two exceptions to this crossover are vision and hearing. In vision, nerves from the left visual field of each eye, rather than from the left eye, pass to the right hemisphere, and those from the right visual field pass to the left hemisphere. Hearing is predominantly contralateral but not exclusively. More on this later.

Your cerebral hemispheres are roughly symmetrical for most functions. For specialized functions, such as language, however, the hemispheres are asymmetrical, and processing is the primary responsibility of one or the other hemisphere.

Each hemisphere consists of white fibrous connective tracts covered by a gray **cortex** of nerve cell bodies approximately a quarter inch thick. The fiber tracts are of three types: association, projection, and transverse. Association fibers run between different areas within each hemisphere; projection fibers connect the cortex to the brainstem and below; and transverse fibers, as the name implies, connect the two hemispheres. The largest transverse tract is the **corpus callosum**.

Your cortex has a wrinkled appearance caused by little hills called gyri and valleys called fissures, or sulci. Each hemisphere is divided into four lobes labeled frontal, parietal, occipital, and temporal (Figure 3.2).

The central sulcus separates your frontal lobe from your parietal lobe. The most anterior, or forward, portion of the frontal lobe is called the **prefrontal cortex**, the newest portion of our brains to evolve. The prefrontal cortex is responsible for executive function, control, organization, and synthesis of sensory and motor information. **Executive function** tones or readies your brain and allocates resources and, as the name implies, is responsible, in part, for control over the entire operation.

Large portions of your cortex serve sensory and motor functions. Immediately in front of the central sulcus is your **motor cortex**, a 2-centimeter-wide strip that controls motor movements. In general, the finer the movement, the larger the cortical area designated for it. In other words, your fingers have a proportionally greater cortical area devoted to motor control than does your trunk (Figure 3.3). Behind and parallel to the motor cortex and in the parietal lobe is your sensory cortex, which receives sensory input from your muscles, joints, bones, and skin. Other motor and sensory functions are found in specialized regions of your cortex. For example, the occipital lobe is primarily concerned with vision, and the temporal lobe processes auditory information.

Despite what you've just read, it is simplistic to conceive of your brain as merely consisting of localized sensory and motor mechanisms. Instead, the integration of sensory and motor information is required for your body to function. Simply stated, your brain does not function based on separate, highly specialized areas. Rather, functions vary as portions of your brain interact with one another (Frackowiak et al., 2004). In general, the higher or more complex the brain function, the more areas involved. For example, problem solving involves more areas than bending your thumb.

FIGURE 3.2 Schematic Lateral Surface of the Left Cerebral Hemisphere

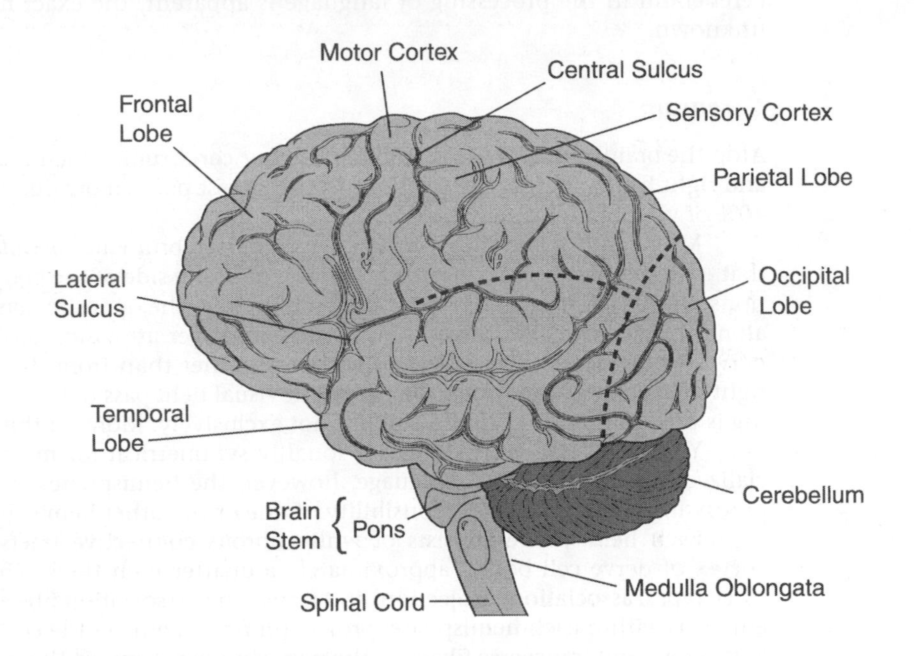

FIGURE 3.3 Schematic of Motor Cortex

Parts of the body drawn to represent the portion of the motor cortex devoted to each.

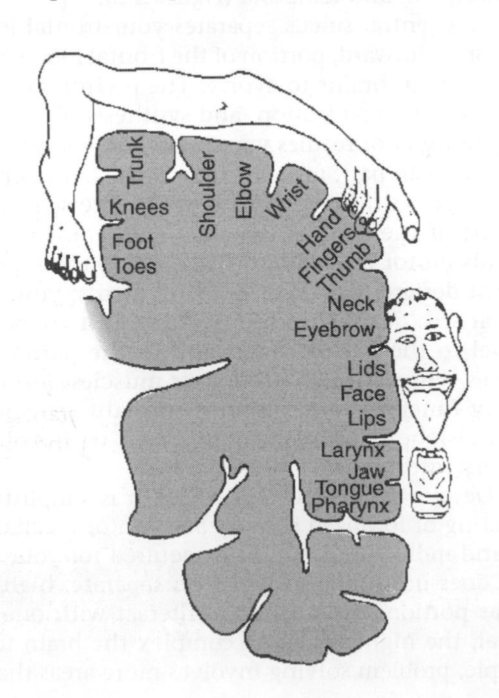

BRAIN FUNCTIONS

Three basic brain functions are regulation, processing, and formulation. The regulation function, located in the reticular formation of the brainstem, is responsible for the energy level and for the overall tone of your cortex. By maintaining the brain at a basic level of awareness and responsivity, this process aids the performance of the other two functions. The regulating process enables you to monitor, evaluate, and flexibly adjust behavior for successful performance.

The processing function, located in the posterior portion of your cortex, controls information analysis, coding, and storage. Highly specialized regions are responsible for the processing of sensory stimuli. Data from each source are combined with those from other sensory sources for analysis and synthesis.

Finally, the formulation process, located in your frontal lobe, is responsible for the formation of intentions and programs for behavior. This function serves primarily to activate the brain for regulation of attention and concentration. Motor behaviors are planned and coordinated, but not activated, within this function.

HEMISPHERIC ASYMMETRY

Although there is symmetry between the hemispheres for many motor and sensory processes, the distribution of specialized functions is usually lateralized to one hemisphere. Though they possess these separate functions, the hemispheres are complementary, and information passes readily between them via the corpus callosum and other transverse bodies. Overall, neither hemisphere is dominant because each possesses specialized talents and brings different skills to a given task. Neither hemisphere is competent to analyze data and program a response alone. In fact, your brain functions as an interconnected whole with activity throughout and differing levels of response with various activities. When a specific ability and primary processing centers are housed primarily in one hemisphere, we generally say that the hemisphere is *dominant* for that ability.

Right Hemisphere

The right hemisphere in humans is specialized for holistic processing through the simultaneous integration of information and is dominant in visuospatial processing, such as depth and orientation in space, and perception and recognition of faces, pictures, and photographs. In addition, the right hemisphere is capable of recognition of printed words but has difficulty decoding information using grapheme–phoneme (letter–sound) correspondence rules. (We'll discuss reading in more detail in Chapter 11.) Other right hemisphere language-related skills include

- comprehension and production of speech prosody and affect,
- comprehension and production of metaphorical language and semantics, and
- comprehension of complex linguistic and ideational material and of environmental sounds.

Environmental sounds include nonspeech sounds, music, melodies, tones, laughter, clicks, and buzzes. Interestingly, individuals who sign, whether deaf or hearing, have better memory for faces and objects than individuals who do not sign, suggesting that at least the visuospatial aspects of sign may be associated with the right hemisphere.

The right hemisphere may play a role in some aspects of pragmatics, including the perception and expression of emotion in language; the ability to understand jokes, irony, and figurative language (i.e., *He hit the roof* or *I could eat an ox*); and the ability to produce and comprehend coherent discourse. These aspects of language processing are especially difficult for adults with right-hemisphere injury.

Left Hemisphere

In almost all humans, the left hemisphere is specialized for language in all modalities (oral, visual, and written), linear order perception, arithmetic calculations, and logical reasoning. Whereas the right hemisphere engages in holistic interpretation, the left is best at step-by-step processing. As such, the left hemisphere is adept at perceiving rapidly changing sequential information, such as the acoustic characteristics of phonemes in speech. Processing these phonemes for meaning, however, involves both hemispheres. Studies using functional magnetic resonance imaging (fMRI) have shown a strong left hemispheric language dominance for auditory comprehension in children as young as 7 years of age (Balsamo et al., 2002).

Variation

Not all human brains are organized as described. In general, almost all right-handers and approximately 60% of left-handers are left-hemisphere dominant for language. The remainder of left-handers, approximately 2% of the human population, are right-hemisphere dominant for language. A minuscule percentage of humans display bilateral linguistic performance, with no apparent dominant hemisphere. Thus, approximately 98% of humans are left-dominant for language. Women seem to be less strongly left-dominant than men, having a slightly more even distribution between the hemispheres. In actuality, lateralization is probably a matter of degree, rather than the all-or-nothing patterns suggested.

BRAIN MATURATION

Language development is highly correlated with brain maturation and specialization. Whether this relationship is based on maturation of specific structures or on the development of particular cognitive abilities is unknown. (In Chapter 4 we'll discuss cognitive growth in the infant.) Two important aspects of brain maturation are weight and organization.

Gross brain weight changes most rapidly during the first two years of life, when the original weight of the brain at birth triples. Average brain weights are presented in Table 3.1. In addition, chemical changes occur and internal pathways become organized, connecting various portions of the brain. By age 12, the brain has usually reached its fully mature weight. The number of neurons does not change appreciably, but they increase in size as dendrites and axons grow to form a dense interconnected web. Disease, malnutrition, or sensory deprivation can result in less density and decreased functioning. Most of the increase in functioning is the result of **myelination**, or the process of sheathing of the nervous system. In general, the myelin areas are the most fully developed and those with the most rapid transmission of neural information. Myelination is controlled, in part, by sex-related hormones, especially estrogen, which enhances the process. This fact may account for the more rapid early neurological development of girls. In general, sensory and motor tracts undergo myelination before higher-functioning areas, such as those processing language.

TABLE 3.1 Gross Brain Weight of Children

Age	Weight (Grams)	Percentage of Adult Brain Weight
Birth	335	25
6 months	660	50
12 months	925	70
24 months	1,065	80
5 years	1,180	90
12 years	1,320	100

Source: Information from Love & Webb (1986).

Neurolinguistics is a specialized study of language and the brain. This video provides a quick review of the relationship of neurology and linguistics. http://www.youtube.com/watch?v=aUFdUiJXS4E

The brain is not simply growing. Microscopic "connections" are being made. Genes determine the basic wiring, and approximately half of the 80,000 genes in your cells are involved in the formation and operation of the CNS. It is experience, however, that determines the pathways. In the first month of life, firings across synapses may increase fiftyfold to more than one thousand trillion. Use of these neural pathways stimulates and strengthens them, making subsequent use more efficient.

Language Processing

It is extremely difficult to identify the exact spot where language and speech reside in your brain. Processing areas often overlap. We are on safer ground to state that language is a complex process performed by many different interconnected areas of your brain rather than a single area.

Recent advances in brain imaging have enabled researchers to monitor cerebral blood flow while a subject is conducting specific linguistic tasks. Such online or "real-time" studies have helped researchers confirm that linguistic processing, such as word retrieval and word and sentence comprehension, often relies on contributions from differing areas of your brain. As a result, brain imagery results have fostered a theoretical move away from processing models based on exclusive sensory input and motor output channels of language processing to an integrated model.

Position emission tomography (PET), a brain-imaging technique, has identified several regions of the brain that are active during speech-sound processing. Although there is greater activation in the left hemisphere during both perception and production, some right-hemisphere involvement also occurs. In general, the frontal and temporal lobes are also more active than other regions in both perception and production, but there is no evidence for a single processing center. Even areas of the frontal lobe important for speech production are not speech-specific, but also participate in nonspeech tasks.

In the 1960s and 1970s, many linguists assumed that language comprehension and production was linear in nature, with processing proceeding in a sequential fashion. For example, comprehension was assumed to flow as follows:

phonetic → phonological → grammatical → semantic

Production ran in the opposite direction. It does seem plausible that words would be selected independently of sentence frames and then put together like cars in a train. But this is not the case.

A more accurate representation of the comprehension process is more complex and would look more like the following:

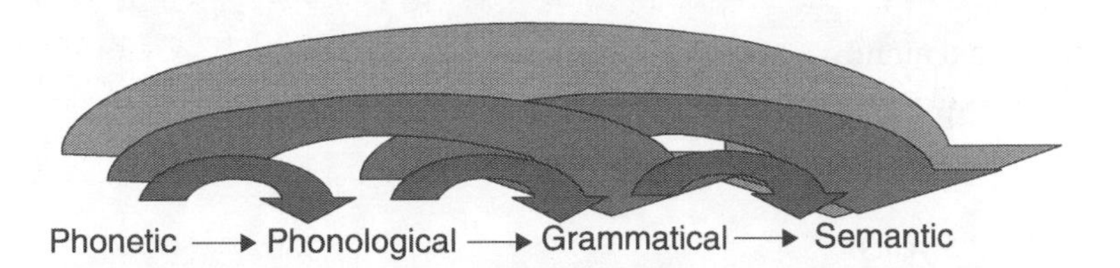

All areas contribute as information becomes available and seemingly earlier or later stages are, in fact, not so. For example, context can penetrate the earliest stages of word identification in comprehension, and speech sounds can affect sentence formation in production.

Linguistic processing, both comprehension and production, depends on your lexicon, or personal dictionary, of stored words and high usage phrases and on your stored linguistic rules. The systems for comprehension and production overlap partially. Brain-imaging techniques indicate that the posterior temporal lobe in the left hemisphere is associated with both comprehension and production (Hickok, 2001).

Many parts of your brain are active in language processing. In addition, the number and location of these activated regions differ across individuals and vary with the task, based on the type of input and output, amount and kind of memory required, the relative level of difficulty and familiarity, attentional demands, and competition from other tasks. Although there is little evidence of a unitary language-processing area, some areas do seem to be more important than others, especially the frontal and temporal regions of the left hemisphere.

Christopher Futcher/E+/Getty Images

Neurological impairment may require that a person find other means of communication.

LANGUAGE COMPREHENSION

Comprehension consists of auditory processing and language decoding and involves many areas of your brain working together. Auditory processing is concerned with the nature of the incoming auditory signal, whereas decoding considers representational meaning and underlying concepts. Processing begins with attending to incoming stimuli. Because it has a limited capacity to process incoming data, your brain must allocate this capacity by focusing its attention on certain stimuli while ignoring or inhibiting others. Think about what happens when you attend to someone talking to you while a TV is blaring in the background.

Location

Auditory signals received in your brainstem are relayed to an area of each auditory cortex called **Heschl's area** (or gyrus). As shown in Figure 3.4, 60% of the signal is received at Heschl's area from the ear on the opposite side of your body. Heschl's area and the surrounding auditory areas separate the incoming information, differentiating significant linguistic information from nonsignificant noise. Linguistic information receives further processing. Linguistic input is sent to your left temporal lobe for processing, while paralinguistic input (intonation, stress, rhythm, rate) is directed to your right temporal lobe. Initial phonological analysis begins in Heschl's area and continues further along in the process (Frackowiak et al., 2004). Figure 3.5 presents receptive linguistic processing.

FIGURE 3.4 **Following the Path of Receptive Processing**

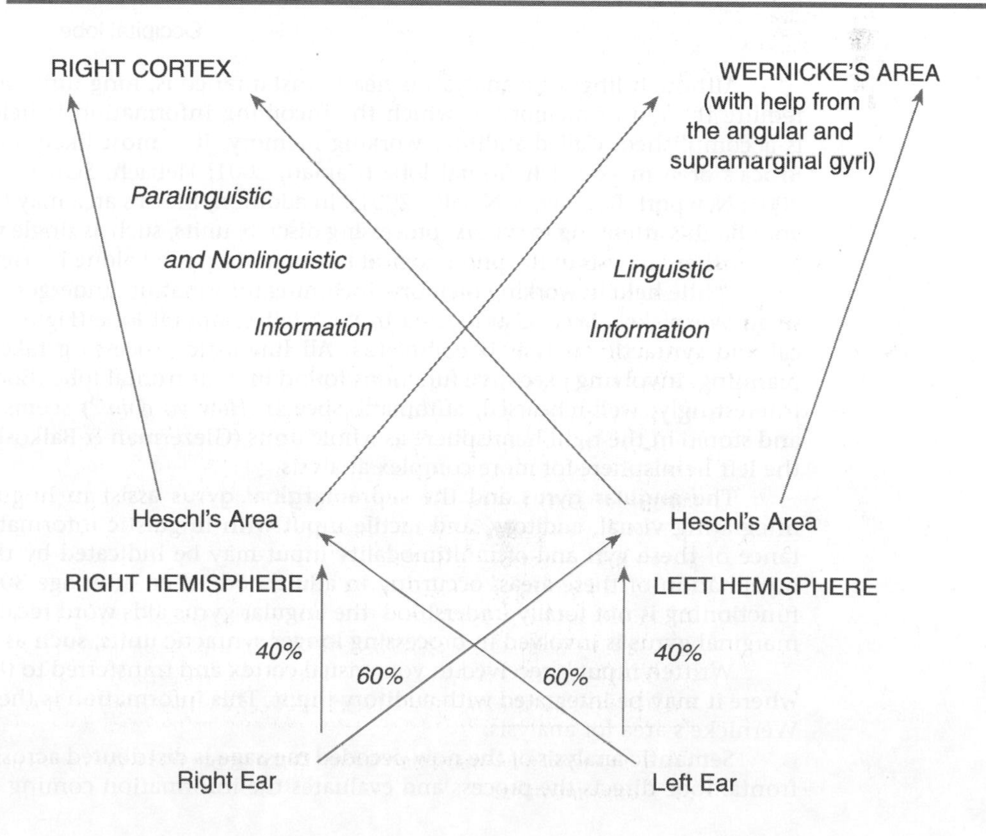

FIGURE 3.5 Receptive Linguistic Processing

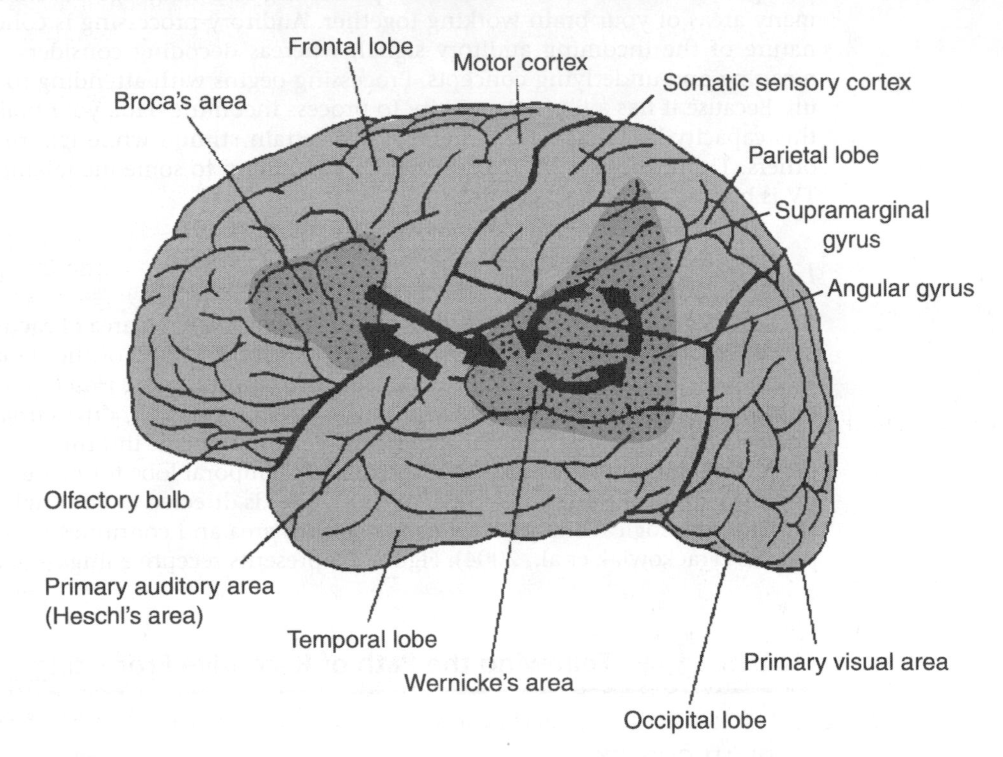

Although linguistic analysis is nearly instantaneous, long units such as sentences require the aid of memory in which the incoming information is held while analysis is accomplished. Called auditory working memory, it is most likely located in or near **Broca's area** in your left frontal lobe (Caplan, 2001; Fiebach, Schlesewsky, & Friedrici, 2001; Newport, Bavelier, & Neville, 2001). In addition, Broca's area may be responsible for your brain's attending to syntax, processing discrete units, such as single words or phrases, and further analysis of the phonological information passed along by Heschl's area.

While held in working memory, incoming information undergoes linguistic analysis in **Wernicke's area**, also located in your left temporal lobe (Figure 3.5). Phonological and syntactic analysis is completed. All linguistic processing takes reasoning and planning, involving executive functions found in your frontal lobe (Bookheimer, 2002). Interestingly, well-rehearsed, automatic speech (*How ya doin'?*) seems to be processed and stored in the right hemisphere as whole units (Glezerman & Balkoski, 1999), freeing the left hemisphere for more complex analysis.

The **angular gyrus** and the **supramarginal gyrus** assist in linguistic processing, integrating visual, auditory, and tactile input with linguistic information. The importance of these gyri and of multimodality input may be indicated by the relatively late myelination of these areas, occurring in adulthood, often after age 30. Although their functioning is not totally understood, the angular gyrus aids word recall, and the supramarginal gyrus is involved in processing longer syntactic units, such as sentences.

Written input is received in your visual cortex and transferred to the angular gyrus, where it may be integrated with auditory input. This information is then transmitted to Wernicke's area for analysis.

Semantic analysis of the now decoded message is distributed across your brain. The frontal lobe directs the process and evaluates the information coming from Wernicke's area where the semantic processing actually occurs. The right hemisphere is also involved in interpretation of figurative and abstract language processing in areas roughly corresponding to Broca's and Wernicke's areas (Bookheimer, 2002). Figurative language (Chapter 10) is nonliteral, as in *My dad hit the roof*. Abstract language represents ideas, intangibles, and concepts such as *beauty* and *love*.

Limited word-recognition and semantic decoding also occurs in your right hemisphere, in addition to paralinguistic processing mentioned previously (Friederici, 2001; Goodglass, Lindfield, & Alexander, 2000). In addition, the right hemisphere may also work to suppress ambiguous or incompatible interpretations (Tompkins, Lehman-Blake, Baumgaertner, & Fassbinder, 2001).

Obviously, analysis for comprehension depends on memory storage of both words and concepts. The store of word meanings required for semantic interpretation is diffusely located, centered primarily in the temporal lobe, although conceptual memory is stored throughout the cortex. Prior to storage, incoming information is transmitted to the *hippocampus* in the left temporal lobe for consolidation.

Finally, pragmatic analysis involves the frontal lobe and integration of paralinguistic information from the right hemisphere. This includes social awareness and intent.

Processing

Although your brain processes sequences of speech sounds approximately seven times faster than nonspeech sounds, the speed of linguistic analysis varies with the linguistic and nonlinguistic complexity of the information and the speed of the incoming information. Each incoming message is processing at both a conversation-meaning and a lexical-syntactic level, with the conversational-meaning process given the very slight advantage of being activated milliseconds before the other (Brown, van Berkum, & Hagoort, 2000).

Let's take a look at sentence processing and different neurological mechanisms at work with two similar sentences. "Ann bumped into Kathy and fell over," in which it is assumed by most listeners that Ann fell, is processed much more rapidly than "Ann bumped into Kathy and she fell over," in which *she* is in doubt. If we measure brain activity using event-related potentials (ERPs), a measure of the electrical activity generated by your brain, we'll find that the first sentence is processed in a section of the brain used for syntactic processing and located near Wernicke's area, while the second is processed in the parietal to right occipital area, used in semantic processing (Streb, Hemighausen, & Rösler, 2004).

LANGUAGE PRODUCTION

When we look at production, we find the same areas of your brain involved in integrated preparation and production of outgoing messages. While many functions are similar, Broca's area has the additional responsibility of programming the motor strip for speech.

Using functional magnetic resonance imaging (fMRI) while participants either imitate or observe speech movements, researchers have found activity in Broca's area for both tasks. It would appear the cortical areas involved in the perception are also used in the execution of speech movements (Paulesu et al., 2003; Skipper, Nusbaum, & Small, 2005). The fact that both functions are located in Broca's area suggests that motor production of speech and phonological analysis are somehow linked (Bookheimer, 2002). Interestingly, there is a right hemisphere area analogous to Broca's area that is also activated in both tasks, although at this time, its role is unclear.

Location

Production processes are located in the same general area of your brain as comprehension functions. The conceptual basis of a message forms in one of the many memory areas of the cortex. The underlying structure of the message is organized in Wernicke's area; the message is then transmitted through the **arcuate fasciculus**, a white fibrous tract running beneath the angular gyrus, to Broca's area, in the frontal lobe (Figure 3.6).

Processing

The message is conceived abstractly and given specific form as it passes through the arcuate fasciculus. Writing follows a similar pathway, passing from Wernicke's area to the angular and supramarginal gyri. From here the message passes to an area similar to and just above Broca's area, called *Exner's area,* for activation of the muscles used for writing.

Like a computer, Broca's area is responsible for preparing and coordinating the motor program for verbalizing the message. Signals are then passed to the regions of the motor cortex that activate the muscles responsible for speech, including respiration, phonation, resonation, and articulation.

FIGURE 3.6 Productive Linguistic Processing

Messages are transmitted from Wernicke's area to Broca's area via the white fibrous tract of the arcuate fasciculus.

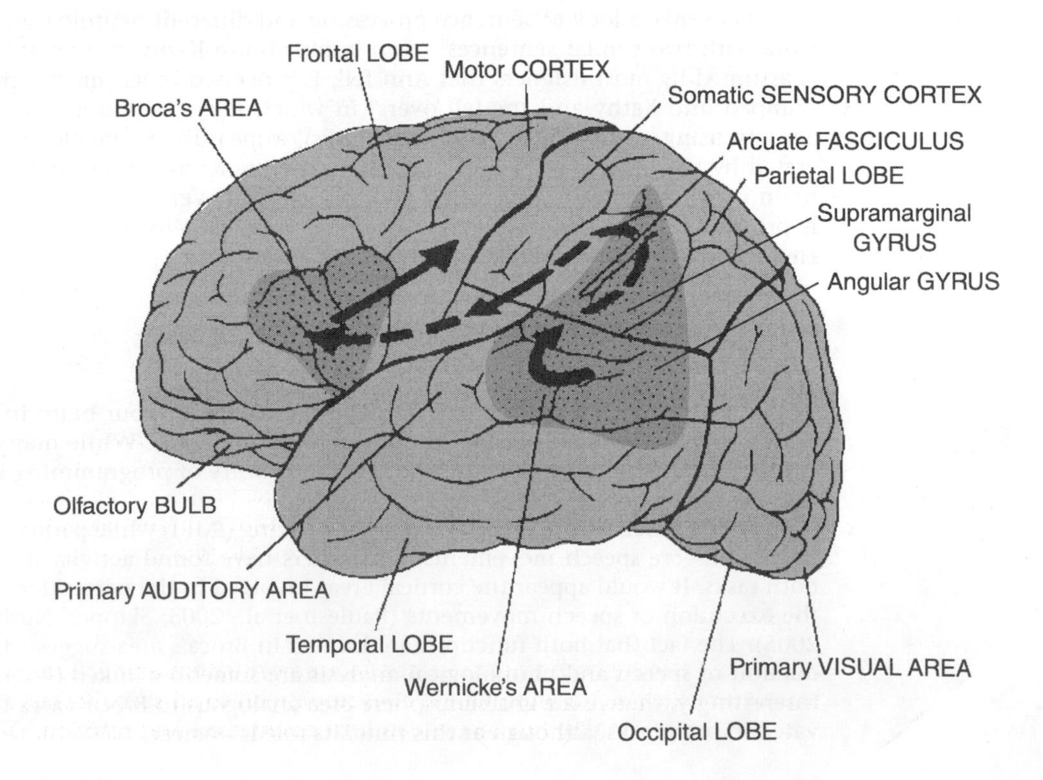

In this video, Dr. James Rilling of Emory University discusses the unique brain features that enable humans to process linguistic information. http://www.youtube.com/watch?v=5nqaPAqOmKQ

Damage to any of these areas results in disruption of linguistic production, but with different effects. Injury to Wernicke's area usually disrupts both expressive and receptive language abilities. If damage occurs to the arcuate fasciculus, speech is unaffected except for repetitive movements, but the resultant speech may not make sense. Finally, damage to Broca's area results in speech difficulties, but writing and language comprehension may be relatively unaffected.

The actual processes are much more complex than our quick overview suggests. Many areas have multiple or as yet unknown functions. Several models of brain functioning have attempted to fill this need.

Models of Linguistic Processing

Several models help explain how cognitive processing in general and specific language processing occurs. The applicable model actually varies depending on the task and the individual language user.

First, we should distinguish between structures and control processes. Structures are the fixed anatomical and physiological features of your CNS. Structures and their functions are similar across most healthy brains. How these structures organize, analyze, and synthesize incoming linguistic information varies by individual and the task involved. The way information is processed represents the voluntary problem-solving strategies of each person, called **information processing**.

INFORMATION PROCESSING

While the structures of your CNS probably vary little from mine, our processes for dealing with incoming stimuli and formulating outgoing responses are more individualized. Although the exact nature of these cognitive processes is unknown, measured intelligence and the speed of such information processing are related.

Qualitative differences may reflect operational or processing differences. For example, there may be differences between types of processing abilities along the following lines:

- Automatic processes are unintentional or have become routinized and thus require very little of the available cognitive capacity and neither interfere with other tasks nor become more efficient with practice.
- Effortful processing requires concentration and attention by your brain and, in general, is slower to develop and requires greater effort.

Both thought and language are managed by your brain's information processing system. This system includes cognitive processes involved in attention, perception, organization, memory, concept formation, problem solving and transfer, and management or executive function (Groome, 1999). As Figure 3.7 shows, tasks such as comprehension of a sentence involve integration of all these processes.

Attention

Attention includes both awareness of a learning situation and active cognitive processing. As in Figure 3.7, the individual does not attend to all stimuli; thus stimulus D does not proceed. Attending can be divided into orientation and reaction. *Orientation* is the

FIGURE 3.7 **Information Processing Model**

Information processing contains the four steps of attention, discrimination, organization, and memory. The process is overseen by the executive function.

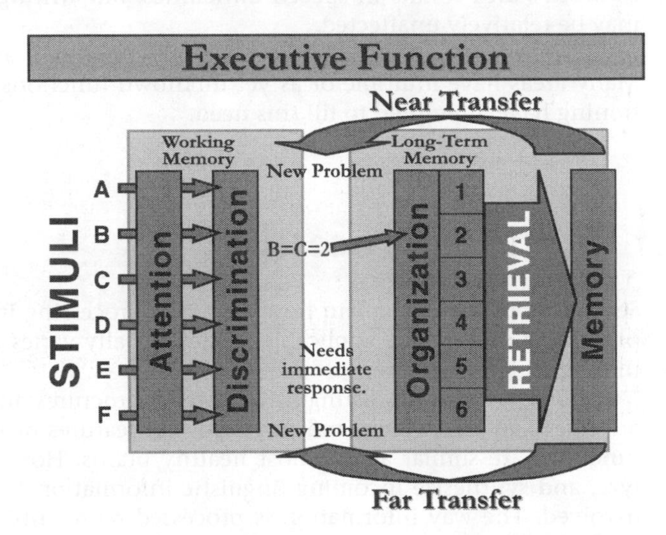

ability to sustain attention over time. Humans attend best when motivated and are especially attracted by high-intensity stimuli that are moving or undergoing change. In part, orientation is related to the individual's ability to determine the uniqueness of the stimulus. *Reaction* refers to the amount of time required for an individual to respond to a stimulus. In part, reaction time is a function of the individual's ability to select the relevant dimensions of a task to which to respond.

In general, less mature individuals are less efficient at attention allocation and have a more limited attentional capacity. These processes are relatively automatic for more mature individuals and require only minimal allocation of the available resources of the brain. Thus, children must allocate more of the limited resources of the brain at this level, leaving fewer resources available for higher-level processes.

Discrimination

Discrimination is the ability to identify stimuli differing along some dimension. If an individual cannot identify the relevant characteristics, she or he will have difficulty comparing the new input with stored information. In the schematic in Figure 3.7, the brain decides that stimuli A and F are new problems. Stimuli B and C are similar and will be stored in bin 2. More on that later. Finally, stimulus E demands an immediate response and the brain does so accordingly.

Working Memory Discrimination, especially for language decoding, requires a special type of memory called **working memory** (WM) that holds a message during processing. Located in Broca's and associated areas, WM is important for higher language and cognitive tasks. WM controls attention and allows limited information to be held in a temporarily accessible state while being processed (Cowan, Nugent, Elliott, Ponomarev,

& Saults, 2005). WM is essential to the acquisition of complex academic skills and knowledge across a variety of language and literacy areas, and is related to the rate at which children learn new vocabulary; comprehend both oral and written language; acquire literacy skills; and become efficient in math, reasoning, and problem solving (Alloway & Alloway, 2010; Bull & Scerif, 2001; Cain, Oakhill, & Bryant, 2004; Passolunghi & Siegel, 2004; Seigneuric, Ehrlich, Oakhill, & Yuill, 2000; Swanson & Sachse-Lee, 2001; Vanderberg & Swanson, 2007; Vukovic & Siegel, 2010).

Children with greater WM capacity show more accurate comprehension than children with low capacity. Speech is fleeting. Once something is said, it disappears. Therefore, it is crucial for decoding of spoken language that your brain be able to hold what was heard when it is no longer present. While held in WM, a sentence can be scanned for words in your lexical storage and for syntactic structure and overall meaning. Older information in the speech stream must also be integrated into the developing concept as speech continues (Lewis, Vasishth, & Van Dyke, 2006; McElree, Foraker, & Dyer, 2003; Van Dyke, 2007). As with any task, each new sentence is not approached by the brain as a totally new problem; rather, linguistic experience seems to aid interpretation (Roberts & Gibson, 2002).

Working memory can be thought of as a multidimensional system with three separable interactive mechanisms (Bayliss, Jarrold, Baddeley, Gunn, & Leigh, 2005; Gavens & Barrouillet, 2004):

1. A *central executive* responsible for coordinating and controlling the flow of information (Lehto, Juujarvi, Kooistra, & Pulkkinen, 2003)
2. A storage device devoted to the temporary retention of verbal material that contains two components:
    a. An *articulatory rehearsal process* in which phonological information is maintained in memory through a process of silent rehearsal
    b. A *phonological short-term memory* (PSTM), which is responsible for temporary storage and processing of phonological representations (Baddeley, Gathercole, & Papagno, 1998; Gathercole & Baddeley, 1993)
3. A device devoted to the temporary retention of *visuospatial storage*

Within PSTM, phonological information quickly decays unless some effort is undertaken to maintain the information. There may also be a fourth mechanism, the *episodic buffer*, that integrates inputs from PSTM and the visuospatial sketchpad into a coherent representation important in the processing and retention of large chunks of connected speech (Baddeley 2000, 2003). Figure 3.8 presents a diagram of WM.

In addition to supervising the system, the central executive controls attention; resource allocation; and processes such as task analysis, strategy selection, and strategy revision (Parente, Kolakowsky-Hayner, Krug, & Wilk, 1999). Tasks that are particularly demanding result in fewer resources available for other aspects of the task.

Phonological short-term memory is an important word-learning and comprehension device that involves matching sound to meaning (Gathercole, 2006). Word learning involves mapping sound to meaning. It is assumed that the ability to hold novel speech material in PSTM permits children to establish a stable, long-term phonological representation of a new word in long-term memory. As a child's vocabulary grows, word entries must become more phonologically refined and better organized. Although the relation of PSTM and word learning weakens after age 8, there is still a significant link through adolescence and into adulthood (Gathercole, Tiffany, Briscoe, Thorn, & the ALSPAC Team, 2005; Gupta, 2003).

In general, processing accuracy increases and storage significantly improves with age. Age-related increases in both STM and processing speed contribute to developmental

Top-down and bottom-up processing differ with the level of informational input. Top-down processing is *conceptually driven*, or affected by your expectations concerning incoming information. In this way, the linguistic and nonlinguistic contexts enable you to predict the form and content of incoming linguistic information. Knowledge, both cognitive and semantic, is used to cue lower functions to search for particular information. For example, when we hear "The cat caught a . . . ," we predict the next word will be *mouse* or *bird*. The initial syllable or sound of the word may be all that is needed for confirmation. The prediction is not confirmed when analysis indicates that the incoming information doesn't fit. At this point the system returns to the stimuli or data, called the *bottom*, for reanalysis and interpretation.

Bottom-up processing is *data driven*. Analysis occurs at the levels of sound and syllable discrimination and proceeds upward to recognition and comprehension. For example, analysis of the word *mouse* would begin at the phoneme level with /m aʊ s/. Partially analyzed data from the perceptual level are passed upward and integrated with predictions from higher levels, which are moving down. For example, if I'm predicting that the cat caught a mouse but I hear another word forming, I need to rely on the phonology to tell me the new word and then I predict what will come next.

Depending on the context, you may use both strategies simultaneously or rely more on one strategy. Incoming speech may be misinterpreted when a listener relies too heavily on words stored in his or her memory rather than on the incoming information. In one example, a small child on his first Halloween had been instructed to say the traditional "Trick or treat," his first exposure to these words. He had no prior reference. His parents were very surprised at the first house when he shouted "Chicken feet!" (Snyder, Dabasinskas, & O'Connor, 2002, p. 4.)

Passive/Active Processing

Passive and active processing are based on recognizing patterns of incoming information. In passive processing, incoming data are analyzed in fragments until enough information can be combined for you to recognize a pattern. This method is similar to bottom-up processing.

The contrasting active process involves the use of a comparator strategy that matches input with either a previously stored or a generated pattern or mental model. World knowledge forms a basis. Because cats typically catch mice, the /m/ sound would predict that *mouse* is the word to follow. This model forms gradually from active engagement with the environment and helps each of us make sense of the world, anticipate or predict, and plan. In actual practice, both processes probably occur simultaneously.

Serial/Parallel Processing

The information processing system can handle more than one task at a time. The different levels of processing may proceed either simultaneously and in parallel with each other or sequentially in a series of separate, autonomous processes.

Processing varies with the speed and volume of information flow. Serial, or successive, processes are one at a time in nature. Located in the left frontal and temporal lobes, successive processes analyze information at one level and then pass it on to the next level. For example, the incoming frequency, intensity, and duration of a signal are synthesized to determine the phonemic features. These features are bundled into phonemic characteristics, then syllables, words, and so on, until the message is understood.

Parallel, or simultaneous, processing accesses multiple levels of analysis at the same time. Located in the occipital and parietal association areas and possibly in the right hemisphere, simultaneous processing deals with underlying meaning and relationships all at once.

In practice, the two processes occur together, with overall comprehension dependent on the one that most efficiently processes incoming information or outgoing signals. Although successive processing is more precise, it necessarily takes more of your brain's processing potential and is relatively slow. It is therefore quickly overwhelmed, so simultaneous processing must carry the bulk of the responsibility for comprehension. When the incoming rate slows, successive processing takes over again.

Imagine that your brain is writing out each message that enters, in the way you do when taking notes. If your professor goes slowly over important points, you can write every word, similar to processing it successively. Because this situation is rare, however, you usually scramble to summarize what your professor has said, recording the overall meaning of the information in a manner similar to simultaneous processing.

Interestingly, signing, unlike speech, has a greater capacity to express information simultaneously. Although signs take longer to produce than words, only a minimal portion is needed to identify a sign. The visual nature of signs provides greater initial information, and few signs have similar initial shapes. Thus, confirmation is more rapid for signs than words.

The Role of Executive Function

The ability to process information is not limitless. In fact, only certain amounts of information can be analyzed and synthesized. This is seen when we multitask. Although it's relatively easy to hold a conversation while walking, it may be difficult to receive and comprehend a lecture while texting in class. Language processing may be limited by the amount of incoming and stored language data, the demands of the task, and your available cognitive resources. As in any system, overloads decrease efficiency.

Aliaksei Lasevich/Fotolia

By about age 4, preschool children recognize that other people can have their own different knowledge and beliefs.

Overseeing the processing system is your brain's central executive or executive function that allocates and coordinates mental resources. Executive function determines cognitive strategies and activities needed for a task and monitors feedback and outcomes in order to reallocate resources if necessary.

Metacognition, or your knowledge of your own cognitive and memory processes, can facilitate encoding and retrieval and the use of problem-solving strategies. Decisions to execute these processes help you to manage their use and guide attending; to make decisions to attempt, continue, or abandon; and to monitor progress.

Conclusion

LANGUAGE PROCESSING, BOTH EXPRESSIVE and receptive, is located primarily in the left hemisphere of the brain in most adults. Anatomical differences between the hemispheres have been noted in the fetus, but specialization for language develops later in the maturing child. Although language-processing functions are situated anatomically within the brain, their exact location and function are not totally understood. The effects on these processes of past learning, problem-solving ability, memory, and language itself are also unclear. It is known, however, that cognition, or the ability to use the resources of the brain, is closely related to the overall language level of each individual.

When I was a child, we used to play "Button, button, who has the button," in which the child in the middle tried to guess which of the children in the circle around him or her held a button. Neurolinguistics can seem like this when we try to discern where language functions reside in the brain. Don't be troubled by the fact that functions may not be located exactly where we've said they are. The human brain is very flexible, and information is often stored in diffuse areas.

Let's do a quick retracing. Comprehension goes from the ear to Heschl's area, with 60% of the information crossing to the opposite hemisphere and 40% staying on the same side; then the two Heschl's areas divide linguistic from paralinguistic data, sending the linguistic to Wernicke's area in the left temporal lobe. Wernicke's area processes the linguistic information with aid from the angular and supramarginal gyri. What do they do? Easy to remember. *Supramarginal* starts with an *s*, and so do *sequential* and *syntax*. The supramarginal gyrus processes units larger than words and the way they're joined together—syntax. The angular gyrus is left with word recall. Good!

Production is easier to remember. Wernicke's area formulates the message and sends it via the arcuate fasciculus to Broca's area in the frontal lobe. Broca's area is a computer that programs the motor strip, which in turn sends nerve impulses to the muscles of speech. Broca's area does not send nerve impulses directly to the muscles. The motor strip does that.

Just as infants must learn to control their muscles, they must also learn to operate their brain. Different parts of the brain become more active during the first year and mature with myelination. As children add more and more information, they must learn to organize that information for access. Information processing helps us describe the process. For example, a child's lexicon, or personal dictionary, will eventually be organized by categories based on word meanings, rhymes, alliteration, synonyms and antonyms, and the like. With improved organization and repeated use, the brain's ability to remember increases, making greater language use possible.

Let me end with a granddaughter story of neurolinguistics. By the young age of 3½, Cassidy had discovered the usefulness of cognitive activity as a manipulative tool. She could sabotage any attempt to hurry her with "Waaaaaaaaaait, I'm thinking . . . I'm thinking." Although she may not have understood the process, she realized that those thoughts, ideas, and words came from somewhere.

Discussion

NO DISCUSSION OF NEUROLINGUISTICS would be complete without the story of Alex, a young man born with a rare brain disorder known as Sturge-Weber syndrome, which resulted in seizure activity and severely limited blood supply to the left hemisphere of his brain (Trudeau & Chadwick, 1997).

As a result, the left hemisphere atrophied, while the right seemed normal. At age 8, when Alex's left hemisphere was removed as a last resort effort to stop his violent seizures, he was nonspeaking and seemingly unable to comprehend language.

Unexpectedly, at age 9, after recovery from surgery, Alex began to speak. Although at first beginning with single words and immature speech, his language began to grow rapidly. In a few months, Alex developed the language of a late preschooler. By age 16 and still improving, his language was equivalent to that of a 10- to 11-year-old.

The experience of Alex calls into question much that we have discussed in this chapter, in addition to the notion of a critical period or age—considered to be the preschool years—for language learning, after which such learning was believed to be extremely difficult. The brain of children is extremely "plastic," or malleable. In other words, functions such as language may be assumed by other areas of the brain whether in the course of normal development or as a result of injury.

As a practicing speech-language pathologist, educator, or psychologist, you will see many children with either brain injury or pathology. While it is important to know the area of injury, we cannot make assumptions about a client's language based on this information. Nor is the size of the damaged area directly related to the resultant deficits, if any. Nothing substitutes for a thorough assessment of speech, language, and communication. It is more important to describe thoroughly what a client can do than to be able to name the site of injury or to name the neurological condition.

Main Points

- It's difficult to pinpoint the neurological location of cognitive processes. Most are diffusely located.
- The left temporal area is specialized for linguistic processing.
- Sound entering each ear is divided; 60% crosses to Heschl's area on the other side of the brain, while 40% is sent to Heschl's on the same side.
- Each Heschl's area sends paralinguistic acoustic information to the right hemisphere and linguistic information to the left hemisphere.
- In the left hemisphere, incoming language is held briefly in Broca's area while processed by Wernicke's area with assistance from the supramarginal gyrus and the angular gyrus.
- Outgoing language is conceived in Wernicke's area, then transferred below the surface via the arcuate fasciculus to Broca's area, which programs the motor cortex to signal the muscles for speech.
- Information processing consists of four steps: attention, discrimination, organization, and memory.

Reflections

1. What are the functions of the thalamus, the cerebellum, and the cerebrum? How do they facilitate the communication process?
2. How would you describe hemispheric asymmetry? What are the functions of the right and left hemispheres of the brain in language development?
3. Few theorists would argue with the notion of brain lateralization for language. Can you explain the major theories on how this lateralization occurs?
4. Explain briefly how language is processed relative to specific areas of the brain.
5. Describe information processing theory and the several models of language comprehension and production processes associated with it.

As the stimulus strength increases, such as becoming louder, so does attention, until a point is attained at which stimulus strength reaches an infant's tolerance threshold. A child will then avert his or her face, become restless, or cry for assistance. If the level of stimulation is too low, an infant loses interest.

Infant Sensation

Many of an infant's behavior-state changes reflect internal changes or intrinsic brain activities, although external stimuli can influence the duration of these states. An infant is most receptive to external stimuli when alert but not overly active. Although the ability to attend is influenced by an infant's internal state, this changes quickly, and, within a few months, the level of external stimulation is a greater determinant of attending than an infant's state. By that time an infant is capable of maintaining a rather stable internal condition.

By 2 months of age an infant exhibits selective attending skills and can remain unresponsive to some background stimulus events. When presented with a stimulus repeatedly, an infant will react less strongly to each successive presentation. Becoming used to a stimulus, a process called **habituation**, is the result of patterns formed as stimuli occur repeatedly. An infant begins to expect the stimulus to occur. If the expectation is fulfilled, then the stimulus does not elicit a significant response. Thus, habituation enables an infant to attend to new stimuli without competition from older, less novel stimuli. Habituation requires sensory learning and perception.

PERCEPTION

Perception is using both sensory information and previous knowledge to make sense of incoming stimuli. The ability to discriminate differences in incoming information is a portion of perception, a process of gaining awareness of what is happening around us. From birth, an infant is an active stimulus seeker who will even work to attain certain types of stimulation.

Auditory Perception

Of most interest for our study of language and speech development are auditory perceptual skills. In order for an infant's perceptual skills in these areas to grow and change, he or she must be exposed to stimulation from the environment. A child must hear speech over and over again. We'll have a lot more to say on this topic later.

Visual Perception

Visually, infants are able to perceive the somewhat blurry human face at birth and learn to direct their attention at faces very quickly. Within a few days, they can discriminate between different facial expressions. By 2 months, infants prefer an "average" face, probably because it matches an internalized concept of a face. When I had a beard—anything but "average"—infants often gave me very quizzical looks. By 3 months, infants can perceive facial differences. Children begin to perceive their own face between 5 and 8 months, although they probably don't yet understand exactly who that vision in the mirror is.

Similarly, recognition of different facial expressions does not imply that an infant understands emotion. In any case, between 4 and 6 months, children respond more positively to a smile.

Parents help their infants explore the world and provide words for the experiences their children are having.

BananaStock/Thinkstock/Getty Images

Some faces are more important than others. Within a few days of birth, infants can recognize their mother's face. Although a stranger's face receives a longer study by an infant at 1 month, mom's face receives a more emotional response.

MOTOR CONTROL

Motor control is muscle movement and the sensory feedback that informs the brain of the extent of that movement. Discernible movement begins at 7 weeks postconception, with isolated limb movement evident 2 weeks later. Hand-to-face contact and body rotation are seen at 10 weeks. This is when mothers-to-be often report feeling movement by the fetus.

Neonatal Reflexes

A neonate is unable to control motor behavior smoothly and voluntarily. Instead, behaviors consist of twitches, jerks, and random movements, most of which involve automatic, involuntary motor patterns called **reflexes**. A newborn's primary oral reflexes, listed in Table 4.1, allow him or her to react to things in the world while

TABLE 4.1 Selected Oral Reflexes of the Newborn

Reflex Name	Stimulation	Response
Phasic bite	Touching or rubbing the gums	Bite-release mouth pattern
Rooting	Stroking cheek at corner of mouth	Head turns toward side being stroked; mouth begins sucking movements
Sucking	Inserting finger or nipple into mouth	Rhythmic sucking

adaptability, and stabilization (Akins & Biederer, 2006; Sheng & Hoogenraad, 2007; Sudhof, 2008).

Experience is essential for the normally occurring regulation of synapse formation. Although cell specification and axon guidance are completed early and relatively rapidly by mid-gestation, the structure of functional areas, growth of dendritic "trees," and the peak formation of synapses are far more time-extensive processes, continuing through the second and third years of life. This growth is highly dependent on stimulation. The slower growth of the cortex continues through puberty with the addition of myelin, dendritic growth, and a complex process of rerouting some synaptic connections.

No two human brains, even those of monozygotic or identical twins, are alike in every way. Instead, the cortex or surface of the upper brain is quite "plastic," meaning it is capable of reorganizing itself in a variety of ways. This is seen in children who sustain brain damage but recover seemingly lost abilities. These abilities are assumed by other portions of the cortex. Thus, children with early brain lesions use a variety of alternative developmental pathways to preserve language functioning (Booth et al., 1999).

Developmental Timing

Timing refers both to when the brain is receptive to certain inputs and to changes in the brain itself as the result of learning. Although timing is sometimes under direct genetic control, it may also be indirect and the result of multiple interactions. As a result, the onset and sequencing of events in development represents both genetic and environmental effects.

Within the first two months postconception, the human brain begins to segment into specific regions. The patterning of the cortex into different functional areas begins as soon as the first neurons are produced. The timing of neuron growth and migration are controlled by genetic factors. Collectively, these events build the early plan for brain architecture. The cerebral cortex is organized to receive information from the environment by integrating information within and across different distinct functional areas and sending this information to other brain centers that generate a response.

Infants are capable of many complex cognitive behaviors.

Experience

Early life events exert a powerful influence on both the pattern of brain organization and behavioral development (see the excellent overview by Fox, Levitt, & Nelson, 2010). The foundations of brain architecture are established early in life by the interaction of genetic influences and environmental conditions and experiences (Friederici, 2006; Grossman et al., 2003; Hensch, 2005; Horn, 2004; Majdan & Shatz, 2006). Although genetics provides a blueprint, environmental factors play a crucial role in coordinating both the timing and pattern of gene expression. For example, the ability to perceive a range of sound frequencies requires exposure to frequency variations in the environment, which later leads to language-processing proficiency (Kuhl, 2004; Newport et al. 2001; Weber-Fox & Neville, 2001). In this interaction, postnatal experiences drive the process of maturation while the ability of developmental processes to occur successfully is largely dependent on the prenatal establishment of basic brain architecture that provides the basis for receiving, interpreting, and acting on incoming information (Hammock & Levitt, 2006).

The role of environment and input to the brain is critical to the bias of neural formation in early life. Each sensory and cognitive system has a unique **sensitive period** (Daw, 1997). Depending on the ages of children, identical environmental input can have very different effects on cognitive development (Amedi et al., 2007; Jones, 2000; Trachtenberg & Stryker, 2001; Tritsch, Yi, Gale, Glowatski, & Bergles, 2007).

The types of experiences encountered in early development can have a profound effect on brain organization and development. In this way, sensitive periods represent a time during which an infant's capabilities can be modified and perhaps enhanced. The quality of experiences during these periods is extremely important. For example, typically developing children institutionalized at birth have IQs in the low 70s. If these children are placed in high-quality foster care before age 2, there are dramatic increases in IQ (Nelson et al., 2007). A similar trend also occurs for language (Windsor, Glaze, Koga, & the BEIP Core Group, 2007), although the sensitive period is later, at around 16 to 18 months of age.

Interestingly, circuits that process lower-level linguistic information, such as speech sounds, mature earlier than those that process higher-level information, such as syntax (Scherf, Behrmann, Humphreys, & Luna, 2007). High-level neural circuits that carry out sophisticated mental functions, such as syntactic processing, depend on the quality of the information they are provided by these lower-level circuits. If low-level circuits are shaped by healthy experiences early in life, they provide high-level circuits with precise, high-quality information.

Overall, changes in experience have a greater impact on younger brains than the same experience has on older more organized brains. Nevertheless, changes in the environment, especially those that are dramatic and pervasive, can alter neural connectivity and cognitive processing. This can be seen in deaf children who receive cochlear implants (Tomblin, Barker, Spencer, Zhang, & Gantz, 2005).

Early learning lays a foundation for later learning. Later development does not seem to be able to overcome the detrimental effects of early deprivation or poor neural development. On the other hand, in cases in which the early cognitive environment of infants is impoverished, early intervention has been shown to improve cognitive, linguistic, and emotional capabilities greatly (Ghera et al., 2009; Nelson et al., 2007; Windsor et al., 2007).

LEARNING

Learning begins early. At 24 weeks postconception, a fetus habituates, or becomes accustomed to, repeated stimuli such as a drumbeat. This requires very limited working memory and recognition that repeated sounds are similar. While habituation does not seem to involve long-term memory and learning, response, such as displaying a preference, to these stimuli do. Thus, newborns exposed to their mothers' voice while in utero express a preference for this sound. Similarly, children exposed to music in the last third of a pregnancy will also prefer this sound.

Both the ability to learn new tasks and to retain this learning increases with age (Rovee-Collier, 1999). For example, a 2-month-old can retain previously learned motor skills for only a few days, while a 6-month-old can recall past learning for two weeks. By 12 months, memory has increased to eight weeks.

The learning context is extremely important for retention, especially for very young infants. A behavior learned in the crib may not be recalled while on grandma's sofa. Also, as in adult learning, infant learning can be enhanced or reduced by the effect of subsequent learning.

Let's demonstrate this interaction through emotional learning. The neural pathways for emotion are established before birth; the rest is environmental. A child experiences the world as it is filtered or mediated by adults and older, more mature children. Reciprocal or shared emotional interactions strengthen the pathways. If the mother fails to respond repeatedly in a reciprocal way, her child can become confused and passive.

The Role of Schemes

As an organism develops, its conceptual system changes. The system consists of schemes, which are organized patterns of reaction to stimuli. **Schemes** are a baby's cognitive structures used for processing incoming sensory information. An event is perceived in a certain way and organized or categorized according to common characteristics. This is an active process involving interpretation and classification. An individual's response to a given stimulus is based on his or her cognitive structures and ability to respond.

A scheme or concept is a mental representation that underlies the ability to categorize, or "chunk," information for storage and retrieval. Concepts or representations are not distinctly separate entities but are linked to related stored information in complex webs called **mental maps**.

The use of concepts frees cognitive resources for higher-order functioning because each new example of the concept can be treated as familiar rather than novel. Concepts also reduce the infinite variety of sensations bombarding the brain into cognitively manageable data. For example, how many colors can you classify? You can perceive approximately 7 million (!) shades of color. Concepts such as *yellow, blue, red,* and the like, simplify information processing and make organized storage possible. When we think or form an idea for communication, concepts are withdrawn from long-term memory and held in working memory while needed.

At a very early age an infant engages in cognitively evaluating and comparing stimuli. A face is insufficient to hold an infant's attention for long periods. Rather, an infant focuses on the contrast between the face and the internal representation of a face. Stimulation is coming from both the stimulus and the representation. These representations provide an infant with an expectation of the properties of objects, events, and people in the environment.

Cognitive development is not a quantitative accumulation of ideas and facts. It is a qualitative change in the process of thought. An individual organizes and stores material in qualitatively different ways as a result. Change occurs through a child's active involvement with the environment as mediated by a mature language user who interprets and facilitates interaction for a child. The motivation for cognitive change or learning is internal as a child attempts to reach a balance between new and previously held schemes.

The Role of Adaptation

All organisms adapt to changes in the environment. These adaptations occur as a result of two related processes: assimilation and accommodation, which we'll explain shortly. Development is the result of adaptation and organization, two complementary processes (Figure 4.1)(Piaget, 1954):

1. **Adaptation** is the function or tendency of all organisms to change in response to the environment.
2. **Organization** is the tendency to systematize or organize processes into systems.

Adaptations can be cognitive as well as physical.

FIGURE 4.1 **Piaget's Cognitive Learning Process**

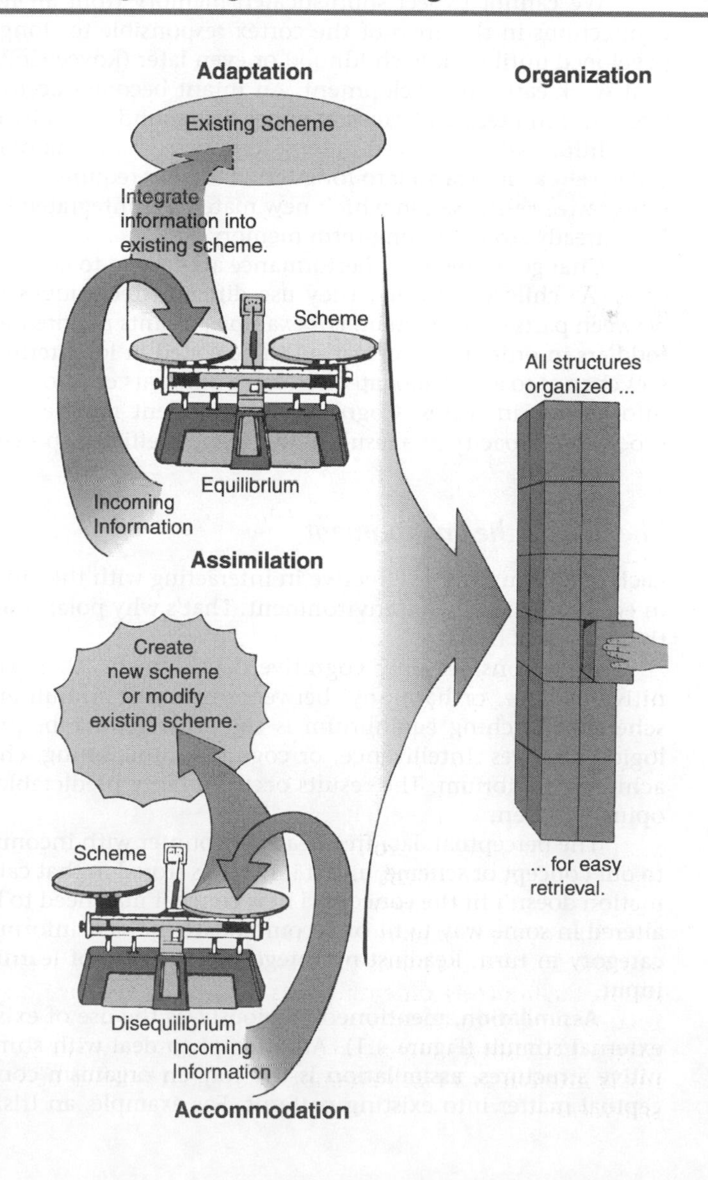

The Role of Organization and Memory

The first step in the long-term memory process involves organizing and storing perceived information. Structuring or organizing incoming information is essential because a child is continually exchanging information with the physical environment and could easily overload his or her cognitive system. This underlying organization can be inferred from the similar way in which infants interact with objects of similar perceptual attributes. Although objects may have an infinite variety of characteristics, an infant has only a limited quantity of motor responses. Therefore, he or she generalizes and classifies objects based on general motor response processes.

Organization is an attempt to bring systematic order to information. Organization is the storing and representing knowledge. If long-term memory capacity is fixed, as assumed in information processing theory, increased organization results in more efficient processing. Through experience, the patterns become better organized, leaving more capacity for other information.

We cannot expect sophisticated memory from an infant. Some of the synaptic connections in the areas of the cortex responsible for long-term memory are not fully developed until middle childhood or even later (Rovee-Collier, 1999). Even so, memory is at work early in development. An infant becomes accustomed to its mother's voice while still in utero and can remember that sound after birth.

Information is placed in long-term storage and maintained by repetition, a process called **rehearsal**. Transfer to long-term memory requires a special type of rehearsal, called **integrative rehearsal**, in which new material is integrated into the structure of information already stored in long-term memory.

Changes in memory performance are related to changes in long-term storage strategies. As children mature, they use different techniques to control information flow between parts of the system. For example, infants require more repetitive rehearsals than toddlers in order for information to be coded in long-term memory. As memory strategies change to accommodate increasing amounts of information, a child's ability to hold information increases. Cognitive development represents an increase in information processing capacity as a result of use of more efficient processing strategies.

The Role of the Environment

Each organism is more effective in interacting with the environment if that organism is in equilibrium with the environment. That's why polar bears survive better in the arctic than do black bears.

If we consider only cognitive development, then **equilibrium** is a state of cognitive balance, or harmony, between incoming stimuli and the organism's cognitive schemes. Reaching equilibrium is the driving force behind cognitive and other biological changes. Intelligence, or cognitive functioning, changes with each attempt to achieve equilibrium. The results occur in fairly predictable patterns in typically developing children.

The perceptual data from each encounter with incoming information is compared to our concept or scheme, and if it fits, it is stored in that category. If the incoming information doesn't fit the concept, a new concept may need to be formed or the old concept altered in some way to fit or accommodate the new information. This change alters the category in turn. Readjusting categories is a form of learning based on environmental input.

Assimilation, mentioned previously, is the use of existing schemes to incorporate external stimuli (Figure 4.1). An attempt to deal with stimuli in terms of present cognitive structures, assimilation is the way an organism continually integrates new perceptual matter into existing patterns. For example, an Irish setter is similar enough to be incorporated into the dog category along with collies and German shepherds. The similarities are great enough to allow their assimilation. Without such categorization, we could make little sense of the environment. Not all stimuli fit into available schemes, however, and mental structures must be adapted to these stimuli.

Accommodation is a transformation process in response to external stimuli that do not fit into any available scheme and, therefore, cannot be assimilated (Figure 4.1). An individual has the option of modifying an existing scheme or developing a new one. The Irish setter could be included in the dog concept; an elephant is sufficiently different to require a new category.

Once the organism has accommodated its schemes to the external stimulus, the new information is assimilated, or incorporated, into the new or modified scheme. Thus, the processes of assimilation and accommodation are complementary and mutually dependent. New or modified structures are created continually and then used to aid the organism's comprehension of the environment. While this explanation has been very simplistic, it does give us a basis for discussing cognition and language development.

Cognition and Communication Development

The same general processes that are at work in cognitive development are also important for development of speech, language, and communication. Let's explore the first two and leave communication for the next chapter because that requires two participants and is better explained along with social development.

SPEECH

Perception of speech and the motor control to produce speech are important factors in communication development. While neither is absolutely necessary and children can use other means, such as sign, to communicate, the typical child's first symbols will take the form of spoken words.

Because of infants' perceptual learning, when they begin to babble, they are well prepared to recognize the related auditory feedback from their own sound production. This feedback allows them to monitor and adjust the vocal tract as they vary their sound production.

Perception

While in utero, a fetus is exposed to many auditory stimuli, especially the sound of the mother's voice. For most newborns, mom's voice is their preferred environmental sound.

A newborn is capable of many types of auditory discrimination. For example, a newborn can discriminate between different sound durations and loudness levels and different consonants in short syllables.

Newborns are also capable of discriminating different pitches or frequencies, especially in the human speech range. In fact, neonates respond to the human voice more often and with more vigor than to other environmental sounds. By 2 months, an infant is also able to discriminate frequency changes, such as high to low. Because intonational patterns are closely related to frequency shifts, we would expect to see this type of discrimination shortly thereafter, and this occurs by 7 months. At about the same time, infants are able to discriminate different words.

When a child hears speech sounds over and over, neurons in the auditory system stimulate connections in the child's temporal lobe. This process is gradual, and sounds must be heard thousands of times before neurons are assigned. Differences and similarities between sounds are noted and recorded. Eventually, different clusters of neurons will respond to each phoneme, firing when the phoneme is heard.

This seemingly early "hardening" of low-level circuits has an effect on language learning. By adulthood, there is a perceptual bias toward certain sounds. Your auditory system is better capable of discriminating phonemes and tones outside the auditory environment in which you were raised. Phonemes that sound close to American English phonemes are harder for American English speakers to discriminate than those that differ more (Frieda, Walley, Flege, & Sloane, 1999; Guion, Flege, Akahane-Yamada, & Pruitt, 2000; Kuhl, 2004). This is why you may think you are saying a word correctly in another language when, in fact, you are butchering it from a native speaker's perspective. All is not lost for those of you learning a second language because neurons seem to be constantly modifying connectivity, allowing learning from new environments to compete against already existing tendencies.

The Formation of Auditory Patterns During the first year, a child lays down a perceptual framework for learning first words. An infant actively encodes the sounds of his or her native language, organizing them into sound patterns.

Learning about speech signals may begin as soon as the auditory system is functional. Thus, it's likely that a fetus is learning something about the rhythms of its soon-to-be native language even while in utero. At birth French newborns seem to prefer listening to French, Japanese infants to Japanese, and so on. Although neonates are especially sensitive to intonation, by 3 months of age they seem to be more attentive to the sound patterns of words (Ferry, Hespos, & Waxman, 2010).

Discrimination of Phonemes Newborns are capable of detecting virtually every phoneme contrast used in human languages, something most adults can no longer easily perceive. The accuracy of children's perceptual ability declines during the first year, as infants learn to lump together sounds that their own language treats as equivalent, such as the /b/ and /v/ in Spanish. In other words, children spend much of the first year losing their ability to perceive contrasts that are not used in the speech around them. Thus, Japanese adults and older children find it very difficult to perceive the difference between "ra" and "la," although Japanese infants have no trouble at all.

Between birth and 6 months of age, infants begin to show a preference for vowel sounds in their native language. Language-specific preference for consonants seems to occur later. An infant's perceptual ability is usually restricted to its native language's speech sounds by 8 to 10 months of age, about the time that most infants start to comprehend words.

Infants' decreasing ability to discriminate most sounds outside their native language results from experience. As an aside, you can now appreciate why it is important for second-language learning to occur early in life.

Beyond Phonemes As they are exposed to their native language, newborns begin to recognize regularities and patterns that occur. This is part of the way in which our minds function; we look for patterns, then form concepts or schemes based on these patterns. The ability to detect patterns and to make generalizations is extremely important for later symbol and language rule learning (Marcus, 2001). Significant correlations exist between speech perception at 6 months of age and later word understanding, word production, and phrase understanding, thus indicating the importance of early perception in language acquisition (Tsao, Liu, & Kuhl, 2004).

Extracting and learning individual speech sounds from the speech stream is difficult, even though newborns are capable of discriminating *individual* phonemes. It is extremely problematic to discern individual words and sounds in the ongoing, multiword utterances of adult speech. Yet by 5 months, most children respond to their own name and, within another month, respond to either *mommy* or *daddy* (Tincoff & Jusczyk, 1999). These are frequently occurring words in a child's world. By 8 months, children can store the sound patterns for words, although meaning is not attached yet.

The period of 8 to 10 months is marked by changes in both perception and production. Timing may be related to brain developments that occur around the same time, including synaptogenesis or a burst in synaptic connections, changes in activity levels in the frontal lobes, and an increase in executive function. In fact, the 8- to 10-month period includes dramatic changes in several cognitive and social domains, such as imitation of others and intentional communication, which will be discussed later. Babies learn patterns of prosody and phonotactic organization of their native language and, at this age, use these skills to help break up and analyze the relative unbroken speech stream of mature speakers into recognizable words.

Prosody Prosody is the flow of language. In English, 80% of words in conversation have stress on the initial syllable. The prosodic pattern in English is characterized as stress-time, meaning that different syllables receive more stress and are held for a longer time, while others receive less of both. Not all languages are so organized. For example, Japanese has short syllables with nearly equal stress and time.

Young infants are sensitive to stress and to rising and falling intonational patterns. Even newborns are capable of discriminating different prosodic patterns and can recognize utterances in their native language from those in languages with different prosodic patterns. Stress patterns are one tool used by infants to determine word boundaries (Jusczyk, Houston, & Newsome, 1999).

As noted, soon after birth, infants prefer their native languages to other languages. Most likely, these preferences emerge from the infant's ability to detect language-specific prosodic or rhythm patterns. From early on, infants seem to be sensitive to the intonation of the language they hear. Even 2-month-olds tend to remember words better when presented with normal sentence intonation. In addition, children tend to perceive and remember stressed or emphasized syllables more readily than unstressed ones. Unfortunately, prosodic cues alone are insufficient to segment speech successfully.

Phonotactic Organization Phonotactic organization consists of syllable structure and sound combinations. For example, /pt/ can appear at the end of both a syllable and a word (stepped) in English but not at the beginning. In contrast, /fh/ and /vt/ are likely to occur across word boundaries, as in *cal**f h**ide* and *glo**ve t**ouches*, respectively. Armed with this information, it's easier for a child to determine word boundaries. Of course, first an infant has to recognize these patterns in the language she or he hears.

Identifying word boundaries in continuous speech is relatively easy for adult listeners. For infants, however, this task can be challenging because words are not consistently separated by pauses. Luckily, there are other types of information embedded in speech that mark word boundaries. These include **phonotactic regularities** or patterns in speech (Jusczyk et al., 1999; Mattys & Jusczyk, 2001).

Young language learners are especially sensitive to frequently occurring patterns in the language of their environment (Werker & Curtin, 2005). These patterns can be thought of as **phonotactic probabilities**, or the likelihood that certain sounds, sound sequences, and syllable types will occur. For example, the likelihood of a word in English ending in /h/—not the letter but the sound—is zero. Nine-month-old infants have a listening preference for nonwords composed of high phonotactic probabilities. In production, infants are better at saying frequent sequences (e.g., /kt/) than infrequent sequences (e.g., /gd/) (Edwards, Beckman, & Munson, 2004).

Think of infants as little statisticians, figuring out the probabilities of certain sound combinations in certain locations in words. Then they apply these probabilities to speech to figure out where word boundaries occur. One regularity available to infants is the probability between syllable sequences or the probability of one syllable type following another.

By 5 months, infants can discriminate their own language from others with the same prosodic patterns (Nazzi, Jusczyk, & Johnson, 2000). Presumably, children use phonemes, frequent phoneme combinations, and syllable structure to reach this decision.

Eight-month-old infants are sensitive to regularities in infant-directed speech (IDS) and can learn them quickly even in another language (Pelucchi, Hay, & Saffran, 2009). Presumably, these infants are using distributional cues. An infant begins to remember certain frequent sound sequences, such as *mommy*, that create representations in the child's long-term memory. When the word is heard again the sound sequence activates this representation and is perceived as a single unit. Use of this sound unit in a sentence helps the child to segment other sentence elements into individual words, as in "Kiss mommy." At this point, a child most likely does not attach meaning to the sound sequence.

At 9 months, children are using both prosodic and phonotactic clues to discern individual speech sounds within connected speech. An infant begins to detect highly probable and recurring sound sequences. High-probability sequences most likely signal words, while low-probability sequences, such ad *tk* or *db*, probably signal word or syllable boundaries (Mattys, Jusczyk, Luce, & Morgan, 1999). Within two months, they are able to recognize allophones and to use variations within individual phonemes to aid in word boundary identification (Jusczyk, Houston, & Newsome, 1999).

A child's phonotactic representations or patterns are also correlated with vocabulary growth. Children with smaller vocabularies have less robust phonological representations, making it more difficult for them to parse or divide words into their sounds and sound sequences. More specifically, vocabulary size seems to be related to young children's (26–32 months) ability to repeat phoneme combinations, especially in the initial position (Zamuner, 2009).

Of course, this doesn't explain how infants figure out these patterns. An infant doesn't need complete knowledge of sound regularities. Instead, an infant only needs some wordlike units with which to figure out regularities. For example, some words, such as a child's name, are frequently heard as single words or in frequent word combinations that would help a child identify them (Bortfeld, Morgan, Golinkoff, & Rathbun, 2005; Brent & Siskind, 2001).

In this video, Dr Patricia Kuhl discusses her research into speech perception in infants. http://www.youtube.com/watch?v=G2XBIkHW954

In summary, throughout the first year an infant tunes out irrelevant speech sounds and tunes in to the phonological characteristics of his or her native language. Now that an infant has some of the patterns of speech, he or she will need to develop oral motor control before talking can occur.

Motor Development and Sound Making

Speech is an extremely complex behavior dependent on the coordination of a number of motor movements. Learning precise control of the oral mechanism continues for years.

Newborn Vocalizations In the neonate, vocalization is controlled by the brainstem and pons, and development may coincide with maturation of portions of the facial and laryngeal areas of the motor cortex of the brain. Newborns produce predominantly reflexive sounds, such as fussing and crying, and vegetative sounds, such as burping and swallowing. Reflexive sounds are primarily produced on exhalation and consist of relatively lengthy vowel-like sounds. In contrast, vegetative sounds are produced on inhalation and exhalation, are both consonant- and vowel-like, and are of brief duration. Production of both types decreases with maturation.

Initially, a newborn cries on both inhalation and exhalation, but there are many individual variations. The expiration phase of breathing gradually increases within crying, which usually occurs most frequently before feeding and bed. Through crying, a child becomes accustomed to airflow across the vocal folds and to modified breathing patterns. Because speech sounds originate at the level of the larynx, where the vocal folds are housed, this early stimulation is important.

Other noncrying sounds typically accompany feeding or are produced in response to smiling or talking by the mother. These noncrying vowel-like sounds with brief consonantal elements have been characterized as **quasi-resonant nuclei (QRN)**. QRNs contain phonation, or vibration of the vocal folds, but a child does not have sufficient control of the vocal mechanism to produce either true consonants or full vowels.

Producing speech sounds is a complicated process that includes the following aspects:

- Respiration of air
- Vibration at the larynx by the exiting air stream
- Resonation or a modification of the vibratory pattern through changes in the size and configuration of the vocal tract, which consists of the nasal cavity, the oral cavity or mouth, and the pharynx or throat
- Articulation of specific phonemes alone or in sequence using the jaw, tongue, teeth, and lips

Initially, production of sounds is caused accidentally by chance movements of the vocal folds. QRNs tend to be individual sounds rather than sound sequences.

The vocal tract of a neonate resembles that of nonhuman primates and differs considerably from that of a human adult. In Figure 4.2, note the relative height of the infant larynx and the close proximity of the larynx and the vocal tract. During crying, the lower jaw and tongue are dropped and the soft palate and pharyngeal wall move rearward, resulting in the vowel-like quality of distress sounds.

FIGURE 4.2 **Comparison of the Oral Structures of the Infant and Adult**

In part, the differences in the sounds of infants and adults can be explained by the physical differences of the two. In this schematic, the infant has been enlarged to the approximate size of an adult.

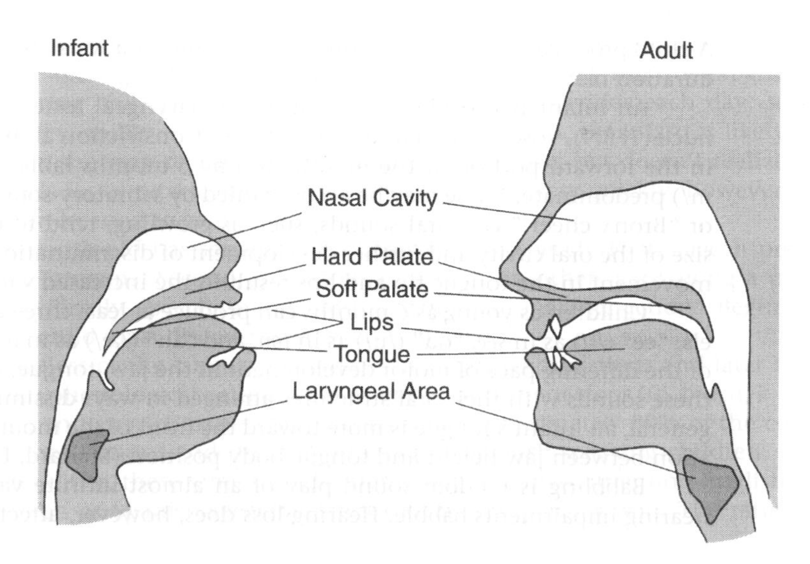

consonants to consonant clusters (/st, gs/)—roughly 9:1—is also similar in babbling and in the first 50 words in both languages. Finally, the ratio of CV to VC syllables is also similar, at roughly 3:1 in both English and Spanish.

Infants whose parents speak to them in languages as different as Korean and English demonstrate similar consonant patterns in their reduplicated babbling (Lee, Davis, & MacNeilage, 2010). The infants' vowel patterns differ, however, and reflect the input language. Syllable structure and the consonant repertoire are also affected.

At around 8 months, other changes occur in an infant's sound patterns. These include echolalia and variegated babbling. Between 8 and 12 months an infant begins to imitate the communication of others. Called echolalic speech, or **echolalia**, it is an immediate imitation of some other speaker. Imitation begins with gestures and intonation, but by 8 months speech exhibits the identifiable pitch and contour patterns of the parent language.

Soon an infant begins to imitate the sounds of others, but at first only those sounds he or she has already produced spontaneously. Within a few months an infant will begin to use imitation to expand and modify his or her repertoire of speech sounds. As you might expect, sounds that are not in the native language decrease in number. An infant will also imitate stressed syllables in certain often-used words. For example, a child may repeat "na-na" when mother says "banana," although he or she may not be associating the sound with the actual referent or thing to which it refers. The number of repeated single sounds and CV syllables increases during reduplicated babbling but appears to plateau immediately prior to the onset of variegated babbling (Fagan, 2009).

In **variegated babbling** adjacent and successive syllables are not identical. Sound sequences may also include VCV and CVC structures. In addition, reduplicated babbling becomes less self-stimulatory and is used more in imitation games with adults. Whatever the babbling, it takes on more of the intonation of speech.

During the first year, the average child utterance is less than a second in duration and contains fewer than three sounds with no repetition. Interestingly, even with the changes mentioned, infant utterances do not become substantially longer and more complex overall. They grow modestly from single sounds to CV syllables and some CV-CV combinations (Fagan, 2009). In their first words, infants will produce only one- and two-syllable utterances (Fagan, 2009).

The Emergence of Speech Patterns There is limited evidence of any direct relationship between early babbling and the language spoken in the environment of an infant prior to 9 months. The seemingly independent development of perception and speech may be related to the different areas of the brain devoted to the two functions.

By 9 months of age, however, there is increasing evidence of a connection. Sound-making changes first occur in intonational patterns. Called **jargon**, it consists of long strings of unintelligible sounds with adultlike prosodic and intonational patterns. Infants 7 to 10 months of age are sensitive to prosodic or rhythmic cues that help them segment speech into smaller perceptual units.

A child's babbling gradually comes to resemble the prosodic pattern of the language to which he or she is exposed. Apparently, the paralinguistic aspects of language are easier for the child to reproduce than the linguistic aspects. Babbling patterns become shorter and phonetically more stable. The resultant jargon may sound like questions, commands, and statements. Many parents will swear at this point that their child is communicating in sentences, although the parents aren't exactly clear on what the child is saying.

Children's early intonation reflects the interaction of biological, affective or emotional, and linguistic influences (Snow, 2006). Although many modifications suggest the importance of linguistic input, the early expression of intonation in infants also points to the role of physiological changes and emotional experience.

Speech recognition and production pose numerous problems for an infant that complicate the process:

- The child is exposed to a variety of speakers and contexts.
- The relationship of spoken words to their meanings is essentially arbitrary and lacks any systematic relationship between the sounds in a word and the word's meaning.
- An infant does not receive any direct instruction is producing comprehensible speech.
- The infant must coordinate the processes of learning to comprehend and to produce speech.

While comprehension involves placing input onto meaning, production involves generating output from a phonological representation in order to convey meaning. To make it even more difficult, this must all be accomplished within ongoing communication.

Phonological representations consist of phonemes and syllable structures of the native language, such as *mommy* or *eat*, that are stored in the brain after repeated exposure. As such, phonological representations of words form a stable template or pattern against which both input and output can be compared to see if it fits. In addition, phonological representations bridge acoustic input, articulatory output, and meaning (Plaut & Kello, 1999).

Many speech sounds will develop sound–meaning relationships. Called **phonetically consistent forms (PCFs)**, these sounds function as words for an infant, even though they are not based on adult words. A PCF is a consistent prosodic and speech-sound pattern, such as "puda," created and used by a child to refer to an entity, such as the family cat. A child may develop a dozen PCFs before he or she speaks first words. PCFs are found across children regardless of the language they will later speak (Blake & deBoysson-Bardies, 1992).

PCFs may be a link between babbling and adultlike speech in that they are more limited than babbling but not as phonologically structured as adult speech. Characterized as meaningful babbling, PCFs display the active and creative role of a child as a language learner. A child does not use PCFs just because adult models are too difficult. Rather, he or she gets the idea that there can be sound–meaning relationships. Thus, the child demonstrates a recognition of linguistic regularities.

Before we move to cognition, it's worth noting that a child's ability to chew and to make sounds is not merely a reflection of the child's developing motor control. Instead, among typically developing infants from 9 to 22 months, lower jaw (mandible) motor control for production of early multisyllabic babbling is influenced by the interaction between linguistic and developing motor systems (Steeve & Moore, 2009). Variation in linguistic complexity changes motor organization to meet these demands. This same effect is noted with chewing and jaw movement. In other words, motor development is in part driven by the requirements of the task, such as babbling or chewing. In 9-month-olds, coordination of the muscles varies with the task. Coordination in babbling lags behind that for sucking and chewing (Steeve, Moore, Green, Reilly, & Ruark McMurtrey, 2008). For 15-month-olds, mandibular control is organized differently across speech and nonspeech tasks and these forms of motor control undergo continuing refinement into adulthood.

In minutes 34:59-39:05 of this video, Dr. Steven Pinker of Harvard University discusses the anatomical and physiological aspects of speech production. http://www.youtube.com/watch?v=Q-B_ONJIEcE

Newly acquired motor skills provide infants with practice prior to the use of similar behaviors in communication. In addition, the emergence of new motor skills changes infants' experience with objects and people in ways that are important for both general communicative development and the acquisition of language (Iverson, 2010). Without a doubt, speech production is a motor act, and there are links among oral-motor physiology, skill acquisition, and oral language (Green & Wilson, 2006; Nip, Green, & Marx, 2009; Thelen, 1991). Gestures, a basis for later language use, are also motor behaviors.

Although the CV pattern in early phonetic development has been found in many languages, by age 1, language-specific patterns have emerged. These include speech-sound combinations and frequency of occurrence (Chen & Kent, 2005).

LANGUAGE

Together, let's try to sift through cognitive development as it relates to the emergence of language. Although Nativists, led by Noam Chomsky, claim that language is innate, that explains very little of the actual process.

Before we begin, we probably need to define one term, **representations**. Representations are our way of describing concepts stored in the brain. Just as a photo or a common sound, such as a dog's bark, can stand for the thing it represents, a representation is a mental image that stands for an external reality. Thinking occurs within a system of representations.

Let's focus our attention on infants' general information processing abilities in memory, processing speed, attention, and representational competence that may account for language growth (Rose, Feldman, & Jankowski, 2004, 2005). We'll discuss each of these areas of cognition briefly.

Memory

Memory is vital for acquiring all forms of knowledge, including language. Infants with better memory are more adept at encoding, storing, consolidating, and retrieving representations of objects and events—skills fundamental to language development. More specifically, infants with better recognition and recall memory are more able to link these words with "referents," the entities to which the words refer.

Good visual *recognition memory*, recognizing entities in the environment, is related to good comprehension and gestural communication in toddlers and better receptive and expressive language in preschoolers (Heimann et al., 2006). Better *recall memory*, bringing information from memory storage, at 9 months is related to better gestural production at 14 months. Together, these two memory abilities, recognition memory and recall, at 12 months predict language skills at 36 months (Rose, Feldman, & Jankowski, 2009).

Over time, with repeated exposure, an infant begins to form a representation of common entities, such as *mommy*. Recognition memory enables the child to identify mommy from incoming stimuli, such as her face or voice. The stimuli are compared to the representation. Mental associations are made between the physical characteristics and the name of the stimulus. Soon, the word *mommy* may elicit the representation.

Finally, a child is able to retrieve the representation at will. A toddler can produce the word *mommy* with no input stimulus, such as the presence of mother. As memory becomes less context-bound, a toddler is free to experiment and to use both objects and symbols in novel ways. With increased memory, a young child is able to understand and produce more than one symbol at a time.

Processing Speed

Processing speed is related to performance on a wide variety of cognitive tasks. Obviously, faster processing speed enables mental operations to be performed more rapidly by the child and thus increases the capacity of working memory. We can assume that limitations in processing speed would make it difficult to keep up with speech input. This in turn would interfere with building internal representations of language essential for development (Leonard et al., 2007).

Language input comes in the form of speech. Infants use working memory to hold information while they segment this auditory speech input into meaningful units, such as words and phrases. With maturation and repeated exposure to the environment, working memory expands and information processing becomes more automatic.

Attention

Attention includes the ability to engage, maintain, disengage, and shift focus. In general, infants with better attention are likely to acquire language more quickly. They are better able to follow the gaze of others, engage in joint or shared attention, and track referents or subjects of others' speech. During the first year, duration of looking, which may reflect more rapid encoding and/or greater facility at disengaging attention, and shift rate, which may reflect more active comparison of targets, change dramatically. In general, the duration of looking becomes shorter and the rate of shifting attention becomes faster (Colombo, Shaddy, Richman, Maikranz, & Blaga, 2004; Frick, Colombo, & Saxon, 1999; Rose, Feldman, & Jankowski, 2001).

There is a correlation between cognitive development and development of joint attention (Mundy et al., 2007). Joint or shared attention occurs when two individuals, such as a mother and infant, attend to the same thing, such as a toy. The ability of an infant to focus on something while his or her mother discusses or manipulates it is important for learning and may be a precursor of focusing on a topic together in a conversation.

Representational Competence

Representational competence is the ability to extract commonalties from experiences and represent them abstractly or symbolically. Representational and symbolic abilities in which an infant establishes relations between words and referents is necessary for language development. These abilities are seen in infants' anticipation of future events, in object permanence, and symbolic play in which one object is used to represent another. These abilities all require an infant to represent things and locations not immediately available to the senses.

Symbolic play and object permanence have long been associated with language development (Tamis-Lemonda, Shannon, Cabrera, & Lamb, 2004). Symbolic play is using an object for other than its intended purpose, such as a slipper being used as a pretend cell phone. Object permanence, seen when an infant searches for a missing object, is knowing that an object exists even when it is not readily visible. The representations are organized and stored in the brain.

The effect of language spoken to a child cannot be overemphasized. There is a direct correlation between the number of words heard by a child during early development and the cognitive abilities of that child even into the late preschool years. In general, the more words a child hears, the faster she or he will learn language.

At about 7 months, an infant begins to "understand" one or two single words. Not only does he or she perceive different sequences of phonemes, but an infant associates them with entities in the environment. Incoming acoustic patterns are compared with stored sound traces and their associated meanings. Within another three months, he or she can recognize a familiar word within a phrase or a short sentence.

At 9 to 13 months, children understand words based on a combination of sound, nonlinguistic and paralinguistic cues, and context. In other words, in certain specific contexts children have limited comprehension of some phonemic sequences. The words are probably not comprehended outside that context. The exceptions are the child's name and *no*, which most children seem to recognize. As a result of continued exposure to recurring speech-sound patterns in context, a child learns these patterns in these situations.

Obviously, memory is important for retention and integration of input in order both to map or form a representation of the entire word connecting semantics and phonology and to retrieve that representation. Acoustic information, even just the initial sounds of a word, likely activates a semantic representation of the entire word, enabling an infant to derive some semantic information from the available input (Plaut & Kello, 1999). When the word is reliably distinguished from others, the semantic network activates the full meaning. While phonological representations of entire words probably build up gradually over time from sequences of acoustic input, semantic representations may begin forming with only one exposure to a word.

It is worth noting that information processing abilities cross different modalities (Rose et al., 2009). In other words, visual memory skills may represent underlying memory abilities that affect auditory memory (Visscher, Kaplan, Kahana, & Sekuler, 2007). This cross-modal transfer can be seen in other areas. For example, advances in symbolic play, using one object to represent another, suggest advances in linguistic representations, using words to represent objects.

ROLE OF THE CAREGIVER

A baby's interaction with the environment is moderated by an adult or a more mature child who uses language to help explain and describe the child's experiences. While not directly teaching the child, this caregiver provides the opportunity for learning.

TABLE 4.2 Maternal Techniques for Infant Participation

Techniques	Behaviors	Examples
Phasing	Monitors infant behavior to determine when to slot her behavior for most impact; must know when to intervene to attain predictable outcome	Mother attains infant's attention to an object before using it in some way. Mother monitors infant's gaze and follows it for clues to infant interest.
Adaptive	Exhibits behaviors that enable infant to assimilate information more rapidly; maintains infant's attention and provides highly ordered, predictable input	Mother uses slower arm movements than with adults. Mother has more emphatic gestures and more exaggerated facial expressions than with adults. Mother's speech is simpler and more repetitive than with adults.
Facilitative	Structures routine and environment to ensure infant success	Mother holds toy so child can explore. Mother assists infant physically. Mother supplies needed materials for task completion.
Elaborative	Allows child to indicate an interest, then elaborates on it; talks following the infant's activities and interests closely	Mother demonstrates play with object of infant's interest. Mother talks about infant's behavior as she performs (parallel talking).
Initiating	Directs infant's attention to objects, events, and persons; follows sequence of gaining infant's attention, directing it, and looking back to ensure that the infant is attending	Mother points to direct attention. Mother brings object into child's view.
Control	Tells infant what she or he is to do; pauses after key words that are emphasized and makes extensive use of gestures	Mother insists that infant eat. Mother stresses what she wants the infant to do.

Source: Information from Schaffer (1977).

The caregiver regulates not only the amount of stimulation but also the timing. Caregiver behavior is not random but fits into the child's behavior. By modifying his or her behavior, the caregiver maintains an interactional dialog with the infant. There are six techniques that mothers and parents use to create opportunities for their children to participate (Schaffer, 1977). These techniques—phasing, adaptive, facilitative, elaborative, initiating, and control—are listed in Table 4.2. The mother monitors her child's behavior continually and adapts her behavior accordingly. Her modifications enable the infant to enter the dialog as a partner. These mutual dialogs seem to reach their greatest frequency when an infant reaches the age of 3 or 4 months.

Conclusion

COGNITION PRECEDES LANGUAGE DEVELOPMENT. At this stage, a child expresses in his or her language only those relationships that are understood intellectually. It seems safe to assert that there are certain levels of cognitive functioning that must precede expressive language. It is also plausible that this relationship changes with maturation.

The child needs perceptual skills to discriminate the smallest units of speech and to process speech-sound sequences. Both skills require good auditory memory. At a linguistic-processing level, these sound sequences are matched with the entities and actions they represent, called referents. These representational abilities develop in the infant during the first two years of life through adaptation to, and organization of, incoming sensory stimuli.

Unfortunately, there are still many unanswered questions about this early relationship of cognition, or thought, and language. The mental processes involved in word–referent association and in the use of true symbols have not been adequately explained.

The cognitive basis of language is best illustrated in early semantic development. Much early expressive language development involves a child's learning how to express the meanings that he or she already knows. Stated somewhat differently, a child must develop a certain number of meanings before he or she can begin to confer information intentionally on the environment. By interacting with objects and persons in the environment, an infant forms primitive definitions that are later paired with the word and the referent.This relationship will be discussed in more detail in Chapters 6 and 7.

In the final analysis, the cognitive and perceptual bases for early language appear to be necessary for early language development but are not adequate for a full explanation of the process. This does not detract from the importance of early perceptual and cognitive development, but it begs consideration of other factors. Language does not develop in a vacuum; rather, it develops within an environment of well-developed communication.

Sociolinguistic studies emphasize environmental influences, especially the social interactions between children and their primary caregiver. It is possible that *event knowledge*, or a child's understanding of daily routines and events, rather than knowledge of objects, forms the conceptual foundation for language (Farrar, Friend, & Forbes, 1993). This possibility will be explored in Chapter 5.

Discussion

LANGUAGE DOESN'T JUST HAPPEN. A child needs certain cognitive perceptual, social, and communicative skills. In the future, you may work with children who lack the cognitive skills to use language. As a group, we might label these children as having mental retardation. A child might also lack perceptual skills. We might say these children have a severe learning disability. Other children may lack the motor skills for speech, such as those with cerebral palsy, or may have a sensory deficit, such as those who have deafness, but they may be able to develop language through some augmentative or alternative method of communication, such as pictures, sign, or the use of computers. As

There is a common assumption that development of language and speech enables children to become communicating beings. This supposition does not reflect the actual behavior of infants, who communicate well before they have language. Actually, acquisition of language depends on the prior development of communication.

In Chapter 4 we discussed how words and symbols take on meaning related to the underlying cognitive representations of a child. This process of associating words to meaning does not occur in isolation. Although a child can, to some degree, understand the entities and relationships in the world by exploring on his or her own, this knowledge can be expanded and labeled only by interacting within a social environment.

As we said in Chapter 1, language is a social tool, and we must look to a child's interactive environment to understand his or her development. Simply put, children learn language in order to communicate better or to maintain better social contact.

The social context in which language occurs helps an infant understand that language. Both the nature of communication situations and the process of communicating aid linguistic development. Caregivers talk about objects that are immediately present in the environment. These communication exchanges have a predictable quality that also facilitates comprehension and learning.

Language represents only a portion of a larger interactional pattern that reflects the way we socialize our children. In short, babies become communicating beings because that's the way they are treated. Within the communication context, the caregiver assumes that the child is attempting to communicate meaningfully.

In this chapter we will discuss infant–caregiver interactions almost exclusively. In middle-class American culture, the mother tends to be her infant's primary caregiver and, therefore, the primary socializing agent, thus nearly all infant interactive studies have focused on the female parent. You should keep in mind as you read that we will be discussing a "generic" mother–child duo and that many variations exist.

In families with lower income (low SES), a mother's need to work, the family structure, and the neighborhood environment may result in older children becoming the primary caregivers. Studies indicate that these children behave in much the same way as middle-class mothers in their communication adaptations. Even so, these older children or mothers from either families with low SES or those from different cultures may interact differently with their children than middle-SES English-speaking mothers in the United States do.

There are many different ways to learn language. In some African cultures, a mother and child have less face-to-face interaction than in the United States. Instead, a mother spends the day reciting ritualized rhymes or songs. Through this process, her child learns that language is predictable. These interactions provide a culturally appropriate language-learning environment.

Within the middle-SES American infant–caregiver exchange, an infant develops the essential skills for learning language. The dialog is one of mutual participation. The infant's contribution is as important as that of the caregiver. The caregiver integrates her or his behavior into the infant's behavior system, and both seem to adjust their behaviors to maintain an optimal level of interaction.

Although the content and intonation of these dialogs has been characterized as "baby talk," the dialog pattern is adult. Naturally, the roles taken by an infant and caregiver are different. The caregiver

- has superior flexibility of timing and anticipates the infant's behavior;
- has an intuitive curriculum and leads the infant's behavior slightly;
- is able to monitor and code changes of expression more rapidly;
- can more readily alternate among different means to attain the desired ends; and
- is more creative in introducing variations of repetitive vocalizations.

Communication is maintained because a mother is socially sensitive to the effect of her behavior on the infant and tailors her speech to the task and to her child's abilities. Mothers learn this skill in order to sustain the exchange and to hold attention. In addition, mothers attribute meaning to their infant's behavior, enabling a dialog to occur.

Much of this early dialog occurs in specific situations, or is situation-dependent. Daily routines also provide predictable patterns of behavior, which aid interpretation. As a result, an infant learns the conventions of conversation. It would be incorrect, however, to assume that a child does not influence the interaction. Mother and child engage as partners in a dialog.

In this chapter we will examine the behavior of both the caregiver and the infant in their early interactions. Of importance are the communication strategies that facilitate later speech and language development. The discussion will be developmental in nature and will specifically concern interaction and communication development in newborns and during the first year. Later in the chapter, we will explore adult communication strategies and interactional behaviors such as joint reference and joint action, game playing, and turn taking. (See also Appendix A, Tables A.1 and A.2.)

Development of Communication: A Chronology

An infant's world is a world of people—people who do things for, to, and with the infant. In the process, an infant learns the conventions of communication into which he or she will eventually place linguistic elements. Every mother will verify the fact that her child began to communicate long before developing language. By the time a child begins to use words, he or she is already able to indicate intentions and to elicit and interpret responses from others.

THE NEWBORN

Perceptual and cognitive abilities might suggest that a neonate is "prewired" for communication. For example, vision attains best focus at about 8 inches, where most infant–caregiver interactions occur. Within a few hours of birth, an infant can follow visually at this close range. During feeding, a mother's eyes are at a distance of almost 7½ inches exactly, and she gazes at her infant 70% of the time. The child is most likely, therefore, to look at and focus on its mother's face, especially the mother's eyes.

Preferences

The newborn's visual preference is for the human face. Newborns prefer visual stimuli with angularity, light and shade, complexity, and curvature. The human face contains all these preferred parameters. Infants find the human face fascinating, and mothers attract as much interest as possible to their faces. Visual preferences suggest that the angles at the corners of the eyes and the dark-light contrast of the eye itself and the eyebrow might be particularly attractive. A caregiver interprets eye contact as a sign of interest or attention.

The importance of eye contact cannot be overstated. Parents of children with congenital blindness or children who avoid eye contact, such as those with autism spectrum disorder (ASD), may have more difficulty relating to their children.

Undoubtedly, a newborn has been exposed in utero to sounds. He or she has also been hearing mother's somewhat muffled voice and experiencing the rhythmic movements that accompany mother's speech. In response to speech, adults make discrete and continuous synchronous movements at the phoneme, syllable, phrase, and sentence levels. This interactional synchronization, called *entrainment*, is also exhibited by a neonate within 20 minutes of birth. In contrast, a neonate will not produce synchronous movements to disconnected vowel sounds or to tapping. A newborn prefers the acoustic patterns of her or his mother's speech.

A neonate's optimal hearing is within the frequency range of the human voice. In fact, a neonate has definite auditory preferences for the human voice, especially his or her mother's voice, over nonspeech sounds.

Infants show a bias for listening to speech from birth (Vouloumanos & Werker, 2007). Genuine conversational speech seems to be an infant's preference. By 3 months, infants show a clear preference for human speech of several varieties (Vouloumanos, Hauser, Werker, & Martin, 2010).

Interactions

Typically, a newborn will search for the human voice and demonstrate pleasure or mild surprise when finding the face that is the sound source. Upon sighting the face, a newborn's eyes widen, his or her face broadens, and he or she may tilt the head toward the source. Body tension increases, but the infant remains quietly inactive. Upon finding a nonhuman sound source, however, an infant does not demonstrate these recognition behaviors. When an infant responds, it is almost impossible for a caregiver not to become "hooked" on the infant.

A newborn will stop crying to attend to its mother's voice. In turn, the mother will stop doing almost anything to attend to her infant's voice.

A newborn's facial expressions demonstrate the high degree of maturity of the facial neuromuscular system, resulting in neonatal expressions resembling displeasure, fear, sorrow, anger, joy, and disgust. Although experts do not attribute these actual emotional states to an infant, caregivers act as if these emotions are present.

Infant head movements also have high signal value for a caregiver. The face and head become important for communication very early on because of the relatively advanced maturational level of these structures compared to the rest of an infant's body. A newborn will turn its head to view a human face. Initially, the head and eyes move together. Three head positions, illustrated in Figure 5.1, are important because the caregiver interprets them as communication signals.

DragonImages/Fotolia

The newborn's visual focus is best at about 8 inches, and the mother's gaze during feeding is about 7½ inches.

FIGURE 5.1 Head Positions of Newborn

Type	Description	Result for Infant and Maternal Interpretation
Central 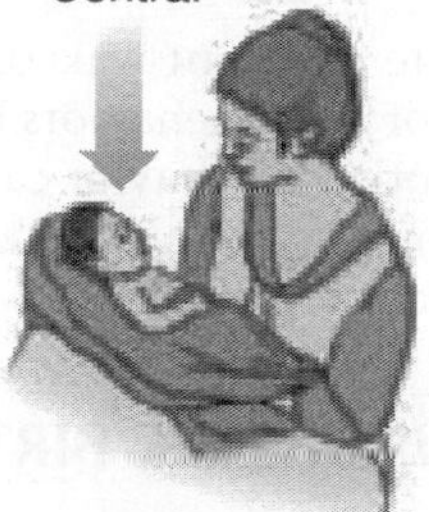	Faces mother or turns away slightly to either side.	Infant: Can discern form. Mother: Interprets as an approach or attending signal.
Peripheral 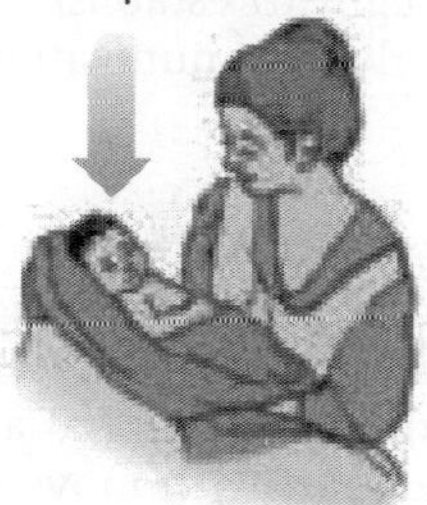	Turns head 15 to 90 degrees.	Infant: Cannot discern mother's facial features so form perception lost; motion, speed, and direction perception maintained, so can monitor mother's head. Mother: Signal of infant aversion or flight.
Loss of Visual Contact 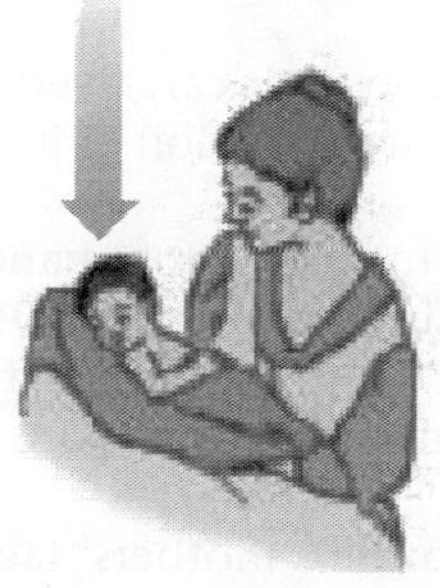	Turns head more than 90 degrees or lowers head.	Infant: Loss of motion, speed, and direction perception. Mother: Termination of interaction; head lowering interpreted as more temporary.

Source: Information from Stern (1977).

Newborns have individual personalities that affect their patterns of interaction. Differences may include an infant's general mood, intensity of activity and response, sensitivity to stimuli and adaptability to change, persistence, distractability, and approach–withdraw. The best interaction is one in which there is a "good fit" between contextual demands and a child's temperament.

Neonates also have a limited set of behaviors that will help them begin to communicate. In fact, newborns communicate unintentionally prior to birth, generally with kicks to express discomfort resulting from the mother's position.

An infant's state of wakefulness influences adults' behaviors. A caregiver learns the appropriate times to play with the neonate and to leave him or her alone. In other words, the caregiver learns the infant's signals for engagement. The refinement of a baby's signals and responsiveness to a caregiver reinforce further communication.

A newborn's states are regulated by bodily processes such as ingestion, elimination, respiration, and hunger. The sleep–awake patterns of a caregiver and child provide shared periods for specific interactions. Under a caregiver's direction, the awake periods fill with specific action sequences such as feeding and dressing. With each successive awakening, a child's and caregiver's interactions become increasingly predictable. This common context aids infant interpretation and becomes the forum for later introduction of new information.

In this video, you'll learn about some early studies of the synchrony between a mother and infant's behavior. http://www.youtube.com/watch?v=dEziPGohFql

A mother appears to maintain an optimal state of infant wakefulness by holding her child in close proximity and by speaking. Both of these behaviors become more frequent in the first two weeks of an infant's life. A mother's behavior can bring an infant back to alertness or facilitate the shift to sleep. Thus, an infant's state influences the mother's behavior, which in turn influences the infant's state.

SOCIALIZATION AND EARLY COMMUNICATION: BIRTH TO 6 MONTHS

Within the first few months, a child and parent begin to establish their relationship. Each learns the patterns of behavior of the other. Early communication begins.

One Month: Getting to Know You

Shortly after birth, an infant becomes actively involved in the interactive process with adults. By 1 month of age, an infant engages in interactional sequences. When awake and in the appropriate position with an adult, an infant will gaze at an adult's face and vocalize and respond to the vocalizations and movements with movement and eye contact. As early as 6 weeks of age, infants are able to coordinate the amount of time spent gazing and will change their gaze patterns based on their partners' gaze (Crown, Feldstein, Jasnow, Beebe, & Jaffe, 2002).

As we noted, infants are especially responsive to their caregivers' voice and face. In fact, a young infant will attend to a human face to the exclusion of just about everything else.

Within the first week of life, infants begin to make gross hand gestures, tongue protrusions, and mouth opening in response to similar behaviors. The caregiver treats this behavior as social in nature, embellishing it with communicational intent. By 1 month of age, an infant may make pitch and speech sound durations similar to those of a caregiver.

In addition, infants respond differentially to their mothers' face and voice. By as early as 2 weeks, an infant is able to distinguish its mother from a stranger. An infant will turn toward its mother and fix its gaze upon her mouth or eyes. The infant's facial expression will be one of interest or mild surprise, followed by a smile. At about 3 weeks of age, this smile of recognition is one of the first examples of a **social smile**, rather than one based on an infant's internal physical state. At around 3 to 6 weeks of age, infants smile in response to the human face and eye gaze, to the human voice (especially if high-pitched), and to tickling. The caregiver, of course, responds in kind.

A young infant is so attuned to the human face that at 3 weeks, he or she will even smile at an oval with two large dots for eyes but will not respond to the outline or to the eyes separately. This preference for eyes increases even more during the second month of life.

Two Months: Increasing Skill

Visual responsiveness and memory are reflected in increased communication skills. Although a 2-month-old will search for its mother's voice, he or she will turn away from strange voices.

By the second month, certain people have become associated with particular behaviors. For example, an infant's mother becomes associated with feeding, and an infant will begin a sucking response upon seeing her. This recognition of familiar people, plus the infant's rapid boredom with other visual stimuli, signify an increase in visual memory.

With maturity, infant cooing increases and is easily stimulated by attention and speech, and by toys moved in front of a baby. An infant coos when not distressed, and this behavior develops parallel to social smiling. By 2 months of age, cooing often occurs in bursts or episodes accompanying other expressions.

Three Months: Big Changes

By 3 months of age, an infant can visually discriminate different people and respond accordingly. This change is reflected in stages of smile development. At the end of the first month, an infant's smile becomes less automatic, but it is still unselective. His or her smile becomes more social and physically broader, with a crinkling around the eyes. This responsiveness is reflected in an infant's selective attention at 4 months of age to specific individuals and to joyful expressions longer than to angry ones. Often he or she will ignore feeding in order to concentrate on "people watching."

A 3-month-old infant's cognitive abilities are such that the expressionless human face alone does not have the stimulus power to hold his or her attention. The stimulus power of any one face resides in that face's similarity to, or difference from, the infant's internal facial schemes. If the mismatch is too great, such as a distorted face, the infant loses interest or gets upset.

To maintain attention, a caregiver must modify her behavior to provide the appropriate level of stimulation. She therefore exaggerates her facial expressions and voice and vocalizes more often. In turn, an infant responds to this new level of stimulation. As the infant develops, there is a "mutual modification" in the infant's and mother's behaviors so that "changes in the baby's development alter the mother's behavior and this, in turn, affects the baby" (Schaffer, 1977, p. 53). In this developmental dance, first one partner leads and then the other.

In very early feeding sessions, a mother adapts her behavior to her infant's rhythms. For example, initially, mothers jiggle the nipple to increase or to elicit feeding. Infants respond by decreasing their sucking behavior. Within two weeks mothers learn to cease their jiggling to elicit sucking. The resultant cycle becomes one in which an infant pause is followed by a jiggle. The jiggling stops. After a short delay, an infant begins to suck. Thus, early feeding behaviors represent a pattern of turn taking.

Both partners affect their interaction. Developmental changes by the infant affect the dynamic relationship between child and caregiver behaviors and the context.

At any given moment, a caregiver must determine the appropriate amount of stimulation based on an infant's level of attention. By 3 months, an infant can maintain a fairly constant internal state, so he or she can be attentive for longer periods. An infant's level of excitation is positively related to the level of incoming stimulation. If a caregiver provides too much stimulation, an infant overloads and turns away or becomes overexcited.

Dialogs become more important and by the third month, although handling has decreased by 30% from that at birth, dialogs have increased. Infants are full partners in this dialog, and their behavior is influenced by the communication behavior of their caregivers.

Infant–caregiver bonding is determined by the quality of their interactions. Several factors influence bonding and an infant's subsequent feelings of security. The levels of maternal playfulness, sensitivity, encouragement, and pacing at 3 months have been found to be positively related to the security of attachment at 9 months.

During the first three months, a caregiver's responding teaches a child the signal value of specific behaviors. The infant learns the stimulus–response sequence. If he or she signals, the caregiver will respond. When the infant cries, the caregiver answers. Thus, the infant develops an expectation that he or she can change or control the environment.

In addition, the child learns that signaling results in a predictable outcome. Possibly as high as 77% of infant crying episodes are followed by maternal responses, while only 6% are preceded by maternal contact. As a result of maternal responses, the cry becomes an infant's means of gaining contact with mother, although this behavior doesn't seem purposeful yet.

Immediate positive parental responsiveness increases a child's motivation to communicate. If motivation is high, an infant will attempt more frequent and varied interactions. Motivation to communicate at 9 months is best indicated by earlier exploration behavior and displays of curiosity.

The degree of parental responsiveness varies with the culture, as does the amount of infant crying. In general, more mobile societies, such as hunter-gatherer cultures, exhibit little child crying. Carried by its mother in a sling, a child is often attended to before crying begins.

Mothers not only respond to their infants' cries but can identify the type of cry produced. Mothers can reliably rate their 3- to 4-month-olds' types of cries.

Later Months

By 3 to 4 months, two additional response patterns have emerged: rituals and game playing. These will be discussed in some detail later in this chapter. Rituals, such as feeding, provide a child with predictable patterns of behavior and speech. A child becomes upset if these rituals are changed or disrupted. Games, such as peekaboo, "this little piggy," and "I'm gonna get you," have all the aspects of communication. There is an exchange of turns, rules for each turn, and particular slots for words and actions.

At 5 months the infant shows more deliberate imitation of movements and vocalizations. Facial imitation is most frequent at 4 to 6 months of age. By 6 to 8 months, however, hand and nonspeech imitation become most frequent for behaviors previously exhibited in the child's spontaneous behavior.

Between 3 and 6 months of age, the period of peak face-to-face play, an infant is exposed to tens of thousands of examples of facial emotions. In interactions with mother, a child mirrors mother's expression, and she, in turn, imitates the infant. The infant's repertoire of facial emotions is listed in Table 5.1.

As infants approach 6 months of age, their interest in toys and objects increases. Prior to this period, an infant is not greatly attracted to objects unless they are noise producing or made mobile and lively by an adult. This change reflects, in part, the development of eye–hand coordination, which is exhibited in reaching, grasping, and manipulation. From this point on, interactions increasingly include the infant, the caregiver, and some object.

A 5-month-old also vocalizes to accompany different attitudes, such as pleasure and displeasure, satisfaction and anger, and eagerness. He or she will vocalize to other people and to a mirror image, as well as to toys and objects.

In this video, note the responsiveness of the mother–child partners and the attunement of each. http://www.youtube.com/watch?v=lGeS7o4FmRI

Both partners are active participants in exchanges. The infant moves face, lips, tongue, arms, hands, and body toward the mother, whose behavior reflects that of the infant. In turn, the infant imitates the mother's movements. Frequently, the behaviors of the mother and infant appear to be so simultaneous as to constitute a single act. The infant frequently leads by initiating the behavior. Mother does not simply follow, however, but maintains a mutual exchange.

DEVELOPMENT OF INTENTIONALITY: AGE 7 TO 12 MONTHS

During the second six months of life, an infant begins to assert more control within the infant–caregiver interaction. He or she learns to communicate intentions more clearly and effectively. Each success motivates an infant to communicate more and to learn to communicate better. The primary modes for this expression are gestural and vocal.

TABLE 5.1 **Infant Emotions**

Emotion	Description	Emergence
Interest	Brows knit or raised, mouth rounded, lips pursed	Present at birth
Distress	Eyes closed tightly, mouth square and angular (as in anger)	Present at birth
Disgust	Nose wrinkled, upper lip elevated, tongue protruded	Present at birth
Social smile	Corners of mouth raised, cheeks lifted, eyes twinkle; neonatal "half smile" and early startle may be precursors	4–6 weeks
Anger	Brows together and drawn downward, eyes set, mouth square	3–4 months
Sadness	Inner corners of brows raised, mouth turns down in corners, pout	3–4 months
Surprise	Brows raised, eyes widened, oval-shaped mouth	3–4 months
Fear	Brows level but drawn in and up, eyes widened, mouth retracted	5–7 weeks

Source: Information from work of Carroll Izard as reported by Trotter (1983).

By 7 months, an infant begins to respond differentially to his or her interactional partner, staying close to the caregiver, following her movements, and becoming distressed if she leaves. Even infant play with objects is influenced by maternal attending. Infants play with toys as long as their mothers look on, but when their mothers turn away, infants leave their toys 50% of the time and attempt to retrieve the lost attention. This maternal attachment is related to the predictability of the mother's behavior.

In recognition of an infant's interest in objects and growing ability to follow conversational cues, the caregiver makes increasing reference to objects, events, and people. Increasingly, the infant demonstrates selective listening to familiar words and compliance with simple requests.

Infants imitate simple motor behaviors by 8 to 10 months, responding to requests to wave bye-bye. Infant responses to maternal verbal and nonverbal requests increase from 39.5% at 9 months to 52.0% at 11 months. Requests for action are answered one and a half times as frequently as requests for vocalization. By modifying forms and frequencies of reply, an infant gains considerable control over the communicative exchange.

Nine-month-olds can also follow maternal pointing and glancing. The infant cues on a combination of maternal head and eye orientation and on eye movement.

Visual orientation of both an infant and mother is usually accompanied by maternal naming to establish the topic. The mother monitors her infant's glance for signs of interest. Mothers of 8- to 14-month-olds look at their infants so frequently that the responsibility for maintaining eye contact really rests with the child. This monitoring by the mother decreases as the infant matures.

Caregivers also monitor infant vocalizations. Parents of 8- to 12-month-olds can consistently recognize infant intonational patterns that convey request, frustration, greeting, and pleasant surprise.

Gaze and vocalization seem to be related. An infant's gaze is more likely to be initiated and maintained when its mother is vocalizing and/or gazing back, and, in turn, the mother is more likely to initiate and maintain vocalization when her infant is looking at her. Although mothers and 1-year-olds exhibit very little vocal overlap, they depart from their turn-taking behaviors when they laugh or join in chorus. The exchange is one of reciprocal actions, intonations, and gestures.

At around 1 year of age, children who have learned to coordinate gaze and vocalization look at their partners at the beginning of a vocal turn, possibly for reassurance. Only six months later, they tend to use a more adult pattern and to look at their partners at the end of a turn to signal a turn shift.

The communication between infant and caregiver is closely related to the infant's behavior state. For example, the infant will vocalize and gesture for attention, then exhibit sadness or grimace and show signs of distress when communication sequences end or fail to materialize.

Communication Intentions

At about 8 to 9 months, an infant begins to develop *intentionality*, or goal-directed behavior, and the ability to share goals with others. Up to this point, the child has focused primarily on either objects or people. Outcomes were rarely predicted by the child. The appearance of gestures signals a cognitive ability to plan and to coordinate that plan to achieve a desired goal rather than the trial-and-error behavior noted earlier.

Intentionality is exhibited when a child begins to encode a message for someone else and for the first time, considers the audience. A child may touch his or her mother, gain eye contact and gesture toward an object, although the order may vary. A bid for attention is coupled with a signal. Initially, a child's **communication intentions** are expressed primarily through gestures. Functions, such as requesting, interacting, and attracting attention, are first fulfilled by prelinguistic means and only later by language. The 9-month-old will use both gestures and vocalizations to accomplish several intentions.

Between 6 and 12 months, infants develop the vocal repertoire to regulate interactions with their caregivers. Emotional or nonintentional vocalizations differ from intentional ones, which are shorter with a lower overall frequency and a greater intensity (Papaeliou, Minadakis, & Cavouras, 2002). Differing pitch patterns in the vocalizations of 10-month-old infants indicate that these vocalizations serve both as a means of purposeful communication when accompanied by nonvocal communicative behavior such as gestures and as a tool of thought when accompanied by explorative activities (Papaeliou & Trevarthen, 2006).

There is a three-stage sequence in the development of early communication functions. In Table 5.2, these stages are related to the infant's cognitive developments.

Initial Stage: Preintentional The initial stage begins at birth and continues into the second half year of life. Throughout this stage, an infant fails to signal specific intentions beyond those behaviors that will sustain an interaction, such as cries, coos, and nonspecific use of the face and body.

Initially, an infant's behavior is characterized by *attentional interactions* in which he or she attends to stimuli and responds to stimuli with diffuse undifferentiated behaviors, such as crying. Crying indicates general pain, discomfort, or need but does not identify the cause of the problem. Mother interprets her infant's behavior and responds differentially. Crying teaches an infant the value of behavior as a signal to communication partners.

The communication system becomes more effective as a caregiver learns to interpret a child's behavior. Interactions become more predictable. Gradually, an infant's greater cognitive ability will enable him or her to understand the outcome of behavior. Soon an infant will begin making deliberate attempts to share specific experiences with caregivers, fully expecting them to respond. Characterized by *contingency interactions*, behavior is directed toward initiating and sustaining interactions (Wetherby & Prizant, 1989). Affective signals, such as crying, will become more conventional and more directed toward and responsive to the communication context.

TABLE 5.2 Development of Intentionality

STAGE	AGE (MONTHS)	CHARACTERISTICS
Pre-intentional	0–8 (approx.)	Intention inferred by adults ***Attentional interactions*** ■ No goal awareness ■ Attends to and responds to stimuli ***Contingency interactions*** ■ Awareness of goal ■ Undifferentiated behavior to initiate or continue a stimulus, anticipates events, vocalizes for attention
Substage 1		Shows self ***Differentiated interactions*** ■ Designs, plans, and adjusts behavior to achieve goal ■ Raises arms to be picked up, pulls string to get object, looks at adult and desired object
Intentional	8–12	Emergence of intentional communication ***Encoded interactions*** ■ Coordinated plan to achieve goals ■ Gestures, brings objects to caregiver for help, climbs for desired objects
Substage 1		Shows objects
Substage 2		Displays a full range of gestures ■ Conventional gestures: requesting, pointing or signaling notice, showing, giving, and protesting ■ Unconventional gestures: tantrums and showing off ■ Functional gestures
Symbolic	12+	Words accompany or replace gestures to express communication functions previously expressed in gestures alone or gestures plus vocalization ***Symbolic interactions***

Sources: Information from Wetherby & Prizant (1989) and Bates, Camaioni, & Volterra (1975).

An infant calls attention to the environment by scanning and searching. The mother follows her infant's visual regard and provides a label or comment.

When aware of a child's desire to continue, a caregiver can sustain their "dialog." When more mature, the child will initiate a behavior and repeat it in order to sustain these interactions.

Toward the end of the initial period, infants become more interested in manipulating objects and begin to use gestures that demonstrate an understanding of object purpose or use and include such behaviors as bringing a cup to the lips or a telephone receiver to the ear. These gestures constitute a primitive form of naming. An infant demonstrates recognition that objects have stable characteristics and functions that necessitate specific behaviors. These early gestures are usually brief and incomplete, and sequences of events are rare.

At this stage, an infant begins reaching for desired objects. For objects that are beyond its grasp, the infant's reach will later become a pointing gesture. In this pre-intentional stage, an infant will exhibit or show self. An infant hides its face, acts coy, raises the arms to be picked up, or plays peekaboo. Behavior becomes coordinated and regulated to achieve goals.

Second Stage: Gestural intentions The second stage of development of intent begins at 8 to 9 months of age. Within this stage an infant uses conventional gestures, vocalizations, or both to communicate different intentions. The emergence of intentional communication is reflected in gestures accompanied by

- eye contact with the child's communication partner
- consistent sound and intonation to signal specific intentions, and
- persistent attempts to communicate.

If not understood, a child may repeat the behaviors or modify them. A child considers both the message and the partner's reception of it, thus exhibiting an intention to communicate.

In the second stage, an infant begins by showing objects, extending them toward the caregiver but not releasing them. A child draws attention to these objects as a way of sharing attention.

Later, an infant displays a full range of gestures, including conventional means of showing, giving, pointing, and requesting (Figure 5.2). Other nonconventional gestures, such as having tantrums and showing off, are also present. In general, each infant develops its own style with nonconventional gestures. Finally, each infant develops one or more functional gestures or gestures that are shaped for specific meaning, such as touching the mouth repeatedly to signal *eat* or running to the door to signal *out*. My daughter would twist her legs around each other to signal *potty*.

The giving gesture, unlike showing, includes a release of the object. Frequently, giving follows a maternal request for the object. A favorite game becomes "the trade," in which the partners take turns passing an object between them.

Pointing may include the whole hand or only a finger with the arm extended. An infant makes only the minimal effort needed to convey the intention. Unlike requesting, pointing is not accompanied by movement of the upper trunk in the direction of the object. Pointing is a widespread, if not universal, pattern cross-culturally (Butterworth, 2003).

By 12 months of age, and possibly earlier, infant pointing to share with others, both attention to a referent and a specific attitude about that referent, is a full communicative act (Liszkowski, Carpenter, & Tomasello, 2007). This is seen in an infant's response to a communication partner's behavior. For example, if a partner responds by attending to something else with positive attitude, an infant will repeat the pointing to redirect the partner's attention, showing both an understanding of the partner's reference and active message repair. In contrast, when a partner identifies an infant's referent correctly ("I see doggie.") but displays disinterest, an infant will not repeat pointing, and there is an overall decrease in pointing behavior. Finally, when the partner attends to an infant's intended referent enthusiastically, there is an overall increase in gesturing by the infant.

Requesting is a whole-hand grasping reach toward a desired object or a giving gesture accompanied by a call for assistance. In its most mature form, each gesture contains a visual check to ensure that the communication partner is attending.

These initial gestures are used to signal two general communication functions: *protoimperatives*, such as requests, and *protodeclaratives*. Protoimperatives or requests generally request objects, participation, or actions. An infant begins to realize with requests that she cannot be unreasonable or ask for something that she can do herself.

FIGURE 5.2 **Infant Standardized Gestures**

Infants develop a set of standardized gestures in addition to nonstandardized and functional gestures.

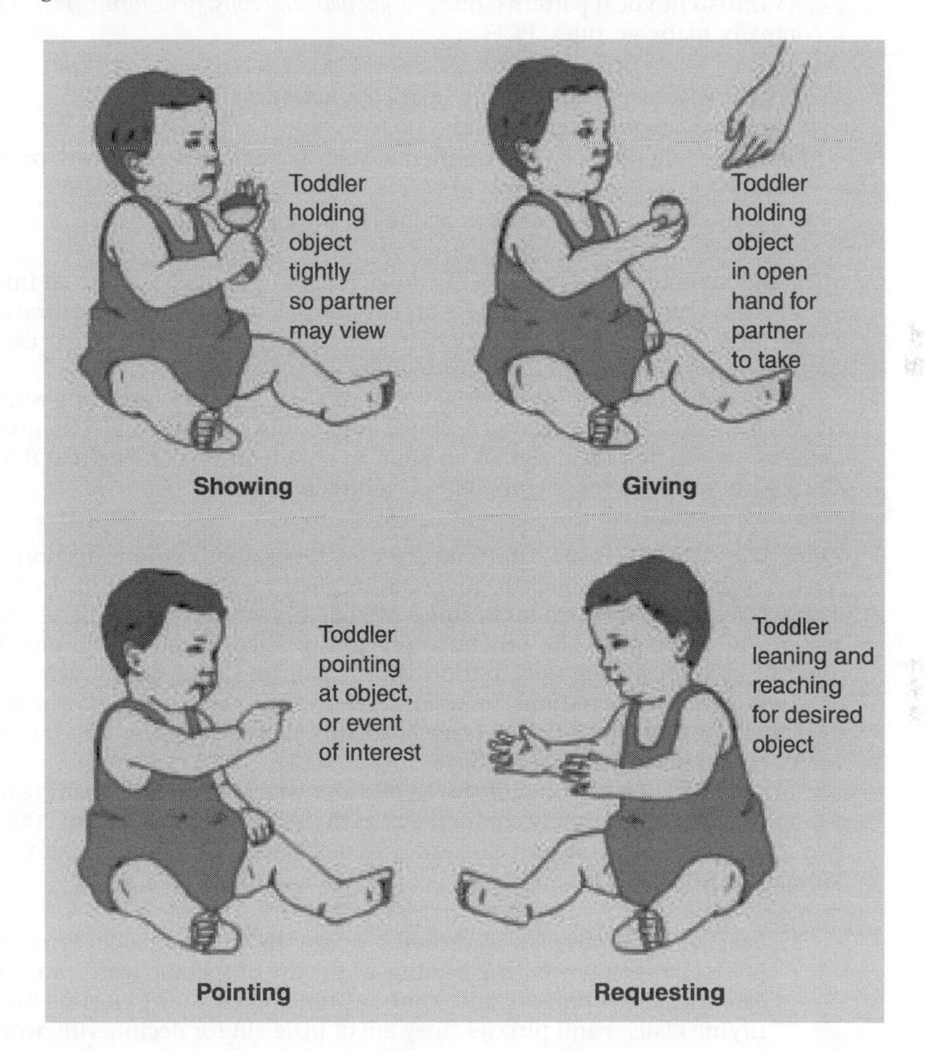

The acquisition of gestures by infants is reflected in maternal speech to these children. For example, the earlier infants produce imperative gestures, such as requesting, the more frequently their mothers talk about the infants' own states, using words such as *want*, *try*, and *need* (Slaughter, Peterson, & Carpenter, 2009). In turn, the mothers' talk about desires and intentions positively influences their infants' early developing communicative abilities.

Protodeclaratives, such as pointing or showing, have the goal of maintaining joint or shared attending. Thus, children communicate to share. Nearly 30% of the communication episodes between presymbolic children and their caregivers are of this type. An infant will point in the presence of a communication partner but not when alone.

Initially, gestures appear without vocalizations, but the two are gradually paired. The prelinguistic vocalization patterns of infants vary based on intent. Social vocalizations, uttered apparently with the intention to communicate, and "private" speech, related to solitary activities, have differing pitch shapes or contours (Papaeliou & Trevarthen, 2006). Thus, prelinguistic vocalizations serve both as means of purposeful communication and as a tool of thought, functions later assumed by language.

Consistent vocal patterns, dubbed *phonetically consistent forms (PCFs)* in Chapter 4, accompany many gestures. PCFs

- occur with pauses that clearly mark boundaries,
- function as words for a child,
- may be imitations of environmental sounds, such as a dog's bark or a car's engine, and
- usually accompany events or actions in the environment.

My granddaughter Cassidy started barking at about 7 months. Once an infant begins to use PCFs, his mother will no longer accept other, less consistent vocalizations. PCFs are a transition to words in a highly creative developmental period when the child is also adept at employing gestures and intonation.

The appearance of intentional communication in the form of gestures requires a certain level of cognitive, as well as social, functioning. Person–object sequences, such as requests, in which a child signals an adult to obtain an object, begin at 8 to 10 months, along with a shift to more complex social interactions.

Third Stage: First Words The final stage of functional communication development is the symbolic stage, which begins with the first meaningful word. In these symbolic interactions, the child's intent becomes encoded in words that are used with or without gestures to accomplish the functions previously filled by gestures alone. For example, pointing develops, then vocalization within pointing, and finally verbalization or use of words. Words and gestures are used to refer to the same content. The gesture, which initially stands for the entire message, gradually becomes the context for more symbolic ways of communicating the message.

During the second six months, a child also begins to attach meaning to symbols. At 8 months, some infants may comprehend as many as 20 words (Fagan, 2009). Infants use two strategies, bracketing and clustering, to segregate speech directed at them (Goodsitt, Morgan, & Kuhl, 1993):

1. **Bracketing** is the use of prosodic or rhythmic cues, such as maternal pauses, pitch changes, vowel lengthening, or the use of specific words, to detect divisions *between* clauses phrases, and words. Although bracketing cues are helpful for identifying clauses and phrases, they are of little aid for deciphering words.
2. **Clustering** is the use of predictable phonotactic units *within* words. Because between words predictability is low, phonotactic predictability can highlight these transitions for infants.

Using a combination of these strategies, an infant is able to divide caregiver speech into manageable units. Predictable, familiar words and phrases become associated with familiar contexts, helping early meanings to form in the infant's brain.

Summary During the first six months of life, an infant learns the rituals and processes of communication through interaction with his or her caregiver (Table 5.3). The caregiver treats the infant as a full conversational partner and acts as if the infant communicates meaningfully. The infant also learns that behavior can have an effect on the environment. At first, the infant's communication is general and unspecified. During the

TABLE 5.3 **Infant Social and Communicative Development**

AGE	BEHAVIORS
Newborn	Vision best at 8 inches; prefers light–dark contrasts, angularity, complexity, curvature
	Hearing best in frequency range of human voice; prefers human voice; exhibits entrainment
	Facial expressions
1 week	"Self-imitation"; reflexive actions but treated as meaningful by caregiver
2 weeks	Distinguishing of caregiver's voice and face
3 weeks	Social smile
1 month	Short visual exchanges with caregiver; prefers human face to all else
2 months	Cooing
3 months	Face alone not enough to hold infant's attention; in response, mother exaggerates her facial movements
	More frequent dialogs; decrease of handling by 30%
	Revocalization likely if caregiver's verbal response immediately follows child's first vocalization
	Vocal turn taking and concurrent vocalization
	Gaze coupling
	Rituals and games
	Face play
5 months	Purposeful facial imitation
	Vocalization to accompany attitude
6 months	Hand and nonspeech imitation
8 months	Gestures
9 months	Imitation of more complicated motor behaviors
	Following of maternal pointing
11 months	Response to about half of maternal verbal and nonverbal requests
12 months	Use of words to fill communicative functions established by gestures

second six months, he or she develops intentional communication, first gesturally, then vocally. When the infant begins to use meaningful speech, it is within this context of gestures and vocalizations.

Maternal Communication Behaviors

As we have noted, infants and caregivers engage in dialog soon after birth. It is a complex interaction between infant character/temperament and maternal speech. Both partners exert some control within this exchange. The infant sets the level of exchange because of limited abilities, and his or her responses are rather rigid and fixed. Only gradually does the infant expand these abilities.

The mother provides the framework and adjusts her behaviors to the information processing limitations of her infant. She also demonstrates a willingness to learn from and respond to her infant's behavior patterns.

Within a given exchange, both partners continually adjust their behavior to maintain an optimum level of stimulation. The mother maintains the infant's attention at a high level by her behavior. In response, the infant coos, smiles, and gazes alertly. Reinforced for her efforts, the mother tries even harder to maintain the infant's level of stimulation. Each party is responsive to the other. For example, the mother helps expand the infant's abilities by deliberately "messing up" more consistently than expected. By slightly exceeding the limits of the infant's behavior, the mother forces the infant to adjust to new stimuli.

The foundation for infant–caregiver face-to-face exchanges is in the modifications made by an adult to accommodate a child. The caregiver monitors the infant's state to determine the right time to begin an exchange, and then obtains the child's attention to optimize the interaction. Once the exchange begins, the mother modifies her behavior to maintain the child's interest.

Table 5.4 describes these maternal behaviors and gives examples of each. Within the exchange, mothers make infantlike modifications such as exaggerated facial expressions, body movements, positioning, timing, touching, prolonged gaze, and modified speech. These modifications also occur in the behavior of other adults and older children as they interact with infants. Neither prior experience with infants nor prior learning

TABLE 5.4 Caregiver Foundations for Face-to-Face Communication

Behavior	Description	Examples
Preparatory activities	Free infant from physiological state dominance	Reduce interference of hunger or fatigue Soothe or calm infant when upset
State-setting activities	Manipulate physical environment to optimize interaction	Move into infant's visual field Attain attention by modifying vocalizations
Maintenance of communication framework	Use of continuates by caregiver	Modulate speech, rhythmic tapping and patting, rhythmic body movements; provide infant with a focus of attention and action, a set of timing markers
Infantlike modifications of adult actions	Variation of caregiver activities in rate, intensity modulation, amplitude, and quality from those of adult–adult	Use baby talk—slowed and exaggerated Imitate baby movements—close, oriented straight ahead, parallel, and perpendicular to plane of infant

Source: Information from Tronick, Als, & Adamson (1979).

seems to explain this adult behavior. Three factors appear important in influencing the initial interactions of a newborn and its mother:

1. Medication used in delivery
2. Number of pregnancies
3. The mother's socioeconomic and cultural background

Maternal sensitivity to her infant is multifaceted and varies with the situation. In general, sensitivity permeates all the parent's behaviors with the infant and promotes rather than interrupts an exchange (van den Boom, 1997). Of most importance is timing of a mother's behaviors and the match between that behavior and the infant's behavior. In general, sensitive mothers vary their rate of noninterruptive speech based on their infant's rate of such behavior (Hane, Feldstein, & Dernetz, 2003). Mothers who are over- or underresponsive tend to undermine the attachment between themselves and their infants (Jafee, Beebe, Feldstein, Crown, & Jasnow, 2001).

In this video, you'll be treated to an example of a positive parent–child interaction. Note the responsive behaviors of both partners. http://www.youtube.com/watch?v=9FeTK7ZxmVI

Most adults respond to the "babyness" of an infant, particularly the face, which they find irresistible. An infant's head is large in proportion to the body, with large eyes and round cheeks. In essence, a baby is cute. To this physical image an infant adds smiles, gazes, an open mouth, and tongue thrusts. Infants with a facial deformity may elicit very different or negative responses.

In the following sections, we will explore the modifications made by caregivers in response to their infants. This behavior varies with culture, class, and gender of an infant.

INFANT-ELICITED SOCIAL BEHAVIOR

Caregiver responses can be characterized as "infant-elicited social behaviors." They appear in response to infants but occur infrequently in adult-to-adult exchanges. These caregiver behaviors have exaggerated physical movement, usually slow or elongated in rate, and form a select, limited repertoire that is used frequently. The purpose of these modifications is to enhance recognition and discrimination by a child. The behaviors of one mother differ from those of another. Each caregiver develops a personal style. Infant-elicited social behavior also consists of maternal adaptations in speech and language, gaze, facial expression, facial presentation and head movement, and proxemics.

Although maternal language to young infants and toddlers reflects the responsiveness and communication of the child, there are additional differences that reflect individual maternal styles (Abraham, Crais, Vernon-Feagans, & the Family Life Project Phase 1 Key Investigators, 2013). These maternal styles are consistent. Maternal language use at 6 months of age significantly predicts maternal language at 15 months.

Infant-Directed Speech (IDS)

The speech and language of adults and older children to infants is systematically modified from that used in regular conversation. This adapted speech and language addressed to infants is called infant-directed speech (IDS) or *motherese*. For our purposes, we will use IDS to signify the speech and language addressed to infants consisting of "babyish-sounding" forms (Table 5.5).

Characteristics IDS is characterized by short utterance length, simple syntax, and use of a small core vocabulary. Mothers also paraphrase and repeat themselves. Topics are limited to the here and now. The mother's choice of content, type of information conveyed, and syntax appear to be heavily influenced by the context as well. In addition, mothers use paralinguistic variations, such as intonation and pause, beyond those found

TABLE 5.5 Characteristics of Infant-Directed Speech

Characteristics
Short utterance length (mean utterance length as few as 2.6 morphemes) and simple syntax
Small core vocabulary, usually object-centered
Topics limited to the here and now
Heightened use of facial expressions and gestures
Frequent questioning and greeting
Treating of infant behaviors as meaningful: Mother awaits infant's turn and responds even to nonturns
Episodes of maternal utterances
Paralinguistic modifications of pitch and loudness
Frequent verbal rituals

in adult-to-adult speech. Employing more frequent facial expressions and gestures and an overall higher pitch, any one of us might engage in the following monolog:

See the dog. (points, turns, looks, pauses)
Big dog. (spreads arms, pauses)
Nice dog. (pauses)
Pet the dog. (pets, pauses)
Can you pet dog? (pauses)
Nice dog. Do you like dog? (pauses)
Un-huh. Nice dog.

This little monolog contains most aspects of IDS.

Maternal utterances often occur in strings of successive utterances referring to the same object, action, or event. These verbal episodes may facilitate understanding because speech is less difficult to understand if a string of utterances refers to the same object. Information gained from preceding utterances assists comprehension of utterances that follow. Most communication episodes with infants begin with object manipulation and a high proportion of naming by the mother. At the beginning of the episode, pauses between utterances are twice as long as pauses within the episode itself. Young children receive help with object reference and *episodic* boundaries. A typical communication episode might proceed as follows:

(shakes doll) Here's baby! (pauses)
Mommy has baby. (cuddles doll, pauses)
Uh-huh, Betsy want baby? (surprised expression, pauses)
Here's baby! (pauses)
Oh, baby scare Betsy? (concerned expression, pauses)

High rates of redundancy also occur in IDS, and there is a great degree of semantic similarity between successive utterances. This high rate of syntactic and semantic redundancy increases the predictability and continuity of each episode. Mothers repeat one out of every six utterances immediately and exactly. These self-repetitions decrease as a child assumes increasing responsibility in the conversation.

Early content tends to be object centered and concerned with the here and now. For a mother, topics are generally limited to what her infant can see and hear. As a child's

Mothers are tuned to the conversational needs of their children and modify their behavior to maximize children's participation.

age approaches 6 months, mothers in the United States tend to use a more informational style and, as a result, talk more about the environment and the infant's behavior.

Both maternal labels and gestures affect a child's acquisition of specific object names. Interestingly, not all gestures have the same effect. Iconic gestures that mime an object's use or action or represent the object, such as two hands being used to represent opening and closing a book, are especially effective (Zammit & Schafer, 2011). In general, a mother's use of iconic gestures predicts earlier learning of the word being represented.

In addition, mothers use paralinguistic variations, varying the manner of presentation. For their part, infants respond to intonation patterns before they comprehend language, preferring a high, variable pitch. Mothers use a broad range of pitch and loudness, although overall, their pitch is higher than in adult-to-adult conversations. This pitch contour has been found in a number of languages. Conversational sequences may include instances of maternal falsetto or bass voice and of whispers or yells. Content words and syllables receive additional emphasis.

The mother modifies her rhythm and timing as well. Vowel duration is longer than in adult-to-adult discourse. The mother also uses longer pauses between utterances. Signing mothers of children with deafness maintain similarly slow rhythms with their hands. Japanese mothers use responding to alter the duration of their infant's vocalizations. The length of maternal pauses is reflected in the child's subsequent response.

There are many similarities in parental intonation across languages as different as Comanche, English, French, Italian, German, Japanese, Latvian, Mandarin Chinese, Sinhala, and Xhosa (South African language). Parents use a higher pitch, greater variability in pitch, shorter utterances, and longer pauses when talking to their preverbal infants than when talking to other adults. In general, regardless of the language, mothers use a wider pitch range than fathers.

Parents who speak American English seem to have more extreme modifications in their speech than do parents in other languages, especially Asian languages. These differences may reflect the more open American style of communicating and the more reticent and respectful Asian style. Regardless of the language, infants seem to prefer the intonational patterns of IDS from a very young age (Cooper & Aslin, 1990).

Maternal speech prior to 6 months can contain fewer than 3 morphemes per utterance, expanding to about 3.5 or more morphemes at 6 months. In part, this rise may reflect the increasingly complex communication of a mother and her infant. After 1 year, average maternal utterance length is reported to be between 2.8 and 3.5 morphemes. These lower values may represent maternal modeling in anticipation of an infant's speech. These adult-to-infant averages are well below the adult-to-adult average, which is around 8 morphemes. In addition, IDS is less complex structurally than adult-to-adult speech. In general, mothers who use more short sentences when their children are 9 months of age have toddlers with better receptive language abilities at 18 months (Murray, Johnson, & Peters, 1990). Such short, simple utterances can be found in the IDS of many languages.

Mothers also use a considerable number of questions and greetings with their infants. These conversational devices enable a mother to treat any infant response as a conversational turn because both questions and greetings require a response. In turn, mothers respond to their infants' behaviors with a meaningful reply. Even an infant's burps, yawns, sneezes, coughs, coos, smiles, and laughs may receive a response from its mother. Over 20% of maternal utterances are greetings such as *hi* and *bye-bye* or acknowledgments such as *sure*, *uh-huh*, and *yeah*. This maternal response pattern does not occur with noncommunication-like infant behaviors, such as arm flapping or bouncing.

After speaking, a mother waits approximately 0.6 second, the average adult turn-switching pause. Next, she waits for the duration of an imaginary infant response and another turn switch. Since many maternal utterances are questions, the duration of an infant response is relatively easy for the mother to estimate. Thus, the infant is exposed to a mature time frame in which later discourse skills will develop.

Maternal input is particularly important for an infant's own communication development. For example, children who are deaf and exposed to maternal signing from birth achieve all linguistic milestones at or before the expected age for hearing children. In a second example, when Korean mothers speak to their infants, they use sounds that closely match their infant's production abilities as well as highlight perceptual differences between sounds (Lee, Davis, & MacNeilage, 2008). In this way, IDS may facilitate infant learning of phonological regularities of the native language.

Appropriate and consistent adult *responsivity* is especially important in the emergence of early communication, although the amount and type of responsivity varies greatly across caregiver–infant pairs. Communication results when the caregiver attributes meaning to a baby's behaviors. Consistently, mothers are able to identify what they perceive as communicatively important behaviors in their infants (Meadows, Elias, & Bain, 2000). Gradually, a child learns that his or her behavior results in consistent, predictable effects.

Caregivers spontaneously respond to 30% to 50% of infants' noncrying vocalizations. When adults fail to respond, 5-month-old infants will increase their vocalizing (Goldstein, Schwade, & Bornstein, 2009). Interestingly, those infants who respond most vigorously have the best language comprehension abilities at 13 months.

For its part, an infant responds selectively. Situational variations are important, and an infant is least likely to vocalize when engaged in activities such as being changed, fed, or rocked, or when its mother watches television or talks to another person. In contrast, some maternal nonvocal behaviors, such as touching, holding close, looking at, or smiling at an infant, increase the likelihood of infant vocalizations.

Within an episode, an infant and mother engage in a dialog in which the infant's new communication abilities can emerge. Certain elements appear over and over in the mother's speech and give her infant the opportunity to predict and engage in the dialog. These predictable maternal behaviors may aid the infant's comprehension, allow the infant to concentrate her or his attention, and provide models of the expected dialog.

One of the most common sequences is that of joint or shared reference. **Referencing** is the noting of a single object, action, or event and is signaled by a mother either following her infant's glance and commenting on the object of its focus, shaking an object, or exaggerating an action to attract her infant's attention.

In elicitation sequences with their infants, mothers use all the behaviors just mentioned in an attempt to get their infants to make sounds. Unlike games, elicitation sequences continue even when an infant does not respond. In such situations, mothers redouble their efforts by increasing their use of IDS. There is no fixed repertoire of behaviors, and mothers are very adaptable.

Purpose of IDS Language development experts differ as to the purpose of IDS. First, a mother probably uses both repetition and variation to capture and maintain her infant's attention. Maternal patterns of repetition are found in nonverbal as well as verbal behaviors. Prosodic and intonational variations reach a peak at 4 to 6 months. This variety helps keep an infant alert and interested. As an infant gets older, his or her mother introduces more vocal and verbal variety, and rhythm declines.

Second, simplified speech helps children learn language. Because maternal modifications differ only slightly from what an infant already knows, stimuli provide an optimal level of training. Although mothers' responses to 2-month-old infants are stimulating and inject meaning into infants' expressions, it seems doubtful at this stage that verbal meaning has any influence on an infant.

Third, maternal modifications may maintain a child's responsiveness at an optimal level. A mother assumes that her infant is a communication partner. Thus, maternal speech modifications are an attempt to maintain the conversation despite the conversational limitations of the infant. With a 3-month-old infant, the mother structures the sequence so that any infant response can be treated as a reply.

Fourth, maternal modifications maintain a conversation in order to provide a context for teaching language use. The mother's modifications are highly correlated with the level of her infant's performance.

Finally, maternal adaptations may reflect our evolutionary history. The long period of offspring dependency found in humans may necessitate the use of such adaptations as an important part of nurturing and survival of the infant.

In a final analysis, IDS adaptations fulfill three functions. First, the mother's speech modifications gain and hold the infant's attention. Second, the modifications aid in the establishment of emotional bonds. Third, maternal speech characteristics enable communication to occur at the earliest opportunity.

Gaze

A mother modifies her typical gaze pattern, as well as her speech, when she interacts with her infant. Mature adult gaze patterns, which rarely last more than a few seconds, can evoke strong feelings if extended. In a conversational exchange, mature speakers look away as they begin to speak and check back only occasionally. When a mother gazes at her infant, however, she may remain in eye contact for more than 30 seconds. During play, maternal gazing may occur up to 70% of the time simultaneous with vocalization.

A mother also monitors her infant's gaze, adjusting her conversational topic accordingly. Gradually, an infant's gaze behavior comes to follow its mother's pointing or naming, although the infant is still free to gaze where it chooses. A mother also learns that her infant will look into her face for interpretation of novel events.

Maternal gaze modifications help maintain an infant's interest and focus attention on mother's face. A mother's monitoring of her infant's gaze enables them to establish joint reference, which we'll discuss later.

Facial Expression

Mothers use facial expression skillfully to complement their talking. Facial expressions can fulfill a number of conversational functions, including initiation, maintenance and modulation of the exchange, termination, and avoidance of interaction. Mock surprise is frequently used to initiate, invite, or signal readiness. In this expression, a mother's eyes open wide and her eyebrows rise, her mouth opens, her head tilts, and she intones an "o-o-o" or "ah-h-h." Owing to the brevity of most interactional exchanges, a mother may use mock surprise every 10 to 15 seconds.

An exchange can be maintained by a smile or an expression of concern. Similar to adult exchanges, a smile signals that communication is proceeding without difficulty. An expression of concern signals communication distress and a willingness to refocus the exchange.

Termination is signaled by a frown, accompanying head aversion, and gaze breaking. Occasionally, the frown is accompanied by a vocalization with decreased volume and dropping pitch.

Finally, avoidance of a social interaction can also be signaled by turning away but with a neutral or expressionless face. There is little in a mother's face, therefore, to hold her infant's attention.

A mother's repertoire includes a full range of facial expressions. Mothers use these expressions to maintain their infants' attention and to facilitate comprehension.

Facial Presentation and Head Movement

Mothers use a large repertoire of head movements to help transmit their messages, including nodding and wagging, averting, and cocking to one side. The sudden appearance of the face, as in peekaboo, is used to capture and hold a child's attention. In a variation of this procedure, a mother lowers her face and then returns to a full-face gaze accompanied by a vocalization. Many games, such as "I'm gonna get you" and "raspberries on your tummy," are accomplished by a full-face presentation. Frequently, a mother also exhibits mock surprise.

Proxemics

Proxemics, or the communicative use of interpersonal space, is a powerful interactional tool. Each person has a psychological envelope of personal space that can be violated only in the most intimate situations. When communicating with her infant, however, a mother acts as if this space does not exist and communicates from a very close distance. As an infant gets older, the American mother communicates more and more from a distance. The resultant decrease in touching is accompanied by an increase in eye contact.

CULTURAL, SOCIOECONOMIC, AND GENDER DIFFERENCES

The interactional patterns just described reflect the infant–caregiver behaviors found in middle-SES American culture. In general, maternal responsiveness is determined by an interplay of the maturational level of the infant and culture-specific interactional patterns (Kärtner, Keller, & Yovsi, 2010). In other cultures, a caregiver provides different types of linguistic input. For example, extended families, common in many cultures, involve multiple caregivers.

Cultural differences are evident in the parent's assumptions about infant intentionality. Mothers in the United States are more information oriented than mothers in

Japan. U.S. mothers are more chatty and use more questions, especially of the yes/no type, as well as more grammatically correct utterances with their 3-month-olds. In contrast, Japanese mothers are more emotion oriented and use more nonsense, onomatopoetic (beginning with the same sound), and environmental sounds, more baby talk, and more babies' names. These differences may reflect each society's assumptions about infants and adult-to-adult cultural styles of talking. In the United States styles are direct and emphasize individual expression. Styles in Japan are more intuitive and indirect and emphasize empathy and conformity.

Japanese mothers also vocalize less with their 3-month-old infants but offer, in turn, more physical contact than do mothers in the United States. This difference is also reflected in more frequent nonverbal responding by Japanese mothers and more frequent verbal responding by U.S. mothers. The types of utterances to which mothers are most likely to respond also differ. U.S. mothers are more likely to respond to their 3-month-old's positive cooing and comfort sounds, while Japanese mothers are more likely to respond to discomfort or fussing sounds. In response, Japanese mothers try to soothe their infants with speech. U.S. mothers are more likely to talk to maintain attention, while Japanese mothers talk more within vocal activities to elicit vocalizations.

Mothers make use of pitch early in their infants' lives. In English, a rising contour is used to gain an infant's attention. This pattern is not universal. For example, mothers speaking Thai to their infants use a falling pitch pattern, and those speaking Quiche Mayan, a native Mexican language, use a flat or falling contour. Maternal speech patterns are acquired behaviors, reflecting the culture in which the mother was raised.

Within North American culture, race, education, and socioeconomic class each influence maternal behaviors toward a child. For example, although inner-city, lower-SES African American mothers reportedly engage in vocal behavior at about the same rate as middle-SES African American mothers, data reveal other more subtle differences (Hammer & Weiss, 1999). Middle-SES mothers incorporate language goals more frequently in their play with their infants. In response, their infants initiate verbal play more frequently and produce twice as many vocalizations as lower-SES infants.

While middle-SES North American mothers ask more questions, seemingly to stimulate language growth, mothers from low-SES backgrounds use more imperatives or directives. Similarly, better educated mothers are more verbal. Siblings and peers are more important in the infant socialization process within the homes of African American and low-SES families, possibly accounting for the decreased talking by the mother.

Within some groups, children may be expected to learn language through observation, not interaction. In one Piedmont, South Carolina, African American community, infants are not viewed as capable of intentional behavior, so their vocalizations are often ignored.

Cultural and socioeconomic differences are not maladaptive. Quite the contrary, they reflect the values and beliefs of an ethnic or other recognizable group. It is not known exactly which aspects of maternal adaptation are most important for a child's communication development. It would be inappropriate, therefore, to suggest that one culture's maternal practices are better than another.

Differences also reflect the gender of the infant. In general, mothers tend to maintain closer proximity to their daughters than to their sons, at least until the age of 4 years. This gender difference is reflected in other ways. At 2 years of age, female infants receive more questions, male infants more directives. With female infants, mothers are more repetitive, acknowledge more child answers, and take more turns. In short, more maternal utterances of a longer length are addressed to daughters than to sons. This difference is not related to the child's linguistic behavior, there being very few if any gender differences in children's language performance at this age.

a positive language-learning environment when measured by the size of the toddler's vocabulary (Benigno, Clark, & Farrar, 2007).

An infant's understanding develops slowly. By 8 weeks an infant is able to visually follow his or her mother's movements. At 3 months infants can distinguish and attend to utterances addressed to them. A 4-month-old infant is able to follow its mother's line of regard or pointing. Within a short time, the infant's response quickens with mother's directives, such as "Look!" When my friend Natalia was an infant, her Spanish-speaking mother, Catalina, continually directed her baby's attention with "Mira!" ("Look!"). Later, mothers use object or event names to establish joint reference. By 6 months a mother's intonational pattern signals her infant to shift attention, although the mother and infant use a number of cues to regulate reference.

The Beginning of Intentional Communication With maturity an infant's interest in objects is accompanied by reaching. With the onset of reaching, objects become the focus of attention and face-to-face contact decreases from 80% to 15% of infant–mother contact time.

Initially, an infant's reach is solely a reach and is not intended to communicate any other meaning. The infant does not look toward mother to see if she has received the message. Instead, the infant orients toward either the object or mother. By 8 months the reach is less exigent, and the infant begins to look at mother while reaching. At this point, the infant has two reaches, a "reach-for-real" and a "reach-for-signal," indicating that he or she expects maternal assistance. The infant's reach-for-signal becomes a gesture. He or she shifts gaze from the object to mother and back again. Mother responds with the object or with encouragement of an even greater effort.

There are also thematic changes in mothers' speech to their infants at 5 to 7 months. Mothers move from a social mode, in which they discuss feelings and states, to an activity mode, in which they discuss both their baby's activities and events outside the immediate context. The concentration is on objects.

Gestures and Vocalizations In the next phase an infant begins to point and to vocalize. Gradually, the full-hand reaching grasp becomes a finger point. The pointing behavior becomes separated from the intention to obtain an object. In response, a mother asks questions and incorporates the child's pointing and interests into the dialog.

Mothers' comments based on the child's action or interest at 9 months seem related to better language comprehension by children later on (Rollins, 2003). Such behaviors indicate that a mother is sensitive to the focus of her child's attention.

Names and Topics Finally, in the last phase an infant masters naming and topicalizing. With this change in a child's behavior there is a corresponding increase in its mother's use of nouns. Increasingly, exchanges involve objects. Initially, the mother provides object and event labels. This strategy is modified when the child begins to talk. The mother attempts to get the child to look, to point, and to verbalize within the ongoing dialog. She uses object-related questions, such as "What do you want?" to elicit these verbalizations. As the child assumes more control of the dialog, the mother's questioning decreases.

Summary

The reference function, established months before meaningful language appears, is the vehicle for the development of naming and establishing a topic. More important, joint reference provides one of the earliest opportunities for the infant to engage in a truly communicative act of sharing information. Specific speech and language skills develop as more precise means to transmit the signal to a communication partner.

JOINT ACTION

Throughout the first year of life, a caregiver and infant develop shared behaviors in familiar contexts. These routine actions, called **joint action**, provide a structure within which language can be analyzed. Routine activities, such as game playing and daily routines, let a child encounter rules within a pleasurable experience. From game playing and routines, a child learns turn-taking and conversational skills.

These social interactions are among the most crucial infant learning and participating experiences. Within these joint action sequences, an infant begins to learn the conventions of human communication. Crying patterns become dialog patterns.

An infant's initial crying is gradually modified into recognizable signals by its mother's repeated response. Crying shifts from a demand mode to an anticipatory request mode. As a mother responds to her infant's demand cry, she establishes an expectation within her infant. The resultant request cry is less insistent. The infant pauses in anticipation of her mother's response. This shift is a forerunner of early dialogs in which a behavior or a vocalization is followed by a response.

Early examples of dialogs can be found in the anticipatory body games of infant and mother, such as peekaboo and "I'm gonna get you." Gradually, the infant's and mother's play evolves into an exchange in which the partners shift roles. For example, when passing an object back and forth, each partner plays the passer and the recipient in turn. Exchange, rather than possession, becomes the goal. Within these exchange games, an infant learns to shift roles, take turns, and coordinate signaling and acting. Role shifting and turn taking become so important that an infant will react with frustration, often accompanied by gestures and vocalizations, if the turn is delayed. In coordinating his or her signals and actions, an infant learns to look at mother's face in anticipation of the mother's signals.

Over time, a reciprocal mode of interaction replaces the exchange mode. With the reciprocal mode, activities revolve around a joint task format, such as play with an object, rather than a turn-taking format.

Game Playing

Infants and caregivers engage in play almost from birth. Each mother and infant develop a unique set of games. As each mother becomes familiar with her infant's abilities and interests, she creates interpersonal games. These games, in turn, become ritualized exchanges.

The most striking feature is the consistency of each mother's behavior both within and between these play sequences, especially the repetitiveness of a mother's vocal and nonvocal behaviors. Approximately one third to two thirds of maternal behavior directed toward an infant occurs in *runs*, or strings of behavior related to a single topic. This form of stimulation may be optimal for holding an infant's attention.

Early face-to-face play occurs in alternating cycles of arousal. An infant is aroused by maternal stimulation. A strong positive correlation exists between the sensory modality of a mother's stimulation and her infant's responses. For example, if a mother stimulates vocally, her child is likely to respond vocally.

An infant as young as 6 weeks old can initiate games by modifying its internal state of alertness. By 13 weeks an infant has adopted a true role in social games and thus signals readiness to begin play. When the mother approaches with a still face, her infant initiates the interaction by performing its repertoire of facial expressions and body movements. If the infant fails to get a response, it turns away. This behavior is modified, in turn, to independent exploration play by 23 weeks.

Over time, an infant's vocalizations accompanying game playing change and reflect the changes seen in overall language development (Rome-Flanders & Cronk, 1995).

The percentage of vocalizations and single syllables gives way to jargon and PCFs, which in turn are pushed aside for single words and multiword expressions. Although vocalizations decrease as a percentage of overall communication, the overall amount of vocalizing remains constant. It is possible that these sounds signal an availability to play and a willingness to participate.

Mothers adjust gradually to these developmental changes and to changes in their infant's internal state. First, a mother adjusts her timing to her infant's arousal to find the appropriate slot for her behavior. By modifying her timing, a mother attempts to alter the interactional pattern, to prolong the interactions, or to elicit a response from the infant. Second, a mother attempts to maintain a moderate level of infant arousal, an optimal state for learning. In turn, the mother is reinforced by her infant's responsiveness. Finally, a mother maintains a balance between her agenda and her infant's behavior. For example, when the infant does not interact for a period of 5 to 10 seconds, the mother responds with her bag of tricks. She makes faces, smiles, protrudes her tongue, moves her limbs, or vocalizes. In so doing, she is careful to leave an opportunity or slot for the infant to respond.

One very popular infant–mother game is "copycat" in which a mother's imitative behavior is dependent on her infant's. The importance of this particular game for later imitation by the infant cannot be overemphasized.

Maternal imitation is not an exact imitation, however, and a mother pulls her child in the direction of the mother's agenda. First, the mother may maximize the imitation by exaggerating her infant's behavior and thus calling attention to it. Second, she may minimize the imitation to a short, quick flash, used to draw her infant back to the mother's ongoing behavior. Third, the mother may perform a modulating imitation such as responding with a mellowed version of the infant's behavior. For example, the mother may perform mellow crying in imitation of the child's wail. This may have a calming effect on the child.

In contrast, infant behaviors that can be interpreted as having communicative intent receive a conversational response. For example, mothers do not usually imitate prespeech or small hand movements such as pointing. Instead, they reply to these with IDS.

Early play consists primarily of social behaviors. During the first six months, the focus of play is social; there are no specific game rules. Social play is usually spontaneous and occurs frequently during routines. Once play begins, all other tasks end.

During the second six months of life, object play increases. Object play is almost nonexistent at 3 months of age. By 6 months, play often begins with the body but is repeated with a toy. Increasingly, infant and mother participate in a ritualized give and take of objects as infant possession time decreases steadily from 30 to 10 seconds over the next four months. By 11 months the child does not need coaxing before releasing an object. Another popular infant game is "retrieve," in which the child drops an object in anticipation that mother will return it. Infants in all cultures seem to enjoy the shared anticipation and the predictable sequence under their own control. Games allow for lots of shared meaningful communication at a nonverbal level. Throughout the first year, play demonstrates many of the characteristics of later conversation.

Sequence of Social Play

In a typical social play period, the "game" begins with a greeting when the partners catch each other's glance. This initiation is followed by a moment of mutual gaze. If either partner breaks the gaze pattern, play ceases momentarily. Maintenance of the gaze signals readiness and is usually followed by a maternal mock surprise, in which she raises her eyebrows, widens her eyes, opens her mouth, and repositions her head. Her infant responds with wide eyes, an open mouth, a smile, and head reorientation. The infant may wag its head or approach mother's face, but the result is a full-face positioning. Play begins.

This initial exchange in play is actually a greeting. The exchange, which may last for only a second, accomplishes two things. First, all other activities stop; second, there is a reorientation to a face-to-face position, in which signals will be most visible. Often the infant is not prepared, and there are false starts.

Two episodes of the play sequence that may occur several times per minute are *engagement* and *time out*. Episodes of engagement are variable-length sequences of social behaviors separated by clearly marked pauses. Each sequence begins with a greeting that is less full than the initial greeting. Within each episode, the rate of caregiver verbal and nonverbal behaviors is relatively constant. These behaviors occur in discrete bursts within each episode. The mother keeps most of her behaviors under half a second in duration.

Tempo can be used to soothe or arouse the infant. For example, the mother increases her rate to exceed that of a fussy child, then gradually slows in order to soothe her infant. Although the rate of maternal behaviors within an episode is constant, the tempo between episodes may vary considerably. For example, the excitement caused by "I'm gonna get you" is due to changes in tempo.

Generally, each episode has one major purpose: to establish attention, to maintain attention, or to enter into play. Within each episode, therefore, the mother's behavior is fairly predictable for her infant. These maternal consistencies, accompanied by slight variations, are ideal for gaining and maintaining the infant's attention.

Maternal behaviors often occur in repetitive runs within each episode. The average run is three or more units in length. For example, the mother may introduce a topic and then vary it systematically, as in the following sequences:

You're so big, aren't you?
So big.
Oh, so big.
No, we can't do that.
No, not that.
Oh, no.

These repetitions have enormous instructional potential. They expand the infant's range of experience and maintain her or his attention.

Episodes of time out consist of rests used to readjust the interaction. Time out, usually lasting for 3 seconds or longer, occurs when the infant signals, often by fussing or averting the gaze, that he or she is no longer excited. Time out provides an opportunity to retune the interaction. The mother changes the focus of the interaction by glancing away or at some other infant body part or by sitting quietly.

Routines

Communication can be dynamic, complex, and difficult to predict. At first, it must seem to an infant that the behaviors of others are random and unrelated. This is not the best learning environment. In contrast, routines, such as bathing or dressing, offer conventionalized, predictable contexts in which caregivers provide order. An infant can rely on the order and on caregiver cues. The frequency of routines increases throughout the infant's first year.

Routines provide **scripts** that have "slots" for the infant's behavior and aid meaningful interpretation of the event. Just as a fast-food restaurant has a script that constrains adult behavior, dressing and feeding have similar scripts for an infant. Gradually, the infant learns a script, and this, in turn, eases participation. The more familiar you are with the script, the more energy you can devote to differing aspects of participation. By providing a framework, scripts reduce the cognitive energy needed to participate and to make sense.

Infants' event knowledge, which is one of the conceptual foundations of later language development, is gained within familiar daily routines and events. Event knowledge includes information on the actors, actions, props, causality, and temporal aspects of an event. Later, this knowledge is translated into the semantic categories of early speech.

In fact, much of the content of a child's language may come from these daily interactions. When children begin to talk, they display greater semantic complexity and range, longer utterances, and more unique words in these familiar situations (Farrar et al., 1993).

Summary

Although each infant–caregiver pair evolves different patterns of interaction, there are similarities that are important for later communication development. These include the "process" of shared communication, the mutual topic/comment, routines, and learning to anticipate partner behavior change. Play is particularly relevant to language acquisition. First, play usually occurs in a highly restricted and well-understood *semantic domain*. Games such as peekaboo and "I'm gonna get you" have a restricted format, limited semantic elements (*hands, face, cover, uncover*), and a highly constrained set of semantic relations (*hands, cover, face*). Mother is frequently the agent of some action upon an object (*mommy roll ball*).

Second, play has a well-defined task structure. The order of events enables the child to predict. Later, the rules of language will provide similar boundaries.

Third, play has a role structure similar to that of conversation. We might call these *plays* and *audience*. The infant learns to recognize and to play various roles. In addition, she or he learns that roles have a property of reversibility.

TURN TAKING

Most of the interactional behaviors discussed so far have contained an element of turn taking. An infant's development of this skill is essential for development of later conversational skills.

Most early infant and mother turns last for less than 1 second. The pattern is like a dance in which the partners know the steps and the music and can dance accordingly. As a result, sequences of infant–mother behavior emerge.

Even body games, such as tickling, lifting, and bouncing, contain pauses for infant responses. The pauses are initially short, but they lengthen as an infant gains the ability to respond more fully. This gradual pause lengthening is also found in the maternal responses of Japanese mothers (Masataka, 1993). At 3 to 6 months of age, the infant responds or attends quietly. Gaze, facial expression, body movement, or vocalization can all fill a turn. A lack of maternal pauses can result in overstimulation and a less responsive infant.

A 12-week-old infant is twice as likely to revocalize if his or her caregiver responds verbally to its initial vocalization rather than responding with a touch, look, or smile. There is a greater tendency for an infant's vocalizations to be followed by caregiver vocalizations, and those of the caregiver by the child's, than would be expected by chance. A caregiver may perceive her role as that of "conversational replier" to the infant's vocalizations and have a preference for babbling that sounds like speech.

This "conversational" turn taking by adults with 3-month-olds benefits an infant's babbling and turn taking. As we have seen, babbling may become more speechlike and mature, containing syllables rather than individual sounds.

There appears to be a shift in the infant–caregiver vocalization pattern from simultaneous to sequential beginning at about 12 weeks, although concurrent vocalizations still occur more frequently. Prior to this, the infant produces vocalizations that overlap with those of its mother, and the child is more likely to initiate vocalizations when the mother is vocalizing. In addition, both interactive partners make extensive use of smiles, head movements, and gestures. Although vocal exchanges are rather simple and contain little useful information, later, more complex messages will necessitate a turn-taking pattern rather than a concurrent one. During alternating vocalization, both American and Japanese infants will pause as if awaiting a response. If none is forthcoming, the child may revocalize.

Mothers begin to imitate their infants' coughing at 2 months of age. Initially, this behavior is performed to attract attention, but eventually an exchange emerges. By 4 months, an infant will initiate the exchange with a smile or a cough.

Eye gaze is also important in these early dialogs. By 6 weeks of age, an infant is able to fix visually on its mother's eyes and hold the gaze, with eyes widening and brightening. An infant is more likely to begin and to continue looking if the caregiver is looking. In return, the caregiver's behavior becomes more social, and play interactions begin. At 3 months of age, an infant has a focal range that almost equals its mother's, and he or she becomes a true interactional partner in this modality.

Two types of gaze patterns have been identified. During joint or shared attending, gaze is directed at objects. Mothers monitor their infants' gaze and follow its orientation. **Mutual gaze**, or looking at each other, may signal intensified attention. At about 3 months, mutual gaze may be modified occasionally into *gaze coupling*, a turn-taking interaction of making and breaking eye contact. Mutual eye gaze may be important for the formation of attachment or bonding. Also called dyadic gaze, its rhythm of mother and infant looking at and looking away from each other's faces seems to be important in enabling infants to predict events and maternal behaviors (Beebe et al., 2008). Of particular importance is the relative lengths of time spent in mutual gaze and looking away and variations from that pattern. In general, both high-stress infants and high-stress mothers use more variation in their gaze patterns, making anticipation of each other's gaze patterns more difficult for both partners. High-stress mothers report more depression, anxiety, self-criticism, and traumatic childhood experiences.

PROTOCONVERSATIONS

There are identifiable interactional phases in routines and game playing. Mothers and their 3-month-old infants exhibit initiation, mutual orientation, greeting, a play dialog, and disengagement, although any given exchange may not contain every phase. To initiate the exchange, a mother smiles and talks to her infant. For its part, the infant vocalizes and smiles at mother when mother has paused too long. When one partner responds with a neutral or bright face, the mutual phase begins, and one partner speaks or vocalizes. The greeting consists of mutual smiles and eye gazes, with little body or hand movement. Turn taking is seen in the play-dialog phase. The mother talks in a pattern of bursts interspersed with pauses, and the infant vocalizes during the pauses. Finally, disengagement occurs when one partner looks away. These interactional exchanges, called **protoconversations**, contain the initial elements of emerging conversation. A set of conversational behaviors evolves from these infant turn-filling behaviors, such as the development of reciprocal and alternating patterns of vocalizations. Gestures and, later, words will develop to fill an infant's turn as true conversations develop.

SITUATIONAL VARIATIONS

Mothers use a variety of naturally occurring situations to facilitate language and communication development. Prelinguistic behaviors may be situationally bound, even at an early age. Certain infant–mother situations occur frequently. Eight interactional situations account for almost all locational activities of the 3-month-old infant. From most to least frequent, these situations are mother's lap, crib/bed, infant seat, table/tub, couch/sofa, playpen, floor, and jumper/swing. Of developmental importance is the frequency of vocalization within each situation.

Within each situation, certain infant–mother behaviors occur regularly. This regularity is the basis for a child's development of meaning, which emerges from nonrandom action sequences, especially vocalization sequences associated with different "situational" locations. For example, the infant is usually placed in the crib to sleep. Therefore, the mother neither responds nor initiates vocalizations. On the other hand, at the table or in the tub, the infant is subjected to many vocalizations and nonrandom maternal behaviors. Situations provide a context within which the child can process the nonrandom content. These nonrandom behaviors of a parent form an early meaning base.

Conclusion

SYMBOLIC COMMUNICATION IN THE FORM of spoken language develops within the context of a very early communication system that is integrated and nonspeech in nature. Presymbolic communication enables a child to learn language. Over the first year, an infant's early behaviors acquire intentionality and serve several communication functions.

A child's initial behavior communicates little, if anything, beyond the immediate behavior itself. Infant behaviors are not as significant overall as a mother's response to these behaviors. Mothers perceive their infants as persons and interpret their baby's behavior as communicative, verbal, and meaningful.

Humans are social animals who live generally within a social network. An infant is dependent on others, especially mother. The mother is controlled to a great extent by the infant's biological needs.

As the infant adapts to the social world, its mother is very responsive to the infant's behavior. Mindful of the infant's current abilities, she accommodates quickly to infant behavior changes, but her own behavior always has a direction. In general, the mother modifies her behavior by simplifying her speech, by increasing the amount and quality of her nonverbal communication, and by relying heavily on the context. She gives linguistic input while providing an opportunity or turn in which the infant can respond.

Both semantic structure and pragmatic functions are derived by an infant from social interaction. A child infers meaning from mother's vocalizations and nonrandom behaviors in interactional situations. Word relationships are learned through joint action routines, such as games, in which a child takes a particular role within the interaction.

The ability to reference or refer to entities derives from joint attention. A mother and child attend jointly to a rather limited array of objects they share in common. These form the initial concepts that are later expressed in words by the child. In addition to reference, other communication functions, such as requesting and giving, are also expressed preverbally.

Intentions or language uses develop as a result of a mother's responsiveness to her child's earliest interactional behaviors. As the infant learns to control the behavior of others, he or she begins to modify and regularize signals in order to communicate more specifically. The particular words that an infant later uses expressively will be determined by pragmatic factors, such as the intentions these words express. An infant will use those words that are most accurate for expressing its intentions.

Social communication is found in mother–infant discourse over the first year of life. In turn, communication skills developed within the mother–infant duo provide a basis for the infant's learning of the linguistic code.

It may not be glaringly obvious, but in both Chapters 4 and 5, we have addressed the *how* of language development but not the *why*. There is a simple explanation for this omission: We don't know why children develop language.

Although behaviors that a child learns may lead to language, we cannot conclude that a child learned them for that reason. An infant does not understand the long-term consequences of learning, nor is the child storing away knowledge for an unknown future. Even if a young infant did sense a need for attaining linguistic competence, he or she is incapable of planning for this eventuality.

The social and communicative bases for language development can be used to explain, in part, the motivation for learning language. A child and caregiver establish strong communicative bonds. Because of the enjoyment or reinforcement each partner receives from these communicative interactions, he or she is desirous of even more communication. The frustration of being misinterpreted and the joy of being understood are strong motivators for both children and caregivers to modify their language. The infant attempts to learn the code used by the caregiver, who, in turn, simplifies that code to enhance the infant's comprehension. The outcome for the infant is that he or she understands and uses more language within communicative interactions as an attempt to participate even more.

Discussion

WITHIN A DISCUSSION OF THE SOCIAL and communicative bases of language, we get to the motivation for learning language in the first place. Language is learned within well-established communication. Learning language makes the learner a better communicator.

Most important, children become communicators because we treat them that way. We expect them to communicate. If a speech–language pathologist or teacher doesn't expect his or her clients or students to communicate, they won't. Not to expect better performance is to give up.

Babies seem prewired for communication, but it is what caregivers—primarily the mother—do with this "predisposition" that is important. Recall how the child progresses to gestures, the first signs of intention to communicate, and how words fulfill the intentions expressed through these gestures. Remember the early learning within joint action routines and game playing that teaches the child about predictability in interactions and about turn taking. Think of all the things an infant can do socially. And don't forget all the intentional communication expressed through the child's gestures. The first word is merely the icing on the cake.

Sadly, some children will not obtain a strong social and communicative base for language. This may be due to environmental or individual factors or both. Children in abusive or neglectful homes may fail to bond with a parent or may become fearful of sound making. Other children, such as those with ASD, may fail to bond with and respond to their caretakers because of a seeming inability to relate to other humans in a way that differs from the way in which the child relates to objects. Whether the factors are environmental or individual, the result may be impaired language and communication.

Main Points

- Children become communicators because we treat them that way.
- Language is acquired to fill the intentions initially expressed in gestures.
- There is a mutual modification in the behavior of the infant and the mother in that changes in the baby's behavior result in changes in the mother's, which in turn affect the infant.
- Newborns seem to prefer the human face and voice over other stimuli.
- Of particular importance for later communication are the early patterns of gaze coupling, turn taking, stimulus-response bonds, routines, and games. Routines teach the child that behavior is predictable and facilitate a child's participation, while games have many of the attributes of conversations.
- Intentions go through stages of development: pre-intentional, intentional, and symbolic. During the intentional stage a child learns to signal intent via gestures, first showing itself, then showing objects, and finally with an array of gestures. Initially, each gesture is silent, then vocalization is added, and finally a word or verbalization accompanies the gesture.
- Mothers modify their behavior to facilitate interactions.

- Cultural differences exist and signify only difference. There are many ways to help children acquire language.
- Of particular importance for early communication are joint or shared reference and joint action.

Reflections

1. Discuss the abilities and behaviors of the newborn that suggest prewiring for communication.
2. Describe the aspects of conversation found in gaze coupling, ritualized behaviors, and game playing.
3. Why are gestures particularly important? Describe the sequence of gestural development.
4. What communicative behaviors does the infant elicit from the mother, and what is the effect of each on communication?
5. Explain why three interactions—joint reference, joint actions, and turn taking—are particularly important for the development of early communication, and trace briefly the development of each.
6. Explain the cultural and socioeconomic differences found in the interactions of caregivers and infants.

Steve Smith/Photodisc/Getty Images

6 Language-Learning and Teaching Processes and Young Children

OBJECTIVES

It's difficult to explain language learning without discussing children's learning strategies and parents' teaching techniques. Although the relationship is not one of pupil and teacher, many of the elements of that relationship exist in a more subtle form.

Learning language is not simply a process of accumulating language structures and content. Children use certain strategies to comprehend the language they hear and to form hypotheses about the underlying language rules. Caregivers also aid linguistic analysis by modifying the speech stream directed at children. When you have completed this chapter, you should understand the following:

- Relationship among comprehension, production, and cognition
- Role of selective imitation and formulas
- Universal language-learning principles
- Characteristics of child-directed speech
- Types of parental prompting
- Effects of parental expansion, extension, and imitation
- Use of parental turnabouts
- Importance of play
- Effects of cultural variation on the language-learning process
- Important terms:

analogy
bootstrapping
contingent query
entrenchment
evocative utterances
expansion
extension
formula
functionally based distributional analysis
hypothesis-testing utterances
intention-reading
interrogative utterances
pattern-finding
preemption
reformulation
request for clarification
schematization
selective imitation
turnabout

In Chapters 4 and 5 we discussed the bases for language development. These bases are inadequate, however, to explain of the extremely complicated process of language learning. Language development is not haphazard. Although large, general changes occur in an orderly, predictable fashion, there is great individual variation that reflects a child's underlying language-learning strategies, linguistic complexity, and cognitive-conceptual growth.

Even though adults do not attempt to teach language directly to children developing typically, we do adapt our language input to a child's level of attention and comprehension. In the process, we provide models of simplified language. We also tend to react to a child's utterances in a way that increases the chance that he or she will repeat the structures later. This reinforcement is not direct but instead includes such indirect behaviors as repeating and responding to a child's utterances. It is also important to remember the context of most language-learning exchanges. As you already know, children engage in conversations with their caregivers throughout the day while engaged in activities and routines that form the backdrop for communication.

In this chapter we will examine issues related to language learning. We begin by exploring the relationship among comprehension, production, and cognitive growth. In addition, we will examine child language-learning strategies and adult teaching strategies. Finally, we will discuss the conversational context in which a child's language develops and the maternal strategies for maintaining a conversation. Naturally, the strategies used by both a child and an adult differ with their culture, the language being learned, and the language maturity of the child.

Comprehension, Production, and Cognitive Growth

There is a strong link among comprehension, production, and cognition. A child's cognitive conceptual development is the primary tool for comprehension. The properties of individual languages also affect development.

COGNITION AND LANGUAGE

Cognitive skills and language abilities are associated. They develop in parallel fashion and are strongly related with underlying factors. For example, cognitive development in infants and toddlers is strongly related to increased memory and to the ability to acquire symbols in many areas, including language and gestures. First words and recognitory gestures, such as sniffing flowers, appear at about the same age. At times, evidence of the correlation between language and cognition is strong, especially during the first two years of life.

A significant difference in the cognitive levels of play exists between children who use no words and those who use single words. Children who do not produce words are more likely to play with toys such as blocks, while children who produce single words are more likely to play with "animate" objects, such as dolls or action figures. The play of children beginning to combine words consists of combining two or more play sequences and/or performing the same action on a sequence of entities.

Cognitive growth may have an especially important influence on early word combinations. Many of the principles of cognitive learning can also be applied to language learning:

- Selectively attending to perceptually important stimuli
- Discriminating stimuli along different dimensions
- Remembering stimuli
- Classifying stimuli according to the results of the discriminations

These principles correspond to the steps taken in information processing presented in Chapter 3.

Children are active learners, forming hypotheses based on patterns in the incoming language stream. Data are tested and incorporated into the system or used to reorganize the system. As a child's mind stores bits of information, she or he tries to organize them based on perceived relationships.

Organization of longer utterances requires better short-term memory and knowledge of syntactic patterns and word classes. Hierarchical word-order organization develops similar to that depicted in Figure 1.5, and individual words become "slot fillers" for various word classes.

Development of many grammatical constructions also reflect cognitive development. For example, reversibility, or the ability to trace a process backward, is strongly related to acquisition of *before* and *after*, *because*, and *why*. In order to respond to a *why* question, a child must be able to use *because* and reverse the order of events.

ADULT: *Why* are you wet?
RESULT: Event_2
CHILD: *Because* I spilled my apple juice.
CAUSE: Event_1

Knowledge structures of two types are assumed to guide word acquisition: *event-based knowledge* and *taxonomic knowledge* (Sell, 1992). Event-based knowledge consists of sequences of events or routines, such as a birthday party, that are temporal or causal in nature and organized toward a goal. These sequences of events contain actors, roles, props, and options or alternatives. A child uses this knowledge to form *scripts* or sets of expectations that aid memory, enhance comprehension, and give the individual child a knowledge base for interpreting events.

Event-based, or world, knowledge influences vocabulary acquisition and may be the basis for taxonomic, or word, knowledge. Words are learned within a social context; their meaning is found in a child's representation of events.

Taxonomic knowledge consists of categories and classes of words. New words are compared categorically and organized for retrieval.

Early words are first comprehended and produced in the context of everyday events. From repeated use, the words themselves become cues for the event. For example, the words *bath* and *soap* become cues for bathing, while *cookie* and *juice* represent snack. As the child acquires more words, *cookie*, *cracker*, *milk*, and *juice* become *things I eat*, which later evolves into the category *food*. Preschoolers rely on event-based knowledge, while kindergarteners use more categorical script-related groupings such as *things I eat*. By age 7 to 10, children are using taxonomic categories, such as *food* (Sell, 1992).

Comprehension and Production

The exact developmental relationship between language comprehension and production is unclear. In comprehension, a child uses both linguistic and conceptual input plus his or her memory. In contrast, production also uses linguistic and conceptual input but relies on linguistic knowledge alone for encoding.

Although comprehension is assumed to occur prior to production, children may employ other strategies. For example, young Thai children seem to employ a distributional strategy. Based on both location of words in sentences and frequency, Thai children use the strategy for production of certain language forms before they comprehend these forms. This may be only one of several strategies used by all children.

The comprehension–production relationship is a dynamic one that changes with rates and levels of development and different linguistic demands. The comprehension of presymbolic infants is difficult to determine. An infant may look where mother looks, act on objects that mother references, and imitate actions. These behaviors represent the infant's strategies. The caregiver interprets the child's behavior as meaningful.

In early phonological development, the relationship is easier to discern. Infant perception of speech-sound differences greatly precedes expression. A child can perceive speech sounds very early on. Intonational patterns are also discriminated early, at around 8 months of age.

Infant acoustic-phonetic comprehension of first words may be less specific. Initially, recognition and comprehension are holistic, such as grossly discriminating *dog* from *cookie*. Rather quickly, however, an infant acquires the detailed perceptual skill needed for more subtle distinctions, such as *hot* and *hit*. Over 50% of the most common monosyllabic words spoken by 1- to 3-year-olds have three or more other words that differ by only one phoneme.

Single Words Comprehension and production of first words pose different problems. Obviously, a child does not fully comprehend the word before he or she produces it. Full comprehension requires a greater linguistic and experiential background than that of a year-old infant. Instead, event-based knowledge is used by toddlers, or 12- to 24-month-olds, to form responses (Paul, 1990). For example, when a caregiver says, "Let's read a book," and hands one to a child, the child responds by opening the book, which is part of the book script.

Up through age 2, comprehension is highly context-dependent (Striano, Rochat, & Legerstee, 2003). Most speech addressed to a toddler is associated with that immediate nonlinguistic context. Adults may overestimate a child's comprehension unless they consider cues available to a child. Later, preschoolers focus on linguistic factors to gain needed information. Event knowledge continues to be important, however, even for adults, and comprehension is easiest within familiar events.

Even though a symbol signifies a particular referent, the meaning of the symbol goes beyond that referent. True meaning refers to a concept, not to individual examples.

After a mother labels an entity, her child forms hypotheses about its nature. In turn, the child tests these hypotheses by applying the label. The mother monitors her child's output and improves her child's accuracy by providing evaluative feedback. Hence, the child's comprehension and production are fine-tuned essentially at the same time.

Within the first 50 words, comprehension seems to precede production. As a group, children understand approximately 50 words before they are able to produce 10, although the range of comprehended words varies greatly across children.

The distribution of syntactic types also varies between comprehension and production (Table 6.1). As children mature, the distribution changes.

TABLE 6.1 Comprehension and Production of Single Words by Syntactic Category

	Comprehension (First 100 Words)	Production (First 50 Words)
Nominals (Nouns)		
Specific	17%	11%
General	39%	50%
Action	36%	19%
Modifiers	3%	10%
Personal-social	5%	10%

Source: Information from Benedict (1979).

In summary, the ability to comprehend words develops gradually, and initially is highly context-dependent. Symbolic comprehension continues to develop through the second year of life (Striano et al., 2003).

Nonlinguistic context is an essential comprehension aid. In addition, comprehension of a simple sentence depends on recognition of highly meaningful words within it. A child need not know syntax if he or she knows the meanings of these words separately. The nonlinguistic context provides additional relational information. Yet children seem to respond best to verbal commands that are slightly above their production level, suggesting comprehension above their level of production.

Toddlers rely on the uses of objects and on routines for comprehension. Two strategies may be used with objects:

1. *Do-what-you-usually-do*. Balls would be rolled, thrown, dropped, or passed back and forth, no matter what the child heard. Young preschoolers use this "probable event" strategy. If there is no obvious probable action, a child may respond randomly or use basic syntactic relationships for comprehension.
2. *Act-on-the-object-in-the-way-mentioned*. Noting the action, the child would throw the ball whether the caregiver said, "Now, you *throw* the ball," or "Remember how Johnny *throws* the ball in the baseball game?" Event knowledge is still important.

Verb comprehension may be acquired one verb at a time, moving from general verbs, such as *do*, to more specific verbs, such as *eat* and *sit*. By 28 months, a child can use word order for limited comprehension.

By late preschool, children learning English consistently use word order for comprehension, although they may still revert to event knowledge. It is not until age 5 or 6 that children begin to rely consistently on syntactic and morphologic interpretation. By age 7 to 9, children are using language to acquire more language, such as word definitions, and are more sensitive to phrases and subordinate clauses and to connectors, such as *before*, *after*, *during*, and *while*.

LESS IS MORE

A child changes throughout the period that he or she is learning language. It would seem logical to suppose that a child's brain would undergo change during this learning. One developmental change occurs in *working memory* and attention. Both are initially limited and increase over time.

The fact that these abilities are limited at first may actually be an advantage for learning language (Elman, 1999). Short, simple sentences are easier to process, and they provide a starting point for discovering words, categories of words, and grammatical patterns in the environment. Once this information has been induced, it provides a basis for moving on. As working memory improves, it can deal with increasingly complex input and, in the process, help a child refine his or her knowledge.

When we view the problem of learning language from this perspective, such maturational limitations are really a plus. The process of deconstructing the language code and mastering it is extremely complex. Beginning small is a good place to start. It seems logical that a child might need cues to help discover grammar. Emergentists suggest that the timing of memory and other cognitive developments have the effect of limiting language processing in exactly the right way to enable a child's brain to solve this problem (Elman, 1999).

Although it seems counterintuitive from an adult perspective, some problems, such as learning language, may be best solved by starting small. We might call this the "less is more" hypothesis.

Maybe we can illustrate how limited cognitive resources can affect the process by looking at young language learners in comparison to older ones. It is well-documented that late learners of a second language exhibit poorer performance relative to early or native learners. While learning language, younger and older children make similar numbers of errors, but the types of errors differ. Late learners make more morphological mistakes and rely more heavily on fixed forms in which internal morphological elements become frozen and are therefore often used inappropriately. For example, *I don't* and *you don't* may result in *he don't*. Similarly, a late learner may rely on *drink-drank-drunk* to produce *think-thank-thunk* or *link-lank-lunk*. In contrast, young native learners make more errors of omission.

These different error patterns may be based on differing ability to analyze the structure of language utterances, with younger learners possibly having an advantage. Although the young learner is handicapped by short-term memory, this reduces the space that can be examined by the child. In contrast, the late language learner's greater storage and computational skills work to his or her disadvantage because the form-meaning (*ed* = past) relationships that underlie morphology are complex.

Summary

During the preschool years, the relationship among comprehension, production, and cognition changes as the child matures. In general, linguistic developments parallel much of the cognitive growth of the preschool child, although this is not a one-to-one relationship. A young child's brain, however, does seem to be uniquely suited for the task of unraveling language and reconstructing it again in his or her own form.

Child Learning Strategies

Although there are many variations in the way in which children learn language, there are ample similarities. These suggest underlying strategies that differ with the language level of a child. In the following section, we consider the language-learning strategies most frequently associated with toddlers and preschoolers.

TODDLER LANGUAGE-LEARNING STRATEGIES

To assume that toddlers, children ages 12 to 24 months, merely speak what they hear is to oversimplify the acquisition of language. A child must use certain learning methods to sort out relevant and irrelevant information in adult and sibling conversations. A child must decide which utterances are good examples of the language for accomplishing his or her communication goals and must hypothesize about their underlying meanings and structures.

Receptive Strategies: When Is a Word a Word?

As toddlers mature, they become increasingly adept at acquiring new words under conditions that are not always ideal. Although 14- to 15-month-olds experience difficulty establishing stable symbol–referent associations even with caregiver assistance, 18- to 19-month-olds are able to establish these links even when the caregiver names entities to which the toddler is not attending.

Before children can recognize words, they must gain a sense of how sounds go together to form syllables of the native language (Jusczyk, 1999). Infants may use lexical, syntactic, phonological, and stress-pattern cues in combination to break the speech stream they hear and facilitate interpretation. These cues are probably used flexibly depending on what's available in any given situation (Sanders & Neville, 2000). For example, English words can begin with a consonant blend, such as *bl* or *str*; Korean words cannot. Armed with these phonological structures gained by listening to speech, the child can more easily locate word boundaries. As a result, the seemingly endless speech flow becomes a series of distinct but, for now, meaningless words. For example, a 6- to 10-month-old child reared in an English-speaking home begins to develop a bias in favor of words with the English pattern of emphasis on the first syllable, such as *mommy*, *daddy*, *doggie*, and *baby*. By 11 months, infants are sensitive to word boundaries and phonological characteristics of their native language (Shafer, Shucard, Shucard, & Gerken, 1998).

Although adults modify their speech to highlight word and sentence boundaries and to hold a child's attention, and although words usually pertain to semantic and pragmatic concepts previously established, these explanations alone are insufficient for describing how toddlers learn words. What do children bring to the task? What assumptions do children make about language they encounter? Although linguists don't really know, they can infer from the language behavior of toddlers that certain lexical principles or assumptions are being used.

Three assumptions of toddlers seem fundamental:

1. People use words to refer to entities.
2. Words are extendable.
3. A given word refers to the whole entity, not its parts. (Golinkoff, Mervis, & Hirsh-Pasek, 1994)

The first or *reference principle* assumes that people refer. Words do not just "go with" but actually "stand for" entities to which they refer. Therefore, a toddler must be able to determine the speaker's intention to refer, the linguistic patterns used, and the entities to which they refer. A subprinciple of mutual exclusivity presupposes that each referent has a unique symbol. In other words, a referent cannot be both a *cup* and a *spoon*. Eventually, as a child gains multiple referents for some words, this assumption will be overridden.

As you will recall from Chapter 1, words are symbols that represent concepts, not specific referents. Using the second or *extendability principle*, an infant assumes that there is some similarity, such as shared perceptual attributes, that enables use of one symbol for more than one referent. Thus, *cup* can refer to the child's cup and to those that the child perceives to be similar, such as other child cups.

There is still some ambiguity, however, because the word *doggie* could refer to the dog's fur, color, bark, four legs, or any number of similarities. The third or *whole-object principle* assumes that a label refers to a whole entity rather than to a part or attribute. In fact, object parts are rare in toddler lexicons. Mothers aid this assumption of their children by providing basic-level terms (*table*) before more restricted terms (*leg*, *top*, *drawer*). Basic-level terms are often accompanied by pointing, thus parental teaching strategies seem to match children's learning preferences.

Three additional assumptions may be needed for the toddler to form hypothetical definitions quickly and to use syntactic information:

1. Categorical assumption
2. Novel name-nameless assumption
3. Conventionality assumption (Golinkoff et al., 1994; Markman, 1992)

The *categorical assumption* is used by children as young as 18 months to extend a label to related entities. Classification is based not just on perceptual attributes but on function, world knowledge, and communication characteristic of the words, such as frequency of use. Unlike the extendability principle, which would apply *cup* to a limited sample, the categorical assumption goes beyond basic-level referents of the same kind. In this case, *cup* may be extended to all objects that hold liquid.

The *novel name-nameless assumption* enables a child to link a symbol and referent after only a few exposures. In short, a child assumes that novel symbols are linked to previously unnamed referents. Use of this assumption seems to correspond to the vocabulary spurt experienced by many children at around 18 months. Caregivers aid children by naming and pointing to, holding, or manipulating novel objects to further specify the referent. As children mature, they rely less on these gestural assists and more on the caregivers' language.

Finally, the *conventionality assumption* leads a child to expect meanings to be expressed by others in consistent conventional forms. In other words, caregivers don't change the word's meaning with each use. A car is consistently called by that name. Conversely, because a child wishes to be understood, he or she is motivated to produce the forms used by the language community.

We are not certain that children actually use these principles or make these assumptions. Toddlers employ these or similar principles, however, in order to make sense of the speech stream directed at them. Children actively attempt to understand adult language and to make word–referent associations. Language learning is not passive.

Expressive Strategies

Young children use at least four expressive strategies to gain linguistic knowledge. These are evocative utterances, hypothesis testing, interrogative utterances, and selective imitation (see Table 6.2). **Evocative utterances** are statements a child makes naming entities. After a child names an entity, an adult usually gives evaluative feedback that confirms or negates the child's selection of exemplars. As a result, the child either maintains or modifies his or her meaning. As you might expect, there is a positive relationship between the amount of verbal input from adults at 20 months and vocabulary size and average utterance length of the child at 24 months. Children are more verbal in homes in which parents are more verbal.

Hypothesis-testing utterances and **interrogative utterances** are more direct methods of acquiring linguistic knowledge. When seeking confirmation of a word meaning,

TABLE 6.2 Examples of Toddler Expressive Strategies

Expressive Strategy	Explanation	Examples
Evocative utterance	Child says a word and may await a response. May be used when child is certain of the word or in trial-and-error mode.	*Horsie.* *Cup.* *Big.*
Hypothesis testing	Child says word with rising intonation awaiting reassurance or confirmation by the conversational partner.	*Doggie?* *Run?* *All-gone?*
Interrogative utterance	Child is unsure of the word, so asks.	*What's that?*

the child may say a word or word combination with rising intonation, such as "doggie↑" or "baby eat↑." This utterance serves as a question seeking a yes/no response. An adult either confirms or denies the child's hypothesis. When unaware of an entity label, a child uses an interrogative utterance, such as "What?" "That?" or "Wassat?" These requests for information are even found in the pointing and vocalizing behaviors of infants prior to first words. At 24 months there is a positive correlation between the number of interrogative utterances used by children and their vocabulary size.

The last strategy, imitation, is selective. Children do not imitate indiscriminately. In fact, they actively select what to imitate. Table 6.3 contains examples of selective imitation. Note that the ends of utterances seem to have particular perceptual importance for children.

Role of Selective Imitation Selective imitation is used in the acquisition of words, morphology, and syntactic-semantic structures. In general, imitation is defined as a whole or partial repetition of an utterance of another speaker within no more than three successive child utterances. Approximately 20% of what toddlers say is an imitation of other speakers, although there are widespread differences across children and situations. For example, the amount of child imitation seems to reflect the amount of maternal imitation of her child.

Usually, imitations are slightly more mature than the production capacities of a child, indicating selective imitation's use as a learning strategy. The role of imitation as a strategy is complex. For example, imitation of others is important for vocabulary growth, while self-imitation seems to be important for the transition from single-word to multiword language production.

The use of selective imitation as a learning strategy decreases with age, especially after age 2. It appears that imitation's usefulness as a language-learning strategy decreases as the learning task becomes more complex.

At the single-word level, selective imitation seems particularly important for vocabulary growth, although conceptual development is certainly central as well. Although the presence of the referent increases the likelihood of imitation, a child's ability to repeat an utterance depends on his or her understanding of its meaning.

Many imitations and much early vocabulary growth take place within the context of daily routines, which may contain predictable or repetitious language. Imitations may appear later in an altered form. For example, when a child goes to the door, his mother may say, "Do you want to go out?" When next the child goes to the door, he may say, "Out." The word is the same, but the intent has changed.

TABLE 6.3 Examples of Selective Imitation

Adult Utterance	Child Response	Explanation
ADULT: Daddy home.	CHILD: Daddy home.	Immediate whole imitation
ADULT: The doggy is sick.	CHILD: Doggie sick.	Immediate partial imitation
ADULT: You want the baby?	CHILD: No.	
ADULT: Okay, mommy want baby.	CHILD: Want baby.	Immediate partial imitation, changed to a child request
ADULT: Want mommy to throw ball?	Child reaches arms forward.	
ADULT: What?	CHILD: Throw ball	Delayed partial imitation, changed to a child request

Initially, children rely on a few rigid syntactic formulas. In English, children become dependent on the SVO (*Mommy is eating a cookie*) sentence form. Later, they learn other forms and develop a flexible system that is adaptable to different discourse situations. This evolution from rigid to flexible systems has been reported in the development of languages as different as English, Chinese, French, Modern Hebrew, Hungarian, and Turkish.

Using knowledge of semantics, a preschooler attempts to *pay attention to how and where semantic distinctions are marked* syntactically. This varies across languages. For example, consonants and the inside of words are important in modern Hebrew, stems and word endings are important in Hungarian, and word and phrase order and relationships are important in English.

In addition to learning words, meanings, and word order, a child learns the classes in which words belong, such as nouns and verbs. Language rules apply to word classes, not to individual words. Most likely a child hypothesizes that words are similar and thus belong together because of the way they are treated linguistically. For example, a child hears certain words in English receive *-ed* and *-ing* markers and begins to "chunk" these words together into what adults call *verbs*. As the child discriminates similarities, words treated in the same manner are organized and linked together. New members are added as they meet the same criteria. Although this explanation is somewhat simplified, it adequately describes an active process by the child that corresponds to our knowledge of information processing and hypothesis building.

Children's grammatical errors do not necessarily reflect a lack of either knowledge or development. Even some children with little knowledge of a grammatical structure may make few errors with that structure because they attempt to produce it infrequently (Rispoli, 2005). Other children—we might call them risk takers—attempt repeatedly to produce these structures with the result that they make frequent errors.

From a cross-linguistic perspective, the development of syntactic and morphological features seems to progress through three phases. First, use of the language feature is context based and dependent on extralinguistic cues. Second, a child relates meanings to forms such as word order, as in "A acts on B," seen in *Mommy eats soup*. In the third phase, a child acquires mature use of the language feature based on internalized rules.

Universal Language-Learning Principles

There are patterns of development that suggest underlying universal syntax learning strategies and operational principles of children (see Table 6.4) (Slobin, 1978). Although we do not know the exact strategies children use, we can infer their presence from

TABLE 6.4 Universal Language-Learning Principles

1. Pay attention to the ends of words.
2. Phonological forms of words can be systematically modified.
3. Pay attention to the order of words and morphemes.
4. Avoid interruption and rearrangement of linguistic units.
5. Underlying semantic relations should be marked overtly and clearly.
6. Avoid exceptions.
7. The use of grammatical markers should make semantic sense.

Source: Information from Slobin (1978).

consistent behaviors of young children learning different languages. The following sections address some of these principles. A caution: The following sections require a lot of thought. Go slow; pause often to digest.

Pay Attention to the Ends of Words Across languages, children acquire linguistic markers that occur at the ends of words, such as the English *-s*, *-er*, *-ed*, before those that appear at the beginnings of words, as in *un-*, *dis-*, *in-*.

A corollary could be stated as follows: *For any given semantic notion, suffixes or post-positions will be acquired earlier than will prefixes or pre-positions.* For example, the comparative *-er* (*costlier*) and superlative *-est* (*costliest*) endings are acquired before the alternative *more* (*more costly*) and *most* (*most costly*) markers. The child is thus more likely to learn *sweeter* than *more sweet.*

Many new or expanded grammatical structures initially occur at the end of sentences, suggesting that the final position in longer structures is also important for learning. Initial word order in children's questions may also reflect attention to the ends of adult utterances. For example, after hearing a parent say, "I don't know where it is," a child may later produce the question form "Where it is?"

Phonological Forms Can Be Systematically Modified Through experimentation, the child learns to vary pronunciation. Gradually, the child recognizes that various sound changes, consistent across several words, such as the final /t/ sound on ***walked*** and ***talked***, can reflect underlying meaning changes.

Pay Attention to the Order of Words and Morphemes The standard order of morphemes used in adult utterances is preserved in child speech. Thus, a child produces "charm*ingly*," not "charm*lying*." In English, general word order (SVO) is maintained by preschoolers, leading to another universal corollary: *Word order in child speech reflects word order in adult forms of the language.* This seems to be especially true in languages such as English, in which word order is important for underlying meaning.

A second universal corollary states: *In early stages of development, sentences that do not have standard word order will be interpreted using standard word order.* Two following

Conversations with adults afford preschoolers chances to make verbal contributions, learn when to speak, and develop cohesiveness between speaker and listener.

examples from English relate to passive sentences and ordering of events. In the first example, English-speaking preschoolers interpret passive sentences as if they represent the common agent-action-object form. The child will therefore interpret "The cat is chased by the dog" as "The cat chased the dog." In a second example, 3-year-old children will ignore the conjunctions *before* and *after* in compound sentences, interpreting the order of the clauses as an order of occurrence. In other words, clause 1 occurred first, then clause 2. For example, the sentence "We'll go to Grandma's after the movie" may be interpreted as "Grandma's, then movie."

Avoid Interruption and Rearrangement of Linguistic Units As mentioned, in English, children learn the SVO form early. Interruption and rearrangement of this form strain a child's processing, especially with sentences that require a child to retain large amounts of information.

A related universal corollary states: *Structures requiring rearrangement of elements will first appear in nonrearranged form.* In other words, a form in English that differs from the predominant SVO format will first appear in the SVO form. In some children's speech, the auxiliary or helping verb in questions ("What *are* you eating?") appears originally in a noninverted form ("What you *are* eating?"), keeping the verb "is eating" together.

A second related corollary states: *Discontinuous morphemes are reduced to, or replaced by, continuous morphemes whenever possible.* In English, this universal is demonstrated again in the progressive verb form, consisting of the auxiliary verb *be* plus a main verb with the inflection *-ing* (*is eating*), which appears initially in children's speech without the auxiliary verb, as in "I eating ice cream."

There is a tendency, states a third axiom, to *preserve the structure of the sentence as a closed entity by sentence-external placement of new linguistic forms.* In other words, new structures may be tacked on to the beginning or, more likely, at the end of the sentence prior to moving within it. For example, in English early negatives are attached to the beginning (*No* eat soup) and, occasionally, to the end of a sentence. Only later does the negative move into the sentence, as in "I *no* eat soup." Initial subordinate clauses and infinitive phrases are attached at the end of the sentence first and develop within the sentence later.

Finally, a fourth universal corollary states: *The greater the separation between related parts of a sentence, the more difficult it is for the child to process adequately.* A sentence containing a phrase or clause is more difficult to interpret if the phrase or clause interrupts the SVO format. A sentence such as "I saw the man *who fell down*" is easier for preschoolers to interpret than "The man *who fell down* ran away." In a sentence such as "The girl who stole the horse ran away," a young child is likely to interpret it as "The girl stole the horse and the horse ran away."

To produce complicated sentences, a preschooler must take some risks (Dale & Crain-Thoreson, 1993). As mentioned, not all children are language risk takers.

Underlying Semantic Relations Should Be Marked Overtly and Clearly As a child listens to and attempts to interpret speech, obvious, consistent morphological markers may help. Not all languages are the same in their use of morphological markers. Both the Tamil and Turkish morphological systems are learned early because of their regularity and clarity of marking. Each affix encodes only one feature, and, by age 2, most children are using them correctly. Compare this to English, in which three phonological forms (/s, z, əz/) are used for plural (*three dogs*), third person singular (*he walks*), and possessive (*daddy's key*) marking.

A related universal corollary states: *A child will begin to mark a semantic notion earlier if its morphological structure is more obvious perceptually.* The development of the passive (*The boy was hit by the girl.*) is illustrative. The concept of the passive form is not difficult for children to learn, but in English the linguistic structure is. Egyptian Arabic-speaking children learn the passive prefix *it-* rather early. In English, a passive sentence requires several syntactic changes and may not be acquired fully until adolescence.

A second universal corollary states: *There is a preference for marking even unmarked members of a semantic category*. This preference may account for some of the overextensions in English. Overextension is when a language feature, such as a morphological ending, is used where it is not required. For example, the clear *-ed* past-tense marker may be used with irregular verbs (*wented*) which may have appeared to a child to have no marking (*went*). Preference for marking may also be seen with the plural as in *mans* and *feets*.

When a child first learns a linguistic entity that can be contracted or deleted, contractions or deletions tend not to be used. In other words, initially a child will use the full form of contractible or deletable forms. In English, young children may respond with "I will" when asked to imitate "I'll" in a sentence. Similarly, the verb *to be* first appears as "he is," although adults use "*he's*" more frequently. It's no surprise, therefore, that for young children it is easier to understand a complex sentence in which material usually deleted is not deleted.

Avoid Exceptions There is a tendency among children to overgeneralize linguistic rules and to avoid exceptions to these rules. As a group, the rules for a larger class, such as past tense (*walked, jumped, asked*), are learned before those for a subclass, such as irregular past tense (*ate, drank, thought*). The stages of linguistic marking of semantic notions are as follows:

1. No marking (walk)
2. Appropriate marking in a small number of cases (walk*ed*)
3. *Overgeneralization of marking*, although limited and with a small number of examples (eat*ed*)
4. Adultlike system (walk*ed*, ate)

For example, initially there is no marking of the English past tense. Next, some irregular past-tense verbs, such as *came* and *fell*, are formed correctly, but the regular past *-ed* is not used. Once learned, the regular past is overextended to irregular verbs, as in *comed* and *falled*, in an attempt to introduce regularity. Finally, full adult usage is acquired.

A related universal corollary states: *Rules for larger classes are learned before rules for subdivisions, and general rules are learned before exceptions*. Most plural nouns, for example, can use the word *many* to indicate quantity, such as *many cookies* or *many blocks*. Children learn this rule quickly. Mass nouns, a smaller class—liquids or granular substances, such as *sand* or *water*—require *much*. It takes children longer to learn to use *much* with the appropriate nouns.

Overextension of morphological or syntactic rules may be related to an increase in number of examples learned. Initial learning, most probably by rote memorization, continues until such time as the number is large enough for a child to synthesize a general rule. Overextension begins at this point.

Grammatical Markers Should Make Semantic Sense Inflectional markers, such as *-s*, *-ed*, or *-ing*, and words, such as *a*, *the*, or *at*, are applied within certain grammatical classes. Thus, the *-ed* morphological marker is applied to words in the verb class. Words are substituted for words from the same class. For example, a child may use *in*, a preposition, incorrectly in place of *at*, another preposition, but he or she will not substitute *in* for *the*, because *the* is not a preposition.

A corollary states: *When selecting an appropriate marker from among a group performing the same semantic function, the child tends to rely on a single form*. For example, the selection of the /s/, /z/, or /əz/ phonological form of the plural is based on the ending

Watch minutes 39:16–44:53 of this video to see Dr. Steven Pinker of Harvard University give you some idea of the challenges a child faces in comprehending the language in his or her environment. http://www.youtube.com/watch?v=Q-B_ONJIEcE

consonant of the stem word as in *cats*/s/, *dogs*/z/, and *wishes*/əz/. Initially, a child relies on only one form of the plural where possible.

Summary It must be stressed these hypotheses attempt to explain the order of acquisition. Using these or other operating principles, a child scans the language code to discover the means of comprehension and production.

CHILDREN'S PROCESSES OF LANGUAGE ACQUISITION

As we'll see in the following discussion, and then again in Chapter 9, children's early linguistic representations are highly concrete and specific pieces of language and are not abstract categories and rules (Savage, Lieven, Theakston, & Tomasello, 2003). From these often word-specific constructions, children's thinking gradually grows more abstract as they encounter more and more examples. Frequency of use and probability in the language that surrounds a child are important factors.

When confronting all the language data around them, children may use two general cognitive processes (Tomasello, 2003): intention-reading and pattern-finding, mentioned in Chapter 2. **Intention-reading** is a uniquely human social cognitive skill for understanding language behavior of others. **Pattern-finding** is a cognitive skill that enables us to find common threads in disparate information, such as seeking underlying rules for language. More specific processes may explain how children learn symbols and categories and the ways in which those categories relate.

Intention-Reading

Cultural learning is basic to language learning and can be explained simply as the ability to do things the way that other people do. In order to learn from those in the culture, a child must determine the intentions of others. As a child is attempting to comprehend the communicative intention of an utterance, he or she may also be attempting to comprehend the functional roles being played by its various components of that utterance. Identifying these roles is only possible if the child has some understanding of the adult's overall communicative intent and discovers how each component contributes. In this way, a child learns the communicative function of words, phrases, and utterance units that will enhance pattern-finding.

Pattern-Finding

It is believed by some linguists that children use several techniques in pattern-finding, among them are (Tomasello, 2003)

- **schematization** and **analogy**, which account for how children create abstract syntactic constructions from concrete pieces of language they have heard;
- **entrenchment** and **preemption**, which account for how children confine these abstractions to those of their linguistic community; and
- **functionally based distributional analysis**, which accounts for how children form linguistic categories, such as nouns and verbs.

Let's look at each briefly.

Schematization and Analogy Young children hear and use the same utterances repeated over and over but with systematic variation. Common expressions are *Where's the X?*, *I wanna X*, *Let's X*, *Can you X?*, *Gimme X*, and *I'm Xing it* (Tomasello, 2003). In short, a child learns these recurrent concrete pieces of language or schemes for specific functions and individual words to fill the slots in each. For example, *Gimme X* is a common way to request something, but the thing being requested changes across situations. Although the slot for *X* is somewhat open, it is constrained by the function of the utterance.

If a child understands the relationship across schemes, as in *He is eating cake* and *Mommy is drinking juice*, then a child realizes that *he* and *mommy* play analogous roles, as do *cake* and *juice*. In this way, different constructions develop their own syntactic roles. This first occurs with each construction, so roles may include *eater* (*he*) and *thing eaten* (*cake*), then by use of analogy become more abstract. Word order and morphological markers may aid this process.

Entrenchment and Preemption When we do something in the same way successfully several times, that way of doing it becomes habitual, as in *subject is verbing object* (*Mommy is drinking juice*). That's entrenchment. Preemption is the notion that if someone communicates to me using one form (*Is subject verbing object?*) rather than another, there was a reason for that choice related to the speaker's specific communicative intention. This motivates a listener to search for that reason and distinguish the two forms and their appropriate communicative contexts. Using both processes together, a child inspects different possible forms expressing different communicative intentions.

Functionally Based Distributional Analysis Over time, concrete linguistic items, such as words or phrases that serve the same communicative function, are grouped together into a category. Thus, noun and verb are categories based on the functions that different words of each type serve within differing constructions. Nouns are defined by what nouns do.

Production

A child's language production consists of constructing utterances out of various already learned pieces of language in a way appropriate to the communication context. This requires a child to focus on both an utterance's form and its function or intent. In other words, a child does not put together utterances from scratch, one morpheme at a time; rather, he or she pieces together the utterance from a ragtag assortment of different preexisting linguistic units (Tomasello, 2003).

This can be seen in the production of preschool children in which as little as one third of their utterances may be novel and of these three quarters may consist of repetitions of some previously used utterance within the last week or so (Lieven et al., 2003). The small number of novel multiword utterances will most likely involve combinations of "fill-ins" and "add-ons" to already well-established constructions.

It would seem, then, that a child has three basic options for producing an utterance on a specific occasion (Lieven et al., 2003):

1. Retrieve a functionally appropriate concrete expression and just say it as it has been heard.
2. Retrieve an utterance-level construction and simultaneously "tweak" it to fit the current communicative situation.
3. Produce an utterance by combining word and phrase schemes without using an utterance-level construction based on the context.

In this way, a child cobbles together a situationally appropriate utterance from pieces of language of various shapes, sizes, and degrees of abstraction rather than gluing together words and morphemes following countless abstract language rules.

Adult Conversational Teaching Techniques

Although parents spend little time directly teaching language, many caregiving and experiential activities facilitate language acquisition. Parental behavior varies with the language maturity of a child and the culture and language involved. While several parental factors may affect children's language development, the level of maternal education seems to be most highly correlated (Dollaghan et al., 1999).

ADULT SPEECH TO TODDLERS

The effect of a mother's behavior on her child's language acquisition varies with the age of the child (Masur, Flynn, & Eichorst, 2005). Around a child's first birthday, nonverbal adult behavior seems to influence an infant's vocabulary growth in a positive way. In contrast, maternal verbal behavior is more important for a child's vocabulary growth from 13 to 17 months, especially a mother's verbal responses to her child and her supportive directions. These changes reflect a child's increasing ability to comprehend and use verbal information. Intrusive verbal directions by the mother negatively influence vocabulary growth.

Throughout the first two years of life, parents talk with their children, label objects and events, and respond to their children's communication. It would be simplistic, however, to assume that a child merely applies the labels heard to his or her preexisting internal concepts. Meaning is also derived from the communication process (Levy & Nelson, 1994). Initially, words are constrained by the conversational context, but later a child encounters words in other contexts and gradually modifies their meaning. Within the conversational context, parents facilitate acquisition by engaging in modeling, cueing, prompting, and responding behaviors that affect the linguistic behaviors of their children.

Modeling: Child-Directed Speech

As a child's communication becomes more verbal, mother unconsciously modifies her own behaviors so that she requires more child participation. Once the child is able to verbalize, the mother "ups the ante" and withholds the names of objects or repeatedly asks the name until the child replies with a word.

First words are learned within interactive contexts. Initially, mothers provide object names, but within a short time they begin to request these names from children. By the middle of the second year, mothers are labeling and requesting at approximately equal rates, and dialog is fully established. This dialog becomes the framework for a new routine. The mother begins to shape the child's speech by distinguishing more sharply between acceptable and unacceptable responses. The child's verbalizations are often responses that fill specific slots within the dialog, such as answering a question. Within the dialog, the mother provides consistency that supports her toddler's learning, including the repetition rate, the rate of confirmation, and the probability of reciprocating.

At age 1, infants are alert to the subtle stress placed on new words by adults and that this stress aids word learning (Curtin, 2009). Early on, 2-year-olds recognize that adults use prosodic features, such as pitch, duration, and loudness, to indicate new referents (Grassmann & Tomasello, 2007). Toddlers use this information in word learning.

Grammatical structures modeled most frequently by mothers are most likely to be used by their children. Data from both English and Modern Hebrew demonstrate that nearly all the utterances of young children mirror patterns used by their mothers.

In addition, mothers make other speech modifications that, taken together, are called child-directed speech (CDS). The characteristics of CDS are listed in Table 6.5.

TABLE 6.5 Characteristics of CDS Compared to Adult-to-Adult Speech

Paralinguistic
Slower speech with longer pauses between utterances and after content words
Higher overall pitch; greater pitch range
Exaggerated intonation and stress
More varied loudness pattern
Fewer dysfluencies (1 dysfluency per 1,000 words versus 4.5 per 1,000 for adult–adult)
Fewer words per minute
Lexical
More restricted vocabulary
Three times as much paraphrasing
More concrete reference to the here and now
Semantic
More limited range of semantic functions
More contextual support
Syntactic
Fewer broken or run-on sentences
Shorter, less complex sentences (approximately 50% are single words or short declaratives)
More well-formed and intelligible sentences
Fewer complex utterances
More imperatives and questions (approximately 60% of utterances)
Conversational
Fewer utterances per conversation
More repetitions (approximately 16% of utterances are repeated within three turns)

Compared to adult-to-adult speech, CDS exhibits (a) greater pitch range, especially at the higher end; (b) lexical simplification characterized by the diminutive ("doggie") and syllable reduplication (consonant-verb syllable repetition); (c) shorter, less complex utterances; (d) less dysfluency; (e) more paraphrasing and repetition; (f) limited, concrete vocabulary and a restricted set of semantic relations; (g) more contextual support; and (h) more directives and questions.

As you know from Chapter 5, mothers use short utterances when conversing with their infants. Interestingly, they use even shorter, less adult utterances with toddlers. The decrease in a mother's utterance, beginning months prior to her child's first words, is positively related to better receptive language skills by her child at 18 months of age, although there seems to be no measurable effect on expressive language. Mothers aid their baby's bootstrapping, mentioned previously, by maintaining semantic-syntactic consistency. For example, in utterances addressed to children, mothers use agents or action causers (*mommy, daddy, boy, dog*) as subjects almost exclusively. Maternal behavior makes it easier for a child to decipher the syntax of its mother's utterances.

As her child's language matures, a mother's speech directed to that child also changes. CDS seems well-tuned to the child's language level.

The overall amount of maternal speech—as well as the frequency of partial repetitions of a child, gestures accompanying speech, and initiated statements commenting on her child's activity or eliciting attention—vary with a child's overall language level. These dynamic elements appear to be strongly related to a child's subsequent development. At age 2, the amount of shared attention and maternal gestures and relevant comments are positively correlated with a child's verbal learning a year later (Schmidt & Lawson, 2002). Clearly, adult input is extremely important.

Slow at first, the rate of both mother's and child's linguistic change increases with the child's age. The length and complexity of a mother's utterances change most between 20 and 27 months, when her child's language changes most rapidly. In contrast, there seems to be little or no change in the structural complexity of CDS between 8 and 18 months. During this period there is also little corresponding change in the complexity of child speech, the changes consisting primarily of the addition of single words.

Mothers fine-tune their language input to their children based primarily on the children's comprehension level. Other factors that influence the level of a mother's language are the conversational situation, the content, and her intent. Overall, adults will simplify their input if a child does not seem to comprehend.

The amount of parental labeling or naming in both English and French varies with the age and development of a child. A positive relationship exists between the amount of adult labeling with young children and a child's subsequent vocabulary growth. As a child's use of noun labels decreases with development, parents replace noun labels with verbs.

Conversational input by mothers provides useful data for children to create early meanings for non-object terms, such as *color, number, and time* (Tare, Shatz, & Gilbertson, 2008). Non-object terms pose a challenge for word learning by children because of the nonobvious word–referent relationship. For example, to what aspect of an object does the word *red* apply?

Undoubtedly, a child's characteristics have an influence on the language input to which a child is exposed. The toys that a child plays with also influence the amount and types of language produced by an adult. In general, toys that encourage role play, such as dolls, elicit more language of a greater variety from parents.

Adults seem not to be conscious of their modifications, nor are they consciously attempting to teach language. Adult-to-child speech seems to be modified in response to the amount of child feedback and participation. Adults simplify their language in order to be understood. Not only is much of the speech addressed to a child adapted for the child's linguistic level, but speech that is not adapted may be simply ignored or not processed by children. In other words, children play an active role in selecting the utterances to which they will attend. A lack of response is important because it informs a parent there has been a breakdown in communication that, in turn, necessitates linguistic changes by that parent. Although the exact nature of child feedback is unknown, children seem to be the key to adult linguistic changes.

The pragmatic aspects of a mother's speech may be related to the talking style of her child. Mothers of children who name frequently use more descriptive words and fewer directions. In addition, these mothers use more utterances within a given situation than mothers of children who name less.

Despite linguistic inadequacies, children can participate effectively because of their mothers' ability to maintain the conversation. The steady, rhythmic flow of the dialog depends on the structural similarity of a mother's and child's utterances and on the correspondence of a mother's speech to events in the environment. She enables her child to participate through her use of turn-passing devices such as questions. She does not use turn-grabbing or turn-keeping behaviors, such as "well . . . ," "but . . . ," or pause fillers.

Mothers maintain control, however, and the dialog is much less symmetrical than it may appear. They maintain the interaction by inferring their children's communication intentions, compensating for the children's communication failures, and providing feedback. After children reach age 2, mothers slowly relinquish their control.

Within the interactional sequence, a mother analyzes, synthesizes, and abstracts language structures for her child. Through word substitutions, she aids her child's learning of language form. A sequence might be as follows:

CHILD: She running.
MOTHER: She's running fast. Oh, she's tired. Now she's running slowly. She's stopping. She's jumping slowly. Now she's jumping quickly.

Note how the mother uses the same forms repeatedly. Much of linguistic analysis, synthesis, and abstraction is performed by, or at least facilitated by, the mother.

Fathers and Other Caregivers These speech modifications are not limited to mothers. Fathers and other caregivers modify their speech in similar ways. In fact, fathers seem to provide even more examples of simplified adult speech than mothers.

The range of vocabulary used by fathers and mothers with their young language-learning children is similar, but fathers use fewer common words. In this way, fathers are more demanding than mothers.

Although fathers make modifications similar to those of mothers, they are less successful in communicating with toddlers, as measured by the amount of communication breakdown. Fathers use more requests for clarification than mothers. In addition, the form of these requests is more nonspecific ("What?") than those of mothers ("You want what?"). Fathers also acknowledge their children's utterances less frequently ("Um-hm," "Yeah," "Okay"). In return, children tend to persist less in conversation with their fathers than with their mothers. It is possible that fathers serve as a bridge for their children between communication with the mother and with other adults. The child learns how to communicate with those less familiar with his or her style and manner.

Even children as young as 4 years of age make language and speech modifications when addressing younger language-learning children. Adult and peer language modifications differ somewhat. In general, peer speech to toddlers is less complex and shorter and contains more repetition than adult-to-toddler speech, although peers elicit fewer language responses than parents. Peer interaction may provide a "proving ground" where younger children can try new linguistic structures.

Children enrolled in daycare centers and preschools also encounter CDS that varies with the size of the group and the age of the children. In general, the larger the group of children, the less individual adaptation by an adult. Larger groups force teachers to concentrate on keeping attention and control. While use of behavior and turn-taking control techniques by teachers results in little toddler language production, use of child-centered strategies, such as adopting a child's topics and waiting for child initiations, and interaction-promoting behaviors result in high levels of talkativeness by toddlers (Girolametto & Weitzman, 2002; Girolametto, Weitzman, van Lieshout, & Duff, 2000). There are clear language-learning advantages for children attending preschool when the curriculum emphasizes language and literacy (Craig, Connor, & Washington, 2003).

The presence of older siblings may also influence the language a younger child hears and produces. For example, an older child will usually respond to more of a parent's questions, thereby reducing the number of responses made by a younger child. The younger child will often respond by imitating the older sibling. In this situation, the mother uses fewer rephrased questions, fewer questions with hints and answers, and fewer questions when the older child is present. In addition, the mother uses more direct repetitions of questions.

Deaf Culture In the Deaf culture, among parents and children who are both deaf and for whom American Sign Language is the primary means of communication, CDS is conveyed by sign and facial expression. Use of sign can present a potential problem because facial expression marks both affect and grammatical structures, such as questions. With only limited use of paralinguistic cues, such as higher pitch and exaggerated intonation and stress, a mother's nonvocal facial expression takes on added importance as a conveyer of her intentions and as a device to hold a child's interest. Prior to a child's second birthday mothers of children with deafness use facial expression primarily for emotion. There is a shift to more grammatical uses after that point (Reilly & Bellugi, 1996).

Summary Parents who use a more conversational style with less direct instructing are more likely to have children who learn language more quickly. In other words, children benefit more from language input when parents are more concerned with understanding and participation and less so with teaching.

The exact effect of CDS on language acquisition is unknown. The modifications made by mothers may facilitate language acquisition by bringing maternal utterances into the "processing range" of a child. If nothing else, these modifications increase a mother's chances of getting a response from her child. Because we find similar modifications in many cultures, we can at least assume that they somehow facilitate communication between adults and children.

The modifications of CDS seem to be maximally effective with the 18- to 21-month-old child. The child attends selectively, focusing on the best examples of various structures.

Prompting

Prompting includes any parental behaviors that require a toddler's response. Three common types are fill-ins, elicited imitations, and questions. In fill-ins, the parent says, "This is a . . . ." No response or an incorrect response from the child will usually result in additional prompts and recueing.

In elicited imitations, the parent cues with "Say X." Young language-learning children respond to slightly over half of the elicited imitations addressed to them.

Questions may be of the confirmational yes/no type, such as "Is this a ball?" or of the *wh-* variety, such as "What's that?" or "Where's doggie?" Unanswered or incorrectly answered questions are usually reformulated by the adult. Approximately 20% to 50% of mothers' utterances to young language-learning children are questions. The individual range varies greatly.

In general, these three types of maternal language-teaching utterances have a shorter average length than the majority of the utterances addressed to a child. Maternal yes/no interrogatives, such as "Are we going home?" appear to correlate with child language-development gains in syntactic complexity, while intonational interrogatives, such as "You going home?" correlate with gains in a child's pragmatic ability. In contrast, maternal directives, such as "Go get your coat," seem to correlate highly with child gains in utterance length and semantic-syntactic complexity but may slow vocabulary growth.

Parents employ an interesting technique to give their toddler an opportunity to produce two related single-word utterances. After a child produces a single-word utterance, his or her parent uses questions to aid the child in producing other elements of a longer utterance. The parent concludes by repeating the whole utterance. The following exchange is an example of this strategy:

> CHILD: Daddy.
> ADULT: Uh-huh. What's Daddy doing?
> CHILD: Eat.
> ADULT: Yeah, *Daddy eat* cookie.

Prompting and cueing are effective teaching techniques.

Responding Behaviors

Parents do not directly reinforce the syntactic correctness of toddler's utterances as in "Good talking" or "You're such a big girl." In fact, less than 10% of children's utterances are followed by verbal approval. Generally, such reinforcement is given for truthfulness and politeness, not for the correctness of the syntax.

Feedback by parents, however, does follow their children's language production. Imitation, topic changes, acknowledgments (*uh-huh, yeah*), or no response are more frequent following grammatically correct child utterances, while reformulations, expansions of the child's utterance, and requests for clarification are more likely following ungrammatical utterances. Different responses may signal a child as to the acceptability of the utterance. For example, Japanese mothers facilitate their infants' transition between sounds and words by repeating poorly formed child words correctly, thus signaling errors for the child and providing an alternative (Otomo, 2001). Let's look at some of the strategies used by English-speaking moms in the United States.

Let's assume that a 30-month-old says to you, "Gran'ma car, go zoo, 'morrow with Nuncle Juan." You might reply, "Yes, tomorrow Uncle Juan and you are going to the zoo in grandmother's car." What you just did is called a **reformulation** or a recast utterance. Your goal is not to teach but to understand the child. That said, what is the effect on the child?

As in this example, children's truncated or ungrammatical utterances can leave caregivers wondering what exactly a child means, so adults frequently check their own understanding against the child's meaning. An adult does this, as you did above, by reformulating the child's utterance into what the adult thinks the child meant to say. In the process, the adult locates the error or errors and embeds a correction. As a result, the child hears a more conventional form for expressing his or her meaning.

With preschoolers, adults reformulate more frequently than they imitate error-free utterances (Chouinard & Clark, 2003). As mentioned previously, imitation among both children and adults decreases markedly as the child passes from toddler to preschooler. In a similar fashion, reformulations decrease as a child passes through the preschool years (Chouinard & Clark, 2003).

We assume from their behavior that children understand reformulations to be corrections. For their part, children either repeat the reformulation, acknowledge the correction with *yeah* or *uh-huh* and continue the conversation, or reject the reformulation because the adult has misunderstood the child's meaning. Reformulation is a great teaching tool because of its immediacy, its timeliness, and the attending of the child.

The type of reformulation used by the mother may have an effect on the particular form being learned. For example, reformulating the child's previous utterance by adding, substituting, or moving a morpheme may aid learning of plurals and progressives (is eat*ing*) but has less effect on the past tense or the verb *to be*, which seem to benefit from removal of morphemes and restatement of correct forms.

Some adult responding behaviors seem to have reinforcing value. Approximately 30% of mothers' responses to 18- to 24-month-old children consist of expansions. An **expansion** is a more mature version of a child's utterance in which the word order is preserved. For example, if a child says "Mommy eat," mother might respond with "Mommy is eating her lunch." The mother assumes that the child intends to communicate a certain meaning. As a child's average utterance length increases beyond two words, the number of expansions by the mother decreases. Approximately one fifth of a 2-year-old's ill-formed utterances are expanded by the mother into more syntactically correct versions.

Children seem to perceive expansions as a cue to imitate. Nearly a third of adult expansions are in turn imitated by the child. These imitations are likely to be more linguistically correct than the child's original utterance. Let's see how it works:

CHILD: Block fall.
ADULT: Um-hm, blocks fall *down*.
CHILD: Block fall down.

Hopefully, spontaneous productions follow, and rules are generalized to conversational use. As spontaneous production of structures occurs, imitation of these structures by the child decreases. Expansion adds meaning to a child's utterance at a time when the child is attending to a topic he or she has established. In addition, expansion provides evaluative feedback. Expansions continue the topic of conversation and encourage a child to take his or her turn and, thus, to maintain the dialog.

Right now expansion and reformulation probably seem like the same thing. Let's sort it out. Expansions, used primarily with younger children, maintain the child's word order while providing a more mature form of the child's utterance. While both expansion and reformulation seek to preserve the child's meaning, reformulation is a strategy for older children who are beginning to create truly complicated sentences. Think of reformulation as the next step in caregiver teaching after expansion. Reformulations go beyond a mere expansion and can involve considerable rearrangement of the sentence elements while preserving the child's meaning.

Extension, a comment or reply to a child's utterance, may be even more helpful. For example, when a child says "Doggie eat," the partner replies, "Doggie is hungry." Thus, extension provides more semantic information. Its value lies in its conversational nature, which provides positive feedback, and in both its *semantic* and *pragmatic contingency*. A semantically contingent utterance is one that retains the focus or topic of the previous utterance. A pragmatically contingent utterance concurs with the intent of the previous utterance; that is, topics invite comments, questions invite answers, requests invite responses, and so on. In short, both types of contingency maintain the conversational flow, which is inherently rewarding to almost all children.

Finally, parents imitate their toddler's speech. In conversations between adults and preschool children, adults repeat to establish that they have understood and children repeat to ratify what adults have said (Clark & Bernicot, 2008). For both adults and children, repetition signals attention to the other's utterances and places the repeated information on common ground. With 2-year-old children, adults combine their repeats with new information. Children then re-repeat the original form about 20% of the time. With older preschool children, adults check on intentions but less frequently, and only occasionally check on form. Older children also re-repeat, but, like adults, add further information.

Summary

Mothers' responses to their infants' verbal imitations are especially interesting and would seem to facilitate language learning (Olson & Frank Masur, 2012). For example, maternal responses to young 1-year-olds include shorter and single-word utterances. The mother's reproduction of her child's imitation provides as extra example for the child.

In the mother's responses to older 1-year-olds, familiar words may be expanded or receive a *reduced + expanded/extended* response. The placement of the mother's reproduction of the child's word usually occurs in a sentence-final position, making the word more salient or obvious. In an expanded/extended response, the mother might follow the child's "Doggie" with "Uh-hm, big doggie," providing her child with additional lexical information.

A reduced + expanded/extended response emphasizes the child's imitation and provides additional information. Here's an example:

MOTHER: See the big doggie. [Mother's model]
CHILD: Doggie. [Imitation]
MOTHER: Doggie. [Reduced from her model] The doggie's barking. [Extended the child's utterance]

In her response, the mother shows her child another way to use the word rather than just repeating the mother's model. The mother has provided the child with contrasting syntax for the familiar word *doggie*. These types of maternal responses increase throughout the child's second year.

In this instructional video, SLP Tracy Kaplan, of the University of Arizona, offers tips for parents on talking with their young language-learning children. http://www.youtube.com/watch?v=bG2RvZVvL5A

All three parental responding behaviors—expansion, extension, and imitation—result in greater amounts of child imitation than either adult topic initiation or nonimitative behaviors. Hence, expansion, extension, and imitation appear to be valuable language-teaching devices. Each reinforces a child's utterance, and expansion and extension also provide models of more mature language. Maternal extending correlates significantly with changes in the length of a child's utterances. The adult utterance is semantically contingent on the preceding child utterance. This characteristic decreases the linguistic processing load on a child because the adult utterance is close to the child's utterance in form and content. Parents do not consciously devise these teaching strategies; rather, they evolve within child–caregiver conversations.

ADULT CONVERSATIONS WITH PRESCHOOLERS

As noted in Chapter 5, caregivers' altered behavior enables infants to engage in successful communication as early as possible. This process continues in the preschool years. Mothers provide opportunities for their children to make verbal contributions, draw them into conversations and provide a well-cued framework for the exchange, show their children when to speak, and thereby develop cohesiveness between the speaker and the listener. Mothers ask children to comment on objects and events within their experience. They also expand information by talking about the same object or event in different ways or by adding new ideas and elaborating on them. These maternal modifications appear to be correlated with advances in the child's language abilities.

What Children Hear

To understand how children acquire language, we need to know something about the language they hear, primarily from their mothers. For example, English-speaking 2- to 3-year-old children hear approximately 5,000 to 7,000 utterances each day, between a quarter and a third of these being questions (e.g., *Where's your crayon?*) and approximately a quarter are imperatives (e.g., *Stop that; Come here*) (Cameron-Faulkner, Lieven, & Tomasello, 2003).

Almost 80% of maternal utterances are full adult sentences. The rest are phrases, most often a noun phrase (e.g., *the big dog, her little pony, the girl in the car*) or prepositional phrase (e.g., *on the phone, at school, with grandma*). About a quarter of the mothers' utterances use the copula or verb *be* (e.g., *am, is, are, was, were*) as the main verb (e.g., *I'm busy now; Mommy's sick today; The doggies are hungry*). Interestingly, only about 15% of maternal utterances have the SVO sentence form characteristic of English, and over 80% of these have a pronoun subject (*I, you, he, she, it, we, they*).

Further analysis indicates highly frequent patterns or frames in maternal utterances, some of which are repeated as many as 40 times per day (Cameron-Faulkner et al., 2003). Most of these patterns consist of two words or morphemes. Approximately 45% of all maternal utterances begin with one of the following words: *what, that, it, you, are/aren't, do/does/did/don't, I, is, shall, a, can/can't, where, there, who, come, look*, and *let's*. In turn, children use many of these same word-based utterance frames in their own speech.

Although a language-learning child is thus faced with the formidable task of acquiring perhaps hundreds of different sentence and phrase constructions based on input, the appearance of these constructions in the speech of their mothers is not random. Acquisition is made a little easier by mothers. The majority of the utterances a child hears are highly repetitive word-based frames that they experience sometimes hundreds of times every day.

Mothers of 3- to 4-year-olds use many techniques to encourage communication. For example, mothers begin twice as many utterances with words such as *well* and *now* as their children do. These signals, plus varied intonation, are used with responses and help a child understand by signaling that a response is coming. In addition, mothers use a high proportion of redundant utterances to acknowledge and reassure children, as in the following:

CHILD: Want cookie.
MOTHER: You want a cookie? Well, let's see. You want a chocolate cookie?
CHILD: Yeah, chocolate.
MOTHER: Okay, one chocolate cookie for Stacy.

A mother frequently acknowledges with "good" or "that's it." This response fills a minimal turn and adds little additional information but encourages the child without being overly disruptive to the child's speech stream. Maternal repetition of a child's utterance seems to be for the purposes of emphasis and reassurance.

Clearly in control, mothers are not equally helpful in all areas of language. For example, mothers are not as facilitative with turn taking as they are with other pragmatic skills. Control of the conversation seems more important to mothers than facilitation. As a child gets older, mother uses more imperatives.

As the dominant conversational partner throughout the preschool years, mothers interrupt their children much more than their children interrupt them. When interrupting, mothers usually omit the politeness markers, such as *excuse me*, seen in adult–adult dialog. The frequency of these interruptions decreases with a child's maturity level. When interrupted, children usually cease talking and then reintroduce the topic. In contrast, mothers usually continue to talk when interrupted by their children and do not reintroduce the topic as often. These actions teach a child to negotiate conversations with others.

Naturally, teaching methods change as a child matures. Expansion of her child's utterances is not as effective a teaching tool with the preschool child as it is with the toddler. Instead, a mother's expansion of her own prior utterances may be more important. This expansion is characterized by a maternal self-repetition followed by an expansion, such as "Want big cookie? Does Maury want a big cookie?" Thus, the mother assists the child in finding the structural similarity by a comparison of adjacent utterances.

Keeping the Conversation Going

Mothers facilitate the structure and cohesiveness of conversations by maintaining and reintroducing the topic. With increasing age, a typical child takes a greater number of turns on each topic, although the number of turns is still low by adult standards and does not change radically until school age.

Maternal speech to 30-month-olds benefits syntactic learning by providing language-advancing data and by eliciting conversation. From a mother's point of view, it seems more important to engage her child in conversation than to elicit advanced syntactic forms from the child. Conversation keeps a child's attention on language input and motivates the child to participate.

The mother sustains her child's interest by the use of mild encouragement ("Oh, that's nice") and praise ("What a lovely picture"). Generally, such elicitation and feedback on the quality of a child's language productions does little to contribute to development beyond keeping her child involved.

The effects of conversation appear to be structure-specific. As might be expected, questions contribute to the development of auxiliary or helping verbs and the verb *to be* because these words are prominently placed at the beginning of the sentence, as in "*Did* you eat the cookies?" and "*Is* he happy or sad?" Mothers also use yes/no questions to reformulate their children's utterances. For example, when the child says, "Mommy eating," the adult might reply in a teasing way, "***Is*** mommy eating?"

Mothers invite child utterances, primarily through the use of questions, often followed by self-responses. This form of modeling is an effective teaching tool. For example, she might ask, "What color should we use?" followed by "I pick red." In turn, her child may respond, "I pick green."

Shared knowledge of events or routines is still important and provides scaffolding for new structures. Scripts that emerge from these shared events, such as going to the park or riding in the car, concentrate a child's attention, provide models, create formats, and limit a child's linguistic options, thus decreasing the amount of child cognitive processing and supporting the topic of conversation. This scaffolding is particularly important when discussing either nonpresent referents or topics. Approximately 85% of 24- to 29-month-old children's information-providing utterances on nonpresent topics occur in such scripted contexts.

Turnabouts

The turn-taking goals of adult–adult and adult–child conversations differ. In adult–adult conversations, the participants try to obtain a turn, whereas the adult goal in adult–child conversations is to get the child to take her or his turn. As with a younger child, mothers rely heavily on the questioning technique of elicitation. One variant of this technique is a **turnabout**, an utterance that both responds to the previous utterance and, in turn, requires a response. Thus, a turnabout fills a mother's turn and then requires a turn by her child. By using turnabouts, a mother creates a series of successful turns that resemble conversational dialog. Here's an example:

> CHILD: We had pizza.
> ADULT: Pizza! Hmmm, I bet you went to a ________
> CHILD: Birthday party!
> ADULT: I love birthday parties. Whose party was it?

Generally, a turnabout consists of some type of response to, or statement about, a child's utterance and a request for information, clarification, or confirmation that serves as a cue to the child. The mother often initiates a topic or an exchange with a question, thus gaining control. If asked a question, she regains control by responding with another question. Resultant dialogs consist of three successive utterances: the mother's first question; the child's response; and the mother's confirmation, which may include another question. For example, the mother might say, "Can you tell me what this is?" and then respond to the child's answer with "Um-hum, and what does it do?" Thus, the mother is now back in control. In general, the child is less likely to respond to the mother without a turnabout.

Repeatedly hearing a caregiver's questions can have a beneficial effect on a preschooler's development of more adultlike questions (Valian & Casey, 2003). Corrective feedback also facilitates development of some syntactic structures.

There are several types of turnabouts, shown with examples in Table 6.6. One type, the **request for clarification** or **contingent query**, is used by both adults and children to gain information that initially was not clearly transmitted or received. Its use requires that both the listener and the speaker attend to prior discourse. Thus, its use may be related to the development of the ability to refer to what has come before. In addition, children receive little negative feedback via contingent queries. Parental requests for clarification are just as likely to be attempts to clarify genuine misunderstandings and miscommunications as to correct production errors.

With 2- to 3-year-olds, mothers most frequently employ yes/no questions in turnabouts. This form requires a confirmation and is easy for children as young as 18 months to process. If a child does not respond appropriately, the conversational expectations of the mother are not fulfilled, and she will ask fewer requests for clarification. It is clear that once again the caregiver's conversational behaviors reflect the feedback she receives from the child.

TABLE 6.6 Turnabouts

Type	Example
Wh- question	When did that happen?
Yes/no question	Does he scratch a lot?
Tag question	I bet he doesn't like fleas, does he?
Request for clarification	
General	What?
	Huh?
Specific	What does your dog have?
Confirming	Fleas?
	Does he have fleas?
Correction	Fleas! (With an expectant tone)
I wonder statement	I wonder where he got them.
Fill-in	Fleas make you . . .
Expansion with (yes/no) turnabout	Your dog has fleas. Did you give him a bath?
Extension with (*wh-*) turnabout	My dog had fleas once. Yukk! What did you do?

Source: Information from Kaye & Charney (1981).

Children age 3 to 5½ are able to produce and respond effectively to requests for clarification from both adults and peers, although younger children are more effective in their use with adults.

Importance of Play

It is easy to forget that much of a child's language develops within the context of play with an adult or with other children. Play can be an ideal vehicle for language acquisition for a number of reasons:

- Play is not goal oriented, so it removes pressure and frustration from the interactive process. It's fun.
- Attention and focus are shared by the interactive partners, so topics are shared.
- Games have structure and variations in the order of elements, as does grammar.
- Games, like conversations, contain turn taking.

In languages as different as English and Japanese, levels of play and language development appear to be similar. Play and language develop interdependently and demonstrate underlying cognitive developments. This relationship is presented in Table 6.7.

Initially, both play and language are concrete and depend on the here and now. With cognition maturity, however, they both become less tangible. At about the time that children begin to combine symbols, they begin to play symbolically, using one play object, such as a spoon, for another, such as a telephone.

Children often attempt to involve their parents in this pretend play. As playmates, parents can show by example how to play. Often, parents contribute running narratives

TABLE 6.7 **Cognition, Play, and Language**

Approx. Age (Months)	Cognitive Development	Play Development	Language Development
Below 12	Association of events with habitual actions	Recognition of objects and functional use	Presymbolic communication
12–15	Global representation of events	Self-pretend: Meaningful actions used playfully	Single words for global referent
15–21	Analysis of represented objects or events	Differentiated pretend play with dolls and other activities Decentered play with reference to others	Reference to a range of entities, parts, and states
21–24	Juxtaposition of symbolic elements	Pretend combinations	Simple language combinations
24–26	Complete event stored with organized component parts	Planning and storage of symbolic goal while trying to accomplish. Combinatorial play episodes with two themes	Store message while parts organized

Source: Information from Bretherton (1984).

poorer language skills than mothers who use high levels of guidance or control alone but without the negativity.

When studies control for the effects of socioeconomic level, preschoolers from single-parent homes appear to have better receptive and expressive language and to have fewer communication problems, especially when compared to children from households with married, working parents. This difference may reflect the more intensive, one-on-one communication between the single parent and the children in these homes. In the absence of another adult, a single parent may spend more time talking to a child.

Socioeconomic Differences

Socioeconomic and cultural factors result in many different child–caregiver interactive patterns. Among low-SES families, the lack of resources may restrict opportunities for children, and parental work schedules may limit parent–child interactions.

Children living in poverty face heightened risks to their cognitive development compared to nonpoor children (Bradley & Corwyn, 2002). For example, the vocabularies of children from low-SES backgrounds develop more slowly than those of children from high-SES backgrounds (Rescorla & Alley, 2001). Poorer development seems especially true for children exposed to chronic poverty early in life (Duncan & Brooks-Gunn, 2000; NICHD Early Child Care Research Network, 2005). Children from low-SES families may be at risk for language development problems because of poor health and poor education. Poverty also affects children's development by increasing family stressors, creating psychological distress, and impairing the quality of parent–child interactions. Although socioeconomic status affects expressive and receptive language performance, it does not seem to influence working memory abilities (Engel, Santos, & Gathercole, 2008).

Early book reading by mothers to infants and toddlers is important for children's language and cognition in the preschool years (Raikes et al., 2006). In general, mothers read more to firstborn and female toddlers, and mothers with higher verbal ability and education read more than other mothers. Among low-SES mothers, white non-Latina mothers read more than African American and Latina mothers.

In this video, we'll explore the effect of parental talking on children's language and cognitive development and the differences found in different socioeconomic groups. http://www.youtube.com/watch?v=qLoEUEDqagQ

On any given day, approximately 634,000 individuals are homeless in the United States (U.S. Dept. of Housing and Urban Development, 2012). Of these about 40% are families (National Coalition for the Homeless, 1999). Language, learning, and cognitive delays are common in preschool children.

Data from mothers and children in homeless shelters is complicated by factors such as poverty, health issues, and race and ethnicity. Nonetheless, we find that both children and mothers in homeless shelters exhibit deficits or delays in at least one of the following: auditory comprehension, verbal expression, reading, and writing (O'Neill-Pirozzi, 2003).

Cultural Differences

Cultural differences may reflect three related factors:

1. the role or status of children,
2. the social organization of caregiving, and
3. folk beliefs about how children learn language.

We must also be careful not to assume that the way middle-SES mothers in the United States interact with their children is the only way or the most correct way. In general, interactive patterns between children and their caregivers have evolved to fulfill the special needs of the populations and cultures in which they occur.

In the middle-SES American family, the child is held in relatively high regard. This is also true among the Kaluli people of New Guinea. In contrast, the relatively lower standing of children reported in Western Samoa and among some African Americans in rural Louisiana results in an expectation that children are to speak only when invited to do so. It is important to remember that low status does not mean a lack of affection for children. Within these same rural southern African American communities, a child is not expected to initiate conversation but to respond to adult questions in the shortest possible form. A child is not expected to perform for adults, and most of a child's requests for information are ignored. What expansion exists is an expansion by adults of their own utterances, not those of the child. It is believed in this culture that children learn by observation, not interaction.

Not all cultures value verbal precocity in children or demonstrate the adult modifications seen in CDS. Among the Kipsigis of Kenya and rural African Americans in Louisiana, for example, comprehension is more important than verbal production in young children; many of the utterances directed to them consist of directives and explanations. Kaluli parents and Samoan parents rarely follow their children's conversational leads. Language acquisition does not seem to be slowed or delayed in any way.

The expectation of a quiet child does not necessarily reflect children's low status. Within the Apache Nation, it is a societal norm to value silence from all people. In general, Japanese parents also encourage less talking by their children, although children are held in very high regard. Nonverbal behavior is more important in Japan than in the United States, and Japanese parents anticipate their children's needs more often, so children have fewer reasons to communicate.

Mothers may use other strategies that seem equally effective as those described in this chapter. For example, Kaluli mothers mentioned previously and some Mexican American mothers provide models of appropriate language for specific situations and direct their young children to imitate these models. In situations with other adults, children are directed by their mothers in the appropriate responses. This recycling of appropriate utterances for recurring situations is a language-learning device. Like semantically related adult utterances found in middle-SES American homes, these predictable situational responses may be highly comprehensible to a child without complete grammatical knowledge.

While Chinese and Western mothers both interpret babbling as meaningful, talk about what their children are doing, do not overtly correct, and recognize that their infants understand some words prior to speaking, Chinese mothers use less expansion and conversational prompting and more direct teaching of language (Johnson & Wong, 2002).

The social organization of caregiving varies widely and reflects economic organization and kinship groupings. In some cultures, such as that of Western Samoa, older siblings are more responsible for caregiving than in middle-SES American homes. This arrangement is also characteristic of many inner-city households in the United States. There is no evidence, however, that children raised by older siblings learn language more slowly than those raised by adults.

Finally, folk "wisdom" on language acquisition affects the language addressed to a child. The Kipsigis of Kenya believe that a child will learn by him- or herself. Thus, there is no CDS as we have described it. A child is encouraged to participate in conversation through imitation of its mother's model of adult speech. The Kaluli of New Guinea also require imitation from a child in certain social rituals, even though the child may not understand what he or she is saying.

Among both middle- and low-SES African American families, a general belief exists that children learn language by listening and watching; thus there is little need to adapt adult behaviors for a child (Scheffner Hammer & Weiss, 2000). Even so, middle-SES African American mothers seem to have a "teaching agenda" that emphasizes production of language by their children. In general, these middle-SES mothers include more language in their child play and use a wider range of words with their children than low-SES mothers (Scheffner Hammer & Weiss, 1999). As a consequence, middle-SES African American infants initiate more verbal play and produce twice as many vocalizations as low-SES infants. In contrast, lower-SES mothers have a very limited teaching agenda and interact less with their children.

Cultural differences are evident in the maternal behavior of Japanese and North American middle-SES mothers. While American mothers talk more with their children and encourage them to respond, Japanese mothers engage in more rocking, carrying, and "lulling." In responding to their infants, American mothers use more facial and vocal behaviors, while Japanese mothers are more nonverbal, responding with touch. With toddlers, Japanese mothers employ more vocalizations similar to the American English *uh-huh*, which is not surprising given the importance of *omoiyari*, maintenance of harmony, in that culture.

The intentions of American mothers are providing information and directing. In contrast, the Japanese mother exhibits fewer of these behaviors, preferring to use nonsense words, sound play, and emphatic routines, such as discussing feelings. Her productions are usually very easy for her child to imitate.

In general, Japanese mothers are less likely to talk about objects; when they do, it is often without the use of the object's name, used more frequently in the United States. Although both American and Japanese mothers use questions frequently, American mothers use them more in the context of labeling. It is not surprising, therefore, that American toddlers have larger noun vocabularies, while Japanese toddlers have more social expressions.

Still, similarities exist across languages. Both American and Japanese mothers use linguistically simple forms when addressing young language-learning children, repeat frequently, and use intonation to engage the infant. The common motivation for these changes seems to be an intuitive sense of the developmental level of the child.

Effects of Media

Children are not limited to direct language input and can acquire language-based knowledge by drawing upon a range of experiences. They can also learn language by indirect means, such as conversational exchanges between other individuals. Children can learn language from speech that is not addressed to them.

Television can also provide limited input. Unlike conversations, television is passive and does not require a response. In addition, the language provided by television is not related to ongoing events within a child's interactive context. Although having adults read to a child positively affects the size of the expressive vocabulary of English- and Spanish-speaking preschoolers, watching television does not have this beneficial effect (Patterson, 2002).

Even with all this variation, children still learn their native languages at about the same rate as middle-SES American children. In general, in the United States, most adults treat a child as a communication partner. The language-learning American child is raised primarily by his or her parent(s) or paid professionals or paraprofessionals who model and elicit language. Even within the United States, however, there is no definitive pattern.

Of most importance among children in the United States are maternal stimulation and the overall quality of the home. For example, among African American families, a strong correlation exists between maternal sensitivity, responsiveness, stimulation, and elaboration and a child's cognitive and communicative skills at age 1 (Wallace, Roberts, & Lodder, 1998). Although socioeconomic differences exist within the African American community, there is strong evidence of these maternal behaviors among all African American mothers.

Conclusion

LANGUAGE LEARNING IS A COMPLEX process that involves linguistic processing and child and adult language-learning strategies. Different cultures employ different strategies.

Comprehension and imitation by a toddler seem to be particularly important. Both appear to be at the cutting edge of language development, although the exact relationship is unknown and seems to change with a child's functioning level.

We do not know the exact language-learning strategies used by young children. These strategies and their underlying cognitive abilities are inferred from children's behaviors. Consistency in a child's language suggests the presence of underlying rule systems. At present, linguists are unsure of the process of rule construction. Undoubtedly, though, comprehension and production are interrelated. This dynamic relationship changes with the level of development and with the structure being learned. The order of acquisition of structures for expressing complex relationships reflects a child's cognitive growth. A child must understand the concept of the relationship and the linguistic forms used to express that relationship before he or she can use this relationship in his or her own language.

Environmental influences strongly affect language development. Adult modeling and responding behaviors are very important, especially for toddlers. Adult–child language provides a simplified model. Certain responding behaviors also reinforce a child's communication attempts.

Although a direct teaching explanation of language development is inadequate, there is a strong indication that modeling, imitation, and reinforcement are central to the learning process. Those elements of maternal speech that change to reflect a child's overall language level seem to be most significant for later language development. The process is much more subtle than that employed in the more direct language training seen in therapeutic intervention.

Although diminished with a child's age, the role of significant caregivers in language development is still critical with preschoolers. Caregivers continue to manipulate the conversational context to maximize language learning by a child. This context and play are important sources of language modeling and use for preschool children.

Discussion

IN THIS CHAPTER, WE'VE SEEN how children approach the learning of language, how they decide what a word is, how they try to decipher the sequential code by applying certain rules to breaking down language, and how they are helped by the environment. If you assume that you are in another culture in which English is never used, you begin to appreciate what the child and caregivers do in order to be understood and to help the child's learning. Look at the child learning strategies again. Wow, what a great way to try to understand language and to attempt to use it! Now look at the adult teaching strategies. We could only hope that those speakers of that other language would be so kind as to use some of these strategies with us until we understand their language.

It is important to recall that caregivers do not decide to teach language. The so-called teaching strategies mostly flow from a desire to be understood. Are they all applicable to intervention with the child with a language impairment? Each SLP and teacher must decide for him- or herself how to best use this developmental knowledge.

We must also remember that, just as language is culturally based, so are the teaching strategies demonstrated by middle-SES mothers in the United States. The French-speaking Haitian mother of a toddler or preschooler with a language impairment may interact very differently. Again the SLP must decide if the mother's interactions are appropriate given her culture and the severity of the child's impairment. The goal is not to create a carbon copy of the middle-SES American mother. Remember that even mothers who exhibit the best CDS can have children with language problems. All professional interactions must be mindful of and sensitive to cultural variability.

Main Points

- In *very general* terms, children's early language follows a pattern in which they "know" something, then comprehend its name, and finally produce the name.
- Several assumptions by an infant may be behind learning a word, including the following:
  - People use words to refer to entities.
  - Words are extendable.
  - A word refers to the whole entity, not the parts.
  - Names refer to categories of things.
  - Novel names refer to previously nameless entities.
  - Adults refer to entities in consistent conventional ways.
- Expressive strategies of toddlers include evocative utterances, hypothesis testing, interrogative utterances, and selective imitation.
- Selective imitation is at the growing or developing edge of a child's language and helps stabilize new forms.
- Bootstrapping, a strategy of preschoolers, is using what you know, such as semantic categories, to figure out what you don't, such as syntactic units.
- Preschooler learning principles are as follows:
  - Pay attention to the ends of words.
  - Phonological forms can be systematically modified.
  - Pay attention to the order of words and morphemes.
  - Avoid interruptions and rearrangement of linguistic units.
  - Underlying semantic relations should be marked overtly and clearly.
  - Avoid exceptions.
  - Grammatical markers should make semantic sense.
- Adult speech to toddlers includes modeling (CDS), prompting, and responding (reformulations, expansions, extensions, and imitations) that collectively facilitate language learning.
- Adult speech to preschoolers includes turnabouts that facilitate the child's turn in a conversation by prompting the child's next response.
- Play is an important area for language growth and trial.
- Cultural differences vary widely but contribute to a child's language learning.

Reflections

1. How do comprehension, production, and cognition help in a child's linguistic development? Explain with examples.
2. State the main principles preschoolers seem to use to learn language from what they hear and give an example of each.
3. Describe the role of imitation for toddlers and the development from repetitious utterances to semantically diverse ones.
4. Mothers and fathers talk differently to their young child than they do to other adults. What are the characteristics of CDS?
5. How can a caregiver use forms of positive reinforcement to help the child's language development?
6. Although parents may not directly reinforce their young language-learning children, they do expand, extend, and imitate. Describe the differences among these three behaviors, and explain the effects of these behaviors on the child.
7. What is a turnabout, and how is it used by caregivers?
8. Describe the importance of play for language development.
9. How do socioeconomic and cultural factors affect the language learning capacities in children? Explain, with examples, how a child learns language by indirect means other than through the regular input of direct language. Provide examples for your answer.

Photodisc/Getty Images

7 First Words and Word Combinations in Toddler Talk

OBJECTIVES

Children's initial language consists of more than the mere accumulation of single words. As with all language, children's initial attempts reflect patterns of production. When you have completed this chapter, you should understand the following:

- Most frequent categories and syllable constructions in first words
- Intentions of early vocalizations/verbalizations
- Bases for early concept development
- Bases for extensions and overextensions
- Two-word combination patterns
- Common phonological rules of toddlers

- Important terms:

associative complex hypothesis
consonant cluster reduction
fast mapping
functional-core hypothesis
holophrase
initial mapping
item-based construction
language socialization
lexicon
neighborhood density
open syllable
otitis media
overextension
pivot schemas
presupposition
prototypic complex hypothesis
reduplication
semantic-feature hypothesis
underextension
word combination

This is it—finally—the place where language is said to begin. But don't expect a change overnight. Words will appear gradually and may be mixed with jargon in long, incomprehensible strings. The child is still experimenting with sounds. Speech may be suddenly interrupted by shrieks or a series of babbles. As a result, a child may talk a great deal without seeming to say very much. (In that way, children resemble some adults I know.) One sound pattern may represent several concepts, or inconsistent production may result in several sound patterns for one word. Words may be changed by deletion of syllables or modification of stress patterns. Whole phrases may be used as single words. If it sounds confusing, it is; but what a wonderful time for the excited family. Before we begin our discussion of language, let's quickly explore the life of toddlers, those little folks who will utter their first words. (See Appendix A, Table A.3 for more information.)

With a beginning realization of self and a new (albeit shaky) method of locomotion called walking, an infant begins the second year of life. During that year he or she will change from a dependent infant to a more independent toddler with the mobility and the linguistic tools to explore.

There is a deceleration in bodily growth rate. Brain growth also decelerates, and head size increases only slightly.

By 15 months, a toddler is experimenting with different forms of walking, such as running and dawdling. Favorite games are hiding and being chased. At 18 months, a toddler is able to walk backward and to stop smoothly but is not able to turn corners very well. There is a rolling, "drunken sailor" quality to these movements. Within six months, he or she progresses to a stable walking rhythm. A 2-year-old is able to walk on tiptoes, stand on one foot with assistance, jump with both feet, and bend at the waist to retrieve an object on the floor.

If allowed by his parents, a toddler will get into everything and initiate active and systematic exploration. As a toddler, my brother went through the house dumping a liberal mound of baby powder into each opened drawer just after my mother had completed cleaning.

Most of a toddler's play and exploration is solitary and nonsocial. A favorite game is carrying objects and handing them to others. During the entire second year, toddlers test objects' qualities by touching, pushing, pulling, and lifting. A toddler enjoys exploring new sights, sounds, and textures.

Increased fine-motor skills and a longer attention span enable a toddler to look at books. By 18 months, a child recognizes pictures of common objects. Six months later, he or she pretends to read books and has the fine-motor skills to turn pages one at a time. A toddler is also capable of holding a crayon and scribbling.

Toys are used increasingly in play. By 18 months, a toddler plays appropriately with toy phones, dishes, and tools and likes dress-up play. Dolls and stuffed animals become more important. My own children loved to pound pegs through a wooden toy workbench and to stack objects. The toddler demonstrates short sequences of role playing at age 2. My son Jason loved to imitate his mother's morning ritual in the bathtub. Toddlers will play near but not usually with other children.

Much of the social interaction of the second year involves a toddler's attempts to be in the spotlight. Having learned to influence others, a toddler will do almost anything for attention.

Increasing self-awareness and the ability to influence others are reflected in a toddler's growing noncompliance. At 16 months, a toddler begins to assert some independence by ignoring or dawdling in response to parental requests. By 21 months, this behavior has evolved into a very defiant "no." The child frequently says "no" even when he or she means *yes*. One little friend, Dean, shouted "no" for *no* and "no" with up-and-down head nodding for *yes*.

A 2-year-old has many self-help skills. For example, a child can usually place food on a spoon and feed him- or herself, undress except for untying shoelaces, wash, turn on simple devices, open easy doors, and straighten a bed. When the child needs help, he or she knows how to request it.

The actual point at which language is said to begin is arbitrary and depends on your definition of *language*. For our purposes, we shall assume that language begins at around the first birthday with the appearance of the first word. To be considered a true word,

1. the child's utterance must have a phonetic relationship to some adult word,
2. the child must use the word consistently, and
3. the word must occur in the presence of a referent, thus implying an underlying concept or meaning.

Therefore, a babbled "dada" would not qualify because there is no referent. Likewise, phonetically consistent forms (PCFs) that do not approximate recognizable adult word likewise don't qualify as words. (See Chapter 4 for a description of PCFs.)

The emergence of first words or verbalizations does not signal the end of babbling, jargon, and PCFs. Individual children exhibit very different patterns of vocalization-verbalization use. Words emerge slowly and often are accompanied by gestures.

Language development in the second year consists of vocabulary growth and word combinations. Vocabulary growth is slow during the first few months. Phrases frequently used by adults in a child's environment may be repeated as single words. For example, many children say, "Wassat?" and "Go-bye." A favorite of the 18-month-old is the "name game" in which a toddler touches an object, queries "Wassat?" and awaits a reply. Each toddler has his or her own **lexicon**, or personal dictionary, with words that reflect, in part, the child's environment.

During the second half of the second year, toddlers begin to combine words and to increase the rate of vocabulary growth. The early word combinations appear to follow predictable patterns, and the toddler is likely to produce phrases such as "More cookie," "Daddy eat," "No night-night," and so on. Within a few months, short-term memory has increased so that the child can attempt a few longer constructions, such as "Daddy eat cookie." By age 2 the toddler has an expressive vocabulary of about 150 to 300 words.

While there are many similarities, the size of expressive vocabularies of children age 2 does vary across different languages and dialects of the same language. For example, the typical 2-year-old Mandarin-speaking child has a vocabulary of about 550 words compared to 307 for an American English child (Fenson et al., 2007; Tardif, Fletcher, Liang & Kaciroti, 2009). The American English-speaking child fares somewhat better against the typical Australian English child, who averages about 262 words in his or her lexicon (Bavin et al., 2008).

A continuity exists between prelinguistic and linguistic skills. Early gesture use is important for communication and also for verbal development. Better gesture and object use at 12 months predicts better vocabulary at 24 months (Bavin et al., 2008). Use of conventional gestures at 14 months is also positively related to receptive language and vocabulary size more than two years later (Rowe, Özçaliskan, & Goldin-Meadow, 2008). In addition, acts for joint attention at 14 months and the number of different consonants at 19 months are positively related to expressive language at 3 years (Watt, Wetherby, & Shumway, 2006).

Table 7.1 presents a conversation between a 22-month-old toddler and her mother. The child's average utterance length is short—only 1.9 morphemes in the entire sample from which this portion is taken—as is the mother's. Note that the mother makes extensive use of imitation, expansion and extension.

TABLE 7.1 Toddler Language Sample

What do you see?

1. Birthday cake Kelly house.
   A birthday cake at Kelly's house? What else was at Kelly's house?
2. Birthday cake mommy.
   Mommy had a birthday cake. What else did you have?
3. Kelly house.
   Kelly's house. Oh, look.
4. Color on the table.
   The man colored on the table. Well, that's all right. What are you making?
5. Doggie.
   Are you making a doggie?
6. Okay.
   All right. Oh, that's nice, T.
7. Where more doggie there?
   Is there another doggie underneath?
8. Yeah.
   Where can you find the picture? Is that what you're looking for, the picture of the doggie?
   Where's the doggie?
9. A doggie.
10. Color a doggie.
    Okay, you color the doggie.
11. Mommy color crayon.
    Mommy has crayons. Mommy's coloring. What's mommy making?
12. Doggie.
    A doggie?
13. Okay.
    All right, I'll make a doggie. Is this the doggie's tail?
14. The doggie's tail.
    Doggie's tail.
15. More.
    More doggie?
16. Okay.
    Can T. color? Hum?
17. More doggie there.
18. More doggie daddy.
    More doggie daddy?
19. Wants a more doggie.
20. More doggie.
21. Put more doggie there.

At first reading, it is obvious that the conversation in Table 7.1 is concrete and concerned with the task of coloring. There is no great variety in the words used, and the child repeats these words frequently. The child engages in turn taking and is focused and responsive. Many of the child's utterances, such as 9 and 14, are whole or partial imitations. The child has a wide range of intentions. Within this segment, she answers (1, 2, 3, 5, 8, 12) and asks questions (7), replies to her mother's utterances (4, 6, 13, 16), makes declarations (10, 18), gives directions to her mother (11, 17, 21), and makes demands (15, 19, 20).

Before you begin this chapter, take a few minutes to think about a 12- to 18-month-old child and what he or she knows. Jot down a short list of 10 to 20 words that he or she might say. Try it; you'll be surprised how much you already know. Much of a child's pronunciation will not mirror adult speech. For that reason, you might want to write possible child pronunciations after applicable words. For example, *water*, an early word for many children, will probably be spoken as "wawa."

Examine your list for patterns. What types of words—nouns, verbs, and so on—predominate? What speech sounds are used most frequently? What syllabic constructions—CV, VC, CVCV-reduplicated, CVCV, CVC, and so on—are most frequent?

In this video Dr. Steven Reznik of Yale University is interviewed about comprehension versus production of young children. http://www.youtube.com/watch?v=g8rOy33sU0k

It is also important to consider the contexts in which first words occur. A child's first words occur as requests for information, or for objects or aid, or as comments. Intentions, previously expressed through gestures and vocalizations, are now expressed through words. There is carryover of pragmatic functions from presymbolic to symbolic communication.

Keep your list handy. As we progress through this chapter, you may be surprised by the accuracy of your responses.

Single-Word Utterances

A toddler's first meaningful speech consists of single-word utterances, such as "doggie," or single-word approximations of frequently used adult phrases, such as "thank you" ("anku") or "what's that?" ("wassat?"). At this point, "words" are phonetic approximations of adult words that a child consistently uses to refer to a particular situation or object. The meaning of the word may be restricted at first and may apply to only one particular referent or thing to which it refers. For example, "doggie" (usually "goggie" or "doddie") may refer only to the family's pet but not to other dogs. As a result of linguistic and "world" experience, a child will gradually modify the definition, and, at some point, it will be close to the generally accepted notion of the word's meaning.

Remember that a word signifies a referent but that the referent is not the meaning of the word. Meaning is found in language users' concepts or mental images, not in individual examples.

In general, a toddler talks about the world he or she knows and will not comment on inflation, unemployment, politics, or international relations. Instead, a toddler may request toys, call people, name pets, reject food, ask for help with clothing, and discuss familiar actions or routines. My own children began speaking with words such as *mama*, *dada*, *pepa* (the dog), *all gone*, and *bye-bye*. Single words are used to make requests, comments, inquiries, and so on.

A child seems to begin speaking by attempting to learn whole adult utterances that represent various communicative purposes. Early utterances seem to represent partial learning of longer, more complex adult utterances. The child's first productions correspond to adult expressions (Tomasello, 2006).

Many linguists believe children's early one-word utterances represent **holophrases** that convey a holistic communicative intention. Functionally speaking, children's early one-word utterances are semantic-pragmatic holophrases that express a single communicative intention (Tomasello, 2006). Usually, these intentions are the same as those of the adult expressions from which they were learned. Many of children's early holophrases are individualistic and will evolve and change over time.

The reason children respond with one-word or one phrase (e.g., *Wassat?*) expressions is unknown. Most likely the child only attends to a part of the adult expression, or because of limited working memory, the child can process only one word or phrase at a time.

Regardless of the language a child is acquiring, early words are used to accomplish several tasks:

- Request or indicate the existence of an object by naming it with a requesting or neutral intonation.
- Request or describe the recurrence of objects or events, using words such as *more*, *'gain* , and *'nother*.
- Request or describe changing events involving objects by *up*, *down*, *on*, *off*, *in*, *out*, *open*, and *close*.
- Request or describe the actions of others with words such as *eat*, *kick*, *ride*, and *fall*.
- Comment on the location of objects and people with words such as *bed*, *car*, and *outside*.
- Ask some basic questions such as *What?*, *What that?*, and *Where mommy?*
- Attribute a property to an object such as *big*, *hot*, and *dirty*.
- Use utterances to mark specific social events and situations or perform some act, as with *hi, bye, and no* (Tomasello, 2006).

Longer utterances are learned as a means of further clarifying the intention. While a young child may say "Doggie" to mean both *See doggie* and *Want doggie*, an older child will clarify these intentions with the addition of "See" and "Want."

What parts of adult expressions children choose for their holophrases depends on the language being learned and on the talking style of adults in a child's life. For example, English has inherited short verb phrases from German that include a verb particle such as *take off*, *pick up*, *put on*, and *get down*. English-speaking children often learn the particle (e.g., *off*, *up*, *on*, *down*) first. In Korean and Mandarin Chinese, which do not have verb particles, children learn fully adult verbs from the onset. Let's explore some qualities of single-word utterances together.

PRAGMATICS

In order to explain early child language fully, we must consider the uses to which these utterances are put. As we noted in Chapter 5, communication is well established before the first word appears. Words are acquired within the established communication system of a child and caregiver.

The repetitiveness of certain daily routines, both verbal and nonverbal, and a mother's willingness to assign meaningful intent to her child's speech facilitate language development. Parent responses also foster word–meaning associations by providing feedback.

The intentions of a child's early utterances are also important. Early words develop to fulfill the intentions originally conveyed by gestures. Novel words may be learned through actual use by a child in conversation (Nelson, 1991; Nelson, Hampson, & Shaw, 1993). A child may say a word in a context where it "sounds right based on what the child has heard." The feedback of others confirms or denies the accuracy of the child's production.

There is a strong relationship between first words and the frequency of maternal use of these words. Many words are used in the same context in which the mother used them previously, such as *bye-bye* while waving and *choo-choo* while playing with a toy train. Not all words are used this way, however, and a significant number are also used to name or label entities or to request something.

Before we continue, return to the fictitious list of first words you generated at the beginning of this chapter. Pause for a moment and consider how these words might be used socially, that is, to attain information, fulfill needs, provide information, and so on. Now, let's see how well you did.

Development of Intent

In Chapter 5 we examined the illocutionary functions or intentions of early gestures. Initially, intentions are signaled by gestures only. To these a child adds vocalizations and then words or verbalizations. Many early words, however, can be interpreted only with consideration of the accompanying gesture. Gradually, a child learns to express intentions more through words and grammar, although gestures remain important, even for adults.

Gestures By the time a child begins producing words, he or she has typically been communicating with others through gestures and sounds for months. A child's first linguistic productions are learned and used in the context of this nonlinguistic communication and for the same basic intentions or purposes. Often, the first intentions expressed are declarations or statements and requests for objects, with requests for information or questions coming shortly thereafter. A child's first declarations are usually about a shared or potentially shared referent.

The child's utterances have intonational patterns indicating requests, comments, or questions, the same intentions as the adults' more complex utterances. This would indicate that a child is not attempting to learn isolated words but to communicate an entire adult utterance (Tomasello, 2006).

During the second year, gestures and words become more coordinated for specific intentions. Reaching increasingly signals a request or demand, while pointing signals a declaration or a reference to something in the environment. Symbolic gestures, such as panting like a dog, appear at about the same time as first words and develop in parallel for several months. Children will continue to use gestures as a backup for speech or as an assist for words that are lacking.

Obviously, not all children are alike. Some rely more on gestures, while others prefer speech, although almost all toddlers use gestures spontaneously with speech and sound making. Young toddlers may rely on caregiver gestures for comprehension.

Vocabulary production in 18- to 28-month-olds appears to be related to the child's ability to make functional gestures (Thal, Tobias, & Morrison, 1991). Functional gestures depict objects through actions demonstrating the object's function, such as pretending to eat from an empty spoon.

In similar fashion, the development of multiword utterances seems to be correlated with the production of gestural combinations. The lengths of "utterances" in both words and gestures are similar.

From age 12 to 18 months, a child increasingly gestures and verbalizes while looking at her or his communication partner. This may be an important transition to the ability to consider both the topic and the listener simultaneously.

Up to this point, a child usually looks at the partner. Initially, a child looks at her or his conversational partner after gesturing. Gradually, the child changes so that the look occurs before, indicating knowledge of the need to have a listener's attention first.

Gestures can be both a source of semantic knowledge and an expression of that knowledge, especially at a time when oral language skills are limited (Capone, 2007). Both infants and toddlers may use gestures to compensate for limitations in articulation and phonology. Gestures may be an efficient means of communicating knowledge or they may facilitate word retrieval at a time when word knowledge is still evolving and weak (Goldin-Meadow & Wagner, 2005). By offering a visual representation of the word, gestures may free cognitive resources for other tasks (Goldin-Meadow, Nusbaum, Kelly, & Wagner, 2001).

From infancy, gestures both supplement and predict speech (Capone & McGregor, 2004). An infant in the one-word stage communicates with deictic gestures, such as pointing or requesting, and some iconic gestures that function as words not yet spoken by the child, such as moving his or her arms to indicate a bird's flight. Pointing and other deictic gestures precede first words, and when first words emerge, pointing gestures and some single iconic gestures are used to communicate. Iconic gestures that convey meaning through the form, action, or spatial position of the body, and hand movements (Goldin-Meadow, 2003). In general, toddlers use deictic gestures more often than iconic ones.

A high proportion of toddlers use gestures to communicate. A toddler's gesture-speech combinations can be characterized as reinforcing combinations convey matching information, such as pointing at dog while saying "Dog." The semantic relations expressed in gesture–speech combinations, such as saying "Daddy" while pointing to his coat, precede similar spoken word combinations, as in "Daddy coat" (Özçaliskan & Goldin-Meadow, 2005).

Both gestures and language are served by the same regions of the brain. When language is activated, motor control areas for both speech and gesture are readied for production.

Gestures and Joint Attending When an adult responds to an infant's point with an emotion but ignores the referent, the infant shows signs of dissatisfaction by repeating the point in an attempt to redirect the adult's attention. If the adult continues to ignore the infant's intent, then over time the infant will point less often (Liszkowski, Carpenter, Henning, Striano, & Tomasello, 2004). When the adult correctly identifies the intended referent, infants simply continue sharing attention and interest, but when the adult identifies the incorrect referent, the infant repeats pointing to the intended referent in an attempt to direct attention (Liszkowski et al., 2007). In these ways, in both their comprehension and production of pointing gestures, 12- to 14-month-olds demonstrate an understanding of both pointing and naming as intentional acts whose purpose is to induce the partner to attend to some entity within a joint-attention context. This process involves much more than simply a gaze or point.

It is entirely possible that when a young infant points for an adult she or he is in some sense trying to influence the adult's intentional/mental states while at the same time engaging in uniquely human skills and motivations for cooperation and shared intentionality (Tomasello, Carpenter, & Liszkowski, 2007). This suggests that early verbal communication and gestures are motivated by shared intentionality.

Infants possess the basic social-cognitive and motivational skills for engaging in human-style cooperative communication by around 12 to 14 months of age. What they possess is an understanding about

- the choices people make in their intentions and attention,
- why people make these choices,
- what knowledge they do and do not share with others based on what they have experienced together with them in joint attention interactions, and
- the basic cooperative motives.

Like gestures, first words are often acquired within everyday routines between children and their caregivers.

From their earliest communicative pointing, infants' intention is to direct others' attention to some entity, suggesting a process of influencing the minds of others. Infants understand quite early on that one achieves one's social intention mainly by making others aware of it, indicating a clear understanding of the mental states of others (Tomasello et al., 2007).

The social-cognitive basis for cooperative communication is mainly joint attention, which requires the ability to know things mutually with others, and the communicative intention to know something together (Tomasello et al., 2007). Even in more traditional societies, such as in rural Nigeria, there is a relationship between toddlers' ability to establish joint reference and language development (Childers, Vaughan, & Burquest, 2007).

The social-motivational part comprises the cooperative motives of helping by informing and sharing emotions and attitudes in a communicative context. These cooperative motives are mutually assumed by both the infant and the infant's partner.

Sound and Word Making There appears to be a pattern in young children's vocalizations and gestures. Gradually, intent moves from being expressed primarily through gesture to being more language dependent. Early, more general vocal-gestural intentions are presented in Table 7.2. Similar, but more specific intentions will be expressed through speech and gestures or speech alone in the second year of life.

As stated, first words fulfill the intentions previously expressed through gestures and vocalizations. Initially, specific words or sounds may be used with each intention. As words increase and intentions diversify, words and utterances become more flexible and multifunctional. The disappearance of specific symbol–intention relationships usually occurs from 16 to 24 months, corresponding to the beginning of multiword combinations.

Six pragmatic categories describe the general purposes of language: control, representational, expressive, social, tutorial, and procedural (Wells, 1985) (see Table 7.2):

1. Speakers use the control function to make demands and requests, to protest, and to direct others.
2. The representational function is used to discuss entities and events and to ask for information.

Initially, speech emerges to accompany action. A child's first words may accompany pointing and be used to display a wish or to express displeasure. A child may draw attention first (*Mommy*), then make a request (*up*) or use *look* for control or *there* to complete a task. As he or she matures, a child may attend to an object and the action associated with it the word, as in saying *eat* when referring to a cookie being eaten. Later, he or she notes object relations or comments on the event, such as asking for a repetition with *again* and *more*. Thus, the child is not just acquiring a stack of words but is using them to build a communication system with that partner.

With two-word speech, content can be communicated more completely without as much dependence on nonlinguistic channels. A single intention can be realized in a variety of grammatical forms. A child can express a request with "Gimme cookie," "Cookie me," or "Cookie please." Conversely, one form can serve a variety of intentions. For example, an utterance such as "Daddy throw" can serve as a descriptor of an event, a request for action, or even a request for information (question).

At around age 2, even as the number of intentions increases, a child begins to combine multiple intentions within a single utterance. For example, on spying some fresh-baked cookies, the child might say, "Mommy, cookies hot?" Even though she is attempting to attain information, she may also be hoping to attain a cookie. Thus, we have a request for information and a request for an entity within the same utterance.

Conversational Abilities

Even at the single-word stage, a child has some knowledge of the information to be included in a conversation, giving evidence of **presupposition**—that is, the assumption that the listener knows or does not know certain information that a child, as speaker, must include or delete from the conversation. For example, as an adult, when you are asked, "How do you want your steak?" you might reply, "Medium rare." There is no need to repeat the redundant information, "I would like my steak. . . ." You omit the redundant information because you presuppose that your listener shares this information with you already. In contrast, you would call your listener's attention to new, different, or changing circumstances that may be unknown to the listener ("Did you know that . . . ?" "Well, let me tell you about. . . .").

Toddlers seem to follow certain rules for presupposition:

- An object not in the child's possession should be labeled.
- An object in the child's possession, but undergoing change, as in being eaten, should be encoded by the action or change.
- Once encoded, an object or action/state change becomes more certain. If the child continues, she or he will encode some other aspect, such as location.

The order of successive single-word utterances ("Doggie. Eat.") reflects these rules. This may explain, in part, the variable order of successive single-word utterances. Sometimes "Eat. Doggie." is perfectly fine. With the onset of two-word utterances, a child learns some word-order rules that may override informational structure. Because children often encode things in the immediate context, it is relatively easy for adults to interpret an utterance in a manner similar to that of a child.

INITIAL LEXICONS

Initial individual vocabularies, or *lexicons*, may contain some of the common words listed in Table 7.4. Although there are many variations in pronunciation, some of the most frequent forms are included in parentheses.

TABLE 7.4 **Representative List of Early Words**

juice (/dus/)	mama	all gone (/ɔdɔn/)
cookie (/tʊti/)	dada	more (/mɔ/)
baby (/bibi/)	doggie (/dɔdi/)	no
bye-bye	kitty (/tɪdi/)	up
ball (/bɔ/)	that (/da/)	eat
hi	dirty (/dɔti/)	go (/d oʊ/)
car (/tɔ/)	hot	do
water (/wʌwʌ)	shoe (/su/)	milk (/mʌk/)
eye	hat	
nose (/n oʊ)		

How does this sample compare with the one you devised earlier?

An analysis of first words indicates that over half consist of a single consonant-vowel (CV) syllable with the remainder split between single vowels and two CV syllables (CVCV) (Fagan, 2009). Nonword vocalizations are similar in structure. The overwhelming majority of words and nonwords contained three or fewer sounds each. For example, in our list in Table 7.4 we find CV words, such as *no* and *car* (/tɔ/); CVCV-reduplicated words, such as *mama, dada*, and *water* (/wʌwʌ/); and CVCV words, such as *doggie* (/dɔdi/). How does your list compare? There are very few CVC words, and many of these will be modified in production. The final consonant may be omitted to form CV or followed by a vowel-like sound approximating a CVCV construction. For example, a word such as *hat* might be produced as *hat-a* (/hatʌ/) similar to a CVCV construction. Front consonants, such as /p/, /b/, /d/, /t/, /m/, /w/, and /n/, and back consonants, such as /g/, /k/, and /h/, predominate. No consonant clusters, such as /tr/, /sl/, or /str/, appear. Clusters are too difficult to produce at this age.

The first words of Spanish-speaking children also demonstrate some of the same characteristic. CV, VC, and CVCV syllable structures. The phonemes /p/, /b/, /m/, and /n/ are also used frequently, plus /g/ and /k/. As a group, these sounds can be found in 70% of the most frequent words of Spanish-speaking children.

A child's first lexicon includes several categories of words. The most frequent words among a child's first 10 words generally name animals, foods, and toys. First words usually apply to a midlevel of generality (*dog*) and only much later to specific types (*spaniel, boxer*) and larger categories (*animal*). Even at this midlevel, however, a child uses the word at first to mark a specific object or event rather than a category. The list in Table 7.4 contains animals (*doggie* and *kitty*), foods (*juice* and *cookie*), and toys (*ball*). How about your own list?

Initial lexical growth is slow, and a child may appear to plateau for short periods. Some words are lost as a child's interests change and production abilities improve. In addition, a child may continue to use a large number of vocalizations that are consistent but fail to meet the "word" criterion. At the center of a child's lexicon is a small core of high-usage words. The lexical growth rate accelerates as a child nears the 50-word mark. Eighteen-month-old infants are capable of learning new words with as few as three exposures (Houston-Price, Plunkett, & Harris, 2005). The second half of the second year is one of tremendous vocabulary expansion, although there is much individual variation.

In general, girls seem to begin to acquire words earlier and have a faster initial trajectory (Bauer, Goldfield, & Reznick, 2002).

By 18 months of age, the toddler will have a lexicon of approximately 50 words. Nouns (*milk, dog, car, mama, dada*) predominate, often accounting for over 60% of a child's lexicon. Most entries are persons and animals within the environment or objects the child can manipulate. Not all noun types are represented; individual objects and beings are most frequent. There are no collections, such as *forest*, or abstractions, such as *joy*.

Again, many of these characteristics are also found in the first words of Spanish-speaking toddlers. *Mama* and *papa* are popular, along with labels for toys, body parts, foods, the names of people, *more* (*mas*), and *yes/no* (*sí/no*) (Jackson-Maldonado, Thal, Marchman, Bates, & Gutierrez-Clellan, 1993).

Growth in the overall size of a child's lexicon does not follow a smooth trend. After acquiring about 100 words, most, but not all, children experience a rapid rise in the rate of acquisition between 18 and 24 months, called a "vocabulary spurt." Words that are learned only in specific contexts and those that are relatively context-free tend to retain so. The specific words learned are determined by a combination of factors, including their relevance for the child and the significance of the referent.

The actual timing of the spurt may depend on the rate of cognitive development. The cause of and the reason for the timing is unknown but could be related to one of the following:

- Development of more articulation control. Once a child has overcome difficulty producing certain phonological forms, she or he is free to produce words that had been too difficult before.
- The role of syntactic patterns. Once a child learns certain syntactic frames used by parents, such as *This is X, Here's the X*, or *Show me your X*, a child can quickly pick up a large quantity of words to fill the "slot" within that frame.
- Underlying growth in cognitive capacities.
- Learning and using words.

We are witnessing the dynamic pairing of semantic learning with quickly developing phonological advances, a system of syntactic patterns, or cognitive advances.

Lexically precocious 2-year-old children—those with larger vocabularies—are also grammatically precocious, with a greater range of grammatical structures and more advanced combinatorial skills (McGregor, Sheng, & Smith, 2005). In general, among 2-year-olds, grammatical development is more closely associated with lexicon size than with chronological age.

Several factors may influence which words children learn:

- Grammatical class. As we'll see, the vocabularies of young children contain a high proportion of nouns. Other early forms include words commonly used in social contexts, such as *hi, bye-bye, uh-oh*, and *no*.
- Frequency of input from adults. Although the effect of input varies according to a word's lexical category, the more a child hears a particular noun, the earlier that word will become part of the child's expressive vocabulary.
- Lexical category. Although words in categories that contain relatively few items, such as pronouns, articles, and prepositions, are the most frequently used by adults with children, these words are acquired relatively late. Nouns, a category with a huge number of words, are acquired early.
- Socioeconomic status (SES). Children from low-SES families are more likely to have a smaller vocabulary than children from high-SES families.

- Phonology of the word. Although there is a relationship between phonology and a child's lexicon, the exact nature of that relationship is unknown. Most likely, the nature of this relationship changes as a child matures. For an in-depth discussion of this topic, see the excellent article by Stoel-Gammon (2011).

We'll explore some of these factors as we proceed.

Nouns Predominate

The proportion of nouns and verbs in a child's lexicon changes with development. There is an initial increase in nouns until a child has acquired approximately 100 words. At this point, verb learning begins to increase slowly. Other word classes, such as prepositions, do not increase proportionally until after acquisition of approximately 400 words, but that won't take long.

Regardless of the language spoken, children's early vocabularies contain relatively greater proportions of nouns than other word classes (Bleses et al., 2008; Bornstein et al., 2004; Dale & Goodman, 2005). In early lexical development, children speaking all languages seem to have a predisposition to learn nouns (Ogura, Dale, Yamashita, Murase, & Mahieu, 2006). As in English, the proportional increase, then decrease, in nouns is also found in the lexicons of Spanish-speaking toddlers.

Among 18- to 36-month-old American English-speaking children and Korean children, vocabulary size is roughly the same (Rescorla, Lee, Oh, & Kim, 2013). In both languages, girls and older children have larger vocabularies (Pae, Chang-Song, Kwak, Sung, & Sim, 2004). Nouns dominate and about half of the most commonly reported words are identical, including *mommy*, *daddy*, *baby*, *hi/hello*, *yes*, and *no*. As you might suspect, there are cultural differences in what children talk about. For example, among the top Korean words are *spicy* and *seaweed*, words that very infrequently appear in lexicons of U.S. children.

There are several possible explanations for the early predominance of nouns in the speech of toddlers learning American English:

- A child may already have a concept of objects from time spent in social interaction around objects and in object exploration.
- Nouns are *perceptually/conceptually distinct*. The "things" that nouns represent are more perceptually cohesive than events or actions, in which perceptual elements are scattered.
- The *linguistic predictability* of nouns makes them easier to use and accounts for their early predominance. Nouns represent specific items and events and thus relate to each other and to other words in specific, predictable ways. For example, they can be *on* or *in*, or other objects can be *on* or *in* them. Some are *eaten*; others *thrown*.
- The frequency of adult use, adult word order, the limited morphological adaptations of nouns, and adult teaching patterns seem to affect children's production. Learning may be made easier by clear parental labeling within context. Maternal naming of objects is most frequent about the time that the first word appears. After that time there is a subtle shift to more action words (Schmidt, 1996).

Effects of Child-Directed Speech (CDS) Although nouns also predominate in the initial words of Korean children, an earlier and proportionally higher use of verbs may reflect both Korean mothers' tendency to use single-word verbs and to use activity-oriented utterances, and the SOV organization of the Korean language that places verbs in a prominent position at the end of the sentence (Kim, McGregor, & Thompson, 2000). In fact, Korean children exhibit their own "verb spurt" not seen in English.

Although word order varies across languages, nouns still form a substantial part of most initial lexicons. Mothers may modify word order to place nouns in more prominent positions. For example, Turkish mothers even violate the SOV order to place nouns last. These changes are reflected in children's initial lexicons. Mandarin caregivers emphasize verbs over nouns, with a resultant higher proportion of verbs in the initial lexicon of Mandarin-speaking toddlers. Likewise, the noun bias of English is not seen in maternal speech in Ngas, a Nigerian language. Ngas-speaking mothers use proportionally more verbs than English-speaking mothers (Childers et al., 2007).

The frequency of nouns in adult-to-adult speech is low, but nouns occur more frequently in CDS, receive more stress than other words, are often in the final position in utterances, and have few morphological markers. Nouns are also frequent in toy play and in short maternal utterances. Verbs are more frequent in non-toy or social play and in conversations.

It is important to note that object-naming games found in American English—"What's that"—are culture based and not found in all cultures. American mothers also prompt their children to produce nouns more frequently than verbs (Goldfield, 2000).

For 16- to 18-month-old toddlers, learning words primes the child's lexical system to learn even more words (Gershkoff-Stowe & Hahn, 2007). In other words, vocabulary development may fine-tune the lexical or vocabulary system in order to increase storage and accessibility to information.

It's easy to see that the effect of frequency of parental input on word learning is not straightforward. Instead, there is a complex interaction with the type of word, receptive and expressive language of the child, and developmental stage (Goodman, Dale, & Li, 2008). Among 8- to 30-month-old children, the frequency of parental input correlates significantly only with the age of acquisition of common nouns.

Child Learning Style Individual children exist along a continuum from a referential style in which they use many nouns ("noun lovers") to an expressive style in which they use few ("noun leavers"), preferring interactional and functional words, such as *hi*, *bye-bye*, and *no*. Children with a referential learning style tend to elaborate the noun portion or noun phrase of their sentences, whereas those with an expressive style prefer to elaborate the verb phrase.

Children with a high proportion of nouns—70% or more—exhibit a rapid increase in the number of words in their lexicons between 14 and 18 months of age. In contrast, children whose lexicons have more balance between nouns and other word types tend to have a more gradual increase in word acquisition. These differences have been found among toddlers in both English and Italian and may indicate two acquisition strategies: (1) naming "things" and (2) encoding a broad range of experiences (D'Odorico, Carubbi, Salerni, & Calvo, 2001).

More than just a high or low proportion of nouns, the referential-expressive continuum represents different learning styles that affect language development. Children with a more referential style seem to have more adult contacts; use more single words; and employ an analytic, or bottom-up, strategy in which they gradually build longer utterances from individual words. In contrast, children with a more expressive style have more peer contacts, attempt to produce longer units, and employ a holistic, or top-down, strategy in which longer utterances are broken into their parts. Although the referential style is usually associated with a faster rate of development, other factors, such as gender, birth order, and social class, seem to be more important (Bates et al., 1994; Lieven & Pine, 1990).

Most children begin language acquisition by learning some adult expressions holistically, such as *I-wanna-do-it*, *Lemme-see*, and *Where-the-doggie*. Children who have an overdependence on this strategy, characterized as "swallowing language whole" or using memorized *formulas*, may be at a real disadvantage in learning language. In order to extract linguistic elements that can be used in other utterances in the future, a child must engage in a process of segmenting or dividing utterances—analyzing, if you will—to determine which components of speech input can be recombined with others. I'm a good example of using formulas. When I go to a country in which I do not speak the language, I memorize a few phrases. This means that I cannot take the phrases apart and form original utterances.

Here Come the Verbs

Twenty-month-olds understand meaning distinctions among several word categories, such as nouns and adjectives (Hall, Corrigall, Rhemtulla, Donegan, & Xu, 2008). Modifiers and verblike words, such as *down*, appear soon after the first word. True verbs, such as *eat* and *play*, occur later. Verbs and other words serve a relational function; they bring together items or events. Unlike objects, actions are not permanent, and verbs may not be accompanied by any consistent maternal gesturing. Thus, a child learning language is less able to guess their meanings after only a brief opportunity to make the symbol–referent connection.

There are several challenges in learning a verb (Hirsh-Pasek & Golinkoff, 2006). To establish a verb's meaning correctly, a child needs to find the underlying concept. The concepts that verbs refer to are abstract and hard to determine from the physical environment. For example, verbs differ greatly depending on who is performing the action. An out-of-shape and not-too-coordinated man looks very different from a ballerina, although both of their actions may be referred to as *dance*. Some verbs describe momentary actions, such as *throw*, while others have more duration, such as *play*. In addition, some nouns can be verbs, as with *skate*, while others cannot, as with *car*.

First, a child must identify a verb in the speech stream. Although 7.5-month-olds can segment nouns from fluent speech, only 13.5-month-olds succeed with verbs. In English, sentences are formed as subject-verb-object. This form may help in identifying verbs if a child can readily identify the nouns or pronouns. For example, Mommy + X + (food), as in *Mommy eat cookie* or *Mommy eat apple*, may provide a format within which the child can identify the action.

In minutes 13:38–15:22 of this video, Dr. Steven Pinker of Harvard University discusses some of the difficulties in learning single words. http://www.youtube.com/watch?v=Q-B_ONJIEcE

Verb learning presents a different situation than noun learning. Noun learning is best in an ongoing condition, in which a child can focus on an adult and still maintain the object within sight. In contrast, as many as 60% of the verbs in maternal speech refer to future action.

Nouns seem to enjoy a natural advantage even among 3- to 5-year-olds. In "verb-friendly" languages such as Chinese and Japanese, children still must depend on both grammatical or sentence support and pragmatic or usage support to learn verbs.

With vocabulary growth and the emergence of grammar, the proportion of verbs increases substantially. This is true for parental speech too. For example, when children begin to combine words, Japanese mothers shift away from a dominance of nouns in their toy play with their children (Ogura et al., 2006).

MEANING OF SINGLE-WORD UTTERANCES

A toddler has spent a year or more organizing the world, making sense of, or giving meaning to, experiences. A child's exact word meaning is unknown. Early lexicons until about 18 months of age seem to follow a principle of mutual exclusivity, which is mentioned in Chapter 6. Stated simply, *if the word means X, it can't mean Y or Z.*

Early object representations are most likely formed by a combination of the word, object parts, and object function (Chaigneau & Barsalou, 2008). Word knowledge may

The short answer to "How do children organize their definitions and on what are they based?" is that we have no idea. It may be all or none of the above theories, and it may vary by word and across child.

Extension: Under, Over, *and* Otherwise

A child's receptive vocabulary precedes her or his expressive vocabulary. Although there is wide individual variation, the receptive vocabulary may be four times the size of the expressive vocabulary between ages 12 to 18 months. A child who understands *motorcycle, bus, truck, car,* and *helicopter* may label all of them *car.*

Usually, a child's meaning encompasses a small portion of the fuller adult definition. For example, a child might hear a mature speaker say "No touch—hot!" as the child approaches the stove. Subsequently, the child may use the phrase as a general prohibition meaning "Don't do it!"

Formation of a link between a particular referent and a new name is called **fast mapping** or **initial mapping**, and it is typically quick, sketchy, and tentative. Most learning occurs after this initial mapping as a child is exposed repeatedly to new instances of a word. Gradually, the word is freed from aspects of the initial context.

In the process of refining meanings, children form hypotheses about underlying concepts and extend current meanings to include new examples. Through this extension process, a child gains knowledge from both examples and nonexamples of the concept.

Concepts may be very restricted or widely extended. Overly restricted meanings are called **underextensions**. Using "cup" for only "my child cup" is an example of underextension. In contrast, **overextensions** are meanings that are too broad when compared to the adult meaning. Calling all men "Daddy" is an example of overextension. Toddlers seem to overextend both receptively and expressively possibly because they fail to differentiate between basic concepts (*dog*) and conceptual categories (*pet*) (Storkel, 2002).

A child receives both implicit and explicit feedback about extensions of both types. Implicit feedback can be found in the naming practices of others, to which a child attends. In contrast, explicit feedback includes direct correction or confirmation of a child's extensions by more mature language users. As a child extends the meaning of *cup* from "my child cup," he or she may include bowls and pots in addition to coffee mugs and tea cups. In the course of daily events, more mature speakers will call bowls and pots by their accepted names and correct the child's attempts more directly.

Over time, words develop a "confirmed core." As long as a child sticks closely to the confirmed core, she or he will tend to undergeneralize a word. In the center are the best instances that display the maximum match. At the periphery, however, are instances that are less clear and compete with closely related words. When a child must communicate about similar entities that are not inside any confirmed core, overgeneralization may occur. Overextensions are common among toddlers in all languages, including those acquiring American Sign Language.

Most overextensions fall into three general types:

1. Categorical overinclusions occur when a child uses a word to label a referent in a related category, such as saying *baby* for all children, *hot* for hot and cold, or *dada* for both parents. The largest number of overinclusions are with people.
2. Analogical overextensions include the use of a word to label a referent based on inferred perceptual, functional, or affective similarity, such as saying *ball* to refer to round objects or *comb* to label a centipede.
3. Predicate statements occur when a child notes the relationship between an object and some absent person, object, property, or state, such as saying "doll" when seeing the empty bed or "door" when requesting adult assistance with opening or closing some object. Types of predicate overextensions are shown in Table 7.5.

TABLE 7.5 **Predicate Extensions**

STATEMENT TYPE	EXAMPLE
Former or unusual state	*Cookie* for empty plate
Anticipations	*Key* while standing in front of door
Elements	*Water* for turned-off hose
Specific activity	*Peepee* for toilet
Pretending	*Nap* while pretending to sleep

Source: Information from Thomson & Chapman (1977).

When we examine extensions of the first 75 words, perceptual similarity seems to account for nearly 60% of both. Most perceptual similarities seem to be visual. Action or functional similarity accounts for about 25% of children's extensions. Thematic or contextual association of an object with the event in which it is used, as when a child uses the word *nap* when referring to a blanket, seems to account for only about 12% of extensions. Finally, a very small number of extensions are based on affective or emotional similarity. More than half of these extensions involve prohibitive or frightening words, such as *hot* or *bad*.

The majority of children use words correctly, often for generalized referents rather than for a single referent. Within one month of acquisition, more than three fourths of words are generalized. Of the remainder, most are names for specific entities, such as *mama*. Words acquired during initial lexical growth are more likely to be both under- and overgeneralized than words acquired later. Much overextension occurs immediately, during the rapid vocabulary growth spurt that accompanies early multiword utterances.

As many as a third of the first 75 words may be overextended. Some categories, such as letters, vehicles, and clothing, are overextended at a greater rate than others. Many children overextend words such as *car, truck, shoe, hat, dada, baby, apple, cheese, ball, dog*, and *hot*.

In summary, it appears that extensions are an aspect of the word-acquisition process. As a child begins to use the acceptable adult meaning, adults become unwilling to accept the child's overinclusiveness, thus overextending decreases.

Early Multiword Combinations

When children begin to combine words into longer utterances at about 18 months of age, they do so in predictable patterns. With increasing memory and processing skills, a child is able to produce longer utterances by recombining some of these early patterns. Language learning in much of the latter half of the second year involves these combinations. It is important to keep in mind, however, that the child still produces a great many single-word utterances and continues to babble and use jargon.

Why does a young child produce short utterances? I'll spare you the long, complicated answer. In short, children's language production is similar to that of adults, meaning that it is a complex interaction of

- syntactic knowledge,
- limited cognitive resources, especially working memory,
- a child's communicative goals, and
- the structure of the conversation (Valian & Aubry, 2005).

TRANSITION: EARLY WORD COMBINATIONS

Prior to the appearance of two-word utterances is a period in which a child produces sequences of words, sounds, and gestures in seeming combination and in a variety of forms. In a gesture-rich culture, such as Italy, a child may make early transitional combinations of a word plus a representational gesture, such as putting a fist to the ear to signal *telephone* or flapping the arms for *bird*. A larger number of such combinations is related to greater verbal production in the later multiword stage.

The types of gesture-speech combinations a child produces during the early verbal stages of language development change with the child's changing cognitive and language skills (Özçaliskan & Goldin-Meadow, 2005). While children and their caregivers produce the same types of gestures and in approximately the same distribution, children differ from caregivers in the way they use gestures accompanying speech. Although caregivers' use of reinforcing (*ball* + point at ball), disambiguating (*that one* + point at ball), and supplementary gesture–word combinations (*push* + point at ball) does not increase during the second year of life, children's use of two-element supplementary gestural-verbal combinations, such as pointing at a car and saying "Go," increases as a child approaches the production of two-word utterances (McEachem & Haynes, 2004).

A second possible transitional form consists of a CV syllable preceding or following a word. The phonology of the extra syllable is inconsistent and has no referent while the word is more consistent. For example, the child might say the following on several different occasions:

ma baby
te baby
bu baby

Other phonological forms may be more consistent but still have no referent. For example, another variation consists of a word plus a preceding or following sound in which the word varies while the vocalization is stable. Examples of these forms are as follows:

beda cookie
beda baby
beda doggie

A third transitional form consists of successive one-word utterances, as in "Mommy" followed by "Eat" as a separate utterance. Mothers may help children construct successive single-word utterances through conversation (Herr-Israel & McCune, 2011). For example, if the child is trying to feed a doll (*Baby*), a conversation may go something like this:

CHILD: Baby
ADULT: Are you trying to make the baby eat?
CHILD: Eat.
ADULT: Oh, baby eat. What's she eating?
CHILD: Soup.
ADULT: The baby eats soup.

Notice that the adult provides the next word in the sequence—a sequence of successive one-word utterances—and then places them together in a longer utterance.

At this point in my language development class, someone always asks about early word combinations such as *all gone*. These seeming combinations, consisting of two words, are learned as a single unit. "Daddybob" was a favorite of my children. Usually, a child does not use the two single-unit words independently as words nor in combination with others. Common examples of single-unit words include:

Watch this video to hear the language of a 2-year-old. http://www.youtube.com/watch?v=UrRKLHq25UA

all-gone
go-bye
so-big
go-potty

Because the words almost always appear together, linguists don's consider these combinations to be true two-word utterances. That's coming next.

MULTIWORD UTTERANCES

Children progress naturally from one-word utterances to two-word ones. At about 18 months of age, many children begin combining words. It is not surprising that children's earliest multiword utterances are produced to talk about many of the same kinds of things they talked about previously in their one-word holophrases. These multiword utterances come in three varieties:

1. Word combinations
2. Pivot schemas
3. Item-based constructions (Tomasello, 2003)

Let's look at each in turn. Examples are presented in Table 7.6.

Word combinations consist of roughly equivalent words that divide an experience into multiple units. For example, a child has learned to label a dog and a bed and then spies the family dog on her bed and says, "Doggie bed." Initially, these utterances may

TABLE 7.6 Multiword Utterance Patterns

Pattern	Explanation	Examples
Word combinations	Equivalent words that encode an experience, sometimes as two successive one-word utterances.	*Water hot* *Wave bye* *Drink cup*
Pivot schema	One word or phrase structures the utterance by determining intent. Several words may fill the "slot," as in "Want + 'things I want'."	*Throw ball* *Throw block* *Throw airplane* *More juice* *More cookie* *More bottle* *Want blanket* *Want up* *Want out*
Item-based constructions	Seem to follow word-order rules for specific rules. May contain morphological markers.	*Baby eat* *Hug baby* *Baby's bed* *Daddy driving* *Drive car* *Drive to gran'ma'*

be expressed as successive single-word utterances with a pause between them and a drop in voice on each. This may be a transition to word combinations in which there is little pause and a drop in voice only on the last word. Often the two words are not combined with other words.

Pivot schemas show a more systematic pattern. Often one word or phrase, such as *want* or *more*), seems to structure the utterance by determining the intent of the utterance as a whole, such as a demand. Often there is an intonational pattern, such as an insistent sound to the utterance, that also signals the intent. Other words, such as *cookie*, or phrases, such as *go-bye*, simply fill in the blank or slot, so to speak, as in *More cookie* or *Want go-bye*. In many of these early utterances, one event-word is used with a wide variety of object labels as in *More cookie*, *More juice*, and *More apple*.

Use of pivot schemas is a widespread and productive strategy for producing many two-word utterances from a limited set of constructions. When 22-month-olds are taught a novel name for an object, they seem to know immediately how to combine that word with pivot-type words in their vocabularies, indicating that they also have the rudiments of grammatical classes for words that will fit into the slot in the pivot schemas. Don't think of these as categories such as nouns and verbs. More likely, the categories reflect "things I want" or "things that disappear." In fact, pivot schemas do not seem to have any internal grammar. For example, "No juice" and "Juice no" seem to have the same meaning.

When there is consistency, however, it most likely reflects the word order children have heard most often in adult speech. Thus, English-speaking toddlers are likely to say "No juice" while Korean-speaking ones are likely to say "Juice no."

Interestingly, and this is an important distinction, novel words used in pivot schemas are not used creatively to make other constructions. For example, if a child is taught a novel action word in one construction, he or she is not likely initially to make novel two-word utterances using that word. We can conclude that at this point in development, each pivot schema is its own grammatical "island," and a child does not have a good command of the grammar of the language.

Under communication pressure, such as being hurried or not knowing the correct word, a child may create utterances that seem unusual to adults . . . and make us smile! For example, a toddler might say "I brooming" as she sweeps or "That a flying" when referring to a helicopter.

Item-based constructions seem to be following word-order rules with specific words. Young children comprehend word order with familiar verbs. A child's word-specific, word-ordered constructions seem to depend on how a child has heard a particular word being used.

Within a specific word's development, there is great continuity. New uses almost always replicate previous uses and then make some small addition or modification. For example, a child may say "Doggie bed" and later produce "Doggie's bed."

Verbs and their grammatical use seem to be learned one verb at a time until children begin to generalize language rules after age 3. In this way, children's syntactic structures are at best relatively independent from each other and dependent on certain words, especially verbs.

Unlike pivot schemas, item-based constructions contain morphological markers (*-ing, -s, -ed*), prepositions (*in, on, to*), and word order to indicate syntactic classes of words that are treated in certain ways. For example, only nouns receive a plural *-s* marker and follow prepositions. These syntactic structures are not generalized. Instead, they are learned and applied word-by-word after hearing similar words used in the same way by adults (Tomasello, 2003).

The toddler is faced with a formidable task trying to form schemes of abstract syntactic rules. It is not surprising, therefore, that this would be accomplished one word at a time.

Social-Cognitive Skills and Multiword Utterances

Children construct multiword utterances from the language they hear around them. The ability to do this rests on a child's underlying social-cognitive skills. To accomplish this task, children must be able to do the following:

- Plan and create a multiple-step procedure toward a single goal.
- Form abstractions across individual items.
- Create item-based constructions (Tomasello, 2003).

Let's discuss each one briefly.

Planning and creating a multistep path to accomplish a goal is seen in the problem-solving behaviors of 14- to 18-month-old toddlers. For example, if a toy is unreachable, a toddler will make a plan and attempt it to retrieve the toy. In addition, toddlers are able to copy sequences of behavior from others.

We see toddlers' ability to form abstractions across items in their play. Certain actions, such as pushing can be performed on several different objects, such as toy cars, balls, the baby stroller, and (to mom's dismay) any food on the highchair tray. This skill would seem to be exactly the kind of cognitive ability needed to create a pivot schema across different utterances, yielding *Push X*. The *X* may be categorized by the child as "pushable things."

At this point, meaning is in words, but in mature speech, many grammatical functions are piggybacked onto these words. Syntactic constructions depend on different semantic elements contained in the words. As children hear a word such as *push* used over and over again, presumably they construct a schema that *push* is structured so that a *pusher* precedes it and a *pushee* follows, regardless of the specific identity of each entity (Tomasello, 2003). We are now ready for syntax, but you'll have to wait until Chapter 9.

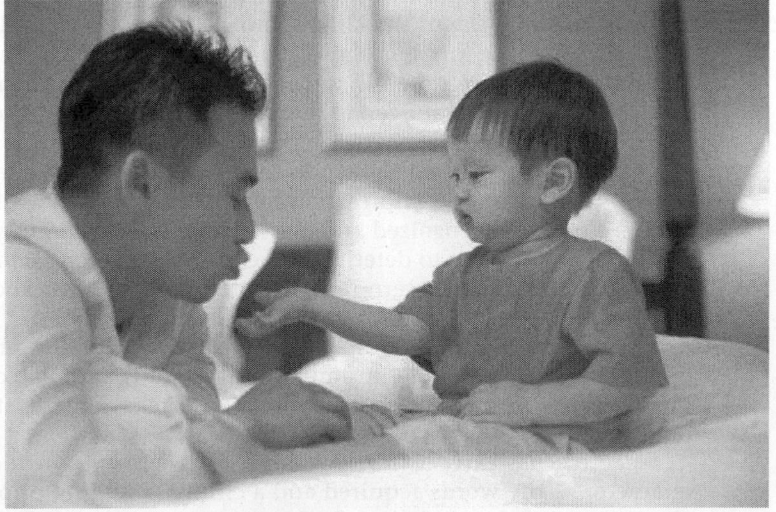

Merzzie/Shutterstock

Parents and siblings are a toddler's primary conversational partners.

Phonological Learning

Phonological development has a strong influence on the first words a child produces. In general, a child will avoid words that he or she cannot pronounce. New words are added when a child develops a "phonological template" or format for those words. For example, when a child acquires a CVC template for final plosive sounds, he or she may add *top*, *pop*, *cat*, *dog*, *bike*, and *cake*, to name a few but still not produce *car*, *knife*, or *bath*. Conversely, lexical development will have a strong influence on the sounds that a child produces. A child's "favorite phonemes" are usually taken from the sounds present in his or her first and favorite words. A child then attempts these sounds in other words. These favorite words and sounds form a kind of language acquisition base from which our little language explorer ventures out but never loses sight of "home."

In the second year, a child faces the task of matching up articulations to auditions, or what he or she says with what he or she hears or has heard. Gaining control of articulation is a major challenge for the 2-year-old. When we break the task down, we find that a child must go from present or stored auditory features to articulation while encoding the sequence and rhythm of each syllable in the word. Although learning auditory sequences requires memory, the learning of articulatory sequences involves memory and rehearsal.

As many as three different representations or maps may be involved in learning a word: auditory, conceptual, and articulatory. Word learning involves the association of elements of all three maps.

AUDITORY MAPS

The learning of a word is an association between the way a word sounds and its meaning. When a child hears a word and sees an object simultaneously, an association is formed. Most likely, at this early juncture, many elements of the two maps are not interconnected. If an initial association is not supported by repeated exposure, the word will be forgotten.

As mentioned, the phonological system of humans is a paired system of incoming and outgoing lexicons (personal dictionaries) (Baker, Croot, McLeod, & Paul, 2001). On the incoming side is the child's knowledge base of stored information about words based on language input and application of the child's learned phonological patterns. Outgoing signals are stored in a parallel branch of the system. There are also semantic avenues for storage that overlap these phonological ones, thus increasing the efficiency of the entire storage system.

Speech perception is based on the child's use of these learned phonological codes to help hold incoming information in working memory while it's analyzed (Nittrouer, 2002). Words are recognized and placed in long-term memory. Although word boundaries often are difficult to determine in connected speech (*Jeat? = Did you eat?*), children, as we know, learn to discern recognizable sound patterns and use these to break down the incoming speech stream.

Production may be stimulated by either side of the phonological system (Baker et al., 2001). For example, in imitation, a child is stimulated by the incoming speech model. In more spontaneous speech, a child relies on the stored lexical items on the outgoing side.

To discuss early lexical development we must consider both the phonological character of the words acquired and a child's emerging phonological system. Lexical characteristics that influence linguistic processing are the word's frequency of use, the **neighborhood density**, and the phonotactic probability (Storkel & Morrisette, 2002).

- Frequently used words are recognized by the child more quickly and accurately and produced more rapidly than infrequent ones. On the other hand, high density or lots of neighbors can result in more confusion and slower, less accurate recognition and production (Vitevitch, 2002; Vitevitch, Luce, & Pisoni, 1999).
- Neighborhood density is the number of possible words that differ by one phoneme. For example, there are very few words in the neighborhood with *the*, thus density is low. Neighbors that differ by one phoneme include *they*, *thee*, *though*, and *thou*. All things being equal, which they never are, words in less dense neighborhoods are easier to learn. For example, a 15- to 17-month-old child will seek out a novel object in response to hearing a novel label provided that the child does not have any familiar words that differ from the novel one by only one phoneme (*cat* vs. *hat*) (Mather & Plunkett, 2011).
- Phonotactic probability is the likelihood of a sound pattern occurring. Sound pattern probability is established for the child through experience each time a sound sequence is encountered. Common sound sequences (/st-, bl-, -ts/) are perceived and produced more quickly than less common ones (/skw-, -lf/) (Vitevitch & Luce, 1999), although it will be years before some consonant sequences are mastered. These stored patterns are used, as we discussed previously, to divide the speech stream into separate words.

Infants attend more readily to frequently occurring words. Because they have few stored words—their *neighborhoods* are sparsely populated—children tend to use global or whole-word recognition strategies. Phonotactic probability emerges at about 9 months as the child learns the likelihood of sound patterns occurring in the speech of others in the environment.

Young children seem to operate at a holistic or whole-word representation level. A transition from holistic to segmental storage of phonological information, while individualistic, begins at about the time when toddlers combine words (Vogel Sosa & Stoel-Gammon, 2006).

Children enter the phonological system at the whole-word or global level when they begin to speak (Beckman & Edwards, 2000). Words are not built phoneme by phoneme but are perceived, learned, and produced as whole-sound-patterned units.

ARTICULATORY MAPS

Language learning, like language teaching, may be both implicit and explicit, reflecting the parallel receptive and expressive phonological systems previously discussed (Velleman & Vihman, 2002). Implicit learning is incidental and unintentional, including mere exposure to the language. Through exposure, an infant gains an expectation for the frequency of occurrence of different phonological patterns, gradually gaining a sense of the language norm. In explicit learning, a child attempts to replicate an adult word heard previously.

An infant gradually becomes familiar with the rhythmic patterns of language by 4 months and with recurring sound distribution patterns by 7 to 8 months. This sound pattern sensitivity occurs at about the same time as a child's production of reduplicated babbling. For the child, this may be the first actual link between the perception and execution portions of his or her phonological system. Gradually, different word shape patterns, such as CV, VC, CVCV, and CVC, evolve from motor practice and the perceived speech of other speakers in the environment. Later, these accessible forms become the templates for a child's first words. In other words, a child unconsciously matches adult words to the phonological patterns that he or she has formed. For example, the adult word *bottle* is fit into the child's CVCV-reduplicated template to form *baba*.

Studies in development of English, French, Japanese, Finnish, Swedish, and Welsh find that first words are similar in form to the child's concurrent babbling (McCune & Vihman, 2001; Vihman & Velleman, 2000). In general, the words match adult forms, but sounds or patterns that do not fit the child's templates or are difficult to produce are omitted.

Toddlers seem to adopt a "frame-and-slot" strategy in which they acquire certain templates or frames, and words selected for expression are similar enough in number of syllables, consonants and location, and syllable stress to fit these frames. Thus, a child integrates words and phrases from the environment with his or her own vocal patterns. This process may account for the large percentage of first words of children that contain similar sounds, sound combinations, and syllable shapes (Coady & Aslin, 2003).

As more words are produced, children demonstrate a bias toward consistency over precision by trying to match adult words to the previously existing templates and sound patterns. Words may be produced correctly at first but later modified to fit a child's templates.

A child's repertoire of individual speech sounds is also important in first-word production. In general, the greater the number of consonants produced at 9 months, the larger a child's lexicon at 16 months (McCune & Vihman, 2001).

Different children exhibit different "favorite sounds" and use these, in part, in selecting the first words that they will produce. Although there is a wide range of individual differences, certain language-based phonetic tendencies are seen in most children, including a preference for monosyllables over longer strings, and stops (/p, b, t, d, k, g/) over other consonants.

Preferences for particular speech sounds at age 1 do not correspond to mastery of these same speech sounds at age 3. Relationships are more subtle. In general, the greater the proportion of true consonants in babbling and true words at age 1, the more advanced the phonological development of a child at age 3 (Vihman & Greenlee, 1987).

Phonological experimentation may exist along a continuum from those children who are very cautious or systematic to those who are more adventurous. More systematic children operate with strong phonetic and structural constraints that are relaxed gradually. In contrast, adventurous speakers have a loose, variable phonological organization and attempt words well beyond their capabilities.

Conclusion

A child learning language auditorily—as almost all of us have done—must map or form both the auditory features and the semantics or concept of a word in parallel (Naigles & Gelman, 1995; Reznick, 1990). A child already possesses fairly well-structured knowledge of the basic objects in the immediate environment (*mommy*, *daddy*, *dog*, *ball*, and so on) and particular activities (*bathe*, *eat*, *fall*, and the like). It is difficult to measure the size of a child's comprehension vocabulary preceding first-word production, but it is probably around 20 words.

With the production of words, a child needs phonological consistency to transmit messages. After the onset of meaningful speech, there is much individual variation in the pattern and rate of speech-sound growth and in the syllable structure of the words acquired.

SINGLE-WORD UTTERANCE PATTERNS

As noted previously, nearly all of the initial words are CV or CVCV constructions. Labial (/p, b, m, w/) and alveolar consonants (/t, d/), mostly plosives (/p, b, t, d, g, k/), predominate, but there are occasional fricatives (/s, f/) and nasals (/m, n/). Vowel production varies widely among children and within each child, but the basic triangle of /a/, /i/, and /u/ is probably established early. Within a given word, the consonants initially tend to be the same, as in *baby, mama, daddy, dawdie* (*doggie*). It is the vowels that initially vary. Consonant contrasts or differences occur more frequently in CVC constructions, such as *cup*.

The order of appearance of the first sounds that children acquire—/m/, /w/, /b/, /p/—cannot be explained by the frequency of their appearance in English. Although not the most frequently appearing English sounds, /m/, /w/, and /p/ are the simplest consonants to produce. The /b/ is relatively more complex, although relatively easy to perceive.

PHONOLOGICAL PROCESSES

Phonological processes are systematic procedures used by children to make adult words pronounceable. They enable children to produce an approximation of an adult model. In other words, for a child, phonological processes are a way of getting from an auditory model to speech production. For example, a child may adopt a CV strategy for CVC words, producing /k^/ for *cup* (/k^p/).

Early phonological processes appear to be word-specific. There is a slow expansion and change in a child's phonological system as rules are created and new words are modified to fit a child's existing sound patterns.

Children's phonological processes exhibit tremendous individual variation for several reasons. First, the entire system of each child is constantly changing. Initially, a child may have one phonemic form for several adult words or several forms for the same word. Thus, *baba* may be used for *baby*, *bottle*, and *rabbit*, or both *doddie* and *goggie* may be used for *doggie*. Gradually, a child develops processes that enable him or her to distinguish between similar adult words. For example, a child with the rule CV = /d/V may produce both *no* and *go* as *do* (/doʊ/). The word *key* becomes *dee* (/di/). Over time, the consonant will broaden to allow for more diverse sound production.

Second, some words are produced consistently, while others vary greatly. Within a given word, there may be trade-offs: The acquisition of one part of a word may, in turn, distort another part, which the child produced correctly in the past.

Third, phonological variation may be the result of toddlers' use of differing phonological production processes, such as reduplication, diminutives, assimilation, CVCV construction, open syllables, and consonant cluster reductions (Table 7.7). **Reduplication** occurs when a child attempts a polysyllabic word (*daddy*) but is unable to produce one syllable correctly. The child compensates by repeating the other syllable (*dada*).

The diminutive is formed by adding the vowel /i/, written as *ie*, *y*, or *ee*, to a CVC word, as in *doggie* for *dog* and *fishy* for *fish*, in an attempt to produce a CVCV word. In assimilation, a child does not change the syllables to become the same (that's reduplication) but changes the consonants only. So the word *doggie* often becomes *dawdie* (/dɔdi/) or *gawgie* (/gɔgi/).

Multisyllabic words or words with final consonants are frequently produced in a CV multisyllable form. For example, *teddy bear* becomes /tedibɛ/ (CVCVCV). **Open syllables**—those that end in a vowel—predominate. Closed syllables—those that end in a consonant—occur only at the ends of early words.

Consonant cluster reduction results in single-consonant production, as in *poon* for *spoon*. Differences exist across languages as to which sound—first or second—is usually omitted. Differences reflect the different sound combinations allowable in each language and that language's rules for syllabification.

A child produces those parts of words that are perceptually most salient or noticeable. Auditory saliency is related to relatively low pitch, loudness, and long duration. For similar reasons, children often delete weak syllables, resulting in *nana* for *banana*.

TABLE 7.7 **Common Phonological Rules of Toddlers**

TYPE	EXAMPLES
Reduplication (CVCV)	*Water* becomes *wawa* (/wɑwɑ/)
	Mommy becomes *mama* (/mɑmɑ/)
	Baby becomes *bebie* (/bibi/)
Assimilation	*Dog* becomes *gog* (/gɔg/)
	Candy becomes *cacie* (/kæki/)
CVCV construction	*Horse* becomes *hawsie* (/hɔsi/)
	Duck becomes *ducky* (/dʌki/)
Open syllables	*Blanket* becomes *bakie* (/bæki/)
	Bottle becomes *baba* (/bɑbɑ/)
Consonant cluster reduction	*Stop* becomes *top* (/tɑp/)
	Tree becomes *tee* (/ti/)

Fourth, variation may reflect multiple processes within the same word. The result may only vaguely resemble the target word. For example, *tee* may be used for *treat*. In this example, a child has deleted the final consonant and simplified the consonant cluster. In similar fashion, suppose that a child has one rule that says that clusters reduce to a front consonant, a second that all initial sounds are voiced, and a third that words with a closed syllable ending receive a final vowel. If the target word is *treat*, it might change as follows:

Target Treat
Apply rule 1 (cluster = front C) Peat
Apply rule 2 (initial C = voiced) Beat
Apply rule 3 (CVC = CVCV) Beatie (/biti/)

Of course, this is neither a conscious nor a step-by-step process for the child. The child reduces the complexity of the adult model to a form he or she can produce, leaving adults to figure out the target word.

A child may even produce the same form for two different words. She or he may interpret adult words as having portions to which different rules apply. For example, suppose that the child produces both *spoon* and *pudding* as *poo* (/pu/). Let's see how this could happen. Assume that consonant clusters, such as *sp*, may be reduced to the plosive sound only and that final consonants, such as *n*, omitted. Thus, *spoon* becomes *poo*. If the child also omits unfamiliar sounds, such as *-ing*, *pudding* would become *pud*, which, in turn, with omission of the final consonant, just as in *spoon*, might also be reduced to *poo* (/pu/).

Finally, individual phonological variation may reflect each child's phonological preferences as well. Such preferences might involve different articulatory patterns, classes of sounds, syllable structures, and location in words. Favorite words may conform to the child's production patterns. As the child learns different phonological patterns, he or she applies them to the production of words.

The most frequent phonological process found in children under 30 months of age is consonant cluster reduction, although there is a dramatic drop in the use of this process after 26 months. Syllabic phonological processes decrease rapidly just prior to the second birthday.

LEARNING UNITS AND EXTENSION

Most likely, whole words function as phonetic units. Only later does a child become aware of speech-sound contrasts. The child's "word" is a representation of its adult model. The primacy of words over individual phonemes is reflected in the wide variation in pronunciation across individual words, and the movement of sounds within but not between words.

A child's earliest words are very limited in the number and type of syllables and phonemes. These restraints are gradually relaxed, resulting in greater structural complexity and phonetic diversity. In this progression, a child frequently generalizes from one word to another. Thus, phonological development occurs with changes in the pronunciation of individual words. Some changes result in improved identification of structures and sounds, others in new skills of production, and still others in the application of new phonological rules governing production.

While constructing his or her own phonological system, a child will extend rule hypotheses to other words. As a result, some child "words" will change to versions that are closer to an adult pronunciation, and others will become more unlike this model. In these cases, the rules have been overextended. These changes reflect the acquisition of underlying phonological rules rather than word-by-word or sound-by-sound development.

At minutes 5:47–8:32 of this video you can watch a 30-month-old child speak. Listen to the language the child uses. http://www.youtube.com/watch?v=2i1z37nYMrM

It appears, then, that a child's first language is governed by phonological rules in addition to those for pragmatics, semantics, and syntax. The child invents and applies a succession of phonological rules reflecting increasing phonological organization via a problem-solving, hypothesis-forming process.

Individual Differences

Individual variation occurs both within and across components of early language. Several additional factors may influence early language acquisition, including overall health, cognitive functioning, environment of the home, **otitis media** (middle ear infection), motor speech problems, socioeconomic status, exposure to television, and international adoption and second language learning. Some of these have been mentioned previously.

Typically developing 16-year-olds enjoy normal friendships, whereas children with either language impairment or delay are more likely to exhibit poorer quality interactions (Durkin & Conti-Ramsden, 2007). Toddlers with language delays exhibit more social withdrawal than do typically developing toddlers (Rescorla, Ross, & McClure, 2007).

Otitis media can negatively affect early language development. Fortunately, these negative consequences on both language comprehension and production appear to resolve by the age of 7 and no lingering effects are seen (Zumach, Gerrits, Chenault, & Anteunis, 2010).

Early, chronic exposure to television may have a negative impact on development of children. Both the quantity and quality of parent–child interaction decrease in the presence of background television (Kirkorian, Pempek, Murphy, Schmidt, & Anderson, 2009). Background TV significantly reduces toy play episode length and focused attention during play of toddlers and young preschool children, even when they pay little overt attention to it (Schmidt, Pempek, Kirkorian, Frankenfield Lund, & Anderson, 2008).

BILINGUALISM

The prevalence of bilingualism reflects the cultural mixing within a nation. In an isolated country, such as Iceland, the rather homogeneous nature of the culture is reflected in the scarcity of bilingualism. In the United States, approximately 20% of the population is bilingual, mostly speaking Spanish and English. Other countries may have large bilingual populations because of a large, influential neighbor with a different language, because the official language differs from the indigenous one, or because of a large immigrant population. In the United States, dual-language children are usually treated as different because the majority culture is monolingual. Worldwide, however, dual or multilingual children are at least as numerous as monolingual ones. Bilingual children seem to have metalinguistic advantages over monolingual children (Bialystock, 2001).

True balanced bilingualism, or equal proficiency in two languages, is rare. Nonbalanced bilingualism, in which an individual has obtained a higher level of proficiency in one of the languages, is more common. The language in which the individual is more proficient may not be the native language, which can recede if devalued or used infrequently.

It is also possible for a person to be semiproficient in both languages. This situation may occur for any number of reasons explained later in the chapter.

Decreased proficiency may reflect mixed input. Children who hear "Spanglish" (Spanish + English) in south Florida and in the southwestern United States or "Franglais" (French + English) in parts of Quebec province can be expected to have more mixing in their own language. Examples of Spanglish among Miami adolescents include *chileado* (chilling out), *coolismo* (ultracool or way cool), *eskipeando* (skipping class), *friquado* (freak out), and *¡Que wow!* More detrimental to the learning of either language is the mixing of syntax as in *¿Como puedo ayudarlo?* literally *How can I help you?*, following English word order—in place of the Spanish *¿Que desea?*

In the United States, speakers of English are in a privileged position because English is widely used and valued, and has institutional support; therefore, it has attained a higher status. Speakers of English form a majority ethnolinguistic community. On the other hand, speakers of Spanish or Tagalog, a Filipino language, each represent a minority ethnolinguistic community whose language is given less support, reflecting its less valued status. These relative status differentials differ across communities. For example, in Miami's Little Havana, Spanish has a relatively higher status than it enjoys in other parts of the southern United States, yet in much of the United States, Spanish enjoys relatively higher minority status than Urdu, a Pakistani language, which has many fewer speakers. In a second example, Canada is officially a bilingual country of two majority languages, although English has relatively higher status in most parts of the country. In Quebec, however, the relative differential is reversed.

There is a not-so-subtle prejudice against other languages in the general U.S. culture, and American English speakers may respond to these languages stereotypically. Unfortunately, recognition of this prejudice can even be seen in the speech of bilingual adults. For example, when talking with a Spanish-speaking Anglo, Latino adults tend to Americanize Spanish words, but they do not do so with a Latino audience.

Bilingual Language Learning

Several factors account for the variability across children in second-language acquisition (Kohnert & Goldstein, 2005; Scheffner Hammer et al., 2012). These include the age at which a child receives input in each language, the environment in which the language occurs, the community support and social prestige of each language, differences and similarities in the languages, individual factors such as motivation and language-learning aptitude, and maternal characteristics. Maternal characteristics, including education, generational status, and language proficiency, are key parental factors. Higher maternal education is associated with the children's better English vocabularies, faster English vocabulary development, and greater knowledge of English (Bohman, Bedore, Peña, Mendez-Perez, & Gillam, 2010; Golberg, Paradis, & Crago, 2008; Portes & Rumbaut, 2001).

A child who learns two languages also learns two cultures, a double learning task, especially if the languages and cultures are particularly dissimilar. Both languages and cultures are learned through interactions with caregivers and others. Language is central to the process of learning culture, and cultural patterns teach children the appropriate way to communicate. The intertwined nature of the process is called **language socialization** (Genesee, Paradis, & Crago, 2004).

Simultaneous Acquisition Simultaneous acquisition is the development of two languages prior to age 3. Simultaneous bilingual acquisition can be characterized by initial language mixing, followed by a slow separation and increasing awareness of the differences. In final separation of the phonological and grammatical systems there may be enduring influence of the dominant system in vocabulary and idioms.

In spite of the bilingual linguistic load, the child acquires both languages at a rate comparable to that of monolingual children. There is little difference in the size and diversity of the lexicons of monolingual and bilingual toddlers, and later syntactic and reading development in both languages appears typical (Abu-Rabia & Siegel, 2002; Junker & Stockman, 2002; Peña, Bedore, & Rappazzo, 2003). The degree of dissimilarity between the two languages does not appear to affect the rate of acquisition. The key to development is the consistent use of the two languages within their primary-use environments.

As you know, the connections between cognition and language are complex and multidimensional. A young child learning two languages simultaneously must be able not only to discriminate speech sounds but also to remember language-related information.

Infants exposed to two languages simultaneously are able to discriminate words in both languages at the same age as children exposed to only one language can discriminate words in that language (Polka & Sundara, 2003). Similarly, the babbling of 10- to 12-month-olds reflects the language or languages to which they have been exposed (Maneva & Genesee, 2002).

There may be three stages in the simultaneous acquisition of two languages in young children. During the first stage, a child has two separate lexical systems, reflecting the child's capacity to differentiate between the two languages prior to speaking (Petitto et al., 2001). Vocabulary words rarely overlap. When there is an overlap, the child does not treat the words as equals. Initially, words from both languages are combined indiscriminately. Rather than signifying a mixing of the two languages, this may be an example of overextension. A child uses whatever vocabulary he or she has available. Mixing of grammatical elements may reflect a lack of development of structures in either language.

In the initial stage of simultaneous bilingual development, children may actually have two different language systems that they are able to use in different contexts or in functionally different ways. Thus, a child may use one system with adults of one language and one with adults of the other.

Although a child may store some words in only one language, approximately 30% of bilingual toddlers' vocabularies consist of word equivalents from both languages. In other words, a toddler has two words for the same referent, such as *gato* in Spanish and *cat* in English (Nicoladis & Secco, 2000; Pearson, Fernandez, & Oller, 1995). Thus, at least in part, bilingual children establish two vocabularies from the beginning.

Although monolingual toddlers can learn minimally different words (e.g., *bih* and *dih*) by 17 months of age, bilingual toddlers take until 20 months (Fennell, Byers-Heinlein, & Werker, 2007). This may indicate the bilingual child's use of phonemic information versus whole-word learning, possibly due to the increased burden of learning two languages. Even so, this delay is minimal and may be helpful in bilingual word learning.

In the second stage, a child has two distinct lexicons but applies the same syntactic rules to both. This lexical generalization process is difficult and occurs slowly. A child must separate a word from its specific context and identify it with the corresponding word in the other language. Each word tends to remain tied to the particular context in which it was learned, and corresponding words are not usually learned simultaneously. The child is able to move between the two lexicons and to translate words freely. Unfortunately, this flexibility is not found at the syntactic level. The nonparallel sequence of syntactic learning reflects the difference in linguistic difficulty of particular syntactic structures within the two languages. In general, a child learns structures common to both languages first, the simpler constructions before the more complex. Thus, if a construction is more complex in one language, it will be learned first in the other language in its simpler form.

Finally, in the third stage, a child correctly produces lexical and syntactic structures from each language. Although there is still a great deal of interference, in which one language affects the other, it is mostly confined to the syntactic level.

Although as preschoolers bilingual children make grammatical errors, there is little evidence of reliance on only one language (Paradis, Nicoladis, & Genesee, 2000). This does not mean that influence by either language is nonexistent. Nor do the languages develop in perfect synchrony. Language dominance, the language in which a child has relatively more proficiency, depends on the amount of input a child receives in that language.

All children acquiring two languages simultaneously exhibit some code mixing, which can include both small units—such as sounds, morphemes, and words—and large units—such as phrases and clauses. Studies involving various combinations of two languages being learned simultaneously indicate that children's code mixing is systematic and conforms to the grammatical rules of the two languages (Allen, Genesee, Fish, & Crago, 2002; Genesee & Sauve, 2000). Individual differences across children include the amount and type of mixing.

As few as 2% of bilingual preschoolers' utterances contain some mixing. In general, mixes are used when a child lacks an appropriate word in one language or when the mixed entry is a more salient word to the child. The child's mixing seems to result from mixed adult input. For Spanish-speaking children in the United States, mixing consists primarily of inserting English nouns into Spanish utterances.

To decrease interference, a child may try to keep the two languages as separate as possible, associating each with a particular person or location. As a child becomes more familiar with the syntactic differences, the tendency to label people with a certain language decreases. A child becomes truly bilingual and can manage two separate languages well by about age 7.

Bilingual children may develop separate language systems that are interdependent (Paradis, 2001). *Interdependence* is seen in the processes of transfer, deceleration, and acceleration in bilingual language acquisition. In transfer, speech sounds specific to one language will transfer to productions of the other language. Transfer has been found to occur in a bidirectional manner. Each language influences the other.

Deceleration occurs when phonological development emerges at a slower rate in bilingual children than in monolingual children. Interaction between the two languages may interfere with acquisition of some linguistic features and thus result in poorer linguistic skills in bilinguals compared with monolinguals (Gildersleeve-Neumann, Kester, Davis, & Peña, 2008; Goldstein & Washington, 2001). At the same time, some aspects of language may be accelerated because interaction between the two languages of bilingual children facilitates the acquisition process and thus results in superior linguistic skills in bilinguals compared with monolinguals (Kehoe, Trujillo, & Lleó, 2001; Lleó, Kuchenbrandt, Kehoe, & Trujillo, 2003). The effects of interdependence will vary with the two languages, specific language features, and the age of the child (Fabiano-Smith & Goldstein, 2010).

When we look at only one language, we find that monolingual 2-year-old children are more advanced in their development of both vocabulary and grammar than bilingual children. When we include data from both languages, bilingual children have comparable vocabularies (Hoff et al., 2012). As you might expect, among bilingual children, development in either language is related to the amount of input in that language.

Bilingual children who may be proficient in both languages as preschoolers often shift dominance later to the majority language, typically the language used in school. If the trend continues, a child may not be a bilingually proficient teen or adult.

The truly bilingual person possesses a dual system simultaneously available during processing. In addition, semantic input may be processed in each language regardless of the language of input. Most information is processed at the semantic level because the interpretation of surface syntax requires much greater proficiency.

My Colombian "granddaughter" Natalia, a very bright preschooler, came to the United States when she was 5 months old with her bilingual Spanish-English, college-educated parents. At home, her parents and their friends spoke Spanish. When she began attending an English-only daycare around age 1, her parents were advised to stop speaking Spanish at home. Luckily, they ignored the recommendation.

At first, Natalia spoke very little at daycare, and, when she did begin to use English, it was often mixed with Spanish. At home her parents continued to speak to her in Spanish. When Natalia was 30 months old, her grandmother (who speaks limited but serviceable English) and her great-grandmother (who speaks only Spanish) came from Bogotá for a visit. To my sheer delight, Natalia conversed easily with her great-grandmother in Spanish, switched to English for me, and negotiated Spanish and English with her grandmother. When her grandmother became confused by English, Natalia smoothly transitioned to Spanish for an explanation, then back to English.

Cross-Language Adoptions: A Special Case

In 2012, approximately 9,000 children were adopted from other countries. Nearly 60% of these children come from China, Ethiopia, Ukraine, and Haiti (U.S. Department of State, 2014). Infants and toddlers adopted from countries with a different language and culture undergo a unique language learning experience. Development in the birth language (L1) is arrested and replaced by development of the adopted language (L2) because adoptive families usually are unable to maintain the birth language (Glennen & Masters, 2002). L1 atrophies very quickly. For example, even in rather late adoptions, such as 4- to 8-year-old Russian-speaking children, most of the expressive language is lost within three to six months (Gindis, 1999). If you want to pursue this unique language acquisition process further, I recommend the excellent review by Glennen (2002).

Up to 88% of these children were initially raised in orphanages, which in itself may pose special challenges. Children raised in developing world orphanages show substantial language delays, with some not yet producing intelligible words in their native language at 30 months of age (Windsor et al., 2007). Subsequent foster care or the presence of a preferred caregiver in an institution can facilitate language growth.

Rapid switching from one language to another is difficult even for an infant. Remember, an infant as early as 10 months of age is able to recognize language patterns in L1. If adopted after that age, a child must learn to discriminate patterns in the new language. Initially, adopted infants lag behind native English-speaking children but they follow the same developmental pattern (Glennen & Masters, 2002). If adopted as infants or toddlers, most children will exhibit the same language abilities as monolingual English-speaking preschoolers after as little as two years (Roberts, Pollock et al., 2005). By early elementary school, most children adopted from China have average to above

several hours' drive apart, my granddaughter Cassidy and I would often take different roles on the phone as we played variations on a favorite movie or book.

The ability to carry a role through story play is reflected in the 4-year-old's language. The child can tell simple stories of his or her own or others' authorship. Increased language skills enable the child to form more complex sentences. Vocabulary has increased to 1,500–1,600 words, with approximately 15,000 used each day.

In general, 4-year-olds are very social beings who have the linguistic skills and the short-term memory to be good, if somewhat limited, conversationalists. My daughter Jessica, now an adult, teasingly asked a 4-year-old for a date. He responded, "No, I'm not grown up yet, but we could go to dinner as a family." Four-year-olds are anxious to exhibit their knowledge and abilities.

Pragmatic Development

In general, children learn language within a conversational context. For most children, the chief conversational partner is an adult, usually a parent. As children broaden their social networks to include those beyond the immediate family, they modify their self-esteem and self-image and become more aware of social standards. Their language reflects this larger network and the need for increased communicative clarity and perspective.

During the preschool years, a child acquires many conversational skills. Still, much of a child's conversation concerns the immediate context, and he or she has much to learn about the conventional routines of conversation. Even though a child has learned to take turns, conversations are short and the number of turns is limited. These skills will be refined during the school years. Notice how creatively the children in Box 8.1 use language within a routine situation.

A longer dialogue is presented in Table 8.1. The child is 32 months old. This conversation was collected in the home and is also a conversation between a child and her mother. The two are engaged in role play with a child's sink, table, and dishes. The mother's speech is complicated by her taking two roles: that of the baby, Michelle, and that of another person in the situation. The child plays herself as the mother of Michelle. The adult uses turnabouts to a greater extent than the mother in the first segment. Expansion is very limited and occurs only after child utterance 24. In general, the child is very responsive. As might be expected, this preschooler's greater output of language compared to the toddler in Table 7.1 also demonstrates many more language features. Both children have much variety in their language and initiate and respond to conversation.

Much of a preschooler's conversation still occurs within mother–child dialogs. This context is a significant influence on language learning. Even though a child is becoming

BOX 8.1

Imaginative Conversation of Two 60-Month-Old Children

J: Let's play house. Okay? This is mine. You're the father and I'm the mother. (To baby) Oh, sweetie. You want me to wash you? (To T) I have to wash her. I'll play with my baby.

T: Pretend this is her liver and the kidney of the . . .

J: (Interrupting) This is our baby's!

T: . . . of the, of the yucky bacon.

J: You're disgusting.

T: Okay. I'm cutting up the liver.

TABLE 8.1 Early Preschool Language Sample

1. She wants some coffee.
   Oh, well, do you have a cup? Where's it at?
2. I don't know where in here.
   Well, just find a cup for her. This is her cereal.
3. Don't know where is it.
   Well, she can't have coffee.
4. Can't have coffee.
5. What's that?
   Coffee.
6. She have coffee?
   Okay. Do you want to feed her and I'll finish ironing?
7. Yeah.
   Okay. Boy, this iron gets hot.
8. What do you do?
   I burned myself.
9. Oh.
   I got burned.
10. Oh, let me . . .
11. No, it's not hot.
    Pshew.
12. It's coldy.
13. I touch it.
    Oh, I think it's hot. Feel it.
14. It's coldy.
    I think it's hot. Okay, the ironing's finished. What are you feeding her?
15. The apple.
16. Michelle eat cereal.
    Gee, okay.
17. She wants some, some, some coffee.
    Oops.
18. That's her coffee.
    Okay, I'll pour some more. Oh, my goodness.
19. It's hot.
    I better put this back on the stove, don't you think?
20. Yeah, don't think.
    Where's the milk?
21. In the refrigerator.
    Okay, let me get some milk. There, got her bottle ready for you.
22. All right.
    Okay.

23. She eated it all-done.

24. She has to go sleep.
    She has to go to sleep. Well well, you better wipe her face.

25. Oh.
    Gee, J., you don't know what you're doing, do you?

26. Yeah.
    Oh, come here, Michelle. Oh, she's still hungry. Can you feed her some more?

27. She wants one that's good.
    Oh.

28. I fix.
    What are you fixing now?

29. I fixing her cereal.
    Oh, the poor little baby's so hungry. Don't you ever feed her?

30. Yeah.
    I think you need to buy her . . .

31. She want some bottle.
    Okay, you color doggie on this.

a fuller conversational participant, mother is still very much in control, creating and maintaining the dialog. This conversational asymmetry continues throughout the preschool period.

Conversational formats and routines provide a scaffolding or support for a preschooler that frees cognitive processing for more linguistic exploration and experimentation. In part, scaffolding and a child's increased cognitive abilities and knowledge enable her or him to talk about nonpresent referents. This more decontextualized language emerges around 18 to 24 months. When a mother discusses past or future events, she tends to rely on their shared knowledge of known, routine, or scripted events, such as going to McDonald's or to a birthday party. This event knowledge is the topic over 50% of the time. With their 2- to 2½-year-olds, mothers talk about specific past events, such as going to the zoo, and future routine events, such as the upcoming bath time.

In addition to conversation, a preschool child engages in monologs. These self-conversations, with no desire to involve others, may account for 20% to 30% of the utterances of 4-year-olds. Although 3-year-olds use monologs in all types of activities when alone, 4-year-olds are more selective and are most likely to use "private speech" only in sustained, focused goal-directed activities such as drawing a picture (Winsler, Carlton, & Barry, 2000).

The presleep monologs of many children are rich with songs, sounds, nonsense words, bits of chitchat, verbal fantasies, and expressions of feelings. Some children engage in presleep self-dialog in which they take on both roles.

Gradually, a child's monologs become more social. In general, throughout the preschool years, audible monolog behavior declines with age, but inaudible self-talk increases. Self-talk decreases after age 10 but doesn't disappear. As adults, most of us still talk to ourselves occasionally, especially when we believe we're alone.

In the following sections, we'll explore the conversational context of preschool language development and a child's conversational abilities and describe the development of narration or storytelling.

THE CONVERSATIONAL CONTEXT

In general, a 2-year-old is able to respond to his or her conversational partner and to engage in short dialogs of a few turns on a given topic. The child can also introduce or change the topic of discussion, although he or she is limited in the choice of topics available. In addition, a 2-year-old has limited conversational skills, although he or she learned turn taking as an infant. Within mother–child conversations, a child learns to maintain a conversational flow and to take the listener's perspective. The preschooler is aided by mother's facilitative behaviors mentioned in Chapter 6. In general, mother and child each engage in roughly 30% opening or initiating and 60% responding behaviors. Initiating behaviors include introductions of a new topic, referrals to a previous one for the purpose of shifting the topic, and deliberate invitations for the partner to respond, such as a question. Responding behaviors include acknowledgments (*I see, uh-huh*), yes/no responses, answers, repetitions, sustaining or reformulated responses, and extensions/replies. Mothers maneuver the conversation by inviting verbal responses.

Let's eavesdrop on a conversation with a 2½-year-old. Notice the pragmatic skills being used. http://www.youtube.com/watch?v=4Y5nbStljel

Child Conversational Skills

When initiating conversations with peers, preschool children mention a person—most often the listener—over 70% of the time with a particular interest in mental states (*think, feel, remember*). This behavior suggests that preschoolers are using their developing Theory of Mind (ToM) in finding common ground with peers (O'Neill, Main, & Ziemski, 2009). Theory of Mind will be discussed in detail in a later section of this chapter, but for now remember that ToM is realizing that others have their own thoughts and perspectives.

A young child is good at introducing topics in which he or she is interested but has difficulty sustaining that topic beyond one or two turns. Frequent introduction of topics results in few contingent responses by the child. Contingent speech is influenced by and dependent on the preceding utterance of the partner, as when one speaker replies to the other. Fewer than 20% of a young preschooler's responses may be relevant to the partner's previous utterance. This percentage increases with a child's age.

Building a bridge between the next and previous speaker's turns is especially difficult. By age 3, a child can engage in longer dialogs beyond a few turns, although spontaneous speech is still easier than the contingent or connected speech found in more mature conversations. With increased age, a preschooler gains the ability to maintain a topic, which in turn results in fewer new topics being introduced within a given conversation. Nearly 50% of 5-year-olds can sustain certain topics through about a dozen turns. Whether they do depends on the topic, the partner, and the intention of the child. The number of utterances within a single turn also varies with a child's intention (Logan, 2003). Multi-utterance turns containing longer, more complex utterances typically serve an assertive function. Note the increase in utterances per turn as the child in Box 8.2 tries to influence her partner's behavior.

Preschool children's reactions to explanatory and nonexplanatory adult information confirm that young children are motivated to seek causal information actively and to use specific conversational strategies in doing so (Frazier, Gelman, & Wellman, 2009). In general, children are more likely to agree and to ask follow-up questions in response to adult explanations and are more likely to re-ask their original question and provide their own explanation following nonexplanations.

There is a large increase in the amount of verbal responding between ages 24 and 30 months. A 30-month-old is, in addition, often successful at engaging her listener's attention and responding to listener feedback. For many children, there is an increase in overall talkativeness at around 36 months of age. Many 3-year-olds and even more 4-year-olds chatter away seemingly nonstop. The largest proportion of their speech is socially directed.

BOX 8.2

Increased Utterances for Control

THE 52-MONTH-OLD CHILD is trying to get the adult to capture some ducks for petting.

CHILD: If we be quiet maybe they'll come up. And if we pretend we're statues maybe they'll come up and try to peck us. And then we can grab them.
ADULT: I don't think that's going to work.
CHILD: I think it is. It might if we stay here for a long time. They'll come peck us, then we can stick out our hands and grab 'em like that.
ADULT: I don't think it is. They're tricky.
CHILD: I think you should go down there and put one on a rope. And then you can tie it in the garage and then we can pet it and . . . hold it for a long time. And they won't be able to get away.

And later . . .

CHILD: Maybe, maybe if we're more quieter and we do it together, we can get 'em. Over there, maybe, if we hold a rock. Let's right up here and maybe when they come up here they can pick it. And we c-can get a leash, then we can grab them when they come near us. And then we'll have one and then we can tie it around the house and the garage. And everyone can see it . . . when they come here.

A 2-year-old considers the conversational partner only in small measure by providing descriptive details to aid comprehension. He or she uses pronouns, however, without previously identifying the entity to which they refer, as in initiating a conversation with "I not like *it*." Between ages 3 and 4, a child seems to gain a better awareness of the social aspects of conversation. In general, utterances addressed to conversational partners are clear, well formed, and well adapted for the listener. By age 4, a child demonstrates a form of child-directed speech (CDS) when addressing very young children. This use of register or style is evidence of a growing awareness of conversational roles.

Becoming more aware of the listener's shared assumptions or presuppositions, a 3- to 4-year-old child uses more *elliptical* responses that omit shared information. The child need not repeat shared knowledge contained in the partner's questions. If mother asks, "What are you doing?" the preschooler's elliptical response, "Playing," omits the *I am* as redundant information.

A 2-year-old's language is used in imaginative ways and in expressions of feeling, often "I'm tired" or "I hungry." By age 4, a child uses twice as many utterances as a child of 3, discussing feelings and emotions. My children constantly amazed me with their affective responses. Once at Christmas, my 4-year-old son Todd comforted a recently widowed elderly neighbor by stating, "I hope our lights will make you happy."

There is also a related shift in verb usage with less use of *go* and *do*. By age 5, a child uses *be* and *do* predominantly. This change indicates that the child is speaking more about state, attitude, or feeling and less about action.

A preschool child appears to be aware of the conventions of turn taking but does not use as many turnabout behaviors as adults. By age 2 simultaneous talking has decreased significantly and the more mature alternating pattern found in conversations is predominant (Elias & Broerse, 1996). Conversational turn taking between mothers and their 2- to

2½-year-old children is very smooth. Less than 5% of the turns of either participant are interrupted by the other partner. As a 3-year-old becomes more aware of the social aspects of discourse, he or she acknowledges the partner's turn with fillers, such as *yeah* and *uh-huh*. Preschool children learning languages as different as Japanese and English find it easy to follow maternal linguistic cues to turn taking.

Throughout the preschool period, about 60% of child–partner exchanges are characterized by a child's attempts to control the partner's behavior or to relay information. Preschool boys are more likely than girls to use the word *no* to correct or prohibit a peer's behavior. Girls use *no* more to reject or deny a playmate's proposition or suggestion. By kindergarten age, a child is able to cloak intentions more skillfully and to use indirect requests. The exchange of information has gained in importance throughout the preschool years, however, and by age 4 is clearly the most important function, accounting for nearly 40% of these exchanges. Other exchanges serve functions such as establishing and maintaining social relations, teaching, managing and correcting communication, expressing feelings, and talking to self.

Register By age 4, children can assume various roles, especially in their play. Roles require different styles of speaking called registers. CDS, discussed in Chapter 6, is a register. Children as young as age 4 demonstrate use of register when they use a form of CDS to address younger children.

Competence with different registers varies with age and experience (Anderson, 1992). The ability to play various family roles, such as mother or baby, appears early in play. Roles outside the family require more skill, possibly even technical-sounding jargon, as when playing a nurse, teacher, or auto mechanic. When my daughter was 5, she loved to play hair salon, using all the terms that accompanied that activity and using me as the customer. Younger children prefer familiar roles.

Pitch and loudness levels are the first variations used by preschoolers to denote differing roles. Often, louder voices are used for adult males. Later variations include the average or mean length of the utterances and the choice of topics and vocabulary.

There are some gender differences. Girls assume more roles, speak more, and modify their register more to fit the roles. Due to socialization, boys may be more conscious of assuming gender roles that might be interpreted as inappropriate.

One aspect of register is politeness, achieved by using polite words (*please, thank you*), a softer tone of voice, and more indirect requests (*May I have a cookie please?* instead of *Gimme a cookie*). Use of these devices varies with the conversational partner and with the age of a child. For example, 2- to 5-year-olds use more commands with other preschoolers and more permission requests (*Can I . . . , May I . . .*) with older children and adults. Imperatives (*sit down, come over here*) also may be used with superiors, and their compliance, followed by a younger child's sly smile, indicates that the child knows she or he has scored a coup. Although even 2-year-olds are capable of using *please* and a softer tone, it is not until age 5 that children recognize that indirect requests are more polite (McCloskey, 1986). This recognition occurs in other languages with indirect forms, such as Italian, at about the same age.

Conversational Repair Young children use questions and contingent queries or requests for clarification (*What? , Huh? , I don't understand*), to initiate or continue an exchange, but not to the extent that adults do when addressing young children. Approximately one fourth of the requests for clarification of 2-year-olds are nonverbal, such as showing a confused expression. As preschoolers mature, nonverbal methods decrease as the primary means of communicating confusion.

Approximately one third of preschoolers' clarification requests seek general or nonspecific information (*What? , Huh?*). A child may lack the ability to state exactly what is desired, however, in part because he or she has difficulty determining what is misunderstood. It is not until mid-elementary school that a child develops the ability to make well-informed specific requests for clarification.

Although 2½-year-olds are able to respond to requests for clarification, they do not respond consistently and do not resolve the breakdown about a third of the time when they do. Young preschoolers have more success with requests for clarification that follow their own requests for action ("Throw the ball at Tobey") rather than to those that follow their assertions or declarations ("I saw a rhinohorserus"). From a purely selfish point of view, they want their requests comprehended correctly.

A preschooler is not always successful in clarifying his or her message. Usually, a preschooler is unable to reformulate the message in response to a facial expression of noncomprehension and must be specifically requested to clarify. The most common clarification strategy among preschoolers is a simple repetition, especially if the request is a nonspecific "Huh?" or "What?" The abilities to clarify and to organize information more systematically do not develop until mid-elementary school. Children as young as 3 do seem to be able to recognize the need to clarify their own gestures, however, and can modify their behavior accordingly (O'Neill & Topolovec, 2000).

If you've listened to a 2½-year-old speak, you know that her or his production is not smooth. Rather, there are revisions and pauses or "stalls" as the child changes the sentence form or searches for the correct word (Rispoli & Hadley, 2001). Understanding children's revisions may be crucial to our knowledge of how sentence production is regulated or monitored.

In monitoring, the intended message is compared with the actual sentence output. In other words, a central monitoring mechanism in the brain receives input from both the produced language and the internal representation. Some revisions, such as phonological ones, may occur as the speech is being produced, while others, such as matching intent with the produced utterance, may take longer and await the entire utterance before the child can make a judgment (Hartsuiker & Kolk, 2001; Oomen & Postma, 2001).

Stalls add or change nothing to the linguistic structure being produced. These pauses or interruptions include

- long silent pauses,
- pauses filled with *um* or *uh,* and
- repetitions of material already produced while a child picks up the lost thread of what he or she was about to say (Rispoli, Hadley, & Holt, 2008).

It is possible that stalls result from the differing processing rates between higher-level linguistic processing and lower-level and quicker speech processing. When a slowdown occurs at a higher level and an individual has already begun to speak, he or she is forced to stall. The sources of stalls are heterogeneous and may result from planning problems that leave a speaker temporarily with nothing to articulate, from an inability to rapidly retrieve a lexical item, or from covert speech repairs.

Developmental changes in revision rate seem to reflect changes in children's ability to monitor their language production (Rispoli et al., 2008). For example, at 27 months of age, revisions occur in approximately 1% of children's sentences, the equivalent of 1 revised sentence in every 100 active declarative sentences, and increase with age. Interestingly, no comparable change is seen in pauses, which are approximately of 9 to 10 stalls per 100 sentences from age 27 to 33 months, although much individual variation exists. Stall rates increase significantly with a sentence's length, whereas revision rate remains constant. It's possible that many short utterances contain rote or memorized phrases, such as *How are you?* or *See you later,* that bypass encoding and monitoring processes used more extensively in longer utterances. In other words, stalls and revisions are different phenomenon representing different processes.

Two-and-a-half-year-old bilingual children are capable of repairing communication breakdowns by switching languages to match that of their partner (Comeau, Genesee, & Mendelson, 2007). Interestingly, they avoided this repair strategy when attempting to repair breakdowns that are not based on language differences. This behavior indicates that even very young bilingual children are capable of identifying their language choice as a cause of a communication breakdown and that they can differentiate these types of breakdown from others. Remember Natalia and her grandmother from Chapter 7?

Topic Introduction, Maintenance, and Closure A **topic** can be defined as the content about which we speak. Topics are identified by name as they are introduced. You might say, "I had escargot last night," in an attempt to establish the topic of eating snails. I might reply, "Oh, did you like them?" Now, we are sharing a topic. My reply was an agreement to accept the topic. Not all topics are as direct. For example, the utterance "Well, what did you think of the rally last night?" might be used to establish several different topics, depending on the manner in which it is stated.

In a larger sense, a topic is the cohesion in a conversation. Through skillful manipulation of the topic, we as participants can make a conversation successful or unsuccessful. For example, the topic of professional sports will work in conversation with many adult males; needlepoint, French cuisine, and American folk art may not. There are conversational partners, however, who could converse on any of these topics for hours.

Once introduced by identification, the topic is maintained by each conversational partner's commenting with additional information; altering the focus of the topic, called *shading*; or requesting more information. The topic is changed by introducing a new one, reintroducing a previous one, or ending the conversation.

At first, an infant attracts attention to self as the topic. By age 1, an infant is highly skilled at initiating a topic by a combination of glances, gestures, vocalizations, and verbalizations, although he or she is limited to topics about items that are physically present. At this age topics typically are maintained for only one or two turns. Only about half of the utterances of children younger than 2 are on the established topic. Child utterances on the topic usually consist of imitations of the adult or of new related information. Extended topic maintenance beyond a turn or two seems to be possible only within well-established routines. These routines, such as bathing or dressing, provide a structure for the discourse, thus relieving a young child of the (for now) nearly impossible task of conversational planning.

By age 2, a child is capable of maintaining a topic in adjacent pairs of utterances. These utterances follow a pattern, such as question/answer. A mature language partner usually offers the toddler choices, as in "Do you like candy or ice cream best?"; asks questions; or makes commands or offers. In this way, the mature partner interprets events for the child and scaffolds or structures the conversation for coherence.

Between ages 2 and 3, a child gains a limited ability to maintain coherent topics. By age 3½, about three fourths of a child's utterances are on the established topic. Topics may last through more turns when children are enacting familiar scenarios or engaging in sociodramatic play, describing a physically present object or an ongoing event, and problem solving. Shorter topics may occur when capturing someone's attention, establishing a play situation, and ensuring cooperation while assigning toys or roles. Notice the rapid topic change in the conversation in Box 8.3.

Repetition is one tactic used by preschoolers to remain on a topic. In the following conversation, the child imitates the adult skillfully:

> ADULT: Later, we'll go to the store for daddy's birthday present.
> CHILD: Go store for daddy's present.
> ADULT: Um-hum, should we get him a new electric razor?
> CHILD: Yeah, new razor.

Even 5-year-olds continue to use frequent repetition to acknowledge, provide cohesion, and fill turns. Still, topics change quickly, and 5-year-olds may discuss as many as 50 different topics within 15 minutes.

BOX 8.3

Rapid Topic Change

DANNY IS 40 MONTHS and Matthew is 34 months.

D: What do you want for dessert? The cake is devil's food.
M: I would pick my cup.
D: Let's play with this. What is it? A puppet? A puppet!
M: I'm pooped. I'm a lion.
D: Oh.
M: I could be a wolf. I could be a wolf. Gr-r-r. I have to eat that food.
D: I'll knife the wolf. You're dead.
M: No.
D: It's my Jello. Look at these toys. Let's pick them up.
M: Oh, the mirror. I see you.
D: Here's a spoon.
M: Let's be cowboys.

Presuppositional: Adaptation to the Listener's Knowledge Presupposition, as we mentioned earlier, is the process whereby a speaker makes background assumptions about a listener's knowledge. This occurs on several levels. The speaker needs to be aware of the listener's word meanings and knowledge of the social context and conversational topic. You and I can't have a meaningful conversation if you don't understand either the words I'm using or the topic. Every one of us has had to stop a speaker—usually someone close to us—at some time and say, "I don't have any idea what you're talking about." We were unable to identify the topic.

In general, a preschool child becomes increasingly adept at knowing what information to include, how to arrange it, and which particular lexical items and linguistic forms to use. This ability emerges gradually. Some linguistic forms are used as presuppositional tools. These include articles, demonstratives, pronouns, proper nouns, some verbs, *wh*-questions, and forms of address. The definite article (*the*), pronouns, demonstratives (*this, that, these, those*), and proper names refer to specific entities that, it is presupposed, both the speaker and the listener can identify.

The form of address used is based on presuppositions relative to the social situation. As speakers, we address only certain people as *dear* or *honey* or by their nicknames. These forms are not used with strangers or with people in positions of authority over us. I remember that when I was a child my grandmother and her sisters used nicknames to relate to each other, but we children were forbidden to follow this practice.

The choice of topic itself is based on an assumption of participant knowledge or at least interest. Once the topic is introduced, each participant generally presupposes that the other knows what the topic is, so there is no need to keep restating it. New topics or information are generally introduced in the final position or near the end of a sentence, marked with the indefinite article *a* or *an*, and emphasized to signal the listener, as in "Did you buy a car?"

Acquiring presuppositional skills requires learning to use many linguistic devices. Thus, the acquisition process extends well into school age.

Prior to age 3, most children do not understand the effect of not providing enough information for their listener. By age 3, however, they are generally able to determine the amount of information a listener needs. Children usually mention the most informative items first, as in the following example:

> ADULT: What happened yesterday?
> CHILD: I went to the doctor and got a needle. (Rather than "I got up, had breakfast, then brushed my teeth, and . . .")

Three-year-olds are able to adjust their answers based on their decisions of what the listener knows and does not know. Thus, the more knowledgeable listener receives even more information and more elaborate descriptions while receiving less redundant information.

Most 3-year-olds also can distinguish between definite (*the*) and indefinite (*a*, *an*) articles. At this age, they use the articles with approximately 85% accuracy. If a preschooler makes errors in usage, it is usually because he or she has assumed erroneously that the listener shares the referent. For example, the child might say, "I liked *the* popsicles," the definite article being used without first introducing the referent. Are we discussing popsicles taken from the freezer or bought from a vendor? When? Where? This same error of assuming a shared referent is also evident in the use of pronouns. For example, the topic in "I liked it" is difficult to determine. Even older preschool children may point to the referent rather than identify it verbally, presupposing that the listener understands. The referent may be even more ambiguous if it is not present.

Some verbs, such as *know* and *remember*, when used before a *that + clause* construction, presuppose the truthfulness of the clause that follows. In the following sentences, the speaker is conveying a belief in the truthfulness of the ending clause:

> I know that you have a red dress.
> I remember that the cat was asleep in this chair.

Not all verbs presuppose the truth of the following clause, as in the case of "I think . . . ." In this instance, the speaker is not as certain as when he says, "I know . . . ."

Verbs such as *know*, *think*, *forget*, and *remember* are used correctly as presuppositional tools by age 4. Prior to age 4 children use *think* and *know* to regulate an interaction (*You know how*) not to refer to a mental state (*I know my letters*). At about age 3½ my granddaughter would ponder great thoughts, then say things like "I think that you look a little darker" (to a suntanned Asian friend) or "I feel like playing Shrek." Children's use of these words reflects that of their mothers (Furrow, Moore, Davidge, & Chiasson, 1992). By age 5 or 6, a child understands the use of other verbs, such as *wish*, *guess*, and *pretend* (Moore, Harris, & Patriquin, 1993). These verbs presuppose that the following clause is false. Thus, when I say, "I wish I had a pony," it is assumed that I do not. Verbs such as *say*, *whisper*, and *believe* are not comprehended by most children until age 7.

Questions are used to gain more information about a presupposed fact. In the example "What are you eating?" it is presupposed that the listener is eating. In "Where is the party?" the speaker presupposes that there is one and that the listener knows its location.

The use of devices, such as word order, stress, and ellipsis, changes with age. In early two-word combinations, toddlers place new information first, as in "Doggie eat," establishing *doggie* as the topic. This practice declines with longer, more adultlike utterances in favor of the more widely used last position, as in "Wasn't that a great picnic?" establishing *picnic* as the topic. Children also use stress at the two-word stage to mark new information for the listener. With age, children become even more reliable in their use of this device.

Ellipsis Ellipsis is used more selectively and with greater sophistication as the child's language and conversations become more complex. Through **ellipsis**, mentioned previously, the speaker omits redundant information that has been previously stated, thereby assuming that the listener knows this information. For example, in response to "Who is baking cookies?" the speaker says, "I am," leaving out the redundant information "baking cookies."

Directives and Requests The purpose of directives and requests is to get others to do things for the speaker. The form can be direct or indirect, conventional, or nonconventional. Examples include:

Stop that! (direct)
Could you get the phone? (indirect, conventional)
Phew, it's hot in here. (indirect, nonconventional)

In the first example, the goal is clearly stated or direct. In the second, the form appears to be a question, although the speaker is not really interested in whether the listener has the ability to perform the task; the ability is assumed. The form is conventional and polite. Finally, in the third, an indirect nonconventional form, the goal is not mentioned and cannot be identified by strict syntactic interpretation. It's unconventional because it's not the typical way in which we ask to turn on the air conditioner.

By 2 years of age, a child is able to use some attention-getting words with gestures and rising intonation; however, he or she is often unsuccessful at gaining attention. A child tends to rely on less specific attention-getting forms, such as "Hey," frequently ignored by adults. Request words such as *more*, *want*, and *mine*, problem statements such as *I'm tired* and *I'm hungry*, and verbal routines are common. Two early directive types are the need statement (*I want/need* . . .) and the imperative (*Give me* . . .). Few, if any, indirect forms are used. The child refers to the desired action or object. These requests become clearer with age, and the child identifies all elements of the request, not just what is desired.

Two- to 3-year-olds make politeness distinctions based on the age or size, familiarity, role, territory, and rights of the listener. Often young children will use *please* in a request, especially if the listener is older or bigger, less familiar, in a dominant role, or the possessor of an object or privilege desired.

KidStock/Blend Images/Getty Images

Preschool children can express an ever-expanding set of intentions and can play a variety of language roles.

Action requests, especially indirect ones, addressed to a child are likely to be answered with the action even when information is sought. Thus, when Grandma says, "Can you sing?" and is seeking a simple yes response, she may get a tuneful rendition that she didn't really want. Interpretation seems to be based on past experience and on a child's knowledge of object uses and locations, activity structures, and roles.

At age 3, a child begins to use some modal auxiliary verbs in indirect requests ("*Could* you give me a . . . ?"), permissive directives ("*Can/may* I have a . . . ?"), and question directives ("*May* I have a . . . ?"). Modals are auxiliary or helping verbs that express the speaker's attitude toward the main verb and include *may, might, must, could, should,* and so on. These forms reflect syntactic developments and a child's increasing skill at modifying language to reflect the social situation. Auxiliary verb development will be discussed in Chapter 9.

A 4-year-old is more skilled with indirect forms although still unsuccessful more than half of the time at getting someone else's attention. Only about 6% of all the requests by 42- to 52-month-olds are indirect in nature, although there is a sharp increase in the use of this form at around age 4½. At around age 4, a child becomes more aware of his or her partner's point of view and role, and of the appropriate form of request and politeness required. Examples include "Why don't you . . ." and "Don't forget to . . . ." The child also offers more explanations and justifications for requests. In addition, a 4-year-old is able to respond correctly to forms such as "You should . . . ," "Please . . . ," and "I'll be happy if you . . ." (Carrell, 1981).

A desired goal may be totally masked in a 5-year-old's directive. For example, as my daughter sped to a nearly missed appointment, my 54-month-old granddaughter asked, "Is there a speed limit on this road?" Sufficiently chastised, her mom slowed accordingly. The form of the request may be very different from a child's actual intention. For example, desiring a glass of juice, a child might say, "Now, you be the mommy and make breakfast." Such inferred requests or other nonconventional forms are infrequent, however, even in the language of 5-year-olds. In general, children rely on conventional forms and the use of markers such as *please*.

Five-year-olds continue to increase use of explanations and justifications, especially when there is a chance of noncompliance by the listener. Often the justifications are self-contained statements, such as "I need it" or "I want it," but they may refer to rights, reasons, causes, or norms. Justifications are initially found in children's attempts to stop an activity. My daughter gained neighborhood notoriety for her very precise "Stop it because I do not like it!"

Although she or he has made tremendous gains, a preschooler is still rather ineffectual in making requests or in giving directives. The child needs to become more efficient at gaining a potential listener's attention, more effective in stating the goal, more aware of social role, more persuasive, and more creative in forming requests. The increased complexity of a school-age child's social interactions and the new demands of the school environment require greater facility with directive and request forms.

Deixis In Greek, **deixis** means indicating or pointing. Deictic terms may be used to direct attention, to make spatial contrasts, and to denote times or participants in a conversation from the speaker's point of view. It is not easy for young children to adopt the perspective of another conversational participant. Thus, correct use of these terms indicates a child's pragmatic and cognitive growth. In this section, we discuss the development of *here/there, this/that,* and personal pronouns. As many as 30% of 7-year-olds may have difficulty comprehending some of these deictic contrasts, even those used in their own speech production.

The development of *this, that, here,* and *there* illustrates the difficulties inherent in learning these terms. Mothers use *that* and *there* more frequently than the other two, although children use all four equally. Mothers use these terms most frequently in directing their child's attention. It is not surprising, then, that children use *that* and *there* for directing attention. *There* is also used to note completion. ("There, I finished.")

Later, children use *this* and *here* for directing attention but make little differentiation based on the location of the object of interest. In mature use *this* is near; *that* is far. A child's comprehension is aided by the gestures used by adults.

Gradually, children begin to realize that these terms denote a contrast in location relative to the speaker, although they still experience difficulty with the actual size of the area covered by terms such as *here*. This is made more difficult by the fact that *here* can be used for a variety of references, from "Come *here*," meaning this very spot, to "We have an environmental problem *here*," meaning on the entire Earth.

There are three problems in the acquisition of deictic terms: point of reference, shifting reference, and shifting boundaries. The point of reference is generally the speaker. Hence, when you say the term *here*, you are speaking of a near area. The child must learn that the speaker is the point of reference. This introduces a potential problem because each new speaker creates a new reference point. Terms that shift most frequently seem to be the hardest to learn.

The boundaries of *this/that* and *here/there* shift with the context and are not generally stated by the speaker. For example, the term *here* has very different boundaries in the following two sentences:

Put your money here, please.
We have a democratic form of government here.

In general, proximal terms, such as *this* and *here*, are usually easier to learn than distal terms, such as *that* and *there*. At least one deictic term—*here, there, this*, or *that*—is usually present in the first 50-word lexicon of most children.

Some deictic pronoun contrasts develop prior to spatial deictic terms, such as *here* and *there*. The contrasts *I/you* and *my/your* develop relatively early, typically by age 2½. These terms may be easier to learn than spatial contrasts because of the relatively distinct boundaries.

Learning of deictic terms has three phases. In the initial phase, there is no contrast between the different dimensions. As previously discussed, terms such as *here* and *there* are used for directing attention or for referencing. In other words, deictic terms are used nondeictically. Among 2½-year-olds, deictic words seem to be used indiscriminately, with a gesture to indicate meaning. As late as age 4, some children exhibit no difference between the use of *this* and *that*. Children seem to prefer to use themselves or a near point as reference.

Look for the pragmatic elements in this phone conversation between 3-year-olds. What pragmatics of phone talking are missing? http://www.youtube.com/watch?v=sL3vqlHabck

Gradually, children develop a partial contrast. A child frequently uses the proximal term (*this, here*) correctly but overuses it for the nonproximal (*that, there*). An alternative pattern is characterized by correct child use only in reference to self or to some inconsistent point.

Finally, a child masters the full deictic contrast. The age of mastery differs for the various contrasts, and some children continue to produce deictic errors into early school age. In general, mastery of *here/there* precedes mastery of *this/that*, possibly because the latter pair contains the notion of *here/there*. Mastery of the full adult system of deixis requires several years.

Intentions

As might be expected, a preschool child's comprehension and production of intentions increases. Although preschoolers become increasingly skilled in comprehending the intentions of others, even 5-year-olds must still rely on gestures for some interpretation (Kelly, 2001). By about 30 months, the relative frequency of the six large pragmatic categories—representational, control, expressive, procedural, social, and tutorial, found in Table 7.3—stabilizes throughout the rest of the preschool period. The control and representational functions account for 70% of all child utterances. Among 30-month-olds, statements or assertions may outnumber direct requests by as much as three to one. Table 8.2 lists the major intentions mastered by preschoolers. Developmental trends are presented in Figures 8.1 and 8.2.

The representational category is dominated by the *statement* function, which gradually increases to 50% of all representational utterances and roughly 20% of all utterances by age 5. The earlier dominance of *naming* in toddler language no longer exists, and these utterances, as might be expected, account for very few representational utterances by age 5. Other representational functions used by at least 90% of 5-year-olds include *content questions* ("What . . . ?" "Where . . . ?"), *content responses* or answers, and *yes/no questions* ("Is this a cheeseburger?").

Within the control function, there is great diversity. The *wanting* function that dominated in toddler language decreases rapidly after 24 months of age. In contrast, *direct requesting* continues a slow increase until around 39 months, when its frequency levels off at 25% of all control utterances but remains the dominant control function throughout the preschool years. Other control intentions used by at least 90% of 5-year-olds include *prohibition* ("Don't do that"), *intention* ("I'm going to put it in"), *request permission* ("Can I have one?"), *suggestion* ("Should we have ice cream?"), *physical justification* ("I can't 'cause the dollie's there"), offer ("Do you want this one?"), and *indirect request* ("Will you pour the juice?").

Expressive functions used by at least 90% of 5-year-olds include *exclamation, expressive state*, and *verbal accompaniment*, all noted previously in toddler language (Table 7.3). Procedural functions used by at least 90% of 5-year-olds include *call, contingent query*, and *elicited repetition*, in which a child repeats the speaker's utterance with a rising intonation ("Daddy will be home soon?"↑). Finally, the *social* and *tutorial* functions together account for less than 4% of the child's utterances at age 5.

TABLE 8.2 Intentions Exhibited by 90% of Children

Intention	Age at Which 90% of Children Use Intention (in Months)
Exclamation and call	18
Ostention (naming)	21
Wanting, direct request, and statement	24
Content question	30
Prohibition, intention, content response, expressive state, and elicited repetition	33
Yes/no question, verbal accompaniment, and contingent query	36
Request permission	45
Suggestion	48
Physical justification	54
Offer an indirect request	57

Source: Information from Wells (1985).

FIGURE 8.1 **Communication Functions as a Percentage of All Utterances**

Note that the representational and control functions predominate throughout the preschool years, accounting for approximately 65% of all utterances by age 5. The representational function includes statements and questions. Within the control function are demands, requests, and statements of prohibition.

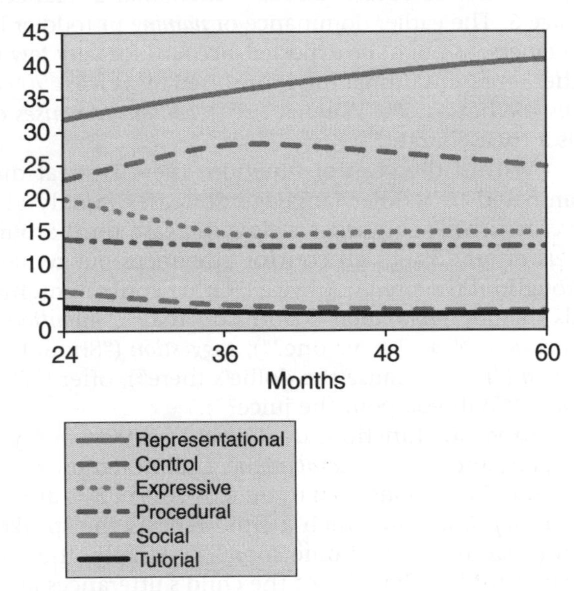

Source: Information from Wells (1985).

NARRATIVES

Oral narratives, or stories, are an uninterrupted stream of language modified by the speaker to capture and hold the listener's interest. Unlike a conversation, the narrator maintains a social monolog throughout, producing language relevant to the overall narrative while presupposing the information needed by the listener. **Narratives** include self-generated stories; telling of familiar tales; retelling of books, movies, or television shows; and recounting of personal experiences. Most adult conversations include narratives of this latter type, possibly beginning with "You'll never believe what happened to me." Common in the conversations of preschoolers, narratives aid children in constructing their own autonomous selves as portrayed in their stories.

Although conversation and narratives share many elements, such as a sense of purpose, relevant information, clear and orderly exchange of information, repair, and the ability to assume the perspective of the listener, they differ in very significant ways. Conversations are dialogs, while narratives are essentially decontextualized monologs. *Decontextualization* means that the language does not center on some immediate experience within the context. Instead, language creates the context of a narrative.

Narratives contain organizational patterns not found in conversation. In order to share the experience, the speaker must present an explicit, topic-centered discussion that clearly states the relationships between events. Thus, events are linked to one another in a predictable manner.

Narratives usually concern people, animals, or imaginary characters engaged in events. Conversations usually involve activities in the immediate context.

FIGURE 8.2 Most Common Intentions as a Percentage of All Utterances

Ostension or naming predominates at age 2 years but quickly decreases. Wanting also decreases as direct requests increase to fill the control function. While other intentions change some between ages 24 and 60 months, the largest change is seen in the increase in statements, which are nearly 20% of all utterances by age 5.

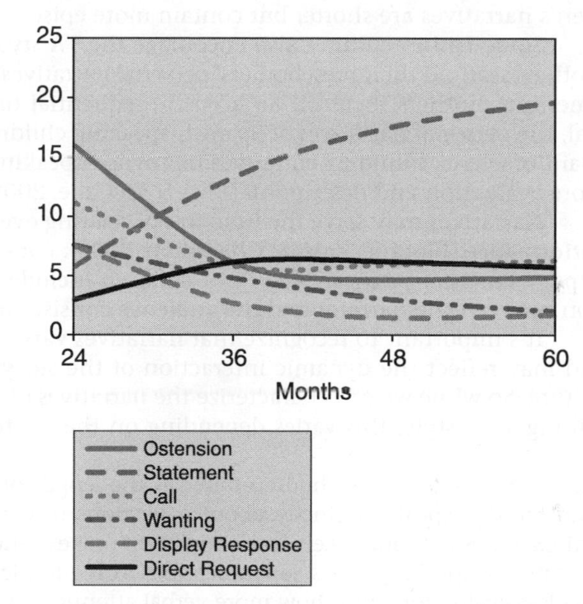

Source: Information from Wells (1985).

Other differences include the narrative use of extended units of story text; introductory and organizing sequences that lead to a narrative conclusion; and the relatively passive role of the listener, who provides only minimal informational support in general American culture. The narrative speaker is responsible for organizing and providing all of the information in an organized whole. It is not surprising, therefore, that narratives are found more frequently in the communication of more mature speakers.

Cultural Differences

Although storytelling is universal, the manner of that telling varies between and within cultures (McGregor, 2000). Narratives may vary in content or the ideas, goals, and themes children express; structural organization; and the function or purpose of the narrative (Gorman, Fiestas, Peña, & Reynolds Clark, 2011). Content usually comes from the experiences a child has and from social interactions in which a child hears the stories of others (Rogoff, 2003). In other words, children's narratives reflect those they hear. As you might expect, narrative content also reflects cultural ideas and perspectives, such as the degree of individualism or collectivism of the culture (Hofstede, 2001). For example, the narratives of Chinese children focus more on social interaction, morals, and authority, emphasizing proper behavior and moral character, than those of American children, who reflect individualism through character autonomy and a personal perspective (Wang & Leichtman, 2000). Similarly, collectivism and family are emphasized in the narratives of young Latino children from Mexico, the Caribbean, and Central and South America (Cristofaro & Tamis-LeMonda, 2008; McCabe & Bliss, 2004–2005). Parents often scaffold the narrative by asking questions about family members, fostering themes of helpfulness and appropriate behavior toward family members.

The organization of narratives is influenced by both context and culture. For example, *topic-associating* (TA) narratives, more characteristic of African American children, are organized around a series of episodes linked to some person or theme. In contrast, *topic-centered* (TC) stories, more characteristic of European American children, are structured around a single topic or closely related topics and emphasize the facts of the narrative in the order of occurrence. Consistent with the TA style, African American children's narratives are shorter but contain more episodes overall (Celinska, 2009).

Some Latino cultures also encourage the TA style. For example, Central American mothers scaffold their preschoolers' personal narratives as a conversation, while European American mothers focus on an accurate sequential organization (Melzi, 2000). In general, the personal narratives of Spanish-speaking children deviate more from a sequential chain of events found in narratives of English-speaking American children, and include more evaluation and description (Bliss & McCabe, 2008; Uccelli, 2008).

Narratives may serve the function of relating events and facts or may function as a performance (Bloome, Katz, & Champion, 2003). For example, the personal narratives of upper elementary African American children include character quotations and interaction between the narrator and the audience consistent with a performance.

It's important to recognize that narratives vary greatly even within the same child and may reflect the dynamic interaction of the story genre (personal or fictional) and culture. So while we can characterize the narratives of African American children as containing a TA style, this varies depending on the content, genre, age, and SES (Gorman et al., 2011).

Japanese and U.S. children differ in the length of personal narratives. Japanese children tend to speak succinctly about collections of experiences, while children from the United States are more likely to elaborate on one experience. A possible link may be found in maternal speaking styles. Japanese mothers request less information from their children, give less evaluation, and show more verbal attention. In response, the conversational turns of Japanese children are shorter than those of children from the United States.

Knowledge of Event Structure

Narratives are event descriptions based on underlying event scripts. Event description, such as explaining how to make cookies, involves more than simply describing single events in a sequential order. To describe the sets of sequences that form the total event, the speaker must be able to describe single events and event combinations and relationships and to indicate the significance of each event within the overall **event structure**. For example, the event structure for a day at the beach involves event sequences for getting ready, preparing the picnic, riding in the car, finding a spot on the beach, and so on.

Descriptions of entire events are based on a framework of scripts. Scripts based on actual events form an individual's expectations about sequences and impose order on event information. These familiar activity sequences or scripts consist of ordered events within routine or high-frequency activities. As such, scripts influence interpretation and telling of events and narratives. By age 3, children are able to describe chains of events within familiar activities, such as a birthday party. Theoretically, scripts are similar across members of the same culture based on their common experiences.

A narrator must have

- knowledge of both single events and connected sequences,
- the linguistic knowledge of the method for describing events, and
- the linguistic and cognitive skill to consider the listener's perspective.

Linguistic devices that speakers use include marking of beginnings and endings, marking of aspect, and modal auxiliary verbs. Beginnings can be marked by words or phrases such as *once upon a time*, *guess what happened to me*, *let's start at the beginning*, and so on. Endings include *the end*, *all done*, and *and that's how it happened*. Aspect and modal auxiliary verbs will be explained in detail in Chapter 9. Let's just say that aspect has to do with referencing time from inside the narrative and modal auxiliary or helping verbs expressing mood or attitude as in *could* versus *should*.

The elements of event knowledge are seen in the narratives of 4-year-olds. Underlying every story is an *event chain*. Events include actions; physical states such as possession and attribution; and mental states such as emotions, dispositions, thoughts, and intentions that may be causally linked as motivations, enablements, initiations, and resultants in the chain.

Development of Narratives

Before the appearance of first words, children have some understanding of familiar events and of the positions of some actions at the beginning, middle, and end of sequences. For example, there's a sequence for taking a bath, with undressing at the beginning and drying at the end. Although 2-year-olds possess basic patterns for familiar events and sequences, called *scripts*, they are not able to describe sequences of events accurately until about age 4.

In the United States, middle-SES children are encouraged to elaborate on their own experiences and to express opinions on these experiences. In contrast, low-SES children are also encouraged to tell personal narratives but are not automatically given the right to express their own views or opinions.

Children as young as age 2 to 3½ talk about things that have happened to them in the past. These early *protonarratives* have five times as much evaluative information ("I didn't like it," "It was yukky," "I cried," "I hate needles") as children's regular conversation. Between ages 2 and 2½, the number of these protonarratives doubles, and children begin to sequence events with very little help from others. Children also begin to tell self-generated, *fictional* narratives between 2 and 3 years of age. Note the short narrative in Box 8.4.

In talking about a book with their mothers and subsequent independent retelling of the story, older preschool children's story retelling skills are related to the extent to which mothers encouraged their active participation during joint book reading (Kang, Kim, & Alexander Pan, 2009). Children's response is closely associated with types of talking used by their mothers.

Narrative Level The overall organization of a narrative is called the **narrative level**. In general, children use two strategies for organization, centering and chaining:

BOX 8.4

A Short Narrative by a 52- Month-Old Child

THE JOKE IS . . . UM . . . I did it this morning on daddy. I said, "Daddy, I pulled my teeth out." He said, "Um, where is it?" And then I said, "April Fools!" It's April Fools Day.

1. **Centering** is the linking of entities to form a story nucleus. Links may be based on similarity of features.
2. **Chaining** consists of a sequence of events that share attributes and lead directly from one to another.

Most of the stories of 2-year-olds are organized by centering. The stories usually focus on certain highlights in a child's life and may have a vague plot. Frequently, children tell of events that they find disruptive or extraordinary. Considering the listener only minimally, a preschooler demonstrates little need to introduce, to explore with, or to orient the audience. Thus, these stories often lack easily identifiable beginnings, middles, and ends.

By age 3, however, nearly half of children use both centering and chaining. This percentage increases, and by age 5, nearly three fourths of the children use both strategies.

Initially, identification of the participants, time, and location may be nonexistent or minimal. Although these elements improve with maturity, even children of 3½ may not identify all story participants. In part, this may result from the fact that most self-generated stories involve individuals well known to the child and to most listeners, thus there is no need to identify them. A sense of time frame is also vague or nonexistent initially but improves with the use of terms such as *yesterday* or *last year*, even though these terms may be used inaccurately. Location is more commonly identified, especially when the narrative events occurred in the home. With maturity, preschool children become better able to identify out-of-home locations.

The organizational strategies of 2-year-olds represent centering *heaps*, sets of unrelated statements about a central stimulus, consisting of one sentence added to another. Although there is no overall organizational pattern, there may be a similarity in the grammatical structure of the sentences:

> The doggie go "woof." The cow go "moo." The man ride tractor—"Bpt-bpt-bpt."

There is no story line, no sequencing, and no cause and effect. The sentences may be moved anywhere in the text without changing the overall meaning. Heaps may also be used to describe a scene.

Somewhat later, preschoolers begin to tell narratives characterized as centering *sequences*. These include events linked on the basis of similar attributes or events that create a simple but meaningful focus for a story. The organization is additive, not temporal or time based, and sentences may be moved without altering the narrative:

> I ate a hamburger (Mimes eating). Mommy throwed the ball, like this. Daddy taked me swimming (Moves hand, acts silly). I had two sodas.

In these early stories, there is a dominance of performance and qualities, such as movement, sound production, and prosody. Gradually, between ages 3 and 7 years, children's narratives increase in the use of prose and plots.

Temporal, or time-based, event chains emerge between ages 3 and 5 years. In these narratives, events follow a logical sequence. *Primitive temporal narratives* are organized around a center with complementary events:

> We went to the parade. There was a big elephant. And tanks (Moves arm like turret). The drum was loud. There was a clown in a little car (Hand gestures "little"). And I got a balloon. And we went home.

Although there is sequencing, there is no plot and no cause and effect or causality.

Narratives characterized as *unfocused temporal chains* lead directly from one event to another while other attributes—characters, settings, and actions—shift. This is the first level of chaining, and the links are concrete. As a result of the shifting focus, unfocused chains have no centers:

> The man got in the boat. He rowed. A big storm knocked over the trees—whish-sh, boom. The doggie had to swim. Fishies jumped out of the water. He had warm milk. And then he went to bed.

Temporal chains frequently include third person pronouns (*he, she, it*); past-tense verbs; temporal conjunctions such as *and, then,* and *and then*; and a definite beginning and ending.

Focused temporal or causal chains generally center on a main character who goes through a series of perceptually linked, concrete events:

> There is this horsie. He eats—munch, munch—hay for breakfast. He runs out of the barn. Then he plays in the sun. He rolls in the warm grass. He comes in for dinner. He sleeps in a bed (mimes sleep).

Notice the pragmatics in this 4-year-old's conversation with Ellen DeGeneres. http://www.youtube.com/watch?v=FmPLI-3IPxg&list=PLOkAMV3eHHjjLPX_vvR7QTOV3k3lB4kIV

Causal chains, in which one event causes or has caused another, are infrequent until age 5 and will be discussed later.

By the time children begin school, most have acquired the basic elements of narratives and can recount sequentially familiar or significant events. These narratives form much of the content of the conversations later encountered in older children and adults.

THEORY OF MIND

Your physical brain is different from your mind, which includes your intellect and your consciousness. Words for the processes of your mind include *thought, perception, memory, will, imagination, reason,* and *emotion.* Development of your mind is a continual process.

When you were born, you had no mental representations or images of anything in the outside world. In other words, objects that were not immediately available to your senses did not exist. This is why a young baby will not search for a toy when it is hidden, even right in front of her or him. From the infant's perspective, the toy no longer exists. The development of mental representations or images of objects is a gradual process that occurs throughout the first year of life as children interact with objects.

In addition to learning about objects, the child gains an awareness that people have an independent existence; have thoughts, beliefs, and feelings; and that these may or may not be the same as the child's. This knowledge is called **Theory of Mind (ToM)**.

ToM is not a psychological theory. Instead ToM is the ability to understand the minds of other people and to comprehend and predict their behavior (Miller, 2006). It's called a theory because we can never really know someone else's mind; we can only guess, using our ToM to theorize what others know, think, or feel. In other words, we each theorize on the mind of other people. Did you ever say, "What could he have been thinking?" If so, you just verbalized Theory of Mind. ToM is not a single, unitary concept. Rather, it consists of several kinds of knowledge and skills (Miller, 2006).

So how do we understand each other? We use many signals to infer the intentions, desires, knowledge, and beliefs of others. In addition, we understand that these thoughts, states, and emotions of others are genuine and real for them, not merely concepts. This inferential process is so automatic and so much a part of our comprehension and predictions about others that it only becomes obvious when something goes wrong.

Of interest for us is the relationship between linguistic abilities and the cognitive ability to understand others as intentional beings with their own beliefs and desires.

Karen Struthers/Shutterstock

The development of narratives, as well as more complicated aspects of semantic development, are generally accomplished by age 5.

After all, language provides us with a means for expressing and understanding meaning and intentionality.

Although Theory of Mind may be an innate potential ability in humans, it requires social and interactional experience over several years to reach fully mature abilities. Even adults' abilities probably represent a continuum, varying from complete and accurate to minimal.

In summary, Theory of Mind is concerned with

- how we gain an understanding that others also have minds, and
- how we learn to recognize and form hypotheses about the different and separate beliefs, desires, mental states, and intentions in others.

Developing Theory of Mind

Although Theory of Mind develops over several years, we may see its beginning in the joint attention or joint reference of infants (Miller, 2006). The capacity to coordinate one's attention with a partner is a critical first step in learning to comprehend and predict the thoughts and actions of other people. When a child shares the experience of attending with its mother, he or she comes to understand that others intend for such sharing to occur. Through words and gestures, a mother singles out objects, events, and actions for attention and specifies aspects for special recognition.

There is a close relationship between ToM and communicative abilities (Astington, 2003). In short, the capacity to consider mental states in others seems to be a key factor that regulates communicative exchanges. Still, the nature of the relationship is not completely understood (Lohmann & Tomasello, 2003). In short, as children grow in their ability to establish relationships between their own mental concepts and those of others, they are more able to understand conversations as a "meeting of the minds" in which being aware of your partner's intentions and informational needs is essential. Although it is difficult to determine whether ToM abilities cause better communication or the opposite, it is clear that both require similar sociocognitive abilities.

Apologies are an interesting example of how children become more attuned to their listener. Children are exposed to apology terms primarily through apologies directed to them and also to a lesser degree through talk about apologies. Before age 2, apologies are rare. Parents play a roll in acquisition in apologetic behavior. As children move through the preschool years into early elementary school, there is a decrease in directly elicited apologies by parents (*Tell John you're sorry*) and an increase in indirectly elicited ones (*How do you think John feels?*). With age children's apologies also became more elaborate (Ely & Berko Gleason, 2006).

Children cannot comprehend the desires or emotions of others until they are aware of their own. Thus, self-awareness develops in parallel with ToM (Eslea, 2002). First, at about 18 months, children learn to recognize themselves and then, about six months later, to express their own emotional states. Ever notice a toddler attempting to "hide" by covering his or her eyes? The child has not made a distinction between self and others. Here's another example from a telephone conversation with a 3-year-old (Eslea, 2002):

ADULT: What have you been doing today?
CHILD: Playing with this.
ADULT: Oh, right. What is it?
CHILD: THIS!!!

It's common for children at this age to fail to realize that other people cannot always see what they can see.

By age 2 children are able to express their own emotions verbally and to begin in pretend play to recognize emotions in others. Most 4-year-olds can relate the emotions of others to desires or intentions and can understand that others may have a different perspective on the world from their own (Eslea, 2002). The understanding that others have knowledge and beliefs different from your own is a major developmental breakthrough.

There is an important change in social cognition in the late preschool years (Wellman, 2002; Wellman & Liu, 2004). Between the ages of 3 and 5 years, children move from an initial incapacity for differentiating between different points of view, through a capacity for making general judgments about what their partners know or do not, to a capacity for taking into account that ignorance or a lack of information may lead to false beliefs by others (Wellman & Liu, 2004). Understanding of false belief seems to be the most powerful predictor of changes in older preschool children's development of communicative competence (Resches & Pérez Pereira, 2007).

As children become more aware of the thoughts and emotions of others, their narrative portrayals change. At age 3, they represent characters in their stories almost exclusively as actors and describe them by physical and external characteristics. By age 4, characters begin to exhibit rudimentary mental states, which are expanded by age 5 (Nicolopoulou & Richner, 2007).

Older children with more mature ToM abilities take part in sophisticated pretend play more frequently, use more mental state terms (*sad, angry*) in their everyday conversations, and are considered by their teachers as having more developed social and interactive abilities.

In general, the language of preschool children with poorer ToM abilities is more ambiguous or incomplete and poorly adapted to the listener's previous knowledge and informational needs. In contrast, children with higher ToM abilities offer clear, simple directions and precise descriptions that are better adapted and more relevant to the aims of the task, the listener's needs, and their own role in the communication task (Resches & Pérez Pereira, 2007). Comments and questions are used to check on the information held by and point of view of the listener. In addition, those children with higher ToM abilities are better at determining their listeners' misunderstandings or lack of understanding and more efficient in repairing them, often with reformulated information rather than simple repetition.

Exhibition of ToM in 4-year-olds corresponds with activation of the anterior medial portion of the frontal lobe and the juncture of the temporal and parietal lobes in the right hemisphere (Figure 8.3) (Sabbagh, Bowman, Evraire, & Ito, 2009). While the right temporoparietal junction in preschool and early elementary children seems to be activated for interpretation of both thought and movement by others, by age 11 this area of the brain seems involved primarily in interpretation of others' thoughts (Saxe, Whitfield-Gabrieli, Scholz, & Pelphrey, 2009).

Maternal speaking style has the potential to promote or hinder children's understanding of the mind and subsequent development of ToM. For example, among 3-year-olds, non-preschool children perform significantly better on mental verb (*think, know, remember*) comprehension task than children in preschool and use fewer mental state statements and more questions, fewer first person utterances (*I, me*) and more second person utterances (*you*), and less use of the verb *think* in its "very certain" form (*I think this so you should*) less often. Greater understanding of the mind was positively associated to maternal mental verb questions (*What do you think?*) and single-clause utterances and negatively associated with maternal statements (Howard, Mayeux, & Naigles, 2008).

FIGURE 8.3 Right Hemisphere and Theory of Mind

Areas of the right hemisphere activated in 4-year-olds and believed to be associated with emergence of Theory of Mind (ToM).

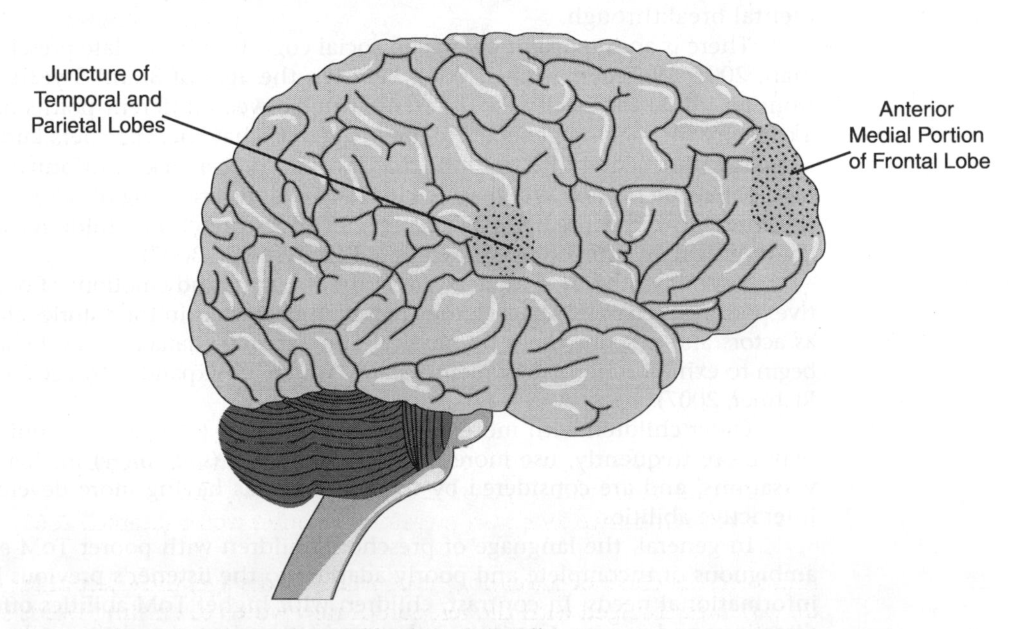

Source: Information drawn from Sabbagh et al. (2009).

SUMMARY

Although there is a considerable difference among families and across cultures in the overall amount of talking, there are certain overall patterns. To some extent, the amount of talking is a function of the energy level of a child and his or her conversational partners. Therefore, the largest proportion of talking occurs in the morning shortly after breakfast. The amount of talking is also related to the activity in progress. Most preschool speech accompanies solitary play or play with others or occurs within activities devoted primarily to conversation. The amount of talking within these latter activities increases throughout the preschool years. In contrast, relatively less talking occurs while either game or role playing, looking at books or television, or doing chores. In general, preschool boys play alone more, talking to themselves and calling bystanders to notice this play. In contrast, girls engage more in household activities and play and are drawn into talk while organizing the task at hand.

Throughout the preschool years, a child learns to become a truer conversational partner, using a greater variety of forms to attain desired ends. In addition, a child expands presuppositional skills and is better able to take the perspective of the other participant. Although he or she can take conversational turns without being prompted with a question, a child still tends to make more coherent contributions to the conversation if discussing an ongoing activity in which engaged at the time. A child is more aware of social roles at age 5 than at age 2 and can adjust his or her speech for younger children or for role playing, but lacks many of the subtleties of older children and adults. As he or she begins to attend school, a child will be under increasing pressure by both teachers and peers to use language even more effectively.

Here's an example of Theory of Mind and the way in which it's tested in young children. http://www.youtube.com/watch?v=8hLubgpY2_w

Semantic Development

When we think about word learning in an abstract way, it seems impossibly difficult. Imagine learning three or four new words every day. Try it. You will soon tire of the task, forget most words, and confuse others. Yet young children continue this process for years.

Do young children confuse words that may seem to them to be similar? Of course. Here are two examples from my grandson Zavier, both from about the age of 3. He asked his mother if she was "five legs tall" instead of five feet tall and he called fireflies "thunder bugs" rather than lightning bugs. In both cases, it's easy to see why he made those word choices.

The preschool period is one of rapid lexical and concept acquisition. It is estimated that a child adds approximately five words to his or her lexicon, or personal dictionary, every day between the ages of 1½ and 6 years. Word meanings are inferred without direct teaching by adults. In general, preschoolers with larger vocabularies are more popular with their peers (Gertner, Rice, & Hadley, 1994).

Several factors influence children's knowledge of words between 16 and 30 months of age. In general, children know

- more words composed of low-probability sounds and sound pairs,
- shorter words with high neighborhood density, and
- words that were semantically related to other words (Storkel, 2009).

Although the effect of phonology is constant across age, the effect of lexical and semantic variables changed with the relation of new words to existing words becoming more important with age.

At age 2, several processes seem to be involved in word learning: word frequency, word segmentation, fast mapping, and a longer, extended process whereby the word meaning is fleshed out (Hoff & Naigles, 2002). For example, there is a strong relationship between the frequency of mothers' use of words at 16 months and the age at which a child produces a word. More frequent words are produced earlier.

Word segmentation or dividing words into phonemes and morphemes is simplified when mothers place words in highly salient or easily noticeable or important positions, such as the final position in an utterance (Aslin, 1999; Choi, 2000). Mothers use the final position to highlight new or unfamiliar words (Cleave & Kay-Raining Bird, 2006; Fernald & Mazzie, 1991). In addition, mothers place unfamiliar nouns in shorter utterances than familiar nouns.

Fast mapping is the initial word–referent relationship or word "meaning" created by a child based on limited exposure to a word (Bedore & Leonard, 2000; Houston-Price et al., 2005; Kay-Raining Bird & Chapman, 1998; Merriman, Marazita, & Jarvis, 1995).

It is possible that a preschool child employs an initial- or fast-mapping strategy that enables him or her to infer a connection between a word and its referent or entity referred to after only one exposure. Initial acquisition is receptive in nature. Obviously, only a small portion of the overall meaning goes into a child's memory after only one exposure. The actual information is affected by both the world and word knowledge of a preschooler. Not all words are learned with the same ease. In general, nouns seem to be easier to fast map than verbs.

Words may be fast-mapped using one or more of the following strategies (Storkel, 2001):

- The range of possible meanings may be constrained by the situation and also by the meanings already possessed by a child. Using reasoning similar to the novel name–no name strategy mentioned in Chapter 6, a child would reason that the definition cannot be the same as one already possessed.
- An associational strategy might be used in which the regularities in the language, such as word order and bound morphemes, give him or her clues as to the meaning.
- A child may use phonotactic probability or the likelihood of occurrence of different sound sequences to aid rapid recall of newly learned words (Storkel, 2002, 2003).

Both neighborhood density and phonotactic probability influence fast mapping but in varying ways (McKean, Letts, & Howard, 2013). Throughout the preschool period, low neighborhood density supports better fast mapping. This suggests that children find it easier to identify words with few neighbors as being novel. Words with many neighbors are harder to discriminate from those that are already in their lexicons, so children do not use their "rapid word-learning mechanism."

In contrast, the influence of phonotactic probability changes across development from a high to a low phonotactic probability advantage, which may represent reorganization in a child's developing lexicon. As a child's lexicon grows, the need to learn words with a wider range of phonotactic patterns becomes more necessary. In addition, the older child is able to segment or divide speech input into words using existing lexical knowledge rather than her or his phonetic and phonotactic knowledge. Identifying word boundaries becomes less critical because in most cases the child can easily accomplish this task.

The effects of neighborhood density and phonotactic probability on new word learning vary with the size of a preschool child's vocabulary (Storkel & Hoover, 2011). This might be expected given that with increasing vocabulary children must find new ways to story and remember novel words.

On one family vacation, my 54-month-old granddaughter commented on my partner's broken "arm." I corrected her with the word *wrist* and offered an explanation. After a few seconds, she added, "I have another wrist," while pointing at her ankle. She had overextended the meaning based on a quick analysis of the physical function of a wrist.

Fast mapping may be the first in a two-step process of lexical acquisition. First, the child roughs out a tentative definition connecting the word and available information. This step may be followed by an extended phase in which a child gradually refines the definition with new information acquired on subsequent encounters. Retrieval may be affected by the nature of the referent, the frequency of exposure to the word, the form and content of the utterance in which it occurs, and the context.

Fuller word meanings are derived from use by both a child and others. Mothers place words in a variety of syntactic forms. For example, greater variety of sentences into which a word is used by mothers is highly correlated with future use of that verb by their children. Similarly, among 2-year-old children, longer maternal utterances are correlated with larger child vocabularies 10 weeks later (Hoff & Naigles, 2002).

Most likely, young children learn single words as unique units, each with its own meaning, probably unrelated to other word meanings. Although these word meanings lack relationship, the system is simple and easy to use.

Children may use two operating principles to establish meanings: *contrast* and *conventionality*. Contrast is the assumption that every form—morpheme, word, syntactic structure—contrasts to every other in meaning. A speaker chooses a form because it means something other than what some other expression means. In other words, it contrasts to other options. Conventionality is the expectation that certain forms will be used to convey certain meanings, such as *-ing* to convey action.

Taken together, the two principles predict that, whenever possible, children will use established forms with conventional meanings that contrast clearly to other forms. Difficulty occurs when a well-established form has a meaning similar to that of a newly learned form. Thus, it may be easier for children to form unrelated unique meanings initially.

In determining the referent of a novel word, preschool children seem to prefer movement (Scofield, Miller, & Hartin, 2011). In other words, in the absence of other clues, preschoolers tend to assume that a novel word applies to an object in motion rather than one that is not.

New word meanings come from both linguistic and nonlinguistic contexts (Au, 1990) and from the surrounding syntactic structure. Let's assume that a child hears the following sentence: "Bring me the *chromium* tray, not the red one" (Gathercole, 1989, p. 694). He or she might proceed through the following steps to differentiate the meaning:

1. Assume that Mommy is trying to communicate with me.
2. Unknown word used in reference to trays as descriptor.
3. Only observable difference between the trays is color.
4. Chromium must be a color.
5. One tray is red.
6. Must not have wanted red tray or would have asked for it.
7. Therefore, must want other than red tray, which is chromium in color.

Preschoolers' noun definitions often include physical properties, such as shape, size, and color; functional properties or what the entity does; use properties; and locational properties, such as *on trees* or *at the beach*. Often missing are superordinate categories, as in *a car is a vehicle*; relationships to other entities, as in *a mouse is much smaller than a cat*; internal constituents, as in *an apple has seeds inside*; origins, as in *hatch from eggs*;

and metaphorical uses, as in *suspicious things are called "fishy."* Adult and older school-age children's definitions contain all these elements.

Preschool verb definitions also differ from those of adults or older children. A preschooler can explain who or what does the action; to what or whom it's done; and where, when, and with what it's done. Usually missing is how and why it's done and a description of the process found in full adult definitions. In languages as different as Korean and English, it appears that preschool children learn novel verbs by noticing the differences, especially the objects used with each verb (Childers & Paik, 2009).

Verbs may be initially mapped based on the number and type of morphological ending applied (Bedore & Leonard, 2000). The number of verb endings varies across languages from English, with very few—making fast mapping of verbs relatively easy—to languages such as Spanish that have many verb inflections.

When gaps exist in preschoolers' vocabularies either because they've forgotten or never knew a word, children invent words. For example, verbs might be created from nouns to produce the following:

> I'm *spooning* my cocoa. (Stirring)
> You *sugared* your coffee. (Sweetened)

In the preschoolers' defense, English allows this practice with some nouns, as in *paddling a canoe*, *shoeing a horse*, and *suiting up*, to name a few. Production of invented words seems to follow from children's construction of compound words from two or more known single ones, as in *doghouse* and *birdhouse*, leading to *fish-house* (aquarium). In both cases, production demonstrates recognition of word formulation.

Late preschool children sometimes invent compound words that are unique in form, such as *drive-trucker*. These may reflect a child's greater familiarity with the verb-object (*drive trucker*) word order when trying to produce the complex object-verb-er (*truckdriver*) order (Murphy & Nicoladis, 2006).

Although vocabulary growth between ages 1 and 3 years is positively related to the diversity of words in the mother's speech and to maternal language and literacy skills, it is not related to the overall amount of maternal talkativeness (Pan, Rowe, Singer, & Snow, 2005).

Children also expand their vocabularies through parental storybook reading. Especially helpful for children are discussions with the reader that accompany the narrative. Even low levels of language participation, such as naming and describing, as well as reasoning and making inferences, can have a positive effect on the child's subsequent language use.

As a child's lexicon expands, the need for better cognitive organization increases and some semantic networks or interrelationships are formed. Relationships may consist of words for referents found in the same context, such as *spoon*, *bowl*, *cup*, and *table*, or word associations, such as *stop and go*, *rise and shine*, and *red, white, and blue*. Preschoolers demonstrate these relationships in their inappropriate use of words and in word substitutions, such as using *spoon* to refer to a fork.

RELATIONAL TERMS

The acquisition of relational terms, such as those for location and time, is a complex process. In general, the order of acquisition is influenced by the syntactic complexity, the amount of adult usage in a child's environment, and the underlying cognitive concept. We shall briefly consider interrogatives or questions, temporal relations, physical relations, locational prepositions, and kinship terms.

Interrogatives

Children's responses to different types of questions and their production of these same types have a similar order of development. Early question forms include *what* and *where*, followed by *who, whose,* and *which*, and finally by *when, how,* and *why*. Most of the later forms involve concepts of cause, manner, or time. Their late appearance can be traced to the late development of these concepts. In other words, a child must have a concept of time in order to comprehend or to answer *when* questions. Occasionally, however, a preschooler responds to or asks questions without fully understanding the underlying meaning. Children seem to be employing the following answering strategy: If the word meaning is unknown, answer on the basis of the verb. Unaware of the meaning of *when*, the child might respond to "When are you going to eat?" with "A cookie!"

Semantic features of the verb are particularly important for certain types of child answers. For example, the verb *touch* is more likely to elicit a response focusing on what was touched, where it was touched, and for what reason regardless of the question. Other verbs elicit different responses, with little regard for the *wh-* question form employed. Preschool children rely heavily on contextual information when answering questions and become increasingly better at integrating this information with linguistic cues (Ryder & Leinonen, 2003).

Even young school-age children have difficulty answering some forms of *wh-* questions that they seem to comprehend. Recognition of the general type of information requested may precede the ability to give acceptable and accurate answers.

Causal, or *why*-type, questions may be especially difficult for a preschool child because of the reverse-order thinking required in the response. The 3-year-old child experiences difficulty reversing the order of sequential events. Yet it is this type of response that is required for the *why* interrogative. For example, "Why did you hit Randy?" requires a response explaining the events that preceded the fist fight. It is not unusual to hear a 3-year-old respond "'Cause he hit me back," a consequence, demonstrating an inability to reverse the order.

Temporal Relations

Temporal terms such as *when, before, since,* and *while* can convey information on the order, duration, and simultaneity of events. The order of acquisition of these terms is related to their use and to the concept each represents. In general, words of order, such as *after* and *before*, precede words of duration, such as *since* and *until*. These, in turn, precede terms of simultaneity, such as *while*. This hierarchy reflects a sequence of cognitive development. Preschool children gain a sense of order before they have a sense of duration. Five-year-olds understand *before* and *after* better than simultaneous terms such as *at the same time* (see Table 8.3).

Temporal terms are initially produced as prepositions and then as conjunctions joining clauses. Thus, the child will produce a sentence such as "You go *after* me" before he says, "You can go home *after* we eat dinner." It is not uncommon for even 6½-year-olds to have difficulty with some of the syntactic structures used with *before* and *after* to link clauses.

When the meaning of a temporal term is unknown, the preschool child tends to rely on the order of mention. Employing this strategy, a 3-year-old will interpret the following sentences as all having the same meaning:

Before you go to school, stop at the store.
Go to school before you stop at the store.
After you go to school, stop at the store.
Go to school after you stop at the store.

TABLE 8.3 **Summary of Comprehension of Locational and Temporal Relationships**

Age (Months)	Relationships Understood
24	Locational prepositions *in* and *on*
36	Locational preposition *under*
40	Locational preposition *next to*
48 (approx.)	Locational prepositions *behind, in back of,* and *in front of;* difficulty with *above, below,* and *at the bottom of;* kinship terms *mother, father, sister,* and *brother* (last two are nonreprocating)
60	Temporal terms *before* and *after*
60+ (school-age)	Additional locational prepositions in temporal expressions, such as *in a week;* most major kinship terms by age 10; more precise locational directives reference the body (*left* and *right*)

In the first and last examples, note that the desired order of occurrence of events is the reverse of the word order stated.

A second interpretive strategy used by older preschool and some school-age children reflects a syntactic approach. The child adopts a strategy in which the main clause becomes the first event. For example, the sentence "After arriving home, *Oz bought a paper*" would be interpreted as "Oz bought a paper, then he arrived home. "Main and subordinate clauses are discussed in more detail in Chapter 9.

When all else fails, a child relies on knowledge of real-life sequences. For example, you wake up before eating breakfast. This strategy of comprehension works as long as the utterance conforms to a child's experiential base.

Physical Relations

Relational terms such as *thick/thin, fat/skinny, more/less,* and *same/different* are frequently difficult for preschool children to learn. In general, a child first learns that the terms are opposites, then the dimensions to which each term refers. The order of acquisition may be based on semantic–syntactic relations, and the cognitive relations expressed with less specific terms are usually learned first. Terms such as *big* and *little* refer to general size on any dimension and would be acquired before more specific terms, such as *deep* and *shallow*, which refer physically to bodies of water.

The positive member, such as *big* or *long,* of each relational pair, as in *big/little* and *long/short,* represents the presence of the entity that it describes (size and length, respectively) and is learned first. The presence of size is *big*, the positive term. The negative aspect or the absence of size is *little.* A general order of acquisition is presented in Table 8.4.

The child seems to learn by accumulating individual examples of each term. Hence, understanding may be restricted to specific objects even if it appears to be more adultlike.

Learning and interpretation of descriptive terms is dependent on context. For example, 2-year-olds understand *big* and *little* used in comparing the size of two objects or judging an object's size for a particular task. It is more difficult for a child to recall the size of a nonpresent entity. This changes, of course, as memory improves.

TABLE 8.4 Order of Acquisition of Physical Relationships

Hard/soft
Big/little, heavy/light
Tall/short, long/short
Large/small
High/low
Thick/thin
Wide/narrow
Deep/shallow

Terms such as *more/less* and *same/different* pose a different problem for a preschool child. There may be an underlying concept for *more/less* in which a young preschool child interprets both terms to mean amount. When presented with a selection task, preschoolers tend to pick the larger grouping, whether cued with *more* or with *less*.

Conceptual development seems equally important for the acquisition of *same* and *different*. The ability to make same/different judgments seems to be related to development of *conservation*, the ability to attend to more than one perceptual dimension without relying strictly on physical evidence. Without this ability, young preschoolers experience difficulty making same/different distinctions.

Locational Prepositions

A child understands different spatial relations before beginning to speak about them. The exact nature of that comprehension is unknown because a child as old as 3½ still relies on gestures to convey much locational meaning. The first English prepositions, *in*, *on*, and *to*, appear at around 2 years of age. When a child does not comprehend these prepositions, he or she seems to follow these interpretive strategies: *If it's a container, something belongs inside and if it's a supporting surface, something belongs on it.* Thus, children may respond in relation to the objects mentioned rather than the prepositions used. Other possible interpretive cues may be the word order of adult utterances and the context. Using these rules, children respond in predictable ways.

Children 18 months of age seem to base their hypotheses about word meanings on these strategies. As a result, they act as if they understand *in* all the time, *on* with surfaces but not containers, and *under* not at all. By age 3, most children have figured out the meanings of all three prepositions. When 3- and 4-year-olds are faced with more complex prepositions such as *above, below, in front of*, or *at the bottom of*, however, they tend to revert to these strategies.

Terms such as *next to* or *in front of* offer special problems. For example, *next to* includes, but is not limited to, *in front of, behind*, and so on. In turn, these terms differ in relation to the locations to which they refer. With fronted objects, such as a chair or a digital monitor, locational terms take their reference from the object. For example, *in front of the TV* means *in front of the screen*. With nonfronted objects, such as a saucer, the term takes its location from the speaker's perspective. Interpretation requires a certain level of social skill on the part of the listener, who must be able to adopt the perspective of the speaker. *Next to* is usually learned at about 40 months, followed by *behind, in back*

Defining words is difficult for all of us. In this video, a 5-year-old has a conversation about the meaning of "discipline." http://www.youtube.com/watch?v=GVYNRUnPpHo

of, and *in front of* around age 4 (see Table 8.3). Children seem to use fronting and the height of the object as cues for initial interpretation.

A 3-year-old child interprets most prepositions of movement to mean *toward.* Hence, the child at first favors *to* over *from, into* over *out of,* and *onto* over *off.* Terms that signal movement *toward* are easier than their opposites.

Syntactic form may also affect acquisition. Prior to age 4, *in, on,* and *over* often are used predominantly as prepositions for object location while *up, down,* and *off* are used both as locational prepositions and verb particles. A *verb particle* is a multiword grammatical unit that functions as a verb, such as *stand up, sit down,* and *take off.* Thus, there is opportunity for confusion and a lack of consistency.

Kinship Terms

A preschooler gains highly selective knowledge of kinship terms that refer to family members, such as *dad, sister,* and *brother.* At first a child treats the term as part of the person's name. I mentioned previously that for a time, my children called me "daddybob." In this stage a child does not possess the components of the kinship term. Initially, for a child, terms are related to specific individuals and to a child's personal experience.

Next, a child gains some features of the definition of the person but not of the relationship; for example, "A grandmother is someone who smells like flowers and wears funny underwear" (an actual child's definition).

A child gains a few of the less complex relationships first (Table 8.5). Complexity may be thought of as the number of shared features. For example, *father* has the features *male* and *parent,* but *aunt,* a more complex term, has *female, sister,* and *parent* of whom she's the sister.

After *Mommy* and *Daddy,* the child learns *brother* and *sister.* Roughly, the meanings are *brother = related boy* and *sister = related girl.* By age 4, a child may understand what a brother or sister is but doesn't realize that he or she can also be a brother or sister to someone else. In other words, the term is not used reciprocally. Eventually, a child will understand all features of the kinship terms and reciprocity. Most of the major kinship terms are understood by age 10.

CONCLUSION

In development, there seems to be a constant interchange between semantic and syntactic development. Grammatical growth is more closely related to vocabulary growth than to chronological age.

There seem to be strong genetic correlations between lexical and syntactical growth from 2 to 3 years of age (Dionne, Dale, Boivin, & Plomin, 2003). This data and that from older preschoolers would suggest a common cognitive mechanism for language development. This does not negate the importance of environmental factors in determining language development. It would appear that both genetic and environmental factors underlie development and account for many of the individual differences across a wide range of linguistic skills (Hayiou-Thomas et al., 2006).

TABLE 8.5 Order of Acquisition of Kinship Terms

Mother, father, sister, brother
Son, daughter, grandfather, grandmother, parent
Uncle, aunt, cousin, nephew, niece

Semantic and Pragmatic Influence on Syntactic Development

Aspects of language do not act independently, and development in one area influences the others. More correctly, the aspects of language develop together.In the next chapter, we'll be discussing preschool development of language form, especially syntax. This does not occur independently of the focus of this chapter, semantics and pragmatics. Let's briefly discuss the influence of semantics and pragmatics on syntax.

SEMANTICS

A central task in learning language acquisition is differentiating how different roles in an event are indicated. In other words, children need both to comprehend and produce the *who-does-what-to-whom* of the event. In part, semantics can be described by **semantic case** or category, such as **agent** (who) and the **patient** (whom) and the relationship between cases expressed through word order and morphological markers. In general, languages differ along a continuum in which highly word-ordered languages, such as English, have fewer morphological markers, and those with a freer word order, such as Italian, have more markers. English-speaking language-learning children rely on several cues to derive meaning, including the following:

- Order of the participants, which is typically agent before patient
- Morphological marking of semantic case marking on pronouns indicating the participants, such as *I, he, she* versus *my, him, her*
- Animacy or the animate nature of agents who cause actions, as in ***Mommy** throw ball*
- Stress or emphasis
- Special markers, such as the passive agent-marker *by* in *The boy was kicked by the horse*

Several crosslinguistic studies have demonstrated that in their spontaneous speech, children learning many different languages generally conform to adult usage and depend on word order to both comprehend and produce sentences (Chan, Lieven, & Tomasello, 2009). Interestingly, Italian-speaking children may ignore word order because word order is quite variable in Italian.

Phonology Affects Semantics

Probably, most discussion of case marking in English has centered around pronoun case errors, such as ***Me** go* and ***Her** eating*. About 50% of English-speaking 2- to 4-year-olds make such pronoun errors, especially substituting patient for agent (***Me** do it*) but rarely the reverse (*Mommy spank **I***). If we examine the most common errors, *her* for *she* and *me* for *I*, we see some interesting phenomena. The female third person singular pronoun is *she* (subjective), *her* (objective), *her* (possessive), and *herself* (reflexive). We might expect, therefore, that children would seek some regularity and substitute *her* for *she* (Rispoli, 1994, 1998). This would follow the phonological regularity found in the first sound of the masculine pronouns *he-him-his-himself* and the third person plural *they-them-their-themselves*. In other words, errors may be based on both semantic and phonological factors, although no one is certain.

PRAGMATICS AND ITS ROLE IN SYNTACTIC DEVELOPMENT

The communicative function of words defines their use. More specifically, articles used with nouns help the listener to locate a referent in actual or conceptual space and verb tense markers help the listener locate a process in actual or conceptual time (Langacker, 1991). In fact, young children use adult nouns early in development to refer to non-object entities such as *kiss, lunch,* and *night* and verbs for nonactions such as *like, feel, want,* and *be* (Nelson et al., 1993). Young children also learn many words that can used as both nouns and verbs, such as *bite, brush, call, drink, help, hug, kiss,* and *walk* (Nelson, 1995).

Instead of understanding abstract syntactic categories such as noun and verb, preschoolers initially understand particular kinds of words based on what those words can and cannot do communicatively. Taught a nonsense word in a format "Look! A wuggie," 2-year-old-children are immediately able to combine the word with verbs (*Hug wuggie*) and to make it plural (*Wuggies*) even though they had never heard these utterances before (Tomasello, Akhtar, Dodson, & Rekau, 1997).

The distinction between nouns and pronouns clearly illustrates the role of pragmatics in development of syntax. Learning the English pronominal system is a complex process. Although a pronoun is a simple device that enables one word to be the equivalent of one or several other words, the listener must understand these equivalences. Typically, speakers use **anaphoric reference**, or referral to what has come before. We can thus decipher *his* and *it* in the sentence, "The boy was watching *his* television when *it* caught fire."

A conversational device, pronouns provide cohesion between old and new information. New information is first identified by name. Then, once identified, it becomes old information and can be referred to by a pronoun. The pronoun refers to what came before or makes anaphoric reference to it. As a kind of shorthand, pronouns facilitate integration of all the complex semantic information in a conversation (Yang, Gordon, Hendrick, Wu, & Chou, 2001). When there is possible confusion, preschool children often use pronominal apposition, as in "My mother, she. . . ." Unless it is a dialectal characteristic, pronominal apposition begins to disappear by school age.

Unlike semantic cases, syntactic roles such as noun and verb are more abstract. While agent-action-object (*Mommy eat cookie*) can be interpreted based on semantic order, syntactic roles of noun-verb-noun (*Mommy eat cookie*) offer less guidance, especially because the two nouns are not morphologically marked in different ways in English. A noun is traditionally defined as a "person, place, or thing" and a verb as an "action word." But nouns can indicate actions, as in the words *discussion* or *biking,* and verbs can indicate nonactions, such as *feel* and *be*. In some cases, even markers, such as use of articles and plural *-s* with nouns (*the cats*) are not appropriate with some proper nouns (*the Mr. Smiths* or the *New York Cities*).

Language Development Differences and Delays

Several factors, such as a child's health, the quality of parent–child interactions, or introduction of a second language, may lead to development that does not follow the outline of this chapter. Let's discuss these briefly.

LANGUAGE DEVELOPMENT DIFFERENCES

In general, language-development differences that are not causes of concern fall into two broad categories, bilingualism and dialectal differences. It is important to stress that these differences are just that. They are differences and not disorders. That is not to say that they do not mask disorders. While a full discussion of language disorders is beyond the scope of this text, suffice it to say that a language disorder would show up in both the native language and in the second language, which in this case is American English. In the previous chapter, we discussed simultaneous development of two languages. Here we shall discuss sequential or successive development. We will also explore dialectal development, focusing on African American English.

Successive Bilingual Acquisition

Most bilingual children develop one language (L_1), such as Spanish, at home and a later second (L_2), such as American English, with peers or in school, usually after age 3. Children who begin learning English at age 5 master comprehension before expression, although English dominance does not occur until middle school (Kohnert & Bates, 2002). Although humans are capable of acquiring a second language at any age, by the late teens it is difficult for a speaker to acquire native-speaker pronunciation characteristics in a second language. In part, this difficulty may reflect the tendency of mature speakers to use processing strategies of their native language to interpret L_2 (Tao & Healy, 1996). Speakers who learn English later in life tend to rely on stress patterns from their native language to interpret English and use English syntax relatively less (Sanders, Neville, & Woldorff, 2002).

The age of arrival in an English-speaking country seems to be critical for second-language learning, especially for East Asians (Jia, Aaronson, & Wu, 2002). For example, Chinese-speaking children who come to the United States before age 9 switch their language preference to English within a year and become more proficient in English than in Chinese (Jia & Aaronson, 2003). Children who immigrate after age 9 usually maintain a preference for Chinese and become less proficient in English than in Chinese. Age of arrival is less of a factor for children immigrating from Europe and may reflect the relative similarity of European language and culture with that of the United States or Canada when compared to East Asian language and culture.

Although young children do not necessarily acquire L_2 faster or more easily than adults, they eventually outperform adults in L_2. In addition, children are less susceptible than adults to interference from L_1. Early exposure to L_2 may result in a delay in L_1 before it is mature. In turn, competence in L_2 may be a function of relative maturity in L_1. Children learning at school age have acquired some metalinguistic skills that may facilitate L_2 learning. There are trade-offs between age and second-language learning.

Success in nonsimultaneous language acquisition is more closely related to a learner's attitude toward and identity with users of the language being acquired, literacy in the home, and his or her positive attitude toward the first language and culture. Need is another strong motivating factor. Interestingly, within limits, intelligence seems to have little effect. Most children acquire a second language rapidly, although the strategies used differ with age, a child's linguistic knowledge, and the nature of the two languages. The more a child's learning style matches the teaching style, the better the development of L_2. Children tend to learn in immediate contexts through sensory activity, while adults prefer explicit rule training.

When children learn two languages successively, they seem to go through easily recognizable stages. In the first stage, a child uses L_1 in the L_2 or English environment even though everyone else is speaking English. A child may persist in this behavior but rapidly realizes that it doesn't work.

A second, nonverbal stage, lasting a few weeks or months, follows, during which a child gains receptive knowledge but says very little in English. Communication is primarily by gesture.

When a child begins to speak, he or she usually uses single words or short phrases or relies on high-usage phrases, such as "Okay," "I don't know," and "Hi, how you doin'?" Gradually, a child begins to produce original phrases and sentences.

as ages 2 to 3 and expands to include a variety of forms and genres, so that by age 5, the basic elements of both fictional and nonfictional narratives are present (Champion, 1998; Price, Roberts, & Jackson, 2006; Sperry & Sperry, 1996).

There are differences too. Let's begin with the language-learning environment. Southern, rural, low-SES African American children are not encouraged to communicate conversationally or to ask questions. In some southeastern Appalachian working-class towns, children are addressed indirectly and are not expected to provide information.

African American children in the rural South are exposed to a wide variety of language through extended families and neighbors who tease and verbally challenge toddlers. The children often begin to speak by imitating the ending phrases of these speakers. Children who try to interrupt adult conversation may be scolded for their speech inaccuracies or for their less mature language. Within other regions, language stimulation may appear in other forms, such as rhymes, songs, or stories.

African American mothers do not feel obligated to teach language. Development differs from that in middle-SES families in the demands for communication placed on the child. Therefore, children differ in their expectations of appropriate communication behavior.

LANGUAGE DEVELOPMENT DELAYS

Several factors seem to predict later speech and language impairments among preschool children. In general, these include

- male gender,
- ongoing hearing problems, and
- a more reactive temperament, consisting of responding negatively to frustration, such as having tantrums.

Factors that could potentially moderate impairment include

- a more persistent and more sociable temperament and
- higher levels of maternal psychological well-being (Harrison & McLeod, 2010).

Significant predictors of late language emergence (LLE) at 24 months of age include family history of LLE and early neurobiological growth (Zubrick, Taylor, Rice, & Slegers, 2007). These factors suggest a strong role for neurobiological and genetic mechanisms of the onset of LLE. In addition, these factors operate across a wide range of maternal and family characteristics, such as parental educational levels, socioeconomic resources, parental mental health, parenting practices, or family functioning.

Delayed language development often predicts a long period of growth difference, particularly for syntax and morphology. Children with a history of LLE at 24 months perform below typical children at age 7 in both speech and language production (Rice, Taylor, & Zubrick, 2008). Even in late adolescence, children with slow language development at 24 to 31 months have weakness in both spoken and written language-related skills (Rescorla, 2009).

Homelessness

The *2012 Annual Homeless Assessment Report* of U.S. Department of Housing and Urban Development estimates that on any given night approximately 630,000 people are homeless and on the streets or in shelters. Within a year as many as 3.5 million people, 1% of the population, may experience homelessness. Within the homeless population, there is an overrepresentation of African Americans, Latino Americans, and Native Americans.

Nearly three fourths of homeless families are headed by a single parent, usually a mother (Lowe, Slater, Wefley, & Hardie, 2002; Weinreb, Buckner, Williams, & Nicholson, 2006). Although, like all parents, these parents care deeply about their children and wish to be good parents, they experience many stressors associated with bureaucratic challenges, shelter living, self-expectations, and the stereotyped perception of women in shelters as unfit mothers.

Preschool children who are homeless are at risk for a combination of language, learning, or cognitive delays (O'Neil-Pirozzi, 2003). In addition, their mothers may exhibit their own language difficulties or deficits. For a variety of reasons, including the mothers' child-rearing beliefs, daily demands on her time, and other life stressors, these mothers also use language strategies sparingly that facilitate young children's language development (Hoff, 2003; O'Neil-Pirozzi, 2006).

Differences in parent language styles are more strongly related to socioeconomic differences than to race or ethnicity (Hammer & Weiss, 2000). In general, parents from low-SES groups use a more directive, less conversational style. Compared with mothers with a high SES, low-SES mothers use a smaller vocabulary, talk less, are more directive, and ask fewer questions of their children (Hoff, Laursen, & Tardiff, 2002). As you might suspect, these characteristics negatively affect young children's syntactic and lexical development (Hoff, 2003; Huttenlocher, Vasilyeva, Cymerman, & Levine, 2002). The use of facilitating language utterances by homeless mothers may be even lower than that of parents who are not homeless (Blom-Hoffman, O'Neil-Pirozzi, Volpe, Cutting, & Bissinger, 2006; O'Neil-Pirozzi, 2006).

Conclusion

BY KINDERGARTEN, A CHILD IS ABLE to uphold his or her end of a conversation. Although a preschooler does not have the range of intentions and subtle conversational abilities or vocabulary of a school-age child, he or she can participate and make valuable conversational contributions. As a child matures socially and cognitively, communication skills and language reflect these developments.

Within a conversational context, a preschool child has progressed from two-, three-, and four-word sentences to longer utterances that reflect adultlike form and content rules. Caregivers continue to treat a child as a conversational partner, and a child's contribution increases in meaningfulness in addition to skill of formation. Increased vocabulary and relational terms enable a child to sustain a conversation on limited topics and to relate action narratives of past and imagined events.

Adults, especially parents, are still the primary conversational partners, although others, such as preschool or daycare friends or siblings, are becoming more important. As a child plays with other children and interacts with adults, he or she learns to modify language for the listener and becomes more flexible. This aspect of language will change greatly throughout the school years.

Discussion

ALTHOUGH TURN TAKING DEVELOPS EARLY, it is a big jump from taking turns passing a ball to becoming a good conversational partner. A preschool child is learning to begin and end conversations; to introduce, maintain, and change topics; and to decide on the right amount of information to provide. In addition, he or she is introducing narratives into the conversation, recalling past events for the conversational partner. It will be many years before conversational and narrative skills reach that of an adult, but we have a strong foundation.

New words and word relationships are also being added to a preschooler's expanding vocabulary. Relational terms such as *better than* and *in front of*

Much of adult morphology, syntax, and phonology has appeared by the time a child goes to kindergarten. This chapter will explain this development and help you understand the course and method of these incredible changes.

Children observe patterns of language use in the environment and gradually—sometimes one word at a time—form hypotheses about the underlying rules. These hypotheses are then tested in the child's speech. Over time, the child's rules change to reflect cognitive and social maturity and greater sophistication in producing and using the linguistic code in conversation. The speed of change varies across linguistic features. Many months or years may be required before the child has complete control of a linguistic element in all contexts. I still make mistakes. How about you?

In this chapter, we'll first relate development of language form to what we learned about semantics in the last chapter. Then we'll discuss development of language.

Given the amount of development that occurs in language form during the preschool years, this chapter is long and complicated. I've tried to shorten it by placing background material in Appendix C. If you don't know a phrase from a clause or never thought about how you form a question syntactically, you might want to read Appendix C before you go any further. I'll wait. If you need further input, ask your professor to suggest a good basic grammar text. Several websites might also be helpful, including

http://en.wikipedia.org/wiki/English_grammar
http://grammar.about.com/od/basicsentencegrammar/a/basicstructures.htm
http://www.grammar.cl/Notes.htm

The Semantic–Syntactic Connection

Although we have discussed the separate domains of language and characterized them as form, content, and use, it is important to recognize that these categories are merely for the convenience of discussion. In the reality of language processing, these aspects of language are interdependent. For example, studies in English and other languages have demonstrated that vocabulary size and syntactic complexity are related in a positive way (Pérez-Leroux, Castilla-Earls, & Brunner, 2012). We noted earlier in the text that vocabulary size among toddlers was a good predictor of later utterance length. Among both preschool and school-age children, a strong correlation exists between vocabulary size and grammatical development (Moyle, Weismer, Evans, & Lindstrom, 2007; Tomblin & Zhang, 2006). These types of findings have led some linguists to propose that there is an underlying, unified learning mechanism for language (MacWhinney, 2005).

The syntax of an utterance emerges from the child's use of language to express meaning (e.g., Atanassova, 2001; Diessel, 2004; Weist, Atanassova, Wysocka, & Pawlak, 1999). When we use specific syntax, we do so in order to facilitate comprehension and expression of the relationship(s) between the concepts we wish to communicate (Diessel, 2004). For example, we can express the addition of two concepts with the word *and*:

Mommy walked to the store *and* daddy drove to school.

This is a different relationship than is expressed in the following sentence:

Mommy walked to the store *because* daddy drove to school.

We can go even further and note that children achieve a way to express meaning about the same time that they acquire the underlying concept. For example, use of syntactic devices to describe temporal relationships (*before, after, first, next, last*) occurs shortly after a child gains the ability to represent temporal concepts cognitively.

The exact manner through which children acquire grammar is unknown. Brain imaging has shown that regular and irregular forms of language rules, as in regular past-tense *walked* and irregular *went*, are processed in different parts of the brain, suggesting that they are not linked in a single rule system. Irregular forms may be associated more closely with semantic information or meaning rather than with morphology. In other words, because we don't seem to access *went* by combining *go* and *-ed*, we might access it directly by a semantic route.

The relationship also flows in the other direction. Individual word learning certainly depends on a word's meaning but also on the role that the word plays in sentences and the ways in which the word is combined with others. Stated another way, word learning is related to syntactic knowledge. It seems logical that children would use all types of reliable information whenever they are available.

Certain types of words, such as nouns and verbs, are treated in distinct ways in sentences. Evidence suggests that children make assumptions about words and that caregivers, usually unintentionally, use conversational strategies that support these assumptions (Hall, Quartz, & Persoage, 2000; Imai & Haryu, 2001; Mintz & Gleitman, 2002; Waxman & Markow, 1999). For example, from adult use a child might correctly assume the following:

if . . . this is an X	must be . . . noun
. . . this is X	. . . proper noun
. . . this is an X one	. . . adjective

When a new word is learned, a child tentatively assigns it to a syntactic category. By noting how the word is used by others, a child confirms the category assignment or makes appropriate changes.

When caregivers read to preschool children, they treat words differently (Hall, Burns, & Pawluski, 2003). Nouns and proper nouns are introduced with little explanation (i.e., *This is an X*). On the other hand, adjectives are introduced and then described or contrasted with other meanings (i.e., *This is an X one. That means . . .*). In this way caregivers help a child acquire words, their meanings, and syntactic categories.

Although nouns are the most easily identifiable word class, words such as *justice* and *love* are so clearly not persons, places, or things that their membership as nouns can only be inferred by their syntactic use as nouns. Thus, both syntactic and semantic factors play a major role in the emergence of language form.

In this video, you'll get a quick overview of language development across the preschool years. http://www.youtube.com/watch?v=QUCcATrW-E8

Sentence processing involves more than just storage of a sequence of words or sounds. The brain predicts the next word in the sentence based on syntactic patterns and grammatical and pragmatic cues. Meaning is found in the individual words and in their combination.

In production, word combinations depend not only on semantics, syntax, and sentence frames but also on templates into which only certain words are acceptable. For example, correct production requires a child to deduce the pattern "V N with N" for words with the semantic features of *fill*, *stuff*, and *cover* ("I filled the tub with water") and the pattern "V N into N" for words with the semantic features *pour*, *dump*, and *empty* ("Pour water in the tub").

Syntactic and Morphologic Development

Before we begin wading through preschool syntactic and morphologic development, we should say something about the way the material will be organized in the following sections. Some changes in preschool language development correspond to increases in a child's average utterance length, measured in morphemes. This value, the **mean length of utterance (MLU)**, is a moderate predictor of the complexity of the language of young English-speaking children. Up to an MLU of 4.0, increases in MLU correspond correct production and comprehension, meaning at first it seems that a child has learned it correctly, but then the child makes more errors, often overgeneralization, and finally correct use returns. Initial use of the bound morpheme may be limited to specific words heard frequently in the child-directed speech of adults. The errors come as a child tries to extend use of the morpheme to words the child has not heard used by others or to infrequently heard words. Gradually, a child begins to abstract a scheme or rule for use of the morpheme.

At any one time, morpheme learning may involve

- perceiving an inflected word (*cats*) and comparing it with the uninflected one (*cat*),
- hypothesizing the function of the morphological marker, and
- placing the morphological marker in a paradigm or model.

Because this must occur while speech is proceeding, processing speed is important. A child must store the novel inflected word in working memory, retrieve its uninflected component from long-term memory, and simultaneously perform a comparative morphological analysis before memory of the marker decays (Tomasello, 2000).

Morphological learning may be made more difficult in English for several reasons (Tomasello, 2006):

- Bound morphemes are phonologically reduced and unstressed monosyllabic bits of language.
- In general, bound morphemes carry very little concrete semantic information and may be redundant.
- Many grammatical morphemes or at least their phonological forms are multifunctional.

Redundancy can also be seen with several bound morphemes. For example, when we say *two kittens*, the number 2 tells us we mean plural, so the plural *-s* is redundant. This isn't always the case, as in *I'll have some cake* (a piece) and *I'll have some cakes* (several). But, of course, this just confuses the issue for a language learner!

The multifunctional quality of some morphemes can be seen in the overworked /s/, /z/, /əz/ markers that can be used for plural (*two cakes*, /s/; *two cards*, /z/; *two cages*, /əz/), possessive (*cat's*, /s/; *dog's*, /z/; *witch's*, /əz/), and third person *-s* (*she kicks*, /s/; *it turns*, /z/; *he kisses*, /əz/). When we compare children's use of the third person present *-s* to the past *-ed*, which is not used to mark any other early morphological distinction, we see the confusion arising from the use of *-s* to also mark plural and possessive. Although all 6-year-old children comprehend *-ed*, it is not until age 7 that all children comprehend *-s* (Beyer & Hudson Kam, 2009). Obviously semantic and phonological distinctions must be explored before a child can use bound morphemes effectively.

Mom's help with some of these grammatical morphemes through the use of recast or reformulated utterances were mentioned in Chapter 7. Thus, mothers provide a child with an immediate comparison of her or his own immature utterance and the corresponding adult form.

As mentioned, a child may also learn a morphologic marker only in specific sentence forms with particular words before going on to learn the general morphologic rule (Wilson, 2003). Even as adults, many of us are not aware of morphological differences, such as the difference between *data* and *datum* or between *uninterested* and *disinterested*.

At an MLU of 2.0 to 2.5, which usually begins around the second birthday, bound morphemes begin to appear. Their development is gradual, and considerable individual variation exists. These and other morphemes may first be learned in specific constructions involving particular words. Most are not fully mastered (used correctly 90% of the time) until much later. Bound morphemes to be discussed are presented in Table 9.1.

TABLE 9.1 Bound Morphemes Acquired in the Preschool Years

Morpheme	Example	Age of Mastery* (in months)
Present progressive *-ing* (no auxiliary verb)	Mommy driv*ing*.	19–28
Regular plural *-s*	Kitti*es* eat my ice cream. Forms: /s/, /z/, and /əz/ *Cats* (/kæts/) *Dogs* (/dɔgz/) *Classes* (/klæsz/), *wishes* (/wIʃəz/)	27–33
Possessive *'s*	Mommy*'s* balloon broke. Forms: /s/, /z/, and /əz/ as in regular plural	26–40
Regular past *-ed*	Mommy pull*ed* the wagon. Forms: /d/, /t/, and /əd/ *Pulled* (/pʊld/) *Walked* (/wɔkt/) *Glided* (/glaIdəd/)	26–48
Regular third person *-s*	Kathy hit*s*. Forms : /s/, /z/, and /əz/ as in regular plural	26–46

*Used correctly 90% of the time in obligatory contexts.

PROGRESSIVE *-ing*

The progressive verb tense is used in English to indicate an activity that is currently or was recently in progress and is of temporary duration, such as I *am swimming*. The progressive form consists of the auxiliary or helping verb *to be* (*am, is, are, was, were*), the main verb, and the *-ing* verb ending. Children initially express this verb tense as *present* progressive, which means the action is happening now, but with only the *-ing* ending. For example, a child might say "Doggie swimming" or "Mommy eating." The progressive verb tense without the auxiliary is the earliest verb inflection acquired in English and is mastered early for most verbs used by young children.

The progressive can be used with action verbs in English but not with verbs of state, such as *need, know,* and *like*. Young children learn this distinction early, and few overgeneralization errors result. (*I am knowing you, He is needing help.*) A child probably learns the rule one verb at a time by applying it to individual verbs to determine whether they are "*-ing* able." Later children abandon this strategy as too cumbersome and adopt an *-ing* rule.

State verbs are not capable of expressing the present progressive meaning of temporary duration. When a child says, "I eating," it is assumed that she'll stop soon. The action is temporary. On the other hand, adults don't say "I am knowing" because

Omission of the third person marker with new verbs may be influenced by adult questions in which the inflection has been transferred to the auxiliary verb, as in the following:

ADULT: Where does it sweep?
CHILD: It sweep here.

Familiar verbs, such as *eat* and *go*, do not seem to be affected by such questions and will appear in a child's answer as *eats* and *goes* (Theakston, Lieven, & Tomasello, 2003).

Development of full understanding of the third person may take even longer than correct production. Speakers of Mainstream American English do not rely on the third person marker alone for either comprehension of tense (*cuts/cut*) or verb–noun distinctions (*the penguin dresses/the penguin dress*) until age 5 and not reliably until age 6 (de Villiers & Johnson, 2007). In contrast, African American English (AAE)–speaking children do not seem to use the information in the third person *-s* at all. This might be expected because the third person marker is rarely used by speakers of AAE.

NOUN AND ADJECTIVE SUFFIXES

During the preschool years, a child begins to acquire a few additional suffixes for nouns and adjectives. These include the adjectival comparative *-er* and the superlative *-est*. By adding these to descriptive adjectives, a child can create forms such as *smaller* or *biggest*. Children understand the superlative by about 3½ years of age; the comparative somewhat later, at age 5. Correct production follows. Specific forms, such as *better* or *best*, which are exceptions to the rule, usually take longer to master.

The derivational noun suffix *-er*, added to a verb to form the name of the person who performs the action, is also understood by age 5 and mastered in production soon after. For example, the person who *teaches* is a *teacher*; the one who *hits* is a *hitter*, and so on. One reason for the late appearance of this marker may be its ambiguous nature. The *-er* is used for both the comparative (*bigger*) and for noun derivation (*teacher*). In addition, several other derivational noun suffixes, such as *-man*, *-person*, and *-ist*, can also be used to designate the person who performs an

Janna Bantan/Shutterstock

Some morphologic developments begin around age 2 and continue well into the school-age years.

action. Two-year-olds tend to rely on the *-man* suffix, often emphasizing it, as in *fisherman*, which contains both the *-er* and the *-man*. Other more creative examples are *busman*, *storewomen*, and *dancerman*.

DETERMINANTS OF ACQUISITION ORDER

The cognitive relationship between the semantic and syntactic complexity of these morphemes and the frequency of use in adult speech help explain further development. The role of English syntactic and semantic complexity becomes evident when we note the order of acquisition in other languages. For example, the concept underlying plural—more than one—is quite simple and is learned as early as age 1 by some children. In Egyptian Arabic, plural marking is very complex, and there are many exceptions to the plural rule. Compared to English-speaking preschoolers, many Egyptian teenagers still have difficulty with the plural.

Initial morphological development of verb markers may be related to the underlying semantic aspects of the verb. A child begins verb development with a few verbs that are general and nonspecific, such as *do*, *go*, and *make*. Once these general forms are developed, the verb markers for these forms appear quickly, suggesting that initial morphological learning may be on a word-by-word basis. In contrast, more specific verbs may be unmarked.

The underlying temporal concept of the verb also seems to be a factor in morphologic learning. For example, the present progressive *-ing* first appears on verbs that display a discrete end with no obvious result, such as *drive*, but not on verbs that describe a discrete event, such as *break*, *hit*, or *drop*. In contrast, the past-tense marker is more likely to appear on verbs that describe a discrete event that expresses a result (Li & Shirai, 2000). Thus, initially a child is more likely to say "Daddy is *driving* the car" and "I *dropped* my cup."

What appears to be working here is the temporal or time properties of situations. The verbs differ in whether the situation has an inherent endpoint. Accomplishments, such as *broke*, express a change of state or location. Activities, such as *playing*, do not. Other aspects include whether the verb implies a dynamic or changing situation, a continuing or singular incident and whether the action is complete or incomplete (Smith, 1997). For example, one study of 2- to 3-year-olds found that children's imitation of verb tenses differed based on the accomplishment versus activity nature of the verb (Johnson & Fey, 2006).

Morphological learning requires that a child correctly segment words into morphemes and correctly categorize words into semantic classes. If a child undersegments, she or he won't break the word or phrase into enough morphemes. The result is creations such as "He *throw-upped* at the party" or "I like *jump-roping*." Most of us learned the alphabet as ". . . J, K, Elemeno, P, Q, . . . ," another good example of undersegmenting. In oversegmenting, the child uses too many morphemes, as in "Daddy, you're *interring-upt* me!" and my son Todd referring to grown-ups as the *dolts*, having oversegmented *adult* into the article *a* and *dolt*. Judging from some of the adults I know, maybe my son was more observant than we gave him credit for being! I've met my share of *dolts*! Two other examples are illustrative. Upon being told her behavior was "inappropriate," a friend's child replied, "No, I'm out of propriate." Last, another friend told of weeks of planning for a trip to Seattle only to find her daughter despondent after three days there. When asked, her daughter pleaded, "I want to see Attle."

Morphemes are not treated the same way by all language-learning children. In polymorphemic languages such as Mohawk, a northern New York and southern Quebec Native language in which words consist of many morphemes, children initially divide words by syllables rather than morphemes. Thus, children are more likely to note and produce stressed syllables than morphemes.

Morphological rules in English apply to classes of words. Hence, *-ing* is used only with action verbs. If the child miscategorizes a word, errors may result. He or she may use inappropriate morphological prefixes and suffixes, as in the following:

> I'm *jellying* my bread. (Using a noun as a verb, although we do say "buttering my bread")
> I got *manys*. (Using a pronoun as a noun)
> He runs *fastly*. (Using an adjective as an adverb)

Often these errors reflect a child's limited descriptive vocabulary. One of my favorites came from my son Jason who, after a fitful sleep, announced, "I hate *nightmaring*." Overgeneralization occurs when a child applies a category rule to subcategories, such as the regular past *-ed* on irregular verbs. Other examples include the following:

> I saw too many *polices*. (Using the plural *-s* inappropriately on a mass noun)
> I am *hating* her. (Using the present progressive *-ing* inappropriately on a state verb)

In another example, a child may apply a limited morpheme to other words, as in *unsad* and *unbig*. Many of the humorous utterances that young children produce reflect errors in segmentation or categorization.

Morphologic rule learning reflects phonologic and semantic rule learning as well. Morphologic rules are learned at an early age, beginning with rules that apply to specific words and continuing through sound-sequence rules. Initial learning may occur on a case-by-case basis. Higher-order rules require more complex integrative learning. Through lexical generalizations, the child learns that a concept may have more than one form and that forms originally construed to be morphologically distinct, such as *more big* and *bigger*, are actually alternatives of the same concept.

Later, morphophonemic rules are required to account for commonalities. For example, the /f/ sound turns to /v/ preceding a plural, as in *knife/knives* and *wolf/wolves*. This rule is not true for all words ending in /f/, such as *cough* or *laugh*. Remember, a preschooler is learning these orally, not in written form. The child recognizes regularity but still must sort out the exceptions. Each of us has heard a small child say a word such as *knifes* (/naIfs/) during this phase.

Phonological variations may influence early morphological use. A child may not recognize the common morpheme beneath variations. For example, a child may not realize that the ending sound on *cats*, *dogs*, and *bridges* signals the same morphologic change, pluralization. Morpheme recognition is easier if the semantic and phonologic variations are minimal, as with *big–bigger–biggest*, rather than *good–better–best*.

In addition to phonologic considerations, the underlying semantic concept may influence morphologic development. For example, cognitive and semantic distinctions may be reflected in the order of acquisition of auxiliary verbs. Initially, the child learns auxiliary verbs concerned with the agent in actual events (*do, have, will*), then with the agent as potential doer (*can, have got to, have to, must, should, had better*), then with a likelihood of events (*might, may*), and finally with inferences about events not experienced (*could*). Thus, a child progresses from a concrete action orientation to a more abstract reference.

Early morphologic development focuses on more concrete relationships, such as plural and possession. Abstract relationships such as person and number markers on the verb tend to take longer to master. The progression from concrete to abstract is also reflected in a developing child's cognitive processing.

Take some time to relax your brain. This is difficult information. When you feel good about bound morphemes, move on.

Phrase Development

Phrases are units of syntax that are used in the construction of longer units, such as sentences. In short, a **phrase** is a group of words that functions as a single distinct syntactic unit that is less than a sentence and does not contain both the subject (noun, pronoun) and the predicate (verb). As such, phrases fill syntactic functions in the sentence, such as noun, verb, or adverb and so on. For example, in the sentence "She was here," *here* is an adverb. I could also say, "She was at our summer cottage." In this case, *at our summer cottage* serves the adverb function. Similarly, in the sentence "Almost everyone on our flight became ill," *Almost everyone on our flight* serves a noun function, and we could replace it with a pronoun to say *They became ill.*

As units of syntax, phrases usually develop within sentences. It seems prudent, however, to pull them out and separately discuss how they develop.

NOUN PHRASE DEVELOPMENT

Noun phrases (NPs) make reference to things in various ways (*your big dog; Derek, my brother; the girl who fell down*). In this way, NPs act as the noun or serve that function in a sentence. NPs can have many elements and become quite complicated. All the elements of NPs are presented in Table 9.2. As you can imagine, it will take several years before a child is able to use all of these easily.

NP elaborations begin when children begin to combine words, but this usually occurs when nouns are in isolation rather than in a longer utterance. The list of early

TABLE 9.2 Elements of the Noun Phrase

INITIATOR	DETERMINER+	ADJECTIVE+	NOUN+	MODIFIER+
Only, a few of, just, at least, less than, nearly, especially, partially, even, merely, almost	Quantifier: *All, both, half, no, one-tenth, some, any, either, each, every, twice, triple* Article: *the, a, an* Possessive: *my, your, his, her, its, our, your, their* Demonstratives: *this, that, these, those* Numerical term: *one, two, thirty, one thousand*	Possessive Nouns: *Mommy's, children's* Ordinal: *first, next, next to last, last, final, second* Adjective: *blue, big, little, fat, old, fast, circular, challenging* Descriptor: *shopping* (center), *baseball* (game), *hot dog* (stand)	Pronoun: *I, you, he, she, it, we, you, they, mine, yours, his, hers, its, ours, theirs* Noun: *boys, dog, feet, sheep, men and women, City of New York, Port of Chicago, leap of faith, matter of conscience*	Prepositional Phrase: *on the car, in box, in the gray flannel suit* Adjectival: *next door, pictured by Renoir, eaten by Martians, loved by her friends* Adverb: *here, there* Embedded clause: *Who went with you, that you saw*
Examples:				
Nearly	*all the one hundred*	*old college*	*alumni*	*attending the event*
Almost all of	*her thirty*	*former brother's*	*clients*	
Nearly	*half of your*	*old baseball*	*uniforms*	*in the closet*

modifiers is generally small (*big, yukky, my*) and only gradually expands as new words are learned. Multiple modifiers are rare among preschoolers.

Children seem to acquire a general rule that adjectives precede nouns in English very early. Around age 2, children also learn that adjectives and articles do not precede pronouns and most proper nouns. It is not acceptable in most situations for mature English speakers to say *little he* or *the Juan*. Of course, children can still make mistakes as they acquire new words.

By age 3, most children produce NP elaboration with the addition of each of the major categories—determiner, adjective, and post-noun modifier—except initiator (Owens, 2013). Although the specific elements used by children differ, most 3-year-olds are using articles, possessive pronouns, and adjectives. Words seen frequently include demonstratives *this, that, these,* and *those*; articles *a* and *the*; and words such as *some, other, more,* and *another*. The most frequent NP elaborations involve one element before the noun as in "*A girl* eated *my cookie*."

Gradually, a child learns the order of different NP elements. As a mature user, you intuitively know that *my big red candy apple* is correct but *red big candy my apple* is not.

Although 3-year-olds seem to understand that pre-noun adjectives (*big dog*) restrict or modify the noun, they do not seem to have the same understanding of post-noun modifiers (*dog* ***in the car***). Nonetheless, the first post-noun modification appears around the third birthday with adverb words, as in "That one *there*" and "This *here*."

By age 4, a child has added quantifiers, demonstratives, and post-noun prepositional phrases (Owens, 2013). These are presented in Table 9.2. Embedded clauses appear in the post-noun position shortly thereafter but are not widely used by most children until school age. Development of clausal embedding will be discussed later.

Articles *a* and *the*

The articles *the* and *a* appear before age 2 but take some time to master. Initially used interchangeably, it is sometimes difficult to ascertain from a child's pronunciation which article is being used.

For adults, the indefinite article *a* is used for nonspecific reference—*a cat* doesn't specify which one—and the definite *the* denotes specific reference. Pragmatic considerations also influence article use. New information is generally marked with *a*, whereas old information is signaled by *the* + noun or use of a pronoun. Of most importance when choosing the appropriate article or use of a pronoun is the speaker's assessment of the knowledge and the expectations of the listener as based on their shared perceptual, previously shared experience, and the immediately preceding discourse. Here's where Theory of Mind comes in.

Correct use of articles and adjectives develops gradually during preschool and kindergarten, possibly as individual words enter a child's lexicon or personal dictionary (Kemp, Lieven, & Tomasello, 2005). Pragmatic correctness, such as use of articles to mark new and old information, usually comes later than the definite-indefinite distinction. Although there are some language differences, Dutch, English, and French 2- to 3-year-old children show a relatively adultlike pattern of association for the distinctions of indefinite/definite and new information/old information (Rozendaal & Baker, 2008). The pragmatic distinction between shared and not shared information appears later.

Initially, the indefinite article *a* tends to predominate. Gradually, children come to use the definite article *the* more frequently. Although most preschoolers follow this path, the rate varies considerably (Abu-Akel et al., 2004).

By 36 months, 90% of children use *a* and *the* correctly, although they tend to overuse the definite article (*the*). This overuse may reflect a child's egocentric assumption that the listener knows more than he or she does. By age 4, a child is more capable of making complicated inferences about the listener's needs. In addition, the 4-year-old knows to use *some* and *any* rather than *a* and *the* with nouns, such as *sand, water,* and *salt,* called *mass nouns* because the name denotes no specific quantity. Some children, especially those with language impairments, will continue to overuse the definite article well into elementary school. Many East Asian languages do not contain articles, so you can imagine the difficulties inherent in learning English as a second language.

VERB PHRASE DEVELOPMENT

A verb is a syntactic element that expresses existence (*I am*), action (*She is jumping*), or occurrence (*We thought of you instantly*). In short, verbs and verb phrases (VPs) say something about people, things, places, and events (*is happy, eats, planted the tree*).

A VP is a construction that includes the verb and all that follows, including noun phrases. The elements of VPs are presented in Table 9.3. Before you begin to read this discussion, you might want to review the discussion on verbs in Appendix C. You might also find this website handy: http://www.examples-help.org.uk/parts-of-speech/verb-tenses.htm

TABLE 9.3 Elements of the Verb Phrase

Modal Auxiliary +	Perfective Auxiliary +	Verb *to Be* +	Negative* +	Passive +	Verb +	Prepositional Phrase, Noun Phrase, Noun Complement, Adverbial Phrase
May, can, shall, will, must, might, should, would, could	*Have, has, had*	*Am, is, are, was, were, be, been*	*Not*	*Been, being*	*Run, walk, eat, throw, see, write*	*On the floor, the ball, our old friend, a doctor, on time, late*
Examples:						
Transitive (may have direct object)						
May	*have*				*wanted*	a cookie
Should			*not*		*throw*	the ball
						in the house
Intransitive (does not take direct object)						
Might	*have*	*been*		*walking*	*to the inn*	
Could			*not*		*talk*	*with you*
Equative (verb *to be* as main verb)						
		Is	*not*			*a doctor*
		was				*late*
		were				*on the sofa*
May		*be*				*ill*

*When modal auxiliaries are used, the negative is placed between the modal and other auxiliary forms, for example, *might not have been going*.

Many verbs appear in the single-word phase of development. At this time, both *transitive* and *intransitive* verbs are produced, but a child does not observe the adult rules for each.

Early in development, children spontaneously produce simple transitive verbs or phrases to describe activities people perform with objects. The main verbs young children use most frequently in these constructions are *break, bring, cut, do, draw, drop, eat, find, get, have, help, hurt, make, open, play, push, put, read, ride, say, take, throw,* and *want.* The primary commonality in intransitive verbs is that they are used for a single participant and action. The most common verbs used in these constructions are *break, come, cry, fall, go, hurt, jump, laugh, open, play, run, see, sing, sit, sleep, stop,* and *swim* (Tomasello, 2003). Note that some words appear on both lists.

A strong correlation exists between the variety of maternal verb usage and a child's development of verbs. The way in which adults use verbs when interacting with children seems to be especially important. Children produce verbs in sentences in much the same way as these verbs were heard in the input (Naigles & Hoff-Ginsberg, 1998). In fact, if young children hear a new verb in a word order that deviates from the typical word order in their language, they often produce the verb in this atypical word order (Akhtar, 1999).

Individual differences among American English-speaking children can, in part, be explained by the language input they receive from parents. More informative parental utterances or those with clearer evidence of tense and person are related to better learning by children and are prime factors, along with a child's gender, in predicting language growth in 2-year-old children (Hadley, Rispoli, Fitzgerald, & Bahnsen, 2011). Directives, such as "Eat your cereal," and reduced questions, such as "Doggie go?" are not informative about tense. The characteristics of parent speech input to young language-learning toddlers is related to development by the child (Fitzgerald, Hadley, & Rispoli, 2013).

A child seems initially to learn verbs as individual items rather than a verb as a member of a category of words. As the child acquires each new verb, he or she observes similarities of syntactic use across items and uses these similarities to predict novel combinations.

Irregular Past Tense

Irregular past-tense verbs, those that do not use the *-ed* ending, such as *ate, wrote,* and *drank*, are a small but frequently used class of words in English. Not all of the approximately 200 irregular verbs in English occur with the same frequency. A small subset of these verbs appears in single-word utterances or by age 2, probably learned individually. For many children, these include *came, fell, broke, sat,* and *went*. Table 9.4 presents the ages at which 80% of preschoolers correctly use certain irregular verbs (Shipley, Maddox, & Driver, 1991). Given the lack of rules for irregular past-tense verbs, it's surprising that preschool children actually make so few errors (Xu & Pinker, 1995). Most errors seem to be based on attempts to generalize from existing irregular verbs as in *sing/sang* influencing *bring* to create *brang*. In similar fashion, knowledge of *drink, drank, drunk* may result in *think, thank, thunk*. Many irregular verbs are not learned until school age.

By 46 months a child has usually mastered both the regular and the irregular past tense in most contexts, as well as other morphemic inflections, such as the third person singular *-s* and the copula or verb *to be* as a main verb. Many verb forms are still to be mastered: past-tense modals and auxiliaries, many irregular past verbs, and the passive voice.

Auxiliary Verbs

Auxiliary or helping verbs *can, do,* and *will/would* first appear in their negative form (*can't, don't, won't*) at 30 months, when MLU is approximately 2.5. Sadly, every parent can attest to the appearance of forms of negatives ("I won't eat it!").

TABLE 9.4 Age of Development of Irregular Past-Tense Verbs

Age (in Years)*	Verb
3–3½	Hit
	Hurt
3½–4	Went
4–4½	Saw
4½–5	Gave
	Ate

*Age at which 80% of children use verb correctly in sentence completion task.
Source: Information from Shipley, Maddox, & Driver (1991).

True auxiliary or helping verbs including *be, can, do,* and *will,* appear later. The verb *to be* may not correctly reflect the verb tense or the number and person of the subject, given its many forms. Thus, a 31- to 34-month-old child may produce "He *am* going," "You *is* running," and so on, although initially she or he will probably overuse *is.* At this age, a child may also begin to overextend the regular past *-ed* marker to irregular verbs, thus producing *eated, goed,* and so on. A sentence may be doubly marked for the past, producing sentences such as "I *did*n't throw*ed* it."

By 40 months the modal auxiliaries *could, would, should, must,* and *might* appear in negatives and interrogatives or questions. Semantically, **modal auxiliaries** are used to express moods or attitudes such as ability (*can*), permission (*may*), intent (*will*), possibility (*might*), and obligation (*must*). Wide variation exists in the acquisition of auxiliary verbs. Table 9.5 presents the ages by which 50% of children begin to use selected auxiliary verbs. Most children use the auxiliaries *do, have,* and *will* by 42 months.

Time and Reference

In English, time and reference to that time are marked by both verb tense and something called aspect. **Tense**, such as past or future, relates the speech time, which is in the present, to the event time, or the time when the event occurs. **Aspect** concerns the dynamics

TABLE 9.5 Auxiliary Verb Use by 50% of Children

Age (in Months)	Auxiliary Verb
27	*Do Have + V-en*
30	*Can Be + V-ing*
	Will
33	*Be going to*
36	*Have got to*
39	*Shall*
42	*Could*

Source: Information from Wells (1979).

of the event relative to its completion, repetition, or continuing duration. Using both time and aspect we can say, "Yesterday my gran'ma said we'll go to the zoo tomorrow." A child's acquisition of tense and aspect reflects both cognitive and linguistic development.

Not all languages use tense and aspect. For example, Mandarin Chinese uses only aspect, and Modern Hebrew uses only tense. In English, tense and aspect, which are intertwined, are acquired later than in Japanese, in which there are distinct suffixes for each.

Children's sense of time and reference to it go through phases of development during the preschool years. These are noted in Table 9.6. Initially, a child talks about things that are occurring now (A). The event time is the same as the speech time. There is no tense or aspect marking. This form is seen in children's use for requests ("Want juice") and to comment ("Doggie run").

Between the age of 18 months and 3 years (B), children speak about the past or present, although the reference point is always in the present. Aspect markers are not combined with tense. Children can distinguish past from nonpast, complete actions from noncomplete, continuative from noncontinuative, and future from nonfuture.

Around age 3 to 3½, a child gains a sense of reference other than the present (C). This occurs at about the same age in very different languages. The notion of referent points can be seen with the following two examples:

1. Kim drove yesterday.
2. We had hoped to go yesterday.

TABLE 9.6 Development of Production of Time and Reference

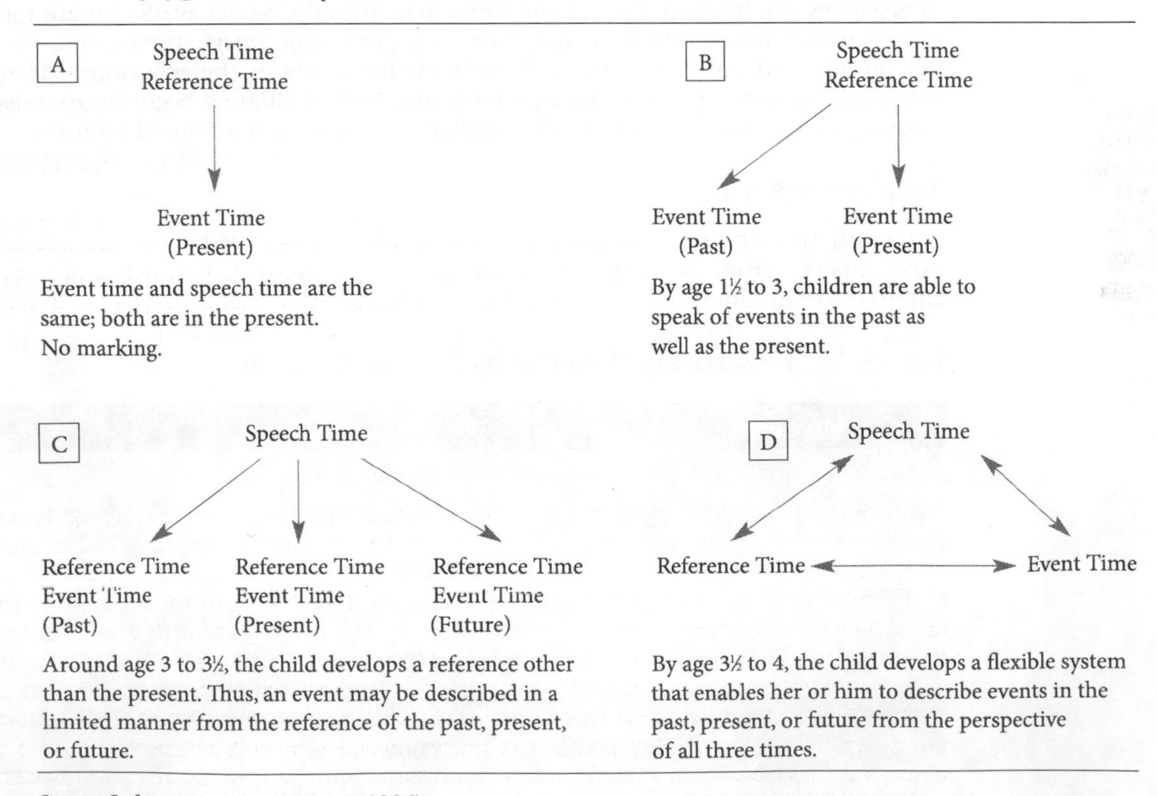

Source: Information from Weist (1986).

In the first, the action was completed in the past but we are describing it from the reference point of the present. In the second, the event is clearly in the past but the reference is some time even earlier, prior to yesterday. Initially, children use adverbs of time such as *yesterday* and *tomorrow*. Only later do they use terms such as *before* and *after*.

Finally, between age 3½ and 4 (D), a child acquires a flexible reference system. This development allows free reference to different points in time. For example, the child might say, "Yesterday, Gran'ma asked, 'Would you like to go to the zoo next week?'" A flexible reference system evolves at about the same time that the child acquires the cognitive skills to arrange things in a series and to reverse this sequential order.

Special Case of the Verb to be

The verb *to be* (*am, is, are, was, were*) may serve as a main verb or as an auxiliary, or helping, verb. As a main verb, it is called the **copula** and is followed by a noun, an adjective, or some adverbs or prepositional phrases. For example, in the sentences "He *is* a teacher," "I *am* sick," and "They *are* late," the verb *to be* is the only verb and hence the main verb or copula. These sentences contain the copula, followed by a noun, *teacher*; an adjective, *sick*; and an adverb, *late*, respectively.

The copula is not fully mastered until around age 4. It takes some time before a child sorts through all the copular variations for person and number (*am, is, are*) and tense (*was, were, will be, been*).

The copula may take many forms to reflect person and number. In general, the *is* and *are* forms develop before *am*. The *is* form tends to be overused, contributing to singular–plural confusion, such as "He *is* fast" and "They *is* big" or "We *is* hungry." The overgeneralization of contractions, such as *'s* and *'re* , also seems to add to the confusion. Contracted forms are short, often unemphasized, and therefore easily missed.

The auxiliary or helping verb *to be* develops more slowly than the copula. Like the copula, the auxiliary *be* is mastered around age 4. The auxiliary *is* and *are* forms precede the *am* form, as in the copula.

There is considerable variation with *it's*. Initially, young children use *it's* and *it* interchangeably, the copula appearing only very gradually.

Young children seem to form their notion of *be* on a word-specific (*am, is, are, was, were*) basis, each variation forming semi-independently (Guo, 2009). Frequency of use of these words seems to influence production accuracy. This would suggest that young children use tense (*am, is, are* vs. *was, were*) and agreement (*I am, she is, they were*) morphemes variably. In order to produce utterances with *be*, young children seem to use highly frequent/word-specific constructions.

PREPOSITIONAL PHRASE DEVELOPMENT

Beginning with their first words, English-speaking toddlers use a variety of location words to express spatial relationships in utterance-level constructions. These include prepositions such as *down, in, off, on, out, to, under*, and *up*, and *verb + particle* constructions, such as *get X down, pick X up*, and *wipe X off*, a holdover from English's German roots. The earliest prepositions are typically *in, on*, and *to* (Owens, 2013). More complex structures might include forms such as "Draw star on me" and "Peoples on their boat" within a few months (Tomasello, 1992b). By age 3, most children have sufficient flexibility to talk explicitly about location in events with three participants as in "*Mommy* put *cereal* in my *bowl*." Notice that the prepositional phrase is at the end of the sentence, which is common in early use. Examples of preschool prepositional phrases are presented in Box 9.1. Development will continue into school age as a child adds ever

BOX 9.1

Examples of Prepositions and Prepositional Phrases of Preschoolers

27 months:	Come **on**.
	Granpa's **in woods**.
36 months:	I'm pouring it **in**.
41 months:	Hi dad, yell **at him** to come back.
42 months:	It's time **for my baby** to go *to bed*.
52 months:	He's doing it **with his feet**.
56 months:	Now it's time **for them** to go **to the store with mommy**.

more complicated prepositional relations and temporal and figurative uses. A full list of prepositions is included in Appendix C.

INFINITIVE PHRASE DEVELOPMENT

Between 2 and 3 years of age, children begin to acquire infinitives. The most frequent error is omission of *to*. These errors seem to be related to different verbs that precede the infinitive, as in "going to" and the frequency with which these verbs are heard by a child (Kirjavainen, Theakston, & Lieven, 2009). At around age 2½ a child develops semi-infinitives such as *gonna* and *wanna*. Occasionally, these forms are followed by a verb, as in "I want (or *wanna*) eat cookie," but at this age, they often are used alone, as in "I wanna." The word *to* is first used at about this time, but as a preposition indicating "direction toward," as in "I walked *to* the store," not as an infinitive. By age 3, forms such as *gonna, wanna, gotta, hafta,* and *sposta* are being used regularly preceding verbs to form infinitive phrases, usually in the object position of the sentence, as in "I want *to eat*." Examples include "I got*ta go*" and "I wan*na play*." As in the examples, almost all of the initial infinitives follow a pattern of *I* + present tense *gotta, hafta,* and so on (Diessel & Tomasello, 2001). Negatives are rare.

From age 2 to 5, infinitive phrases change in several ways (Tomasello, 2003). First, single nouns and third person pronouns (*he, she, it*) are used in place of *I* (*He wants to eat now; Mommy want to drink that*). Second, negative infinitives appear (*I don't like to eat mustard*). Third, a wider range of verbs, such as *remember* and *forget* is used prior to the infinitive phrase (*I forgot to buy candy*). Fourth, other tenses are used as noted in the previous example. Fifth, children learned more complex constructions with a noun phrase between two verbs (*I want mommy to do it*). Finally, children develop *wh-* infinitives, such as *I forget when to go to school*.

More complex infinitives typically appear at the ends of sentences. For example, the child develops *wh-* infinitives, such as "I know *how to do it*" and "Show me *where to put it*." The child also begins to use unmarked infinitive phrases—those without *to*—following verbs such as *help, make,* and *watch,* as in "She can help me *pick these up*." This form is more difficult for a child because the infinitive is not clearly marked. Infinitives are initially learned and used with a small set of verbs, such as *see, look, know, think, say,* and *tell,* as in "I want *to see it*" or "I don't have *to tell you*."

Around 3½, a child begins to use infinitives with nouns other than the subject. For example, a child may say, "This is the right way *to do it*" or "I got this *to give to you*." Most

BOX 9.2

Examples of Embedded Infinitive Phrases of Preschoolers

24 months:	He **gonna get** this.
37 months:	I'm **gonna clean** my room up.
39 months:	Mom, I want **to watch** *Shrek*.
	It's **gotta go** in here.
53 months:	That's where his shoes are supposed **to go**.
	Sissy knows how **to play** a game.
59 months:	We're **gonna make** pizza together.
60 months:	There's nothing else I do **to help** my friends.

children with MLUs above 4.5 continue to use simple but true infinitives with the same subject as the verb. Examples of the infinitive of preschoolers are presented in Box 9.2.

GERUND PHRASE DEVELOPMENT

Gerund development generally parallels that of infinitives. This would seem logical given that gerunds can generally be used where infinitives are, as in "I love to paint" and "I love painting." Gerunds appear after age 4. They first appear in the object position at the end of the sentence. These forms are used infrequently. The most common forms of gerunds are *See X verb-ing* and *Watch X verb-ing*.

Sentence Development

Preschool sentence development can be gauged by an increase in the number of sentence elements and in the diversity of sentence forms. Increases in the number of elements usually occur in declaratives before occurring in other sentence types. The emergence of adult forms takes some time. The majority of English-speaking children, however, possess these sentence types by age 5.

As we might expect, the learning a new syntactic form facilitates acquisition of other sentences that follow the same form. Thus, if a child uses *is* and *are* in declarative sentences and learns to place one in an interrogative, learning to place the second one should be easier. Similarly, placing *is* and *are* copulas in an interrogative should facilitate learning to place auxiliary *is* and *are* in interrogatives. In similar fashion, the learning of more complex sentences seems to facilitate the learning of others even though the structure is different (Keren-Portnoy & Keren, 2011).

Before reading further, you might want to consult Appendix C, especially on the making of negative and interrogative sentences. The development of each is included in Table 9.7.

DECLARATIVE-SENTENCE FORM

Declarative sentences or statements gradually increase in complexity and in number of elements or constituents throughout the preschool years. A child develops the basic *subject + verb + object* sentence format by about 30 months.

TABLE 9.7 **Acquisition of Sentence Forms***

Age (in Months)	MLU	Declarative	Negative	Interrogative	Embedding	Conjoining
12–22	MLU: 1–1.5	Agent + action; Action + object	Single word—*no, all gone, gone; negative* + *X*	*Yes/no* asked with rising intonation on a single word; *what* and *where*		Serial naming without *and*
22–26	MLU 1.5–2.0	Subj. + verb + obj. appears	*No* and *not* used interchangeably	*That X?* *What* + NP + (doing)?	*In* and *on* appear	*And* appears
27–28	MLU: 2.0–2.25	Subj. + copula + complement appears		*Where* + NP + (going)?		
28–30	MLU: 2.25–2.5	Basic subject-verb-object used by most children	*No, not, don't,* and *can't* used interchangeably	*What* or *where* + subj., + pred. Earliest inversion appears	*Gonna, wanna, gotta*, etc., appear	
31–32	MLU: 2.5–2.75	Subj. + aux. + verb + obj. appears; auxiliary verb forms *can, do, have, will,* and *be* appear	Negative element placed between subject and predicate	with copula in *What/where* + copula + subj.		*But, so, or,* and *if* appear
33–34	MLU: 2.75–3.0	Auxiliary verb appears with copula in subj. + aux. + copula + *X*	*Won't* appears	Auxiliary verbs *do, can,* and *will* begin to appear in questions; inversion of subject and auxiliary verb appears in yes/no questions		

Age (in Months)	MLU	Declarative	Negative	Interrogative	Embedding	Conjoining
35–37	MLU: 3.0–3.5		Negative appears with auxiliary verbs (subj. + aux. + neg. + verb)	Inversion of auxiliary verb and subject in *wh-* questions	Object-noun-phrase complements appear with verbs such as *think*, *guess*, and *show*; embedded *wh-* questions	Clausal conjoining with *and* appears (most children cannot produce this form until late stage V); *because* appears
38–40	MLU: 3.5–3.75	Double auxiliary verbs appear in subj. + aux. + aux. + verb + *X*	Adds *isn't*, *aren't*, *doesn't*, and *didn't*	Inversion of copula and subject in yes/no questions; adds *do* to yes/no questions; adds *when* and *how*	Infinitive phrases appear at the ends of sentences	
41–46	MLU: 3.75–4.5	Indirect object appears in subj. + aux. + verb + ind. obj. + obj.	Adds *wasn't*, *wouldn't*, *couldn't*, and *shouldn't*; negative appears with copula in subj. + copula + neg.	Adds modals; stabilizes inverted auxiliary; some adultlike tag questions appear	Relative clauses appear in object position; multiple embedding appear by late stage V; infinitive phrases with same subject as the main verb	Clausal conjoining with *if* appears; three-clause declaratives appear
47+	MLU: 4.5+		Adds indefinite forms *nobody*, *no one*, *none*, and *nothing*; has difficulty with double negatives	Questions other than one-word *why* questions appear; negative interrogatives beyond age 5	Gerunds appear; relative clauses attached to the subject; embedding and conjoining appear within same sentence above an MLU of 5.0	Clausal conjoining with *because* appears with *when*, *but*, and *so* beyond an MLU of 5.0; embedding and conjoining appear within the same sentence above an MLU of 5.0

*Based on approximately 50% of children using a structure.

Older preschool children are able to express complicated relationships about location and talk about the past, present, and future.

By an MLU of 2.5–3.0 or about 33 months, a child has added the auxiliary verb forms *do, have, can, be,* and *will.* The *subject + auxiliary + verb + object* form ("Mommy *is* eating ice cream"; "*I'll* drive that") appears before forms such as "*will* be." Declaratives with double auxiliaries, as in "You *will have* to do it," appear around 3½ but are exceptionally rare.

Finally, close to age 4, a child acquires indirect objects. The *subject + verb + indirect object + object* form ("He gave *me* the ball") appears prior to the *subject + verb + object + to + indirect object* form ("He gave the ball *to me*").

Indirect objects occur in three forms in English, *to + object* (*I gave it to mommy*), *for + object* (*We bought it for daddy*), and double-object (*I bringed mommy flowers*). Although many verbs, such as *bring, give,* and *offer,* can occur in the *to + object* and double-object format, a great many are *to + object* only (*donate*) or double-object only (*cost, deny, fine*). The verbs young children use most frequently in the double-object format are *being, buy, find, get, give, make, read, send, show, take,* and *tell* (Campbell & Tomasello, 2001).

By age 5, a child is capable of saying "She could have given a gift to me." Impressive! But you won't hear it often.

INTERROGATIVE-SENTENCE FORM

Through the use of intonation, children learn to ask questions early on. By age 4, the child seems to do nothing else but ask questions. Questioning is a unique example of using language to gain information about language and about the world in general. I recall my own sense of loss when I replied, "I used to" to my 4-year-old daughter's query "Do you ever talk to the trees?"

Questions are prevalent in the speech adults address to children. Although the amount of questioning doesn't change much in the first 18 months for each parent–child pair, the types of questions and the topics do. At first, questions are used to comment on where the child is gazing (*Are you looking at a birdie?*) or to direct the child's attention to the mother's activity (*What's mommy doing?*). By 18 months, the questions are mostly tutorial or genuine requests for information.

A preschool child's ability to answer questions is influenced by both the type of question and the verb in the question (Salomo, Lieven, & Tomasello, 2013). A third factor is the amount of information requested. For example, questions that focus on the person or thing (agent) providing the action, such as "Who is running?" and questions that focus on the action, such as "What is the boy doing?" are easier for children younger than 4 to answer than more open-ended questions requiring a sentence response, such as "What happened?" Ease in answering also depends on the verb. Answers involving intransitive verbs, such as *sit* and *walk*, that do not require a direct object are easier than those with transitive verbs, such as *want* and *break*, that do require an object.

The difficulty in answering grows with an increase in the amount of information requested. Intransitive answers would require the one-word verb (*jumping*), transitive would require a phrase with the verb and the object (*drawing pictures*), and open-ended questions would require something approaching a sentence (*The boy is drawing pictures*).

Subject-Verb Inversion

Children begin to ask questions at the one-word level through the use of rising intonation (*Doggie?* ↑), through some variation of *what* (*Wha?, Tha?* , or *Wassat?*), or through phonetically consistent forms. There appear to be three phases of question development in young children (Table 9.7). The first phase, which corresponds to an MLU of 1.75 to 2.25 and occurs shortly after the second birthday, is characterized by the following three types of question form:

Nucleus + intonation	That horsie?
What + noun phrase + (*doing*)	What that?
	What doggie (doing)?
Where + noun phrase + (*going*)	Where ball?
	Where man (go)?

These questions are confined to a few routines in which a child requests the names of objects, actions, or locations. The child neither comprehends nor asks other *wh-* questions, although *why* may be used alone (*why?*) as a turn filler to keep the conversation going. *What* and *where* may appear early because they relate to the child's immediate environment. *What* is used to gain labels; *where*, to locate objects. In addition, both are heavily used by parents to encourage a child's speech and are related to the early semantic categories of nomination and location.

By an MLU of 2.25 to 2.75, around 30 to 32 months, a child uses both a subject and a predicate in questions, as in "What doggie eat?" and "Where Johnnie go?" Other questions, such as the yes/no type, may still be identified by rising intonation alone, as in "Daddy go work?"↑.

Subject-verb inversion occurs at the end of this phase in *wh-* interrogatives with the copula (*wh-* + *copula* + *subject* as in *Where is daddy?*). Not surprisingly, the first *wh-* words used in this construction are *what* and *where*.

At an MLU of 2.75 to 3.5 or 33 to 37 months, a child begins to invert subjects and auxiliary verbs. During this phase a child also is acquiring the auxiliary verb in other sentence types, although some errors will persist. Here are two examples of noninversion by a 34- and 53-month-old child, respectively: "What we can do?" and "We going on a froggy hunt?" At about the same time or shortly after, a child begins to invert the copula *be* within *wh-* and yes/no and to add *do* when no auxiliary exists (*Megan likes cookies* becomes *Does Megan like cookies?*) (Santelmann, Berk, Austin, Somashekar, & Lust, 2002).

In *wh-* questions, the type of *wh-* word may influence whether the auxiliary is inverted. In general, the earlier the *wh-* word is acquired, the more likely the verb is to be inverted. Hence, a child would be more likely to invert the verb in *what* (*What is daddy doing?*) questions than in *why* (*Why are we going?*) questions. Correct inversion of the subject and the auxiliary verb also varies with specific verbs (Rowland, Pine, Lieven, & Theakston, 2005). For example, *are, have, do,* and modal auxiliary verbs were significantly more difficult for children to invert than auxiliary verbs *is* and *has*. See Appendix C for an explanation of modal auxiliaries.

To add to your confusion, noninverted questions such as "He's eating clams?" or "He's eating what?" are acceptable in some contexts even for adults. Say these sentences out loud and you'll note that you would use these to obtain clarification of a previous statement or an indication of surprise, as in the following exchange:

> SPEAKER 1: *I just saw Mike at the Fish Shack eating clams!*
> SPEAKER 2: *He was eating what?*

Contrast this with inverted interrogatives, such as "What was Mike eating?" One other exception to inversion occurs when the *wh-* word is the subject of the sentence, as in "Who *can* go with her?"

The acquisition of auxiliary *do* and modal auxiliaries is complex. The auxiliary *do* usually does not occur in positive declarative sentences except for emphasis, as in "I love roller coasters" contrasted with "I *do* love roller coasters." The auxiliary *do* tends to occur in its positive form only in interrogatives, as in "*Does* she run track?" The negative *do*, on the other hand, can occur in both declaratives, as in "He *doesn't* eat dairy products," and in interrogatives, as in "*Doesn't* she want to go?"

It should be obvious why it takes English-speaking children time to master many of these rules, especially those governing interrogatives. Most preschool children will produce both correct and incorrect interrogatives for a relatively long period of time. In general, we can make several generalizations:

- Error rates in *wh-* questions vary with the specific *wh-* word used. For example, most children make more errors in *why* questions.
- Errors occur with some auxiliaries more than others. For example, in both declaratives and interrogatives of children ages 34 to 42 months, *can* tends to be produced correctly most often, followed by *will* and then *does* (Rowland & Theakston, 2009). This order may reflect the additional knowledge regarding how to mark tense, person, and number required to allow correct use of *do*.
- Higher error rates tend to occur in negative questions.

At all ages, use of auxiliary verbs in declaratives is significantly better than in questions. Taken together, these trends suggest a complex interaction among sentence type, negative–positive polarity, and type of auxiliary verb.

Children seem to understand the relation between positive and negative forms of auxiliary *can, will,* and *does* in declaratives by age 3. Although children seem to recognize the relationship, this alone is not sufficient to ensure correct use of negative forms in their own questions. Negative interrogatives pose particular problems for children in the earliest stages of auxiliary verb acquisition around age 3. By 41 months, however, this difference is negligible (Rowland & Theakston, 2009).

To some extent, input from adults seems to affect acquisition order, although this alone does not explain the process. For example, adult yes/no questions starting with *can* are more frequent than questions beginning with *will* and *does*.

Although all forms of *do* (*do, does, did*) occur at a high frequency in yes/no questions, this does not appear to be reflected in high levels of accurate use of *does*. This suggests a lack of generalizing across auxiliary forms and may reflect the difficulty in learning multiple forms.

When children produce auxiliary verb substitutions in interrogatives, they predominantly use either *can* or *is* in the inverted position. These two auxiliaries are very frequent in yes/no questions of mothers. This suggests that children rely on high-frequency forms in their own production of original questions.

Auxiliary substitution errors might arise for two reasons:

1. Children lack syntactic knowledge and have not learned how to produce declaratives and/or interrogatives correctly with some auxiliaries, and therefore make substitution errors more often with forms with which they are less familiar.
2. Children lack semantic knowledge and do not understand the meaning of more subtle distinctions between some auxiliaries.

By 35 months, nearly half of the errors are double marking or two forms of the auxiliary. The resultant utterances include two auxiliary verbs, as in "*Is* the boy *doesn't* ride his bike?" or "*Is* the girl *will* jump over it?"

Most children attain the basic adult question form by 40 months. In addition, *who*, *when*, and *how* interrogatives appear, although the child still has some difficulty with the temporal or time aspects of the last two. Examples of child questions are presented in Box 9.3.

The general order of acquisition of *wh-* question types is determined primarily by the frequency of use by caregivers and to a lesser degree by the elements in the declarative form of the sentence that each *wh-* word replaces (Rowland, Pine, Lieven, & Theakston, 2003). Words such as *what*, *where*, and *who* are pronoun forms for the sentence elements they replace. For example, in the sentence "Mother is eating ice cream," we can substitute *what* for *ice cream*. The resultant question is "What is mother eating?" In contrast, words such as *how* and *when* are used to ask for semantic relations within the sentence (*How did you make it?*). These semantic relations are more difficult than simple

BOX 9.3

Examples of Interrogative Sentences of Preschoolers

26 months:	Want on?
30 months:	What is that thing?
	Where's my sticker book?
42 months:	Chalk used to be here but where did it go? (Conjoining)
46 months:	Does yours smell like this?
	Does this go this way?
50 months:	How do you put these on?
	Let's show the women that's in here, okay? (Immature tag with embedded clause)
	Can I have a little bit, too?
61 months:	Why are you gonna be back in a little while? (Embedded phrases)
64 months:	Do you know what person this is? (Embedded clause)
	What happens if we break this? (Conjoining)
	Looks like soap, doesn't it? (Mature tag)
	I wonder what that is? (Embedded clause)

noun substitutions; they develop later and usually cannot be replaced by a single word. The late development of *why* interrogatives can be explained in similar fashion. Unlike the other *wh-* types, *why* interrogatives affect the entire clause rather than sentence elements or relationships.

Between an MLU of 3.75 to 4.5 interrogative development is mainly concerned with tensing and modals. In addition, the almost 4-year-old child stabilizes the use of the inverted auxiliary.

Negative interrogatives appear after age 5. In general, negative interrogatives, such as "Aren't you going?" are first acquired almost exclusively in the uninverted form, as in "You aren't going?"

Tag Questions

Mature tag questions appear at a relatively late point due to their relative complexity and infrequent usage in American English. Less complex forms—using tags such as *okay, huh,* and *aye,* as in "I do this, okay?"—develop earlier. These forms are more commonly used among English-speaking populations of Canada and Australia in sentences such as "Nice day, aye?"

Three phases have been identified in the development of tag questions. At first, grammatically simple tag forms, such as *okay* and *right,* are used. Truer tags are added later, but with no negation of the proposition. For example, the child might ask, "You like cookies, *do* you?" Finally, the full adult tag, as in "You like cookies, *don't you*?" or "You don't like cookies, *do you*?" is acquired during early school age. Mature tags require complex syntax, so simple tags predominate until age 5.

American English-speaking children acquire the adult form of tag questions later than do British and Australian children because of its infrequent use in American English. Canadian children may also be somewhat late in mastering the full adult form because of the colloquial use of *aye,* as in "You bought a new jacket, *aye*? Just right for this snow, *aye*?" I usually tease my Canadian students that it is impossible for them to make a declaration because they always attach *aye* to the end of every sentence. (Which, of course, they don't.)

IMPERATIVE-SENTENCE FORM

Adult imperative sentences appear around age 2½. In the imperative form the speaker requests, demands, asks, insists, commands, and so on, that the listener perform some act. The verb is uninflected and the subject, *you,* is understood and therefore omitted. Examples include the following:

> Gimme a cookie, please.
> Throw the ball to me.
> Pass the peas, please.

It is somewhat difficult to recognize the imperative in English because there are no morphologic markers. Younger children will produce early forms that mirror imperative sentence form, such as "Eat cookie." These are not true imperatives, however, because young children often omit the subject from sentences clearly intended to be declarative. For example, "Eat cookie" may refer to what mommy is doing. These omissions reflect cognitive processing limitations. This is not meant to imply that toddlers cannot demand of or command others. Even at a prelinguistic level, infants are very adept at expressing their needs. At age 18 months, my granddaughter would demand, "Juice NOW."

NEGATIVE-SENTENCE FORM

Five adult forms of the negative exist in English:

1. *not* and *-n't* attached to the verb;
2. negative words, such as *nobody* and *nothing;*
3. the determiner *no* used before nouns or nounlike words, as in "*No* cookies for you";
4. negative adverbs, such as *never* and *nowhere;* and
5. negative prefixes, such as *un-, dis-,* and *non-.*

The different forms develop at different times.

The earliest negative to appear is the single-word form *no,* which is frequently found within the first 50 words. Syntactic negation appears in longer utterances. The negative element appears prior to the verb, as in "No eat ice cream."

Utterances in which *no* appears before the subject, as in "No Daddy eat" occur less frequently. This *negative + sentence nucleus* form is usually confined to rejection of a proposed or current course of action. For example, if the father were in the process of leaving and the child objected, he or she might state, "No Daddy go bye-bye."

The specific negative element(s) the child uses seems to reflect parental use with the child. Some parents prefer to control behavior with *no;* others employ *don't.* In general, children prefer to use certain forms to fulfill specific intentions. Since this is an individual preference, there is great variety. Examples of negative sentences from several different children are presented in Box 9.4.

There seem to be three periods of syntactic development of negation (Table 9.7). The first period, just discussed, occurs up to an MLU of 2.25 or about 28 months. In the second period, around age 30 months, the negative structure is placed between the subject and the predicate or main verb. A child uses the contractions *can't, don't, no,*

BOX 9.4

Examples of Negative Sentences of Preschoolers

27 months: I **not** make mess.
42 months: I'm **not nothing** of yours (Double negative, but then a self-correction); I'm **not having anything** of yours.
52 months: I think he's **never** probably done it before.
57 months: But I **can't** tell you when I'm back from vacation.

Negative conversation between 54-month-old E and 32-month-old B.

B: Look what I found. A mitten. I found a mitten.
E: That's **not** a mitten.
B: What is it?
E: He's a puppet.
B: Puppet. And that's a puppet. That's a puppet.
E: This is **not** a puppet. This is a big soft worm.
B: Throw it on the floor. I **don't** want it.

and *not* interchangeably. The child does not differentiate these forms, and their positive elements, *can* and *do*, appear only later. Hence, the sentences "I don't eat it" and "I can't eat it" may mean the same thing. *Won't* appears shortly thereafter and, for a brief period, may also be used interchangeably with *no, not, don't,* and *can't.*

In the final period, an MLU of 2.75 to 3.5, a 3-year-old child develops other auxiliary forms. The child develops the positive elements *can, do, does, did, will,* and *be.* These are used with *not* followed by a main verb in negative sentences, as in "She *cannot go.* " Contracted forms also continue to occur in *don't, can't,* and *won't.*

It will be some time before the child correctly uses all the morphologic markers for person, number, and tense with auxiliary verbs. Because use of auxiliaries is a relatively new behavior for the child, he or she may continue to make errors, such as double tense markers, as in "I didn't did it."

By an MLU of 3.5 to 3.75 or 38 to 40 months of age, a child begins to use more negative contractions, including *isn't, aren't, doesn't,* and *didn't.* This development of negative forms continues with the addition of the past tense of *be* (*wasn't*) and modals such as *wouldn't, couldn't,* and *shouldn't.* These forms appear infrequently at first.

Four-year-olds comprehend many negatives, especially with descriptive terms, such as *big,* to mean the opposite, thus, "He's not big; he's little." Not all negatives can be interpreted in this manner. For example, "He's not walking" has no opposite and could mean that he's crawling, running, rollerblading, biking, or driving, to name just a few possibilities. Even though children have a preference for a strong negative interpretation, they are capable of using semantic characteristics of objects, aspects of the verb, and experience to modify their interpretations (Morris, 2003).

It would be incorrect to assume that children master the negative within the preschool period. Negative interrogatives do not appear until after age 5. In addition, indefinite forms, such as *nobody, no one, none,* and *nothing,* prove troublesome even for some adults. It is not uncommon to hear

I *don't* want *none.*
Nobody don't like me.
I *ain't* scared of *nothing.*
I *didn't* get *no* cookies.

Some of these double negatives occur so frequently in the speech of children and some adults that they almost seem acceptable.

SUBORDINATE CLAUSE DEVELOPMENT

Subordinate or dependent clauses, described in detail in Appendix C, are used to combine clauses in a certain way that forms a complex sentence. Among preschool children we see two types primarily, object-noun-phrase complements and relative clauses.

Object-Noun-Phrase Complements

Object-noun-phrase complements first appear around age 3. These subordinate clauses generally have the form of simple sentences, as in

I know *that you can do it.*
I think *that I like stew.*

At first, the basic *I know* format appears alone meaning something akin to *maybe* (Diessel & Tomasello, 2001). The *I know* phrase is then pieced with a subordinate clause.

BOX 9.5

Examples of Embedded Noun-Phrase Complement Clauses of Preschoolers

32 months:	Oh, look **what I found.**
52 months:	Sometimes I forget **what animals they are.**
	I think **the problem is the duckies don't like coming here.**
54 months:	Actually, I'm pretending **it's paint.**
59 months:	I think **that's funny.**
	You know **what I'm going to be when I grow up?** (Embedding and conjoining)
60 months:	You know **how people leave out something sometimes.**
	I remember **that I fell down outside.**
	I don't know **where mom put it,** but I think **it's in my room.** (Multiple embedding)

In general, the subordinate clause fills an object role for verbs, such as *think, guess, see, say, wish, know, hope, like, let, remember, forget, look*, and *show*. The verb in the main clause is most often *think*, as in "I think that I saw a cat." Above an MLU of 4.5, the child may omit the conjunction *that*. Other examples are presented in Box 9.5.

A second object-noun-phrase type of embedding occurs with the attention-getting verbs like *look* and *see*, followed by a clause. This type is almost exclusively imperative. Both the *I know* and *look/see* formats suggest that initially a child's learning may be word-specific rather than representing adultlike understanding.

Later subordinating words in embedded *wh-* complements include *wh-* words such as *what, where*, and *when*, with *what* being used most frequently. Since this form appears at about the same time that the child begins to acquire the adult interrogative form, some initial confusion may exist. Resultant forms may include

I know *what is that.*
Tell me *where does the smoke go.*

Other examples are presented in Box 9.5.

Relative Clause Embedding

Almost all of children's initial relative clauses appear at the end of the sentence and take two forms (Diessel & Tomasello, 2001):

1. *Here's the X that verbs*
2. *That's the X that verb-s*

The main clause basically introduces a new topic using *Here/That* plus *is*. The complex relative clause construction is based in a simpler set of word-specific or item-based constructions.

Many early relative clauses modify empty or nonspecific nouns—*one, kind, thing, place, way*—to form sentences such as "This is the one (*that*) *I want*" or "This is the way

BOX 9.6

Examples of Embedded Relative Clauses of Preschoolers

41 months:	That's all the kites **I bought**.
52 months:	I love birdies **that do tricks.**
53 months:	Well, there's other things **that go in it.**
54 months:	That's a pretty necklace **that you have on.**
	This is **where we get it out from.**
60 months:	That's one of God's things **that he doesn't like.**

(*that*) *I do it.* " In these examples, the object of the sentence is *one* or *way*, and the subordinate clause specifies *which one* or *which way*. Later, relative clauses are used to modify common nouns, as in "Chien Ping has the book (that) I bought."

Full relative clauses appear close to the fourth birthday, although partial forms may appear earlier. They develop gradually, accounting for less than 15% of the two-clause utterances of 5-year-olds. As with other types of embedding, expansion begins at the end of the sentence, as in the following:

This is the kind *what I like*.
This is the toy *that I want*.

In these examples, the relative clause is attached to and modifies the object of the sentence. Some examples of relative clauses attached to the subject include

The one *that you have* is big.
The boy *who lives in that house* is a brat.

Relative clauses attached to the subject do not develop until after 5 years of age, although these forms are still rare by age 7. Examples are presented in Box 9.6.

Connective Words

Many connective words used to join clauses are first learned in nonconnective contexts. For example, *what* and *where* appear in interrogatives prior to their use as relative pronouns. The connective *when* is an exception. *When* is used as a connector to mark temporal relations before the *when* question form develops. Thus, children are likely to produce "I don't know *when* he went" before "*When* did he leave?" Most preschool errors involve use of the wrong relative pronoun as in the following examples (McKee, McDaniel, & Snedeker, 1998, p. 587):

The potato what she's rolling.
Those plates why the elephants are eating them.
The chairs who are flying.

Mature English speakers can omit some relative pronouns, such as *that*, without changing the meaning of the sentence. At first, a preschool child needs these pronouns in order to interpret the sentence. By age 4, however, she or he can comprehend a sentence that omits the relational word. Most children begin to omit some relative pronouns in production soon after, although this form is rare in the speech of preschool children:

This is the candy *that* Hasan likes. (Relative pronoun present)
This is the candy Hasan likes. (Relative pronoun omitted)

Most 4-year-old children can produce multiple embeddings within a single sentence, although such forms are rare even throughout the early school years. For example, a child may combine a subordinate clause (italicized) with an infinitive (underlined) to produce

I think *we gotta go home now*.

Later forms also include conjoined clauses and embedding in the same sentence.

COMPOUND SENTENCE DEVELOPMENT

Cognitively, children are able to form collections of things early on. Most children have appropriate production of *and* to list entities (*dogs and cats and . . .*) between 25 and 27 months of age. Around age 3, individual sentences within an ordered series may begin with *and*, as in the following:

And I petted the dog. And he barked. And I runned home.

In this example, *and* fills a temporal function meaning *and then*.

At an MLU of approximately 3.5, around age 3, the conjunction *because* appears, either alone or attached to a single clause, as in the following examples:

ADULT: Scott, why did you do that?
CHILD: Because.
ADULT: Scott, why did you do that?
CHILD: Because Roger did.

Initially, utterances with *because* demonstrate the inability of young children to give reverse order. Because a 3- or 4-year-old child has difficulty recounting events nonsequentially, a child will respond to questions with a result response rather than a causal one (see the discussion of 4-year-olds in Chapter 8). In response to "Why did you fall off your bicycle?" the child is likely to respond, "'Cause I hurted my leg"—a result, not a cause.

The first clausal conjoining occurs with the conjunction *and* around age 3½ (Table 9.7). For example, a child might say, "I went to the party *and* Jimmie hit me." It is not until closer to age 4, however, that most children can use this form. In general, *and* is used as the all-purpose conjunction, as in the following:

We left *and* mommy called. (meaning *when*)
We had a party *and* we saw a movie. (meaning *then*)
She went home *and* they had a fight. (meaning *because*)

Depending on the child, *and* may be used 5 to 20 times as frequently as the next most common conjunction in the child's repertoire. Even in the narratives of 5-year-olds and school-age children, *and* is the predominant connector of clauses.

Clausal conjoining with *if* appears shortly after *and*, followed quickly by *because*, and *when, but*, and *so* even later. Most children are capable of conjoining clauses with *if* during this latter period. These are not usually complicated sentences; they are more likely to be of the "I can *if* I want to" form. The order of conjunction acquisition reported for American English seems to be true for other languages as well and may reflect the underlying cognitive relationship.

Initially, the causal relationship may be signaled by *that's why*, as in "They were running; that's why they broke the window." Note that the order of the clauses is as they happened and not the reverse order we would find if the child had used *because*.

The conjunctions *because* and *so* are initially used to mark psychological causality or statements of people's intentions. For example, use of *because* might explain "He hit me *because he's mean*" rather than "The bridge fell *because the truck was too heavy*." If the child was to discuss the bridge falling, he or she might explain, "The bridge fell *because it was tired*," using feeling or intention to explain the event.

Increasingly, children recount the past as they become older, and, as noted, narratives become more causally related. With this recounting, there is a greater necessity to discuss the intentions preceding behaviors, as in Box 9.7.

At around age 4, a child may begin to exhibit conjoining and embedding of both phrases and clauses within the same sentence. Most children are using this type of structure, although sparingly, by age 5. Such multiple embedding plus conjoining might result in the following:

Sally wants to stay on the sand but *Carrie is scared of crabs*.

Inf. Ph. Prep. Ph.	Prep. Ph.
Independent Clause	Independent Clause

Three-clause sentences, both embedded and conjoined, appear at about the same age. The child might join three main clauses, as in the following:

Julio flew his kite, *I ate a hot dog*, and *papa took a nap*.

BOX 9.7

Examples of Conjoining Clauses of Preschoolers

32 months:	I'm gonna see **if** I can turn the light off.
46 months:	The first time **when** I went one wave catched me.
52 months:	Maybe both of us can try and run down there **and** try to catch one.
	If he would've been a person **then** he would have been able to scratch himself like that.
	And shut the cage door **so** they can't get out.
	I don't know *what's gonna happen* **but** I think *it's gonna work*. (*Embedding* and **conjoining** of clauses)
57 months:	We better let this stay out **when** I need to go on vacation.
60 months:	And Colin said *he won't lie* **but** then he did lie. (*Embedding* and **conjoining** of clauses)
	I had something for you but I don't know *where it is*. (*Embedding* and conjoining of clauses)
	We went to Pizza Hut **but** we were going to the movies **so** we didn't know *what happened*. (*Embedding* and three-clause **conjoining**)

Another variation might include the embedding and conjoining of three clauses, as in the following:

I saw Spider-Man, and *Clarita saw the one that had that other guy*.
Indep. Clause Indep. Clause Dependent Clause

By age 4½ to 5, multiple embeddings and three-clause sentences may account for about 11% of all child utterances.

Pragmatic and semantic factors seem to affect conjoining as well. Clausal conjoining occurs when two referents must be clearly distinguished for the listener, as in "Katie is little but Pedro is big." A child encodes only what he or she presupposes the listener needs to interpret the sentence.

Conjunctions

The semantic relations between clauses, as expressed in the conjunction, form a hierarchy that affects the order of acquisition: additive, temporal, causal, or contrastive. Initial clausal conjoining is additive; no relationship is expressed, as in "Irene went on the hike and Robyn was at Grandma's." Next, conjoining is used to express either simultaneous or sequential events, as in "Diego went to school and then he went shopping." Causal relationships with *and* and *that's why* appear first, as in "*X and* [led to] *Y*" (*Julia jumped too high and she fell.*) Later *because* is used and the order of the clauses is reversed. Finally, the child expresses a contrasting relationship, usually with the use of *but*. The late appearance of the conjunction *but* in clausal conjoining is probably related to the complex nature of such propositions. The expectation that is set up in the first clause is not confirmed in the second, as in "I went to the zoo, but I didn't see any tapirs."

SUMMARY

The syntactic development of the preschool child is rapid and complex. In essence, the preschool child is trying to discover syntactic regularity that can be used in his or her own speech. Note the conversation in Table 9.8.

As in many aspects of learning, syntactic acquisition is facilitated by practice (Keren-Portnoy, 2006). Early learning facilitates subsequent learning. The language-learning principles discussed in detail in Chapter 6 are evident in the acquisition process.

Language input plays a significant role in shaping children's grammatical development. Children exposed to more complex input show greater comprehension of complex sentences than children exposed to fewer examples of complex sentences (Huttenlocher et al., 2002).

As you will note when you talk with young children, their sentences are often disruptive and filled with false starts and revisions. These behaviors indicate similar aspects of development. First, disruptions tend to occur in the longest, most complex sentences, indicating that these sentences are at the leading or growing edge of the child's language, much as imitation was earlier (Rispoli & Hadley, 2001). In these sentences, a child is at increased risk for difficulties.

By age 5, most children have mastered the basics of syntax. Notice the rich syntax of the 5-year-old in this video. http://www.youtube.com/watch?v=105g5KvRN8E

As a child's language develops, the rate of disruptions followed by revision also increases (Rispoli, 2003). Revision involves self-monitoring and rapid replacement of words and structures with linguistic alternatives. Thus, increasing revision demonstrates more skill not less.

TABLE 9.8 Late Preschool Language Sample

1. Oh, this almost looks like the other one.
2. See?
   But it has the same hat.
3. Hey, I'm gonna put the sticker right here, okay?
4. Put your stickers right here.
   So we can pretend these are the TVs.
5. Okay.
   I'm making dinner.
6. Oh, onions.
   Oh.
7. Oh, let me toast it.
   No way.
8. I'm gonna cook, okay?
9. While you do your stuff, okay?
   I'm toasting. I'm making a piece of bread.
10. I'm eating this bread.
11. Good bread.
12. I think I'm gonna go to work soon.
13. Get this orange out of here.
    Honey . . .
14. What?
15. Let's get married now.
16. Just a place to get married . . . under the table.
    We have to have our toast under. . . . You be married too. Don't touch me.
17. Mine.
    No, you can touch me, you can touch me. I just kidding. . . .
18. I know you just kidding.
    Why'd you say "bye"?
19. Because.
20. I said "bye." . . .
    Here have a piece of bread.
21. I said "bye" just because . . . I said "bye" 'cause I had to go to work and you won't let me.
22. That's why.
    Go to work, honey.
23. Mmmm.
24. It got real leaves.

25. This is a real leaves.	
26. They're real leaves, you know?	
27. See?	What? 'Cause they come off?
28. Uh-huh.	
29. Wanna see?	Don't do it. You'll break their toys.
30. Mmmm, bye, I'm going to work.	Bye-bye. Pretend you came back with that hat on from work and I made you a piece of bread and put a piece of bread.
31. And I won't eat it.	Okay. When you came back from work, I'll give you a piece of bread.
32. Okay, then I won't eat it.	
33. Bye.	Bye-bye, hon.

Phonemic and Phonologic Development

As mentioned, many of the morphologic and syntactic changes in the preschool years are related to phonologic development and reflect the child's underlying phonologic rule system. In addition to developing speech sounds, a preschool child is also developing phonologic rules that govern sound distribution and sequencing.

As with other aspects of language, a child's phonologic development progresses through a long period of language decoding and hypothesis building. The child uses many learning processes that will later be discarded or modified. These natural processes simplify adult forms of speech for young children. During the preschool years, as a child acquires speech sounds and a phonologic system, she or he develops the ability to determine and signal differences in meaning through speech sounds. It appears that perception of speech sounds precedes production but that the two aspects are not parallel.

SPEECH-SOUND ACQUISITION

Speech is a very complicated acoustic event. No other meaningful environmental sounds, not even music, achieve speech's level of complexity. In perception of fluent connected speech, listeners use many different parts of the phonemic context to decode the signal. If we separate the /t/ in *tea* (/ti/) from the /i/, it sounds like a very short "tsch." Yet our brain is able to integrate the signal as it comes in, creating the unified perception of *tea*. To further complicate this process, the /t/ in *tea* is very different from the /t/ in *toe*, but we are able to perceive the same sound across these different phonemic contexts.

Several studies have attempted to establish an order of phoneme acquisition by young children learning English. Comparing the results of these studies (Figure 9.2), we can make the following six statements:

1. As a group, vowels are acquired before consonants. English vowels are acquired by age 3.
2. As a group, the nasals are acquired first, followed by the plosives, approximants, lateral approximants, fricatives, and affricatives.

FIGURE 9.2 Average Age of Acquisition of English Consonants

Representing the ages at which 50% of English-speaking children can produce a sound correctly in all positions in conversation and formal testing.

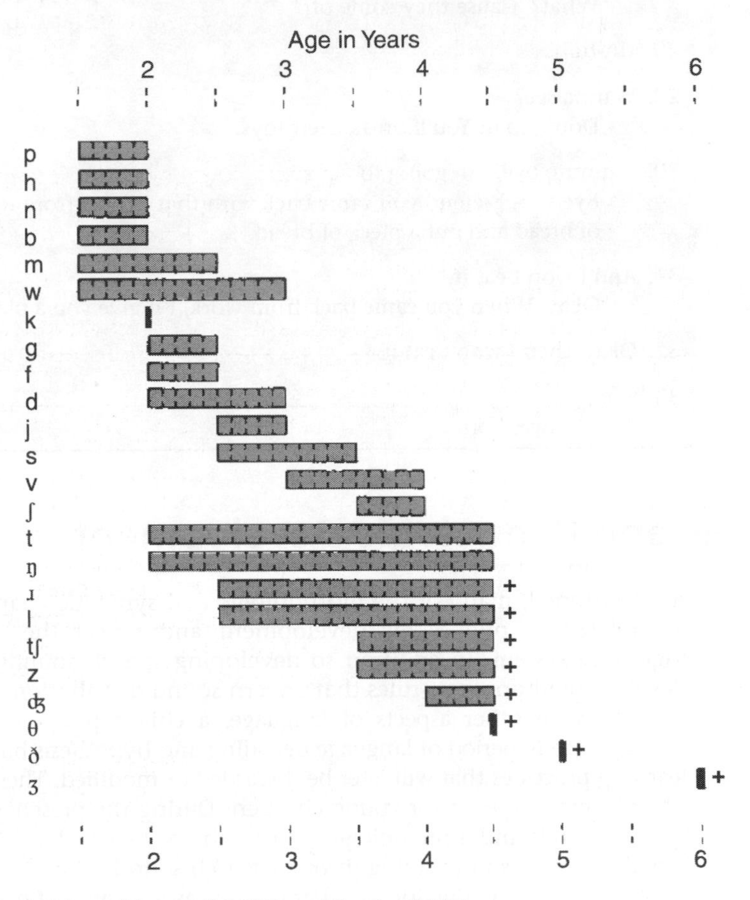

Source: Compiled from Olmstead (1971) and Sander (1972).

3. As a group, the glottals are acquired first, followed by the bilabials, velars, alveolars and post-alveolars, dentals and labiodentals, and palatals.
4. Sounds are first acquired in the initial position in words.
5. Consonant clusters and blends are not acquired until age 7 or 8, although some clusters appear as early as age 4. These early clusters include /s/ + nasal, /s/ + approximant, /s/ + stop, and stop + approximant in the initial position and nasal + stop in the final position.
6. There are great individual differences, and the age of acquisition for some sounds may vary by as much as three years.

By age 2, most children are producing single consonants and simple consonant clusters in their spontaneous speech, including the 15 frequently occurring English consonants /m/, /n/, /p/, /b/, /t/, /d/, /k/, /g/, /w/, /j/, /f/, /s/, /h/, /l/, /r/ (Bland-Stewart, 2003). Most 3-year-olds have mastered the vowel sounds and the consonants /p/, /m/, /h/, /n/, /w/, /b/, /k/, /g/, and /d/. There is much individual variation in speech-sound development, however, and at least 50% of 3-year-olds are also proficient in their use of /t/, /ŋ/, /f/, /j/, / r /, /l/, and /s/ (Figure 9.2). By age 4, most children have added /t/, /ŋ/, /f/, and /j/. At least 50% of all 4-year-olds can produce /r/, /l/, /s/, /tʃ/, /ʃ/, and /z/ (Figure 9.2). By the fifth birthday, most children add /r/, /l/, /s/, /tʃ/, /ʃ/, /z/, /dʒ/, and /v/. At least 50% can also produce the /ð/ ("th" in *there*) sound correctly (Figure 9.2). But 5-year-olds still have difficulty with a few consonant sounds and with consonant blends, as in "*str*eet" or "*cl*ean."

Cross-Language Studies

Although there is considerable agreement across diverse languages on the order of consonant development, no universal ordering exists. That said, there is data from languages as different as English and Korean that stops are acquired before affricates and fricatives (Kim & Stoel-Gammon, 2011).

Consonant development is the result of a complex interplay of motor control factors and each sound's articulatory difficulty, frequency of occurrence in a language, and functional load or the relative importance of a phoneme in contrast to other phonemes. For example, the voiced "th" or /ð/ phoneme (*this, that*) in English could be replaced with /d/ in all instances with very little confusion, so the informational load is low. In contrast, the /w/ phoneme in English is used in a variety of phonemic contexts and would be difficult to replace; thus, its load is high. Load seems to be particularly important for the acquisition of American English consonants, while frequency is more important in the acquisition of Cantonese (Stokes & Surendran, 2005).

Still, surprising similarity exists in speech-sound acquisition across languages. The specific use patterns of different languages influence both the order and speed of acquisition. The acquisitional order of phonemes common to several languages is presented in Table 9.9. Although all English consonants are acquired by age 8, some Arabic consonants are not acquired until later in their standard form, although more casual forms are acquired earlier (Amayreh, 2003).

Compared to monolingual Spanish and monolingual English preschoolers, the speech sound development of bilingual Spanish-English 3- to 4-year-olds is slower and shows the effects of transfer from Spanish (L_1) to English (L_2) (Fabiano-Smith & Goldstein, 2010). The frequency of use of the sound does not predict acquisition of either similar or dissimilar sounds, indicating both separation and interaction between the bilingual children's two languages.

TABLE 9.9 Acquisitional Order of Consonant Sounds Across Languages

Age	English	Spanish	Cantonese	Arabic
By 3 years	t, d, k, f, m, n, w	k, m, n, j	t, n, p, j, m, w	t, k, f, m, n, w
3–4	j, s	d, f, t	k	d
4–5		w	f, s	
5–6		s		s
6+				J

Note: Only phonemes used in all four languages are presented. Despite some glaring differences, there is considerable similarity across languages.

PHONOLOGIC PROCESSES

We will discuss only the phonologic processes most common for the preschool child (Table 9.10). Most of the processes introduced in Chapter 7 have been discarded or modified by age 4.

TABLE 9.10 Phonologic Processes of Preschool Children

Processes	Examples
Syllable structure	
Deletion of final consonants	*cu* (/kʌ/) for *cup*
Deletion of unstressed syllables	*nana* for *banana*
Reduplication	*mama, dada, wawa* (water)
Reduction of clusters	/s/ + consonant (*stop*) = delete /s/ (*top*)
Assimilation	
Contiguous	
Between consonants	*beds* (/bɛdz/), *bets* (/bɛts/)
Regressive VC (vowel alters toward some feature of C)	nasalization of vowels: *can*
Noncontiguous	
Back assimilation	*dog* becomes *gog*; *dark* becomes *gawk*
Substitution	
Obstruants (plosives, fricatives, and affricatives)	
Stopping: replace sound with a plosive	*this* becomes *dis*
Fronting: replace palatals and velars (/k/ and /g/) with alveolars (/t/ and /d/)	*Kenny* becomes *Tenny* go becomes *do*
Nasals	
Fronting (/O/ becomes /n/)	*something* becomes *somethin*
Approximants replaced by	
Plosive	*yellow* becomes *yedow*
Glide	*rabbit* becomes *wabbit*
Another approximant	*girl* becomes *gaul* (/gɔl/)
Vowels	
Neutralization: vowels reduced to /ə/ or /a/	*want to* becomes *wanna*
Deletion of sounds	*balloon* becomes *ba-oon*

Source: Information from Ingram (1976).

TABLE 9.11 Phonologic Development

Age in Months	Syllable Structure	Number of Syllables
24	CV, VC CVC	2
36	CV, VC, CVC, CC___, ___CC	2
48	CV, VC, CVC, CC___, ___CC, CC___CC	3
60	CV, VC, CVC, CC___, ___CC, CC___CC	3+

Syllable Structure Processes

During the preschool years, the child frequently attempts to simplify production by reducing words to this form or to the CVCV structure. The most basic form of this process affects the final consonant. Final-consonant processes usually disappear by age 3.

In addition, a child may delete unstressed syllables to produce, for example, *way* for *away*. Initially, any unstressed syllable may be eliminated, although over time a child typically adopts a pattern of deleting only initial unstressed syllables. Syllable reduction may be more complex than simply deleting the unstressed syllable and may reflect the interaction of syllable stress, location within the word, and phrase boundaries (Snow, 1998).

My grandson Zavier at age 4 gave me a perfect example of deletion of unstressed syllables in the following exchange:

ME: Your mom says you talked about dinosaurs in preschool! What did you learn?
ZAVIER: Stinked.
ME: Well, yeah, they didn't take baths like you, so they probably stunk.
ZAVIER: No, stinked! Stinked!
ME: Oh, extinct. Extinct! Yeah, dinosaurs are extinct. What does that mean?
ZAVIER: All gone.

This deletion process continues until age 4. Development of syllables, word shapes, and consonant cluster types are presented in Table 9.11.

Reduplication is a third process for simplifying syllable structure in which one syllable becomes the same as another in the word, resulting in the reduplicated structure, as in *wawa* for *water*. This process disappears for most children before 30 months of age. The final syllable is usually deleted or changed. Otherwise, the clearly stressed syllable is most often reproduced. The final position is not particularly important for preschoolers unless it is preceded by an *un*stressed syllable, as in *elephant* or *ambulance*.

Consonant Cluster Reduction Preschoolers reduce or simplify consonant clusters, usually by deleting one consonant. English has a large variety of clusters that can make production of many words difficult for young children. Cluster reduction is also one of the most common phonologic processes seen in the speech of Spanish-speaking Puerto Rican preschoolers. While deletions differ based on the parent language and the individual child, we can predict with some certainty how preschoolers will simplify many clusters. Here are some examples from English:

Cluster	*Deletion*	*Example*
/s/+ plosive	/s/	*stop* becomes *top*
plosive or fricative +	liquid or glide	*bring* becomes *bing*
liquid or glide	*swim* becomes *sim*	

A child may exhibit **epenthesis**, or vowel insertion, producing both consonants with a vowel between them. Thus, ***tree*** becomes ***teree***. This vowel-insertion process is infrequent. The specific strategy used and the speed of consonant cluster development vary with the sounds involved.

Nasal clusters are more complex. If a nasal (/m, n, ŋ/) plus a plosive or fricative is reduced, younger children will delete the nasal. Thus, ***bump*** becomes ***bup***. Older preschoolers will delete the plosive if it is voiced (/b, d, g/). Employing this rule, the older child reduces ***mend*** to ***men***.

Clusters emerge in the speech of children at around age 2 (Lleó & Prinz, 1996). Emergence is probably related to having more mature motor control and to experiencing a spurt in vocabulary that necessitates more specific production as a means of distinguishing different words. Although most 2-year-olds can produce consonant clusters, few do so correctly (McLeod, van Doorn, & Reed, 2001a). Individual differences reflect the sounds, types of clusters, and the locations within words. Development is slow, and by 30 months only half of children are producing some clusters correctly.

Children's earliest attempts to produce clusters are inconsistent (McLeod, van Doorn, & Reed, 2001b). Over time, nonpermissible combinations, such as /pw/, give way to permissible ones, usually in the final position in words first. By age 3, children are producing final clusters, such as /nd/, /ts/, /nz/, /ŋk/, /ps/, and /nts/. Word-initial clusters may offer a greater challenge because of the greater variety. As a group, *s*-blends in the initial position (/sp, sk, sm/) are mastered before blends with /l/ and /ɾ/ (/pl, gl, br, kr/), which, in turn, precede three-consonant blends (/skw, spl, θr/).

Most children stop using the cluster-reduction strategy by age 4. Consonant clusters are mastered by age 6 or 7.

Assimilation Processes

Assimilation processes simplify production by producing different sounds in the same way. In general, one sound becomes similar to another in the same word. Assimilation processes may be contiguous or noncontiguous and progressive or regressive. Contiguous assimilation occurs when the two elements are next to each other; noncontiguous assimilation, when apart. Progressive assimilation occurs when the affected element follows the element that influences it; regressive assimilation, when the affected element precedes. For example, children generally produce two varieties of *doggie*. One, *doddie*, exemplifies progressive assimilation, while the other, *goggie*, is regressive.

Regressive contiguous assimilation is exhibited in both CV and VC syllables. The consonant in CV structures may be affected by the voicing of the vowel, as when the voiceless *t* in *top* is produced as a voiced *d*, resulting in *dop*. In regressive VC assimilation, the vowel alters toward some feature of the consonant, as in the nasalized vowels in *can* and *ham*. Progressive contiguous assimilation is much less common.

The most common type of noncontiguous assimilation is back assimilation, in which one consonant is modified toward another that is produced farther back in the oral cavity. The *d* in *dark*, for example, may become a *g* to produce *gawk* (/gɔk/) to conform with the back consonant /k/.

Substitution Processes

Many preschoolers substitute sounds in their speech. These substitutions are not random and usually are in only one direction. The /w/ is often substituted for /ɹ/, for example, but only rarely does the opposite occur. In addition, when a child masters a phoneme, it does not overgeneralize to words in which the substituted sound is the correct sound. For example, the child may say *wabbit* until mastering /ɹ/. Although the child can now produce *rabbit*, the /ɹ/ does not overgeneralize to the /w/ in *what* and *wanna*, in which /w/ is correct.

Sound-for-sound substitutions are usually articulatory in nature. Phonological processes, on the other hand, involve substitutions of classes of sounds, such as all or most back consonants.

Types of substitution processes can be described according to the manner of production of the target sound. For example, obstruant sounds, which include fricatives and affricates, may experience *stopping*, in which a plosive is substituted. Stopping is most common in the initial position in words, as in *dat* for *that* or *dis* for *this*. This process decreases gradually as the child masters fricatives, although stopping with *th* sounds (/ð, θ/) may persist until early school age. Early production of nasal sounds may also be accompanied by stopping. This denasalization, similar to "head cold" speech, substitutes a plosive from a similar position in the oral cavity for a nasal (*Sam* becomes *Sab*).

Another frequent process is *fronting*, a tendency to replace palatals and velars with alveolar sounds. Thus, /t/ and /d/ are substituted for /k/ and /g/, producing *tan* for *can* and *dun* for *gun*. Slightly fewer than 25% of 3-year-olds demonstrate fronting. This percentage decreases rapidly, so that by age 4½ fewer than 4% of children still exhibit this behavior. Fronting is also evident in nasal sounds. The /n/ may be substituted for /ŋ/, as in *sinin* for *singing*.

Although approximants /l/ and /ɹ/ may also experience stopping initially, they are usually replaced by another approximant. Another process, *gliding*, in which /j/ or /w/ replaces /l/ or /ɹ/, may last for several years. I recall one example of gliding that occurred after I had broken my leg in a bicycling accident. Out of concern, my son Jason inquired, "How your yid?" (leg). Not only does this demonstrate gliding on the /l/; the /g/ is fronted as well. This /j/ for /l/ process was also evident in his production of "little" (/jIdə/) and most other words with /l/.

Multiple Processes

In actual practice, it may be difficult to decipher the phonologic processes a young child is using. Often, several processes will be functioning at once. For instance, my children all called our family dog "Peepa" (/pipə/). Her real name was Prisca (/pɹIskə/). We see reduction of the *pr* cluster (in a *stop* + *liquid* cluster, the liquid is deleted). The second cluster, *sc*, also experiences reduction; but even more important, it demonstrates progressive noncontiguous assimilation, becoming a /p/. Finally, the first vowel, /I/, is replaced by /i/, which may be the result of the vowel's altering toward some feature of /p/, another assimilation effect. Whew! And that's only one word!

Perception and Production

Speech-sound perceptual skills in conversations develop relatively late. Although 3- and 4-year-olds can be taught to separate the sounds in words, these skills are very limited. Children do not perform well when asked to make judgments of the appropriateness of sounds. For instance, when K.C., the child of a friend, was in kindergarten, he drew a painting with streaks of bright color and put a big *W* on it. His mother was delighted. "Is that 'W' for 'Whalen'?" (his last name), she inquired. He looked at her with scorn. "No silly, wainbow!"

Preschool children probably do not perceive spoken language as containing phoneme-size units. Yet they seem able to make different speech sounds. Children may know that words are different or similar before they know the basis of those differences and similarities. Through slow evolution, speech sounds gradually change into more deliberate productions that focus on phonological segments and their relationships.

Another important factor in perception and production is phonological working memory. Preschoolers with good phonological memory skills tend to produce language that contains more grammatical complexity, a richer array of words, and longer utterances than preschoolers with poor memory skills.

Although a 5-year-old has good physical reasoning abilities, he or she still believes in magic as an explanation for much that happens. When my son Todd turned 5, he asked for a magic kit. Mom and Dad complied. After opening it, he turned to us for a demonstration. We dutifully explained each trick and showed him how it was done. When we finished, he cried in a very disillusioned voice, "No, no, I wanted *real* magic."

Five-year-olds use very adultlike language, although many of the more subtle syntactic structures are missing. In addition, the child has not acquired some of the pragmatic skills needed to be a truly effective communicator. Expressive vocabulary has grown to about 2,200 words. Word definitions still lack the fullness of adult meanings, however, and this aspect continues to be refined throughout life.

Although there are still many aspects of speech, language, and communication to be mastered, the 5-year-old has made spectacular progress in only a few years. The child of 5 is able to use language to converse and to entertain. He or she can tell stories, has a budding sense of humor, and can tease and discuss emotions. Over the next few years, language development will slow and begin to stabilize but will be nonetheless significant.

In the first six years of school, a child develops cognitive and communicative skills that by age 12 almost equal those of the adult. Increasingly, a child becomes less home centered, as school and age peers become more important.

Physically, the school-age child gains greater coordination of gross- and fine-motor movements. Throughout the period, physical coordination enables a child to perform more motor acts at one time and therefore to enjoy sports and coordinated games. With more mature motor skills, he or she gains more self-help skills and increased independence.

Cognitive skills change markedly during the first six years of school. The brain is nearly adult in size by age 8, but development is not complete. Intrabrain pathways must be better developed. Brain weight and size change little; growth is internal. During the first six years of school, a child's mental abilities mature from concrete problem solving, requiring sensory input, to abstract thought.

A school-age child is also a highly social being, and peers, especially same-gender peers, become very important. This can be a trying period for parents, as children begin to establish an identity separate from their family. One afternoon my son Todd stormed into the house from his friend's house and demanded to know "the truth." "There's one thing you'll never tell me," he challenged. Fearing the worst, I suggested that he ask anyway. What a relief when he shot back, "Is there a real Easter Bunny?" With this peer socialization comes a less egocentric perspective. As Theory of Mind continues to develop, a child begins to realize that his or her own reality is not the only one.

A child also learns to manipulate and influence others, especially through the use of language. During the early school-age years, the child refines the conversational skills needed to be a truly effective communicator. This communication development reflects the child's growing appreciation for the perspective of others.

In addition, a child's vocabulary continues to grow. A first-grader has an expressive vocabulary of approximately 2,600 words but may understand as many as 8,000 to 10,000 root English words and 14,000 when various derivations are included. Aided by school, this receptive vocabulary expands to an understanding of approximately 50,000 words by sixth grade. Multiple word meanings are also acquired.

In part, the school-age child's relatively slower language growth compared to the preschooler's reflects the systematic development and stabilization of word-formation and sentence-structuring rules. The school years are a period of stabilization of rules previously learned and the addition of new rules. Let's explore this development together.

Pragmatic Development

The area of most dramatic linguistic growth during the school-age years is language use, or pragmatics (Table 10.1). It is in pragmatics that we see the interaction of language and socialization.

Although environment is important, twin studies indicate that over half of the variance in young school-age children's conversational language skills may be accounted for by genetic effects (DeThorne et al., 2008). The stability of some conversational measures, such as MLU and total number of words, between first and second grades are almost entirely based on genetic effects (Segebart DeThorne, Harlaar, Petrill, & Deater-Deckard, 2012). In contrast, environmental effects seem less stable across time. Of course, genetic effects are not constant, and there is evidence of genes being turned on and turned off over time and of their influences being modified by environmental effects (Rutter, 2006).

A preschool child does not have the skill of a masterful adult storyteller or even of a junior high student who wants something. No adult is fooled by the adolescent's compliment, "Gee, Mom, those are the best-looking cookies you've ever made," but both parties understand the request, however indirect it may be.

Preschool children frequently begin a conversation assuming that *here* for them is *here* for everyone or without announcing the topic. Once, in imaginative play, my preschool daughter shifted characters on me with no announcement. As the Daddy, I was being told to go to my room! When I balked, she informed me that now I was a child—an abrupt demotion. It had not occurred to her to prepare me for this shift in conversation.

The demands of the classroom require major changes in the way a child uses language. Very different rules for talking apply between the classroom and conversation. A child must negotiate a turn by seeking recognition from the teacher and responding in a highly specific manner to questions, which may represent over half the teacher's utterances. "Text-related" or ideational language becomes relatively more important than social, interpersonal language. A child is held highly accountable for responses and is required to use precise word meanings. A child who comes to school with different language skills and expectations may suffer as a consequence.

Throughout the school years, the cognitive processes of nonegocentrism and decentration increase and combine to enable a child to become a more effective communicator. **Nonegocentrism** is the ability to take the perspective of another person. As a child gains greater facility with language structure, he or she can concentrate more on the audience.

Decentration is the process of moving from rigid, one-dimensional descriptions of objects and events to coordinated, multiattributional ones, allowing both speaker and listener to recognize that there are many dimensions to and perspectives on any given topic. Younger children's descriptions are more personal and do not consider the information available to the listener. Their accuracy depends on what is being conveyed, with abstract information being communicated least accurately by children.

In this section, we first shall consider two aspects of language use: narratives and conversations.

NARRATIVES

Narratives reflect the storyteller's experience. The scripts formed by experiences are the foundations for narratives. In turn, the ability to relate well-formed narratives affects the judgments others make about a speaker's communicative competence. As a consequence, narratives help children maintain a positive self-image and a group identification within their families and communities.

Five- and 6-year-olds produce many different types of narratives. Anecdotal narratives of a personal nature predominate, possibly accounting for as many as 70% of all narratives at this age. In contrast, fantasy stories are relatively rare.

Children learn about narratives within their homes and their language communities. Emerging narratives reflect different cultures. Although every society allows children to hear and produce at least four basic narrative types, the distribution, frequency, and degree of elaboration of these types vary greatly. The four genres are as follows:

1. The **recount** tells about past experiences in which a child participated or observed or about which a child read and is usually requested by an adult.
2. The **eventcast** is an explanation of some current or anticipated event and may be used to direct others in imaginative play sequences, as in *You're the daddy; and you pretend to get dressed; you're going to take the baby to the zoo.*
3. **Accounts** are highly individualized spontaneous narratives in which children share their experiences ("You know what?") and thus are not reporting information requested by adults.
4. **Stories**, although fictionalized and with seemingly endless content variation, have a known and anticipated pattern or structure in which the main character must overcome some problem or challenge.

In middle- and high-SES families in the United States, the earliest narratives are eventcasts that occur during nurturing activities, such as play, and reading. Within these activities, caregivers share also many accounts and stories.

By age 3, children are expected to appreciate and use all forms of narration. Parents invite children to give recounts. These invitations decrease as the child ages.

By the time most children in the United States begin school, they are familiar with all four forms of narration. In the classroom, children are expected to use these forms. This expectation may be unrealistic for some children. For example, Chinese American children are encouraged to give accounts within their families but not outside the immediate household.

In some white low-SES Southern communities, children's recounts are tightly controlled by the interrogator and seem to be the predominant form during the preschool years. Accounts do not begin until children attend school. In these same communities, children are not encouraged to tell stories, a form predominantly used by older, higher-status adults. In contrast, Southern African American low-SES children produce mostly accounts or eventcasts and have minimal experience with recounts.

Development of Narratives

Most 6-year-olds can convey a simple story or recount a movie or television show, often in the form of long, rambling sequential accounts. During the school-age period, these narratives undergo several changes, primarily in their internal structure.

As noted in Chapter 8, children gradually learn to link events in linear fashion and, only later, with causal connectives. Generally, by age 6, children's narratives gain causal coherence. The conjunction *and* continues to be used as frequently in the narratives of 9-year-olds as it was in those of preschoolers. The purpose seems to be cohesion (*And then . . . And then . . .*) rather than conjoining (clause + *and* + clause).

Causality involves descriptions of intentions, emotions, and thoughts and the use of connectives, such as *because, as a result of*, and *since*, to name a few. To some degree, use of causality requires the speaker to be able to go forward and backward in time, something most preschoolers have difficulty doing.

Although 2- and 3-year-olds have mastered some causal expressions, they are unable to construct coherent causal narratives. Causality can be seen, however, in 2- and

3-year-olds' use of plans, scripts, and descriptions of their own behavior and thoughts. A *plan* is a means, or series of actions, intended to accomplish a specified end. *Scripts* are dialogs that accompany familiar routines in the child's everyday environment. Children incorporate these into their narratives. By age 2½, a child has acquired the words to describe perceptions (*see, hear*), physical states (*tired, hungry*), emotions (*love, hate*), needs, thoughts (*know*), and judgments (*naughty*).

Between ages 2 and 10, children's stories begin to contain more mental states and more initiations and motivations as causal links. Initially, psychological causality, such as motives, is more frequently used than physical causality or the connection between events. At around age 4, children's stories begin to contain more explicit physical and mental states. By age 6, children describe motives for actions.

In mature narratives, the center develops as the story progresses. Each incident complements the center, follows from previous incidents, forms a chain, and adds some new aspect to the theme. Causal relationships move toward the ending of the initial situation called the *climax*:

> There was a girl named Ann. And she got lost in the city. She was scared. She looked and looked but couldn't find her mommy and daddy. She slept in a cardboard box by the corner. And one day the box got blowed over and a police lady found her sleeping. She took her home to her mommy and daddy.

Mature narratives may consist of a single episode, as above, or of several episodes. An episode contains a statement of the problem or challenge, and all elements of the plot are directed toward its solution.

Although 4- and 5-year-olds include many elements of narration in their conversations, they lack the linguistic skill to weave a coherent narrative. Between ages 5 and 7, plots emerge. Gradually, these simple plots are elaborated into a series of problems and solutions or are embellished from within.

Both adults and children prefer stories directed toward a goal, such as the overcoming of an obstacle or problem. Narratives of a 7-year-old typically involve a beginning, a problem, a plan to overcome the problem, and a resolution.

The development of causal chains is a gradual process. Initially, the narrative may be truncated so that the problem is solved, but it is unclear how this happened. This occurs in the following:

> And there was this bad guy with a—"k-k-k-k" (gun noise)—death ray. And he was gonna blow up the city. So, the Power Rangers snuck in to his house and stopped him. The end.

In another early form, the problem is resolved without the intervention of the characters in the story. A common device is to have the main character awaken from a dream, resulting in the disappearance of the problem:

> . . . He was in the middle of all these hungry lions. And he lost his gun. He couldn't get away. And then he woke up. Wasn't that funny?

By second grade, a child uses beginning and ending markers in fictional narratives (*once upon a time, lived happily ever after, the end*) and evaluative markers (*that was a good one*). Throughout elementary school, use of both beginning and ending markers increases. Evaluative markers also occur more frequently and increase in use even more (Ukrainetz et al., 2005). Story length increases and becomes more complex with the aid of syntactic devices such as conjunctions (*and, then*), locatives (*in, on, under, next to, in front of*), dialog, comparatives (*bigger than, almost as big as, littlest*), adjectives, and causal statements. Although disquieting events, such as getting a needle or losing a toy, are still central to the theme, characters tend to remain constant throughout the narrative.

Distinct episodes have been replaced by a multiepisodic chronology, although the plot is still not fully developed.

The sense of plot in fictional narratives is increasingly clear after age 8. Definite character-generated resolution of the central problem is present. The narrative presentation relies largely on language rather than on the child's accompanying use of actions and vocalizations. Like a good storyteller, a child manipulates the text and the audience to maintain attention.

In general, older children's narratives are characterized by the following:

- Fewer unresolved problems and unprepared resolutions
- Less extraneous detail
- More overt marking of changes in time and place
- More introduction, including setting and character information
- Greater concern for motivation and internal reactions
- More complex episode structure
- Closer adherence to the story grammar model

These changes represent a child's growing awareness of story structure and increasing understanding of the needs of the audience.

Story Grammar Development Like much in language, narratives are organized in predictable, rule-governed ways that differ with culture. The structure of the narrative consists of various components and the rules underlying the relationships of these components. Components and rules, collectively called a **story grammar**, form a narrative framework, the internal structure of a story.

Formed from reading and listening to stories and from participating in conversations, story grammars can aid information and narrative processing, as well as narrative interpretation and memory. The competent storyteller constructs the story and the flow of information to maximize comprehension.

The typical story in English involves an animate or inanimate protagonist in a particular setting who faces some challenge to which he or she responds. The character makes one or more attempts to meet the challenge and, as a consequence, succeeds or fails. The story usually ends with the character's emotional response to the outcome. This brief outline contains the main components of a story grammar in English.

A story grammar in English and most Western languages consists of the setting plus the episode structure (*story grammar = setting + episode structure*). Each story begins with an introduction contained in the setting, as in "A long, long time ago, in a far off galaxy . . ." or "You'll never guess what happened on the way to work this morning; I was crossing Main Street . . . ." An episode in English consists of an initiating event, an internal response, a plan, an attempt, a consequence, and a reaction. Each component is described in Table 10.2. While only 50% of kindergarten children can retell narratives with well-formed episodes, this percentage increases to 78% by sixth grade. Like clauses, episodes may be linked additively (*and*), temporally (*and then, next*), causally (*because*), or in a mixed fashion. A mature story may consist of one or more interrelated episodes.

There appears to be a sequence of stages in the development of story grammars. The resultant narratives can be described as *descriptive sequences, action sequences, reaction sequences, abbreviated episodes, complete episodes, complex episodes*, and *interactive episodes*. The structural qualities of each type of story grammar are listed in Table 10.3.

Descriptive sequences consist of descriptions of characters, surroundings, and habitual actions. There are no causal or temporal links. The entire story consists of setting statements:

> There was this magician. He had a big hat like this. He turned elephants into mice. And he had birds in his coat. The end.

TABLE 10.2 Story Grammar Components

COMPONENT	DESCRIPTION	EXAMPLE
Setting statement (S)	Introduce the characters; describe their habitual actions and the social, physical and/or temporal contexts; introduce the protagonist.	There was this boy and
Initiating event (IE)	Event that induces the character(s) to act through some natural act, such as an earthquake; a notion to seek something, such as treasure; or the action of one of the characters, such as arresting someone.	. . . he got kidnapped by these pirates.
Internal response (IR)	Characters' reactions, such as emotional responses, thoughts, or intentions, to the initiating events. Internal responses provide some motivation for the characters.	He missed his dog.
Internal plan (P)	Indicates the characters' strategies for attaining their goal(s). Young children rarely include this element.	So he decided to escape.
Attempt (A)	Overt action(s) of the characters to bring about some consequence, such as to attain their goal(s).	When they were all eating, he cut the ropes and
Direct consequence (DC)	Characters' success or failure at attaining their goal(s) as a result of the attempt.	. . . he got away.
Reaction (R)	Characters' emotional response, thought, or actions to the outcome or preceding chain of events.	And he lived on an island with his dog. And they played in the sand every day.

TABLE 10.3 Structural Properties of Narratives

STRUCTURAL PATTERN	STRUCTURAL PROPERTIES
Descriptive sequence	Setting statements (S) (S) (S)
Action sequence	Setting statement (S) + attempts (A) (A) (A)
Reaction sequence	Setting statement (S), initiating event (IE) + attempts (A) (A) (A)
Abbreviated episode	Setting statement (S), initiating event (IE) or internal response (IR) + direct consequence (DC)
Complete episode	Setting statement (S); two of the following: initiating event (IE), internal response (IR), or attempt (A); + direct consequence (DC)
Complex episode	Multiple episodes Setting statement (S); two of the following: initiating event (IE_1), internal response (IR_1), or attempt (A_1); direct consequence (DC_1); followed by another episode Expanded complete episode Setting statement (S), initiating event (IE), internal response (IR), internal plan (IP), attempt (A), direct consequence (DC), and reaction (R)
Interactive episode	Two separate but parallel episodes that influence each other

This type of structure is characteristic of the initial narratives of preschool children, described earlier as *heaps*.

Action sequences have a chronological order for actions but no causal relations. The story consists of a setting statement and various action attempts:

> We got up early on Christmas morning. We lighted the tree. We opened gifts. Mommy made cinnamon buns. Then we played with the toys.

This type of story grammar is the type seen in early sequential and temporal chain narratives of preschool children.

Reaction sequences consist of a series of events in which changes cause other changes with no goal-directed behaviors. The sequence consists of a setting, an initiating event, and action attempts:

> There was a little puppy. He smelled a kittie. The kittie scratched the puppy. The puppy ran away. He smelled a girl. The girl took the puppy home and gave the pu . . . him milk. And that's the end.

In contrast, *abbreviated episodes* contain an implicit or explicit goal. At this level, the story may contain either an event statement and a consequence or an internal response and a consequence:

> This girl hated spinach. And she had a big plate of it. And she fed the spinach to the dog under the table. After her plate was all clean, she got a big dessert. That's all.

Although the character's behavior is purposeful, it is usually not premeditated or planned; instead, the characters react. Reaction sequences and abbreviated episodes are characteristic of the narratives of school-age children until approximately age 9.

Complete episodes contain an entire goal-oriented behavioral sequence consisting of a consequence statement and two of the following: initiating event, internal response, and attempt:

> Once this man went hunting. He woke up a big bear. The bear chased him up a tree and climbed up. To get away, the man waved at a helicopter. The helicopter gave the man a rope. He climbed up and got away from the bear. The end.

Complex episodes are expansions of the complete episode or contain multiple episodes:

> Spiderman saw a bank robber. He jumped down and captured one of them with a punch. And he called the police. One bank robber got away in his truck. Spiderman ran after the truck. He threw his net over the truck and got the bank robber. And that was the end of the bank robbers.

Finally, *interactive episodes* contain two characters who have separate goals and actions that influence the behavior of each other:

> Mary decided to build a doghouse. She bought all the wood she needed. Her cat got jealous. Mary cut all the wood and hammered it. The cat rubbed her leg and meowed. Mary was too busy to stop and she painted it. The cat meowed more. When Mary was all done, she let the dog go to sleep. And then she hugged the kitty too.

Complete, complex, and interactive story grammars are seen in the narratives of mid- and late-elementary school children, adolescents, and adults. Most children produce all the elements of story grammar, although not necessarily in the same narrative, by age 9 or 10.

Cultural Differences

As might be expected, not all children of a given age exhibit the same levels of narrative competence. The narratives of underachieving children may be shorter, have less internal organization and cohesion, and contain fewer story grammar components and less sentence complexity.

Narration varies with the context or situation and with the culture of the speaker. Situational variables may influence the type of storytelling as much as the developmental level of the narrator. Constraints include the type and size of the audience, the goal, time allotment, and competition for the floor. The more familiar the audience, the longer the clauses and the more use of embedded clauses.

Narratives of children in the United States reflect cultural differences (McCabe & Bliss, 2003), which are summarized in Table 10.4. For example, in comparison to the sequentially organized narratives of European American children, the stories of African American children seem less focused and less organized. This reflects the expectation of African Americans for the telling of more rambling, multievent tales that are performed for the enjoyment of the listeners.

By comparison, the narratives of Japanese American children seem concise. This reflects the cultural expectation of *omoiyari* or empathy. The storyteller is expected to get to the point and not to be too garrulous, which would be disrespectful of the listener.

TABLE 10.4 Typical Features of Children's Narratives

Features	European American	African American	Spanish-Speaking Mexican American	Japanese American
Focus	Single experience of child	May contain several experiences; preference for lengthy narratives that are expected and enjoyed	Frequent mention of family members as reference to who narrator is and where; frequent code switching with reference to characters and when events occurred	Preference for concise narratives; poor behavior to concentrate on self too much
Events	Told in simple past and in chronological sequence by age 5	Occasionally combine numerous experiences into single narrative	De-emphasize sequencing, emphasize flow of conversation; less emphasis on past events	Frequently several experiences in one narrative rather than elaborating on event
Resolution	Problem or goal resolved or not by end of narrative	May or may not be resolution	Often resolution but not as important as in European American narratives	Concise, get to the point readily; make every effort to be understood
Organization	Topic-centered, setting explained, sequence of actions, culminating in high point or crisis that is evaluated, resolution, and relationship to present conversation	Both topic-centered and thematic (topic-associating) formats with several experiences related by a theme; each experience may have different tempo and tone	Conversation-focused; emphasis more on relationships; emphasis on habitual activities (*we ran* vs. *we were running*)	Sequential, although adults favor nonsequential format; value implication rather than explication; omission of pronouns

Source: Information from McCabe & Bliss (2003).

Finally, in Mexican American homes, completing a narrative is secondary to conversational interaction. In other words, the process of telling is more important than the product. Often a main event in the home, narratives frequently are told by children while meals are being prepared. The mother maintains the exchange and facilitates the process but is not intent on obtaining a narrative of sequential events.

Linguistic differences will account for differing methods of introducing new elements, referring to old information, and providing cohesion. Still, we find that narratives become increasingly more complex and more coherent in all languages. More characters and dialog and multiple and complex episodes are used. Across languages, the number of characters varies with the style and purpose of the narrative.

The narratives of some African American children, especially girls, have a distinct structure that differs from the story grammar model presented. Characterized as *topic-associating*, these narratives consist of theme-related incidents that make an implicit point, such as the need to help your baby brother or to avoid someone. These narratives often lack clear indicators of characters, place, or shifts in time.

As Spanish-speaking children mature, their narratives become more detailed and contain longer sentences with more embedding, a higher proportion of grammatically acceptable sentences, and more complete episodes, although overall story length increases little (Muñoz, Gillam, Peña, & Gulley-Faehnle, 2003). These narratives exhibit an increase in cohesion, ellipsis, and more accurate reference, and a decrease in ambiguities and redundancies. Cohesion is achieved through the use of articles and nouns (*un niño/a boy*), pronouns (*ella/she*), ellipsis (*El fue a la tienda, cogio un poco de comida/He went to the store, got some food*) and demonstratives (*este/this*). In fact, ellipsis may be even more pronounced than in English because Spanish verb endings indicate person, eliminating the need for pronouns. For example, *hablo* means "I speak," the *o* signaling the first person singular pronoun. The increasing use of ellipsis with locations is consistent with that noted in the narratives of English-speaking children. Props in Spanish narratives are usually referenced by name as in English, as "He put on *his coat.*"

Italian-speaking children also use nouns to introduce new information. Although pronouns and inflected verbs are also used, school-age Italian-speaking children rely more on nouns, thus reducing ambiguity on the part of the listener.

Across languages such as English, German, French, and Mandarin, clear marking of new information in the form of a noun does not emerge until age 7. Because languages differ in form, it might be expected that the development of sentence structure to indicate newness would also differ. For example, in English, new information is often placed at the end of the sentence, but this practice does not emerge fully until adulthood. In contrast, use of sentence structure to introduce newness is used more frequently by French-speaking children. An interplay exists between discourse factors governing information flow, cognition relative to narrative complexity, and language-specific forms.

Dialog is increasingly used within narratives as children mature. As in English, children developing other languages, such as Turkish, gain increasing ability to relate conversations by adopting different roles within their narratives, switching from character to narrator and back again.

CONVERSATIONAL ABILITIES

Successful communication rests on the participants' knowledge of people, relationships, and events. Participants must be actively involved, asking and answering questions, making voluntary replies and statements, and being sensitive to the contributions of others. They collaborate to ensure mutual understanding. Great individual variability exists, and some 7-year-olds are more adept than the least effective adults.

The most successful communicators use questions to probe before introducing a possibly unfamiliar topic. Although the number of questions does not increase with age, more successful communicators use more questions and have more answered than do the least successful. In addition, regardless of age, more successful school-age communicators are quick to recognize communication breakdown and to offer further explanation or to repair.

Adults still exercise control over much of the conversation with a young school-age child by asking questions. Role, power, and control relationships are evident in children's responses. In general, responses to adult queries by first-graders are brief, simple, and appropriate, with little elaboration. In contrast, responses to peer questions are more complex and more varied.

Social perspective-taking, the ability to understand and adopt varying points of view, is necessary for successful communication and is used to persuade, comfort, and to be polite. The largest gains in social perspective-taking and subsequent tailoring of individualized messages occur in middle childhood (ages 7 to 9). As you well know, however, even adults don't always behave in a partner-oriented way and often fail to consider the perspectives of others (Buhl, 2002).

In the following section, we'll explore many of the important conversational changes seen in childhood. These will include language uses; speaking style; topic introduction and maintenance; and use of indirect requests, conversational repair, and deictic terms.

Language Uses

Almost from the time a child begins to speak, he or she is able to provide information and to discuss topics briefly. Language functions increase greatly with the demands of the classroom. Children are required to explain, express, describe, direct, report, reason, imagine, hypothesize, persuade, infer cause, and predict outcomes. New vocabulary and syntactic forms accompany these functions. For example, hypothesizing uses *how about . . .*, *what if . . .*, and so on, while persuading uses *yes but*, *on the other hand*, *because if . . . then . . .*, and the like.

Because of cultural difference, the expectations of the classroom teacher may differ from that of a child. For example, majority English-speaking teachers may prefer individual recitation, while children from populations such as the native Canadian Inuit participate best within cooperative group interactions, the cultural norm. The reluctance of Inuit children to respond individually may be misinterpreted by the teacher as being uncooperative. Similarly, Algonquin narration is a cooperative group effort that may not be appreciated by the teacher demanding individual storytelling. In addition, the teacher's stopping of a narrative to correct grammar may violate the function of narratives in Algonquin culture, which is to amuse or tell a troubling experience.

Speaking Style

The style-switching behavior reported for 4-year-olds is even more pronounced by age 8. When speaking with peers, a child makes more nonlinguistic noises and exact repetitions and engages in more ritualized play. With adults, a child uses different codes for his parents and for those outside the family. In general, parents are the recipients of more demands and whining, and of shorter, less conversational narratives.

Andy Dean Photography/Shutterstock

Peer interaction supplies chances for middle-childhood-aged children to make gains in social perspective taking and tailoring of individual messages.

Topic Introduction and Maintenance

A school-age child is able to introduce a topic into the conversation, sustain it through several turns, and close or switch the topic. These skills develop only gradually throughout elementary school and contrast sharply to preschool performance. The 3-year-old, for example, sustains the topic only 20% of the time if the partner's preceding utterance was a topic-sharing response to one of the child's prior utterances. In other words, topics change rapidly. Four-year-olds can remain on topic when explaining how a toy works but still cannot sustain dialog.

In general, the proportion of introduced topics maintained in subsequent turns increases with age, with the most change occurring from late elementary school to adulthood. A related decrease in the number of different topics introduced or reintroduced occurs during this same period. Thus, there is a growing adherence to the concept of relevance in a conversation. An 8-year-old's topics tend to be concrete. Sustained abstract discussions emerge around age 11.

Indirect Requests

One verbal strategy adults use widely is the indirect request that does not refer directly to what the speaker wants. For example, "The sun sure is a scorcher today" may be an indirect request for a drink. Development of indirect requests is particularly noteworthy because such requests represent a growing awareness of the importance of both socially appropriate requests and the communication context.

Indirect requests are first produced in the preschool years. The proportion of indirect to direct requests increases between ages 3 and 5. This proportion does not change markedly between ages 5 and 6, although the internal structure of requests develops. In general, the 5-year-old is successful at directly asking, commanding, and forbidding. By age 7, he or she has acquired greater facility with indirect forms. Flexibility in indirect request forms increases with age. For example, the proportion of hints—"That's a beautiful jacket, and it would go so well with my tan"—increases from childhood through adulthood.

A school-age child seems to be following two rules: Be brief and be devious (or avoid being demanding). More creative and more aware of social roles than the preschooler, a school-age child knows that overpoliteness is inappropriate. As with preschoolers, however, an 8-year-old is more polite to adults and to those perceived as uncooperative than he or she is to his or her peers.

After age 8, a child increasingly takes others' intentions into consideration. When compared to a preschool child, an 8-year-old is more polite when not from the listener's peer group, when interrupting the listener's activities, and when the task requested is difficult. Although a child's use of requests is similar to that of adults, he or she still has some difficulty with indirect requests and may interpret them literally.

Although 6-year-olds generally respond best to literal meanings, 8-year-olds and adults recognize most nonliteral requests for action as well. For example, the 6-year-old who is asked "Can you pass the cup?" may respond "Yes" but not follow through, treating the request as a question.

More mature language users consider the context more fully and deduce that these questions are indirect requests for action. By age 11, children are able to use the utterance and context to infer the speaker's intent accurately.

There seems to be a general developmental pattern to the comprehension of indirect requests. As a child matures, comprehension of most types of indirect request increases. Interrogative forms, such as *shouldn't you?* and *should you?* are more difficult than declarative forms, such as *you shouldn't* and *you should*.

Negative forms, such as *please don't* and *you shouldn't*, are more difficult for 4- to 7-year-olds to interpret than positive forms, such as *please do* and *you should*. Polarity is a strong factor, especially when it differs from the literal meaning. *Shouldn't you?*, for example, is in a negative form but is a prod for positive action, as in "Shouldn't you leave?" In contrast, *Must you?*, although positive in form, conveys caution or cessation, as in "Must you stop now?" These levels of relative difficulty change little from childhood to adulthood and reflect the same comprehension difficulties experienced by adults.

In part, development of comprehension also reflects the words used. Four- and 5-year-olds understand most simple indirect requests containing *can* and *will* but have difficulty with others, such as *must* and *should*.

Conversational Repair

More mindful of the listener's needs, a school-age child attempts to clarify the conversation through a variety of strategies. Rather than merely repeating, as most 3- to 5-year-olds do, a 6-year-old may elaborate some elements in the repetition, thus providing more information. Although the predominant repair strategy is repetition, a 9-year-old often provides additional input for the listener or addresses the perceived source of breakdown by defining terms, providing more background context, and talking about the process of conversational repair.

Deictic Terms

By school age, most children can produce deictic terms (*here, there*) correctly. By about age 7, a child should be able to produce and comprehend both singular and plural *demonstratives* (*this, that, these, those*) or words that indicate to which object or event the speaker is referring.

Children under age 7 do not incorporate all semantic features of demonstratives. First, a child must understand that *this* and *that* are pronouns when used alone, as in "See *that*," and articles when followed by a noun, as in "*That* one's big." Second, a child must comprehend the feature of more or less far, that is, of distance. Third, a child must realize that the speaker is the referent, the deictic aspect of demonstratives. The last two features overlap with those of *here* and *there*.

An initial strategy for the production of deictic verbs, such as *bring* and *take*, is to use them with locational terms for directionality, as in *bring it here* or *bring it there*. The causal meaning of the verb—it causes something to happen—is acquired first. Later, a child learns the deictic meaning.

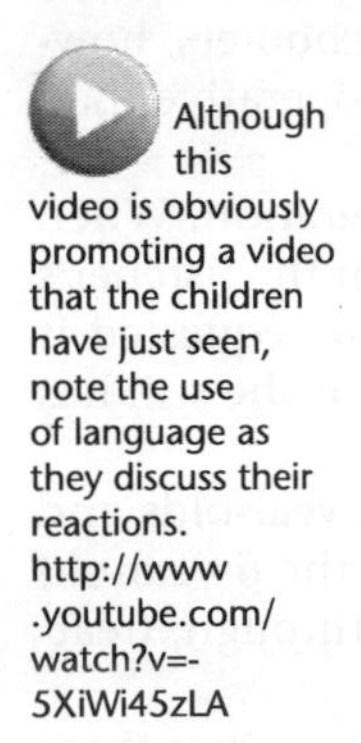

Although this video is obviously promoting a video that the children have just seen, note the use of language as they discuss their reactions. http://www.youtube.com/watch?v=-5XiWi45zLA

SUMMARY

As a child gains greater facility with the form and content aspects of language, he or she is able to concentrate more on language use in narratives and in conversational give and take. As he or she develops, a child requires less and less of his or her limited-capacity system for planning and encoding the message. More capacity is therefore available for adapting messages to specific audiences and situations. Gradually, a child is able to reallocate these limited resources and so to increase the effectiveness of his or her communication system.

Semantic Development

During the school-age period, a child increases the size of his or her vocabulary and the specificity of definitions. Gradually, a child acquires an abstract knowledge of meaning that is independent of particular contexts or individual interpretations. In the process, she or he reorganizes the semantic aspects of language (Table 10.1). The new organization is reflected in the way the child uses words. One outgrowth is the creative or figurative use of language for effect. This entire process of semantic growth, beginning in the early school years, may be related to an overall change in cognitive processing.

VOCABULARY GROWTH

The school-age years are a period of continued growth in the understanding of words and relationships. It is estimated that, by graduation from high school, a young adult may understand as many as 80,000 words. The expressive vocabulary may be considerably smaller. Actually, this number of words is increased with the addition of morphological prefixes and suffixes that change word meanings. Elementary school children appear to store words based on root words (e.g., *day*) and morphological variations (e.g., *days, daily*) (Rabin & Deacon, 2008). Many words are added from context, often while reading, especially after fourth grade.

Word Definitions

Adding lexical items is only a portion of the change. Vocabulary growth is not the same as depth of understanding. Real change comes in interrelated semantic concepts, semantic classes, synonyms, homonyms, and antonyms. These are all part of a child's understanding of a word.

More than other areas of language, development of semantics varies widely with educational level, socioeconomic status, gender, age, and cultural background. In general, middle-SES urban and suburban youngsters have more complete definitions than low-SES rural children (Walker, 2001). Definitional skill is highly correlated with involvement in an academic culture. As a result, some low-SES fourth-graders outperform their parents in providing oral definitions.

During school-age and adult years, there are two types of increases in word meanings. First, a child adds features to the definition that are common to the adult definition of a word. In other words, a child *slow maps* word definitions beyond the functional and physical properties that are core aspects of the definitions of children as old as 5 (McGregor, Friedman, Reilly, & Newman, 2002). Second, a child brings together all the definitions that can fit a single word. The multiple meanings of school-age children and the less flexible semantic systems of younger children are illustrated in the following closing retort of an argument between my two nieces Michelle, then 11, and Katie, age 7:

> MICHELLE: Well, when I have children, I hope they don't get any of your genes.
> KATIE (AFTER A SHORT PAUSE): No, and they won't get any of my sneakers, either.

Definitional skills—the ability to provide definitions of words—are related to the acquisition of metalinguistics, which is discussed at the end of the chapter. Both increase as a function of age and educational level (Benelli, Belacchi, Gini, & Lucangeli, 2006).

Semantic constraints may delay full mature use of even seemingly simple words such as *in*, *on*, and *at*. Many prepositions can mark locative, temporal, and figurative relationships. For example, prepositions such as *in* and *on* represent periodicity of duration, whereas *at* represents a moment in time. Although *in* and *on* are acquired at age 2 to mark location, they are also used for periods of time, such as days (*on Monday*) or parts of days (*in the morning*), or for months (*in May*). In contrast, *at*, another locational preposition, is used for specific moments (*at midnight, at 9:15*). The temporal concept of periodicity develops much later than the locative—not until about age 10. A child is into the teenage years before he or she can explain the periodicity/moment distinction.

As discussed in Chapter 7, words refer to concepts. As he or she matures, a child acquires more features of the concept. Some instances are more typical than others and are easier for children to learn. In general, a child's definition is less well delineated and relies more on perceptual knowledge. In contrast, adult definitions reflect both perceptual attributes and functions.

A child's ability to define words may progress in two ways during the early school years. First, a child progresses conceptually from definitions based on individual experience to more socially shared meaning. Second, he or she moves syntactically from single-word action definitions to sentences expressing complex relationships. This shift in form occurs at around second grade. Similar shifts in definition content occur throughout grade school. Supplying precise semantic content seems to develop prior to using correct syntactic form to provide a definition (Johnson & Anglin, 1995).

As a school-age child's definitions gradually become more literate or dictionary-like, they share certain characteristics. The definitions become more explicit. Around age 11, a child acquires all the elements of the conventional adult definition. The developmental sequence of elements of definitions is presented in Table 10.5. A preschooler's

TABLE 10.5 Developmental Sequence of Definitions

ELEMENTS REQUIRED	EXAMPLE
Noun phrase$_1$ . . .	*Dogs* have yukky breath.
NP$_1$ is . . .	*Dogs are* always barking and breathing.
NP$_1$ is NP$_2$ . . .	*Dogs are things* with four legs, a tail, bad breath, and barking.
NP$_1$ is NP$_2$ (superordinate category)	*Dogs are animals* that usually live in people's houses.

individual, experientially based definition thus shifts to the more conventional, socially shared one of older children and adults.

Vocabulary knowledge is highly correlated with general linguistic competence. A relationship may exist between stored word knowledge and comprehension of discourse. Throughout the school years, the child becomes better at deducing word meaning from context. Older elementary school children seem to rely on syntax for clues to word meaning, but far from relying on the narrow sentence use, 11-year-olds abstract and synthesize meaning to form a definition (Marinellie, 2010).

New Words

Between the ages of 7 and 11, there are significant increases in comprehension of spatial, temporal, familial, disjunctive, and logical relationships. A child acquires many dictionary-like and multiple meanings during this period. The rate of growth slows and stabilizes during the teen years.

New words may reflect the cognitive and linguistic activities of education, such as *remember, doubt, conclude, assert, interpret,* and *predict*. Others, such as connectives—*but, although, however*—are used for narratives and in reading and writing. Full understanding of most connectives occurs gradually, and some are still not mastered by eighth grade. Finally, as the child attempts to be more precise, he or she adds adverbs of magnitude, such as *slightly, somewhat,* and *unusually*. Acquisition of these terms continues into adulthood.

Providing a definition is difficult, as demonstrated by these school-age kids with some help from a few preschoolers. http://www.youtube.com/watch?v=goq740IF1vg

In the early years of elementary school, a change occurs in the use of spatial relational terms. There is a decrease in the use of nonspecific and general terms and a corresponding increase in the use of specific spatial terms from ages 4 to 7. For example, usage shifts gradually from nonspecific deictic terms, based on the speaker's perspective (*here, there*), through environmental-based terms (*away from the window, toward the door*), to spatial terms (*top, up, left*). Increasing precision of use continues into adulthood.

These new relations also require new, more complex syntactic structures. Although *first* and *last* can be applied to single words, newly acquired *before* and *after* are clausal or phrasal connectives requiring a more complex structure.

CONCEPTUAL CHANGE

Adults organize language, especially object concepts, in various ways. Two prominent organizational schemes are taxonomies and themes. *Taxonomies* are categories of objects that share a common essence, such as trees or tools. Objects related by *themes* are bound by an event. For example, gifts, a birthday cake, and party hats are part of a birthday party scheme. Objects are related based on space, such as cake and presents in the same room; cause, such as candles and the birthday child to blow them out; and function, such as knife and cake (Lin & Murphy, 2001). Although mature definitions contain both taxonomic and thematic information, taxonomic knowledge is more readily accessible for both children and adults (Whitmore, Shore, & Hull Smith, 2004).

It appears that both thematic and taxonomic relations are present from an early age. In young children, more abstract taxonomic relations are more fragile than thematic ones in their mental representation. For example, a category such as tools includes objects that are dissimilar in appearance and have several different functions. The fragility of these categories may result in a reliance on more thematic organization when demands are high. As a result, preschoolers switch between organizational strategies depending on the task and context (Blaye & Bonthoux, 2001; Nguyen & Murphy, 2003). By age 6, children organize concepts in ways similar to adults (Hashimoto, McGregor, & Graham, 2007). Within two years, categorical relations seem to be the preferred method of organization. Over time and with more encounters with the word, thematic knowledge gradually increases (Chaffin, Morris, & Seeley, 2001).

Education may play a part as well. For example, uneducated adults seem to rely less on taxonomic organization than do children who have completed grade school. With development and education, taxonomic structures strengthen and are less affected by the task or context. Taxonomic organization is promoted by compare and contrast activities in the classroom and by exercises requiring synonyms and antonyms. Likewise, verbal definitions may increase categorical knowledge because definitions often begin with categorical affiliation, as in "An apple is a fruit."

RELATED COGNITIVE PROCESSING

During the school years, there appears to be a change in cognitive processing, storage, and retrieval that reflects a shift in categorization. The initial change occurs in elementary school, with a shift from concrete to abstract during adolescence. The increasing reliance on linguistic categorization allows the child to process greater amounts of linguistic information.

Several factors affect vocabulary acquisition. First, both children and adults use a strategy of "chunking" semantically related information into categories for remembering. Thus, seventh-graders rely more on chunking for recall than do first-graders. Second, the use of semantic relations resolves word ambiguities. For example, *there, their*, and *they're* sound quite similar and could be confused, except for the very different semantic relations they represent. Third, categorical structures are stored hierarchically, seen in a progression from *Fido* to *dog* to *pet* to *animal*. Fourth, facilitative neural networks connect related word-concept structures. Thus new vocabulary acquisitions are associated with previous knowledge.

Individuals may use several levels of linguistic processing simultaneously:

Surface—syntactic rules and phonetic strings
Deep—semantic categories and relations
Contextual—situation or image

The mode or modes of processing relied on reflect the properties of the sentence and the maturation of the processor.

During early school years, children show a shift in linguistic processing from reliance on surface to reliance on deep strategies. This shift may mirror gradually decreasing cognitive reliance on visual input for memory and recall, a gradual change from visual encoding by preschoolers to overt naming as the dominant memory process of school-age children.

The processing shift may also reflect a child's increasing ability to integrate situational nonlinguistic information with linguistic information. These abilities are needed for effective daily communication. An example is the use of stress or emphasis in sentence decoding. There is a progression in the ability to use stress cues throughout elementary school and into the teenage years. As adults, we may use the following sequence of processing strategies:

1. Segment the message into the underlying sentences.
2. Mark the relations between the underlying sentences.
3. Determine the semantic relations of the lexical items.
4. Determine the semantic probabilities of co-occurrence.
5. Label the functions and properties of specific lexical items.

Children may begin to employ these strategies as early as age 5.

FIGURATIVE LANGUAGE

A school-age child also develops figurative language, which enables use of language in a truly creative way. Figurative language is words used in an imaginative sense, rather than a literal one, to create an imaginative or emotional impression. Figurative language enriches and enlivens our communication and is used to convey information that may be inexpressible or less effectively expressed in literal language. Use is indicative of higher language functions and correlates with adolescent literacy skills (Dean Qualls, O'Brien, Blood, & Scheffner Hammer, 2003). Conversation, classroom teaching, and reading use figurative expressions frequently.

Accuracy in interpreting figurative language slowly increases throughout late childhood and adolescence. Although 5-year-olds interpret most figurative expressions literally, even they can interpret some idioms in context. When compared to adults, however, children's understanding of idioms is less sophisticated, more concrete and incomplete (Nippold & Duthie, 2003).

Of course, development of individual figurative expressions varies widely and depends on, among other things, world knowledge, learning context, and metaphoric transparency. World knowledge is related to a general ability to interpret figurative expressions. For example, *smooth sailing* and *fishing for a compliment* have more meaning if you've sailed or fished.

Figurative expressions are easier for adolescents to comprehend in context than in isolation, possibly because figurative language is learned in context. Frequency of exposure, in contrast, has only a minor effect.

A figurative expression may be learned and stored as a large single lexical item—just as a word is learned and stored—rather than as individual words within the expression. As with single words, the meanings of figurative expressions are inferred from repeated exposure to these expressions in different contexts. For example, after the election, Grandpa says of the side with the poor showing, "They better *throw in the towel.* " After working hard at her job, Mom sighs exhaustedly and says, "I'm *throwing in the towel.*" Soon the child infers that the expression means something akin to *quitting in defeat.* This task is an analytical one in which a child must actively think about the meaning of the expression in context and perceive the metaphoric comparisons.

The figurative and literal interpretations of figurative language may be processed in simultaneous but separate processes. The figurative meaning most likely is stored in the child's lexicon as a single unit. The less frequently the expression is accessed, the more difficult it is to locate.

With interpreting, the literal process occurs as it would with any incoming signal. Meanwhile, lexical figurative analysis of the entire expression occurs. If the context supports the figurative interpretation, literal interpretation is interrupted and does not proceed.

Preschool children do not understand the nonliteral meanings of sarcasm and irony. Sarcasm is directed at a target, usually another person, "*Those* are nice shoes," indicating dislike. A preschooler is likely to reply, "Thanks, my mommy got 'em for me." Irony is not directed specifically as in "Great weather" when it is pouring rain. Although 5- to 6-year-olds are beginning to understand sarcasm and irony, it is not until age 9 or 10 that children become accurate at understanding a speaker's intention, rating sarcastic criticism as more "mean" than irony (Glenwright & Pexman, 2010).

The primary types of figurative language include idioms, metonyms, metaphors, similes, and proverbs. Idioms are short expressions that cannot be analyzed grammatically. These colorful terms are not learned as part of a rule system and cannot be interpreted literally. For example, *hit the road* does not mean to strike a sharp blow to the asphalt but, rather, to leave. Table 10.6 presents some American English idioms. They are acquired through continual use, and their meanings are inferred from context. Idiom

TABLE 10.6 Common American English Idioms

strike a bargain	jump the gun	superior *to* (better *than*)
hit the road	break a date	in search *of* (search *for*)
take a cab	hop a plane	throw a party
robbed blind	do lunch	off the wall
in the pink	on a lark	

learning is closely associated with familiarity and with reading and listening comprehension skills (Nippold, Moran, & Schwarz, 2001).

Metaphorically transparent idioms are easier for children and adults to interpret than metaphorically opaque ones. **Metaphoric transparency** directly affects ease of interpretation. Idioms, such as *hold your tongue*, have closely related literal and figurative meanings or are metaphorically transparent because the meanings relate to speaking and to the tongue. In contrast, *beat around the bush* and *kick the bucket* do not have closely related meanings and are therefore metaphorically opaque.

Idioms and Metonyms

Regional and cultural differences affect idiom understanding. Although high-use idioms, such as *to put their heads together*, are easy for all American English-speaking children, low-use idioms, such as *to paper over the cracks*, are more easily understood by children who represent the majority culture (Qualls & Harris, 1999).

Metonyms are figures of speech in which an individual example stands in for a whole category of things, such as "All hands on deck," in which *hands* stands for sailors. Similarly, the word *Washington* may be used to represent the U.S. government. In this case, we might say, "Washington is in crisis." The utterance does not mean that everyone in the capital is panicked.

Metaphors and Similes

Metaphors and similes are figures of speech that compare actual entities with a descriptive image. In a metaphor, a comparison is implied, such as "She kept a *hawk-eyed* surveillance." In contrast, a simile is an explicit comparison, usually introduced by *like* or *as*, such as "He ran *like a frightened rabbit*." To form a metaphor or a simile, the speaker must perceive a resemblance between two separate elements. The basis of the similarity is not literally true.

Preschool children produce many inventive figures of speech, such as the following examples (Gardner & Winner, 1979):

> A bald man is described as having a "barefoot" head.
> A stop sign is described as a "candy cane."
> A folded potato chip is described as a "cowboy hat."

I recall my daughter Jessica's description of the Lincoln Memorial, with its many columns, as "Lincoln's crib." My son Jason referred to his bruise as a "rotten spot." One of my students reported her daughter crying because she had hurt her "foot thumb," meaning big toe. The same child requested "ear gloves," or earmuffs, for her cold ears. Heather

Leary, a student's child, upon seeing snow for the first time, described it as "white rain like bubbles," a rather poetic image. These early figures of speech are usually based on physical resemblance or on similarities of use or function.

Metaphors become less frequent, if more appropriate, in spontaneous speech after age 6. Two possible reasons for this decline are, first, that the child now has a basic vocabulary and is less pressured to stretch his or her vocabulary to express new meanings and, second, that the rule-guided linguistic training of school leaves little room for such creativity. The remaining figures of speech, although less numerous, are more adultlike. The decline in what children produce spontaneously, however, does not reflect a decline in what they are capable of producing. Both the quantity and quality of metaphors in creative writing increases in later elementary school.

Comprehension of figurative language increases with age. Some idioms are comprehended during late preschool. Even at age 7, however, comprehension seems to be context-dependent, and production by the child lags well behind. The 5- to 7-year-old avoids crossing from physical into psychological domains and prefers to associate two terms rather than equate them. For example, "She is a cold person" may be interpreted as "She lives at the North Pole." In contrast, the 8- to 9-year-old is beginning to appreciate the psychological process. A child still misinterprets the metaphor, however, because he or she does not fully understand the psychological dimension of "cold."

In contrast, the older school-age child is able to make metaphoric matches across several sensory domains. For example, colors can be used to describe psychological states, as in "I feel *blue*."

Proverbs

Proverbs are short, popular sayings that embody a generally accepted truth, useful thought, or advice. Often quite picturesque, proverbs are very difficult for young school-age children to comprehend. Examples of proverbs follow:

Don't put the cart before the horse.
A new broom sweeps clean.
You can't have your cake and eat it, too.
Look before you leap.

The 6-, 7-, or 8-year-old child interprets proverbs quite literally. Development of comprehension continues throughout adolescence and adulthood.

The ability to comprehend proverbs is strongly correlated with perceptual analogical reasoning ability. Analogical reasoning problems follow the format "______ is to ______ as ______ is to ______." In similar fashion, a child attempting to comprehend a proverb must understand the underlying relationships between the proverb and the context. Both figurative language comprehension and analogical reasoning are strongly related to receptive vocabulary development, underscoring the semantic link between these skills.

Syntactic and Morphologic Development

Among school-age children, language productivity and syntactic complexity are strongly influenced by the type of speaking task and familiarity with the topic (Nippold, 2009). Language development consists of simultaneous expansion of existing syntactic forms and acquisition of new forms (Table 10.7). A child continues with internal sentence expansion by elaborating the noun and verb phrases. Conjoining and embedding

TABLE 10.7 Summary of School-Age Child's Development of Language Form

Age in Years	Syntax/Morphology	Phonology
5	■ Produces short passives with *lost, left,* and *broken*	
6	■ Comprehends parallel embedding, imperative commands, *-man* and *-er* suffix ■ Uses many plural nouns	■ Identifies syllables ■ Masters rule for /s/, /z/, and /əz/ pluralization ■ Is able to manipulate sound units to rhyme and produce stems
7	■ Comprehends *because* ■ Follows adult ordering of adjectives	■ Recognizes unacceptable sound sequences
8	■ Uses full passives (80% of children) ■ Uses *-er* suffix to mark initiator of an action (*teacher*) ■ Is able to judge grammatical correctness separate from semantics	■ Is able to produce all American English sounds and blends
9	■ Comprehends and uses *tell* and *promise*	
10	■ Comprehends and uses *ask* ■ Consistently comprehends *because* ■ Uses pronouns to refer to elements outside immediate sentence ■ Understands differences among *definitely, probably,* and *possibly*	
11	■ Comprehends *if* and *though* ■ Creates *much* with mass nouns ■ Uses *-er* for instrument (*eraser*)	
12		■ Uses stress contrasts

functions also expand. Additional structures include the passive sentence form. During the school-age years, adolescence, and early adulthood, syntactic development is characterized by gradual increases in the length and complexity of utterances produced in spoken and written communication (Nippold, 2007).

Both language productivity and syntactic complexity are greater when children talk in an expository genre than in a conversational genre (Nippold, 2009). In addition, during conversation, syntactic complexity is greater when they talk about an area of expertise, such as chess, compared with other topics. Further, children produce substantially greater amounts of language and higher levels of syntactic complexity during an explanation task ("What is a simultaneous match?") compared with either conversation about their expertise ("Why do you enjoy chess?") or general conversation.

Although a child has achieved basic sentence competence by age 5, fewer than 50% of first-graders can produce correct pronouns, "cause" clauses, and gerunds. Fewer than 20% can produce *if* and *so* clauses and participles. You will recall that gerunds are verbs to which *-ing* has been added to produce a form that fulfills a noun function. For example,

He enjoys *fishing*.
Running is her favorite exercise.

In participles, the same form fills an adjectival role, as in

We bought *fishing* equipment.
Do you like your new *running* shoes?

Participial phrases also contain other adjectives ending in *-ed* (*bearded* scholar), *-t* (*unkept* house), and *-en* (*broken* arrow).

MORPHOLOGIC DEVELOPMENT

Learning to use a morphological rule begins with the hypothesis that a small set of words is treated in a certain way grammatically. The first uses of a morphological marker are probably the result of memorization acquired one word at a time. This is followed by morphological generalizations about phonological marking (/d, t/) and meaning (past tense). Gradually, a child forms a rule.

There is individual variation. Difference does not equate to disorder. Although 6-year-old children from low- and middle-income backgrounds who speak African American English have patterns for marking past tense that differ for non-AAE-speaking children, these patterns do not conform to that found in children with language impairment (Oetting & Pruitt, 2009).

While some inflectional suffixes are refined during the school-age years, the main developments occur in the addition of inflectional prefixes (*un-*, *dis-*, *non-*, *ir-*) and derivational suffixes. The development of inflectional prefixes is gradual and protracted, continuing into adulthood. I, for one, know that *flammable* written on a truck means *keep your distance*, but I'm easily confused by *inflammable*.

Derivational suffixes—those that change word classes—are a much larger set of bound morphemes and are usually used to change the part of speech of the base word. Many inflectional suffixes appear during the preschool years on a word-by-word basis. As a group, derivational suffixes have a relatively small range of use and many irregularities. Refer to Figure 1.6 for a list of derivational suffixes. Often, use is highly restricted, as in the use of *-hood* or *-ment*. For example, *-ment* changes the verb *attach* to the noun *attachment* but cannot be used with common verbs, such as *talk*, *eat*, *drink*, and *sit*. To make it all the more confusing, over 80% of English words with derivational suffixes do not even mean what the parts suggest. Despite this fact, knowledge of derivational suffix meaning is a significant factor in interpreting novel words.

Derivational suffixes are first learned orally, although reading strengthens learning, especially for more complex forms. A very limited general order of school-age acquisition is *-er*, *-y*, noun compounds, and *-ly*. Mastery continues into late adolescence. The *-y* marker used to form adjectives such as *sticky* and *fluffy* is not fully acquired until age 11, and the *-ly* marker used to form adverbs such as *quickly* is mastered only in adolescence.

Difficulty in learning is related to *morphophonemic processes*, discussed later in the chapter, and to semantic distinctions. For example, the *-er* suffix has several semantic uses and is initially acquired to mark the initiator of some action, such as paint*er* for the person who paints and teach*er* for the person who teaches. Although this suffix may appear in late preschool with some specific words, children are not able to use it generatively to create words until age 8.

A second *-er* used to mark the instrument for accomplishing some action is acquired even later, around age 11. Examples of the instrumental *-er* include cleaning the shower with a clean*er* or erasing with an eras*er*. In part, the late development of the instrumental *-er* can be explained by the child's use of other more common words in place of the

Box 10.1

Examples of Morphology

Comparative and Superlative

59 months	He might think of something funn*er*.
62 months	This is a bigg*est* one here.
73 months	I don't like school, 'cause it's *more fun* at home.

"verb + *er*" form, such as the more appropriate *stove* for *cooker* and *shovel* for *digger*. Some words have no non-*er* equivalent.

A third type of -er ending is used in the comparative, as in *taller*. Young elementary school children show no preference for either the *adjective* + *er* (*bigger*) or the *more adjective* (*more big*) form of the comparative, using each indiscriminately (Graziano-King & Smith Cairns, 2005). During mid-elementary school, they prefer the *adjective* + *er* form. Finally, by adulthood, English speakers follow more rule-based usage (see Box 10.1).

Although only a few hundred word definitions are taught directly, children generalize their morphologic knowledge to new words for semantic decoding. This process becomes increasingly important with maturity as less frequently used words are encountered more.

NOUN- AND VERB-PHRASE DEVELOPMENT

Children of 5 to 7 years use most elements of noun and verb phrases but frequently omit these elements, even when they are required. Even at age 7, they may omit some elements (. . . *some of cake*) but expand others redundantly (*Nico, who is more bigger than you* . . .). The rhythm of a sentence seems to be more salient, and children often miss small, unstressed words. In addition, school-age children still have difficulty with some prepositions, verb tensing and modality, and plurals. Unique instances or rule exceptions, such as irregular past and plural, are particularly difficult.

Noun Phrases

Within the noun phrase, development continues with additional modifiers and mastery of the pronoun system. At 60 months, children add descriptors in which a noun serves as a modifier (e.g., *the penguin school, the pumpkin patch*). This element is in addition to articles (e.g., *the, a*), possessive pronouns (e.g., *his, her, my*), and adjectives (e.g., *big, little*), quantifiers (e.g., *many, some*), demonstratives (e.g., *this, that*), and post-noun prepositional phrases (e.g., *at school*) (Owens, 2013). The predominant forms are

Article + Adjective + Noun (*a pink coat, the coolest playground*)
Article + Descriptor + Noun (*the pumpkin patch, the party stuff*)
Article + Noun + Prepositional phrase (*a house for your little daughter*)

Most children produce three-element NPs only. Examples of NPs are presented in Box 10.2.

The post-noun embedded clause is added by 72 months. There also are changes in three-element elaborated noun phrases (ENPs). At this age, most children are producing four-element NPs, although no form predominates (Owens, 2013).

Box 10.2

Examples of Noun Phrases

60 months	
Article + Adjective + Noun	*a little daughter, a good cat*
Article + Descriptor + Noun	*a bear workshop, the party stuff, the goat sound, the brake station*
Article + Noun + Prepositional phrase	*a picture of Damien, the bottom of it*
72 months	
Article + Adjective + Adjective + Noun	*a little furry spot*
Article + Adjective + Descriptor + Noun	*a big kid room, the little baby chicks*
Article + Adjective + Noun + Prepositional phrase	*a big cloud of dust, a red mark on his stomach*
Article + Adjective + Noun + Embedded clause	*the new one I like*
Article + Adjective + Noun + Adverb	*a little heart right here*

Source: Information from Owens (2013).

At 84 months, children add numerical terms to the *determiner category*. The *initiator category*, the possessive noun and ordinal elements of *adjective category*, and the post-noun *modifier* elements of adjectival and adverbial are not used by most children or are used infrequently.

With pronouns, a child learns to better differentiate between subject pronouns, such as *I*, *he*, *she*, *we*, and *they*, and object pronouns, such as *me*, *him*, *her*, *us*, and *them*, and to use reflexives, such as *myself*, *himself*, *herself*, and *ourselves*. In addition, a child learns to carry pronouns across sentences and to analyze a sentence to determine to which noun a pronoun refers. For example, a child must perform some complex analysis in order to interpret the following sentences:

> Mary's mother was very sick. Mary knew that *she* must obtain a doctor for *her*.

The child must be able to hold more than one dimension of the noun phrase or of an entire clause and to comprehend or use a pronoun in its place. This pronoun-for-clause usage is demonstrated in the following sentences:

> The earth began to tremble shortly before rush hour, reaching full force 40 minutes later. *It* was devastating.

By age 10, a child is able to use pronouns to make this type of reference outside the immediate sentence.

Adjective ordering also becomes evident within the noun phrase. In English, multiple properties are generally described by a string of sequentially ordered adjectives. As noted in Table 9.2, different semantic classes of adjectives have definite positions based on a complex rule system. During school age, the most evident change comes in the addition of post-noun modifiers in the form of embedded phrases (The blond girl *by the window* . . .) and clauses (The blond girl *who is standing by the window* . . .).

Even 3-year-olds display the same ordering preference as adults for the first adjective in a sequence (*small sour green apples, overgrown ugly pink flowers*). A child does not show adult-type ordering for the other adjectives until school age. Earlier ordering preferences may reflect an imitative strategy rather than the analytical approach of adults. The period from ages 5 to 7 marks a phase of improved cognitive ability to discriminate perceptual attributes and their relationships expressed in adjectives.

The distinction between mass and count nouns and their quantifiers is acquired only slowly throughout the school years. Mass nouns refer to homogeneous, nonindividual substances, such as *water*, *sand*, and *sugar*. Count nouns refer to heterogeneous, individual objects, such as *cup*, *bicycle*, and *house*. Mass nouns take quantifying modifiers, such as *much* and *little*, as in *much sand*, while count nouns take quantifiers, such as *many* and *few*, as in *many cups*. The reverse, *much cups*, sounds awkward. Prior to learning the distinction, a child discovers a way around the quantifier difference by using *lots of* with both types of nouns.

Children must also learn to use the plural determiner (*these*, *those*) with count nouns and not with mass nouns. By early elementary school, the child has learned the correct noun forms of most mass and count nouns, so words like *monies* and *mens* are more characteristic of preschool language. *Many* then appears with plural count nouns, as in "many houses." *Much* is usually learned by late elementary school, although adolescents still make errors.

Verb Phrases

Verbs appear to offer greater difficulty for school-age children than nouns. These difficulties may be related to varied syntactic marking. For example, verb action can be reversed in three ways:

1. Use of the prefix *un-*: "She is tying her shoe. She is *un*tying her shoe."
2. Use of a particle following the verb: "Pull *on* your boots. Pull *off* your boots."
3. Use of separate lexical items: "She *opened* the door. She *closed* the door."

Certain forms may be used only with specific verbs. A child's resultant confusion produces sentences such as these (Bowerman, 1981):

> I had to untake the sewing. (take out the stitches)
> I'll get it after it's plugged out. (unplugged)

The difficulty of learning how to state underlying verb relationships may account for the greater amount of time needed for acquisition of verbs compared to common nouns.

During the school years, a child adds verb tenses, such as the perfect [*have + be + verb(en/ed)* as in *has been eaten*, or *have + verb(en/ed)* as in *has finished*], additional irregular past-tense verbs (see Table 10.8), and modal auxiliary verbs.

Modals express a semantic notion of possibility, obligation, permission, intention, validity, truth, and functionality. Some modal auxiliaries appear in preschool. In addition, school-age children and adults also express the notion of modality in adverbs (*possibly*, *maybe*), adjectives (*possible*, *likely*), nouns (*possibility*, *likelihood*), verbs (*believe*, *doubt*), and suffixes (*-able*). Not all forms of modality develop simultaneously, and the process is a lengthy one. In general, the possibility, obligation, permission, and intention forms develop before the validity, truth, and functionality forms. Even 12-year-olds do not have an adult sense of modality.

Adverbs of likelihood, such as *definitely*, *probably*, and *possibly*, can pose a problem even for school-age children. In general, preschoolers don't understand the distinctions among the terms. By fourth grade, however, most children know the difference. The terms are not learned at the same time; *definitely* is learned first and understood best by most children. And, of course, preschool language is filled with *really* and *actually*.

TABLE 10.8 **School-Age Development of Irregular Verbs**

Age	Verbs
5–0 to 5–5	*took, fell, broke, found*
5–6 to 5–11	*came, made, threw, sat*
6–0 to 6–5	*ran, flew, wore, wrote, cut, fed, drove, bit*
6–6 to 6–11	*blew, read, shot, rode*
7–0 to 7–5	*drank*
7–6 to 7–11	*hid, rang, slept, drew, dug, swam*
8–0 to 8–5	*left, caught, slid, hung*
8–6 to 8–11	*sent, shook, built*

Note: Nine words did not reach criterion by 8–5 through 8–11 years. These were *bent, chose, fought, held, sang, sank, stood, swang,* and *swept*.

Source: Information from Shipley, Maddox, and Driver (1991).

Listen to this fun conversation with an 8-year-old. Note the sentence development and the way in which she plays with language. http://www.youtube.com/watch?v=kTAtg7mvbs4

Even within a form, such as the word *will*, different functions develop at different rates. Cognitively, *will-do* (I will go) seems to develop before *will-happen* ("It will take time"). This is true in languages as different as English, Greek, and Turkish.

SENTENCE TYPES

In general, comprehension of linguistic relationships expressed in sentences improves throughout the school years (Table 10.7). The comparative relationship, as in *as big as*, *smaller than*, and *more fun than*, is the easiest one for young school-age children to interpret. The cognitive skills needed for comparative relationships develop during the preschool years but must await linguistic development. Other sentential relations, such as passive, are more difficult even for school-age children to interpret.

Syntax does not fully represent the organization of a spoken sentence. Prosody—rate and pausing—seems to aid mature listeners by segmenting linguistic units, just as it helps language-learning children. When speakers pause at inappropriate boundaries, they interfere with their listeners' syntactic processing. It is possible that the rhythmic outline of a sentence forms a frame in auditory working memory into which the syntactic elements are placed for analysis. In fact, prosodic information can aid older children and adults in identifying sentence elements, even when these elements are jumbled or misplaced.

Sentence production continues to expand during school-age through adult years across individuals at all socioeconomic levels and of all racial/ethnic groups. In both English and Spanish, sentences become longer with the addition of more words, embedded phrases, and embedded clauses. As might be expected, in both English and Spanish, children with low school achievement have less complex syntax.

Passive Sentences

Passive sentences are troublesome, both receptively and expressively, for English-speaking children in large part because of the syntactic form. The passive form is acquired earlier in non-Indo-European languages, such as Inuktitut; Sesotho, a West African language;

Zulu; and Quiche Mayan, a native Mexican language. In English passive sentences, the agent or cause of action and the patient or recipient are reversed, so in "Deshon was pushed by Trevor," we focus on Deshon and not on Trevor's act. In another variation, an instrument used to complete an action, as in *ball,* becomes the focus in "The ball was thrown by mommy." American English-speaking adults use the passive form infrequently. As you might imagine, then, 5-year-old children rarely produce full passive sentences.

Children do not truly comprehend some forms of passive sentences until about age 5½. Prior to this age, children use extralinguistic strategies, such as contextual support, to interpret passive sentences. Children may also rely on action verbs for interpretation.

An additional clue for passive interpretation may be the presence of a preposition. In general, young school-age children interpret a sentence as passive when *from* or *by* is present and as active when *to* is used. Thus, "The picture was painted *by* Mary" is passive, and "The picture was given *to* John" is active.

Production of passives begins in the late preschool years with short sentences containing noun + *be/get* + verb(*-en/-ed*), such as "It got broken" or "It was crushed." In these early passives, the noun or pronoun subject is almost always inanimate. Verbs of state, such as *lost, left,* and *broken,* tend to predominate in these short passives. Later, a child uses action verbs, such as *killed, hit,* and *crashed,* in both short and full passives (*He got hit*).

In fact, children form passives with *get* and *be* quite distinctively. For example, *got* is most often used when an animate patient is negatively affected by a nonagent, as in "I got sick from the french fries." On the other hand, *be* is used when an inanimate entity undergoes a neutral change of state, as in "The hamburger was cooked on the grill."

Although use of the past-tense *-ed* (He *kicked* the ball) is acquired by most children by age 4, development of the morpheme participles *-ed* (He was *kicked* by his friend) and *-en* (We were *beaten* by East High School) used in passive sentences takes until school-age to be mastered (Redmond, 2003). Commission errors—applying the morphological marker where it is not needed (He was *cutted* by the axe. It was *boughten* by her.)—may persist into early adolescence.

In general, low-SES African American children lag behind their middle-SES peers in passive participle learning (Pruitt et al., 2011). Even though low-SES African American children have the past tense forms (*bumped*) used in these sentences, they still perform more poorly than might be expected. This difference may be related to poorer vocabulary development.

Approximately 80% of 7½- to 8-year-olds produce full passive sentences. In general, a full passive contains some form of *be* or *got,* a verb with past-tense marker, and a preposition followed by a noun phrase as in "The window *was broken by Diego.*" Some passive forms do not appear until 11 years of age.

Passives are of three general types: *reversible, instrumental nonreversible,* and *agentive nonreversible.* In the reversible type, either noun could be the actor or the object: "The dog was chased by the cat" could be reversed to read "The cat was chased by the dog." In the nonreversible type, the nouns cannot be reversed. Two types of nonreversible passives include the instrumental type in which the action is brought about by an inanimate instrument, as in "The window was broken by the *ball,*" and the agentive type in which the action occurs because of an agent, as in "The window was broken by the *boy.*" Both are nonreversible because we could not say, "The ball/boy was broken by the window." These semantic distinctions appear to be important for development of the passive form.

As a group, children use about an equal number of reversible and nonreversible passives. Prior to age 4, children produce more reversible passives and with considerable word-order confusion. Children say "The boy is chased by the girl" when in fact the boy is in pursuit. This confusion is reflected in sentence interpretation as well. Only about 50% of 5-year-olds can correctly interpret reversible passives.

A marked increase in nonreversible passive production occurs just prior to age 8. The type of nonreversible passive that is most prominent changes with age. Agentive nonreversibles appear at age 9. Instrumental nonreversible passives are the most frequent nonreversibles for 11- to 13-year-olds. For this age group, semantic distinctions are also signaled by preposition use. Reversible passives use *by*, whereas nonreversibles use *with*. Adults may use either *by* or *with* in the instrumental nonreversible type. Both children and adults use *by* with the agentive nonreversible passive. Children's passives thus seem to be semantically different from those of adults and reflect a lengthy period of acquisition.

Conjoining

A child's repertoire of embedded and conjoined forms increases throughout the school years. Syntactic rules for both forms are observed more frequently. Examples are presented in Box 10.3. Clausal conjoining expands with the use of the following conjunctions:

Type	***Examples***
Causal	*because, so, therefore*
Conditional	*if*
Disjunctive	*but, or, although*
Temporal	*when, before, after, then*

The conjunction of choice for narration, however, remains *and*. Between 50% and 80% of the narrative sentences of school-age children begin with *and*. This percentage decreases as children mature. By 11 to 14 years of age, only about 20% of narrative sentences begin with *and*. This percentage decreases to 5% under the somewhat more formal constraints of writing.

Other conjunctions are more frequently used for clausal conjoining. Up to age 12, *because* and *when* predominate, with *if* and *in order to* also used frequently.

Even though *if*, *so*, and *because* are produced relatively early in the late preschool years, full understanding does not develop until much later. Semantic concepts of time and pragmatic aspects of propositional truth may affect comprehension.

BOX 10.3

Examples of Embedding and Conjoining

61 months	I think *I don't know what this is.* (Multiple embedded clauses)
	The frog could just gulp you up you know cause look how big it is. (Clausal conjoining and embedding)
64 months	Nicky said it wasn't real but mommy said it was because she tried to hit it and she broke it. (Embedded and conjoined clauses)
72 months	I got hit *in the eye with a baseball bat from the gym.* (Multiple prepositional phrases embedded)
73 months	The people *across the street* are going too. (Post-noun modifier)

Learning to understand and use *because* is not an easy task. To understand a sentence with *because*, a child must comprehend not only the relationship between two events but also their temporal sequence. This sequence is not the same as the order presented in the sentence. In "I went because I was asked," the speaker was invited before he or she actually left, although the linguistic ordering is the reverse. At first, a child tends to confuse *because* with *and* and *then*, using them all in a similar fashion. In both comprehension and production, the preschool child appears to follow an order-of-mention strategy. Although the causal relationship appears to be understood prior to age 7, knowledge of the ordering role of *because* seems to be weak.

True comprehension of *because* does not seem to develop until age 7. Consistently correct comprehension of *because* sentences may not occur until around age 10 or 11.

The long developmental period for conjunctions may be related to an interesting finding. Experimental results suggest that semantic understanding of the relations expressed by conjunctions continues to develop long after children begin to use these terms correctly in their speech (Cain, Patson, & Andrews, 2005).

Pragmatic factors may also affect the development of conjunctions. Children are more accurate at judging the speaker's meaning if the speaker expresses belief in the truthfulness of the utterance and if the two clauses are related positively. The conjunction *because* expresses both strong belief and a positive relationship. Other conjunctions express different relations. For example, both *because* and *although* presuppose that the speaker believes the two expressed propositions to be true:

It is a block because it is cubical.
It is a block, although it is made of metal.

In contrast, *unless* and *if* presuppose speaker uncertainty about at least one of the propositions:

It is a block unless it is round.
It is a block if it is wooden.

Similarly, *because* and *if* express a positive relationship between the two clauses, while *although* and *unless* express a negative relationship. *Although* expresses an exception or an illogical relationship. *Unless* requires that the truth of one proposition be denied in order for the relationship to be logical. Figure 10.1 expresses these concepts. In general, the more positive the relationship, the easier it is to comprehend the conjunction. Thus *because* is learned before *if* and *although*, which in turn are followed by *unless*. Even fifth-graders may have difficulty understanding *unless*. Younger children do not understand the appropriate pragmatic cues for disbelief and uncertainty. Therefore, they rely on syntactic cues.

Embedding

By 5 years of age, most children can easily produce sentences containing all types of subordinate clauses (Diessel, 2004). From this point on, development focuses on

- increased efficiency with which complex structures are accessed,
- multiple and embedded subordinate clauses, and
- integration of these utterances into organized and sustained discourse (Bates, 2003; Berman & Verhoeven, 2002; Nippold, Hesketh, Duthie, & Mansfield, 2005; Nippold, Mansfield, & Billow, 2007; Verhoeven et al., 2002).

FIGURE 10.1 **Concepts Expressed by Conjunctions**

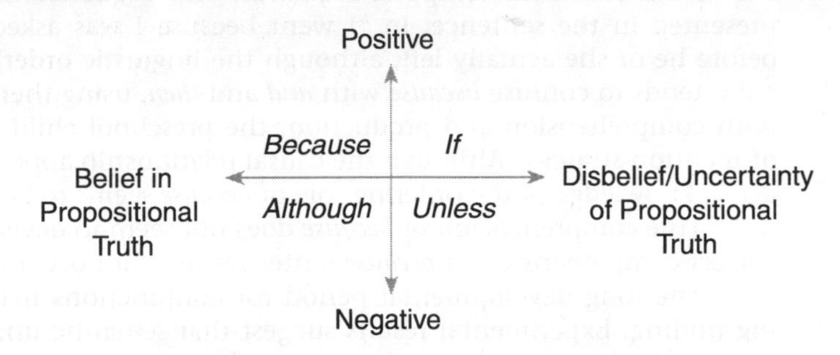

Source: Information from Wing & Scholnick (1981).

Developmental changes in syntactic complexity are influenced in part by intellectual stimulation and expanded knowledge. For example, academically stronger children produce longer sentences with greater amounts of subordination in both speaking and writing than do academically weaker ones. We could go so far as to say that "complex thought is driving the development of complex language" (Nippold et al., 2005, p. 1048).

The percentage of embedded sentences increases steadily to 20% to 30% in children's narratives throughout the school years. Relative pronoun use is expanded with the addition of *whose, whom,* and *in which.* Multiple embeddings also increase with maturity and are one of the most significant differences between the narrative syntactic structure of 6- to 8-year-olds and 10- to 12-year-olds.

Although school-age clausal embeddings include relative pronoun deletions and center or subject–relative clause embedding, these forms are rarely produced prior to age 7. Examples of each of these forms include the following:

> I'm engaged to someone (*whom*) you know. (Relative pronoun deletion)
> The book (*that*) *Reggie read* was exciting. (Center or subject–relative clause embedding)

Center embedding is particularly difficult for young school-age children.

Semantic role is an important factor in interpretation. If the object of a center embedding is inanimate, it is less likely to be misinterpreted than an animate object is. In the following, *window* cannot *run,* so there is no confusion in the first sentence, but the second may be misinterpreted:

> The boy who broke the window ran away. (Interpreted correctly)
> The boy who hit the girl ran away. (Could be interpreted by a child to mean that the girl ran away)

Faced with confusion, a child resorts to a *subject* + *verb* + *object* interpretation strategy.

Comprehension of embedded clauses also seems to be based on the place and manner of the embedding. Embeddings may occur at the end of a sentence or in the center. The two clauses may be parallel, in which both share the same subject or object, or nonparallel, in which they do not:

> The *boy who* lives next door gave me a present. (Parallel central embedding: The same subject—*boy*—serves both clauses.)

He gave me a *present that* I didn't like. (Parallel ending embedding: The same object—*present*—serves both clauses.)
He gave me the *present that* is on the table. (Nonparallel ending embedding: The object of one—*present*—is the subject of the other.)
The *dog that* was chased by the boy is angry. (Nonparallel central embedding: The subject of the main clause—*dog*—is the object of the embedded clause.)

This order is the general developmental sequence from easiest to most difficult. The relative difficulty of center embedded clauses may be due to limitation in auditory working memory. As a child matures, auditory working memory is able to hold more items for longer periods of time.

Working memory is significantly involved in school-age children's comprehension of complex sentences (Montgomery, Magimairaj, & O'Malley, 2008). Simple sentence comprehension does not seem to require extensive use of working memory. Of most importance for comprehension of complex sentences are both processing speed and control and allocation of attention.

First-graders rely heavily on word order for interpretation and are confused by semantic class reversals between subject and object class. By seventh grade, a child has little difficulty interpreting these sentences and relies primarily on grammatical cues. This change probably reflects a child's underlying cognitive development.

SUMMARY

During the school-age years, a child adds new morphologic and syntactic structures and expands and refines existing forms. These developments enable expression of increasingly complex relationships and use of more creative language. Underlying semantic concepts are often the key to this complex learning.

Phonologic Development

During the early school years, a child completes the phonetic inventory (Table 10.7). By age 8 he or she can produce all English speech sounds competently. Sounds in longer words or blends may still be difficult. The acquisition of sounds, however, is only one aspect of a child's phonological competence.

By age 5, a child can identify syllables. Very few 4-year-olds are able to identify these units. A 4-year-old child is able to decide if a sound sequence conforms to the phonological rules of English. He or she will repeat words that contain possible sequences, even when the words are not real, but will modify impermissible sequences when repeating them in order to produce sequences more like English. A 7-year-old tends to replace the meaningless words with actual words. These changes most likely reflect the child's increasing metalinguistic skills, which we will discuss later.

MORPHOPHONEMIC DEVELOPMENT

Morphophonemic changes are phonological or sound modifications that result when morphemes are placed together. For example, the final /k/ in *electric* changes to a /s/ in *electricity*. Several rules for morphophonemic change are learned gradually throughout elementary school.

One rule, usually learned by first grade, pertains to the regular plural *-s* mentioned in Chapter 9. The 5- to 6-year-old has learned the rule for /s/ and /z/ but not for /əz/ in all cases. Even in third grade, some students may have difficulty pluralizing nouns ending in *-sk* and *-st* clusters. Is the plural of *desk* /desks/ or /deskəz/?

During the school years, a child also learns the rules for vowel shifting. For example, the /aI/ sound in *divine* changes to an /I/ in *divinity*. Other examples are as follows:

/aI/—/I/	/eI/—/æ/	/i/—/ɛ/
div*i*ne—div*i*nity	expl*ai*n—expl*a*nation	ser*e*ne—ser*e*nity
coll*i*de—coll*i*sion	s*a*ne—s*a*nity	obsc*e*ne—obsc*e*nity

Knowledge of vowel shifting is gained only gradually. A 5-year-old child does not understand the rules, and it is not until age 17 that most individuals learn to apply all the rules.

Stress, or emphasis, is also learned during the school years. The stress placed on certain syllables or words reflects the grammatical function of that unit. In English, stress varies with the relationship between two words and with the word's use as a noun or verb. For example, two words may form a phrase, such as *green house*, or a compound word, such as *greenhouse*. If you repeat the two, you will find that you stress *house* in the phrase and *green* in the compound word. Here are some other examples:

Phrase	*Compound Word*
red *head*	*red*head
black *board*	*black*board
high *chair*	*high*chair

Noun–verb pairs also differ. In the noun *record*, emphasis is on the first syllable, whereas the verb *record* is pronounced with stress on the last. Other examples:

Noun	*Verb*
*pre*sent	pre*sent*
*con*duct	con*duct*

Initially acquired on isolated words, pitch contours are gradually integrated into larger units. The period from age 3 to 5 seems to be particularly important in several languages for the acquisition of stress patterns. It is not until age 12, however, that the full adult stress and accent system is acquired (Ingram, 1986).

SPEECH PRODUCTION

Increased sentence length and complexity requires increased speech motor planning. Although there is a protracted course of speech motor development that lasts well into adolescence, around age 9 years, children begin to use adultlike prespeech processes to plan the timing of sentence phrases (Sadagopan & Smith, 2008). Although younger children vary considerably in their movement, such as lip-rounding, to produce sounds, these movements may affect and extend across an entire utterance. For both young children and adults, broad chunks of speech have been planned by the time they initiate production of a sentence (Goffman, Smith, Heisler, & Lo, 2008).

Say the following sentence as both a statement and a declarative and then again as a question or interrogative but do not change the word order: *John's going to the party*. Note the different rhythmic or prosodic patterns in each and the different intonation. Although children as young as age 4 are capable of modifying their lip and jaw

Comstock/Stockbyte/Getty Images

By late elementary school, the language use differences of boys and girls are readily apparent.

movements to mark this declarative–interrogative contrast, refinement of these movements will continue throughout childhood (Grigos & Patel, 2007).

SUMMARY

Throughout the school years, a child learns rules for permissible combinations and for the use of stress, which is related to syntactic and semantic growth as well. Thus, the child is again forming rule systems that bring order to the linguistic world. The child is not simply mirroring the speech heard around him or her.

Metalinguistic Abilities

Metalinguistic abilities enable a language user to think about language independently of comprehension and production abilities. As such, a child focuses on and reflects on language as a decontextualized object. It is these "linguistic intuitions" that let us make decisions about the grammatical acceptability of an utterance. Thus, a child treats language as an object of analysis and observation, using language to describe language. This metalinguistic ability develops only gradually throughout the school years.

In adults, comprehension and production are almost automatic, and processing occurs at the rate of communication. There is no inordinate burden. Even school-age children's comprehension strategies seem to be unconscious. Controlled, conscious processes tend to be minimal because comprehension includes the total linguistic and nonlinguistic contexts.

Although metalinguistic abilities appear in the preschool years, full awareness is not achieved until age 7 to 8 years. Prior to this age, children view language primarily as a means of communication and do not focus on the manner in which it is conveyed. After age 7 or 8, the development of decentration enables a child to concentrate on and process simultaneously two aspects of language: message meaning and linguistic correctness. Thus, a child is able to judge grammatical correctness without being influenced by semantics.

Preschool children tend to make judgments of utterance acceptability based on the content rather than on the grammatical structure. Thus, a 4-year-old might judge "Daddy painted the fence" as unacceptable because, in the child's realm of experience, "Daddies don't paint fences; they paint houses." By kindergarten, a child is just beginning to separate what is said from how it is said, to separate referents from words, and to notice structure. Even so, school-age children may still judge correctness more on semantic intent or meaning than on grammatical form.

The ability to detect syntactic errors develops first. A school-age child demonstrates an increasing ability to judge grammatical acceptability and to correct unacceptable sentences.

Ability to perform judgment tasks differs with age, but especially with working memory span and phonological ability (McDonald, 2008). Although school-age children can easily make judgments about grammatical structures, such as word order and article omissions, even 11-year-old children differ from adults on others, such as past tense and third person singular (*she walks*) agreement. Results of several studies indicate a rough developmental order of mastery of grammatical structures in judgment tasks may be (1) simple word order changes; (2) the present progressive morpheme; (3) omitted determiners and auxiliaries; (4) agreement errors, especially third person singular subject–verb agreement and plural agreement; and (5) irregular forms.

Working memory increases throughout the elementary school years and among third-graders is significantly correlated with both grammaticality judgment and the ability to correct ungrammatical sentences. Similarly, working memory is correlated with receptive syntax ability and sentence comprehension in young elementary school children (Ellis Weismer, Evans, & Hesketh, 1999; Montgomery, 2000b).

Metalinguistic abilities usually emerge after a child has mastered a linguistic form. Therefore, it is possible that a young school-age child becomes aware at a metalinguistic level of language forms and content unconsciously used in the preschool years. Some metalinguistic abilities are an almost unconscious or implicit aspect of feedback, whereas others are extremely explicit and conscious. An order of development based on this continuum is presented in Table 10.9.

Metalinguistic awareness may be essential to changes in semantic organization discussed earlier and are important for the development of reading. Morphological awareness of root words, such as *like*, and derived forms, such as *likable*, *unlike*, *likely*, and *unlikely*, is necessary for the formation of associational networks. These networks are constructed of highly similar words, and activation of one opens access to others.

Like emerging pragmatic skills, metalinguistic abilities depend on development of all aspects of language. With increased structural and semantic skills, a child is freed from the immediate linguistic context and can attend to how a message is communicated. In addition, metalinguistic skill development is related to language use, cognitive development, reading ability, academic achievement, IQ, environmental stimulation, and play (Kemper & Vernooy, 1993).

Language Difference

Bilingual and nonmajority dialectal speakers may or may not experience difficulty developing American English. Children who learned two languages simultaneously should experience no difficulty by school age and may actually be at an advantage in school. Children who are learning English successive to a first language may experience some difficulty in school depending on when they began to learn English. Some of these issues have been explored earlier. Let's discuss two specific issues, code switching among bilingual children and the prejudice some speakers of African American English (AAE) or other dialects may face.

TABLE 10.9 **Development of Metalinguistic Skills and Awareness**

Approximate Age	Abilities
Toddler	1. Monitors own utterances ■ Repairs spontaneously ■ Adjusts speech to different listeners
Preschool	2. Checks the result of own utterance ■ Checks whether the listener has understood; if not, repair or try again ■ Comments explicitly on own utterances and those of others ■ Corrects others
	3. Tests for reality ■ Decides whether a word or sentence "works" in furthering listener understanding
	4. Attempts to learn language deliberately ■ Applies appropriate inflections to "new" words ■ Practices speech styles of different roles
School age	5. Predicts the consequences of using particular forms (inflections, words, phrases, sentences) ■ Judges utterances as appropriate for a specific listener or setting ■ Corrects word order and wording in sentences judged as "wrong"
	6. Reflects on an utterance (structure independent of use) ■ Identifies specific linguistic units (sounds, syllables, words, sentences) ■ Provides definitions of words ■ Constructs puns, riddles, or other forms of humor ■ Explains why some sentences are possible and how to interpret them ■ Judges utterance correctness

Source: Drawn from Clark (1978).

CODE SWITCHING DEVELOPMENT

Bilingual speakers often exhibit code switching, or shifting from one language to another, especially when both languages are used in the environment, as in the southwestern United States, in Quebec, or in sections of many major U.S. cities. The behavior is not random, nor does it reflect an underlying language deficit. Rather, code switching is the result of functional and grammatical principles and is a complex, rule-governed phenomenon that is systematically influenced by the context and the situation. Code switching is confined almost exclusively to free morphemes, most frequently nouns, and tends to occur where the surface structures are similar. Children begin by code switching single words from one language to another. In contrast, adults tend to substitute whole sentences. Certain words and phrases tend to be switched predictably across different conversations by the same speaker. Individuals vary based on their proficiency in both languages.

Rather than representing the integration of both grammars into a third, new grammar, code switching rules demonstrate the continuing separation of the two languages. For example, code switching occurs only when words are positioned according to the rules for the language from which the word is selected. In other words, code switching occurs at natural word and phrase boundaries that correspond to monolinguals' processing units. Although adults do not code switch within words, this practice is frequently violated by children under 10.

For children, systematic code switching appears to be a function of the participants in a conversation. Three characteristics of the participants are important: their perceived language proficiency, their language preference, and their social identity. In general, children under age 5 combine proficiency and preference decisions. A listener either knows a language or does not, they reason. Older children make finer distinctions and may, therefore, consider their speaker more often. Their behavior reflects the developing presuppositional skills seen in school-age children. Children also identify certain people with certain languages. If unsure, they try to use physical characteristics as a guide. For example, in the southwestern United States, Anglo teachers may be addressed in English even though they are proficient in Spanish.

Other functional variables also influence code switching. Although physical setting alone has little influence, the type of discourse is a factor. Interviews and narratives contain few switches, instead remaining in one language or the other. Conversations, in contrast, are characterized by frequent switches. Adults are more likely to code switch in casual conversations than in public settings in which speech is usually more formal (Zentella, 1999). In addition, code switching can be a stylistic device used for direct quotes, emphasis, clarification or repetition, elaboration, focus on a particular portion of a message, attention getting and maintenance, and personal interjections or asides. Although topics alone do not usually influence switching, the language of a specific group may be used when discussing that group, and code switching may signal topic changes. In the southwestern United States, for example, Spanish-speaking families may use English when discussing Anglos even though no Anglos are present.

The function of code switching may be twofold. First, it may be an aid for retention of the first language while a second is learned. Second, once the two languages are learned, code switching may ensure that both are used.

AFRICAN AMERICAN ENGLISH SPEAKERS AND SOCIETY

For an individual child, the main effects of African American English (AAE) are social and educational. To the extent that AAE is stigmatized within our multidialectal society, a child may also be stigmatized. Unfortunately, many people attach relative values to certain dialects and to the speakers of those dialects and tend to respond in terms of their stereotypes. This response may, in turn, affect other judgments. Employment and educational opportunities may be denied because of dialectal differences. In general, AAE speakers are granted shorter employment interviews, offered fewer positions, and offered lower-paying positions than speakers of dialects with more typical features. Apparently, this discrimination does not significantly affect the self-concept of AAE speakers. African American children who speak AAE seem to have a higher self-concept than those who do not.

Unfortunately, some educators exhibit a bias in favor of a regional or majority dialect. Teachers may use any of the following reasons for assuming that minority students are less capable:

Lack of verbal capacity in formal or threatening situations.
Poor school performance is a result of this verbal deficit.
Middle-class speech habits result in better school achievement.
Dialectal differences reflect differences in the capacity for logical analysis.
Logical thinking can be fostered by teaching children to mimic the formal speech patterns of their teachers.
Children who adopt these formal patterns think logically and thus do better in reading and arithmetic.

Scores on norm-referenced tests, usually based on majority language usage, can be, and often are, used to bolster this position.

Although preschool African American children from homes using AAE do not develop all forms of the dialect, there is a marked increase in use during school age, especially from grades 3 to 5. Prepubescent boys are especially likely to use AAE.

Teachers may assume that students who speak AAE do not understand the predominant regional dialect. But this does not appear to be the case. African American children's comprehension seems to be similar for both dialects. In fact, African American students perform better at sentence completion when cued in the majority dialect. Finally, there is no difference between African American low-SES and white middle-SES children in imitation of sentences in the majority dialect. The ability of African American children to comprehend both dialects continues into adulthood. African American adults find child speakers of both dialects equally intelligible, whereas adult majority speakers find children speakers significantly more intelligible in the majority dialect.

Speakers of AAE may have difficulty with reading and spelling. In general, children read orally in accordance with their dialects. The resultant differences are not errors, but phonemic differences that may make it difficult for the teacher to interpret a child's oral reading. Surface phonemic differences may also account for a child's spelling errors. Morphological and syntactic features of AAE are found in the writing of African American school-age children but to a lesser degree than found in their speech (Thompson, Craig, & Washington, 2004).

AAE speakers may not recognize the significance of the grammatical markers that they omit. This suggests that the AAE-speaking child may not hear a difference or may not understand its significance. In one study, 4- to 6 year-old AAE speakers did not understand the third person singular *-s* as a number agreement marker (*he-they take-takes*) nor were they sensitive to its use as a clue to the subject number (Johnson, 2005). It is easy to see how this difficulty could be transferred to other academic areas. Among 5- to 8-year-old African American children, higher familiarity with school English encountered in academic materials and settings is associated with better reading achievement (Charity, Scarborough, & Griffin, 2004).

Conclusion

WITHIN TWELVE YEARS, THE CHILD develops from a dependent newborn to an adolescent. The overall rate of development is amazing.

By kindergarten age, a child has acquired much of the structure of the mature oral language user. Development continues, however, as a child adds new forms and gains new skills in transmitting messages. The process continues throughout life, especially in the semantic and pragmatic aspects of language.

With increased age, a child sharpens word definitions and relationships, resulting in more accurate communication. At the same time, he or she learns to use language figuratively to create nonliteral relationships. As a result of both processes, communication is both more precise and more creative. The language user has gained increased flexibility.

Discussion

PRAGMATIC DEVELOPMENT IS SEEN in conversational and narrative skills. Narratives focus on internal narrative development called story grammars.

Vocabulary expands rapidly, thus requiring increasingly better organization. There is a shift from a word-order type of organization to a categorical, semantic-based organization. The result is flexibility and easy access. New items in the vocabulary are multiple definitions and figurative language.

Syntactic development has slowed, and many forms, such as conjunctions and passive voice, take a long time to develop fully. The development of language form has become intricate as sentence complexity increases and as morphophonemic changes occur in the child's expanding vocabulary.

At about the time the child begins school, he or she gains an increased ability to manipulate language out of the physical context. Thus, the language

FIGURE 11.2 **Dynamic Relationship of Reading and Phonological Awareness**

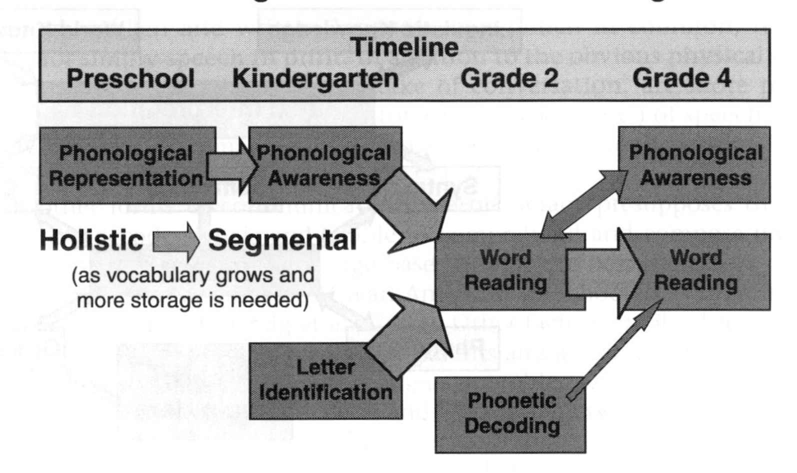

Note: Arrow thickness approximates amount of effect.
Sources: Information from Hogan, Catts, and Little (2005); Sutherland and Gillon (2005).

predictor is reading itself (Hogan, Catts, & Little, 2005). At this point, word reading influences phonological awareness.

Socioeconomic status (SES), age, speech-sound accuracy, and vocabulary make unique contributions to phonological awareness for children between the ages of 2 and 5. In short, the effects of SES and speech-sound accuracy on phonological awareness become increasingly important as children get older (McDowell, Lonigan, & Goldstein, 2007).

The dynamic relationships among vocabulary size, storage and processing components of working memory, and phonological awareness (PA) development is evident in both languages of English language learners (ELLs) (Gorman, 2012). Among bilingual children, language experience affects phonological awareness in either language (Ibrahim, Eviatar, & Aharon-Peretz, 2007). PA instruction in Spanish (L1) results in gains in both L1 and in English (L2).

Reading ability for bilingual children is also affected by the visual complexity of the script. For example, Arabic script seems particularly complex for bilingual children compared to Latin, Cyrillic, and Hebrew script. Examples of several types of script are presented in Table 11.1.

COMPREHENSION

Meaning is actively constructed by the interaction of words and sentences with personal meanings and experiences. Several levels of text comprehension exist. At the basic level, a reader is primarily concerned with decoding. Above this level is **critical literacy** in which a reader actively interprets, analyzes, and synthesizes information and is able to explain the content. A reader actively bridges the gaps between what is written and what is meant (Caccamise & Snyder, 2005). At the highest level of **dynamic literacy**, a reader is able to relate content to other knowledge. Dynamic literacy is relating information

TABLE 11.1 Examples of Written Scripts

Arabic:	جثرنثظققكلقوى
Greek:	ΠΡΣΦβγδ
Latin:	ABCDabcd
Kanji:	明清強雄
Hebrew:	בגדהףפצקש
Cyrillic:	ДЕЖЗèђѓє
Hangul:	한글 집현전

across multiple texts, comparing and contrasting, integrating and using ideas for problem raising and solving (Westby, 2005).

A reader's meaning is composed of the text and the mental model the reader creates through the comprehension process. Comprehension occurs as a reader builds models based on the text and his or her knowledge and experience.

Reading is a goal-directed activity. Knowing what to do and how to do it is called **metacognition**, knowledge about knowledge and about cognitive processes. Metacognition has two aspects important for reading: self-appraisal, or knowledge of one's own cognitive processes and how you are using them, and executive function. Executive function, mentioned in Chapter 3, is self-regulation and includes the ability to attend; to set reasonable goals; to plan and organize to achieve each goal; to initiate, monitor, and evaluate one's performance in relation to the goal; and to revise plans and strategies based on feedback.

During reading, the efficient reader uses self-regulation. Speed changes with the difficulty of the material. The reader makes hypotheses and predictions and confirms or does not confirm these.

We can describe reading by two processes. Dubbed *bottom-up* and *top-down*, they describe distinct processes for print.

Within the bottom-up process, reading is translating written elements into speech. Hence, bottom-up emphasizes lower-level perceptual and phonemic processes and their influence on higher cognitive functioning. Knowledge of both perceptual features in letters and grapheme–phoneme (letter–sound) correspondence, as well as lexical retrieval, facilitate word recognition and decoding.

In contrast, the top-down, or problem-solving, process emphasizes the cognitive task of deriving meaning. Higher cognitive functions, such as concepts, inferences, and levels of meaning, influence the processing. A reader generates hypotheses about the written material based on his or her knowledge, the content, and the syntactic structures used. Sampling of the reading confirms or does not confirm these hypotheses.

For a skilled reader, printed words are represented only briefly for processing. Automatic and usually below the level of consciousness, each word is represented for less than one quarter of a second while the brain retrieves all information about that word.

confirmation. At first, a child will learn to recognize high-usage words, such as *the* and *is*, on sight and then use them plus the overall text to form hypotheses regarding unknown words. In other words, a child uses his or her knowledge of language to help figure out the word, much as in speech, when the listener predicts the next word, phrase, or clause.

A mature silent reader, such as you, doesn't even read whole words. Rather, you sample enough of a word to confirm your hypothesis and recognize others quickly by sight. In this manner, you can read rapidly for overall meaning.

Most likely, mature reading consists of parallel processes, both top-down and bottom-up, that provide information simultaneously at various levels of analysis. This information is then synthesized. The processes are interactive, and relative reliance on each varies with the material being read and the skill of a reader. By third or fourth grade, children employ both a bottom-up strategy when reading isolated words and a top-down strategy when reading text. Thus, faster top-down processes are used with textual material, and slower, bottom-up processes when such support is lacking.

The complex process of reading is closely related to linguistic processing. In addition to the initial use of two input modes, a reader processes material on at least two levels: bit by bit and holistically. The relative reliance of the reader on each level varies with reading competence.

Reading Development

Like speech and language, prereading in our culture is acquired through social interaction rather than formal instruction. Reading together is a highly social activity in which both parents and children participate. While reading to a child, the adult uses many of the conversational techniquesdescribed in Chapter 6, including focusing attention, asking questions, and reinforcing the child's attempts at reading.

EMERGING READING

There are several phases of reading development. In the emerging phase, which occurs prior to age 6, a child gains an awareness of print and sounds while gradually learning to make associations between the two.

Reading development begins within social interactions between a child and caregiver(s) at around age 1, as adults begin to share books with toddlers. Book sharing is usually conversational in tone with the book serving as the focus of communication. Here's an example:

ADULT: This book is about a . . .
CHILD: Cow.
ADULT: Well, yes. You found a cow. That's right. What do cows say?
CHILD: Moo!
ADULT: Um-hm, cows say, "Moo." Can you find another cow?

Reading the story is secondary to and will be included in the conversation. A parent or caregiver mediates the process by modeling responses for a child, by providing feedback, and by talking about both the text and the pictures (van Kleeck & Beckley-McCall, 2002).

Actual reading by parents usually begins late in a child's second year. A relationship exists between the age of onset of home reading routines and a child's oral language skills, especially oral comprehension.

Parent–child reading is not the only way of developing a concept of literacy. Television shows, such as *Sesame Street*, and parental activities, such as the use of cookbooks and TV schedules or bill paying, and using the Internet, are also important. A child learns that books and writing or print convey information. In short, the child gains a notion of literacy.

By age 3, most children in our culture are familiar with books and can recognize their favorites. Through book sharing they have gained the rudiments of **print awareness**, such as knowing the direction in which reading proceeds across a page and through a book, being interested in print, and recognizing some letters (Snow et al., 1999). Later the child will learn that words are discrete units and will be able to identify some letters and use literacy terminology, such as *letter*, *word*, and *sentence*.

At this age, words may be stored by their visual features, or the way they look, but children lack knowledge of the phoneme–grapheme (sound–letter) correspondence. The connections in the child's memory for printed words are relatively unsystematic at this point.

For most children, emergent story reading in which a child pretends to read a book or uses a book to tell a story begins between ages 2½ and 4 (Kaderavek & Sulzby, 2000). A child uses the vocabulary and syntax associated with specific books and written elements, such as printed words, in this process, even if the words are not interpreted correctly. Gradually, a child moves from language about the text to language that recreates the text. At this age, my granddaughter could recite several of her favorite books, many of the simple ones word for word.

Most 4-year-olds are "consumers" of print and are able to recognize their names and a few memorized words. Words learned within one context, such as environmental signs and package labels, gradually become decontextualized until they are recognized in print alone. Approximately 60% of 3-year-olds and 80% of 4- and 5-year-olds recognize the word *stop*, and they all probably know McDonald's golden "M." In addition, they gain some general concept that print in books is distinct from the pictures and that books are used in certain ways.

Children who have been exposed to a home literacy environment and to print media have better phoneme awareness, letter knowledge, and vocabulary (Foy & Mann, 2003). Some home literacy practices seem to affect later language and literacy skills more than others. For example, among low-SES African American children, these factors are overall support from the home environment, responsiveness, sensitivity, and acceptance of children's behavior that provides structure, organization, and a positive general emotional climate at home along with stimulating toys and interactions (Roberts, Jurgens, & Burchinal, 2005).

Mothers vary their book-sharing behaviors based on a preschool child's age (van Kleeck & Beckley-McCall, 2002). For example, mothers use more complex books and more sentences with higher levels of abstraction and spend more time sharing books with older preschoolers. High levels of abstraction include summarizing, making judgments and comparisons, predicting, and explaining. In contrast, mothers use more mediating strategies and spend more time getting and maintaining attention with younger children. In mediating strategies, the parent goes beyond the book to provide a context for the child, as in Jonathan lived on a farm. Remember when we went to the farm to pet the animals?

As early as age 2 some children show awareness of sounds in their speech, in rhyming, and in sound play (Kamhi & Catts, 1999). Rhyming activities also increase awareness of syllables and smaller units. Although children are aware of sounds, most will require some formal instruction in order to break down words into individual phonemes. Most 3-year-olds are unable to segment words into smaller units.

Phonologic awareness progresses gradually from an awareness of larger segments to smaller ones. By age 4, children are beginning to attend to the internal structure of words such as phonologic similarities and syllable structure.

Syllables are the organizing units for sounds. Each syllable can be divided into its initial phonemes, called the *onset*, and the remaining part of the word or *rime*, which, in comprehension skills become evident. Meaningful words in context are read faster than random words. At this stage, a child begins by relying heavily on visual configuration for word recognition by paying particular attention to the first letter and to word length, ignoring letter order and other features. A child is aware of the importance of the letters but is unable to use them in analyzing the word. Next, a child learns sound–spelling correspondence rules and is able, using this phonetic approach, to sound out novel words. Thus, segmental detail, or the arrangement of sound and letter sequences, becomes more important. In addition, a child learns that the text, not the reader, is the bearer of the message and that the text does more than just describe the pictures. Successful first-grade oral readers are able to use the text to analyze unknown words. Along with phonology and orthographics, semantics is also an important factor in word decoding. Poor readers tend to guess wildly.

By age 7 or 8, most children have acquired the graphemic (sound–symbol), syllabic, and word knowledge they need to become competent readers. This knowledge is acquired in school in most cultures. Among the Vai, a Liberian population, however, knowledge of written syllabic symbols is learned informally within the family.

In the second or orthographic phase of reading development, roughly third and fourth grades, the child is able to analyze unknown words using orthographic patterns and contextual references. In third grade, the child is expected to use silent independent reading and to use reading texts in different content areas. There is a shift from *learning to read* to *reading to learn* (Snow et al., 1999).

As a child improves, reading becomes more automatic or fluent, especially for familiar words. Fluency is aided by the use of grapheme–phoneme patterns in the child's memory and by analogy, the process of relating unfamiliar words to familiar ones based on similar spelling.

Grades 4 to 8 seem to be a major watershed in which the emphasis in reading shifts to comprehension. Thus, a child's scanning rate continues to increase steadily.

Children with poor reading comprehension are impaired in their use of supportive context to aid their understanding of opaque idioms (Cain & Towse, 2008). Their difficulty does not seem to result from poor semantic analysis skills.

By secondary school, the adolescent uses higher-level skills such as inference and recognition of viewpoint to aid comprehension. Lower-level skills are already firmly established. Finally, at the college level and beyond, you are able to integrate what you read into your current knowledge base and make critical judgments about the material.

The differences between the 7-year-old and the adult reader seem more quantitative than qualitative, although there are some obvious differences. Adults have a larger, more diverse vocabulary and a more flexible pronunciation system, and they are able to comprehend larger units than elementary school children.

Comprehension for all readers is aided by cohesion within the text. In general, the more cohesive ties in the text, the more understandable it is. More explicit texts are more readable. As in oral development, more mature readers interpret ties more readily and have less difficulty with complex, intersentential cohesion.

Not all children follow the same progression. Children have different cognitive styles that influence the manner in which they approach tasks. In addition, which language is being read and whether it is a reader's first or second language will influence the processes emphasized.

Literacy achievement gaps can be attributed to factors such as oral language; emergent and conventional literacy skills; family; schooling; instructional variables; and dialect (Connor, Morrison, Fishman, Schatschneider, & Underwood, 2007; Connor, Son, Hindman, & Morrison, 2005; National Early Literacy Panel, 2009; National Reading Panel, 2000; Spira, Bracken, & Fischel, 2005). Although frequent Nonmainstream American English (NMAE) production is not always associated with poor reading achievement, there is a significant relationship between a child's frequent use of NMAE in school at the end of kindergarten and poorer reading achievement by the end of first grade (Patton

Terry & McDonald Connor, 2012; Terry, Connor, Thomas-Tate, & Love, 2010). Although there is a significant increase in children's production of Mainstream American English (MAE) forms during this period, this change does not seem to be associated with change in letter–word reading and phonological awareness skills.

MATURE READING

Mature readers use very little cognitive energy determining word pronunciation. At a higher level of processing, language and world knowledge or experiences are used to derive an understanding of the text, which is monitored automatically to ensure that the information makes sense (Snow et al., 1999). A skilled reader then predicts the next word or phrase and glances at it to confirm the prediction. Printed words are processed quickly, automatically, and below the level of consciousness most of the time.

Mature readers like you don't so much simply read the text as dialog with it. Reading is an active process in which ideas and concepts are formed and modified, details remembered and recalled, and information checked. Although much of this is the unconscious process of the brain partaking of new information, other activities, such as looking up a definition, are decidedly conscious.

As you mature, the types and purposes of reading change, but you can continue to enjoy the process throughout your life. Reading skill will continue to be strong through adulthood if you exercise your ability and do not experience any neuropathologies. Reading is one of the primary ways by which adults increase both their vocabulary and their knowledge.

The Process of Writing

Writing is a social act, and like a speaker, the writer must consider his or her audience. This demands more cognitive resources for planning and execution than does speaking because no audience is present.

Nor is written language the simple transcription of oral language. Children must learn to use constructions other than those they use in speech and to represent phonemes with letters.

In short, writing is using knowledge and new ideas combined with language knowledge to create text. It's a complex process that includes generating ideas, organizing and planning, acting on that plan, revising, and monitoring based on self-feedback (Scott, 1999).

Writing is more abstract than speech and more decontextualized than conversation, requiring internal knowledge of different writing forms, such as narratives and expository writing. When we write, the entire context is contained in the writing. We create the context from our own language without the help of conversational partners.

The difference between writing and speech fosters two distinct styles of discourse. Spoken communication is usually produced under the pressure of rapid processing. In contrast, writing allows for more planning and monitoring (Strömqvist, Nordqvist, & Wengelin, 2004). In addition, spoken language is often more personalized and interactive, while written language is more detached and less interactive, with increased time for linguistic encoding (Berman, Ragnarsdöttir, & Strömqvist, 2002; Biber, 1995; Ravid & Zilberbuch, 2003).

Initially, the overall structure of both speech and writing is very close, but children display less maturity in the written form. This is probably because the physical process is so laborious. Once writing becomes more automatic, however, the grammar in writing becomes more advanced than that in speech.

Some structures are common to both speech and writing, while others occur rarely, if at all, in writing. Other structures are more typical of writing than of speech. Structures found almost exclusively in speech include dysfluencies, fillers (*well, you know*), vague expletives (*. . . and all, . . . and everything*), *this* and *these* used for new information (*And there was this man . . .*), and pronoun apposition (*My dog, he got a bath*). Dysfluencies, such as false starts, reformulations, redundant repetitions, and ungrammatical strings of words, are nine times as frequent in the speech of 10-year-olds as in their writing. No doubt this reflects the additional time that writers have to plan, reflect upon, and modify their message. Studies of elementary children who speak majority dialects indicate that dialectal structures also do not occur in written communication.

The ability of elementary school children who speak African American English (AAE) to dialect shift to the majority dialect has significant implications for educational achievement (Craig, Zhang, Hensel, & Quinn, 2009). In short, AAE-speaking students who learn to use a more standard dialect in literacy tasks outperform their peers who do not make this linguistic adaptation. Lower rates of use of AAE in writing also accounted for higher achievement in reading.

When we examine the use of African American English (AAE) grammatical features in spoken and written language, we find a difference across literacy development. Although third-graders have comparable dialectal use in both speech and writing, eighth-graders use more dialectal features in their speech, indicating an increased ability to dialect switch with maturity (Ivy & Masterson, 2011).

Writing consists of several processes: text construction, handwriting, spelling, executive function, and memory (Berninger, 2000). Text construction is the process of going from ideas to written texts of words and sentences that support the ideas of the writer. Executive function is the self-regulatory aspect of writing. It's the ability to select and sustain attention, organize perception, and flexibly shift perceptual and cognitive setup, as well as control social and affective behavior (Ylvisaker & DeBonis, 2000).

In general, writing is more formal and more complex than speech, and the structures found more frequently in writing reflect this quality. The writing of 9- or 10-year-olds is free of many of the features of speech and becomes more mature than speech. By ages 12 to 13, the syntax used in writing far exceeds that used in speech. This is a gradual process. For example, post-noun modifiers (*the boy at* my school) become more numerous in writing than in speech at about age 8 and embedded clauses at about age 10.

While complex subjects are rare in speech, they are found more frequently in the writing of 9-year-olds than in the speech of adults. This reflects the use of embedded phrases and clauses, some of which, such as those beginning with *whose, whom, on which,* and *in which,* occur almost exclusively in writing. In addition, written sentences include more prepositional and adverbial phrases (*opposite the drug counter, about 5 miles down the beach*).

For most of childhood and adolescence, writing ability lags behind reading comprehension. This asymmetry cannot be totally explained by English orthography. Although the sound–letter correspondence is not found in kanji, a Japanese writing system using Chinese characters for words and concepts, the reading–writing asymmetry still persists even in children there.

ORTHOGRAPHIC KNOWLEDGE

Orthographic knowledge is information stored in memory that tells us how to represent spoken language in written form. As such, orthographic knowledge plays an important role in literacy acquisition. Exactly what we mean by orthographic knowledge can be confusing. I refer you to the excellent tutorial by Ken Apel (2011) for a discussion of the term and clarification.

Let's try to clarify some. In part, orthographic knowledge consists of the following elements:

- Stored mental representations of specific written words or word parts called *mental graphemic representations* (MGRs) (Apel, 2010; Wolter & Apel, 2010). MGRs consist of specific sequences of graphemes or letters representing written words.

- *Orthographic patterns* that govern how speech must be represented in writing, including knowledge of how a letter or letters may represent speech sounds, called alphabetic knowledge or letter-to-sound correspondence rules; how we represent sounds that go beyond one-to-one correspondence, such as long vowels; how letters can and cannot be combined; and rules that govern in what word positions letters may or may not be used.

Despite its many irregularities, English orthography is a highly regular, pattern-based system (Hayes, Treiman, & Kessler, 2006; Pacton, Fayol, & Perruchet, 2005; Share, 2008). Both components of orthographic knowledge are used in reading and spelling. You read and spell either by accessing previously stored knowledge of the specific words found in MGRs or by using your knowledge of orthographic patterns.

Orthographic processing refers to the ability to acquire, store, and use both MGR and orthographic pattern knowledge. The acquisition of these two aspects of orthographic knowledge are different and occur at different ages. Some regularities based on the probability or frequency of occurrence are learned by children as young as age 5 (Apel, Wolter, & Masterson, 2006; Wolter & Apel, 2010).

SPELLING

Spelling of most words is self-taught using a trial-and-error approach. It is estimated that only 4,000 words are explicitly taught in elementary school and yet you can spell tens of thousands of words.

Reading and writing are essential for academic success. In this video a Kenyan boy with a winning smile uses his foot to write. http://www.youtube.com/watch?v=dAqihb8DIzU

Learning to spell is not simply memorizing words. Good spellers use a variety of strategies. More specifically, mature spellers, like you, rely on a combination of memory; spelling and reading experience; phonological, semantic, and morphological knowledge; orthographic knowledge and mental grapheme representations; and analogy (Apel & Masterson, 2001). Semantic knowledge is concerned with the interrelationship of spelling and meaning, while morphological knowledge is knowing the internal structure of words, affixes (*un-*, *dis-*, *-ly*, *-ment*) and the derivation of words (*happy*, *unhappily*). Mental grapheme representations are best exhibited when you ask yourself, "Does that word look right?" Your representations are formed through repeated exposure to words in print. Finally, through analogy, a speller tries to spell an unfamiliar word using prior knowledge of words that sound the same.

Writing Development

There is only a moderate amount of overlap between writing and reading. Rather than creating meaning from the text and integrating it with background knowledge as in reading, the writer creates text from concepts.

Writing development is really the development of many interdependent processes. The mechanics of forming letters and learning to spell develops first, with text generation and executive function developing much later.

Although spelling knowledge is working knowledge, not just the applying of memorized rules, it requires a large amount of information to be extracted from memory (Ehri, 2000). Sometimes a speller relies on memory; at other times, on invention based on spelling and reading experience; and at still others, on analogy to familiar words already in memory. Thus, spelling competes for cognitive processing capacity. Excessive energy expended on low-level processing comes at the cost to higher language functions. In other words, poor or inexperienced spellers generally produce poorer, shorter texts.

EMERGING WRITING

Initially, children treat writing and speaking as two separate systems on the page; writing and drawing are mixed. Three-year-olds, for example, will "write" in their own way but don't yet realize that writing represents sounds. By age 4, some real letters may be included. Figure 11.5 is a drawing by a 4-year-old that shows the beginning stage of graphical communication.

As with reading, in early writing, children expend a great deal of cognitive energy on the mechanics, such as forming letters. Over time, spelling, like reading, becomes more accurate and automatic.

Gradually, the spoken and written systems converge, and children write in the same manner as they speak, although speech is more complex. As mentioned earlier, around age 9 or 10, talking and speaking become differentiated as children become increasingly literate. Written sentences slowly become longer and more complex than speaking. Children display increasing awareness of their use of syntax, vocabulary, textual themes, and attitude.

MATURE WRITING

In a phase not achieved by all writers, speaking and writing become consciously separate. The syntactic and semantic characteristics of writing are consciously recognized as somewhat different from those of speech, and the writer has great flexibility of style. You may or may not have achieved this phase yet.

DEVELOPMENT OF ORTHOGRAPHIC KNOWLEDGE

Children acquire orthographic knowledge through both implicit and explicit means. Most likely development of the two aspects of orthographic knowledge influence each other.

FIGURE 11.5 A 4-Year-Old's Self-Portrait

With drawings such as this (entitled Me), children begin to communicate information graphically prior to the development of writing.

Initial MGR acquisition by preschool and kindergarten-age children demonstrates that they learned initial mental graphemic representations (MGRs) implicitly as they began to read and spell (Apel, 2010; Apel et al., 2006; Apel, Thomas-Tate, Wilson-Fowler, & Brimo, 2012; Wolter & Apel, 2010). Preschool and kindergarten-age children learn some letter–sound correspondence and are sensitive to some orthographic regularities as they develop initial spelling abilities (Apel, 2010; Bara, Gentaz, & Cole, 2007; Shatil, Share, & Levin, 2000; Treiman & Kessler, 2004, Wolter & Apel 2010). In general, an understanding of how to represent consonant sounds develops prior to understanding of how to represent vowel sounds.

Knowledge of orthographic patterns develops early and continues over the elementary school years. Interestingly, first-graders are sensitive to how an initial consonant influences the spelling of the vowel that follows but do not become sensitive to how vowel spelling is influenced by the following, final position consonant until fourth grade (Apel et al., 2006; Apel et al., 2012; Wolter & Apel, 2010).

Although orthographic knowledge contributes uniquely to reading and spelling development, the specific contributions of MGR and pattern knowledge to this process are unknown. Even in the earliest stages of reading development, young children are sensitive to orthographic regularities independent of phonological awareness (Apel, 2010; Levy, Gong, Hessels, Evans, & Jared, 2006; Ouellette & Sénéchal, 2008a, 2008b; Wolter & Apel, 2010).

SPELLING DEVELOPMENT

Spelling development is a long, slow process. Initial *preliterate* attempts at spelling consist mostly of scribbles and drawing with an occasional letter thrown in (Henderson, 1990). Later, children use some phoneme–grapheme knowledge along with letter names. Gradually, they become aware of conventional spelling and are able to analyze a word into sounds and letters. As mentioned earlier, mature spellers are able to call on multiple learning strategies and different types of knowledge (Rittle-Johnson & Siegler, 1999).

As knowledge of the alphabetic system emerges, a child connects letters and sounds and devises a system called "invented spelling" in which the names of letters may be used in spelling, as in *SKP* for *escape* or *LFT* for *elephant*. One letter may represent a group

Pressmaster/Shutterstock

Practice in all facets of the writing process helps build proficiency.

of sounds, as in *set* for ***street***. Children have difficulty separating words into phonemes (Treiman, 1993). Here are some examples (Pflaum, 1986):

Use vowel names if the vowel is long:

DA = day *LIK = like*

But do not use vowel names if the vowel is short:

FES = fish *LAFFT = left*

Spell the word the way it's pronounced:

BEDR = better *WOODR = water* *PREDE = pretty*

Spell according to placement of the tongue (Temple, Nathan, & Burris, 1982) (note that different vowels are used for *a* and that medial *n* is often omitted):

PLAT = plant *WOTED = wanted*

Do not use vowels with medial and final nasals (/m/, /n/) or liquids (/r/, /l/):

GRDN = garden *LITL = little*

Write past and plural endings generally as they are heard (*T* is used first, then both *T* and *D*):

STOPT = stopped *DAZ = days* *FESEZ = fishes* *PLATS = plants*

Interestingly, invented spelling demonstrates an analytical approach to spelling and facilitates the integration of phonological and orthographic knowledge, which seems to facilitate the acquisition of reading (Ouellette & Sénéchal, 2008a-b).

In a later phase of inventive spelling, called *phonemic spelling*, a child is aware of the alphabet and the correspondence of sound and symbol. Note the spelling in the following short story (Temple et al., 1982):

HE HAD A BLUE CLTH. IT TRD IN TO A BRD.
(He had a blue cloth. It turned into a bird.)

With school instruction, a child develops a more conventional system.

It appears that 6-year-olds initially learn morphological rules for spelling on a word-by-word basis (Chliounaki & Bryant, 2007). This forms a base for later adoption and use of morphological spelling rules.

A child who possesses full knowledge of the alphabetic system can segment words into phonemes and know the conventional phoneme–grapheme (/p/-p) correspondences. As a child begins to recognize more regularities and consolidate the alphabetic system, she or he becomes a more efficient speller (Ehri, 2000). Increased memory capacity for these regularities is at the heart of spelling ability.

Even beginning spellers are sensitive to multiple dimensions of spelling. Although 6-year-olds seem to rely on orthographic regularity, 7- to 9-year-olds are sensitive to both the orthographic and morphological aspects of the word (Deacon, LeBlanc, & Sabourin, 2011).

As spelling becomes more sophisticated, children learn about spacing, sequencing, various ways to represent phonemes, and the morpheme–grapheme relationship. Parallel developments in reading aid this process.

Many vowel representations, phonological variations, such as *later–latter*, and morphophonemic variations, such as *sign–signal*, will take several years to acquire. Gradually, children learn about consonant doubling, stressed and unstressed syllables (***report–report***), and root words and derivations (*add–addition*).

Sensitivity to both orthography and morphology can lead to spelling errors when these two dimensions conflict. For example, in the word *sitter*, the morphological marker is added as a simple *–er* but orthographic regularity is a doubling of the final *t*, as in *hitter* and *knitter*.

Most spellers shift from a purely phonological strategy to a mixed one between second and fifth grade. Typical spelling development takes a long time, is word-specific, and is nonlinear, meaning that the growth is uneven across orthography, phonology, and morphology.

Children may initially form separate representations of a word based on all three orthographic, phonologic, and morphologic representations. These representations are gradually coordinated into the correct spelling of the word (Bahr, Silliman, & Berninger, 2009; Berninger, Garcia, & Abbott, 2009; EGarcia, Abbott, & Berninger, 2010). Orthographic errors predominate in the writing of children and young teens. For example a child who writes *mist* for *missed* has noted both the phonologic and morphologic change but cannot consistently mark that information orthographically. Between fourth and fifth grade morphological errors increase in relative frequency, probably due to a combination of word-formation issues (*submit–submission*) and vocabulary growth (Huntley Bahr, Silliman, Berninger, & Dow, 2012).

In general, the order in which children learn to spell inflectional suffixes is similar to the order in which they learn to express them in oral language during preschool (Turnbull, Deacon, & Kay-Raining Bird, 2011). Variations reflect English spelling patterns, which introduce variables not present in oral language. Although individual children will differ, the overall order of spelling mastery is progressive, regular plural, possessive, third person singular and regular past tense.

Writing is more than putting letters on a page. Here's a young woman who understands. http://www.youtube.com/watch?v=kkbfAE3qmxU

Although the late mastery of the regular past tense seems odd, learning may be complicated by correct spelling of the past marker (*-ed*) usually requiring a morphological spelling that is not phonetic. In the irregular past, using *-t* or *-d* to spell the final consonant sound /t/ or /d/ is correct, as in *kept* and *held*. But phonetic spelling does not lead to a correct spelling in the regular past tense. This confusion does not seem to exist with /s/ and /z/, which are usually spelled as *–s*.

As words and strategies are stored in long-term memory, the load on cognitive capacity is lessened and access becomes fluent. A child can now focus on other writing tasks.

TEXT GENERATION AND EXECUTIVE FUNCTION

Writing, of course, involves more than spelling. Young writers, like preschool speakers, are often oblivious of the needs of the reader.(See the discussion of presuppositional skills in Chapter 8.) A 6-year-old pays very little attention to format, spacing, spelling, and punctuation.

Often, other aspects of writing will deteriorate when one aspect is stressed. Writing on a difficult topic may result in spelling, handwriting, or text deterioration.

Text generation begins with oral narratives. Children become proficient in representing absent entities and events and in describing the internal states, thoughts, and feelings of characters in their narratives at about age 4. These skills are important for writing in which a child must create a context through language.

The written stories of young children are often direct and beautiful in their simplicity, as evidenced by the short story that follows. It's from my granddaughter Cassidy, written when she was in second grade.

> One day a man went to a hotel and said I am in room 222! oh you're the man. do you like cats? No. he said. ok. here's your room key. go to your room. he opened the door and Saw a Kitten. he shut the door and ran. Meow THE END

Another story by Cassidy is presented in Box 11.1.

Once children begin to produce true spelling, even if it is unconventional, they begin to generate text. In first grade, text may consist of only a single sentence, as in *My sister is yukky* or *Today is Halloween.*

Early text formats are usually of the topic-comment type, as in Cassidy's story and the following:

> *I like my birthday parties. I get presents. I eat cake and ice cream.*

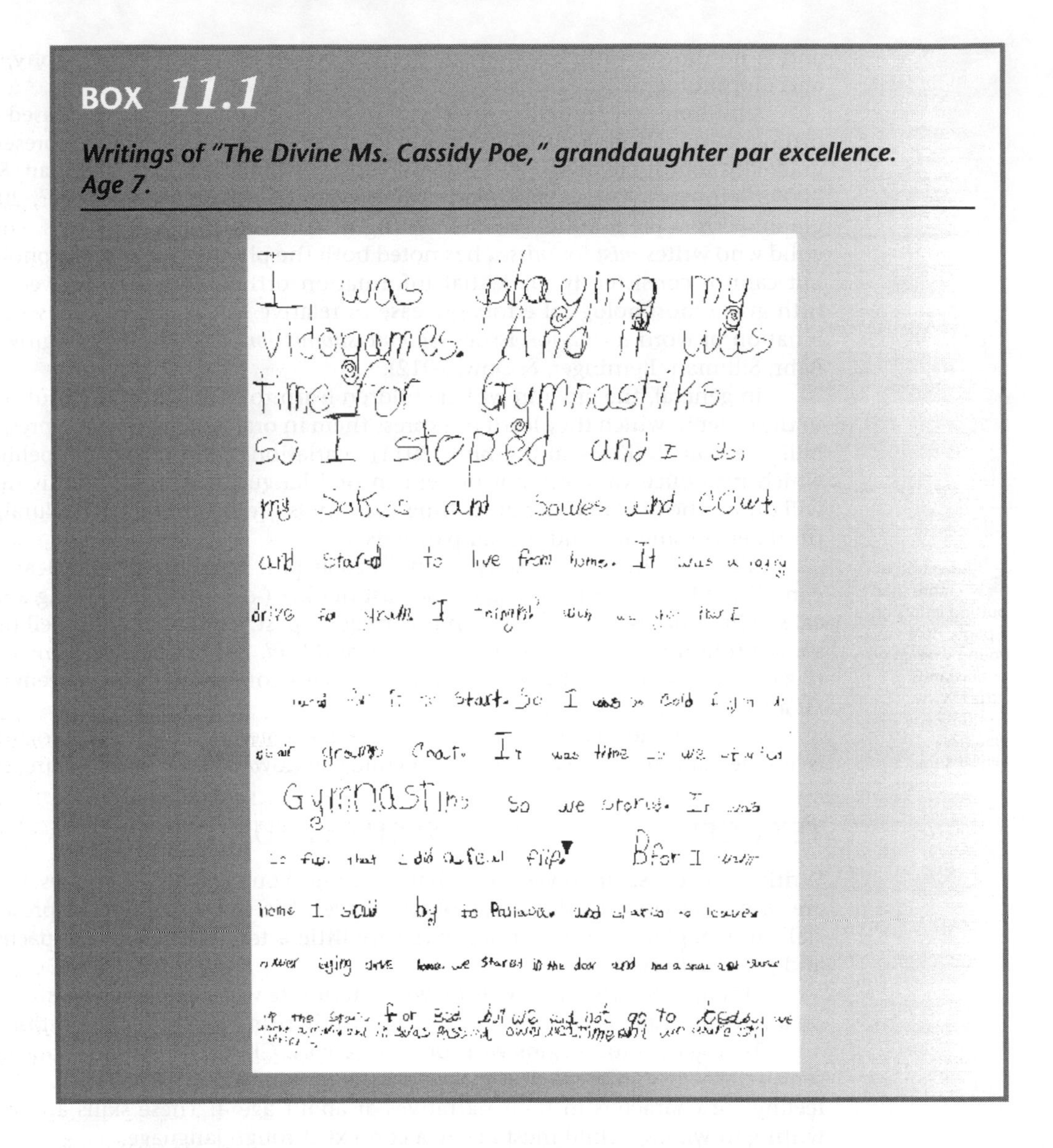

BOX 11.1

Writings of "The Divine Ms. Cassidy Poe," granddaughter par excellence. Age 7.

Early compositions usually lack cohesion and use structures repeatedly, as in the following:

> *I like going to the zoo. I like monkeys. I like elephants. I like the petting zoo.*

Notice both of these patterns in Cassidy's story. More mature writers use additional variety for dramatic effect.

The facts and events characteristic of young writers evolve into the more mature writer's use of judgments and opinions, parenthetical expressions, qualifications, contrasts, and generalizations (Berninger, 2000). Initially, composition lacks coherence and ideas may be joined with little underlying organization. With the longer writing required in school comes increasing cognitive demands on the child for coherence of ideas.

At first, drawings may be used to highlight important portions and to help organize the text. Later, as in Cassidy's story, ideas may relate to a central idea, similar to the centering narratives of young children. Very simple narratives, consisting of a list of sequential events, and expository texts emerge next. Early expository writing, seen in essays and reports, includes a unifying sentence to provide coherence. Text forms, such as the letter-writing format, help organize material.

By the middle school years, the length and diversity of children's productions increase. Advanced narratives and expository text develop. Narratives contain temporal events unified by a topic sentence and the narrative elements of story grammar, character development, plot, and dialog. Expository essays include a unifying topic sentence, comments referenced to the topic, and elaborations on the comments.

Accompanying increasing length in both sentences and text are increases in complexity and variety of sentence types. For example, the types of sentences change. There is a threefold increase in the number of written passive sentences between ages 8 and 13.

At the sentence level, clause length increases in writing, as it does in speech. The mean length of the written clause is 6.5 words for the 8-year-old writer, 7.7 for the 13-year-old, 8.6 for the 17-year-old, and 11.5 for the adult. As in speech, there is also an increase in embedded subordinate clauses and a decrease in coordination or compound sentences. Relative clauses double in frequency between ages 7 and 17 and continue to increase into adulthood. Adverbial clauses, especially those signifying time (*when* . . .), also increase and diversify.

At the noun phrase level, there is an increase in pre- and post-noun modifiers. By adolescence, writers are modifying nouns with adverbs as well as adjectives and are often using four or more modifiers with a noun. Verb phrases are expanded by increasing use of modality, tense, and aspect.

It is not until early adulthood that most writers develop the cognitive processes and executive functions needed for mature writing (Berninger, 2000; Ylvisaker & DeBonis, 2000). Children begin to proofread and revise as early as third grade. The process is influenced by a writer's syntactic knowledge. Until adolescence, however, young writers need adult guidance in planning and revising their writing. By junior high school, teens are capable of revising all aspects of writing.

Conclusion

ONCE CHILDREN HAVE GAINED a working knowledge of spoken language, most adapt to the new mode of written language with relative ease. Initial difficulties with symbol relationships slow the first stages. The underlying linguistic relationships between spoken and written language, however, make eventual success possible and help explain the process. In addition to a child's linguistic knowledge, emerging metalinguistic skills (mentioned in Chapter 10) enable him or her to use decontextualized language and to understand language in another mode of communication.

Although a child's first introduction to print is informal and conversational, a child learns this new mode of communication by formal instruction, usually in school. Reading and writing open new avenues of exploration and learning for a child and are essential skills in our modern literate society.

Discussion

AS MUCH AS 70% of children with oral language impairments will later exhibit written language impairments. In other words, a child's success in school may be determined to a large extent by toddler and preschool language development. For children at risk, the importance of early intervention cannot be overstressed.

Development slows in adulthood but continues throughout one's lifetime unless hindered by poor health, accident, or injury. As adults, hopefully some of us are examples for children and set the standards for mature behavior.

The body usually continues to grow slowly through early adulthood, then steadies, and finally goes into a long, slow decline that can be forestalled somewhat with proper diet and moderate exercise. Likewise, cognitive growth also slows but can continue throughout life. As an adult, a person adds new skills, new words, and new problem-solving skills to the formidable ones already possessed.

Measurement of regional cerebral blood flow in the brain suggests that brain maturation continues. Myelination or nerve sheathing is not complete until early adulthood. Dendritic pruning or trimming, begun in utero and important in increasing neural efficiency, continues into adolescence in higher-order cognitive areas, such as the angular gyrus (Devous et al., 2006). In healthy brains engaged in simple language tasks, such as naming, we find that brain activation continues to increase into the senior years in Broca's and Wernicke's areas as well as the correspondingly similar area to Broca's in the right hemisphere (Fridriksson, Morrow, Moser, & Baylis, 2006).

Social and communicative abilities adapt subtly to the many different environments in which we adults function. With development of a truly impressive set of pragmatic and interactional skills, an adult learns to maneuver in the complex worlds of family, profession, and community, and increasingly in the international multiethnic realm in which we live.

As a language user, an adult gains increasing flexibility. The organization of his or her huge vocabulary enables an adult to access concepts both effectively and efficiently. Increased social skills help an adult to choose the most appropriate words and syntactic structures for any given situation. This doesn't mean that language will be error-free or that an adult is an effective communicator in every situation—especially cross-cultural ones—but as you mature you will be even more skilled than you already are.

With aging, there is a slow decline in both oral and written language comprehension, understanding syntactically complex sentences, and inferencing. Decline may be related to either overload or processing difficulties in working memory. Although comprehension of figurative language seems unimpaired in healthy older adults, the ability to explain figurative expressions does decline.

The evolution of processing strategies may be reflected in the shifting recall patterns that occur with adult changes. The free recall of complex linguistic material decreases with age. These changes in cognitive operations may be more quantitative than qualitative. The elderly have more difficulty with linguistic processing that requires greater organization in order to recall. In general, the elderly are more sensitive to theme or underlying meaning but are less able than young adults to recall syntax.

The incidence of hearing loss increases with age, being both more common and more severe for those in their 80s than in their 70s. In addition, men are more affected than women and Caucasian Americans more than African Americans. Other factors, such as education, income, smoking, and cardiovascular disease histories, do not seem to be significant (Pratt et al., 2009).

The language difficulties of children with deafness are well documented, but even those with mild-to-moderate hearing loss exhibit language deficits in adolescence (Delage & Tuller, 2007). As adolescents, whatever the cause, children with language impairments tend to be less independent than their typically developing peers, due in part to poor early language and poor later literacy skills (Conti-Ramsden & Durkin, 2008).

In the remainder of the chapter, we'll examine all aspects of language and describe the changes evident in adolescence and adulthood. We'll pay special attention to gender differences and phonological skills.

Pragmatics

Adolescents and adults have the linguistic skills to enable them to select, from among several available communication strategies, the one best suited to a specific situation. Mature language is more efficient and appropriate than child language. It is efficient because words are more specifically defined and because forms do not need repetition or paraphrasing in order to be understood. It is appropriate because utterances are selected for the psychosocial dynamics of the communication situation. Less mature language users are less able to select the appropriate code because they have a limited repertoire of language forms.

The communication experiences and needs of adults result in a language system characterized by many special *registers*, or styles of speech, not found in childhood. For example, most adults have jobs that require specific language skills—talking on the phone, writing, giving directives—or terminology, called *professional jargon*. Also, special communication rules reflect the power structure of the workplace. Selective styles exist for those with whom an adult is intimate, such as pet names (*poobear, sweet pea*) or terms of endearment (*honey, dear*), that are distinct from those reserved for strangers or business associates. Many adults also belong to ethnic, racial, or sexual-orientation minorities or to social groups that require still other styles. These act as a bond for these groups, whether they are African American teenage males, Jewish elders, lesbians, avid CB or shortwave radio enthusiasts, computer geeks, or wine connoisseurs. Adults also engage in diverse social functions, such as funerals, public speaking, sports, or even card playing, that require special lexicons and manners of speaking. It is even possible to detect political orientation from the adult's choice of terms. For example, in the present political climate, the contrasts between *women's lib–women's movement*, *Negroes–African Americans*, and *pro-life–antiabortion* signal conservatism by the first term, liberalism by the second. Most adults use several different registers. Exposure and need are the determining factors in acquisition, and registers disappear from a person's repertoire with infrequent use.

Mature speakers of African American English (AAE) make systematic alternations in dialect use characterized as changes within the dialect rather than dialect switching (Wolfram, 2004). Although there is some variation in the use of AAE across gender and employment status, educational achievement is the strongest factor related to the less frequent use of AAE (Craig & Grogger, 2012). Interestingly, the race of a conversational partner does not seem to affect AAE usage.

One of the main differences between young children and adults may be in the development of narration and of special styles of communicating found only in adulthood. In general, adult narratives seem to improve steadily in terms of main themes and details into middle age and the early senior years, then display decreasing abilities after the late 70s (Marini, Boewe, Caltagirone, & Carlomagno, 2005). Those over 75 have less flexibility and ease with word retrieval and make more morpho-grammatical errors.

NARRATIVES

When we examine healthy adults' ability to comprehend and tell narratives, we find some differences based on age. In general, although adults of varying ages are similar in their ability to retell narratives, older adults are less accurate than younger and middle aged adults in answering questions about narratives they have heard or retold. Text comprehension may consist of three levels (Stine-Morrow, 2007):

1. Surface text or wording
2. Meaning or content
3. Integration of the text with one's own background knowledge

Interestingly, younger and older adults do not seem to differ in their ability to integrate the text (Ferstl, 2006). A difference does exist in the ability to process the surface text and the meaning, with older adults performing less well than younger (Ferstl, 2006; Radvansky, Copeland, & Zwaan, 2003). These differences may be due to decline in working memory with age, even among cognitively healthy seniors (Chapman et al., 2002; Ferstl, 2006; Radvanksy et al., 2003). Older adults may be less sensitive to the details presented in the text.

Decline in working memory may also explain why the narratives of cognitively healthy seniors in their 70s and 80s have fewer clauses in their utterances and fewer cohesive ties. Although the narratives of older seniors contain more words and utterances than those of middle-age adults, they also have more irrelevant content (Juncos-Rabadán et al., 2005). In narrative retelling tasks, the narratives of younger adults are more accurate, complete, and informative than those of older adults (Capilouto, Wright, & Wagovich, 2005; Duong & Ska, 2001; Marini et al., 2005; Wright, Capilouto, Wagovich, Cranfill, & Davis, 2005). These differences may be related to comprehension of the narrative (Harris Wright, Capilouto, Srinivasan, & Fergadiotis, 2011).

SPEAKING STYLES

Styles of speaking are socially conditioned and characterized by differences in syntactic complexity, word choice, phonological from, and the phonetic realization or clarity and speed of speech. Style shifting, or changing from one style to another, is in part determined by the social distance, context, and listener feedback. For example, we might switch to a slower, clearer speaking style if the other person is very old, speaks English as a second language, or indicates comprehension difficulties. Style shifting in adults is rapid and unconscious. If you have ever talked with a 2-year-old, you have probably noticed that she or he did not change speaking styles in the way that adults do.

Children must acquire relevant social and pragmatic skills before they can develop distinct speaking styles. More specifically, they must be aware that they can adjust their speech to help a listener understand what they are trying to say. Although this awareness may be in place by the end of the second year, being able to style shift depends in part on acquiring adultlike control strategies (Ferrier, Dunham, & Dunham, 2000).

Children acquire distinct speaking styles over several years in early childhood. For example, listeners are unable to differentiate between 3-year-olds' clear speaking style and casual word productions (Redford & Gildersleeve-Neumann, 2009). Listeners are better able to differentiate between those produced by 4-year-olds and are especially able to distinguish between the clear and casual words produced by 5-year-olds (Redford & Gildersleeve-Neumann, 2009).

Children may not develop adultlike styles until they have acquired expert articulatory control and the ability to highlight the internal structure of words. Clear speech in adults, for example, is listener oriented and used on formal occasions or when they wish to have no misunderstanding. Adults shift from a casual to a clear speaking style by manipulating some basic control parameters. For example, clearer, more intelligible speech is slower than casual, less intelligible speech. An overall slower rate may lead to secondary changes in articulation, such as decreased overlap in sound production and increased likelihood of attaining the specific sounds desired (Munhall, Kawato, & Vatikiotis-Bateson, 2000). Clear speech also typically has more pauses and greater pitch range than casual speech. These pauses are not uniform and tend to highlight linguistic boundaries (Frazier, Carlson, & Clifton, 2006). Initial and final sounds in words may also be emphasized or more fully produced (Krause & Braida, 2004; Smiljanic & Bradlow, 2008).

Zohra Sehgal, an Indian senior, demonstrates her wonderful acting skills and a range of communication behaviors. http://www.youtube.com/watch?v=rRtxy06_TBo

Communication skills flourish in adulthood and continue into the senior years unless a person experiences a neuropathology, other health-related issue, or accident.

CONVERSATIONAL ABILITIES

Through middle and high school, adolescents spend an increasing amount of time with peers. Communication occurs largely in conversations. Management of these interactions becomes increasingly important for peer acceptance and notions of self-worth. The diversity of communication partners increases as adolescents and young adults enter the workforce or pursue higher education.

In conversations, adolescents frequently gaze at their partner, especially during listening; nod and show neutral and positive facial expressions; use feedback; and give contingent responses (Turkstra, Ciccia, & Seaton, 2003). When conversing with their peers, most teens in the United States, regardless of race, are careful to direct their partners' attention, to give positive verbal and nonverbal feedback, and to make responses based on their partner's statements. Verbal feedback occurs on approximately 20% of the utterances and includes words such as *yeah, so yeah,* and *uh-huh* that indicate agreement with or understanding of the previous utterance and encouragement to continue. In contrast, teens rarely show negative emotions, turning away, requests for clarification, or failure to answer questions in conversations with peers.

The overwhelming majority of teen utterances are contingent on—that's related to—the previous utterance. In other words, the adolescent conversation hangs together.

The delay markers *uh* and *um* are often used by adult speakers to indicate an upcoming pause, not the end of a conversational turn. Both markers are used in distinct ways. In general, *uh* is used to signal a short delay and *um* to signal a longer one. See if this is true in conversation or when your professor lectures. Both sounds indicate searching for a word, thinking of the next word to say, or holding or ceding the floor in speaking. Three- and 4-year-old children appear to understand the basic use of both markers, but do not yet differentiate between them by the length of the pauses that follow (Hudson Kam & Edwards, 2008).

With more contingent responses, fewer topic changes occur, and, when they do, topics are often related in subtle ways. Adults effectively use *shading*, or modifying the focus of the topic, as a means of gradually moving from one topic to another while maintaining some continuity in the conversation. The topic-shading utterance includes some aspect of the preceding utterance but shifts the central focus of concern.

Although requests for clarification are rare, the ability to detect communication breakdown improves with age and metalinguistic skill. By adulthood, linguistic anomalies are detected almost instantaneously.

Interestingly, despite young adults' contentions that multitasking does not affect their performance, resource allocation does affect sentence processing. Among typical young adult females, auditory distractions negatively affected judgments of grammatical correctness in narrative tasks. Distractions had less effect in more explicit, deliberate tasks, such as self-paced reading (Smith, 2011). Judging grammatical correctness requires linguistic, metalinguistic, and memory skills, so auditory distraction creates an extra cognitive burden. Grammatical judgment is not merely an academic exercise. It is part of communication used to make judgments about a speaker's SES, status, education, proficiency, primary language, and intelligence, to name a few.

Finally, there is an increase in the variety of intentions expressed with maturity. Mastery of these intentions comes gradually and varies with the type of intention. Even though 13-year-old adolescents are able to synthesize information rather than parrot what they have heard or read, some 17-year-olds still have difficulty offering and supporting their opinions in a well-formed, logical fashion.

The high-schooler uses language creatively in sarcasm, jokes, and double meanings. These begin to develop in the early school years. It can be a memorable event when a child devises her or his first joke. I remember my daughter's first one very well. We were discussing groupings of animals, such as *herds* of cattle, *flocks* of chickens, *packs* of wolves, and so on, when someone asked about bees. One son ventured *hive*, another *school*. At this point Jessica, age 7, chimed in with "If bees went to school, they'd have to ride the school *buzz*!" Even if she heard it elsewhere, and it was pretty lame, she gets some credit for good timing.

High-schoolers also make deliberate use of metaphor and can explain complex behavior and natural phenomena. These changes reflect overall development within all five aspects of language.

GENDER DIFFERENCES

In the early elementary school years, the language of boys and girls begins to reflect the gender differences of older children and adults. These differences can be noted in vocabulary use and conversational style. Although the changing status of women in our society may lessen these differences, they nonetheless exist currently. See how many you note among your peers.

It is important to remind ourselves that males and females have more similarities than differences in their language use. In addition, other factors such as the context and topic have a greater influence on conversational style than gender.

Other differences may be physiological. For example, gender differences in the production of some phonemes (/f, θ, s, ʃ) exist as early as age 6 but are more pronounced in postpubescent adolescents and young adults (Fox & Nissen, 2005). These differences most likely reflect vocal tract variation between men and women. These differences decrease for adults as they age.

Finally, any communicative act must be interpreted in light of context, the conversational style of the participants, the interaction of these styles, and the cultural background of the participants. Interrupting may be interpreted by some speakers as rudeness or pushiness and by others as enthusiastic participation.

Vocabulary Use

The lexical differences between men and women are generally quantitative rather than qualitative. In general, women use less swearing and coarse language in conversation and tend to use more polite words, such as *please, thank you,* and *good-bye*. Other descriptive words, such as *adorable, charming, sweet, lovely,* and *divine,* are also associated with women. In addition, women use a fuller range of color terms.

Considerable differences can be found in emphatic or emotional expressions. Women tend to use expressions, such as *oh dear, goodness,* and *gracious me,* while men tend to use expletives like *damn it.* Even when experimenters digitally equalize speakers' pitch, first-graders are reasonably accurate at selecting the gender of a speaker who says, "Damn it, you broke the TV" or "My goodness, you broke the TV." In emergency situations in which an active, assertive response is needed, interjections, such as *oh dear,* are rare even for women.

Conversational Style

The caricature of the wife and husband at the breakfast table, she talking while he reads the newspaper, has its basis in adult conversational styles. In short, men talk more in public and less at home. The most frequent reason for divorce given by women in the United States is lack of communication between the two spouses.

Although American English-speaking men and women may possess the same language, they use and understand it in very different ways. While women tend to be more indirect, to seek consensus, and to listen carefully, men tend to lecture and may seem inattentive to women. Women see their role as conversation facilitators, while men see theirs as information providers. Thus, women face their conversational partners, giving vocal or verbal feedback and often finishing the listener's thought. Men, on the other hand, often do not face their partners, instead looking around the room and making only fleeting eye contact. Body posture differences can be observed in young teens, with males more distant and not facing each other. In contrast, girls sit closer and may touch during the conversation.

Much of this difference stems from the different expectations of men and women in conversation. Men see conversations as an opportunity for debate or competition, and thus act combative. When listening, they are silent, giving little vocal feedback, which they may consider to be interruptive.

For men, conversations are events in which talk maintains status and independence. The goal, therefore, becomes "scoring" on one's opponent and protecting oneself. To score, a man may dismiss the topic and, by association, the conversational partner as trivial or unimportant.

Among men in the United States, topics are changed often and rarely involve personal issues or feelings. One unfortunate result may be a lack of intimacy reported by some men throughout adulthood. It is difficult to build intimate relationships based only on talk of sports, work, and politics with no personal element.

In contrast, women see conversations as a way to share. For women, intimacy is built through talking. The topics discussed are not as important as the closeness and sharing of feelings and emotions. Topics are often shared at length and explored thoroughly. In general, girls' and women's topics are more focused, less diffuse than those of boys and men. At all ages, females have less difficulty finding something to talk about, and topics are changed less frequently. As good conversationalists, women see their role as an agreeable and supportive one. When possible, they try to avoid anger and disagreement. Women maintain more eye contact and smile more often than men.

It is not surprising to find that men and women differ in the amount of talking, in nonlinguistic devices used, and in turn-taking behaviors. In general, men tend to be more verbose than women. In a conversational context, the longest speaking time occurs when men speak with other men. Contrary to contemporary "wisdom," women's conversations with men or with other women are shorter.

Within a conversation, men and women use different turn-taking styles. In general, adult listeners of either sex are more likely to interrupt a female speaker than a male. Men typically interrupt to suggest alternative views, to argue, to introduce new topics, or to complete the speaker's sentence. In contrast, women interrupt to clarify and support the speaker. In general, however, interrupting is more related to the context than to the gender of the interrupter.

Women relinquish their conversational turns more readily than men. A frequently used device is a question, compliment, or request. Women ask more questions, thus indirectly introducing topics into the conversation. In male–female conversations, only about 36% of these topics become the focus of conversation. In contrast, 96% of male-introduced topics are sustained.

Given these characteristics and the societal roles of men and women, men may feel no need to talk at home because there are no other men to whom they must prove themselves. In contrast, women may feel secure within the home and feel that they are free to talk without offending or being seen as combative.

Development

These differences may reflect how children are raised. Parental speech to children of different sexes varies. As early as 2 years of age, daughters are imitated more by their mothers and talked to longer than are sons. Fathers use more imperatives and more insulting terms, such as *butthead*, with their sons and address their daughters as *honey* and *sweetie*. These terms may reflect the nature of adult male conversations. Fathers use the diminutive form (adding a suffix to denote smallness or affection) more frequently with daughters and interrupt them more often than sons. The overall effects of these parental behaviors are not known.

Preschool boys seem more aware of the differences between male and female adults than girls do. As early as kindergarten, boys' topics tend to be space, quantity, physical movement, self, and value judgments. In contrast, kindergarten girls talk more about "traditional" female roles. Boys begin to talk about sports and girls about school possibly as early as age 4.

From early childhood, boys' relationships are based less on talking and more on doing. Boys' groups tend to be larger and more hierarchical than those of girls. Actions and talking are used in the struggle to avoid subordination. The listener role is seen as one of passivity and submissiveness, while the talker role is assertive.

In contrast to boys, young girls usually play in pairs, sharing the play, talking, and telling "secrets." Personal problems and concerns are shared, with agreement and understanding by the participants. In this cooperative environment, girls spend considerable time talking, reflecting, and sharing. Their language is more inclusive than that of boys, with frequent use of words such as *let's* and *we*.

Here's an amusing video on genderlect. Note the differences you observe. http://www.youtube.com/watch?v=Laa-KPZ9dw0

In the competitive environment of preadolescence and adolescence, however, both girls and boys posture and counterposture, using verbal aggression such as practical jokes, put-downs, and insults. The sense of competition is one in which speech is used by both sexes to hold attention, to assert dominance, and to bully.

Genderlect, as the collective stylistic characteristics of men and women is called, is well established by mid-adolescence. Communicative competence is valued by adolescents as a way of presenting themselves to peers when great pressure exists to conform.

Conclusion

The communication behaviors of men and women may reflect the traditional status of women within our society. As in other cultures, words associated with masculinity are judged to be better or more positive than those associated with femininity.

Women demonstrate nonlinguistic behaviors, such as increased eye contact, which could also suggest that they hold a less dominant position within conversations. The freedom to interrupt and the sustaining of male-introduced topics reflect a higher relative status for males. In addition, women's use of "feminine" exclamations, such as *oh dear*, suggests a lack of power or a lack of conviction in the importance of the message. Traditionally, the behaviors to which they are expected to conform deny women interactional control and send a devaluing message.

The actual basis for these gender differences has not been determined. It will be interesting to see the effects of more women in the workplace and in college on the communicative behavior of both sexes.

It is impossible to separate conversational behaviors from culture. Men and women around the world interact in very different manners. For example, in Greece, both men and women use indirect styles of address at about the same rate as U.S. women (Tannen, 1994). Nor is the interrupting behavior of U.S. men universal among males. In Africa, the Caribbean, the Mediterranean, South America, Jewish and Arab cultures, and Eastern Europe, women interrupt men far more frequently than in the majority U.S. culture. Finally, many cultures, such as Thai, Japanese, Hawaiian, and Antiguan, exhibit a cultural style of overlapping speech that is cooperative rather than interruptive.

Semantics

Throughout life, the average healthy person will continue to add new words to his or her lexicon. Other than for reasons of poor health, language growth should continue, albeit at a slower rate.

Typical seniors experience some deficits, primarily in the accuracy and speed of word retrieval and naming. When compared to younger adults, seniors use more indefinite words, such as *thing* and *one* in place of specific names. These deficits reflect accompanying deficits in working memory and, in turn, affect ability to produce grammatically complex sentences (Kemper, Thompson, & Marquis, 2001). There does not seem to be loss in ability to produce simple sentences when words are provided, possibly because working memory is not taxed in this situation (Davidson, Zacks, & Ferreira, 2003).

In this video, two seniors engage in an interview and conversation. http://www.youtube.com/watch?v=H_vmSUsr80

The popular image of the incoherent, rambling older adult with poor word memory is untrue and unfair to most seniors. As Larry, a senior friend of mine, says, "Gettin' old ain't for sissies!"

Senior citizens tend to use older terminology, which makes them appear to be less adept at using language. Newer terms may be more difficult for them to recall. Thus, the older adult might use the terms *dungarees* and *tennis shoes* in place of *jeans* and *sneakers*.

WORD DEFINITIONS

Although the ability to access or recall words, especially newly learned ones, may rapidly decline for some after age 70, lexical items are not lost. In fact, older adults are as able as younger language users to define words appropriately. While the language performance of older adults may seem to be deteriorating, it may reflect other factors, such as decreased hearing ability. Seniors may miss critical pieces of information, making it more difficult to participate.

Age, metalinguistic ability, and educational level are all important for the production of well-structured formal definitions (Benelli et al., 2006). In general, adult definitions are more abstract than child definitions. They tend to be descriptive, with concrete terms or references to specific instances used to modify the concept. In addition, adult definitions include synonyms, explanations, and categorizations of the word defined.

During adolescence, a number of changes occur in definitions, with the inclusion of category membership, the sharpening of core features of a word, and the addition of subtle aspects of meaning (Nippold, Hegel, Sohlberg, & Schwarz, 1999). Frequency of a word's use may be a relatively more important factor in development of definitions by teens and young adults for some types of words, such as adjectives (Marinellie & Johnson, 2003).

Unlike child meanings, adult definitions are exclusionary and also specify what an entity is not. Adult definitions also reflect an individual's personal biases and experiences.

Supplying word definitions is a metalinguistic skill. In general, both quantitative and qualitative improvement in definitions occurs in adolescence. Synonym-type definitions increase. A greater tendency exists to include categorical membership (*an apple is a fruit*), function, description, and degree (*almost, nearly*). High-quality definitions develop for root words prior to inflected or derived words.

Figurative Language

Figurative language will be a challenge into adulthood. For preteens and adolescents, idioms that are more familiar, supported by context, and more transparent are easier to understand than those that are less familiar, isolated or out of context, and more opaque. These factors are also important in the interpretation of proverbs. Language experience and the development of metalinguistic abilities (see Chapter 10) are important determiners of individual skill with proverbs. For adults in their 20s, concrete proverbs are still easier to interpret than abstract. This difference is not seen in older adults, where the ease of interpreting is related to a person's overall level of education.

Ability to define idioms increases with age as does familiarity with idioms (Chan & Marinellie, 2008). As children move from childhood through adolescence to adulthood, definitions include more critical elements and related or associated concepts.

Syntax and Morphology

The length and syntactic complexity of oral sentences increases into early adulthood and stabilizes in middle age, although there are differences across individual speakers and contexts (Nippold, Hesketh, et al., 2005). Much of the increase in complexity is in the use of dependent clauses. Individual variability exists at all ages with some children using elaborate sentences and some adults simple ones. In general, all speakers produce more complex sentences when explaining how to do something than when in conversational give and take. Cohesion in explanations is obtained by relating one sentence to another through the use of various conversation devices, such as articles and use of pronouns and nouns.

Acquisition of increasingly abstract thought enables an adolescent to integrate new information into existing knowledge systems. This is accomplished to support the production of dialogues, such as conversations, and, with increased maturity, the production of social monologs.

Expository monologs are especially challenging because they require production that taps a speaker's knowledge of the topic—however limited or extensive that may be (Nippold et al., 2007). Expository speech places greater demands on a speaker because there is an expectation of an informative monolog in contrast to the more interactive dialog found in conversation.

When children, adolescents, and adults speak in an expository genre, they use greater syntactic complexity than when they are speaking in conversations or relating narratives (Berman & Verhoeven, 2002; Nippold, Hesketh, et al., 2005; Nippold, Mansfield, Billow, & Tomblin, 2008; Scott & Windsor, 2000; Verhoeven et al., 2002). Complex thought, supported by a knowledge base, seems to drive the use of complex language.

NOUN PHRASES

The density and variety of nouns and noun phrase types increases dramatically in adolescence and on into adulthood (Ravid, 2006). Because older children do not repeat the same word over and over as do infants and toddlers, the greater density of nouns means more variety and higher linguistic complexity (Hickmann, 2003).

As children grow older and mature cognitively, they increase their knowledge, which, in turn, enables them to express increasingly complex concepts in abstract terms (Seroussi, 2004). Even mid-elementary school children, ages 9–10, use fewer concrete nouns, such as *ball, backpack, a new car, boy in my class*, than preschool children, and this change continues into adolescence. Through the teen years, there is an increase in categorical and abstract nouns and noun phrases, such as *road to peace, conclusion, authority, his opinion, the teacher's feedback, an annoyance, intervention, prejudices*. Defining abstract nouns, however, is difficult for adolescents, even for 18-year-olds (Nippold et al., 1999). Full mastery of abstract and morphologically complex nouns consolidates only in adulthood.

These changes in types of nouns are affected by linguistic, cognitive, and social development, and by modality (spoken vs. written) and text genre (narrative vs. expository). Beginning in late elementary school, as noted in Chapter 10, narratives become increasingly rich compared to speech in the types of nouns used, especially in adulthood (Ravid & Cahana-Amitay, 2005). There is an increase in the level of abstraction and in the complexity of the syntactic structures in which such nouns occurred.

With increased age and education, written texts became richer in complex noun structures (*the small boy from next door who goes to my school*), especially in written expository texts. Crosslinguistic studies report a consistent increase in complex noun phrases (NP) from childhood to adulthood, again more so in written expository texts (Ravid, van Hell, Rosado, & Zamora, 2002).

CONJUNCTS AND DISJUNCTS

In conversation, a child or adolescent slowly learns to link sentences with devices that are peripheral to the clause. By bridging utterances, these devices provide continuity. The devices consist of *adverbial disjuncts*, which comment on or convey the speaker's attitude toward the content of the connected sentence, such as *frankly, to be honest, perhaps, however, yet*, and *to my surprise*, and *adverbial conjuncts*, which signal a logical relation between sentences, such as *still, as a result of*, and *to conclude*. The following are examples of adverbial disjuncts used in conversation:

Honestly, I don't know why you bought that car.
In my opinion, it was a bargain.
Well, to be honest, I think it's a lemon.

Adverbial conjuncts are cohesive and connective devices and may be concordant (*similarly, moreover, consequently*) or discordant (*in contrast, rather, but, nevertheless*).

Conjuncts express a logical intersentential relationship and are more common in literature than in conversation. In the following example, the conjunct *as a result of* signals the relationship of the two sentences:

We were up all night. As a result of our effort, our group won the competition.

Development of conjuncts occurs gradually from school age into adulthood. Both production and understanding increase with age, although comprehension exceeds production even in young adults. By age 6, a child uses the adverbial conjuncts *now, then, so,* and *though,* although disjuncts are rare. By age 12, a youth has added *otherwise, anyway, therefore,* and *however,* plus the disjuncts *really* and *probably.* This development continues well into the adult years, with adults using 12 conjuncts per 100 utterances compared to the 12-year-old's 4 conjuncts.

Phonology

It's important to note that even though the phonetic inventory is mastered by around age 8, finer aspects of speech development extend to the late teens for both males and females (Smith & Goffman, 2004). For example, male–female differences in the laryngeal or formant frequency of speech become evident as early as age 4 but become more apparent later in childhood. Although jumps in the formant frequency accompany growth spurts in the vocal tract, there is an overall decrease in this frequency into adulthood, with the most rapid decreases occurring during early childhood and adolescence (Vorperian & Kent, 2007).

Adult phonological knowledge—what they know about American English speech sounds—is multidimensional. It consists of acoustic-perceptual and articulatory knowledge, knowledge of higher-level phonological categories, and social-indexical knowledge, which is related to styles of talking (Munson, Edwards, & Beckman, 2005a). Let's discuss each briefly.

The characteristics of a phoneme vary as a function of both (1) the phonetic context or the adjacent speech sounds and (2) the social factors, such as sexual orientation, class, race, regional dialect, gender, and age (Munson, 2004; Munson, Edwards, & Beckman, 2005b). Adults are able to perceive speech sounds with little difficulty; they know the sound characteristics of /s/ and don't confuse it with other speech sounds.

ACOUSTIC-PERCEPTUAL KNOWLEDGE

Adults' perceptual knowledge may be based on perception of very fine acoustic characteristics and on knowledge of categories of sounds. For example, adults may base their judgments of a sound on such parameters as frequency, intensity, and duration of the sound. Even children as old as 10 years do not use this variety of perceptual cues (Hazan & Barret, 2000). Children also lack the adult ability to recognize words and sounds from different speakers, suggesting that children have incomplete auditory–perceptual knowledge.

You will recall that very young children process new words holistically rather than breaking them down into separate sounds. In this situation, high neighborhood density or a greater number of words that differ by one sound can make word learning more difficult. In contrast, among adults high neighborhood density may positively influence the integration of new word representations (Storkel, Armbrüster, & Hogan, 2006). Among both children and adults, phonotactic probability or the likelihood of sound and syllable construction may aid in new word learning.

ARTICULATORY KNOWLEDGE

Articulatory knowledge is knowing the movements needed to produce different speech sounds. These movements vary with the phonetic and prosodic context and such word-specific factors as frequency of use and word similarity. An individual's sound production accuracy depends on recognizing these factors and being sufficiently flexible to adapt to different contexts and task demands.

Acquisition of articulatory knowledge is an extended process. Even adolescent speech differs from adult speech in the length of sounds and words and in characteristics that differentiate one sound from another (Lee, Potamianos, & Naryanan, 1999).

As the development of speech continues into the adult years, there is a steady increase in fluency. This is aided by **coarticulation**, a speech process in which sounds that will be produced later in an utterance are anticipated and the mouth is moved into position on an earlier speech sound. For example, the /k/ in *coat* and *cat* are produced in qualitatively different ways as the speaker anticipates the sound to follow. Produce both words and notice the lip rounding on the /k/ in *coat* that is absent in *cat*.

Adult phonological knowledge also involves the way speech-sound categories are used to convey meaning through morphophonemic changes and the admissible speech-sound combinations in American English. Obviously, such knowledge varies with the language being spoken.

Children do not possess adultlike knowledge that words are composed of strings of phonemes. Such knowledge is acquired throughout childhood and into adolescence. In general, children with larger vocabularies have more higher-level phonological skills (Edwards et al., 2004). Most likely, as a child's vocabulary increases, and he or she must store more and more words with similar sound and syllable combinations, the child uses acoustic-perceptual representations and articulatory representations to refine knowledge of word formations. Words become strings of sounds.

SOCIAL-INDEXICAL KNOWLEDGE

Social-indexical knowledge includes knowing how linguistic variability conveys or is perceived to convey a speaker's membership in different social groups (Clopper & Pisoni, 2004; Smyth, Jacobs, & Rogers, 2003). A person's speech may identify group membership and influence a listener's perceptions.

Social-indexical variation, such as gender and dialectal differences, is present even in the speech of very young children. Ability to comprehend speech in an unfamiliar dialect requires greater facility and develops throughout childhood and adolescence (Nathan, Wells, & Donlan, 1998).

Literacy

The incidence of pleasure reading seems to decrease through adolescence, especially among males (Nippold, Duthie, & Larsen, 2005). Although a moderately popular free-time activity, reading is less desirable than listening to music/going to concerts, watching television or videos, playing sports, or playing computer or video games. The most popular reading materials are the Internet, magazines, novels, and comics.

Adults read somewhat more than adolescents, often in work-related settings. This generational difference may decrease as more and more individuals from the computer generation enter adulthood. It must not be forgotten, however, that access to the Internet requires considerable literacy skill. Even spell-checkers, grammar-checkers, and word-prediction programs require minimal writing ability to engage their programs.

While adults continue to refine both their writing and reading abilities, these changes are not dramatic. The biggest change in adolescence and adulthood is in executive function, the ability to engage actively with print and to write and read with purpose.

It is not until early adulthood—about where most of you are right now—that writers develop the cognitive processes and executive functions needed for mature writing (Berninger, 2000; Ylvisaker & DeBonis, 2000). It takes this long because of the protracted period of anatomical and physiological development of your brain's frontal lobe where executive function is housed.

Although we don't know what effect technology will have on language learning and use, it's an important topic to discuss. This video begins to explore the possibilities. http://www.youtube.com/watch?v=0vbMWDtc4ms

Until adolescence, young writers need adult scaffolding or guidance in planning and revising their writing. By junior high school, teens are capable of revising all aspects of writing, which, added to improved long-term memory, results in improved overall compositional quality.

If you find yourself using an enlarged vocabulary when writing or pondering how sentences flow from one to the next, then you are probably a mature writer. As with reading, practice results in improvement, which should continue throughout the life span. In general, the writing of adults as compared to adolescents is longer, with longer, more complex sentences; uses more abstract nouns, such as *longevity* and *kindness*; and contains more metalinguistic and metacognitive words, such as *reflect* and *disagree* (Nippold, Ward-Lonergan, & Fanning, 2005).

Bilingualism

Immigrant children tend to score lower on English language tests than nonimmigrant children, but their language growth in English continues into adolescence more than nonimmigrant children (Leventhal, Xue, & Brooks-Gunn, 2006). Family SES affects performance as well. Poorer children do not have language skills as high as more affluent children.

Although it varies with the brain function in question, there does seem to be a "sensitive" period or a time during development in which the brain is particularly responsive to experiences or patterns of activity. In the area of speech and language, native language proficiency cannot be obtained when learning begins after puberty (Bruer, 2001; Werker & Tees, 2005). For example, adults exposed to a second language in early childhood have nativelike accents and intonation, while those not exposed until adulthood or late adolescence do not achieve nativelike speech (Birdsong & Molis, 2001; Gordon, 2000; Stein et al., 2006). Similarly, early exposure to a second language leads to better judgments of grammatical correctness (Flege, MacKay, & Meador, 1999; Komarova & Nowak, 2001). We should add that these data are complicated somewhat by the differing cognitive processing of adults and children that may enhance the child's ability to learn language (Newport et al., 2001).

Nonnative child and adult listeners seem to rely less on grammatical analysis for interpretation than native listeners (Felser & Clahsen, 2009). These second-language learners may rely more on other cues, such as social. The difference can be explained in part by slower processing speed and cognitive resource allocation by nonnative listeners. For example, relatively more cognitive resources may be allocated to lower-level phonological analysis, leaving fewer for higher-order comprehension processing.

Learning of single words in a second language is affected by several variables, such as familiarity with the language and with the sounds of that language. Phonological familiarity only appears to help word learning of familiar referents but not unfamiliar ones, such as culture-specific referents (Kaushanskaya, Yoo, & Van Hecke, 2013).

Congratulations!

Well, you made it! You reached the end of this text. Congratulations! And like the folks discussed in this chapter, you have your entire adult life before you. Make it a great one. Take what you've learned from this book and course and use it with your own children and children in school or those who need special services.

For those of you who will go on to work with children with special needs, you now have a firm foundation to begin to discuss language impairments. Keep an open mind. New ideas come along all the time. Evaluate each in light of research and your knowledge of language development. Good luck. Be well and safe.

Conclusion

BY ADULTHOOD, EACH INDIVIDUAL is a truly versatile speaker who can tailor his or her message to the context and the participants. Adults are able to move flexibly from work to the gym to a cocktail party and home to tuck in the kids and alter their language effortlessly as needed. Within these contexts and many more, the mature communicator can change style and topic rapidly or remain in both almost indefinitely.

The conversational and literacy abilities of adults continue to diversify and to become more elaborate with age if health is maintained. Except for the small percentage of older adults who have suffered some brain injury or disease, most continue to be effective communicators throughout their lives.

Discussion

MOST OF THE QUANTITATIVE DEVELOPMENT of language is behind you, but you can still refine and improve your language as your life progresses. To do so, you must remain actively involved in life and open to new ideas and change. When I began the first edition of this text, I had no more idea how to write a book than many of you. It continues to be a learning experience, and you can judge for yourself how much I have learned and how far I still need to go.

Many of you will be able to participate again in the developmental process through your own children or those of others. Those of you who go into education will help children with the formal aspects of learning language, while those who select special education or speech-language pathology will be involved with children and adults who are experiencing difficulties. Just because a person has matured into adulthood, it does not follow that speech and language disorders mature into nondisordered communication. In addition, some adults will experience difficulties because of illness or injury and will also require intervention. You now have some of the knowledge you need to make judgments on the appropriateness of communication among children and adults.

Main Points

- Development continues slowly through adolescence and adulthood, although there are some declines in the senior years.
- Teens and adults are adept and flexible communicators with various styles of talking.
- In the U.S. majority culture, gender differences are obvious in adulthood but may begin as early as late preschool. In general, men and women use different vocabularies and styles of talking that may reflect societal

TABLE A.1 **The Examiner: 1 to 6 Months *(Continued)***

Age (Months)	Motor	Cognition	Socialization	Communication
4	Can turn head in all directions; complete rollover On stomach: Raises head and chest on arms Occasionally opposes thumb and fingers; grasps small objects put in hand; brings objects to mouth	Localizes to sound Stares at place from which object is dropped Remembers visually for 5–7 seconds Recognizes mother in group; senses strange places and people	Pays attention to faces; discriminates different faces Looks in direction of person leaving room Anticipates being lifted; laughs when played with	Babbles strings of consonants Varies pitch Imitates tones Smiles at person speaking to him or her
5	Sits supported for up to half an hour Rolls from stomach to back Can be easily pulled to stand Has partial thumb opposition; swaps objects from hand to hand	Recognizes familiar objects; anticipates whole object after seeing a part, is capable of 3-hour visual memory Explores by mouthing and touching Remembers own actions in immediate past	Discriminates parents and siblings from others Imitates some movements of others Frolics when played with Displays anger when objects taken away	Vocalizes to toys Discriminates angry and friendly voices Experiments with sound Imitates some sounds Responds to name Smiles and vocalizes to image in mirror
6	Turns head freely Sits straight when slightly supported or in chair Balances well Reaches with one arm Turns and twists in all directions Creeps	Looks and reaches smoothly and quickly Inspects objects Reaches to grab dropped objects	Differentiates social responses Prefers people games, such as peekaboo Feeds self finger food Explores face of person holding	Varies volume, pitch, and rate Vocalizes pleasure and displeasure: squeals with excitement, intones displeasure

TABLE A.2 The Experimenter: 7 to 12 Months

Age (Months)	Motor	Cognition	Socialization	Communication
7	Transfers object from hand to hand; bangs objects together Cuts first tooth; has better chewing and jaw control; can eat some strained solids Pushes up on hands and knees; rocks	Visually searches briefly for toy that disappears Imitates a physical act if in repertoire Remembers that jack pops up at the end of jack-in-the-box song	Resists Teases (beginning of humor); laughs at funny expressions Raises arms to be picked up	Plays vocally Produces several sounds in one breath Listens to vocalization of others Recognizes different tones and inflections
8	Uses thumb–finger apposition Manipulates objects to explore Pulls up to stand but needs help to get down Crawls Drops and throws objects	Recognizes object dimensions Prefers novel and relatively complex toys Explores shape, weight, texture, function, and properties (example: in/out)	Acts positively toward peers Is clearly attached to mother Shouts for attention Responds to self in mirror May reject being alone	Recognizes some words Repeats emphasized syllable Imitates gestures and tonal quality of adult speech; echolalia
9	Stands alone briefly; gets down alone; cruises Sits unsupported; gets into and out of sitting position alone Removes and replaces bottle Puts objects in containers	Uncovers object if observes act of hiding first Anticipates outcome of events and return of persons	Explores other babies "Performs" for family ("so big") Imitates play Plays action games	Produces distinct intonational patterns Imitates nonspeech sounds Uses social gestures Uses jargon May respond to name and "no" Attends to conversation
10	Holds and drinks from cup Sits from a standing position Momentary unsupported stand	Points to body parts Attains a goal with trial-and-error approach Searches for hidden object in a familiar place	Helps dress and feed self Becomes aware of social approval and disapproval	Imitates adult speech if sounds in repertoire Obeys some commands

(continued)

TABLE A.2 **The Experimenter: 7 to 12 Months *(Continued)***

Age (Months)	Motor	Cognition	Socialization	Communication
11	Stands alone; gets up from all-fours position by pushing up Climbs up stairs Feeds self with spoon	Imitates increasingly Associates properties with objects	Seeks approval Anticipates mother's goal and tries to change it by protest or "persuasion"	Imitates inflections, rhythms, facial expressions, etc.
12	Stands alone; pushes to stand from squat Climbs up and down stairs Uses spoon, cup, and crayon; releases objects willfully Takes first steps with support	Can reach while looking away Uses common objects appropriately Searches in location where an object was last seen	Expresses people preferences Expresses many different emotions	Follows simple motor instructions, if accompanied by a visual cue ("bye-bye"); reacts to "no" Speaks one or more words Mixes word and jargon

TABLE A.3 **The Explorer: 12 to 24 Months**

Age (Months)	Motor	Cognition	Socialization	Communication
15	Walks with rapid runlike gait Walks a few steps backwards and sideways Dumps toys in container Takes off shoes and socks Picks up small objects with index finger and thumb	Imitates small motor acts Uses toy phone like real one	Likes music and dancing Pushes toys Imitates housework Plays in solitary manner but likes to act for an audience Begins make-believe play Laughs when chased	Points to clothes, persons, toys, and animals named Uses jargon and words in conversation Has four- to six-word vocabulary
18	Walks up stairs with help; walks smoothly, runs stiffly Drinks unassisted Throws ball with whole arm Throws and catches without falling Jumps with both feet off floor Turns pages	Recognizes pictures Recognizes self in mirror Remembers places where objects are usually located Uses a stick as a tool Imitates adult object use	Explores reactions of others; tests others Enjoys solitary play Pretends to feed doll Responds to scolding and praise Little or no sense of sharing	Begins to use two-word utterances Has approximately 20-word vocabulary Identifies some body parts Refers to self by name "Sings" and hums Plays question-answer with adults
21	Walks up and down stairs with help of railing or hand Jumps, runs, throws, climbs; kicks large ball; squats to play; running is stiff Fits puzzle together Responds rhythmically to music with whole body	Knows shapes Sits alone for short periods with book Notices little objects and small sounds Matching objects with owners Recalls absent objects or persons	Hugs spontaneously Plays near but not with other kids Likes toy telephone, doll, and truck for play Enjoys outings Becomes clingy around strangers	Likes rhyming games Pulls person to show something Tries to "tell" experiences Understands some personal pronouns Uses *I* and *mine*
24	Walks watching feet Runs rhythmically but unable to start or stop smoothly Walks up and down stairs alone without alternating feet Pushes tricycle Eats with fork Transitions smoothly from walk to run	Matches familiar objects Comprehends *one* and *many* Recognizes when picture in book is upside down	Can role-play in limited manner Engages in pretend play constrained by the objects Enjoys parallel play predominately Prefers action toys Cooperates with adults in simple household tasks Communicates feelings, desires, and interests	Has expressive vocabulary of 200–300 words Uses short, incomplete sentences

TABLE A.4 The Exhibitor

Age (Years)	Motor	Cognition	Socialization	Communication
3	Walks up and down stairs without assistance; uses nonalternating step Walks without watching feet, marches to music Balances momentarily on one foot Rides tricycle Can spread with knife Explores, dismantles, dismembers	Creates representational art Matches primary colors and shapes Can show two objects: understands concept of two Enjoys make-believe play; is less constrained by objects Knows age but no concept of length of a year	Labels some coins Plays in groups, talks while playing, selects with whom to play Shares toys for short periods Takes turns Insists on being in the limelight	Has expressive vocabulary of 900–1,000 words; creates three- to four-word sentences Uses "sentences" with subject and verb, but simple sentence construction Plays with words and sounds Follows two-step commands Talks about the present
4	Walks up and down stair with alternating steps Jumps over objects Hops on one foot Can copy block letters	Categorizes Counts rotely to five; can show three objects; understands concept of three Knows primary colors	Plays and cooperates with others Role-plays	Has 1,500-word expressive vocabulary Asks many, many questions Uses increasingly more complex sentence forms Recounts stories and the recent past Has some difficulty answering how and why Relies on word order for interpretation
5	Has gross-motor control, good body awareness; plays complex games Cuts own meat with a knife Draws well, colors in lines; creates more recognizable drawings Prints simple words Dresses without assistance Has established hand preference	Carries a rule through a series of activities Knows own right and left, but not those of others Counts to 13; can show four or five objects Accepts magic as an explanation Develops time concepts Recognizes relationship of parts to whole	Plays simple games Selects some playmates based on sex Enjoys dramatic play Shows interest in group activities Plays purposefully and constructively	Has expressive vocabulary of 2,100 to 2,200 words Discusses feelings Understands *before* and *after*, regardless of word order Follows three-step commands Has 90% grammar acquisition

TABLE A.5 The Expert: The School-Age Child

Age (Years)	Motor	Cognition	Socialization	Communication
6	Has better gross-motor coordination; rides bicycle Throws ball well Begins to get permanent teeth	Has longer attention span Is less distracted by additional information when problem solving Remembers and repeats three digits	Enjoys active games Is competitive Identifies with sex peers in groups Transforms egocentric reality to more complex and relative reality view	Has expressive vocabulary of 2,600 words, receptive of 20,000 to 24,000 words Has many well-formed sentences of a complex nature
8	Has longer arms, larger hands Has better manipulative skills Has nearly mature-size brain Has more permanent teeth	Knows left and right of others Understands conservation Knows differences and similarities Reads spontaneously	Enjoys an audience Learns that others have different perspectives Has allegiance to gang but also strong need for adult support	Talks a lot Verbalizes ideas and problems readily Communicates thought
10	Has eyes of almost mature size Has almost mature lungs and digestive and circulatory systems	Plans future actions Solves problems with only minimal physical input	Enjoys games, sports, hobbies Discovers that he or she may be the object of someone else's perspective	Spends lots of time talking Has good comprehension
12	Experiences "rest" before adolescent growth (girls usually taller and heavier, may have entered puberty) Begins rapid muscle growth with puberty	Engages in abstract thought	Has different interests than those of the opposite sex	Has 50,000-word receptive vocabulary Constructs adultlike definitions

Appendix B

Computing MLU

In general, 50 to 100 utterances are considered a sufficient sample from which to generalize about a speaker's overall production. An utterance may be a sentence or a shorter unit of language that is separated from other utterances by a drop in the voice, a pause, and/or a breath that signals a new thought. Once transcribed, each utterance is analyzed by morphemes; the total sample is then averaged to determine the speaker's MLU.

When analyzing the language of young children, several assumptions about preschool language must be made. Let's use the past tense as an example. The regular past tense includes the verb stem plus *-ed*, as in *walked* or *opened*. Hence, the regular past equals two morphemes, one free and one bound. In contrast, the irregular past is signaled by a different word, as in *eat/ate* and *sit/sat*. As adults, we realize that *eat* plus a past-tense marker equals *ate*. It could thus be argued that *ate* should also be counted as two morphemes. It seems, however, that young children learn separate words for the present and the irregular past and are not necessarily aware of the relationship between the two. Therefore, the irregular past counts as one morpheme for young children. A similar logic exists for words such as *gonna* and *wanna*. As adults, we can subdivide these words into their components: *going to* and *want to*. Young children, however, cannot perform such analyses. Therefore, *gonna* counts as one morpheme for the child, not as the three represented by *going to*.

Although we may not agree with this rationale, for uniformity's sake we must adopt it if we are to discuss language development across children. Guidelines for counting morphemes are presented in Table B.1 (Brown, 1973). Applying these rules, we would reach the following values:

Daddy bring me choo-choo-s. = 5 morphemes
Mommy eat-ed a-a-a sandwich. = 5 morphemes
Doggie-'s bed broke baboom. = 5 morphemes
Paddington Bear go-ing night-night. = 4 morphemes
He hafta. = 2 morphemes

Once the morphemes for each utterance are counted, they are totaled and then divided by the total number of utterances. The formula is very simple:

$$\text{MLU} = \frac{\text{Total number of morphemes}}{\text{Total number of utterances}}$$

Thus, if the total number of morphemes for a 100-utterance sample is 221, the MLU will equal 2.21 morphemes per utterance. Remember that this is an average value and does not identify the length of the child's longest utterance. In other words, an MLU of 2.0 does *not* mean that the child uses only two-word utterances.

TABLE B.1 Brown's Rules for Counting Morphemes

Rule	Example
Count as one morpheme:	
Reoccurrences of a word for emphasis	*No! No! No!* (3 morphemes)
Compound words (two or more free morphemes)	*Railroad, birthday*
Proper names	*Billy Sue*
Ritualized reduplications	*Night-night, choo-choo*
Irregular past-tense verbs	*Went, ate, got, came*
Diminutives	*Daddie, doggie*
Auxiliary verbs and catenatives	*Is, have, do, gonna, hafta*
Irregular plurals	*Men, feet*
Count as two morphemes (inflected verbs and nouns):	
Possessive nouns	*Sam's, daddie's*
Plural nouns	*Doggies, kitties*
Third person singular, present-tense verbs	*Walks, eats*
Regular past-tense verbs	*Walked, jumped*
Present progressive verbs	*Walking, eating*
Do not count:	
Dysfluencies, except for most complete form	*C-c-c-candy, bab-baby*
Fillers	*Um-m, ah-h, oh*

Source: Information from Brown (1973).

Appendix C

Background Grammar

Verb Types

Verb phrases are of three types: *transitive, intransitive,* and *stative*. In mature language, transitive verbs take a direct object and include words such as *love, hate, make, give, build, send, owe,* and *show*. With few exceptions—verbs such as *have, lack,* or *resemble*—transitive verbs can be changed from active to passive voice by exchanging the positions of the two noun phrases.

Active Voice	*Passive Voice*
Mary sent a letter.	A letter was sent by Mary.
Sue loves Fran.	Fran is loved by Sue.

In contrast, intransitive verbs do not have a passive form, nor do they take direct objects. Examples include *swim, fall, look, seem,* and *weigh*. Although we say, "She swam the river," it is awkward to say, "The river was swum by her." Some verbs may be both transitive and intransitive:

I *opened* the door slowly. (Transitive: *door* is direct object)
The door *opened* slowly. (Intransitive: no direct object)

Overall, transitive verb phrases are more common in English than in other languages.

Intransitive verbs are easier to learn because they don't require a direct object (Valian, 1991). Likewise, verbs that are transitive are first produced by children without a direct object as in *Mommy give* or *I make*. Of interest, this is the way that mothers use these verbs when talking to their young language-learning children (Theakston, Lieven, Pine, & Rowland, 2001).

Stative verbs, such as the copula *to be*, are followed by a *complement*, an element that sets up an equality with the subject. In "She is a doctor," *doctor* complements or describes what *she* is. In other words, she = doctor.

Auxiliary Verbs

Auxiliary, or helping, verbs in English can be classified as primary, such as *be, have,* and *do*, or as secondary or modal, such as *will, shall, can, may,* and *must*. In general, auxiliary verbs and the copula *be* are the only verbs that can be inverted with the subject to form questions or that can have negative forms attached. Examples of auxiliary forms include the following:

Are you running in the race? (Inverted from the statement "You are running . . . .")
What *have* you done? (Inverted from the statement "You have done . . . .")
I *can't* help you. (Negative form)
I *may* not be able to go. (Negative form)

The copula can also be inverted and made into a negative form, as in *Is she sick?* or *This isn't funny.*

In addition, auxiliary verbs are used to avoid repetition in elliptical responses that omit redundant information and for emphasis. For example, when asked, "Who can go with me?" a respondent avoids repetition by the elliptical reply "I *can.*" To affirm a statement emphatically, a speaker emphasizes the auxiliary verb, as in "I *do* like to dance."

Phrases and Clauses

Sentences are strings of related words or larger units containing a noun subject and a verb or predicate. For example, the sentence "She ate cookies" is a string of words related in a certain way. *She* has acted on *cookies*.

The units within sentences are composed of words, phrases, and clauses. A phrase is a group of related words that does not include both a subject and a predicate and is used as a noun substitute or as a noun or verb modifier. For example, the phrase *to fish*, an infinitive, can take the place of a noun. In the sentence "I love candy," *to fish* can be substituted for *candy*, a noun, to form "I love to fish." Other phrases modify nouns, as in "The man *in the blue suit*," or verbs, as in "Loren fought *with a vengeance*." These phrases are said to be embedded within a sentence.

In contrast to a phrase, a **clause** is a group of words that contains both a subject and a predicate. A clause that can stand alone as grammatically complete is a **simple sentence**. Thus, the shortest Biblical verse, "Jesus wept," is a simple sentence. Occasionally, a sentence may contain more than one clause. When a sentence is combined with another sentence, they each become **main clauses**. A **compound sentence** is made up of two or more main clauses joined as equals, as in "*Mary drove to work*, and *she had an accident*." Both "Mary drove to work" and "She had an accident" are simple sentences serving as main clauses in the larger compound sentence. Main clauses may be joined by conjunctions, such as *and, but, because, if*, and so on, to form compound sentences. This process is called **conjoining** or coordinating.

Some clauses, such as *whom we met last week*, cannot stand alone even though they contain a subject and a predicate. In this example, *we* is the subject and *met* is the predicate, or main verb. When embedded, such clauses, called **subordinate** clauses, function as nouns, adjectives, or adverbs in support of the main clause. For example, *she is the girl*, a simple sentence, or main clause, can embed the above subordinate clause within it to form "She is the girl whom we met last week."

A sentence such as this, made up of a main clause and at least one subordinate clause, is called a **complex sentence**. The subordinate clause is said to be *embedded* within the main clause even if it's just attached. In general, subordinate clauses are introduced by subordinating conjunctions, such as *after, although, before, until, while*, and *when*, or by relative pronouns, such as *who, which*, and *that*. For example, the sentence "He doesn't know when it began to rain" contains the subordinate clause *when it began to rain*, which serves as the object of the verb *know*. In "the man who lives here hates children," *who lives here* is a subordinate clause modifying *man* and identifying which one.

In the following sections, we'll discuss the development of both embedding and conjoining. As you can imagine, multiple embeddings can produce extremely complicated sentences.

Types of Phrases

Phrases other than the noun and verb types can be formed in four ways: (1) with a preposition, (2) with a participle, (3) with a gerund, and (4) with an infinitive. A prepositional phrase contains a preposition, such as *in*, *on*, *under*, *at*, or *into*, and its object, along with possible articles and modifiers, as in *on the roof* or *at the school dance*. Prepositions include the following:

about	among	beneath	except	instead of	onto	through	up
above	around	beside	for	into	out of	to	upon
across	at	between	from	near	outside	toward	with
after	before	by	in	next to	over	under	within
against	behind	down	in front of	of	past	underneath	without
along	below	during	inside	on	since	until	

Many words have other functions. For example, *since* can also be a conjunction, *down* can be an adverb, *past* can be a verb form.

A participial phrase contains a participle (a verb-derived word ending in *-ing*, *-ed*, *-t*, *-en*, or a few irregular forms) and serves as an adjective. Examples of participles include the *setting* sun, a *lost* cause, a *broken* promise, and a *fallen* warrior. In the sentence "The boy riding the bicycle is athletic," *riding the bicycle* is a participial phrase describing or modifying *boy*.

In contrast, a gerund, which also ends in *-ing*, functions as a noun. Gerunds may be used as a subject ("*Skiing* is fun"), as an object ("I enjoy *skiing*"), or in any other sentence function that may be filled by a noun.

Finally, an infinitive phrase may function as a noun but also as an adjective or adverb. An infinitive consists of *to* plus a verb, as in "He wanted *to open* his present." The entire phrase *to open his present* is an infinitive phrase serving as the object of the sentence. The *to* may be omitted after certain verbs, as in "He helped *clean up the mess*" or "He dared not *speak aloud*."

Interrogative Form

There are three general forms of questions: those that assume a yes/no response; those that begin with a *wh-* word and assume a more complex answer; and those that are a statement to which agreement is sought by adding a tag, such as "isn't he?" Yes/no questions seek confirmation or nonconfirmation and are typically formed by adding rising intonation to the end of a statement, as in "You're eating snails?" ↑; by moving the auxiliary verb or copula from its position in a declarative sentence (You *are* eating snails) to form "*Are* you eating snails?"; or by adding the auxiliary verb *do* to a position in front of the subject, as in "Do you like eating snails?"

Typical *wh-* or constituent questions begin with words such as *what*, *where*, and *who*. The verb and subject are inverted, as in yes/no questions, and the *wh-* word appears before the subject (What do you want?) unless it is the subject, as in *who* questions (Who is here?).

In tag questions, a proposition is made, such as "He loves sweets," then negated in the tag: "He loves sweets, doesn't he?" An equally acceptable reverse order might produce "He doesn't love sweets, does he?"

Inverted forms, whether in yes/no or *wh-* questions, require a child to learn the following three rules:

1.	The auxiliary verb is inverted to precede the subject.	She can play house. *Can* she play house? Tom is eating candy. What *is* Tom eating?
2.	The copula is inverted to precede the subject.	They are funny. *Are* they funny? Mary is in school. Where *is* Mary?
3.	The do is inserted before the subject if no copula or auxiliary exists.	Todd loves Joanie. *Does* Todd love Joanie? Mike drank a soda. What *did* Mike drink?

Subordinate Clause Embedding

Three primary types of subordinate clauses include the following:

1. Nominal ("The dogs knew their master had arrived"), which we'll call *object noun phrase complements* and *embedded wh- complements*
2. Relative ("The dogs that were hungry ran to the door")
3. Adverbial ("When they heard their master, the dogs ran to the door")

Object noun-phrase complements consist of a subordinate clause that serves as the object of the main clause. For example, we could say "I know *X* (something)" in which *X* is the object. We could replace *X* with a noun phrase (*a story*) or with a subordinate clause, such as (*that*) *I like it* to form "I know (*that*) *I like it*."

Indirect or **embedded *wh-* complements** are similar to object noun-phrase complements. In the following sentences, the *wh-* subordinate clause fills the object function, as in "I know *X*":

I know *who did it*.
She saw *where the kitty went*.

Relative clauses are subordinate clauses that follow and modify nouns. Rather than take the place of a noun, these clauses are attached to a noun with relative pronouns, such as *who*, *which*, and *that*. The earliest relative pronouns are *that*, *what*, and *where*.

Adverbial subordinate clauses serve as adverbs. For example, in the sentence "Later, they were all sad," *later* is an adverb of time. We could replace it with a clause to form "After we left, they were all sad."

Compound Sentences or Conjoining

Unlike complex sentences in which one clause is subordinate and cannot stand alone, compound sentences consist of two independent clauses. Each could serve as a sentence. The two clauses are joined by a conjunction, such as one of these:

after	because	in order that	than	when
although	before	now that	that	whenever
as	even if	once	though	where
as if	even though	rather than	till	whereas
as long as	if	since	unless	wherever
as though	if only	so that	until	while

Conjunctions are small overworked words and may have other syntactic functions. Some also serve as prepositions.

Conjoining may include whole clauses or clauses with deleted common elements, called **phrasal coordination**, as in "Mary ran and fell." In full clausal or **sentential coordination**, such as "Mary ran and Mary fell," *Mary* is redundant and may be deleted, as in the first example. Obviously, sentential coordination, such as "Mary ran and John fell," does not lend itself to such shortening. Conjoining by children is relatively independent of the length of the two units to be conjoined, although, obviously, a very young child is not capable of producing adult-length utterances. Initially, sentential coordination seems to be used for events that occur at different times in different locations, while phrasal coordination is used for simultaneous or near-simultaneous events in the same location.

In phrasal coordination, forward reductions are more common and appear earlier than backward reductions. In *forward reductions*, the full clause is stated first, followed by a conjunction, plus the nonredundant information. "Reggie made the cookies by himself and ate them before dinner" is an example of forward reduction. *Reggie* would be redundant in the second clause. Conversely, in *backward reductions* the full clause follows the conjunction, as in "Reggie and Noi baked cookies." Ease of processing may be more closely related to the amount of information a child is required to hold than to the direction of reduction. Preschool children have great difficulty with a sentence such as "The sheep patted the kangaroo and the pig the giraffe" because of the amount of information they must hold in short-term memory, especially from the first clause, while deciphering this sentence.

Glossary

Accommodation Process of reorganizing cognitive structures or schemes or creating new schemes in response to external stimuli that do not fit into any available scheme. Piagetian concept.

Account A type of narrative in which the speaker relates a past experience in which the listener did not share.

Adaptation Process by which an organism adapts to the environment; occurs as a result of two complementary processes, assimilation and accommodation. Piagetian concept.

Agent Semantic case characterized by causing action, as in ***Daddy*** *is fixing my bike.*

Allophone Perceptual grouping of phones of similar speech sounds. Together, allophones form a phoneme.

Analogy A pattern-finding technique that accounts for how children create abstract syntactic constructions from concrete pieces of language by understanding the relationship across schemes. For example, if *X is Y-ing the Z* and the *A is B-ing the C*, then a child sees that X and A play analogous roles, as do C and Z.

Anaphoric reference Grammatical mechanism which notifies the listener that the speaker is referring to a previous reference. Pronouns are one type of word used in anaphoric reference.

Angular gyrus Association area of the brain, located in the posterior portion of the temporal lobe, responsible for linguistic processing, especially word recall.

Antonym A word that differs only in the opposite value of a single important feature.

Archiform One member of a word class used to the exclusion of all others. For example, *a* may be used for all articles or *he* for all third person pronouns.

Arcuate fasciculus White, fibrous tract of mostly axons and dendrites underlying the angular gyrus in the brain. Language is organized in Wernicke's area and transmitted through the arcuate fasciculus to Broca's area.

Aspect The dynamics of an event, noted by the verb, relative to the event's completion, repetition, or continuing duration.

Assimilation Process by which external stimuli are incorporated into existing cognitive structures or schemes. Piagetian concept.

Associative complex hypothesis Theory that each example of a meaning category shares something with a core concept. In other words, there are common elements in the meanings of *pants*, *shirt*, *shoes*, and *hat* that classify each as clothing. Vygotskyan concept.

Babbling Long strings of sounds that children begin to produce at about 4 months of age.

Bilingual Fluent in two languages; uses two languages on a daily basis.

Blending Creating a word from individual sounds and syllables and being able to compare initial phonemes in words for likeness and difference.

Bootstrapping Process of learning language in which a child uses what he or she knows to decode more mature language. For example, the child may use semantic knowledge to aid in decoding and learning syntax.

Bound morpheme Meaning unit that cannot occur alone but must be joined to a free morpheme; generally includes grammatical tags or markers that are derivational, such as *-ly*, *-er*, or *-ment*, or inflectional, such as *-ed* or *-s*.

Bracketing Process of breaking a speech stream into analyzable units by detecting end points or divisions through the use of intonational cues.

Broca's area Cortical area of the left frontal lobe of the brain responsible for detailing and coordinating the programming of speech movements.

Centering The linking of entities in a narrative to form a story nucleus. Links may be based on similarity or complementarity of features, sequence, or causality.

Central nervous system (CNS) Portion of the nervous system consisting of the brain and spinal cord.

Cerebellum The "little brain," consisting of right and left hemispheres and a central region; has considerable influence on language processing and on higher-level cognitive and emotional functions.

Cerebrum Upper brain, consisting of the cortex and the subcortical structures.

Chaining Narrative form consisting of a sequence of events that share attributes and lead directly from one to another.

Child-directed speech (CDS) Adult speech adapted for use when talking with young children.

Clause Group of words containing a subject and the accompanying verb; used as a sentence (independent clause) or attached to an independent clause (dependent clause).

Clustering Process of breaking speech stream into analyzable units based on predictability of syllables and phoneme structures.

Coarticulation Co-occurrence of the characteristics of two or more phonemes as one phoneme influences another in perception or in production; may be forward (anticipatory) or backward (carryover).

Code switching Process of varying between two or more languages.

Cognates Phoneme pairs that differ only in voicing; manner and place of articulation are similar. For example, /f/ and /v/ are cognates, as are /s/ and /z/.

Communication Process of encoding, transmitting, and decoding signals in order to exchange information and ideas between the participants.

Communication intention Purpose of an utterance, that is, to gain information, request permission, or provide information.

Communicative competence Degree of success in communicating, measured by the appropriateness and effectiveness of the message.

Complex sentence Sentence consisting of a main clause and at least one subordinate clause.

Compound sentence Sentence consisting of two or more main clauses.

Conjoining Joining two or more main clauses with a conjunction.

Consonant cluster reduction Phonological process seen in preschool children in which one or more consonants are deleted from a cluster of two or more (/tɹ, stɹ, sl, kɹ) in order to simplify production.

Constructivist approach Linguistic theory that argues that children learn language from their environment one construction at a time versus rule learning.

Contingent query Request for clarification, such as "What?" or "Huh?"

Copula Form of the verb *to be* as a main verb. Signifies a relationship between the subject and a predicate adjective (*fat, tired, young*) or another noun (*teacher, farmer, pianist*).

Corpus callosum Main transverse tract of neurons running between the two hemispheres of the brain.

Cortex Outermost gray layer of the brain, made up of neuron cell bodies.

Critical literacy Above the basic reading level, critical literacy involves active interpretation, analysis, and synthesis of information and the ability to explain the content.

Decentration Process of moving from one-dimensional descriptions of entities and events to coordinated multiattributional ones.

Decoding The first step in interpreting print, decoding consists of breaking a word into its component sounds and then blending them together to form a recognizable word.

Deficit approach Notion that only one dialect of a language is inherently correct or standard and that others are substandard or exhibit some deficit.

Deixis Process of using the speaker's perspective as a reference. For example, deixis can be seen in words such as *this, that, here, there, me,* and *you*.

Dialects Subcategories of a parent language that use similar but not identical rules.

Diphthong Vowel-like speech sound produced by blending two vowels within a syllable.

Discourse Aspect of language concerned with how a set of utterances is used to convey a message.

Dynamic literacy At the highest level of reading, the ability to relate content to other knowledge.

Echolalia Immediate, whole or partial vocal imitation of another speaker; characterizes the child's speech beginning at about 8 months.

Ellipsis Conversational device of omitting redundant information. For example, when asked, "Who saw the movie?" we reply, "I did," not "I saw the movie."

Embedded *wh-* complement Object noun-phrase complement using a *wh-* word as a connector for the dependent clause.

Emergentism Linguistic theory that argues that language is a structure arising from existing interacting patterns in the human brain.

Entrenchment A pattern-finding technique that accounts for how children confine abstractions about language by doing something in the same way successfully several times, thus making it habitual.

Epenthesis Process of inserting a vowel sound where none is required.

Equilibrium State of cognitive balance or harmony between incoming stimuli and cognitive structures. Piagetian concept.

Eventcast A type of narrative that explains some current or anticipated event. Eventcasts often accompany the play of young children.

Event structure Set of event sequences including the events, relationships, and relative significance.

Evocative utterance Toddler language-learning strategy in which the child names an entity and awaits adult evaluative feedback as to the correctness of the name or label.

Executive function The self-regulatory aspect of writing that enables the writer to plan, write according to that plan, and proofread and revise as needed.

Expansion Adult's more mature version of a child's utterance that preserves the word order of the original child utterance. For example, when a child says, "Doggie eat," an adult might reply, "The doggie is eating."

Extension Adult's semantically related comment on a topic established by a child. For example, when a child says, "Doggie eat," an adult might reply, "Yes, doggie hungry."

Fast mapping Quick, sketchy, and tentative formation of a link between a particular referent and a new name that enables a child to have access to and use the word in an immediate although somewhat limited way. Gradually, the meaning of the referent widens as the word is freed from aspects of the initial context.

Formula Memorized verbal routine or unanalyzed chunk of language often used in everyday conversation.

Free alternation Variable use of members of a word class without consideration of different meanings; for example, *the* and *a* may be used randomly.

Free morpheme Meaning unit that can occur alone, such as *dog, chair, run,* and *fast.*

Fully resonant nuclei (FRN) Vowel-like sounds that are fully resonated laryngeal tones.

Functional-core hypothesis Theory that word meanings represent dynamic relationships, such as actions or functional uses, rather than static perceptual traits. Concept usually associated with Nelson.

Functionally based distributional analysis A pattern-finding technique that accounts for how children form linguistic categories, such as nouns and verbs, based on communicative function. Over time, linguistic items that serve the same communicative function are grouped together into a category based on what these units do.

Genderlect The style of talking used by men and women.

Generative approach Also called Nativist, the generative approach assumes that children are able to acquire language because they are born with innate rules or principles related to structures of human languages.

Habituation Over time, with repeated exposure, organisms react less strongly to successive presentation of a stimulus.

Heschl's area (or gyrus) Area located in the auditory cortex of each hemisphere of the brain that receives incoming auditory signals from the inner ear.

Holophrases Early one-word utterances that convey a holistic communicative intention.

Hypothesis-testing utterance Toddler language-learning strategy in which the child seeks confirmation of the name of an entity by naming it with rising intonation, thus posing a yes/no question.

Information processing Theoretical model of brain function that stresses methods employed in dealing with information.

Initial mapping See *fast mapping.*

Integrative rehearsal Use of repetition or rehearsal to transfer information to long-term memory. Information-processing concept.

Intention-reading A uniquely human social cognitive skill used in understanding language behavior of others.

Interlanguage Transitional system in which a person uses rules from two or more languages simultaneously.

Interrogative utterance Toddler language-learning strategy in which the child attempts to learn the name of an entity by asking *What? That?* or *Wassat?* Not to be confused with adult-like interrogative sentences, which are more varied (*what, where, who, why, how, when*).

Item-based construction Two-word utterance seemingly based on word-order rules with specific words influenced by how a child has heard a particular word being used.

Jargon Strings of unintelligible speech sounds with the intonational pattern of adult speech.

Joint action Shared action sequences of mother and child, often routines; provides basis for many scripts.

Language A socially shared code or conventional system for representing concepts through the use of arbitrary symbols and rule-governed combinations of those symbols.

Language socialization Process of learning language and culture through interactions with caregivers and others. Language is central to the process of learning culture, and cultural patterns teach children the appropriate way to communicate.

Lexicon Individual dictionary of each person containing words and the underlying concepts of each. The lexicon is dynamic, changing with experience.

Linguistic competence Native speaker's underlying knowledge of the rules for generating and understanding conventional linguistic forms.

Linguistic performance Actual language use, reflecting linguistic competence and the communication constraints.

Literacy Use of visual modes of communication, specifically reading and writing.

Main clause Clause within a multiclause sentence that can occur alone.

Mean length of utterance (MLU) Average number of morphemes per utterance.

Mental maps Complex organizational webs that link concepts within the cognitive systems.

Metacognition Knowing what to do cognitively and how to do it—knowledge about knowledge and about cognitive processes.

Metalinguistics Consideration of language in the abstract, stepping back from language to make judgments about correctness or appropriateness. Metalinguistics is important for reading and writing.

Metaphoric transparency Amount of literal-figurative relationship. High or strong relationships result in easy interpretation.

Modal auxiliary Auxiliary or helping verb used to express mood or attitude, such as ability (*can*), permission (*may*), intention (*will*), possibility (*might*), and obligation (*must*).

Morpheme Smallest unit of meaning; indivisible (*dog*) without violating the meaning or producing meaningless units (*do*, *g*). There are two types of morphemes, free and bound.

Morphology Aspect of language concerned with rules governing change in meaning at the intraword level.

Morphophonemic Referring to changes in sound production related to meaning changes.

Motor cortex Posterior portion of the frontal lobe responsible for sending nerve impulses to the muscles.

Mutual gaze Eye contact with a communication partner; used to signal intensified attention.

Myelination Process of maturation of the nervous system in which the nerves develop a protective myelin sheath, or sleeve.

Narrative Consists of self-generated story; familiar tale; retelling of a movie, television show, or previously heard or seen story; and personal experience recounting.

Narrative level Overall organization of a narrative.

Nativist approach Linguistic theory associated with Chomsky and his followers, who emphasize innateness of language and contend that there are special mechanisms in the human brain dedicated to the acquisition and use of language.

Neighborhood density The number of possible words that differ by one phoneme and a factor characteristic in shaping a child's emerging lexical system.

Neonate Newborn.

Neurolinguistics Study of the anatomy, physiology, and biochemistry of the brain responsible for language processing and formulation.

Neuron Nerve cell; basic unit of the nervous system.

Neuroscience The study of neuroanatomy or where structures are located and neurophysiology or how the brain functions.

Nonegocentrism Ability to take another person's perspective.

Nonlinguistic cues Coding devices that contribute to communication but are not a part of speech. Examples include gestures, body posture, eye contact, head and body movement, facial expression, and physical distance or proxemics.

Object noun-phrase complement Subordinate clause that serves as the object of the main clause, as in "I remember *what you did to me*."

Open syllable Syllable, usually consonant-vowel (CV), ending in a vowel.

Organization Tendency for all living things to systemize or organize behaviors. Piagetian concept.

Otitis media Middle ear infection.

Overextension Process in which a child applies a word's meaning to more exemplars than an adult would. The child's definition is too broad and is thus beyond acceptable adult usage.

Paralinguistic codes Vocal and nonvocal codes that are superimposed on a linguistic code to signal the speaker's attitude or emotion or to clarify or provide additional meaning.

Patient Semantic case characterized as those for whom action is performed, as in *Give the flowers to* ***mommy***.

Pattern-finding A cognitive skill humans share with other primates that enables us to find common threads in disparate information, such as seeking underlying rules for language.

Peripheral nervous system (PNS) All elements of the nervous system outside the skull and spinal cord.

Phone Actual produced speech sound.

Phoneme Smallest linguistic unit of sound, each with distinctive features, that can signal a difference in meaning when modified.

Phonemic awareness An aspect of phonological awareness, phonemic awareness is the specific ability to manipulate sounds, such as blending sounds to create new words or segmenting words into sounds.

Phonetically consistent forms (PCFs) Consistent vocal patterns that accompany gestures prior to the appearance of words.

Phonics Sound–letter or phoneme–grapheme relationship; the primary way in which most children are taught to read.

Phonological awareness Consideration of phonology at a conscious level, including syllabification; sound identification, manipulation, segmentation, and blending; rhyming; and alliteration. A metalingistic skill, phonological awareness is necessary for the development of reading.

Phonology Aspect of language concerned with the rules governing the structure, distribution, and sequencing of speech-sound patterns.

Phonotactic probability The likelihood of phonemes appearing together and/or in certain locations in words.

Phonotactic regularities Phonemes, phoneme combinations, and syllable structures typical of the native language and noticed by young children.

Phrasal coordination Process of conjoining clauses and deleting common elements.

Phrase Group of words that does not contain a subject or predicate and is used as a noun substitute or as a noun or verb modifier.

Pivot schemas Two-word utterances in which one word or phrase, such as *want* or *more*, seems to structure the utterance by determining the intent of the utterance as a whole, such as a demand. In many of these early utterances one event-word is used with a wide variety of object labels as in *More cookie, More juice,* and *More apple*.

Pragmatics Aspect of language concerned with language use within a communication context.

Preemption A pattern-finding technique that accounts for how children confine abstractions about language based on the notion that if someone communicates to me using one form, rather than another, there was a reason for that choice related to the speaker's specific communicative intention.

Prefrontal cortex Most anterior or forward portion of the frontal lobe of the brain.

Presupposition Process of assuming which information a listener possesses or may need.

Priming When a sentence produced by one speaker influences the sentences of a second speaker even though the second speaker's productions do not contain the same words or semantic themes.

Print awareness Knowledge of letters and words, ability to identify some letters by name, and knowledge of the way in which words progress through a book.

Protoconversation Vocal interactions between mothers and infants that resemble the verbal exchanges of more mature conversations.

Prototypic complex hypothesis Theory that word meanings represent an underlying concept exemplified by a central referent, or prototype, that is a best exemplar or a composite of the concept.

Quasi-resonant nuclei (QRN) Partial resonance of speech sounds found in neonates.

Recount A type of narrative that relates past experiences of which the child and the listener partook, observed, or read.

References

Abbot-Smith, K., & Tomasello, M. (2006). Exemplar-learning and schematization in a usage-based account of syntactic acquisition. *The Linguistic Review, 23*, 275–290.

Abraham, L. M., Crais, E., Vernon-Feagans, L., & the Family Life Project Phase 1 Key Investigators. (2013). Early maternal language use during book sharing in families from low-income environments. *American Journal of Speech-Language Pathology, 22*, 71–83.

Abu-Akel, A., Bailey, A. L., & Thum, Y. (2004). Describing the acquisition of determiners in English: A growth modeling approach. *Journal of Psycholinguistic Research, 33*, 407–424.

Abu-Rabia, S., & Siegel, L. S. (2002). Reading, syntactic, orthographic, and working memory skills of bilingual Arabic-English speaking Canadian children. *Journal of Psycholinguistic Research, 31*, 661–678.

Akhtar, N. (1999). Acquiring basic word order: Evidence for data-driven learning of syntactic structure. *Journal of Child Language*, 26, 339–356.

Akhtar, N., Dunham, F., & Dunham, P. J. (1991). Directive interactions and early vocabulary development: The role of joint attentional focus. *Journal of Child Language, 18*, 41–49.

Akins, M. R., & Biederer, T. (2006). Cell–cell interactions in synaptogenesis. *Current Opinion in Neurobiology, 16*, 83–89.

Alcamo, E. A., Chiriella, L., Dautzenberg, M., Dobreva, G., Fariñas, I., Grosschedl, R., et al. (2008). Satb2 regulates callosal projection neuron identity in the developing cerebral cortex. *Neuron, 57*, 364–377.

Alexander, D., Wetherby, A., & Prizant, B. (1997). The emergence of repair strategies in infants and toddlers. *Seminars in Speech and Language, 18*, 197–213.

Allen, K., Filippini, E., Johnson, M., Kanuck, A., Kroecker, J., Loccisano, S., Lyle, K., Nieto, J., Feenaughty, L., Sligar, C., Wind, K., Young, S., & Owens, R. E. (2010). Noun phrase elaboration in children's language samples. GREAT Day presentation. SUNY Geneseo, Geneseo, NY.

Allen, S., Genesee, F., Fish, S., & Crago, M. (2002). Patterns of code-mixing in English-Inuktitut bilinguals. In M. Andronis, C. Ball, H. Elston, & S. Neuvel (Eds.), *Proceedings of the 37th Annual Meeting of the Chicago Linguistics Society* (Vol. 2, pp. 171–188). Chicago, IL: Chicago Linguistics Society.

Alloway, T. P. (2009). Working memory, but not IQ, predicts subsequent learning in children with learning difficulties. *European Journal of Psychological Assessment, 25*, 92–98.

Alloway, T. P., & Alloway, R. C. (2010). Investigating the predictive roles of working memory and IQ in academic attainment. *Journal of Experimental Child Psychology, 106*, 20–29.

Alloway, T. P., Gathercole, S. E., Adams, A. M., Willis, C., Eaglen, R., & Lamont, E. (2005). Working memory and other cognitive skills as predictors of progress toward early learning goals at school entry. *British Journal of Developmental Psychology, 23*, 417–426.

Alloway, T. P., Gathercole, S. E., Kirkwood, H., & Elliott, J. (2009). The Working Memory Rating Scale: A classroom-based behavioral assessment of working memory. *Learning and Individual Differences, 19*, 242–245.

Amayreh, M. M. (2003). Completion of the consonant inventory of Arabic. *Journal of Speech, Language, and Hearing Research, 46*, 517–529.

Amayreh, M. M., & Dyson, A. T. (1998). The acquisition of Arabic consonants. *Journal of Speech, Language, and Hearing Research, 41*, 642–653.

Amedi, A., Stern, W. M., Camprodon, J. A., Bermpohl, F., Merabet, L., Rotman, S., et al. (2007). Shape conveyed by visual-to-auditory sensory substitution activates the lateral occipital complex. *Nature Neuroscience, 10*, 687–689.

Anderson, E. (1992). *Speaking with style: The sociolinguistic skills of children*. London, England: Routledge.

Anglin, J. M. (1993). Vocabulary development: A morphological analysis. *Monographs of the Society for Research in Child Development, 58*, 10.

Anglin, J. M. (1995a). Classifying the world through language: Functional relevance, cultural significance, and category name learning. *International Journal of Intercultural Relations, 19*, 161–181.

Anglin, J. M. (1995b, April). *Word knowledge and the growth of potentially knowable vocabulary*. Paper presented at the biennial meeting of the Society for Research in Child Development, Indianapolis, IN.

Apel, K. (2010). Kindergarten children's initial spoken and written word learning in a storybook context. *Scientific Studies in Reading, 14*(5), 440–463.

Apel, K. (2011). What Is orthographic knowledge? *Language, Speech, and Hearing Services in Schools*, 42, 592–603.

Apel, K., & Masterson, J. (2001). Theory-guided spelling assessment and intervention: A case study. *Language, Speech, and Hearing Services in Schools, 32*, 182–194.

Apel, K., Thomas-Tate, S., Wilson-Fowler, E. B., & Brimo, D. (2012). Acquisition of initial mental graphemic representations by children at risk for literacy development. *Applied Psycholinguistics, 33*(2), 365–391.

Apel, K., Wolter, J. A., & Masterson, J. J. (2006). Effects of phonotactic and orthotactic probabilities during fast-mapping on five-year-olds' learning to spell. *Developmental Neuropsychology, 29*(1), 21–42.

Aslin, R. A. (1999, April). *Utterance-final bias in word recognition by eight-month-olds*. Poster session presented at the biennial meeting of the Society for Research in Child Development, Albuquerque, NM.

Aslin, R. N. (1992). Segmentation of fluent speech into words: Learning models and the role of maternal input. In B. deBoysson-Bardies, S. DeSchonen, P. Jusczyk, P. MacNeilage, & J. Morton (Eds.), *Developmental neurocognition: Speech and face processing in the first year of life*. Dordrecht: Kluwer.

Aslin, R. N., Saffran, J. R., & Newport, E. L. (1998). Computation of conditional probability statistics by 8-month-old infants. *Psychological Science, 9*, 321–324.

Astington, J. W. (2003). Sometimes necessary, never sufficient: False belief understanding and social competence. In B. Repacholi & V. Slaughter (Eds.), *Individual differences in Theory of Mind: Implications for typical and atypical development*. New York, NY: Psychology Press.

Astington, J. W., & Jenkins, J. (1995). Theory of mind development and social understanding. *Cognition and Emotion, 9*, 151–165.

Astington, J. W., & Jenkins, J. (1999). A longitudinal study of the relation between language and theory of mind development. *Developmental Psychology, 35*, 1311–1320.

Atanassova, M. (2001). On the acquisition of temporal conjunctions in Finnish. *Journal of Psycholinguistic Research, 30*, 115–134.

Au, K. (1990). Children's use of information in word learning. *Journal of Child Language, 17*, 393–416.

Axtell, R. E. (1991). *Gestures: The do's and taboos of body language around the world*. Baltimore, MD: Wiley.

Backus, A. (1999). Mixed native language: A challenge to the monolithic view of language. *Topics in Language Disorders, 19*(4), 11–22.

Baddeley, A. (1996). Exploring the central executive. *The Quarterly Journal of Experimental Psychology, 49*, 5–28.

Baddeley, A. (2000). The episodic buffer: New component of working memory? *Trends in Cognitive Sciences, 4*, 417–423.

Baddeley, A. (2003). Working memory and language: An overview. *Journal of Communication Disorders, 36*, 189–208.

Baddeley, A. D. (1986). *Working memory*. Oxford, United Kingdom: Oxford University Press.

Baddeley, A. D. (1992). Is working memory working? The fifteenth Bartlett lecture. *Quarterly Journal of Experimental Psychology, 44*, 1–31.

Baddeley, A. D. (2000). Short-term and working memory. In E. Tulving & F. I. M. Craik (Eds.), *The Oxford handbook of memory* (pp. 77–92). Oxford, United Kingdom: Oxford University Press.

Baddeley, A. D., Gathercole, S. E., & Papagno, C. (1998). The phonological loop as a language learning device. *Psychological Review, 105*, 158–173.

Bahr, R. H., Silliman, E. R., & Berninger, V. W. (2009). What spelling errors have to tell about vocabulary learning. In C. Wood & V. Connelly (Eds.), *Reading and spelling: Contemporary perspectives* (pp. 109–129). New York, NY: Routledge.

Baker, C. L., & McCarthy, J. J. (1981). *The logical problem of language acquisition*. Cambridge, MA: MIT Press.

Baker, E., Croot, K., McLeod, S., & Paul, R. (2001). Psycholinguistic models of speech development and their application to clinical practice. *Journal of Speech, Language, and Hearing Research, 44,* 685–702.

Balsamo, L. M., Xu, B., Grandin, C. B., Petrella, J. R., Braniecki, S. H., & Elliott T. K., et al. (2002). A functional magnetic resonance imaging study of left hemisphere language dominance in children. *Archives of Neurology,* 59, 1168–74.

Bara, F., Gentaz, E., & Cole, P. (2007). Haptics in learning to read with children from low socioeconomic status families. *British Journal of Developmental Psychology, 25*(4), 643–663.

Baratz, J. C. (1969). A bi-dialectal task for determining language proficiency in economically disadvantaged Negro children. *Child Development, 40,* 889–901.

Barker, J., Nicol, J., & Garrett, M. (2001). Semantic factors in the production of number agreement. *Journal of Psycholinguistic Research, 30,* 91–114.

Barsalou, L. W., Simmons, W. K., Barbey, A. K., & Wilson, C. D. (2003). Grounding conceptual knowledge in modality-specific systems. *Trends in Cognitive Science, 7,* 84–91.

Bates, E. (1976). *Language and context: The acquisition of pragmatics*. New York, NY: Academic Press.

Bates, E. (1997). On the nature and nurture of language. In E. Bizzi, P. Catissano, & V. Volterra (Eds.), *Frontiers of biology: The brain of* Homo sapiens. Rome, Italy: Giovanni Trecani.

Bates, E. (2003). On the nature and nurture of language. In R. Levi-Montalcini, D. Baltimore, R. Dulbecco, F. Jacob, E. Bizzi, P. Calissano, & V. Volterra (Eds.), *Frontiers of biology: The brain of* Homo sapiens (pp. 241–265). Rome, Italy: Istituto della Enciclopedia Italiana fondata da Giovanni Trecanni.

Bates, E., Camaioni, L., & Volterra, V. (1975). The acquisition of performatives prior to speech. *Merrill-Palmer Quarterly, 21,* 205–216.

Bates, E., Marchman, V., Thal, D., Fenson, L., Dale, P., Reznick, J., Reilly, J., & Hartung, J. (1994). Developmental and stylistic variation in the composition of early vocabulary. *Journal of Child Language, 21,* 85–123.

Bauer, D. J., Goldfield, B. A., & Reznick, J. S. (2002). Alternative approaches to analyzing individual differences in the rate of early vocabulary development. *Applied Psycholinguistics, 23,* 313–335.

Bavin, E. L., Prior, M., Reilly, S., Bretherton, L., Williams, J., Eadie, P., Barrett, Y., & Ukoumunne, O. C. (2008). The Early Language in Victoria Study: Predicting vocabulary at age one and two years from gesture and object use. *Journal of Child Language, 35,* 687–701.

Bayliss, D., Jarrold, C., Baddeley, A., Gunn, D., & Leigh, E. (2005). Mapping the developmental constraints on working memory span performance. *Developmental Psychology, 41,* 579–597.

Beckman, M., & Edwards, J. (2000). The ontogeny of phonological categories and the primacy of lexical learning in linguistic development. *Child Development, 71,* 240–249.

Bedore, L., & Leonard, L. B. (2000). The effects of inflectional variation on fast mapping of verbs in English and Spanish. *Journal of Speech, Language, and Hearing Research, 43,* 21–33.

Beebe, B., Badalamenti, A., Jaffe, J., Feldstein, S., Marquette, L., Helbraun, E., Demetri-Friedman, D., Flaster, C., Goodman, P., Kaminer, T., Kaufman-Balamuth, L., Putterman, J., Stepakoff, S., & Ellman, L. (2008). Distressed mothers and their infants use a less efficient timing mechanism in creating expectancies of each other's looking patterns. *Journal of Psycholinguistic Research, 37,* 293–308.

Behrens, H. (1998). *Where does the information go?* Paper presented at MPI workshop on argument structure. Nijmegen, the Netherlands.

Bencini, G. M. L., & Valian, V. V. (2008). Abstract sentence representations in 3-year-olds: Evidence from language production and comprehension. *Journal of Memory and Language, 59,* 97–113.

Benedict, H. (1979). Early lexical development: Comprehension and production. *Journal of Child Language, 6,* 183–200.

Benelli, B., Belacchi, C., Gini, G., & Lucangeli, D. (2006). "To define means to say what you know about things": The development of definitional skills as metalinguistic acquisition. *Journal of Child Language, 33*, 71–97.

Benigno, J. P., Clark, L., & Farrar, M. J. (2007). Three is not always a crowd: Contexts of joint attention and language. *Journal of Child Language, 34*, 175–187.

Berman, R. A. (1982). Verb-pattern alternation: The interface of morphology, syntax, and semantics in Hebrew child language. *Journal of Child Language, 9*, 169–91.

Berman, R. A. (1986). A crosslinguistic perspective: Morphology and syntax. In P. Fletcher & M. Garman (Eds.), *Language acquisition* (2nd ed.). New York, NY: Cambridge University Press.

Berman, R. A., Ragnarsdöttir, H., & Strömqvist, S. (2002). Discourse stance. *Written Language and Literacy, 5*, 255–291.

Berman, R. A., & Verhoeven, L. (2002). Cross-linguistic perspectives on the development of text-production abilities: Speech and writing. *Written Language and Literacy, 5*(1), 1–43.

Berninger, V. W. (2000). Development of language by hand and its connections with language by ear, mouth, and eye. *Topics in Language Disorders, 20*(4), 65–84.

Berninger, V. W., Abbott, R. D., Billingsley, F., & Nagy, W. (2001). Processes underlying timing and fluency of reading: Efficiency, automaticity, coordination, and morphological awareness. In M. Worf (Ed.), *Dyslexia, fluency, and the brain* (pp. 383–413). Timonium, MD: York.

Berninger, V. W., Abbott, R. D., Nagy, W., & Carlisle, J. (2010). Growth in phonological, orthographic, and morphological awareness in grades 1 to 6. *Journal of Psycholinguistic Research, 39*, 141–164.

Berninger, V. W., Cartwright, A., Yates, C., Swanson, H. L., & Abbott, R. (1994). Developmental skills related to writing and reading acquisition in the intermediate grades: Shared and unique variance. *Reading and Writing: An Interdisciplinary Journal, 6*, 161–196.

Berninger, V. W., Garcia, N. P., & Abbott, R. D. (2009). Multiple processes that matter in writing instruction and assessment. In G. A. Troia (Ed.), *Instruction and assessment for struggling writers: Evidence-based practices* (pp. 15–74). New York, NY: Guilford.

Beyer, T., & Hudson Kam, C. L. (2009). Some cues are stronger than others: The (non)interpretation of 3rd person present *-s* as a tense marker by 6- and 7-year-olds. *First Language, 29*, 208–227.

Bialystock, E. (2001). *Bilingualism in development: Language, literacy, and cognition.* New York, NY: Cambridge University Press.

Biber, D. (1995). *Dimensions of register variation: A crosslinguistic comparison.* Cambridge, United Kingdom: Cambridge University Press.

Bickerton, D. (2003). Symbol and structure: A comprehensive framework. In M. H. Christiansen & S. Kirby (Eds.), *Language evolution* (pp. 77–93). Oxford, United Kingdom: Oxford University Press.

Birdsong, D., & Molis, M. (2001). On the evidence for maturational constraints in second-language acquisition. *Journal of Memory and Language, 44*, 235–249.

Blake, J., & deBoysson-Bardies, B. (1992). Patterns of babbling: A cross-linguistic study. *Journal of Child Language, 19*, 51–74.

Bland-Stewart, L. M. (2003). Phonetic inventories and phonological patterns of African American 2-year-olds: A preliminary investigation. *Communication Disorders Quarterly, 24*, 109–112.

Blaye, A., & Bonthoux, F. (2001). Thematic and taxonomic relations in preschoolers: The development of flexibility in categorization choices. *British Journal of Developmental Psychology, 19*, 395–412.

Bleses, D., Vach, W., Slott, M., Wehberg, S., Thomsen, P., Madsen, T. O., & Basbøll, H. (2008). Early vocabulary development in Danish and other languages: A CDI-based comparison. *Journal of Child Language, 35*, 619–650. doi:10.1017/S0305000908008714.

Bliss, L. S. (1992). A comparison of tactful messages by children with and without language impairment. *Language, Speech, and Hearing Services in Schools, 23*, 343–347.

Bliss, L. S., & McCabe, A. (2008). Personal narratives: Cultural differences and clinical implications. *Topics in Language Disorders, 28*, 162–177.

Blom-Hoffman, J., O'Neil-Pirozzi, T. M., Volpe, R., Cutting, J., & Bissinger, E. (2006). Instructing parents to use dialogic reading strategies with preschool children: Impact of a video-based training program on caregiver reading behaviors and children's related verbalizations. *Journal of Applied School Psychology, 23*, 117–131.

Bloom, L. (1973). *One word at a time: The use of single-word utterances before syntax*. The Hague, the Netherlands: Mouton.

Bloom, L. (1983). Of continuity, nature, and magic. In R. Golinkoff (Ed.), *The transition from preverbal to verbal communication*. Hillsdale, NJ: Erlbaum.

Bloom, L. (1993). *The transition from infancy to language: Acquiring the power of expression*. Cambridge, MA: Cambridge University Press.

Bloom, P. (1990). Subjectless sentences in child language. *Linguistic Inquiry, 21*, 491–504.

Bloom, P. (2000). *How children learn the meanings of words*. Cambridge, MA: MIT Press.

Bloome, D., Katz, L., & Champion, T. (2003). Young children's narratives and ideologies of language in classrooms. *Reading & Writing Quarterly, 19*, 205–223.

Bock, J. K., & Griffin, Z. M. (2000). The persistence of structural priming: Transient activation or implicit learning? *Journal of Experimental Psychology: General, 129*, 177–192.

Bohman, T., Bedore, L. M., Peña, E. D., Mendez-Perez, A., & Gillam, R. B. (2010). What they hear and what they say: Language performance in young Spanish–English bilinguals. *International Journal of Bilingualism and Bilingual Education, 13*, 325–344.

Bookheimer, S. (2002). Functional MRI of language: New approaches for understanding the cortical organization of semantic processing. *Annual Reviews of Neuroscience, 25*, 151–168.

Booth, J. R., MacWhinney, B., Thulborn, K. R., Sacco, K., Voyvodic, J., & Feldman, H. (1999). Functional organization of activation patterns in children: Whole brain fMRI imaging during three different cognitive tasks. *Progress in Neuropsychopharmocology and Biological Psychiatry, 23*, 669–682.

Bornstein, M. H., Cote, L. R., Maital, S., Painter, K., Park, S., Pascual, L., Pêcheux, M., Ruel, J., Venuti, P., & Vyt, A. (2004). Cross-linguistic analysis of vocabulary in young children: Spanish, Dutch, French, Hebrew, Italian, Korean, and American English. *Child Development, 75*, 1115–1139.

Bornstein, M. H., Haynes, O. M., Painter, K. M., & Genevro, J. L. (2000). Child language with mother and with stranger at home and in the laboratory: A methodological study. *Journal of Child Language, 27*, 407–420.

Bornstein, M. H., & Hendricks, C. (2012). Basic language comprehension and production in >100,000 young children from sixteen developing nations. *Journal of Child Language, 39*, 899–918.

Bornstein, M. H., Painter, K. M., & Park, J. (2002). Naturalistic language sampling in typically developing children. *Journal of Child Language, 29*,687–699.

Bortfeld, H., Morgan, J. L., Golinkoff, R. M., & Rathbun, K. (2005). Mommy and me: Familiar names help launch babies into speech-stream segmentation. *Psychological Science, 16*, 298–304.

Bosch, L., & Sebastián-Gallés, N. (1997). Native-language recognition abilities in 4-month-old infants from monolingual and bilingual environment. *Cognition, 65*, 33–69.

Boswell, S. (2006, January 17). Signs from the desert. *The ASHA Leader, 11*(1), 12.

Bourgeois, J.-P., Goldman-Rakic, P. S., & Rakic, P. (1999). Formation, elimination, and stabilization of synapses in the primate cerebral cortex. In M. S. Gazzaniga (Ed.), *The new cognitive neurosciences* (pp. 45–53). Cambridge, MA: MIT Press.

Bowerman, M. (1981). *The child's expression of meaning: Expanding relationships among lexicon, syntax and morphology*. Paper presented at the New York Academy of Science Conference on Native Language and Foreign Language Acquisition, New York, NY.

Bowerman, M. (1988). The "no negative evidence" problem. In J. Hawkins (Ed.), *Explaining language universals* (pp. 73–104). London, England: Blackwell.

Bowerman, M. (1993). Learning a semantic system: What role do cognitive predispositions play? In P. Bloom (Ed.), *Language acquisition: Core readings*. Cambridge, MA: MIT Press.

Bradley, R. H., & Corwyn, R. F. (2002). Socioeconomic status and child development. *Annual Review of Psychology, 53*, 371–399.

Brent, M. R., & Siskind, J. M. (2001). The role of exposure to isolated words in early vocabulary development. *Cognition, 81*, B33–B44.

Bretherton, I. (1984). Representing the social world in symbolic play: Reality and fantasy. In I. Bretherton (Ed.), *Symbolic play: The development of social understanding*. New York, NY: Academic Press.

Brown, C. M., van Berkum, J. J. A., & Hagoort, P. (2000). Discourse before gender: An event-related brain potential study on the interplay of semantic and syntactic information during spoken language understanding. *Journal of Psycholinguistic Research, 29*, 53–68.

Brown, R. (1973). *A first language: The early stages.* Cambridge, MA: Harvard University Press.

Bruer, J. T. (2001). A critical and sensitive period primer. In D. Ailer Jr., J. T. Bruer, F. J. Symons, & J. W. Lichtman (Eds.), *Critical thinking about critical periods* (pp. 3–26). Baltimore, MD: Brookes.

Bruner, J. (1975). The ontogenesis of speech acts. *Journal of Child Language, 2*, 1–19.

Bruner, J. (1977). Early social interaction and language acquisition. In R. Schaffer (Ed.), *Studies in mother–infant interaction.* New York, NY: Academic Press.

Bruner, J. (1983). *Child's talk.* New York, NY: Norton.

Buhl, H. M. (2002). Partner orientation and speaker's knowledge as conflicting parameters in language production. *Journal of Psycholinguistic Research, 30*, 549–567.

Bull, R., & Scerif, G. (2001). Executive functioning as a predictor of children's mathematics ability: Shifting, inhibition, and working memory. *Developmental Neuropsychology, 19*, 273–293.

Butterworth, G. (2003). Pointing is the royal road to language for babies. In S. Kita (Ed.), *Pointing: Where language, culture, and cognition meet* (pp. 9–33). Mahwah, NJ: Erlbaum.

Bybee, J. (1995). Regular morphology and the lexicon. *Language and Cognitive Processes, 10*, 425–455.

Bybee, J. (2002). Word frequency and context of use in the lexical diffusion of phonetically conditioned sound change. *Language Variation and Change*, 14, 261–290.

Caccamise, D., & Snyder, L. (2005). Theory and pedagogical practices of text comprehension. *Topics in Language Disorders, 25*(1), 1–20.

Cain, K., & Towse, A. S. (2008). To get hold of the wrong end of the stick: Reasons for poor idiom understanding in children with reading comprehension difficulties. *Journal of Speech, Language, and Hearing Research, 51*, 1538–1549.

Cain, K., Oakhill, J., & Bryant, P. (2004). Children's reading comprehension ability: Concurrent prediction by working memory, verbal ability, and component skills. *Journal of Educational Psychology, 96*, 31–42.

Cain, K., Patson, N., & Andrews, L. (2005). Age- and ability-related differences in young readers' use of conjunctions. *Journal of Child Language, 32*, 877–892.

Calkins, S. D., Hungerford, A., & Dedmon, S. E. (2004). Mothers' interactions with temperamentally frustrated infants. *Infant Mental Health Journal, 25*, 219–239.

Cameron-Faulkner, T., Lieven, E., & Tomasello, M. (2003). A construction based analysis of child directed speech. *Cognitive Science, 27*, 843–873.

Campbell, A., & Tomasello, M. (2001). The acquisition of English dative constructions. *Applied Psycholinguistics, 22*, 253–267.

Capilouto, G. J., Wright, H. H., & Wagovich, S. A. (2005). CIU and main event analysis of the structured discourse of older and younger adults. *Journal of Communication Disorders, 38*, 431–444.

Caplan, D. (2001). Functional neuroimaging studies of syntactic processing. *Journal of Psycholinguistic Research, 30*, 297–320.

Capone, N. C. (2007). Tapping toddlers' evolving semantic representation via gesture. *Journal of Speech, Language, and Hearing Research, 50*, 732–745.

Capone, N. C., & McGregor, K. K. (2004). Gesture development: A review for clinical and research practices. *Journal of Speech, Language, and Hearing Research, 47*, 173–186.

Carrell, P. (1981). Children's understanding of indirect requests: Comparing child and adult comprehension. *Journal of Child Language, 8*, 329–345.

Celinska, D. K. (2009). Narrative voices of early adolescents: Influences of learning disability and cultural background. *International Journal of Special Education, 24*, 150–172.

Chaffin, R., Morris, R., & Seeley, R. (2001). Learning new meanings from context: A study of eye movement. *Journal of Experimental Psychology, 27*, 225–235.

Chaigneau, S. E., & Barsalou, L. W. (in press). *The role of function in categorization.* Theoria et Historia Scientiarum.

Champion, T. B. (1998). "Tell me somethin' good": A description of narrative structures among

African American children. *Linguistics and Education, 9*(3), 251–286.

Chan, A., Lieven, E., & Tomasello, M. (2009). Children's understanding of the agent–patient relations in the transitive construction: Cross-linguistic comparisons between Cantonese, German, and English. *Cognitive Linguistics, 20*, 267–300.

Chan, Y.-L., & Marinellie, S. A. (2008). Definitions of idioms in preadolescents, adolescents, and adults. *Journal of Psycholinguistic Research, 37*, 1–20.

Chapman, S. B., Zientz, J., Weiner, M., Rosenberg, R., Frawley, W., & Burns, M. H. (2002). Discourse changes in early Alzheimer' disease, mild cognitive impairment, and normal aging. *Alzheimer Disease and Associated Disorders, 16*, 177–186.

Charity, A. H., Scarborough, H. S., & Griffin, D. M. (2004). Familiarity with school English in African American children and its relation to early reading achievement. *Child Development, 75*, 1340–1356.

Chen, L., & Kent, R. D. (2005). Consonant–vowel co-occurrence patterns in Mandarin-learning infants. *Journal of Child Language, 32*, 507–534.

Cheng, L. (1987, June). Cross-cultural and linguistic considerations in working with Asian populations. *ASHA, 29*(6), 33–38.

Childers, J. B., & Paik, J. H. (2009). Korean- and English-speaking children use cross-situational information to learn novel predicate terms. *Journal of Child Language, 36*, 201–224.

Childers, J. B., Vaughan, J., & Burquest, D. A. (2007). Joint attention and word learning in Ngas-speaking toddlers in Nigeria. *Journal of Child Language, 33*, 199–225.

Chliounaki, K., & Bryant, P. (2007). How children learn about morphological spelling rules. *Child Development, 78*, 1360–1373.

Choi, S. (2000). Caregiver input in English and Korean: Use of nouns and verbs in book-reading and toy-play contexts. *Journal of Child Language, 27*, 69–96.

Chomsky, N. (1965a). *Aspects of the theory of syntax*. Cambridge, MA: MIT Press.

Chomsky, N. (1965b). Three models for the description of language. In R. Luce, R. Bush, & E. Galanter (Eds.), *Readings in mathematical psychology* (Vol. II, pp. 105–124). New York, NY: Wiley.

Chomsky, N. (1980). Rules and representations. *Behavioral and Brain Sciences, 3*, 1–61.

Chouinard, M. M., & Clark, E. V. (2003). Adult reformulations of child errors as negative evidence. *Journal of Child Language, 30*, 637–669.

Christiansen, M. H., & Charter, N. (1999). Toward a connectionist model of recursion in human linguistic performance. *Cognitive Science, 23*(2), 157–205.

Clahsen, H., Aveledo, F., & Roca, I. (2002). The development of regular and irregular verb inflection in Spanish child language. *Journal of Child Language, 29*, 591–622.

Clancy, P. M. (2000). *Exceptional casemarking in Korean acquisition: A discourse-functional account.* Paper presented at Conceptual Structure, Discourse, and Language Conference, University of California, Santa Barbara.

Clark, E. V. (1978). Awareness of language: Some evidence from what children say and do. In A. Sinclair, R. Jarvella, & W. Levelt (Eds.), *The child's conception of language*. New York, NY: Springer-Verlag.

Clark, E. V., & Bernicot, J. (2008). Repetition as ratification: How parents and children place information in common ground. *Journal of Child Language, 35*, 349–371.

Cleave, P. L., & Kay-Raining Bird, E. (2006). Effects of familiarity on mothers' talk about nouns and verbs. *Journal of Child Language, 33*, 661–676.

Clopper, C., & Pisoni, D. (2004). Some acoustic cues for the perceptual categorization of American English dialects. *Journal of Phonetics, 32*, 111–140.

Coady, J. A., & Aslin, R. N. (2003). Phonological neighborhoods in the developing lexicon. *Journal of Child Language, 30*, 441–469.

Colombo, J., Shaddy, D. J., Richman, W. A., Maikranz, J. M., & Blaga, O. M. (2004). The developmental course of habituation in infancy and preschool outcome. *Infancy, 5*, 1–38.

Comeau, L., Genesee, F., & Mendelson, M. (2007). Bilingual children's repairs of breakdowns in communication. *Journal of Child Language, 34*, 159–174.

Committee on Language, American Speech-Language-Hearing Association. (1983). Definition of language. *ASHA, 25*, 44.

Connor, C. M., Morrison, F. J., Fishman, B. J., Schatschneider, C., & Underwood, P. (2007,

January 26). The early years: Algorithm-guided individualized reading instruction. *Science, 315*, 464–465.

Connor, C. M., Son, S. H., Hindman, A., & Morrison, F. J. (2005). Teacher qualifications, classroom practices, and family characteristics: Complex effects on first graders' language and early reading. *Journal of School Psychology, 43*, 343–375.

Cooper, R. P., & Aslin, R. N. (1990). Preference for infant-directed speech in the first month after birth. *Child Development, 61*, 1584–1595.

Coplan, R. J., Barber, A. M., & Lagace-Seguin, D. G. (1999). The role of child temperament as a predictor of early literacy and numeracy skills in preschoolers. *Early Childhood Research Quarterly, 14*, 537–53.

Coulson, A. (1999, August 20). Language is more than words and sentences. Rochester, NY, *Democrat & Chronicle*, p. 8A.

Cowan, N., Nugent, L., Elliott, E., Ponomarev, I., & Saults, S. (2005). The role of attention in the development of short-term memory: Age differences in the verbal span of apprehension. *Child Development, 70*, 1082–1097.

Craig, H. K., Connor, C. M., & Washington, J. A. (2003). Early positive predictors of later reading comprehension for African American students: A preliminary investigation. *Language, Speech, and Hearing Services in Schools, 34*, 31–43.

Craig, H. K., Zhang, L., Hensel, S. L., & Quinn, E. J. (2009). African American English–speaking students: An examination of the relationship between dialect shifting and reading outcomes. *Journal of Speech, Language, and Hearing Research, 52*, 839–855.

Craig, H. K., & Grogger, J. T. (2012). Influences of social and style variables on adult usage of African American English features. *Journal of Speech, Language, and Hearing Research,* 55, 1274–1288.

Cristofaro, T. N., & Tamis-LeMonda, C. S. (2008). Lessons in mother–child and father–child personal narratives in Latino families. In A. McCabe, A. L. Bailey, & G. Melzi (Eds.), *Spanish-language narration and literacy: Culture, cognition and emotion* (pp. 54–91). New York, NY: Cambridge University Press.

Crnic, K. A., & Low, C. (2002). Everyday stresses and parenting. In M. Bornstein (Ed.), *Handbook of parenting: Volume 5, Practical issues in parenting* (2nd ed., pp. 243–268). Mahwah, NJ: Erlbaum.

Crown, C. L., Feldstein, S., Jasnow, M. D., Beebe, B., & Jaffe, J. (2002). The cross-modal coordination of interpersonal timing: Six-week-old infants' gaze with adults' vocal behavior. *Journal of Psycholinguistic Research, 31*, 1–23.

Cupples, L., & Iacono, T. (2000). Phonological awareness and oral reading skill in children with Down syndrome. *Journal of Speech, Language, and Hearing Research, 43*, 595–608.

Curtin, S. (2009). Twelve-month-olds learn novel word–object pairings differing only in stress pattern. *Journal of Child Language, 36*, 1157–1165.

Cutting, J., & Ferriera, V. (1999). Semantic and phonological information flow in the production lexicon. *Journal of Experimental Psychology: Learning, Memory, and Cognition, 25*, 318–344.

Dąbrowska, E. (2000). From formula to schema: The acquisition of English questions. *Cognitive Linguistics, 11*(1/2), 83–102.

Dąbrowska, E., & Lieven, E. (2005). Towards a lexically specific grammar of children's question constructions. *Cognitive Linguistics, 16*(3), 437–474.

Dale, P. S., & Crain-Thoreson, C. (1993). Pronoun reversals: Who, when, & why? *Journal of Child Language, 20*, 573–589.

Dale, P. S., & Goodman, J. (2005). Commonality and individual differences in vocabulary growth. In M. Tomasello & D. I. Slobin (Eds.), *Beyond nature-nurture: Essays in honor of Elizabeth Bates* (pp. 41–78). Mahwah, NJ: Erlbaum.

Davidson, D. J., Zacks, R. T., & Ferreira, F. (2003). Age preservation of the syntactic processor in production. *Journal of Psycholinguistic Research, 32*, 541–566.

Daw, N. W. (1997). Critical periods and strabismus: What questions remain? *Optometry and Vision Science, 74*, 690–694.

de Villiers, J. (2001). Continuity and modularity in language acquisition and research. *Annual Review of Language Acquisition, 1*, 1–64.

de Villiers, J., & Johnson, V. E. (2007). The information in third-person /s/: Acquisition across dialects of American English. *Journal of Child Language, 34*(1), 133–158.

Deacon, S. H., & Kirby, J. R. (2004). Morphological awareness: Just "more phonological"? The roles of morphological and phonological awareness in reading development. *Applied Psycholinguistics, 25*, 223–238.

Deacon, S. H., LeBlanc, D., & Sabourin, C. (2011). When cues collide: Children's sensitivity to letter- and meaning-patterns in spelling words in English. *Journal of Child Language, 38*, 809–827.

Dean Qualls, C., O'Brien, R. M., Blood, G. W., & Scheffner Hammer, C. (2003). Contextual variation, familiarity, academic literacy, and rural adolescents' idiom knowledge. *Language, Speech, and Hearing Services in Schools, 34*, 69–79.

Delage, H., & Tuller, L. (2007). Language development and mild-to-moderate hearing loss: Does language normalize with age? *Journal of Speech, Language, and Hearing Research, 50*, 1300–1313.

DeThorne, L. S., Petrill, S. A., Hart, S. A., Channell, R. W., Campbell, R. J., Deater-Deckard, K., Thompson, L. A., & Vandenbergh, D. J. (2008). Genetic effects on children's conversational language use. *Journal of Speech, Language, and Hearing Research, 51*, 423–435.

Devescovi, A., Caselli, C. M., Marchione, D., Pasqualetti, P., Reilly, J., & Bates, E. (2005). A crosslinguistic study of the relationship between grammar and lexical development. *Journal of Child Language, 32*, 759–786.

Devous, M. D., Altuna, D., Furl, N., Cooper, W., Gabbert, G., Ngai, W. T., Chiu, S., Scott, J. M., Harris, T. S., Payne, J. K., & Tobey, E. A. (2006). Maturation of speech and language functional neuroanatomy in pediatric normal controls. *Journal of Speech, Language, and Hearing Research, 49*, 856–866.

Diessel, H. (2004). *The acquisition of complex sentences*. Cambridge, MA: Cambridge University Press.

Diessel, H., & Tomasello, M. (2001). The acquisition of finite complement clauses in English: A corpus-based analysis. *Cognitive Linguistics, 12*, 1–45

Dionne, G., Dale, P. S., Boivin, M., & Plomin, R. (2003). Genetic evidence for bidirectional effects of early lexical and grammatical development. *Child Development 74*, 394–412.

Dodd, B., & Carr, A. (2003). Young children's letter-sound knowledge. *Language, Speech, and Hearing Services in Schools, 34*, 128–137.

Dore, J. (1974). A pragmatic description of early language development. *Journal of Psycholinguistic Research, 3*, 343–350.

Dore, J. (1975, April). Holophrases, speech acts, and language universals. *Journal of Child Language, 2*(1), 33.

Duncan, G. J., & Brooks-Dunn, J. (2000). Family poverty, welfare reform, and child development. *Child Development, 71*, 188–196.

Duong, A., & Ska, B. (2001). Production of narratives: Picture sequence facilitates organizational but not conceptual processing in less educated subjects. *Brain and Cognition, 46*, 121–124.

Durkin, K., & Conti-Ramsden, G. (2007). Language, social behavior, and the quality of friendships in adolescents with and without a history of specific language impairment. *Child Development, 78*, 1441–1457.

Edwards, J., Beckman, M. E., & Munson, B. (2004). The interaction between vocabulary size and phonotactic probability effects on children's production accuracy and fluency in nonword repetition. *Journal of Speech, Language, and Hearing Research, 47*, 421–436.

Ehri, L. C. (2000). Learning to read and learning to spell: Two sides of a coin. *TLD, 20*(3), 19–36.

Elias, G., & Broerse, J. (1996). Developmental changes in the incidence and likelihood of simultaneous talk during the first two years: A question of function. *Journal of Child Language, 23*, 201–217.

Ellis Weismer, S., Evans, J., & Hesketh, L. J. (1999). An examination of verbal working memory capacity in children with specific language impairment. *Journal of Speech, Language, and Hearing Research, 42*, 1249–1260.

Elman, J. L. (1999). Origins of language: A conspiracy theory. In B. MacWhinney (Ed.), *The emergence of language*. Hillsdale, NJ: Erlbaum.

Elman, J. L., Bates, E. A., Johnson, M. H., Karmiloff-Smith, A., Parisi, D., & Plunkett, K. (1996). *Rethinking innateness: A connectionist perspective on development*. Cambridge, MA: MIT Press.

Ely, R., & Berko Gleason, J. (2006). I'm sorry I said that: Apologies in young children's discourse. *Journal of Child Language, 33*, 599–620.

Emmorey, K. (1993). Processing a dynamic visual-spatial language: Psycholinguistic studies of American Sign Language. *Journal of Psycholinguistic Research, 22*, 153–187.

Engel, P. M. J., Santos, F. H., & Gathercole, S. E. (2008). Are working memory measures free of socioeconomic influence? *Journal of Speech, Language, and Hearing Research, 51*, 1580–1587.

Eslea, M. (2002). *Theory of mind,* PS2200 "Virtual Lecture." Retrieved from http://www.uclan.ac.uk/psychology/bully/tom.htm. Last modified August 30, 2002.

Fabiano-Smith, L., & Goldstein, B. A. (2010). Phonological acquisition in bilingual Spanish–English speaking children. *Journal of Speech, Language, and Hearing Research, 53*, 160–178.

Fagan, M. K. (2009). Mean length of utterance before words and grammar: Longitudinal trends and developmental implications of infant vocalizations. *Journal of Child Language, 36*, 495–527.

Farrar, M. J., Friend, M. J., & Forbes, J. N. (1993). Event knowledge and early language acquisition. *Journal of Child Language, 20*, 591–606.

Fasold, R. W., & Wolfram, W. A. (1970). Some dialectal features of Negro dialect. In R. W. Fasold & R. W. Shuy (Eds.), *Teaching standard English in the inner city*. Washington, DC: CAL.

Felser, C., & Clahsen, H. (2009). Grammatical processing of spoken language in child and adult language learners. *Journal of Psycholinguistic Research, 38*, 305–320.

Fennell, C. T., Byers-Heinlein, K., & Werker, J. F. (2007). Using speech sounds to guide word learning: The case of bilingual infants. *Child Development, 78*, 1510–1525.

Fenson, L., Marchman, V., Thal, D., Dale, P., Rezni ck, S. & Bates, E. (2007). *MacArthur-Bates Communicative Development Inventories: User's guide and technical manual* (2nd ed.). Baltimore, MD: Brookes.

Fernald, A., & Mazzie, C. (1991). Prosody and focus in speech to infants and adults. *Developmental Psychology, 27*, 209–21.

Ferrier, S., Dunham, P., & Dunham, F. (2000). The confused robot: Two-year-olds' responses to breakdowns in conversation. *Social Development, 9*, 337–347

Ferry, A. L., Hespos, S. J., & Waxman, S. R. (2010). Categorization in 3- and 4-month-old infants: An advantage of words over tones. *Child Development, 81*, 472–479.

Ferstl, E. C. (2006). Text comprehension in middle aged adults: Is there anything wrong? *Aging, Neuropsychology, and Cognition, 13*, 62–85.

Fiebach, C. J., Schlesewsky, M., & Friedrici, A. D. (2001). Syntactic working memory and the establishment of filler-gap dependencies: Insights from ERPs and FMRI. *Journal of Psycholinguistic Research, 30*, 321–338.

Fitzgerald, C.E., Hadley, P.A, & Rispoli, M. (2013). Are Some Parents' Interaction Styles Associated With Richer Grammatical Input? *American Journal of Speech-Language Pathology*, 22, 476–488.

Flege, J. E., MacKay, I. R., & Meador, D. (1999). Native Italian speakers' perception and production of English vowels. *Journal of Acoustical Society of America, 106*, 2973–2987.

Forbes, J. N., & Poulin-DuBois, D. (1997). Representational change in young children's understanding of familiar verb meaning. *Journal of Child Language, 24*, 389–406.

Fox, R. A., & Nissen, S. L. (2005). Sex-related acoustic changes in voiceless English fricatives. *Journal of Speech, Language, and Hearing Research, 48*, 753–765.

Fox, S. E., Levitt, P., & Nelson, C. A. (2010). How the timing and quality of early experiences influence the development of brain architecture. *Child Development, 81*, 28–40.

Foy, J. G., & Mann, V. (2003). Home literacy environment and phonological awareness in preschool children: Differential effects for rhyme and phoneme awareness. *Applied Psycholinguistics, 24*, 59–88.

Frackowiak, R. S. J., Friston, K. J., Frith, C. D., Dolan, R. J., Price, C. J., Zeki, S. I., et al. (2004). *Human brain function* (2nd ed.). San Diego, CA: Academic Press.

Frazier, B. N., Gelman, S. A., & Wellman, H. M. (2009). Preschoolers' search for explanatory information within adult–child conversation. *Child Development, 80*, 1592–1611.

Frazier, L., Carlson, K., & Clifton, C. (2006). Prosodic phrasing is central to language comprehension. *Trends in Cognitive Science, 10*, 244–249.

Frick, J. E., Colombo, J., & Saxon, T. F. (1999). Individual and developmental differences in disengagement of fixation in early infancy. *Child Development, 70*, 537–548.

Fridriksson, J., Morrow, K. L., Moser, D., & Baylis, G. C. (2006). Age-related variability in cortical activity during language processing. *Journal of Speech, Language, and Hearing Research, 49*, 690–697.

Frieda, E. M., Walley, A. C., Flege, J. E., & Sloane, M. E. (1999). Adults' perception of native and nonnative vowels: Implications for the perceptual magnet effect. *Perception & Psychophysics, 61,* 561–577.

Friederici, A. D. (2001). Syntactic, prosodic, and semantic processes in the brain: Evidence from event-related neuroimaging. *Journal of Psycholinguistic Research, 30,* 237–250.

Friederici, A. D. (2006). The neural basis of language development and its impairment. *Neuron, 52,* 941–952.

Furrow, D., Moore, C., Davidge, J., & Chiasson, L. (1992). Mental terms in mothers' and children's speech: Similarities and relationships. *Journal of Child Language, 19,* 617–631.

Galasso, J. (2003). A note on pedagogy, topics and ways of understanding child language acquisition: A working paper. Retrieved from http://www.csun.edu/~galasso/hoff.htm. Posted 2003.

Gardner, H., & Winner, E. (1979, May). The child is father to the metaphor. *Psychology Today,* 81–91.

Gathercole, S. E. (2006). Nonword repetition and word learning: The nature of the relationship. *Applied Psycholinguistics, 27,* 513–543.

Gathercole, S. E., & Baddeley, A. D. (1993). Phonological working memory: A critical building block for reading development and vocabulary acquisition. *European Journal of Psychology of Education, 8,* 259–272.

Gathercole, S. E., Tiffany, C., Briscoe, J., Thorn, A., & the ALSPAC Team. (2005). Developmental consequences of poor phonological short-term memory function in childhood: A longitudinal study. *Journal of Child Psychology and Psychiatry, 46,* 598–611.

Gathercole, V. (1989). Contrast: A semantic constraint? *Journal of Child Language, 16,* 685–702.

Gavens, N., & Barrouillet, P. (2004). Delays of retention, processing efficiency and attentional resources in working memory span development. *Journal of Memory and Language, 51,* 644–657.

Genesee, F., & Sauve, D. (2000, March 12). *Grammatical constraints on child bilingual code-mixing.* Paper presented at the Annual Conference of the American Association for Applied Linguistics, Vancouver, Canada.

Genesee, F., Paradis, J., & Crago, M. (2004). *Dual language development and disorders.* Baltimore, MD: Brookes.

Gerken, L., & Asline, R. N. (2005). Thirty years of research on infant speech perception: The legacy of Petter W. Jusczyk. *Language Learning and Development, 1,* 5–21.

Gershkoff-Stowe, L., & Hahn, E. R. (2007). Fast mapping skills in the developing lexicon. *Journal of Speech, Language, and Hearing Research, 50,* 682–697.

Gertner, B. L., Rice, M. L., & Hadley, P. A. (1994). Influence of communicative competence on peer preferences in a preschool classroom. *Journal of Speech and Hearing Research, 37,* 913–923.

Ghera, M., Marshall, P., Fox, N., Zeanah, C., Nelson, C. A., & Smyke, A. (2009). Social deprivation and young institutionalized children's attention and expression of positive affect: Effects of a foster care intervention. *Journal of Child Psychology and Psychiatry, 50,* 253–256.

Gildersleeve-Neumann, C., Kester, E., Davis, B., & Peña, E. (2008). English speech sound development in preschool-aged children from bilingual Spanish-English environments. *Language, Speech, and Hearing Services in Schools, 39,* 314–328.

Gillam, R. B., & Gorman, B. K. (2004). Language and discourse contributions to word recognition and text interpretation. In E. R. Silliman & L. C. Wilkinson (Eds.), *Language and literacy learning in schools* (pp. 63–97). New York, NY: Guilford.

Gindis, B. (1999). Language-related issues for international adoptees and adoptive families. In T. Tepper, L. Hannon, & D. Sandstrom (Eds.), *International adoption: Challenges and opportunities* (pp. 98–107). Meadowlands, PA: First Edition.

Girolametto, L., & Weitzman, E. (2002). Responsiveness of child care providers in interactions with toddlers and preschoolers. *Language, Speech, and Hearing Services in Schools, 33,* 268–281.

Girolametto, L., Weitzman, E., van Lieshout, R., & Duff, D. (2000). Directiveness in teachers' language input to toddlers and preschoolers in day care. *Journal of Speech, Language, and Hearing Research, 43,* 1101–1114.

Gleitman, L. R. (1993). The structural sources of verb meanings. In P. Bloom (Ed.), *Language acquisition: Core readings.* Cambridge, MA: MIT Press.

Glennen, S. L. (2007). Predicting language outcomes for internationally adopted children. *Journal of Speech, Language, and Hearing Research, 50,* 529–548.

Glennen, S. L., & Masters, M. G. (2002). Typical and atypical language development in infants and toddlers adopted from Eastern Europe. *American Journal of Speech-Language Pathology, 11,* 417–433.

Glenwright, M., & Pexman, P. M. (2010). Development of children's ability to distinguish sarcasm and verbal irony. *Journal of Child Language, 37*, 429–451.

Glezerman, T. B., & Balkoski, V. (1999). *Language, thought and the brain*. New York, NY: Kluwer.

Goffman, L., Smith, A., Heisler, L., & Ho, M. (2008). The breadth of coarticulatory units in children and adults. *Journal of Speech, Language, and Hearing Research, 51*, 1424–1437.

Gogate, L. J., Bolzani, L. E., & Betancourt, E. (2006). Attention to maternal multimodal naming by 6- to 8-month-old infants and learning of word-object relations. *Infancy, 9*(3), 259–88.

Golberg, H., Paradis, J., & Crago, M. (2008). Lexical acquisition over time in minority L1 children learning English as a L2. *Applied Psycholinguistics, 29*, 1–25.

Goldberg, A. E. (2006). *Constructions at work: The nature of generalization in language*. Oxford, United Kingdom: Oxford University Press.

Golder, C., & Coirier, P. (1994). Argumentative text writing: Developmental trends. *Discourse processes, 18*, 187–210.

Goldfield, B. A. (2000). Nouns before verbs in comprehension vs. production: The view from pragmatics. *Journal of Child Language, 27*, 501–520.

Goldin-Meadow, S. (2003). *Hearing gesture: How our hands help us think*. Cambridge, MA: Harvard University Press.

Goldin-Meadow, S. (2005). *The resilience of language*. New York, NY: Psychology Press.

Goldin-Meadow, S., & Wagner, S. M. (2005). How our hands help us learn. *Trends in Cognitive Sciences, 9*, 234–241.

Goldin-Meadow, S., Nusbaum, H., Kelly, S. D., & Wagner, S. (2001). Explaining math: Gesturing lightens the load. *Psychological Science, 12*, 516–522.

Goldstein, B., & Washington, P. S. (2001). An initial investigation of phonological patterns in typically developing 4-year-old Spanish-English bilingual children. *Language, Speech, and Hearing Services in Schools, 32*, 153–164.

Goldstein, B. A., Fabiano, L., & Swasey Washington, P. (2005). Phonological skills in predominantly English-speaking, predominantly Spanish-speaking, and Spanish-English bilingual children. *Language, Speech, and Hearing Services in Schools, 36*, 201–218.

Goldstein, M. H., Schwade, J. A., & Bornstein, M. H. (2009). The value of vocalizing: Five-month-old infants associate their own noncry vocalizations with responses from caregivers. *Child Development, 80*, 636–644.

Golinkoff, R. M. (1993). When is communication a "meeting of the minds"? *Journal of Child Language, 20*, 199–207.

Golinkoff, R. M., Mervis, C. B., & Hirsh-Pasek, K. (1994). Early object labels: The case for a developmental lexical principles framework. *Journal of Child Language, 21*, 135–155.

Gomez, R. (2002). Variability and detection of invariant structure. *Psychological Science, 13*(5), 431–436.

Goodglass, H., & Lindfield, K. C., & Alexander, M. P. (2000). Semantic capacities of the right hemisphere as seen in two cases of pure word blindness. *Journal of Psycholinguistic Research, 29*, 399–422.

Goodman, J. C., Dale, P. S., & Li, P. (2008). Does frequency count? Parental input and the acquisition of vocabulary. *Journal of Child Language, 35*, 515–531.

Goodsitt, J. V., Morgan, J. L., & Kuhl, P. K. (1993). Perceptual strategies in prelingual speech segmentation. *Journal of Child Language, 20*, 229–252.

Gordon, N. (2000). The acquisition of a second language [Review]. *European Journal of Pediatric Neurology, 4*, 3–7.

Gorman, B. K. (2012). Relationships between vocabulary size, working memory, and phonological awareness in Spanish-speaking English language learners. *American Journal of Speech-Language Pathology, 21*, 109–123.

Gorman, B. K., Fiestas, C. E., Peña, E. D., & Reynolds Clark, M. (2011). Creative and stylistic devices employed by children during a storybook narrative task: A cross-cultural study. *Language, Speech, and Hearing Services in Schools, 42*, 167–181.

Grassmann, S., & Tomasello, M. (2007). Two-year-olds use primary sentence accent to learn new words. *Journal of Child Language, 34*, 677–687.

Graziano-King, J., & Smith Cairns, H. (2005). Acquisition of English comparative adjectives. *Journal of Child Language, 32*, 345–373.

Green, J. R., & Wilson, E. M. (2006). Spontaneous facial motility in infancy: A 3D kinematic analysis. *Developmental Psychobiology, 48*, 16–28.

Grice, H. (1975). Logic and conversation. In D. Davidson & G. Harmon (Eds.), *The logic of grammar*. Encino, CA: Dickenson Press.

Grigos, M. I., & Patel, R. (2007). Articulator movement associated with the development of prosodic control in children. *Journal of Speech, Language, and Hearing Research, 50*, 119–130.

Groome, D. (1999). *An introduction to cognitive psychology: Processes and disorders*. London, England: Psychological Press.

Grossman, A. W., Churchill, J., McKinney, B. C., Kodish, I. M., Otte, S. L., & Greenough, W. T. (2003). Experience effects on brain development: Possible contributions to psychopathology. *Journal of Child Psychology and Psychiatry, 44*, 33–63.

Guion, S. G., Flege, J. E., Akahane-Yamada, R., & Pruitt, J. C. (2000). An investigation of current models of second language speech perception: The case of Japanese adults' perception of English consonants. *Journal of the Acoustical Society of America, 107*, 2711–2724.

Guo, L.-Y. (2009). *Acquisition of auxiliary and copula be in young English-speaking children*. Unpublished doctoral dissertation, University of Iowa.

Gupta, P. (2003). Examining the relationship between word learning, nonword repetition, and immediate serial recall in adults. *Quarterly Journal of Experimental Psychology, 5A*, 1213–1236.

Guttierrez-Clellen, V. F. (1998). Syntactic skills of Spanish-speaking children with low school achievement. *Language, Speech, and Hearing Services in Schools, 29*, 207–215.

Haas, A., & Owens, R. (1985). *Preschoolers' pronoun strategies: You and me make us*. Paper presented at the annual convention of the American Speech-Language-Hearing Association.

Hadley, P. A. (1999). Validating a rate-based measure of early grammatical abilities: Unique syntactic types. *American Journal of Speech-Language Pathology, 8*, 261–272.

Hadley, P. A., Rispoli, M., Fitzgerald, C., & Bahnsen, A. (2011). Predictors of morphosyntactic growth in typically developing toddlers: Contributions of parent input and child sex. *Journal of Speech, Language, and Hearing Research, 54*, 549–566.

Hall, D. G., Burns, T. C., & Pawluski, J. L. (2003). Input and word learning: Caregivers' sensitivity to lexical category distinctions. *Journal of Child Language, 30*, 711–729.

Hall, D. G., Corrigall, K., Rhemtulla, M., Donegan, E., & Xu, F. (2008). Infants' use of lexical-category-to-meaning links in object individuation. *Child Development, 79*, 1432–1443.

Hall, D. G., Quartz, D., & Persoage, K. (2000). Preschoolers' use of syntactic cues in word learning. *Developmental Psychology, 36*, 449–462.

Hammer, C. S., & Weiss, A. L. (1999). Guiding language development: How African American mothers and their infants structure play interactions. *Journal of Speech, Language, and Hearing Research, 42*, 1219–1233.

Hammer, C. S., & Weiss, A. L. (2000). African American mothers' views of their infants' language development and language-learning environment. *American Journal of Speech-Language Pathology, 9*, 126–140.

Hammock, E. A. D., & Levitt, P. (2006). The discipline of neurobehavioral development: The emerging interface that builds processes and skills. *Human Development, 49*, 294–309.

Hane, A. A., Feldstein, S., & Dernetz, V. H. (2003). The relation between coordinated interpersonal timing and maternal sensitivity in four-month-olds. *Journal of Psycholinguistic Research, 32*, 525–539.

Hardin, E. E., O'Connell, D. C., & Kowal, S. (1998). Reading aloud from logographic and alphabetic texts: Comparisons between Chinese and German. *Journal of Psycholinguistic Research, 27*, 413–439.

Harlaar, N., Hayiou-Thomas, M. E., Dale, P. S., & Plomin, R. (2008). Why do preschool language abilities correlate with later reading? A twin study. *Journal of Speech, Language, and Hearing Research, 51*, 688–705.

Harrison, L. J., & McLeod, S. (2010). Risk and protective factors associated with speech and language impairment in a nationally representative sample of 4- to 5-year-old children. *Journal of Speech, Language, and Hearing Research, 53*, 508–529.

Harris Wright, H., Capilouto, G. J., Srinivasan, C., & Fergadiotis, G. (2011). Story processing ability in cognitively healthy younger and older adults. *Journal of Speech, Language, and Hearing Research*, 54, 900–917.

Hart, B., & Risley, T. R. (1995). *Meaningful differences in the everyday experience of young American children*. Baltimore, MD: Brookes.

Hartsuiker, R. J., Bernolet, S., Schoonbaert, S., Speybroeck, S., & Vanderelst, D. (2008). Syntactic priming persists while the lexical boost decays: Evidence from written and spoken dialogue. *Journal of Memory and Language, 58,* 214–238.

Hartsuiker, R., & Kolk, H. (2001). Error monitoring in speech production: A computational test of the perceptual loop theory. *Cognitive Psychology, 42,* 113–157.

Hashimoto, N., McGregor, K. K., & Graham, A. (2007). Conceptual organization at 6 and 8 years of age: Evidence from the semantic priming of object decisions. *Journal of Speech, Language, and Hearing Research, 50,* 161–176.

Hayes, H., Treiman, R., & Kessler, B. (2006). Children use vowels to help them spell consonants. *Journal of Experimental Child Psychology, 94,* 27–42.

Hayiou-Thomas, M. E., Harlaar, N., Dale, P. S., & Plomin, R. (2010). Preschool speech, language skills, and reading at 7, 9, and 10 years: Etiology of the relationship. *Journal of Speech, Language, and Hearing Research, 53,* 311–332.

Hayiou-Thomas, M. E., Kovas, Y., Harlaar, N., Plomin, R., Bishop, D. V. M., & Dale, P. S. (2006). Common aetiology for diverse language skills in $4\frac{1}{2}$ -year-old twins. *Journal of Child Language, 33,* 339–368.

Hazan, V., & Barret, S. (2000). The development of phonemic categorization in children aged 6–12. *Journal of Phonetics, 28,* 377–396.

Heimann, M., Strid, K., Smith, L., Tjus, T., Ulvund, S. E., & Meltzoff, A. N. (2006). Exploring the relation between memory, gestural communication, and the emergence of language in infancy: A longitudinal study. *Infant and Child Development, 15,* 233–249.

Henderson, E. H. (1990). *Teaching spelling* (2nd ed.). Boston, MA: Houghton Mifflin.

Hensch, T. K. (2005). Critical period mechanisms in developing visual cortex. *Current Topics in Developmental Biology, 69,* 215–237.

Herr-Israel, E., & McCune, L. (2011). Successive single-word utterances and use of conversational input: a pre-syntactic route to multiword utterances. *Journal of Child Language, 38,* 166–180.

Hickmann, M. (2003). *Children's discourse: Person, space, and time across languages.* Cambridge, United Kingdom: Cambridge University Press.

Hickok, G. (2001). Functional anatomy of speech perception and speech production: Psycholinguistic implications. *Journal of Psycholinguistic Research, 30,* 225–235.

Highnam, C. L., & Bleile, K. M. (2011). Language in the Cerebellum. *American Journal of Speech-Language Pathology,* 20, 337-347.

Hinton, L. N., & Pollock, K. E. (2000). Regional variation in the phonological characteristics of African American vernacular English. *World Englishes, 19*(1), 39–58.

Hirsch, E. D. (2006). Building knowledge: The case for bringing content into the language arts block and for a knowledge-rich curriculum core for all children. *American Educator, 30*(1), 8–51.

Hirsh-Pasek, K., & Golinkoff, R. M. (Eds.). (2006). *Action meets word. How children learn verbs.* Oxford, United Kingdom: Oxford University Press.

Hoff, E. (2003). The specificity of environmental influence: Socioeconomic status affects early vocabulary development via maternal speech. *Child Development, 74,* 1368–1378.

Hoff, E., Core, C., Place, S., Rumiche, R., Señor, M., & Parra, M. (2012). Dual language exposure and early bilingual development. *Journal of Child Language, 39,* 1–27.

Hoff, E., Laursen, B., & Tardif, T. (2002). Socioeconomic status and parenting. In M. H. Bornstein (Ed.), *Handbook of parenting* (2nd ed., pp. 231–252). Mahwah, NJ: Erlbaum.

Hoff, E., & Naigles, L. (2002). How children use input to acquire a lexicon. *Child Development, 73,* 418–33.

Hoff-Ginsberg, E. (1990). Maternal speech and the child's development of syntax: A further look. *Journal of Child Language, 17,* 85–99.

Hoffner, C., Cantor, J., & Badzinski, D. (1990). Children's understanding of adverbs denoting degree of likelihood. *Journal of Child Language, 17,* 217–231.

Hofstede, G. (2001), *Culture's Consequences: International Differences in Work Related Values,* 2001 edition, Thousand Oaks, CA: Sage Publications, Inc.

Hogan, T., & Catts, H. W. (2004). *Phonological awareness test items: Lexical and phonological characteristics affect performance.* Paper presented at the Annual Convention of the American Speech-Language-Hearing Association, Philadelphia, PA.

Hogan, T. P., Catts, H. W., & Little, T. D. (2005). The relationship between phonological awareness and reading: Implications for the assessment of phonological awareness. *Language, Speech, and Hearing Services in Schools, 36*, 285–293.

Hollich, G., Hirsh-Pasek, K., & Michnick Golinkoff, R. M. (2000). Breaking the language barrier: An Emergentist coalition model for the origins of word learning. *Monographs of the Society for Research in Child Development, 65* (3, Serial No. 262).

Hood, J., & Rankin, P. M. (2005). How do specific memory disorders present in the school classroom? *Pediatric Rehabilitation, 8*, 272–282.

Horn, G. (2004). Pathways of the past: The imprint of memory. *Nature Reviews Neuroscience, 5*, 108–120.

Hornstein, D., & Lightfoot, N. (1981). *Explanation in linguistics*. London, England: Longman.

Houston-Price, C., Plunkett, K., & Harris, P. (2005). Word-learning wizardry at 1;6. *Journal of Child Language, 32*, 175–189.

Howard, A. A., Mayeux, L., & Naigles, L. R. (2008). Conversational correlates of children's acquisition of mental verbs and a theory of mind. *First Language, 28*, 375–402.

Hudson Kam, C. L., & Edwards, N. A. (2008). The use of *uh* and *um* by 3- and 4-year-old native English-speaking children: Not quite right but not completely wrong. *First Language, 28*, 313–327.

Huntley Bahr, R., Silliman, E. R., Berninger, V. W., & Dow, M. (2012). Linguistic pattern analysis of misspellings of typically developing writers in grades 1–9. *Journal of Speech, Language, and Hearing Research, 55*, 1587–1599.

Hurtado, N., Marchman, V. A., & Fernald, A. (2007). Spoken word recognition by Latino children learning Spanish as their first language. *Journal of Child Language, 33*, 227–249.

Huttenlocher, J., Vasilyeva, M., Cymerman, E., & Levine, S. (2002). Language input at home and at school: Relation to child syntax. *Cognitive Psychology*, *45*, 337–374.

Ibrahim, R., Eviatar, Z., & Aharon-Peretz, J. (2007). Metalinguistic awareness and reading performance: A cross language comparison. *Journal of Psycholinguistic Research, 36*, 297–318.

Imai, M., & Haryu, E. (2001). Learning proper nouns and common nouns without clues from syntax. *Child Development, 72*, 787–802.

Ingram, D. (1976). *Phonological disability in children*. London, England: Arnold.

Ingram, D. (1986). Phonological development: Production. In P. Fletcher & M. Garman (Eds.), *Language acquisition* (2nd ed.). New York, NY: Cambridge University Press.

Iverson, J. M. (2010). Developing language in a developing body: The relationship between motor development and language development. *Journal of Child Language, 37*, 229–261.

Ivy, L. J., & Masterson, J. J. (2011). A comparison of oral and written English styles in African American students at different stages of writing development. *Language, Speech, and Hearing Services in Schools*, 42, 31–40.

Jackson, S. C., & Roberts, J. E. (2001). Complex syntax production of African American preschoolers. *Journal of Speech, Language, and Hearing Research, 44*, 1083–1096.

Jackson-Maldonado, D., Thal, D., Marchman, V., Bates, E., & Gutierrez-Clellan, V. (1993). Early lexical development in Spanish-speaking infants and toddlers. *Journal of Child Language, 20*, 523–549.

Jafee, J., Beebe, B., Feldstein, S., Crown, C. L., & Jasnow, M. D. (2001). Rhythms of dialogue in infancy. *Monographs of the Society for Research in Child Development, 66* (2, Serial No. 265).

Jia, G., & Aaronson, D. (2003). A longitudinal study of Chinese children and adolescents learning English in the United States. *Applied Psycholinguistics, 24*, 131–161.

Jia, G., Aaronson, D., & Wu, Y. (2002). Long-term language attainment of bilingual immigrants: Predictive variables and language group differences. *Applied Psycholinguistics, 23*, 599–621.

Johnson, B. W., & Fey, M. E. (2006). Interaction of lexical and grammatical aspect in toddlers' language. *Journal of Child Language, 33*, 419–435.

Johnson, C. J., & Anglin, J. M. (1995). Qualitative developments in the content and form of children's definitions. *Journal of Speech and Hearing Research, 38*, 612–629.

Johnson, J. R., & Wong, M. Y. (2002). Cultural differences in beliefs and practices concerning talk to children. *Journal of Speech, Language, and Hearing Research, 45*, 916–926.

Johnson, N. S. (1983). What do you do when you can't tell the whole story? The development of summarization skills. In K. E. Nelson (Ed.), *Children's language* (Vol. 4, pp. 315–383). Hillsdale, NJ: Erlbaum.

Johnson, V. E. (2005). Comprehension of third person singular /s/ in AAE-speaking children. *Language, Speech, and Hearing Services in Schools, 36*, 116–124.

Joiner, C. (F. Supp. 1979). *Martin Luther King Junior Elementary School vs. Ann Arbor School District*, 1371–1391.

Jones, E. G. (2000). Cortical and subcortical contributions to activity-dependent plasticity in primate somatosensory cortex. *Annual Review of Neuroscience, 23*, 1–37.

Juncos-Rabadan, O., Pereiro, A. X., & Rodriguez, M. S. (2005). Narrative speech in aging: Quantity, information content, and cohesion. *Brain and Language*, 95, 423–434.

Junker, D. A., & Stockman, I. J. (2002). Expressive vocabulary of German-English bilingual toddlers. *American Journal of Speech-Language Pathology, 11*, 381–394.

Jusczyk, P. W. (1997). Finding and remembering words: Some beginnings by English-learning infants. *Current Directions in Psychological Science, 6*(6), 170–174.

Jusczyk, P. W. (1999, September 30). *Making sense of sounds: Foundations of language acquisition*. Presentation at State University of New York, Geneseo.

Jusczyk, P. W., & Hohne, E. A. (1997). Infants' memory for spoken words. *Science, 277*, 1984–1986.

Jusczyk, P. W., Houston, D., & Newsome, M. (1999). The beginning of word segmentation in English-learning infants. *Cognitive Psychology, 39*, 159–207.

Jusczyk, P. W., Jusczyk, A. M., Kennedy, L. J., Schomberg, T., & Koenig, N. (1995). Young infants' retention of information about bisyllabic utterances. *Journal of Experimental Psychology: Human Perception and Performance, 21*, 822–836.

Jusczyk, P. W., Luce, P. A., & Charles-Luce, J. (1994). Infant's sensitivity to phonotactic patterns in the native language. *Journal of Memory and Language, 33*, 630–645.

Kachru, B. B. (2005). *Asian Englishes: Beyond the canon*. Hong Kong: Hong Kong University Press.

Kaderavek, J. N., & Sulzby, E. (2000). Narrative production by children with and without specific language impairment: Oral narratives and emergent readings. *Journal of Speech, Language, and Hearing Research, 43*, 34–49.

Kamhi, A. G., & Catts, H. W. (2005). Language and reading: Convergences and divergences. In H. W. Catts & A. G. Kamhi (Eds.), *Language and reading disabilities* (2nd ed., pp. 1–25). Boston, MA: Allyn & Bacon.

Kan, P. F., & Kohnert, K. (2005). Preschoolers learning Hmong and English: Lexical-semantic skills in L1 and L2. *Journal of Speech, Language, and Hearing Research, 48*, 372–383.

Kang, J. Y., Kim, Y.-S., & Alexander Pan, B. (2009). Five-year-olds' book talk and story retelling: Contributions of mother–child joint book reading. *First Language, 29*, 243–265.

Karmiloff, K., & Karmiloff-Smith, A. (2001). *Pathways to language from fetus to adolescent*. Cambridge, MA: Harvard University Press.

Karmiloff-Smith, A. (1986). Some fundamental aspects of language development after age 5. In P. Fletcher & M. Garman (Eds.), *Language acquisition* (2nd ed.). New York, NY: Cambridge University Press.

Karrass, J., Braungart-Rieker, J. M., Mullins, J., & Lefever, J. B. (2002). Processes in language acquisition: The roles of gender, attention, and maternal encouragement of attention over time. *Journal of Child Language, 29*, 519–543.

Kärtner, J., Keller, H., & Yovsi, R. D. (2010). Mother–infant interaction during the first 3 months: The emergence of culture-specific contingency patterns. *Child Development, 81*, 540–555.

Katzir, T., Kim, Y., Wolf, M., O'Brien, B., Kennedy, B., Lovett, M., & Morris, R. (2006). Reading fluency: The whole is more than the parts. *Annals of Dyslexia, 56*, 51–82.

Kaushanskaya, M., Yoo, J., & Van Hecke, S. (2013). Word learning in adults with second-language experience: Effects of phonological and referent familiarity. *Journal of Speech, Language, and Hearing Research*, 56, 667–678.

Kaye, K., & Charney, R. (1981). Conversational asymmetry between mothers and children. *Journal of Child Language, 8*, 35–49.

Kay-Raining Bird, E., & Chapman, R.S. (1998). Partial representations and phonological selectivity in comprehension. *First Language, 18*, 105–127.

Kehoe, M., Trujillo, C., & Lleó, C. (2001). Bilingual phonological acquisition: An analysis of syllable structure and VOT. In K. F. Cantone & M. O. Hinzelin (Eds.), *Proceedings of the colloquium on structure, acquisition and change of grammars: Phonological and syntactic aspects* (Vol. 27, pp. 38–54). Universität Hamburg, Germany: Arbeiten zur Mehrsprachigkeit.

Kelly, S. D. (2001). Broadening the units of analysis in communication: Speech and nonverbal behaviors in pragmatic comprehension. *Journal of Child Language, 28*, 325–349.

Kemp, N., Lieven, E., & Tomasello, M. (2005). Young children's knowledge of the "determiner" and "adjective" categories. *Journal of Speech, Language, and Hearing Research, 48*, 592–609.

Kemper, R. L., & Vernooy, A. R. (1993). Metalinguistic awareness in first graders: A qualitative perspective. *Journal of Psycholinguistic Research, 22*, 41–57.

Kemper, S., Thompson, M., & Marquis, J. (2001). Longitudinal change in language production: Effects of aging and dementia on grammatical complexity and prepositional content. *Psychology and Aging, 16*, 600–614.

Keren-Portnoy, T. (2006). Facilitation and practice in verb acquisition. *Journal of Child Language, 33*, 487–518.

Keren-Portnoy, T., & Keren, M. (2011). The dynamics of syntax acquisition: Facilitation between syntactic structures. *Journal of Child Language, 38*, 404–432.

Kim, M., & Stoel-Gammon, C. (2011). Phonological development of word-initial Korean obstruents in young Korean children. *Journal of Child Language, 38*, 316–340.

Kim, M., McGregor, K. K., & Thompson, C. K. (2000). Early lexical development in English- and Korean-speaking children: Language-general and language-specific patterns. *Journal of Child Language, 27*, 225–254.

Kirjavainen, M., Theakston, A., & Lieven, E. (2009). Can input explain children's me-for-I errors? *Journal of Child Language, 36*, 1091–1114.

Kirkorian, H. L., Pempek, T. A., Murphy, L. A., Schmidt, M. E., & Anderson, D. R. (2009). The impact of background television on parent-child interaction. *Child Development, 80*, 1350–1359.

Kohnert, K. J., & Bates, E. (2002). Balancing bilinguals ii: Lexical comprehension and cognitive processing in children learning Spanish and English. *Journal of Speech, Language, and Hearing Research, 45*, 347–359.

Kohnert, K., & Goldstein, B. (2005). Speech, language, and hearing in developing bilingual children: From practice to research. *Language, Speech, and Hearing Services in Schools, 36*, 169–171.

Komarova, N. L., & Nowak, M. A. (2001). Natural selection of the critical period for language acquisition. *Proceedings of the Royal Society of London, Series B, Biological Sciences, 268*, 1189–1196.

Konopka, A., & Bock, K. (2005, March). *Helping syntax out: How much do words do?* Paper presented at the CUNY Conference on Human Sentence Processing, Tucson, AZ.

Krause, J. C., & Braida, L. D. (2004). Acoustic properties of naturally produced clear speech at normal speaking rates. *The Journal of the Acoustical Society of America, 115*, 362–378.

Kuhl, P. K. (2004). Early language acquisition: Cracking the speech code. *Nature Reviews Neuroscience, 5*, 831–843.

Langacker, R. (1991). *Foundations of cognitive grammar, Volume 2*. Stanford, CA: Stanford University Press.

Language Sample Analysis Made Quick & Easy: Sampling Utterances & Syntactic Analysis Revisited (SUGAR). (2013, November). American Speech-Language-Hearing Association Convention, Chicago.

Lee, S. S., Davis, B., & MacNeilage, P. (2010). Universal production patterns and ambient language influences in babbling: A cross-linguistic study of Korean- and English-learning infants. *Journal of Child Language, 37*, 293–318.

Lee, S. S., Davis, B. L., & MacNeilage, P. F. (2008). Segmental properties of input to infants: A study of Korean. *Journal of Child Language, 35*, 591–617.

Lee, S. S., Potamianos, A., & Naryanan, S. (1999). Acoustics of children's speech: Developmental changes of temporal and spectral parameters. *Journal of the Acoustical Society of America, 105*, 1455–1468.

Legerstee, M., Anderson, D., & Schaffer, A. (1998). Five- and eight-month-old infants recognize their faces and voices as familiar and social stimuli. *Child Development, 69*, 37–50.

Lehto, J., Juujarvi, P., Kooistra, L., & Pulkkinen, L. (2003). Dimensions of executive functioning: Evidence from children. *British Journal of Developmental Psychology, 21*, 59–80.

Lenneberg, E. (1967). *Biological foundations of language*. New York, NY: Wiley.

Leonard, L. B., Weismer, S. E., Miller, C. A., Francis, D. J., Tomblin, J. B., & Kail, R. V. (2007). Speed of processing, working memory, and language impairment in children. *Journal of Speech, Language, and Hearing Research, 50*, 408–428.

Leventhal, T., Xue, Y., & Brooks-Gunn, J. (2006). Immigrant differences in school-age children's verbal trajectories: A look at four racial/ethnic groups. *Child Development, 77*, 1359–1374.

Levy, B. A., Gong, Z., Hessels, S., Evans, M. A., & Jared, D. (2006). Understanding print: Early reading development and the contributions of home literacy experiences. *Journal of Experimental Child Psychology, 93*, 63–93.

Levy, E., & Nelson, K. (1994). Words in discourse: A dialectal approach to the acquisition of meaning and use. *Journal of Child Language, 21*, 367–389.

Lewis, M., & Freedle, R. (1973). Mother-infant dyad: The cradle of meaning. In P. Pilner, L. Kranes, & T. Alloway (Eds.), *Communication and affect: Language and thought.* New York, NY: Academic Press.

Lewis, R. L., Vasishth, S., & Van Dyke, J. A. (2006). Computational principles of working memory in sentence comprehension. *Trends in Cognitive Sciences, 10*, 447–454.

Li, P., & Shirai, Y. (2000). *The acquisition of lexical and grammatical aspect.* New York, NY: Mouton de Gruyter.

Lieven, E., & Pine, J. M. (1990). Review of *From first words to grammar: Individual differences and dissociable mechanisms* by E. Bates, I. Bretherton, & L. J. Snyder. *Journal of Child Language, 17*, 495–501.

Lieven, E., Behrens, H., Speares, J., & Tomasello, M. (2003). Early syntactic creativity: A usage-based approach. *Journal of Child Language, 30*, 333–370.

Lieven, E. V. M., Pine, J. M., & Baldwin, G. (1997). Lexically based learning and early grammatical development. *Journal of Child Language, 24*, 187–219.

Lillo-Martin, D. (1991). *Universal grammar and American Sign Language: Setting the null argument parameters.* Dordrecht, the Netherlands: Kluwer.

Lin, E. L., & Murphy, G. L. (2001). Thematic relations in adults' concepts. *Journal of Experimental Psychology: General, 130*, 3–28.

Lisker, L., & Abramson, A. (1965). Voice onset time in the production and perception of English stops. *Speech Research, Haskins Laboratories, 1.*

Liszkowski, U., Carpenter, M., Henning, A., Striano, T., & Tomasello, M. (2004). Twelve-month-olds point to share attention and interest. *Developmental Science, 7*, 297–307.

Liszkowski, U., Carpenter, M., & Tomasello, M. (2007). Reference and attitude in infant pointing. *Journal of Child Language, 34*, 1–20.

Lleó, C., & Prinz, M. (1996). Consonant clusters in child phonology and the directionality of syllable structure assignment. *Journal of Child Language, 23*, 31–56.

Lleó, C., Kuchenbrandt, I., Kehoe, M., & Trujillo, C. (2003). Syllable final consonants in Spanish and German monolingual and bilingual acquisition. In N. Müller (Ed.), *(In)vulnerable domains in multilingualism* (pp. 191–220). Amsterdam, the Netherlands: John Benjamins.

Lloyd, P., & Banham, L. (1997). Does drawing attention to the referent constrain the way in which children construct verbal messages? *Journal of Psycholinguistic Research, 26*, 509–518.

Logan, K. J. (2003). Language and fluency characteristic of preschoolers' multiple-utterance conversational turns. *Journal of Speech, Language, and Hearing Research, 46*, 178–188.

Lohmann, H., & Tomasello, M. (2003). The role of language in the development of false belief understanding: A training study. *Child Development, 74*, 1130–1144.

Love, R., & Webb, W. (1986). *Neurology for the speech-language pathologist.* Boston, MA: Butterworth's.

Lowe, E., Slater, A., Wefley, J., & Hardie, D. (2002). *A status report on hunger and homelessness in America's cities 2002: A 25-city survey*. Washington, DC: U.S. Conference of Mayors.

Maas, E., & Nailend, M. (2012). Speech planning happens before speech execution: Online reaction time methods in the study of apraxia of speech. *Journal of Speech, Language, and Hearing Research, 55*, S1523–S1534.

MacWhinney, B. (2002). Language emergence. In P. Burmeister, T. Piske, & A. Rohde (Eds.), *An integrated view of language development—Papers in honor of Henning Wode* (pp. 17–42). Trier, Germany: Wissenshaftliche Verlag.

MacWhinney, B. (2004). A multiple process solution to the logical problem of language acquisition. *Journal of Child Language, 31*, 883–914.

MacWhinney, B. (2005). A unified model of language acquisition. In J. F. Kroll & A. DeGroot (Eds.), *Handbook of bilingualism* (pp. 49–67). Oxford, United Kingdom: Oxford University Press.

Majdan, M., & Shatz, C. J. (2006). Effects of visual experience on activity-dependent gene regulation in cortex. *Nature Neuroscience, 9*, 650–659.

Maneva, B., & Genesee, F. (2002). Bilingual babbling: Evidence for language differentiation in dual language acquisition. In B. Skarabela et al. (Eds.), *The proceedings of the 26th Boston University Conference on Language Development* (pp. 383–392). Somerville, MA: Cascadilla Press.

Marcus, G. F. (2001). *The algebraic mind.* Cambridge, MA: MIT Press.

Marinellie, S. A. (2010). The understanding of word definitions in school-age children. *Journal of Psycholinguistic Research, 39*, 179–198.

Marinellie, S. A., & Johnson, C. J. (2003). Adjective definitions and the influence of word frequency. *Journal of Speech, Language, and Hearing Research, 46*, 1061–1076.

Marini, A., Boewe, A., Caltagirone, C., & Carlomagno, S. (2005). Age-related differences in the production of textual descriptions. *Journal of Psycholinguistic Research, 34*, 439–463.

Markman, E. M. (1992). The whole object, taxonomic, and mutual exclusivity assumptions as initial constraints on word meanings. In J. P. Byrnes & S. A. Gelman (Eds.), *Perspectives on language and cognition: Interrelations in development.* New York, NY: Cambridge University Press.

Masataka, N. (1993). Effects of contingent and noncontingent maternal stimulation on the vocal behavior of three- to four-month-old Japanese infants. *Journal of Child Language, 20*, 303–312.

Masur, E. F., Flynn, V., & Eichorst, D. L. (2005). Maternal responsive and directive behaviours and utterances as predictors of children's lexical development. *Journal of Child Language, 32*, 63–91.

Mather, E., & Plunkett, K. (2011). Mutual exclusivity and phonological novelty constrain word learning at 16 months. *Journal of Child Language, 38*, 933–950.

Mattys, S. L., & Jusczyk, P. W. (2001). Phonotactic cues for segmentation of fluent speech by infants. *Cognition, 78*, 91–121.

Mattys, S. L., Jusczyk, P. W., Luce, P. A., & Morgan, J. L. (1999). Phonotactic and prosodic effects on word segmentation in infants. *Cognitive Psychology, 38*(4), 465–94.

McCabe, A., & Bliss, L. S. (2003). *Patterns of narrative discourse: A multicultural life span approach.* Boston, MA: Allyn & Bacon.

McCabe, A., & Bliss, L. S. (2004–2005). Narratives from Spanish-speaking children with impaired and typical language development. *Imagination, Cognition and Personality, 24*(4), 331–346.

McCloskey, L. A. (1986). *Prosody and children's understanding of discourse.* Unpublished doctoral dissertation, University of Michigan, Ann Arbor.

McCune, L., & Vihman, M. M. (2001). Early phonetic and lexical development: A productivity approach. *Journal of Speech, Language, and Hearing Research, 44*, 670–684.

McDonald Connor, C., & Craig, H. K. (2006). African American preschoolers' language, emergent literacy skills, and use of African American English: A complex relation. *Journal of Speech, Language, and Hearing Research, 49*, 771–792.

McDonald, J. L. (2008). Grammaticality judgments in children: The role of age, working memory and phonological ability. *Journal of Child Language, 35*, 247–268.

McDowell, K. D., Lonigan, C. J., & Goldstein, H. (2007). Relations among socioeconomic status, age, and predictors of phonological awareness. *Journal of Speech, Language, and Hearing Research, 50*, 1079–1092.

McEachem, D., & Haynes, W. O. (2004). Gesture-speech combinations as a transition to multiword utterances. *American Journal of Speech-Language Pathology, 13*, 227–235.

McElree, B., Foraker, S., & Dyer, L. (2003). Memory structures that subserve sentence comprehension. *Journal of Memory and Language, 48*, 67–91.

McGowan, R. W., McGowan, R. S., Denny, M., & Nittrouer, S. (2013). A longitudinal study of very young children's vowel production. *Journal of Speech, Language, and Hearing Research, 56.* doi:10.1044/1092-4388(2013/12-0112)

McGregor, K. K. (2000). The development and enhancement of narrative skills in a preschool classroom: Towards a solution to clinician–client mismatch. *American Journal of Speech-Language Pathology, 9*, 55–71.

McGregor, K. K., Friedman, R. M., Reilly, R. M., & Newman, R. M. (2002). Semantic representation and naming in young children. *Journal of Speech, Language, and Hearing Research, 45*, 332–346.

McGregor, K. K., Sheng, L., & Smith, B. (2005). The precocious two-year-old: Status of the lexicon and links to the grammar. *Journal of Child Language, 32*, 563–585.

McKean, C., Letts, C., & Howard, D. (2013). Functional reorganization in the developing lexicon: Separable and changing influences of lexical and phonological variables on children's fast-mapping. *Journal of Child Language, 40*, 307–335.

McKee, C., McDaniel, D., & Snedeker, J. (1998). Relatives children say. *Journal of Psycholinguistic Research, 27*, 573–596.

McLeod, S., van Doorn, J., & Reed, V. A. (2001a). Consonant cluster development in two-year-olds: General trends and individual difference. *Journal of Speech, Language, and Hearing Research, 44*, 1144–1171.

McLeod, S., van Doorn, J., & Reed, V. A. (2001b). Normal acquisition of consonant clusters. *American Journal of Speech-Language Pathology, 10*, 99–110.

Meadows, D., Elias, G., & Bain, J. (2000). Mothers' ability to identify infants' communicative acts consistently. *Journal of Child Language, 27*, 393–406.

Mealings, K. T., Cox, F., & Demuth, K. (2013). Acoustic investigations into the later acquisition of syllabic *-es* plurals. *Journal of Speech, Language, and Hearing Research, 56*, 1260–1271.

Melzi, G. (2000). Cultural variations in the construction of personal narratives: Central American and European American mothers' elicitation style. *Discourse Processes, 30*, 153–177.

Ménard, L., Davis, B. L., Boë, L-J., & Roy, J.-P. (2009). Producing American-English vowels during vocal tract growth: A perceptual categorization study of synthesized vowels. *Journal of Speech, Language, and Hearing Research, 52*, 1268–1285.

Merriman, W. E., Marazita, J., & Jarvis, L. (1995). Children's disposition to map new words onto new referents. In M. Tomasello & W. E. Merriman (Eds.), *Beyond names for things: Young children's acquisition of verbs*. Hillsdale, NJ: Erlbaum.

Miller, C. A. (2006). Developmental relationships between language and theory of mind. *American Journal of Speech-Language Pathology, 15*, 142–154.

Mills, M. T., Edwards, J., & Beckman, M. (2005, November). *Child-directed speech in African American vernacular English*. Poster presented at the annual convention of the American Speech-Language-Hearing Association, San Diego, CA.

Minear, M., & Shah, P. (2006). Sources of working memory deficits in children and possibilities for remediation. In S. E. Pickering & G. D. Phye (Eds.), *Working memory and education* (pp. 273–297). Mahwah, NJ: Erlbaum.

Mintz, T., & Gleitman, L. (2002). Adjectives really do modify nouns: The incremental and restricted nature of early adjective acquisition. *Cognition, 84*, 267–293.

Montgomery, J. W. (2000b). Verbal working memory and sentence comprehension in children with specific language impairment. *Journal of Speech, Language, and Hearing Research, 43*, 293–308.

Montgomery, J. W., Magimairaj, B. M., & O'Malley, M. H. (2008). Role of working memory in typically developing children's complex sentence comprehension. *Journal of Psycholinguistic Research, 37*, 331–356.

Moore, C., Angelopoulos, M., & Bennett, P. (1999). Word learning in the context of referential and salience cues. *Developmental Psychology, 35*, 60–68.

Moore, C., Harris, L., & Patriquin, M. (1993). Lexical and prosodic cues in the comprehension of relative certainty. *Journal of Child Language, 20*, 153–167.

Morales, M., Mundy, P., Delgado, C. E. F., Yale, M., Neal, R., & Schwartz, H. K. (2000). Gaze following, temperament, and language development in 6-month-olds: A replication and extension. *Infant Behavior & Development, 23*, 231–236.

Morgan, J. L. (1994). Converging measures of speech segmentation in prelingual infants. *Infants' Behavior and Development, 17*, 387–400.

Morgan, J. L., & Saffran, J. R. (1995). Emerging integration of sequential and suprasegmental information in preverbal speech segmentation. *Child Development, 66*, 911–936.

Morris, B. J. (2003). Opposites attract: The role of predicate dimensionality in preschool children's processing of negations. *Journal of Child Language, 30*, 419–440.

Moyle, M. J., Weismer, S. E., Evans, J. L., & Lindstrom, M. J. (2007). Longitudinal relationships between lexical and grammatical development in typical and late-talking children. *Journal of Speech, Language, and Hearing Research, 50*, 508–528.

Mundy, P., Block, J., Delgado, C., Pomares, Y., Vaughan Van Hecke, A., & Venezia Parlade, M. (2007). Individual differences and the development of joint attention in infancy. *Child Development, 78*, 938–954.

Munhall, K. G., Kawato, M., & Vatikiotis-Bateson, E. (2000). Coarticulation and physical models of speech production. In M. B. Broe & J. B. Pierrehumbert (Eds.), *Papers in laboratory phonology*

V: Acquisition and the lexicon (pp. 9–28). Cambridge, United Kingdom: Cambridge University Press.

Muñoz, M. L., Gillam, R. B., Peña, E. D., & Gulley-Faehnle, A. (2003). Measures of language development in fictional narratives of Latino children. *Language, Speech, and Hearing Services in Schools, 34*, 332–342.

Munson, B. (2004). Variability /s/ production in children and adults: Evidence from dynamic measures of spectral mean. *Journal of Speech, Language, and Hearing Research, 47*, 58–69.

Munson, B., Edwards, J., & Beckman, M. E. (2005a). Phonological knowledge in typical and atypical speech-sound development. *Topics in Language Disorders, 25*, 190–206.

Munson, B., Edwards, J., & Beckman, M. E. (2005b). Relationships between nonword repetition accuracy and other measures of linguistic development in children with phonological disorders. *Journal of Speech, Language, and Hearing Research, 48*, 61–78.

Murphy, V. A., & Nicoladis, E. (2006). When answer-phone makes a difference in children's acquisition of English compounds. *Journal of Child Language, 33*, 677–691.

Murray, A., Johnson, J., & Peters, J. (1990). Fine-tuning of utterance length to preverbal infants: Effects on later language development. *Journal of Child Language, 17*, 511–525.

Naigles, L. (1990). Children use syntax to learn verb meanings. *Journal of Child Language, 17*, 357–374.

Naigles, L. G., & Gelman, S. A. (1995). Overextensions in comprehension and production revisited: Preferential looking in a study of dog, cat, and cow. *Journal of Child Language, 22*, 19–46.

Naigles, L. R., & Hoff-Ginsberg, E. (1998). Why are some verbs learned before other verbs? Effects of input frequency and structure on children's early verb use. *Journal of Child Language, 25*, 95–120.

Nathan, L., Wells, B., & Donlan, C. (1998). Can children with speech difficulties process an unfamiliar accent? *Applied Psycholinguistics, 22*, 343–361.

Nation, K., & Norbury, C. F. (2005). Why reading comprehension fails: Insights into developmental disorders. *Topics in Language Disorders, 25*(1), 21–32.

National Coalition for the Homeless. (1999). *Homeless families with children: National Coalition for the Homeless fact sheet #7*. Washington, DC: Author.

National Early Literacy Panel. (2009). *Developing early literacy: Report of the National Early Literacy Panel*. Jessup, MD: National Center for Family Literacy, the National Institute for Literacy, U.S. Department of Health and Human Services.

National Reading Panel. (2000). *Teaching children to read: An evidence-based assessment of the scientific research literature on reading and its implications for reading instruction* (NIH Pub. No. 00-4769). Washington, DC: U.S. Department of Health and Human Services, Public Health Service, National Institutes of Health, National Institute of Child Health and Human Development.

Nazzi, T., Bertoncini, J., & Mehler, J. (1998). Language discrimination by newborns: Towards an understanding of the role of rhythm. *Journal of Experimental Psychology: Human Perception and Performance, 24*, 756–766.

Nazzi, T., Jusczyk, P.W. & Johnson, E.K. (2000). Language discrimination by English-learning 5-month-olds: Effects of rhythm and familiarity. *Journal of Memory and Language, 43*, 1–19.

Nelson, C. A., Zeanah, C. H., Fox, N. A., Marshall, P. J., Smyke, A., & Guthrie, D. (2007). Cognitive recovery in socially deprived young children: The Bucharest Early Intervention Project. *Science, 318*, 1937–1940.

Nelson, K. E. (1991). The matter of time: Interdependencies between language and concepts. In S. A. Gelman & J. P. Byrnes (Eds.), *Perspectives on language and thought: Interrelations in development*. New York, NY: Cambridge University Press.

Nelson, K. E. (1995). The dual category problem in the acquisition of action words. In M. Tomasello & W. Merriman (Eds.), *Beyond names for things: young children's acquisition of verbs*. Hillsdale, NJ: Erlbaum.

Nelson, K. E., Hampson, J., & Shaw, L. K. (1993). Nouns in early lexicons: Evidence, explanations, & implications. *Journal of Child Language, 20*, 61–84.

Nelson, L. K., & Bauer, H. R. (1991). Speech and language production at age 2: Evidence for tradeoffs between linguistic and phonetic processing. *Journal of Speech and Hearing Research, 34*, 879–892.

Newport, E. L. (1988). Constraints on learning and their role in language acquisition: Studies of the acquisition of American Sign Language. *Language Sciences, 10*, 147–172.

Newport, E. L. (1990). Maturational constraints on language learning. *Cognitive Science, 14*, 11–28.

Newport, E. L., Bavelier, D., & Neville, H. J. (2001). Critical thinking about critical periods: Perspectives on a critical period for language acquisition. In E. Doupoux (Ed.), *Language, brain and cognitive development: Essays in honor of Jacques Mehler* (pp. 481–502). Cambridge, MA: MIT Press.

Nguyen, S. P., & Murphy, G. L. (2003). An apple is more than just a fruit: Cross-classification in children's concepts. *Child Development, 74*, 1783–1806.

NICHD Early Child Care Research Network. (2005). Duration and developmental timing of poverty and children's cognitive and social development from birth through third grade. *Child Development, 76*, 795–810.

Nicoladis, E., & Genesee, F. (1996). Word awareness in second language learners and bilingual children. *Language Awareness, 5*(2), 80–89.

Nicoladis, E., & Secco, G. (2000). Productive vocabulary and language choice. *First Language, 20*(58), 3–28.

Nicolopoulou, A., & Richner, E. S. (2007). From actors to agents to persons: The development of character representation in young children's narratives. *Child Development, 78*, 412–429.

Nip, I. S. B., Green, J. R., & Marx, D. B. (2009). Early speech motor development: Cognitive and linguistic considerations. *Journal of Communication Disorders, 42*, 286–98.

Nippold, M. A. (1991). Evaluating and enhancing idiom comprehension in language-disordered children. *Language, Speech, and Hearing Services in Schools, 22*, 100–106.

Nippold, M. A. (2007). *Later language development: School-age children, adolescents, and young adults* (3rd ed.). Austin, TX: Pro-Ed.

Nippold, M. A. (2009). School-age children talk about chess: Does knowledge drive syntactic complexity? *Journal of Speech, Language, and Hearing Research, 52*, 856–871.

Nippold, M. A., & Duthie, J. K. (2003). Mental imagery and idiom comprehension: A comparison of school-age children and adults. *Journal of Speech, Language, and Hearing Research, 46*, 788–799.

Nippold, M. A., Duthie, J. K., & Larsen, J. (2005). Literacy as a leisure activity: Free-time preferences of older children and young adolescents. *Language, Speech, and Hearing Service in Schools, 36*, 93–102.

Nippold, M. A., & Haq, F. S. (1996). Proverb comprehension in youth: The role of concreteness and familiarity. *Journal of Speech, Language, and Hearing Research, 39*, 166–176.

Nippold, M. A., Hegel, S. L., Sohlberg, M. M., & Schwarz, I. E. (1999). Defining abstract entities: development in pre-adolescents, adolescents, and young adults. *Journal of Speech, Language, and Hearing Research, 42*, 473–481.

Nippold, M. A., Hesketh, L. J., Duthie, J. K., & Mansfield, T. C. (2005). Conversational vs. expository discourse: A study of syntactic development in children, adolescents, and adults. *Journal of Speech, Language, and Hearing Research, 48*, 1048–1064.

Nippold, M. A., Mansfield, T. C., & Billow, J. L. (2007). Peer conflict explanations in children, adolescents, and adults: Examining the development of complex syntax. *American Journal of Speech-Language Pathology, 16*, 179–188.

Nippold, M. A., Mansfield, T. C., Billow, J. L., & Tomblin, J. B. (2008). Expository discourse in adolescents with language impairments: Examining syntactic development. *American Journal of Speech-Language Pathology, 17*, 356–366.

Nippold, M. A., Moran, C., & Schwartz, I. E. (2001). Idiom understanding in preadolescents: Synergy in action. *American Journal of Speech-Language Pathology, 10*, 169–179.

Nippold, M. A., Schwarz, I. E., & Undlin, R. (1992). Use and understanding of adverbial conjuncts: A developmental study of adolescents and young adults. *Journal of Speech and Hearing Research, 35*, 108–118.

Nippold, M. A., & Taylor, C. L. (1995). Idiom understanding in youth: Further examination of familiarity and transparency. *Journal of Speech, Language, and Hearing Research, 38*, 426–433.

Nippold, M. A., Taylor, C. L., & Baker, J. M. (1995). Idiom understanding in Australian youth: A cross-cultural comparison. *Journal of Speech, Language, and Hearing Research, 39*, 442–447.

Nippold, M. A., Uhden, L. D., & Schwarz, I. E. (1997). Proverb explanation through the lifespan: A developmental study of adolescents and adults. *Journal of Speech, Language, and Hearing Research, 40*, 245–253.

Nippold, M. A., Ward-Lonergan, J. M., & Fanning, J. L. (2005). Persuasive writing in children, adolescents, and adults: A study of syntactic, semantic, and pragmatic development. *Language, Speech, and Hearing Service in Schools, 36*, 125–138.

Nittrouer, S. (2002). From ear to cortex: A perspective on what clinicians need to understand about speech perception and language processing. *Language, Speech, and Hearing Services in Schools, 33*, 237–252.

Noel, M., Peterson, C., & Jesso, B. (2008). The relationship of parenting stress and child temperament to language development among economically disadvantaged preschoolers. *Journal of Child Language, 35*, 823–843.

Oetting, J., & Pruitt, S. (2009). Past tense marking by African American English–speaking children reared in poverty. *Journal of Speech, Language, and Hearing Research, 52*, 2–15.

Oetting, J. B., & Newkirk, B. L. (2008). Subject relatives by children with and without SLI across different dialects of English. *Clinical Linguistics and Phonetics, 22*(2), 111–125.

Oetting, J. B., & Wimberly Garrity, A. (2006). Variation within dialects: A case of Cajun/Creole influence within child SAAE and SWE. *Journal of Speech, Language, & Hearing Research, 49*, 16–26.

Ogura, T., Dale, P. S., Yamashita, Y., Murase, T., & Mahieu, A. (2006). The use of nouns and verbs by Japanese children and their caregivers in book-reading and toy-playing contexts. *Journal of Child Language, 33*, 1–29.

Olmstead, D. (1971). *Out of the mouths of babes*. The Hague, the Netherlands: Mouton.

Olson, J., & Frank Masur, E. (2012). Mothers respond differently to infants' familiar versus non-familiar verbal imitations. *Journal of Child Language, 39*, 731–752.

O'Neill, D. K., & Topolovec, J. C. (2000). Two-year-old children's sensitivity to the referential (in) efficacy of their own pointing gestures. *Journal of Child Language, 28*, 1–28.

Oomen, C., & Postma, A. (2001). Effects of increased speech rate on monitoring and self-repair. *Journal of Psycholinguistic Research, 30*, 163–184.

Otomo, K. (2001). Maternal response to word approximation in Japanese children's transition to language. *Journal of Child Language, 28*, 29–57.

Ouellette, G., & Sénéchal, M. (2008a). Pathways to literacy: A study of invented spelling and its role in learning to read. *Child Development, 79*(4), 899–913.

Ouellette, G., & Sénéchal, M. (2008b). A window into early literacy: Exploring the cognitive and linguistic underpinnings of invented spelling. *Scientific Studies of Reading, 12*, 195–219.

Owens, R. (1978). *Speech acts in the early language of non-delayed and retarded children: A taxonomy and distributional study*. Unpublished doctoral dissertation, The Ohio State University.

Özçaliskan, S., & Goldin-Meadow, S. (2005). Do parents lead their children by the hand? *Journal of Child Language, 32*, 481–505.

Pacton, S., Fayol, M., & Perruchet, P. (2005). Children's implicit learning of graphotactic and morphological regularities. *Child Development, 76*, 324–339.

Pae, S., Chang-Song, Y., Kwak, K., Sung, H., & Sim, H. (2004). MCDI-K referenced expressive word development of Korean children and gender differences. *Korean Journal of Communication Disorders, 9*, 45–56.

Pan, B. A., Rowe, M. L., Singer, J. D., & Snow, C. E. (2005). Maternal correlates of growth in toddler vocabulary production in low-income families. *Child Development, 76*, 763–782.

Papaeliou, C., Minadakis, G., & Cavouras, D. (2002). Acoustic patterns of infant vocalizations expressing emotions and communicative functions. *Journal of Speech, Language, and Hearing Research, 45*, 311–317.

Papaeliou, C. F., & Trevarthen, C. (2006). Prelinguistic pitch patterns expressing "communication" and "apprehension." *Journal of Child Language, 33*, 163–178.

Paradis, J. (2001). Do bilingual two-year-olds have separate phonological systems? *International Journal of Bilingualism, 5*, 19–38.

Paradis, J., & Genesee, F. (1996). Syntactic acquisition in bilingual children: Autonomous or interdependent? *Studies in Second Language Acquisition, 18*, 1–25.

Paradis, J., Nicoladis, E., & Genesee, F. (2000). Early emergence of structural constraints on code-mixing: Evidence from French-English bilingual children. *Bilingualism: Language and Cognition, 3*, 245–261.

Parente, R., Kolakowsky-Hayner, S., Krug, K., & Wilk, C. (1999). Retraining working memory after traumatic brain injury. *NeuroRehabilitation, 13*, 157–163.

Passolunghi, M. C., & Siegel, L. S. (2004). Working memory and access to numerical information in children with disability in mathematics. *Journal of Experimental Child Psychology, 88*, 348–367.

Patterson, J. L. (2002). Relationships of expressive vocabulary to frequency of reading and television experience among bilingual toddlers. *Applied Psycholinguistics, 23*, 493–508.

Patton Terry, N., & McDonald Connor, C. (2012). Changing Nonmainstream American English Use and Early Reading Achievement from Kindergarten to First Grade. *American Journal of Speech-Language Pathology, 21*, 78–86.

Patton Terry, N., McDonald Connor, C., Thomas-Tate, S., & Love, M. (2010). Examining relationships among dialect variation, literacy skills, and school context in first grade. *Journal of Speech, Language, and Hearing Research, 53*, 126–145.

Paul, R. (1990). Comprehension strategies: Interactions between world knowledge and the development of sentence comprehension. *Topics in Language Disorders, 10*(3), 63–75.

Paulesu, F., Perani, D., Blasi, V., Silani, G., Borghese, N. A., De Giovanni, V., et al. (2003). A functional-anatomical model for lip reading. *Journal of Neurophysiology, 90*, 2005–2013.

Pearson, B. Z., Fernandez, S., & Oller, D. K. (1995). Cross-language synonyms in the lexicons of bilingual infants: One language or two? *Journal of Child Language, 22*, 345–368.

Pelucchi, B., Hay, J. F., & Saffran, J. R. (2009). Statistical learning in a natural language by 8-month-old infants. *Child Development, 80*, 674–685.

Peña, E., Bedore, L. M., & Rappazzo, D. (2003). Comparison of Spanish, English, and bilingual children's performance across semantic tasks. *Language, Speech, and Hearing Services in Schools, 34*, 5–16.

Pérez-Leroux, A.T., Castilla-Earls, A.P., & Brunner, J. (2012). General and Specific Effects of Lexicon in Grammar: Determiner and Object Pronoun Omissions in Child Spanish. *Journal of Speech, Language, and Hearing Research, 55*, 313–327.

Perez-Pereira, M. (1994). Imitations, repetitions, routines, and the child's analysis of language: Insights from the blind. *Journal of Child Language, 21*, 317–337.

Peterson, C. (1990). The who, when and where of early narratives. *Journal of Child Language, 17*, 433–455.

Petitto, L. A., Katerelos, M., Levy, B. G., Gauna, K., Tétreault, K., & Ferraro, V. (2001). Bilingual signed and spoken language acquisition from birth: Implications for the mechanisms underlying early bilingual language acquisition. *Journal of Child Language, 28*, 453–496.

Petitto, L. A., & Marentette, P. F. (1990, October). *The timing of linguistic milestones in sign language acquisition: Are first signs acquired earlier than first words?* Paper presented at the 15th Annual Boston University Conference on Language Development, Boston, MA.

Petitto, L. A., & Marentette, P. F. (1991, April). The timing of linguistic milestones in sign and spoken language acquisition. In L. Petitto (Chair), *Are the linguistic milestones in signed and spoken language acquisition similar or different?* Symposium conducted at the Biennial Meeting of the Society for Research in Child Development, Seattle, WA.

Pflaum, S. (1986). *The development of language and literacy in young children* (3rd ed.). Columbus, OH: Merrill.

Piaget, J. (1954). *The construction of reality in the child.* New York, NY: Basic Books.

Piaget, J. P. (1952). *The origins of intelligence in children.* New York, NY: International Universities Press.

Pillon, A., Degauquier, C., & Duquesne, F. (1992). Males' and females' conversational behavior in cross-sex dyads: From gender differences to gender similarities. *Journal of Psycholinguistic Research, 21*, 147–172.

Pine, J. M. (1990). *Non-referential children: Slow or different?* Paper presented at the Fifth International Congress for the Study of Child Language, Budapest, Hungary.

Pine, J. M., Conti-Ramsden, G., Joseph, K. L., Liebergott, J., & Serratrice, L. (2008). Tense over time: Test the Agreement/Tense Omission Model as an account of the pattern of tense-marking provision in early child English. *Journal of Child Language, 35*, 55–75.

Pine, J. M., & Lieven, E. V. M. (1990). Referential style at thirteen months: Why age-defined cross sectional measures are inappropriate for the study of strategy differences in early language development. *Journal of Child Language, 17*, 625–631.

Pine, J. M., & Lieven, E. V. M. (1993). Reanalysing rote-learned phrases: Individual differences in the transition to multiword speech. *Journal of Child Language, 20*, 551–571.

Pine, J. M., Lieven, E. V. M., & Rowland, C. F. (1998). Comparing different models of the development of the English verb category. *Linguistics, 36*, 807–830.

Pinker, S. (1984). *Language learnability and language development.* Cambridge, MA: Harvard University Press.

Pinker, S. (1994). *Language and instinct.* New York, NY: Morrow.

Pinker, S., & Ullman, M. (2002). The past and future of the past tense. *Trends in Cognitive Science, 6*(11), 456-463.

Plaut, D. C., & Kello, C. T. (1999). The emergence of phonology from the interplay of speech comprehension and production: A distributed connectionist approach. In B. MacWhinney (Ed.), *The emergence of language*. Mahwah, NJ: Erlbaum.

Plunkett, K. (1993). Lexical segmentation and vocabulary growth in early language acquisition. *Journal of Child Language, 20*, 43–60.

Plunkett, K., & Marchman, V. (1993). From rote learning to system building: The acquisition of morphology in children and connectionist nets. *Cognition, 48*, 21–69.

Polka, L., & Sundara, M. (2003). Word segmentation in monolingual and bilingual infant learners of English and French. In M. J. Solé, D. Recasens, & J. Romero (Eds.), *Proceedings of the International Congress of Phonetic Sciences, 15*, 1021–1024.

Polka, L., & Werker, J. F. (1994). Developmental changes in perception of non-native vowel contrasts. *Journal of Experimental Psychology: Human Perception and Performance, 20*, 421–435.

Portes, A., & Hao, L. (1998). E pluribus unum: Bilingualism and loss of language in the second language. *Sociology of Education, 71*, 269–294.

Portes, A., & Rumbaut, R. (2001). *Legacies: The story of immigrant second generation.* Berkeley, CA: University of California Press.

Prasada, S., & Ferenz, K. S. (2002). Singular or plural? Children's knowledge of the factors that determine the appropriate form of count nouns. *Journal of Child Language, 29*, 49–70.

Pratt, S. R., Kuller, L., Talbott, E. O., McHugh-Pemu, K., Buhari, A. M., & Xu, X. (2009). Prevalence of hearing loss in black and white elders: Results of the cardiovascular health study. *Journal of Speech, Language, and Hearing Research, 52*, 973–989.

Price, J. R., Roberts, J. E., & Jackson, S. C. (2006). Structural development of the fictional narratives of African American preschoolers. *Language, Speech, and Hearing Services in Schools, 37*, 178–190.

Pruitt, S. L., & Oetting, J. B. (2009). Past tense marking by African American English–speaking children reared in poverty. *Journal of Speech, Language, and Hearing Research, 52*, 2–15.

Pruitt, S. L., Oetting, J. B., & Hegarty, M. (2011). Passive participle marking by African American English–speaking children reared in poverty. *Journal of Speech, Language, and Hearing Research, 54*, 598–607.

Qualls, C. D., & Harris, J. L. (1999). Effects of familiarity on idiom comprehension in African American and European American fifth-graders. *Language, Speech, and Hearing Services in Schools, 30*, 141–151.

Rabin, J., & Deacon, H. (2008). The representation of morphologically complex words in the developing lexicon. *Journal of Child Language, 35*, 453–465.

Radvansky, G. A., Copeland, D. E., & Zwaan, R. A. (2003). Brief report: Aging and functional spatial relations in comprehension and memory. *Psychology and Aging, 18*, 161–165.

Raikes, H., Alexander Pan, B., Luze, G., Tamis-LeMonda, C. S., Brooks-Gunn, J., Constantine, J., Banks Tarullo, L., Raikes, H. A., & Rodriguez, E. T. (2006). Mother-child book reading in low-income families: Correlates and outcomes during the first three years of life. *Child Development, 77*, 924–953.

Ravid, D. (2006). Semantic development in textual contexts during the school years: Noun Scale analyses. *Journal of Child Language, 33*, 791–821.

Ravid, D., & Avidor, A. (1998). Acquisition of derived nominals in Hebrew: Developmental and linguistic principles. *Journal of Child Language, 25*, 229–266.

Ravid, D., & Cahana-Amitay, D. (2005). Verbal and nominal expression in narrating conflict situations in Hebrew. *Journal of Pragmatics, 37*, 157–183.

Ravid, D., van Hell, J., Rosado, E., & Zamora, A. (2002). Subject NP patterning in the development of text production: Speech and writing. *Written Language and Literacy, 5*, 69–94.

Ravid, D., & Zilberbuch, S. (2003). Morphosyntactic constructs in the development of spoken and written Hebrew text production. *Journal of Child Language, 30*, 395–418.

Reali, F., & Christiansen, M. H. (2005). Uncovering the richness of the stimulus: Structure dependence and indirect statistical evidence. *Cognitive Science, 29*, 1007–1028.

Redford, M. A., & Gildersleeve-Neumann, C. E. (2009). The development of distinct speaking styles in preschool children. *Journal of Speech, Language, and Hearing Research, 52*, 1434–1448.

Redmond, S. M. (2003). Children's productions of the affix *-ed* in past tense and past participle contexts. *Journal of Speech, Language, and Hearing Research, 46*, 1095–1109.

Reilly, J., & Bellugi, U. (1996). Competition on the face: Affect and language in ASL motherese. *Journal of Child Language, 23*, 219–239.

Resches, M., & Pérez Pereira, M. (2007). Referential communication abilities and Theory of Mind development in preschool children. *Journal of Child Language, 34*, 21–52.

Rescorla, L. (2002). Language and reading outcomes to age 9 in late-talking toddlers. *Journal of Speech, Language, and Hearing Research, 45*, 360–371.

Rescorla, L. (2009). Age 17 language and reading outcomes in late-talking toddlers: Support for a dimensional perspective on language delay. *Journal of Speech, Language, and Hearing Research, 52*, 16–30.

Rescorla, L., & Alley, A. (2001). Validation of the Language Development Survey (LDS): A parent report tool for identifying language delay in toddlers. *Journal of Speech, Language, and Hearing Research, 44*, 434–45.

Rescorla, L., & Fechnay, T. (1996). Mother-child synchrony and communicative reciprocity in late-talking toddlers. *Journal of Speech, Language, and Hearing Research, 39*, 200–208.

Rescorla, L., Lee, Y. M., Oh, K. J., & Kim, Y. A. (2013). Lexical development in Korean: vocabulary size, lexical composition, and late talking. *Journal of Speech, Language, and Hearing Research, 56*, 735–747.

Rescorla, L., Ross, G. S., & McClure, S. (2007). Language delay and behavioral/emotional problems in toddlers: Findings from two developmental clinics. *Journal of Speech, Language, and Hearing Research, 50*, 1063–1078.

Reznick, J. S., & Goldfield, B. A. (1994). Diary vs. representative checklist assessment of productive vocabulary. *Journal of Child Language, 21*, 465–472.

Reznick, S. (1990). Visual preference as a test of infant word comprehension. *Applied Psycholinguistics, 11*, 145–166.

Rice, M. L., Smolik, F., Perpich, D., Thompson, T., Rytting, N., & Blossom, M. (2010). Mean Length of Utterance levels in 6-month intervals for children 3 to 9 years with and without language impairments. *Journal of Speech, Language, and Hearing Research, 53*, 333–349.

Rice, M. L., Taylor, C. L., & Zubrick, S. R. (2008). Language outcomes of 7-year-old children with or without a history of late language emergence at 24 months. *Journal of Speech, Language, and Hearing Research, 51*, 394–407.

Rispoli, M. (1994). Structural dependency and the acquisition of grammatical relations. In Y. Levy (Ed.), *Other children, other languages: Issues in the theory of language acquisition*. Hillsdale, NJ: Erlbaum.

Rispoli, M. (1998). Patterns of pronoun case error. *Journal of Child Language, 25*, 533–544.

Rispoli, M. (2003). Changes in the nature of sentence production during the period of grammatical development. *Journal of Speech, Language, and Hearing Research, 46*, 818–830.

Rispoli, M. (2005). When children reach beyond their grasp: Why some children make pronoun case errors and others don't. *Journal of Child Language, 32*, 93–116.

Rispoli, M., & Hadley, P. (2001). The leading edge: The significance of sentence disruptions in the development of grammar. *Journal of Speech, Language, and Hearing Research, 44*, 1131–1143.

Rispoli, M., & Hadley, P. (2011). Toward a theory of gradual morphosyntactic learning. In I. Arnon & E. Clark (Eds.), *Experience, variation and generalization: Learning a first language* (pp. 15–33). Amsterdam, the Netherlands: John Benjamins.

Rispoli, M., Hadley, P., & Holt, J. (2008). Stalls and revisions: A developmental perspective on sentence production. *Journal of Speech, Language, and Hearing Research, 51*, 953–966.

Rispoli, M., Hadley, P., & Holt, J. (2009). The growth of tense productivity. *Journal of Speech, Language, and Hearing Research, 52*, 930–944.

Rispoli, M., Hadley, P. A., & Holt, J. K. (2012). Sequence and system in the acquisition of tense and agreement. *Journal of Speech, Language, and Hearing Research, 55*, 1007–1021.

Rittle-Johnson, B., & Siegler, R. S. (1999). Learning to spell: Variability, choice, and change in children's strategy use. *Child Development, 70*, 332–348.

Roberts, J., Jurgens, J., & Burchinal, M. (2005). The role of home literacy practices in preschool children's language and emergent literacy skills. *Journal of Speech, Language, and Hearing Research, 48*, 345–359.

Roberts, J. A., Pollock, K. E., Krakow, R., Price, J., Fulmer, K. C., & Wang, P. P. (2005). Language development in preschool-age children adopted from China. *Journal of Speech, Language, and Hearing Research, 48*, 93–107.

Roberts, R., & Gibson, E. (2002). Individual differences in sentence memory. *Journal of Psycholinguistic Research, 31*, 573–598.

Rogoff, B. (2003). *Cultural nature of human development*. New York, NY: Oxford University Press.

Rollins, P. R. (2003). Caregivers' contingent comments to 9-month-old infants: Relationships with later language. *Applied Psycholinguistics, 24*, 221–234.

Rome-Flanders, T., & Cronk, C. (1995). A longitudinal study of infant vocalizations during mother-infant games. *Journal of Child Language, 22*, 259–274.

Rose, S. A., Feldman, J. F., & Jankowski, J. J. (2001). Attention and recognition memory in the first year of life: A longitudinal study of preterms and full-terms. *Developmental Psychology, 37*, 135–151.

Rose, S. A., Feldman, J. F., & Jankowski, J. J. (2004). Dimensions of cognition in infancy. *Intelligence, 32*, 245–262.

Rose, S. A., Feldman, J. F., & Jankowski, J. J. (2005). The structure of infant cognition at 1 year. *Intelligence, 33*, 231–250.

Rose, S. A., Feldman, J. F., & Jankowski, J. J. (2009). A cognitive approach to the development of early language. *Child Development, 80*, 134–150.

Ross, S., Oetting, J. B., & Stapleton, B. (2004). Preterite had + v-ed: A developmental narrative structure of African American English. *American Speech, 79*(2), 167–193.

Rovee-Collier, C. K. (1999). The development of infant memory. *Current Direction in Psychological Science, 8*, 80–85.

Rowe, M. L., Özçaliskan, S., & Goldin-Meadow, S. (2008). Learning words by hand: Gesture's role in predicting vocabulary development. *First Language, 28*, 182–199.

Rowland, C. F., Pine, J. M., Lieven, E. V. M., & Theakston, A. L. (2003). Determinants of acquisition order in *wh-* questions: Re-evaluating the role of caregiver speech. *Journal of Child Language, 30*, 609–635.

Rowland, C. F., Pine, J. M., Lieven, E. V. M., & Theakston, A. L. (2005). The incidence of error in young children's *wh*-questions. *Journal of Speech, Language and Hearing Research, 48*, 384–404.

Rowland, C. F., & Theakston, A. L. (2009). The acquisition of auxiliary syntax: A longitudinal elicitation study. Part 2: The modals and auxiliary DO. *Journal of Speech, Language, and Hearing Research, 52*, 1471–1492.

Rozendaal, M. I., & Baker, A. E. (2008). A cross-linguistic investigation of the acquisition of the pragmatics of indefinite and definite reference in two-year-olds. *Journal of Child Language, 35*, 773–807.

Rutter, M. (2006). *Genes and behaviour: Nature–nurture interplay explained*. London, England: Blackwell.

Ryan, J. (1974). Early language development: Towards a communicational analysis. In P. Richards (Ed.), *The integration of a child into a social world*. London, England: Cambridge University Press.

Ryder, N., & Leinonen, E. (2003). Use of context in question answering by 3-, 4-, and 5-year-old children. *Journal of Psycholinguistic Research, 32*, 397–416.

Sabbagh, M., & Gelman, S. (2000). Buzzsaws and blueprints: What children need (or don't need) to learn language. *Journal of Child Language, 27*, 715–726.

Sabbagh, M. A., Bowman, L. C., Evraire, L. E., & Ito, J. M. B. (2009). Neurodevelopmental correlates of Theory of Mind in preschool children. *Child Development, 80*, 1147–1162.

Sadagopan, N., & Smith, A. (2008). Developmental changes in the effects of utterance length and complexity on speech movement variability. *Journal of Speech, Language, and Hearing Research, 51*, 1138–1151.

Salomo, D., Lieven, E., & Tomasello, M. (2013). Children's ability to answer different types of questions. *Journal of Child Language, 40*, 469–491.

Sander, E. (1972). When are speech sounds learned? *Journal of Speech and Hearing Disorders, 37*, 55–63.

Sanders, L. D., & Neville, H. J. (2000). Lexical, syntactic, and stress-pattern cues for speech segmentation. *Journal of Speech, Language, and Hearing Research, 43*, 1301–1321.

Sanders, L. D., Neville, H. J., & Woldorff, M. G. (2002). Speech segmentation by native and non-native speakers: The use of lexical, syntactic, and stress-pattern cues. *Journal of Speech, Language, and Hearing Research, 45*, 519–530.

Santelmann, L., Berk, S., Austin, J., Somashekar, S., & Lust, B. (2002). Continuity and development in the acquisition of inversion in yes/no questions: Dissociating movement and inflection. *Journal of Child Language, 29*, 813–842.

Savage, C., Lieven, E., Theakston, A., & Tomasello, M. (2003). Testing the abstractness of children's linguistic representations: Lexical and structural priming of syntactic constructions in young children. *Developmental Science, 6*, 557–567.

Saxe, R. R., Whitfield-Gabrieli, S., Scholz, J., & Pelphrey, K. A. (2009). Brain regions for perceiving and reasoning about other people in school-aged children. *Child Development, 80*, 1197–1209.

Scaife, M., & Bruner, J. (1975). The capacity of joint visual attention in the infant. *Nature, 253*, 265–266.

Scarborough, H., Wyckoff, J., & Davidson, R. (1986). A reconsideration of the relationship between age and mean utterance length. *Journal of Speech and Hearing Research, 29*, 394–399.

Scarborough, H. S. (1998). Predicting the future achievement of second-graders with reading disabilities: Contributions of phonemic awareness, verbal memory, rapid naming, and IQ. *Annals of Dyslexia, 48*, 115–136.

Schafer, G. (2005). Infants can learn decontextualized words before their first birthday. *Child Development, 76*, 87–96.

Schafer, G., & Plunkett, K. (1998). Rapid word learning by fifteen-month-olds under tightly controlled conditions. *Child Development, 69*, 309–320.

Schaffer, R. (1977). *Mothering*. Cambridge, MA: Harvard University Press.

Schane, S. (1973). *Generative phonology*. Englewood Cliffs, NJ: Prentice Hall.

Scheffner Hammer, C., & Weiss, A. L. (1999). Guiding language development: How African American mothers and their infants structure play interactions. *Journal of Speech, Language, and Hearing Research, 42*, 1219–1233.

Scheffner Hammer, C., & Weiss, A. L. (2000). African American mothers' views on their infants' language-development and language-learning environment. *American Journal of Speech-Language Pathology, 9*, 126–140.

Scheffner Hammer, C., Komaroff, E., Rodriguez, B. L., Lopez, L. M., Scarpin, S. E., & Goldstein, B. (2012). Predicting Spanish–English bilingual children's language abilities. *Journal of Speech, Language, and Hearing Research, 55*, 1251–1264.

Scherf, K. S., Behrmann, M., Humphreys, K., & Luna, B. (2007). Visual category-selectivity for faces, places and objects emerges along different developmental trajectories. *Developmental Science, 10*, F15–F30.

Schlesinger, I. (1971). Production of utterances and language acquisition. In D. Slobin (Ed.), *The ontogenesis of grammar*. New York, NY: Academic Press.

Schmidt, C. L. (1996). Scrutinizing reference: How gesture and speech are coordinated in mother–child interaction. *Journal of Child Language, 23*, 279–305.

Schmidt, C. L., & Lawson, K. R. (2002). Caregiver attention-focusing and children's attention-sharing behaviours as predictors of later verbal IQ in very low birth weight children. *Journal of Child Language, 29*, 3–22.

Schmidt, M. E., Pempek, T. A., Kirkorian, H. L., Frankenfield Lund, A., & Anderson, D. R. (2008). The effects of background television on the toy play behavior of very young children. *Child Development, 79*, 1137–1151.

Scofield, J., Miller, A., & Hartin, T. (2011). Object movement in preschool children's word learning. *Journal of Child Language, 38*, 181–200.

Scopesi, A., & Pellegrino, M. (1990). Structure and function of baby talk in a day-care center. *Journal of Child Language, 17*, 101–114.

Scott, C. M. (1987). *Summarizing text: Context effects in language disordered children.* Paper presented at the First International Symposium, Specific Language Disorders in Children, University of Reading, England.

Scott, C. M. (1988). Producing complex sentences. *Topics in Language Disorders, 8*(2), 44–62.

Scott, C. M. (1999). Learning to write. In H. W. Catts & A. G. Kamhi (Eds.), *Language and reading disabilities* (pp. 224–258). Boston, MA: Allyn & Bacon.

Scott, C. M., & Windsor, J. (2000). General language performance measures in spoken and written narrative and expository discourse of school-age children with language learning disabilities. *Journal of Speech, Language, and Hearing Research, 43*, 324–339.

Scott, C. M., Nippold, M. A., Norris, J. A., & Johnson, C. J. (1992, November). *School-age children and adolescents: Establishing language norms.* Paper presented at the annual convention of the American Speech-Language-Hearing Association, San Antonio, TX.

Scott, K. A., Roberts, J. A., & Glennen, S. (2011). How well do children who are internationally adopted acquire language? A meta-analysis. *Journal of Speech, Language, and Hearing Research, 54*, 1153–1169.

Scott, K. A., Roberts, J. A., & Krakow, R. (2008). Oral and written language development of children adopted from China. *American Journal of Speech-Language Pathology, 17*, 150–160.

Segebart DeThorne, L., Harlaar, N., Petrill, S. A., & Deater-Deckard, K. (2012). Longitudinal stability in genetic effects on children's conversational language productivity. *Journal of Speech, Language, and Hearing Research, 55*, 739–753.

Seigneuric, A., & Ehrlich, J. (2005). Contributions of working memory capacity to children's reading comprehension: A longitudinal investigation. *Reading and Writing, 18*, 617–656.

Seigneuric, A., Ehrlich, M-F., Oakhill, J., & Yuill, N. (2000). Working memory resources and children's reading comprehension. *Reading and Writing: An Interdisciplinary Journal, 13*, 81–103.

Sell, M. A. (1992). The development of children's knowledge structures: Events, slots, and taxonomies. *Journal of Child Language, 19*, 659–676.

Senechal, M. (1997). The differential effect of storybook reading on preschoolers' acquisition of expressive and receptive vocabulary. *Journal of Child Language, 24*, 123–138.

Seroussi, B. (2004). Hebrew derived nouns in context: A developmental perspective. *Folia Phoniatrica et Logopaedica, 56*, 273–290.

Shafer, V. L., Shucard, D. W., Shucard, J. L., & Gerken, L. (1998). An electrophysiological study of infants' sensitivity to the sound patterns of English speech. *Journal of Speech, Language, and Hearing Research, 41*, 874–886.

Shapiro, L., Swinney, D., & Borsky, S. (1998). Online examination of language performance in normal and neurologically impaired adults. *American Journal of Speech-Language Pathology, 7*, 49–60.

Share, D. L. (2008). On the anglocentricities of current reading research and practice: The perils of overreliance on an "outlier" orthography. *Psychological Bulletin, 134*, 584–615.

Shatil, E., Share, D. L., & Levin, I. (2000). On the contribution of kindergarten writing to grade 1 literacy: A longitudinal study in Hebrew. *Applied Psycholinguistics, 21*(1), 1–21.

Shatz, M., & O'Reilly, A. (1990). Conversational or communicative skill? A reassessment of two year-olds' behavior in miscommunication episodes. *Journal of Child Language, 17*, 131–146.

Sheng, M., & Hoogenraad, C. C. (2007). The post-synaptic architecture of excitatory synapses: A more quantitative view. *Annual Review of Biochemistry, 76*, 823–847.

Shimpi, P. M., Gámez, P. B., Huttenlocher, J., & Vasilyeva, M. (2007). Syntactic priming in 3- and 4-year-old children: Evidence for abstract representations of transitive and dative forms. *Developmental Psychology, 43*, 1334–1346.

Shipley, K., Maddox, M., & Driver, J. (1991). Children's development of irregular past tense verb forms. *Language, Speech, and Hearing Services in Schools, 22*, 115–122.

Short-Meyerson, K. J., & Abbeduto, L. J. (1997). Preschoolers' communication during scripted interactions. *Journal of Child Language, 24*, 469–493.

Singer, B. D., & Bashir, A. S. (1999). What are executive functions and self-regulation and what do they have to do with language-learning disorders? *Language, Speech, and Hearing Services in Schools, 30*, 265–273.

Singson, M., Mahony, D., & Mann, V. (2000). The relation between reading ability and morphological skills: Evidence from derivational suffixes. *Reading and Writing: An Interdisciplinary Journal, 12*, 219–252.

Ska, B., Duong, A., & Joanette, Y. (2004). Discourse impairments. In R. D. Kent (Ed.), *The MIT encyclopedia of communication disorders* (pp. 302–304). Cambridge, MA: MIT Press.

Skinner, B.F. (1957). *Verbal Behavior*. Boston: Copley Publishing Group.

Skipper, J. I., Nusbaum, H. C., & Small, S. L. (2005). Listening to talking faces: Motor cortical activation during speech perception. *NeuroImage, 25*, 76–89.

Slaughter, V., Peterson, C. C., & Carpenter, M. (2009). Maternal mental state talk and infants' early gestural communication. *Journal of Child Language, 36*, 1053–1074.

Slobin, D. (1970). Universals of grammatical development in children. In G. Flores D'Arcais & W. Levelt (Eds.), *Advances in psycholinguistics*. Amsterdam, the Netherlands: North Holland.

Slobin, D. (1978). Cognitive prerequisites for the development of grammar. In L. Bloom & M. Lahey (Eds.), *Readings in language development*. New York, NY: Wiley.

Slobin, D. I. (1973). Cognitive prerequisites for the development of grammar. In C. Ferguson & D. Slobin (Eds.), *Studies of child language development*. New York, NY: Holt, Rinehart, & Winston.

Smiljanic, R., & Bradlow, A. R. (2008). Stability of temporal contrasts across speaking styles in English and Croation. *Journal of Phonetics, 36*, 91–113.

Smith, A., & Goffman, L. (2004). Interaction of motor and language factors in the development of speech. In B. Maassen, R. Kent, H. Peters, P. van Lieshout, & W. Hulstijn (Eds.), *Speech motor control in normal and disordered speech* (pp. 227–252). Oxford, United Kingdom: Oxford University Press.

Smith, C. S. (1997). *The parameter of aspect* (2nd ed.). Norwell, MA: Kluwer.

Smith, P.A. (2011). Attention, Working Memory, and Grammaticality Judgment in Typical Young Adults. *Journal of Speech, Language, and Hearing Research, 54*, 918–931.

Smitherman, G. (1994). *Black talk: Words and phrases from the hood to the amen corner*. New York, NY: Houghton-Mifflin.

Smyth, R., Jacobs, G., & Rogers, H. (2003). Male voices and perceived sexual orientation: An experimental and theoretical approach. *Language in Society, 32*, 329–350.

Snow, C. E., Scarborough, H. S., & Burns, M. S. (1999). What speech-language pathologists need to know about early reading. *Topics in Language Disorders, 20*(1), 48–58.

Snow, D. (1998). A prominence account of syllable reduction in early speech development: The child's prosodic phonology of *tiger* and *giraffe*. *Journal of Speech, Language, and Hearing Research, 41*, 1171–1184.

Snow, D. (2006). Regression and reorganization of intonation between 6 and 23 months. *Child Development, 77*, 281–296.

Snyder, L. E., Dabasinskas, C., & O'Connor, E. (2002). An information processing perspective on language impairment in children: Looking at both sides of the coin. *Topics in Language Disorders, 22*(3), 1–14.

So, L. K., & Dodd, B. J. (1995). The acquisition of phonology by Cantonese-speaking children. *Journal of Child Language, 22*, 473–495.

Song, J. Y., Sundara, M., & Demuth, K. (2009). Phonological constraints on children's production of English third person singular *–s*. *Journal of Speech, Language, and Hearing Research, 52*, 623–642.

Sperry, L. L., & Sperry, D. E. (1996). Early development of narrative skills. *Cognitive development, 11*, 443–465.

Spira, E. G., Bracken, S. S., & Fischel, J. E. (2005). Predicting improvement after first-grade reading difficulties: The effects of oral language, emergent literacy, and behavior skills. *Developmental Psychology, 41*, 225–234.

Stanwood, G. D., & Levitt, P. (2007). Prenatal exposure to cocaine produces unique developmental and long-term adaptive changes in dopamine D1 receptor activity and subcellular distribution. *Journal of Neuroscience, 27*, 152–157.

Stark, R. (1986). Prespeech segmental feature development. In P. Fletcher & M. Garman (Eds.), *Language acquisition* (2nd ed.). New York, NY: Cambridge University Press.

Steeve, R. W., & Moore, C. A. (2009). Mandibular motor control during the early development of speech and nonspeech behaviors. *Journal of Speech, Language, and Hearing Research, 52*, 1530–1554.

Steeve, R. W., Moore, C. A., Green, J. R., Reilly, K. J., & Ruark McMurtrey, J. (2008). Babbling, chewing, and sucking: Oromandibular coordination at 9 months. *Journal of Speech, Language, and Hearing Research, 51*, 1390–1404.

Stein, M., Dierks, T., Brandeis, D., Wirth, M., Srtik, W., & Koenig, T. (2006). Plasticity in the adult language system: A longitudinal electrophysiological study on second language learning. *Neuroimage, 33*(2), 774–783.

Stern, D. N. (1977). *The first relationship.* Cambridge, MA: Harvard University Press.

Stine-Morrow, E. A. L. (2007). The Dumbledore hypothesis of cognitive aging. *Current Directions in Psychological Sciences, 16*, 295–299.

Stockman, I. (2006a). Alveolar bias in the final consonant deletion patterns of African American children. *Language, Speech, and Hearing Services in Schools, 37*, 85–95.

Stockman, I. (2006b). Evidence for a minimal competence core of consonant sounds in the speech of African American children: A preliminary study. *Clinical Linguistics & Phonetics, 20*(10), 723–749.

Stockman, I. (2007, October). *Acquisition of "go copula" in African American English*, Poster presented at the annual conference of New Ways to Analyze Language Variation, University of Pennsylvania, Philadelphia.

Stockman, I. (2008). Toward validation of a minimal competence phonetic core for African American children. *Journal of Speech, Language, and Hearing Research, 51*, 1244–1262.

Stockman, I. J. Guillory, B. Seibert, M. Boult, J. (2013). Toward validation of a minimal competence core of morphosyntax for African American children. *American Journal of Speech-Language Pathology, 22*, 40–56

Stockman, I., Karasinski, L., & Guillory, B. (2008). The use of conversational repairs by African American preschoolers. *Language, Speech, and Hearing Services in Schools, 39*, 461–474.

Stoel-Gammon, C. (2011). Relationships between lexical and phonological development in young children. *Journal of Child Language, 38*, 1–34.

Stoel-Gammon, C. & Sosa, A. V. (2007). Phonological development. In Hoff, E., & Schatz, M. (Eds.), *Handbook of child language*, 238–56. Oxford, United Kingdom: Blackwell.

Stokes, S. F., & Surendran, D. (2005). Articulatory complexity, ambient frequency, and functional load as predictors of consonant development in children. *Journal of Speech, Language, and Hearing Research, 48*, 577–591.

Storkel, H. L. (2001). Learning new words: Phonotactic probability in language development. *Journal of Speech, Language, and Hearing Research, 44*, 1321–1337.

Storkel, H. L. (2002). Restructuring of similarity neighbourhoods in the developing mental lexicon. *Journal of Child Language, 29*, 251–274.

Storkel, H. L. (2003). Learning new words II: Phonotactic probability in verb learning. *Journal of Speech, Language, and Hearing Research, 46*, 1312–1323.

Storkel, H. L. (2009). Developmental differences in the effects of phonological, lexical and semantic variables on word learning by infants. *Journal of Child Language, 36*, 291–321.

Storkel, H. L., Armbrüster, J., & Hogan, T. P. (2006). Differentiating phonotactic probability and neighborhood density in adult word learning. *Journal of Speech, Language, and Hearing Research, 49*, 1175–1192.

Storkel, H. L., & Hoover, J. R. (2011). The influence of part-word phonotactic probability/neighborhood density on word learning by preschool children varying in expressive vocabulary. *Journal of Child Language, 38*, 628–643.

Storkel, H. L., & Morrisette, M. L. (2002). The lexicon and phonology: Interactions in language acquisition. *Language, Speech, and Hearing Services in Schools, 33*, 24–37.

Streb, J., Hemighausen, E., & Rösler, F. (2004). Different anaphoric expressions are investigated by event-related brain potentials. *Journal of Psycholinguistic Research, 33*, 175–201.

Striano, T., Rochat, P., & Legerstee, M. (2003). The role of modeling request type on symbolic comprehension of objects and gestures in young children. *Journal of Child Language, 30*, 27–45.

Strömqvist, S., Nordqvist, A., & Wengelin, A. (2004). Writing the frog story: Developmental and cross-modal perspectives. In S. Strömqvist & L. Verhoeven (Eds.), *Relating events in narrative: Typological and contextual perspectives*. Mahwah, NJ: Erlbaum.

Sudhof, T. C. (2008). Neurotransmitter release. *Handbook of Experimental Pharmacology, 184*, 1–21.

Sulzby, E., & Zecker, L. B. (1991). The oral monologue as a form of emergent reading. In A. McCabe & C. Peterson (Eds.), *Developing narrative structure* (pp. 175–214). Hillsdale, NJ: Erlbaum.

Sundara, M., Demuth, K., & Kuhl, P. K. (2011). sentence-position effects on children's perception and production of English third person singular *–s*. *Journal of Speech, Language, and Hearing Research, 54*, 55–71.

Sutherland, D., & Gillon, G. T. (2005). Assessment of phonological representations in children with speech impairment. *Language, Speech, and Hearing Services in Schools, 36*, 294–307.

Tamis-Lemonda, C. S., Shannon, J. D., Cabrera, N. J., & Lamb, M. E. (2004). Fathers and mothers play with their 2- and 3-year olds: Contributions to language and cognitive development. *Child Development, 75*, 1806–1820.

Tannen, D. (1990). *You just don't understand: Talk between the sexes*. New York, NY: Ballantine.

Tannen, D. (1994). *Gender and discourse*. New York, NY: Oxford University Press.

Tao, L., & Healy, A. F. (1996). Cognitive strategies in discourse processing: A comparison of Chinese and English speakers. *Journal of Psycholinguistic Research, 25*, 597–616.

Tardif, T. (1996). Nouns are not always learned before verbs: Evidence from Mandarin speakers' early vocabularies. *Developmental Psychology, 32*, 492–504.

Tardif, T., Shatz, M., & Naigles, L. (1997). Caregiver speech and children's use of nouns versus verbs: A comparison of English, Italian, and Mandarin. *Journal of Child Language, 24*, 535–565.

Tardif, T., Fletcher, P., Liang, W. & Kaciroti, N. (2009). Early vocabulary in Mandarin (Putonghua) and Cantonese. *Journal of Child Language, 36*, 1115–1144.

Tare, M., Shatz, M., & Gilbertson, L. (2008). Maternal uses of non-object terms in child-directed speech: Color, number and time. *First Language, 28*, 87–100.

Taylor, N., Donovan, W., Miles, S., & Leavitt, L. (2009). Maternal control strategies, maternal language usage and children's language usage at two years. *Journal of Child Language, 36*, 381–404.

Temple, C., Nathan, R., & Burris, N. (1982). *The beginnings of writing*. Boston, MA: Allyn & Bacon.

Terry, N. P., Connor, C. M., Thomas-Tate, S., & Love, M. (2010). Examining relationships among dialect variation, literacy skills, and school context in first grade. *Journal of Speech, Language, and Hearing Research, 53*, 126–145.

Thal, D. J., Bates, E., Goodman, J., & Jahn-Samilo, J. (1997). Continuity of language abilities: An exploratory study of late- and early-talking toddlers. *Developmental Neuropsychology 13*, 239–273.

Thal, D., Tobias, S., & Morrison, D. (1991). Language and gesture in late talkers: A one-year follow-up. *Journal of Speech and Hearing Disorders, 34*, 604–612.

Theakston, A. L., Lieven, E. V. M., Pine, J. M., & Rowland, C. F. (2001). The role of performance limitations in the acquisition of verb-argument structure: An alternative account. *Journal of Child Language, 28*, 127–152.

Theakston, A. L., Lieven, E. V. M., Pine, J. M., & Rowland, C. F. (2005). The acquisition of auxiliary syntax: BE and HAVE. *Cognitive Linguistics, 16*(1), 247–277.

Theakston, A. L., Lieven, E. V. M., & Tomasello, M. (2003). The role of the input in the acquisition of third person singular verbs in English. *Journal of Speech, Language, and Hearing Research, 46*, 863–877.

Thelen, E. (1991). Motor aspects of emergent speech: A dynamic approach. In N. Krasnegor (Ed.), *Biobehavioral foundations of language* (pp. 339–362). Hillsdale, NJ: Erlbaum.

Theodore, R.M., Demuth, K., & Shattuck-Hufnagel, S. (2011). Acoustic evidence for positional and complexity effects on children's production of plural *–s*. *Journal of Speech, Language and Hearing Research, 54*, 539–548.

Thompson, C. A., Craig, H. K., & Washington, J. A. (2004). Variable production of African American English across oracy and literacy contexts. *Language, Speech, and Hearing Services in Schools, 35*, 269–282.

Thomson, J., & Chapman, R. (1977). Who is "Daddy" revisited: The status of two-year-olds' over-extensioned words in use and comprehension. *Journal of Child Language, 4*, 359–375.

Tincoff, R., & Jusczyk, P. W. (1999). Some beginning of word comprehension in 6-month-olds. *Psychological Science, 10*, 172–175.

Tomasello, M. (1992a). *First verbs: A case study of early grammatical development*. Cambridge, United Kingdom: Cambridge University Press.

Tomasello, M. (1992). The social bases of language acquisition. *Social Development, 1*, 67–87.

Tomasello, M. (2000). Do young children have adult syntactic competence? *Cognition, 4*, 209–253.

Tomasello, M. (2003). *Constructing a language: A usage-based theory of language acquisition*. Cambridge, MA: Harvard University Press.

Tomasello, M. (2005). Beyond formalities: The case of language acquisition. *The Linguistic Review, 22*, 183–197.

Tomasello, M. (2006). Acquiring linguistic constructions. In W. Damon, R. M. Lerner, D. Kuhn, & R. Siegler (Eds.), *Handbook of child psychology, Vol. 2: Cognitive perception and language* (pp. 255–298). Hoboken, NJ: Wiley.

Tomasello, M. (2008). *Origins of human communication*. Cambridge, MA: MIT Press.

Tomasello, M., Akhtar, N., Dodson, K., & Rekau, L. (1997). Differential productivity in young children's use of nouns and verbs. *Journal of Child Language, 24*, 373–387.

Tomasello, M., & Cale Kruger, A. (1992). Joint attention on actions: Acquiring verbs in ostensive and non-ostensive context. *Journal of Child Language, 19*, 311–333.

Tomasello, M., & Call, J. (1997). *Primate cognition*. New York, NY: Oxford University Press.

Tomasello, M., Carpenter, M., Call, J., Behne, T., & Moll, H. (2005). Understanding and sharing intentions: The origins of cultural cognition. *Behavioral and Brain Sciences, 28*, 675–735.

Tomasello, M., Carpenter, M., & Liszkowski, U. (2007). A new look at infant pointing. *Child Development, 78*, 705–722.

Tomasello, M., Conti-Ramsden, G., & Ewert, B. (1990). Young children's conversations with their mothers and fathers: Differences in breakdown and repair. *Journal of Child Language, 17*, 115–130.

Tomasello, M., Strosberg, R., & Akhtar, N. (1996). Eighteen-month-old children learn words in non-ostensive contexts. *Journal of Child Language, 23*, 157–176.

Tomblin, J. B., Barker, B. A., Spencer, L., Zhang, X., & Gantz, B. J. (2005). The effect of age at cochlear implant initial stimulation on expressive language growth in infants and toddlers. *Journal of Speech, Language and Hearing Research, 48*, 853–867.

Tomblin, J. B., & Zhang, X. (2006). The dimensionality of language ability in school-age children. *Journal of Speech, Language, and Hearing Research, 49*, 1193–1208.

Tompkins, C. A. (1995). *Right hemisphere communication disorders: Theory and management*. San Diego, CA: Singular.

Tompkins, C. A., Lehman-Blake, M. T., Baumgaertner, A., & Fassbinder, W. (2001). Mechanisms of discourse comprehension impairment after right hemisphere brain damage: Suppression in inferential ambiguity resolution. *Journal of Speech, Language, and Hearing Research, 44*, 400–415.

Torgesen, J. K., Rashotte, C. A., & Alexander, A. W. (2001). Principles of fluency instruction in reading: Relationships with established empirical outcomes. In M. Wolf (Ed.), *Dyslexia, fluency and the brain* (pp. 332–355). Timonium, MD: York Press.

Towse, J., Hitch, G., & Hutton, U. (1998). A re-evaluation of working memory capacity in children. *Journal of Memory and Language, 39*, 195–217.

Trachtenberg, J. T., & Stryker, M. P. (2001). Rapid anatomical plasticity of horizontal connections in the developing visual cortex. *Journal of Neuroscience, 15*, 3476–3482.

Treiman, R. (1993). *Beginning to spell*. New York, NY: Oxford University Press.

Treiman, R., & Cassar, M. (1997). Spelling acquisition in English. In C. A. Perfetti, L. Rieben, & M. Fayol (Eds.), *Learning to spell: Research, theory, and practice across languages* (pp. 61–80). Mahwah, NJ: Erlbaum.

Treiman, R., & Kessler, B. (2004). The case of case: Children's knowledge and use of upper and lowercase letters. *Applied Psycholinguistics, 25*(3), 413–428.

Treiman, R., & Kessler, B. (2006). Spelling as statistical learning: Using consonantal context to spell vowels. *Journal of Educational Psychology, 98*, 642–652.

Treiman, R., Kessler, B., Zevin, J. D., Bick, S., & Davis, M. (2006). Influence of consonantal context on the reading of vowels: Evidence from children. *Journal of Experimental Child Psychology, 93*, 1–24.

Tritsch, N. X., Yi, E., Gale, J. E., Glowatski, E., & Bergles, D. E. (2007). The origin of spontaneous activity in the developing auditory system. *Nature, 450*, 50–55.

Tronick, E., Als, H., & Adamson, L. (1979). Structure of early face-to-face communicative interactions. In M. Bullowa (Ed.), *Before speech*. New York, NY: Cambridge University Press.

Trotter, R. (1983, August). Baby face. *Psychology Today, 17*(8), 14–20.

Trudeau, M., & Chadwick, A. (1997, February 7). *Language development.* National Public Radio.

Tsao, F., Liu, H., & Kuhl, P. K. (2004). Speech perception in infancy predicts language development in the second year of life: A longitudinal study. *Child Development, 75,* 1067–1084.

Turkstra, L., Ciccia, A., & Seaton, C. (2003). Interactive behaviors in adolescent conversation dyads. *Language, Speech, and Hearing Services in Schools, 34,* 117–127.

Turnbull, K., Deacon, S. H., & Kay-Raining Bird, E. (2011). Mastering inflectional suffixes: A longitudinal study of beginning writers' spellings. *Journal of Child Language, 38,* 533–553.

U.S. Department of Housing and Urban Development. (2008, July). *The third annual homeless assessment report to Congress.* Washington, DC: Author.

U.S. Department of Housing and Urban Development. (2012). The 2012 Annual Homeless Assessment Report. Retrieved September 5, 2014, from https://www.hudexchange.info/resources/documents/2012AHAR_PITestimates.pdf

U.S. Department of State. (2002). *Number of immigrant visas issued to orphans coming to the U.S.* Retrieved October 10, 2002, from http://travel.state.gov/orphan_numbers.html.

U.S. Department of State. (2013). *FY 2013 Annual Report on Intercountry Adoption.* (2014, March). Bureau of Consular Affairs, Retrieved September 2, 2014, from http://adoption.state.gov/content/pdf/fy2013_annual_report.pdf

U.S. Department of State. (2012). *Fact Sheet: The decline in U.S. Fertility.* Population Reference Bureau. Retrieved September 5, 2014, from http://www.prb.org/Publications/Datasheets/2012/world-population-data-sheet/fact-sheet-us-population.aspx.

Uccelli, P. (2008). Beyond chronicity: Evaluation and temporality in Spanish-speaking children's personal narratives. In A. McCabe, A. L. Bailey, & G. Melzi (Eds.), *Spanish-language narration and literacy: Culture, cognition and emotion* (pp. 175–212). New York, NY: Cambridge University Press.

Ukrainetz, T. A., Justice, L. M., Kaderavek, J. N., Eisenberg, S. L., Gillam, R. B., & Harm, H. M. (2005). The development of expressive elaboration in fictional narratives. *Journal of Speech, Language, and Hearing Research, 48,* 1363–1377.

Ulatowska, H. K., & Olness, G. S. (2004). Discourse. In R. D. Kent (Ed.), *The MIT encyclopedia of communication disorders* (pp. 300–302). Cambridge, MA: MIT Press.

Valian, V. (1991). Syntactic subjects in the early speech of American and Italian children. *Cognition: International Journal of Cognitive Science, 40,* 21–81.

Valian, V., & Aubry, S. (2005). When opportunity knocks twice: Two-year-olds' repetition of sentence subjects. *Journal of Child Language, 32,* 617–641.

Valian, V., & Casey, L. (2003). Young children's acquisition of *wh-* questions: the role of structured input. *Journal of Child Language, 30,* 117–143.

van den Boom, D. C. (1997). Sensitivity and attachment: Next step for developmentalists. *Child Development, 64,* 259–294.

Van Dyke, J. (2007). Interference effects from grammatically unavailable constituents during sentence processing. *Journal of Experimental Psychology: Learning, Memory, and Language, 33,* 407–430.

van Kleeck, A., & Beckley-McCall, A. (2002). A comparison of mothers' individual and simultaneous book sharing with preschool siblings: An exploratory study of five families. *American Journal of Speech-Language Pathology, 11,* 175–189.

van Kleeck, A., Gillam, R. B., Hamilton, L., & McGrath, C. (1997). The relationship between middle-class parents' book sharing discussion and their preschoolers' abstract language development. *Journal of Speech, Language, and Hearing Research, 40,* 1261–1271.

Vanderberg, R., & Swanson, H. L. (2007). Which components of working memory are important in the writing process? *Reading and Writing, 20,* 721–752.

Velleman, S. L., & Vihman, M. M. (2002). Whole-word phonology and templates: Trap, bootstrap, or some of each? *Language, Speech, and Hearing Services in Schools, 33,* 9–23.

Verhoeven, L., Aparici, M., Cahana-Amitay, D., van Hell, J., Kriz, S., & Viguie-Simon, A. (2002). Clause packaging in writing and speech: A cross-linguistic developmental analysis. *Written Language and Literacy, 5,* 135–162.

Vihman, M. M., & Greenlee, M. (1987). Individual differences in phonological development: Ages one and three years. *Journal of Speech and Hearing Research, 30*, 503–521.

Vihman, M. M., & Velleman, S. L. (2000). Phonetics and the origins of phonology. In N. Burton-Roberts, P. Carr, & G. Docherty (Eds.), *Phonological knowledge: Conceptual and empirical issues* (pp. 305–399). Oxford, United Kingdom: Oxford University Press.

Visscher, K. M., Kaplan, E., Kahana, M. J., & Sekuler, R. (2007). Auditory short-term memory behaves like visual short-term memory. *Plos Biology, 5*, 0001–0011.

Vitevitch, M. S. (2002). The influence of phonological similarity neighborhoods on speech production. *Learning, Memory, and Cognition, 28*, 735–747.

Vitevitch, M. S., & Luce, P. A. (1999). Probabilistic phonotactics and neighborhood activism in spoken word recognition. *Journal of Memory and Language, 40*, 374–408.

Vitevitch, M. S., Luce, P. A., & Pisoni, D. B. (1999). Phonotactics, neighborhood activation and lexical access for spoken words. *Brain and Language, 68*, 306–311.

Vogel Sosa, A., & Stoel-Gammon, C. (2006). Patterns of intra-word phonological variability during the second year of life. *Journal of Child Language, 33*, 31–50.

Vorperian, H. K., & Kent, R. D. (2007). Vowel acoustic space development in children: A synthesis of acoustic and anatomic data. *Journal of Speech, Language, and Hearing Research, 50*, 1510–1545.

Vouloumanos, A., Hauser, M. D., Werker, J. F., & Martin, A. (2010). The tuning of human neonates' preference for speech. *Child Development, 81*, 517–527.

Vouloumanos, A., & Werker, J. F. (2007). Listening to language at birth: Evidence for a bias for speech in neonates. *Developmental Science, 10*, 159–164.

Vukovic, R. K., & Siegel, L. S. (2010). Academic and cognitive characteristics of persistent mathematics difficulty from first through fourth grade. *Learning Disabilities Research & Practice, 25*, 25–38.

Walker, S. J. (2001). Cognitive, linguistic, and social aspects of adults' noun definitions. *Journal of Psycholinguistic Research, 30*, 147–161.

Wallace, I. F., Roberts, J. E., & Lodder, D. E. (1998). Interactions of African American infants and their mothers: Relations with development at 1 year of age. *Journal of Speech, Language, and Hearing Research, 42*, 900–912.

Walley, A. (1993). The role of vocabulary development in children's spoken word recognition and segmentation ability. *Developmental Review, 13*, 286–350.

Walsh, M., Richardson, K., & Faulkner, D. (1993). Perceptual, thematic, and taxonomic relations in children's mental representations: Responses to triads. *European Journal of Psychology of Education, 8*, 85–102.

Walton, G. E., Bower, N. J. A., & Bower, T. G. R. (1992). Recognition of familiar faces by newborns. *Infant Behavior and Development, 15*, 265–269.

Wang, Q., & Leichtman, M. D. (2000). Same beginnings, different stories: A comparison of American and Chinese children's narratives. *Child Development, 71*, 1329–1346.

Washington, J. A., & Craig, H. K. (1994). Dialectal forms during discourse of poor, urban, African American preschoolers. *Journal of Speech and Hearing Research, 37*, 816–823.

Washington, J. A., & Craig, H. K. (1998). Socioeconomic status and gender influences on children's dialectal variations. *Journal of Speech, Language, and Hearing Research, 41*(3), 618–626.

Washington, J. A., & Craig, H. K. (2002). Morphosyntactic forms of African American English used by young children and their caregivers. *Applied Psycholinguistics, 23*, 209–231.

Washington, J. A., & Craig, H. K. (2004). A language screening protocol for use with young African American children in urban settings. *American Journal of Speech-Language Pathology, 13*(4), 329–340.

Watt, N., Wetherby, A., & Shumway, S. (2006). Prelinguistic predictors of language outcome at 3 years of age. *Journal of Speech, Language, and Hearing Research, 49*, 1224–1237.

Waxman, S., & Booth, A. (2003). The origins and evolution of links between word learning and conceptual organization: New evidence from 11-month-olds. *Developmental Science, 6*, 128–135.

Waxman, S. R., & Markow, D. B. (1999). Object properties and object kind: 21-month-old infants' extension of novel adjectives. *Child Development, 69*, 1313–1329.

Weber-Fox, C., & Neville, H. J. (2001). Sensitive periods differentiate processing of open- and closed-class words: An ERP study of bilinguals. *Journal of Speech, Language, and Hearing Research, 44*, 1338–1353.

Weinreb, L. F., Buckner, J. C., Williams, V., & Nicholson, J. (2006). A comparison of the health and mental health status of homeless mothers in Worcester, Mass: 1993 and 2003. *American Journal of Public Health, 96*, 1444–1448.

Weist, R. M. (1986). Tense and aspect. In P. Fletcher & M. Garman (Eds.), *Language acquisition* (2nd ed.). New York, NY: Cambridge University Press.

Weist, R. M., Atanassova, M., Wysocka, H., & Pawlak, A. (1999). Spatial and temporal systems in child language and thought: A cross-linguistic study. *A First Language, 19*, 267–311.

Wellman, H. M. (2002). Understanding the psychological world: Developing a Theory of Mind. In U. Goswami (Ed.), *Handbook of childhood cognitive development*. Oxford, United Kingdom: Blackwell.

Wellman, H. M., & Liu, D. (2004). Scaling of theory of mind tasks. *Child Development, 75*, 523–541.

Wells, G. (1979). Learning and using the auxiliary verb in English. In V. Lee (Ed.), *Language development*. New York, NY: Wiley.

Wells, G. (1985). *Language development in the preschool years*. New York, NY: Cambridge University Press.

Werker, J. F., & Curtin, S. (2005). PRIMIR: A developmental framework of infant speech processing. *Language Learning and Development, 1*, 197–234.

Werker, J. F., & Tees, R. C. (1994). Cross-language speech perception: Evidence for perceptual reorganization during the first year of life. *Infant Behavior and Development, 7*, 49–63.

Werker, J. F., & Tees, R. C. (2005). Speech perception as a window for understanding plasticity and commitment in language systems of the brain. *Developmental Psychobiology, 46*, 233–251.

Westby, C. E. (2005). Assessing and remediating text comprehension problems. In H. W. Catts & A. G. Kamhi (Eds.), *Language and reading disabilities* (2nd ed., pp. 157–232). Boston, MA: Allyn & Bacon.

Wetherby, A. M., & Prizant, B. M. (1989). The expression of communicative intent: Assessment guidelines. *Seminars in Speech and Language, 10*, 77–91.

Wexler, K. (1998). Very early parameter setting and the unique checking constraint: A new explanation of the optional infinitive stage. *Lingua, 103*, 23–79.

Wexler, K. (2003). Lenneberg's dream: Learning, normal language development, and specific language impairment. In Y. Levy & J. Schaeffer (Eds.), *Language competence across populations: Toward a definition of specific language impairment*. Mahwah, NJ: Erlbaum.

Whitehurst, G. J., & Lonigan, C. J. (2001). Emergent readers: Development from prereaders to readers. In S. B. Neuman & D. K. Dickinson (Eds.), *Handbook of early literacy research* (pp. 11–29). New York, NY: Guilford.

Whitmore, J. M., Shore, W. J., & Hull Smith, P. (2004). Partial knowledge of word meanings: Thematic and taxonomic representations. *Journal of Psycholinguistic Research, 33*, 137–164.

Wiley, A. R., Rose, A. J., Burger, L. K., & Miller, P. J. (1998). Constructing autonomous selves through narrative practices: A comparative study of working-class and middle-class families. *Child Development, 69*, 833–847.

Wilson, E. (2003). Lexically specific constructions in the acquisition of inflections in English. *Journal of Child Language, 30*, 75–115.

Windsor, J., Glaze, L. E., Koga, S. F., & the BEIP Core Group. (2007). Language acquisition with limited input: Romanian institution and foster care. *Journal of Speech, Language, and Hearing Research, 50*, 1365–1381.

Wing, C., & Scholnick, E. (1981). Children's comprehension of pragmatic concepts expressed in "because," "although," "if" and "unless." *Journal of Child Language, 8*, 347–365.

Winsler, A., Carlton, M. P., & Barry, M. J. (2000). Age-related changes in preschool children's systematic use of private speech in a natural setting. *Journal of Child Language, 27*, 665–687.

Wolf, M. (2007). *Proust and the Squid: The story and science of the reading brain*. New York, NY: HarperCollins.

Wolf, M., & Katzir-Cohen, T. (2001). Reading fluency and its intervention. *Scientific Studies of Reading, 5*, 211–239.

Wolfram, W. (1986). Structural variability in phonological development: Final nasals in vernacular Black English. In R. W. Fasold & D. Schiffrin (Eds.), *Current issues in linguistic theory: Language change and variation* (pp. 301–332). Philadelphia, PA: John Benjamins.

Wolfram, W. (2004). Social varieties of American English. In E. Finegan & J. R. Rickford (Eds.), *Language in the USA: Themes for the twenty-first century* (pp. 58–75). Cambridge, United Kingdom: Cambridge University Press.

Wolter, J. A., & Apel, K. (2010). Initial acquisition of mental graphemic representations in children with language impairment. *Journal of Speech, Language, and Hearing Research, 53*, 179–195.

Wright, H. H., Capilouto, G. J., Wagovich, S. A., Cranfill, T. B., & Davis, J. E. (2005). Development and reliability of a quantitative measure of adults' narratives. *Aphasiology, 19*, 263–273.

Xu, F., & Pinker, S. (1995). Weird past tense forms. *Journal of Child Language, 22*, 531–556.

Yang, C. (2002). *Knowledge and learning in natural language*. New York, NY: Oxford University Press.

Yang, C. (2004). Universal grammar, statistics, or both? *Trends in Cognitive Sciences, 8*, 451–456.

Yang, C. L., Gordon, P. C., Hendrick, R., Wu, J. T., & Chou, T. L. (2001). The processing of coreference for reduced expression in discourse integration. *Journal of Psycholinguistic Research, 30*, 21–35.

Ylvisaker, M., & DeBonis, D. (2000). Executive function impairment in adolescence: TBI and ADHD. *Topics in Language Disorders, 20*(2), 29–57.

Zammit, M., & Schafer, G. (2011). Maternal label and gesture use affects acquisition of specific object names. *Journal of Child Language, 38*, 201–221.

Zamuner, T. S. (2009). Phonotactic probabilities at the onset of language development: Speech production and word position. *Journal of Speech, Language, and Hearing Research 52*, 49–60.

Zentella, A. C. (1999). *Growing up bilingual*. Malden, MA: Blackwell.

Zubrick, S. R., Taylor, C. L., Rice, M. L., & Slegers, D. W. (2007). Late language emergence at 24 months: An epidemiological study of prevalence, predictors, and covariates. *Journal of Speech, Language, and Hearing Research, 50*, 1562–1592.

Zumach, A., Gerrits, E., Chenault, M., & Anteunis, L. (2010). Long-term effects of early otitis media on language development. *Journal of Speech, Language, and Hearing Research, 53*, 34–43.

Author Index

Subject Index

H

I

J

K

L